AF598737

JUDY FRATER

ARTISANS by Design

An Odyssey of Education for Textile Artisans in India

With photos by **NEVADA WEIR**

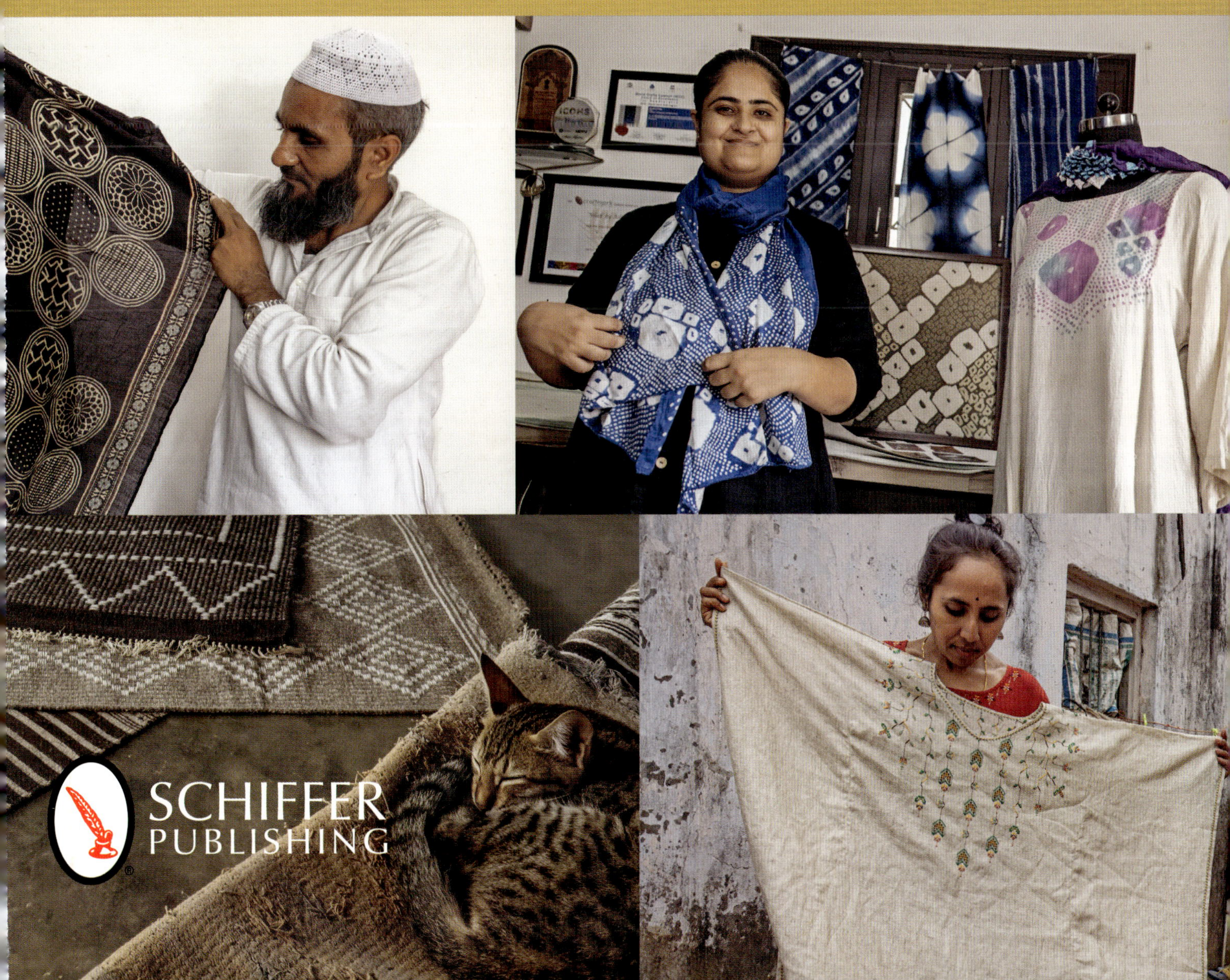

Money comes and goes; education stays with you forever.

~Pachanbhai Premji Siju, weaver designer

Other Schiffer Books on Related Subjects:

In Search of Wild Silk: Exploring a Village Industry in the Jungles of India, Karen Selk, ISBN 978-0-7643-6497-6

The Pigment Trail: Inspiration from the Colors, Textures, and People of India, Debra Luker, ISBN 978-0-7643-6756-4

The Art and Science of Natural Dyes: Principles, Experiments, and Results, Joy Boutrup and Catharine Ellis, ISBN 978-0-7643-5633-9

Library of Congress Control Number: 2024932160

Designed by Lori Malkin Ehrlich
Type set in Daydreamer/Minion Pro
ISBN: 978-0-7643-6843-1
Printed in India

Published by Schiffer Publishing, Ltd.
4880 Lower Valley Road
Atglen, PA 19310
Phone: (610) 593-1777; Fax: (610) 593-2002
Email: info@schifferbooks.com
Web: www.schifferbooks.com

CONTENTS

ACKNOWLEDGMENTS

It takes a village—in this case, a lot of villages. And I think it also takes vision and faith. Many people contributed to making the dream of relevant education for artisans a reality.

Foundation support came from Prakashbhai Bhanani, who recognized that it was a good idea; Ashoka, whose belief in my idea gave me courage to begin; and the late Jan Baker, the late Chip Morris, Krishnaben Patel, and Aleta Margolis, who brainstormed with me to initiate curriculum development. Jolene Holten, through Ashoka, worked with me on the BMA curriculum. Arjo Klamer, though I met him later, provided the core concept of a Creative Craft Culture.

The senior artisan advisors—Dr. Ismailbhai Mohmed Khatri, the late Alimamadbhai Isha Khatri, the late Umarbhai Faruk Khatri, Gulambhai Husen Umar Khatri, the late Laljibhai Vankar, and Shamjibhai Vishramji Siju—helped keep the program relevant. Special mention goes to Vishramjibhai Valji Siju, who also taught me much about cultural history.

I received big-picture guidance and support from the late M. P. Ranjan, Ashoke Chatterjee, Ritu Sethi and Craft Revival Trust, James Ferreira, and Hiteshbhai Bhatt. I thank the Sir Misha Black Awards Committee, the Crafts Council of India, the Association of Designers of India and JKLU Institute of Design, the Rotary Club of Delhi Premier, and the Muslim Khatri Khidmat Trust for their very fortifying recognition.

A program relies on funding to prosper. Initial funding came from the American India Foundation, UNESCO, and the Indian Government Office of the Development Commissioner Handicrafts. Over the years, Eileen Fisher, Bestseller Foundation, Como Foundation, the Sohanlal Trust, the Anjana Somany Foundation, the Sheela Kanoria Foundation, Geeta Ram, Eicher Good Earth, Tata Trusts, Narotam Sekhsaria Foundation, CTC Geotechnical Pvt Ltd., Cloth Roads, Somaiya Vidyavihar, Global Giving, and many individual donors contributed invaluable financial support.

Architect Hemen Sanghvi designed and built two exquisite campuses with painstaking care and detail, giving the program a presence.

The staff kept our campuses and programs vital. Lakhabhai Paba Rabari, office manager; Nilanjan Mondal, Pallavi Gaur, and other program coordinators; Sangabhai P. Rabari; and the late Lakhmirbhai P. Rabari and Lakhabhai Rabari, buildings and grounds managers, and our drivers and cooks over the years, worked with dedication and creativity. I have a special thank-you for the village of Bhopani Vandh, who supported Kala Raksha Vidhyalaya in various ways for eight years.

A curriculum is realized through syllabus development and instruction. Lokesh Ghai, the late Shwetha Shettar, Shweta Dhariwal, and Bishakha Shome were founding visiting faculty who gave life to curriculum concepts and wholeheartedly nurtured students. Many other visiting faculty contributed equally creatively. The resident faculty—Harishbhai Bhanani, Bharatbhai Goradia, Virendrabhai Vegad, and design graduates Dahyabhai Kudecha, Laxmiben Parmar, Tulsiben Puvar, Taraben Puvar, Mukhtarbhai Soneji, and Muskanben Khatri—served as liaisons between visiting faculty and artisan students, ensuring that courses were effective.

The annual convocation was the face of the design education program, creating value for tradition among

Opposite: Faradi, 2022. Tulsiben embroiders her brand Liti (Line) on each piece she creates. The design education program enables individual artisans to be recognized. *Photo: Nevada Wier*

DEDICATION

To all the artisan graduates who gave time, heart, and soul to nurturing their traditions, and to Lakhabhai, the voice of reason, who was there throughout.

artisan communities and motivating future students. Jayaben Chakravarty designed and developed its first avatar as the Kala Raksha Vidhyalaya Mela. Nilanjanbhai Mondal re-branded it as Kala Umang! Utsav Dholakia choreographed extremely popular fashion shows at the KRV Mela. At Kala Umang!, Achla Sachdev, teaming with lighting designer Urvish Jalgaonkar, took fashion shows to the next level with joyous enthusiasm. Ketanbhai and Hemantbhai Pomal documented it all for posterity.

Thanks to Dr. Priyatej Kotipalli for conducting a value-based impact assessment of fourteen years of the program, which provided invaluable quotes for this book.

Samirbhai Somaiya, Amritaben Somaiya, and the trustees of the K. J. Somaiya Gujarat Trust made it possible to develop a range of new programs and take the design program to an institute. Pandurang Hoti and Rashmiben Bharati hosted Outreach programs, enabling design education to take on new forms and broader reach. And Nishitbhai Sangomla, current director of Somaiya Kala Vidya, is staying the course and taking artisan design into the future.

The story has become a book thanks to Al Tafoya, who taught me how to write; Linda Ligon, who guided its creative form; Nevada Wier, who created amazing images; Ravibhai Mejar Rabari and team, who provided ground support for our 2022 photography sojourn; and Schiffer Publishing Ltd., who not only brought the book to light but also created studio images, and Sandra Korinchak and Karla Rosenbusch, who contributed incisive editing.

Last and most of all, I want to thank all the artisan students and families who together made Artisan Design a reality.

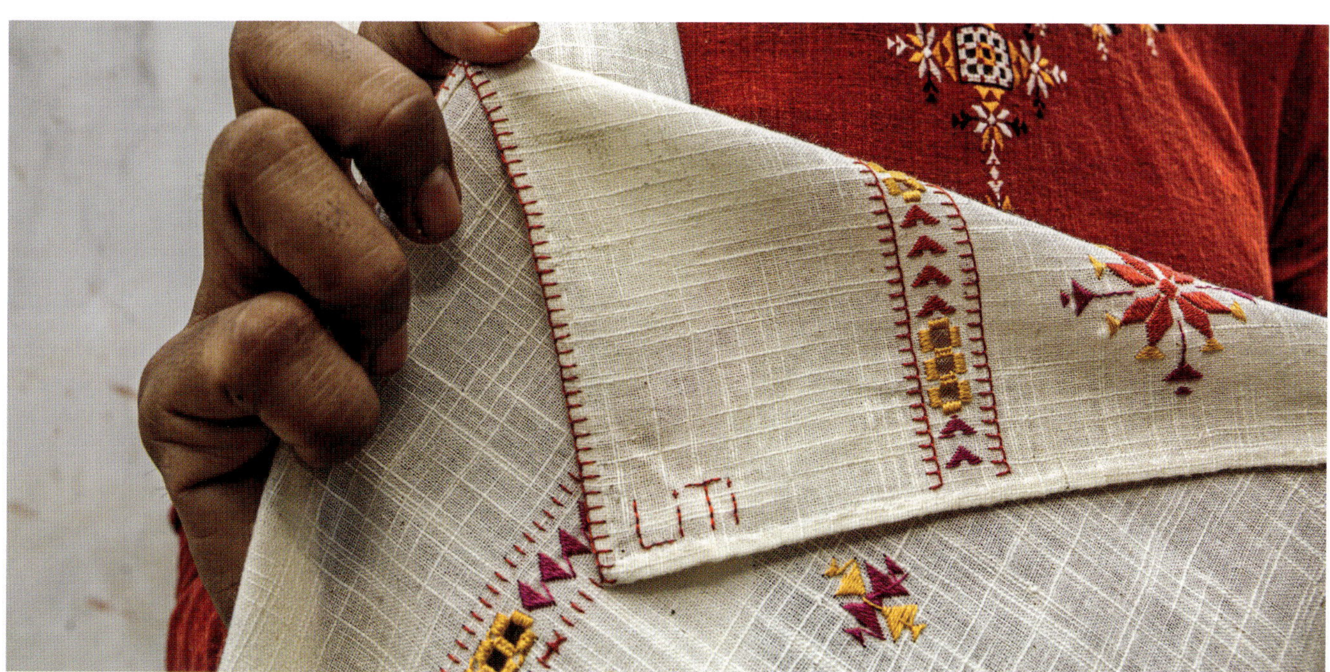

FOREWORD

I have always been captivated by virtuosity—not just skill, but the depth of knowing that enables the virtuoso to express poetically and timelessly. The art becomes an extension of the self, allowing the virtuoso to play. So when I had the chance to come to India in 1970, it was traditional art that I wanted to study.

Studying traditional art has been a journey of fifty-four years—so far. The journey took on a life of its own. I never said, "Now I'm going to live in India." It just happened. Pursuit of a deeply engaging topic introduced me to other equally compelling issues. It was organic. I do remember one evening, however, speeding through the impossibly choked and wondrous lanes in Chandni Chowk, Delhi, everything imaginable lit by golden light whizzing by, and thinking, "I'm going to be here for a while."

I began with the expressive quality of embroidery traditions in Kutch. Two levels seemed to operate simultaneously: historical elements of identity, and women artisans' pictorial narrations of their own lives. I pursued that from a prescribed distance, in an academic way. Then one day, Dayaben, a young and confident embroiderer, boldly asked me with exasperation, "Why are you studying us? Why don't you help us?" I heard her. And so, we began Kala Raksha, a social enterprise for women embroiderers.

As a participant, I was learning by doing and doing while learning, peeling away layers of the realities in which traditional artisans work. "Realities" are colored by one's own experiences, and it was my perceptions that drove me. As I pondered what I perceived as problems, trying to find solutions, the best answers always seemed to be education.

Working closely with artisans, I realized that they have far more capacity than is usually acknowledged by the development professionals, designers, and clients who deal with them. I would observe young design students struggling to get artisans to work on designs that had little relation to their own work, and think, "They should start a design school for artisans."

It took an earthquake for me to take my thought seriously. On January 26, 2001, a massive earthquake devastated Kutch. Days later, I was camped in the freezing cold in Sumrasar, and at 6 a.m. a reporter woke me to ask what I wanted to see come out of the earthquake. "A design school for artisans!" I blurted. Immediately, I realized that now I would have to do it—because there was no "they."

This book details my journey of learning what tradition means and understanding how that continuously evolves as societies evolve. It is a story of finding—and sometimes creating—opportunities for artisans to realize potential and reach capacity, a struggle with which I empathize in my own parallel story.

Kachhi Rabari nolo, Nakhatrana taluka, Kutch, ca. 1950. 4" x 20". Collection of the author. Rabari embroidery fascinated me most, with its bold pictorial motifs. This money belt, worn by a man during a wedding ceremony, is embroidered with motifs of elephants and trees. *Photo: Schiffer Publishing Ltd.*

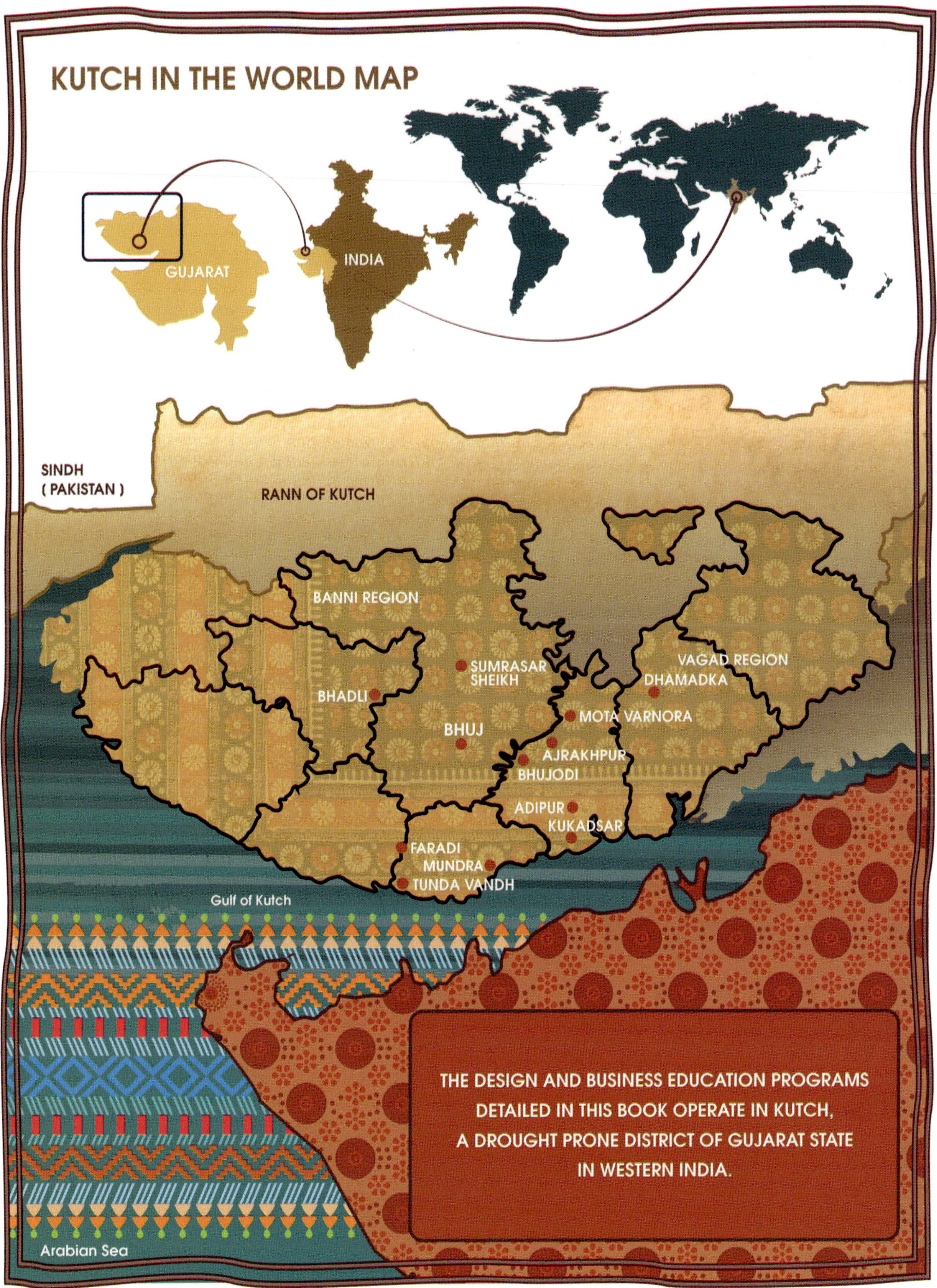

Photo: If the Art Cafe

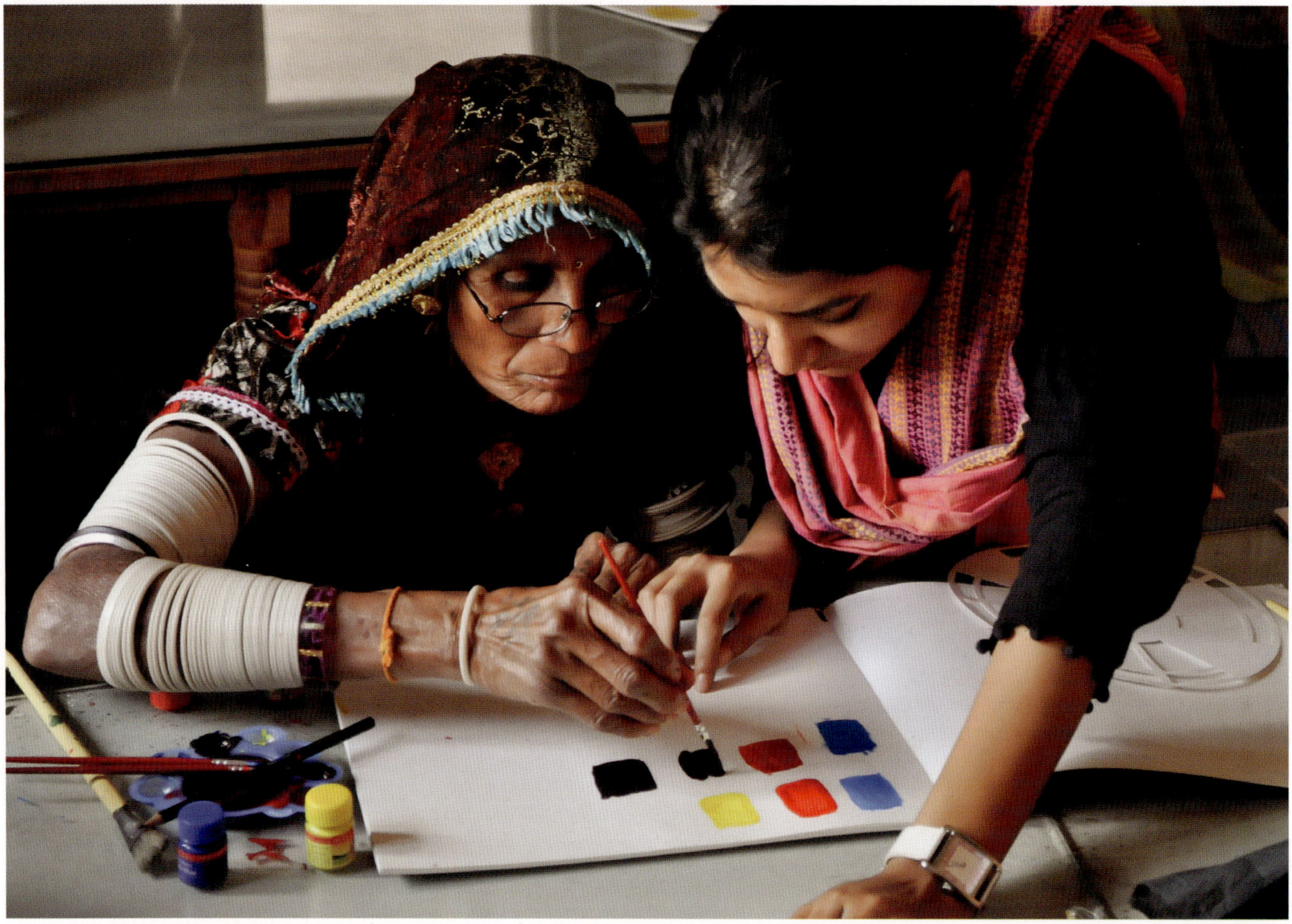

Against many odds, but with wonderful, serendipitous support, I began the first institute of design education for artisans. This immersed me in the magic of education. Over the years, I have learned about learning and innovated on the curriculum and methodology to respond to shortcomings I observed, trying always to hear the goals of artisan participants and provide the most genuine, appropriate, and effective experience.

In the fifteen years that I directed the program, we enjoyed dramatically positive results—not only for the participants but for artisan communities in which they live. Today in all of India, Kutch artisans exemplify vibrant design and social as well as economic success.

Most importantly, I will share with you some of the many amazing stories of artisans who have studied design—and business. Each individual has a tale, and all are truly inspirational.

Top: Kala Raksha Vidhyalaya, 2010. Babraben Moru Bhanani learns color theory by painting. Kala Raksha Vidhyalaya, the first program of education for artisans, taught design to traditional artisans of Kutch. *Photo: Judy Frater*

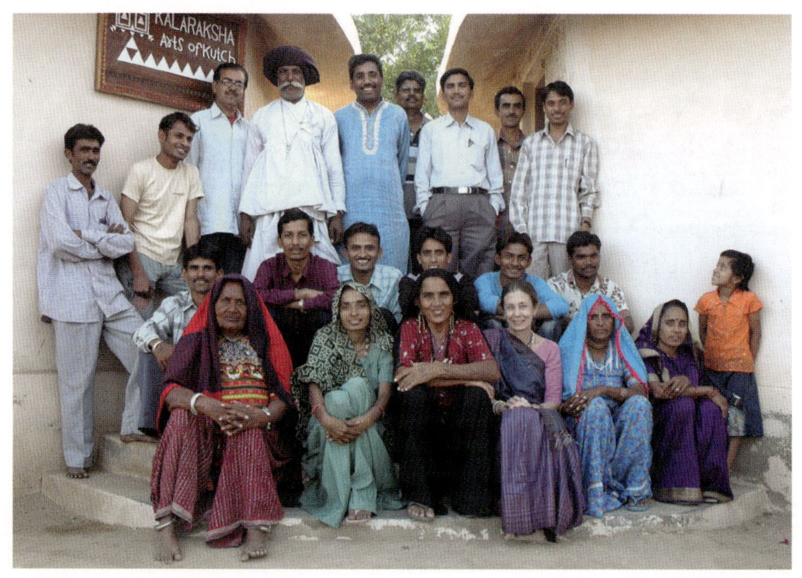

Right: Sumrasar Sheikh, 2007. The Kala Raksha team comprised traditional village artisans, their families, and me. *Photo: a visitor to Kala Raksha*

Chapter 1

MY MUSE: ARTISAN DESIGNERS OF NEW HOPE, PENNSYLVANIA

I grew up in the country, in Bucks County, Pennsylvania. Our address was New Hope, RD2 (rural delivery).

We didn't go to New Hope for household needs. It wasn't that kind of town. A village of about a thousand people, New Hope had been an artists' colony since the end of the nineteenth century and had evolved into a bohemian haven for artisans and nonconformists of all orientations. I loved browsing the tiny streets of New Hope, exploring antique shops and open studios where artists designed and created. I chatted with artists working in silver, leather, and clay and marveled that they could imagine and make the jewelry, sandals, plates, and cups in their shops.

Although this was not a mainstream world, it was a reality that coexisted comfortably enough with the shopping centers and housing developments that were springing up in other towns of Bucks County in the 1960s. The artists and antique dealers of New Hope were patronized by the gentlemen farmers of Bucks Country and busloads of weekend tourists from New York. Tourism shaped a world in which the mood was holiday and income was mostly reliable, and when the tourists left, the small community bonded in response.

The craftwork of New Hope was studio craft. It was created as functional art—useful, with beautiful design. Production was limited edition or one of a kind. The work was authenticated by the fact that the artist from whom you purchased it was making similar craft right before your eyes. And the artist, a designer-maker, signed his or her work as any artist would. No doubt this kind of craft owed a large part of its appreciation to Bauhaus thought, which had influenced the Western world from 1919 into the 1960s. The New Hope designer-makers embodied Bauhaus founder Walter Gropius's idea "to create a new guild of craftsmen, without the class distinctions which raise an arrogant barrier between craftsman and artist."

I had not known that arrogant barrier. So for me, the designer-maker was simply a wonderful reality abundant in the town nearby.

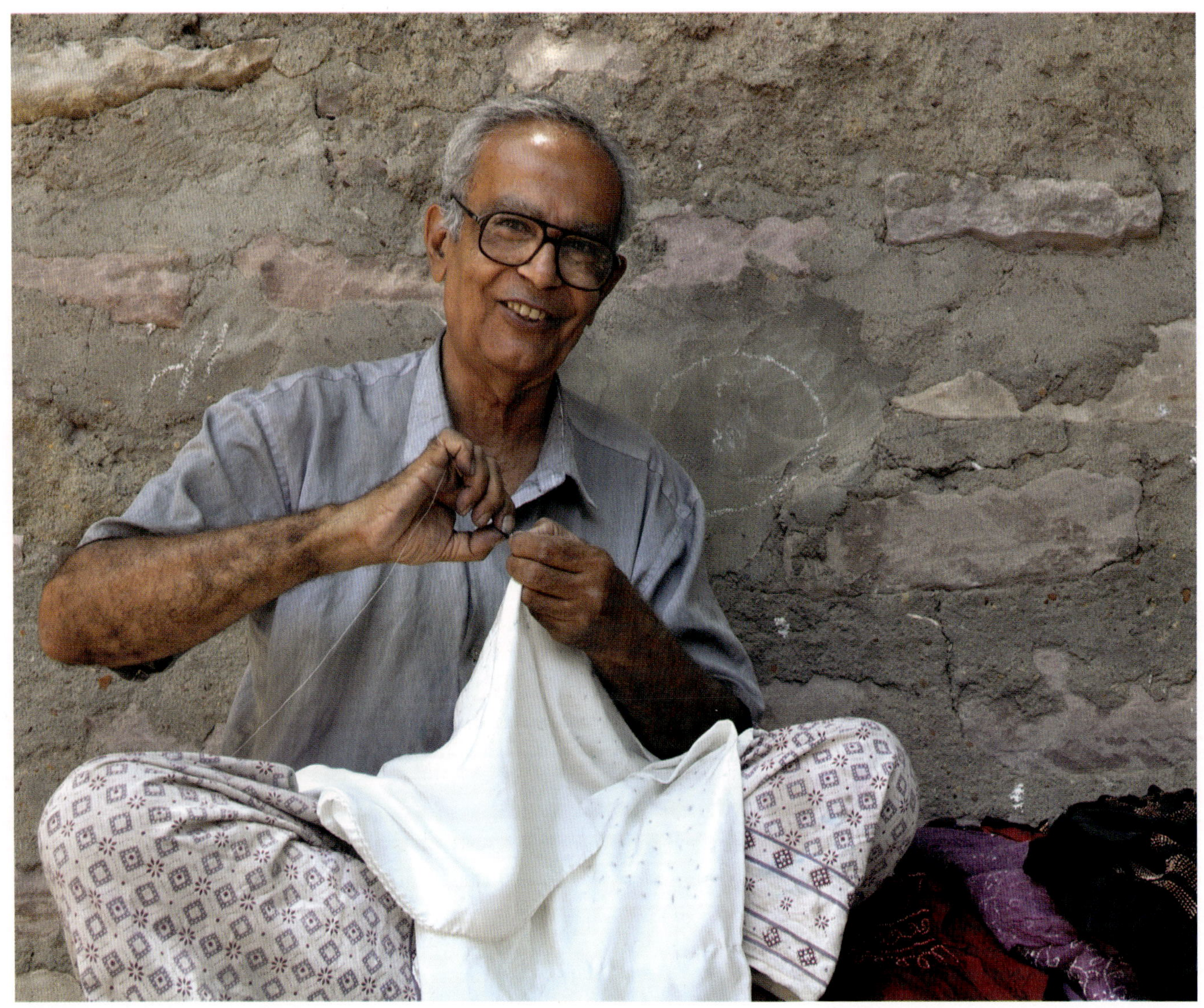

My philosophy is that whatever I make should have something of me in it—myself. If not, I won't like it.

~Alimamadbhai Isha Khatri

Above: Bhuj, 2010. Alimamad Isha Khatri ties bandhani at his home. Although men traditionally tied bandhani, he was one of the few men who continued to tie even after the craft became commercialized. *Photo: Judy Frater*

Opposite: Bhuj, 2022. Bandhani is a resist-dyeing technique in which minute portions of fabric are tightly tied with fine cotton yarn. The dye cannot penetrate the tie, and a dotted pattern is created. *Photo: Nevada Wier*

Chapter 2

ALIMAMADBHAI ISHA KHATRI: AN ORIGINAL ARTISAN DESIGNER IN KUTCH

In the 1950s, India began nation building. Leaders focused on rapid industrialization. Inflation coupled with an influx of cheaper industrially produced products, and villagers, the traditional consumers of handcraft, began to prefer plastics, synthetics, and mill-made fabrics. Artisans were forced to seek alternative clients, and they looked to more-distant, unknown markets.

At the same time, the industrial concept of design as an entity was introduced to India. Designers sought inspiration from artisans, and artisans found aid in their quest for remote markets in designers as well as traders.

The commercialization of craft used an industrial model in which the assumed goals are to manufacture faster, cheaper, and in a more standardized way. By the 1970s, shops in Bhuj, the capital of Kutch, were filled with inexpensive bandhani saris for the urban mass market.

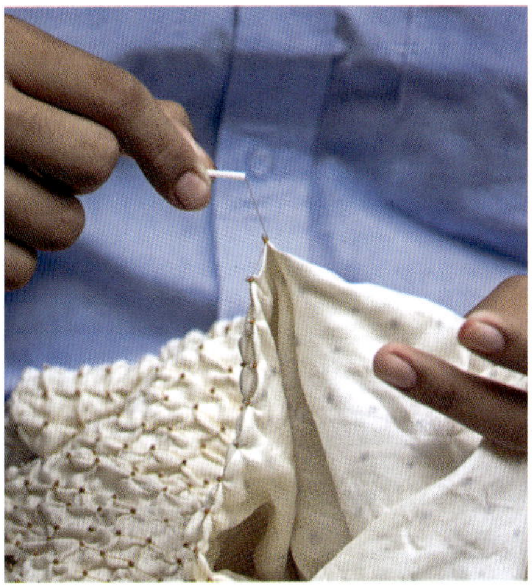

But in the crowded Khatri Chakla neighborhood of Bhuj, bandhani artist Alimamd Isha Khatri lived in a special world—with a large old neem tree right in the middle of his tiny home. Alimamadbhai[1] had no interest in commercial bandhani. “I make one piece at a time,” he said, “and each one is a masterpiece. My philosophy is that whatever I make should have something of me in it—myself. If not, I won’t like it.” A designer-maker, an artisan designer, was alive and well in postindustrial Kutch.

Alimamad Isha was a fifth-generation bandhani artist. His father, a bandhani artist, died when he was six. At age seven, he learned bandhani from his uncle, mother, and grandmother. He studied until 1965 and then got a job in the government land records office in Bhuj. At the time, he didn’t want to get his hands dirty, he reminisced, laughing. But sitting in the office, he realized this was not him. He married in 1967. In 1973, he was transferred to Dhrangadhra. He was in the office there for ten days, planning to bring his family there, but he got a message from home—“Come home.”

His uncle offered to rent him a shop in Bhuj for RS 6 a month, so he left his job and began a bandhani business. He started with honesty and good relations, he noted. He worked in cotton at first and then learned silk dyeing from the governmental Weavers' Service Center.

In 1975, his mother and wife were invited to Delhi for the first International Women's Day to demonstrate bandhani. Alimamadbhai accompanied them. Prime Minister Indira Gandhi came to the exhibition, and she was so impressed that she authorized a national award for the two women on the spot. They did not even have to submit a sample. This was the second national award ever given for bandhani. "They got the award for continuing their tradition," Alimamadbhai reflected. "It was different then—not about doing the most-elaborate work."

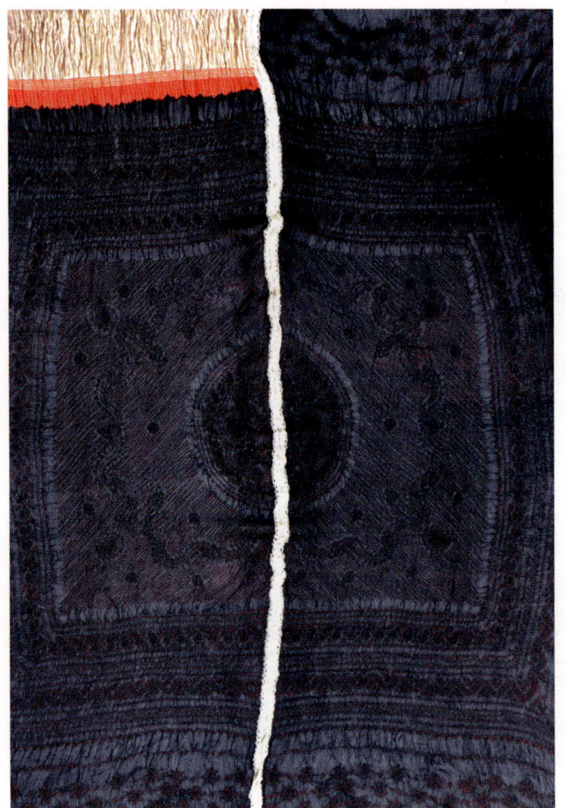

One award is enough for the family, he said. The award brought the family recognition, and Alimamadbhai also became known. He got invitations to travel to Japan, Singapore, Finland, Scotland, and Australia. Only America is left, he joked. But he didn't want to just travel. He wanted to show his work.

An earthquake ravaged Bhuj in 2001. Alimamadbhai lost his house with the neem tree. Commercialization of craft ramped up exponentially. But Alimamadbhai remained the quintessential artisan designer.

He had a wonderful understanding of color and composition, and excellent tying skill. He tied much of his own work, rare today, rather than giving it to workers as most bandhani artisans do.

He was a philosopher with imagination and humor.

"Bandhani is very old work," he said. "I think it is older than printing because it doesn't require equipment or space or up-front expense. We use our hands and decorate fabric. In short, we give life to fabric.

"I heard that bandhani originated with a humble dyer of plain cloth. One day a fakir came to him and said if you feed me, God will protect you. The dyer fed him and gave him some money. The fakir was happy, so he thought to give the dyer something in return—a piece of cloth with a knot in it. The dyer immediately dyed it. When it was dried, he noticed the knot, and when he opened it, there was a design. He thought, why not make designs this way? So if we see, this was a gift of God . . ."

Artisans traditionally made a range of bandhani textiles for many different ethnic groups of different social strata. They are primarily used for auspicious occasions, but among some communities bandhani was also used to cover people who died.

Hand art, bandhani was created in the context of personal relations, Alimamadbhai emphasized. "Originally, artisans made for their own family members or for those with whom they had close relations. For example, a mother made something for her daughter. What is made with such a relationship will be excellent because the relation is of love. The feeling was 'I'll make you something that no one else can make.' Today craft is made for commerce. It is for earning money. The traditional work was for earning love."

Above: Chandrokhani, Mundra, ca. 1920. 67" x 77". Collection of Adil and Zakiya Khatri. A *chandrokhani*, a traditional black silk veil cloth with red bandhani, is worn by the bride at her wedding. *Photo: Ketan Pomal, L.M. Studio*

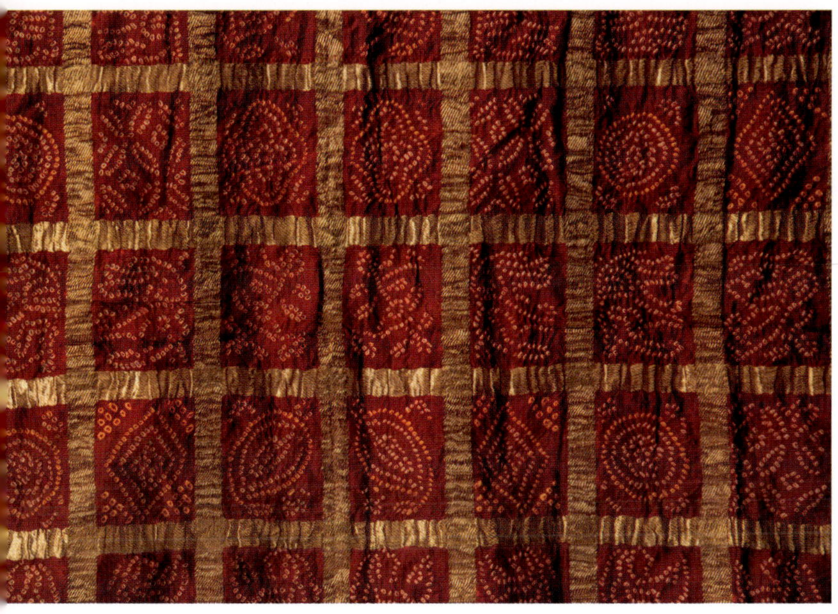

Gharcholu, Bhuj, ca. 1994. By Alimamad Isha Khatri. Silk, azo-free acid dyes, bandhani, with metallic yarns. 42" x 110". Collection of the author. A *gharcholu* can be a veil cloth or a sari. Traditionally cotton with a grid of real gold *zari*/metallic threads, it has a series of bandhani patterns in the squares and is worn for engagements or other auspicious occasions. *Photo: Schiffer Publishing Ltd.*

Alimamadbhai knew traditional work well and had analyzed it. Many traditional bandhani textiles are red. "Whenever we see red, we can understand that it is a happy occasion," he said. However, the traditional Khatri bandhani, *chandrokhani*, was black with red dots. "If anyone says 'chandrokhani,' it means a design of red dots on black. That's the identity. I believe these two colors are the best for showing bandhani. The two dark colors look good on skin, and everyone all over the world likes them. The name comes from the circle in the center, which looks like the moon."

A *gharcholu* is characterized by squares. "All the squares in a gharcholu are homes," he continued. "In this square is an elephant, so it is an elephant's home. This is a flower, so we know it's a garden. This is a peacock; a peacock lives here. And these are people's homes. That way the piece shows all homes. That's why it's called gharcholu [home garment]."

In a *bagido* or a *sabot*, the border always has a quarter circle and half circle. "This makes the textile evoke a whole city, or a village," he explained. "The border is the fort—*gadhrang*. There was a heavier border on one side, the part that covered a woman's head. We believe that covering your head shows respect."

Pattern and composition also considered technical limitations. "The size of motifs relates to the technique," he explained. "It depends on the size of the dot. So the artisan had to know the capacity of his tiers and design accordingly. Traditionally, the women of his home tied and each did an entire piece. So he knew the style of tying. It is better if one person does it all."

Perhaps because he tied, slowly, patiently, Alimamadbhai thought a lot. He got ideas as he worked, he said, a concept shared by many designers. Asked about art and craftsmanship, he said that art is the original work, the tradition that is still going on. Craftsmanship is when an

Sabot, Mundra ca. 1920. Collection of Adil and Zakiya Khatri. 70" x 74". A sabot is a traditional veil cloth characterized by a border and central medallions filled with bandhani. It is worn by a bride on the day that she returns to her family home after her marriage. *Photo: Ketan Pomal, L.M. Studio*

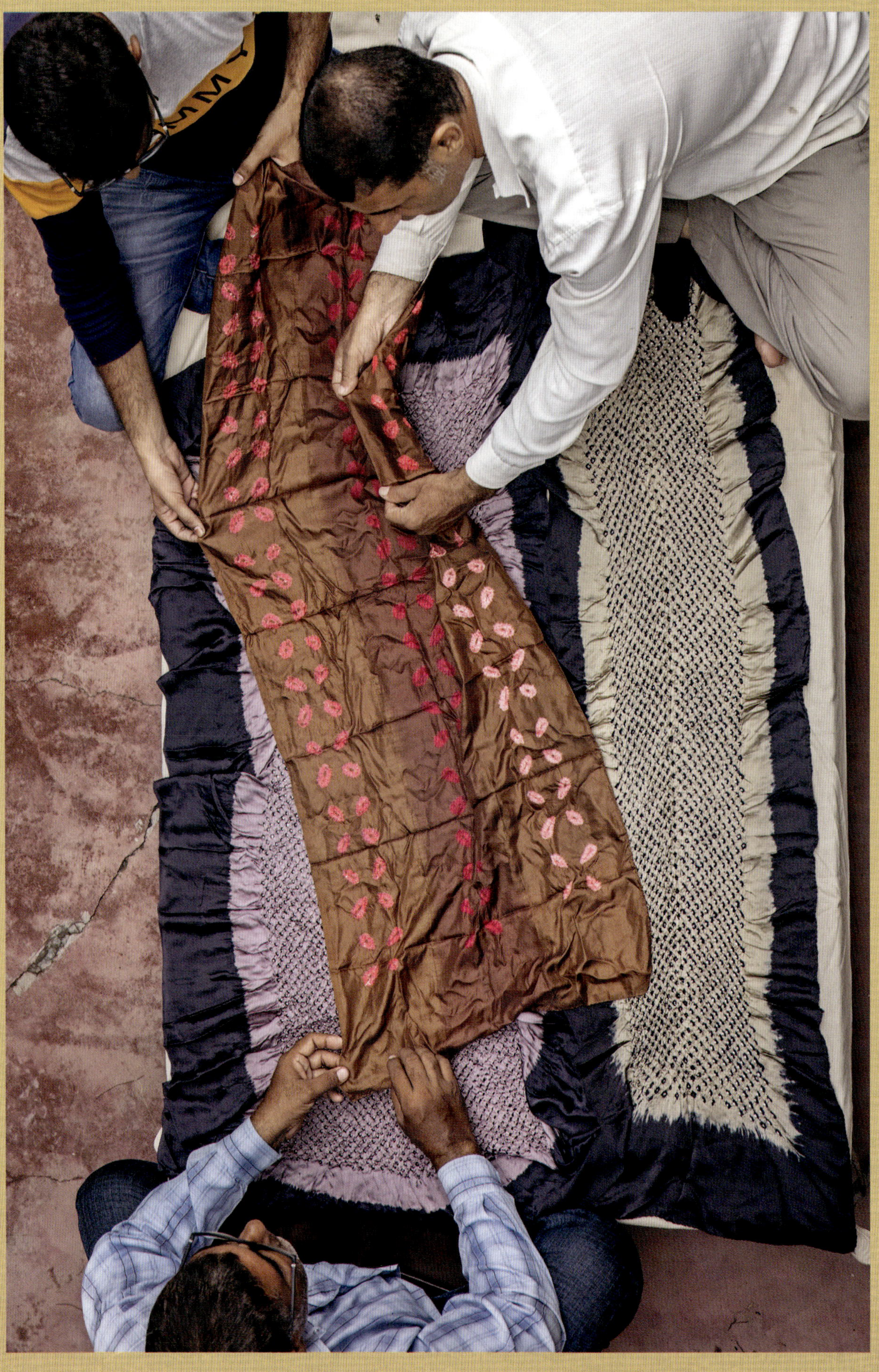

artisan adds, takes knowledge and experience into his work, and makes something new.

"An artisan is one who is learning," he said. "I'm still learning. There is no end to education. There is an Arabian story about a flying carpet. What was it made of? We've not thought of that. I think it was bandhani. Maybe there was a color or some other quality that made it fly. We can still reach that height. We will make a flying carpet. If there is an idea, it can be possible. An artisan has to find out how it is possible. I experiment from my understanding and my ideas. You learn by experience, not by books. I try to constantly find new possibilities in bandhani."

Alimamadbhai had a few extraordinary examples of his craftsmanship. In one, he made a *dupatta* with double dots of white and a dark ring and a dark border. He covered the dark edges and bleached the center to off-white, then opened the covered part and put the *dupatta* in boiling water. The excess color of the dark ran onto the off-white area, resulting in a color that emanates from the dark color. The combination is harmonious, and all the excess color is absorbed into the center area. The craftsmanship is in mixing the dark color. He used three colors—red, yellow, and green or blue in correct proportion. Carefully, he used excess of the color he wanted to migrate to the center. He understood how color behaves, which colors migrate faster at which temperatures. In another piece, he controlled temperature so skillfully that the bandhani dots were white on one side and red on the other.

Alimamadbhai lived what he believed. He understood proportion and balance in terms of his own capacity, and the importance of remaining an artist.

"By choice I work in limited quantity," he said. "I make less, but when a client takes my work, she returns and says your work is good."

In 1994, he met the renowned fashion designer Ritu Kumar in Delhi. She asked him to make a traditional *abho*, which he did. She loved it and asked him how many he could make. He told her three per month.

That isn't enough, she told him.

Opposite: Bhuj, 2022. Alimamad Isha passed away in 2021. A year later, his sons and grandson view his work. Alimamadbhai's bandhani is apart—glowing. It is art among commerce, living on as it was created. *Photo: Nevada Wier*

Above: Magic Dots scarf, by Alimamad Isha ca. 2018. Silk, azo-free acid dyes, bandhani. 22" x 56". Collection of the author. Alimamadbhai invented this design, in which the dots are white on one side and pink on the other, by thinking about the carbon paper used in typing. The great knowledge and skill in dyeing the design are astonishing. *Photo: Schiffer Publishing Ltd.*

He answered, "That is my capacity."

That year, Ritu Kumar dressed Sushmita Sen in Alimamadbhai's *abho* for the Miss Universe pageant. She told him she had bought *abhas* from him for RS 5,000 and with some value addition sold them for RS 60,000.

"Good for you," he answered, "But that does not change my capacity."

"If we are greedy and try to do more," Alimamadbhai said, "the quality changes and the whole art suffers. People say, 'Tie dye is bad . . . the color runs.' The client loses interest. The market goes down. Artisans become poor and the craft will be ruined. I believe in doing less but good. This is hand art, not a machine. The more patiently we work, the better we earn. When people see the art, they should realize it is worth it. Many times, people feel my work is underpriced. I take what is correct, and not more. I have never been told to make it cheaper."

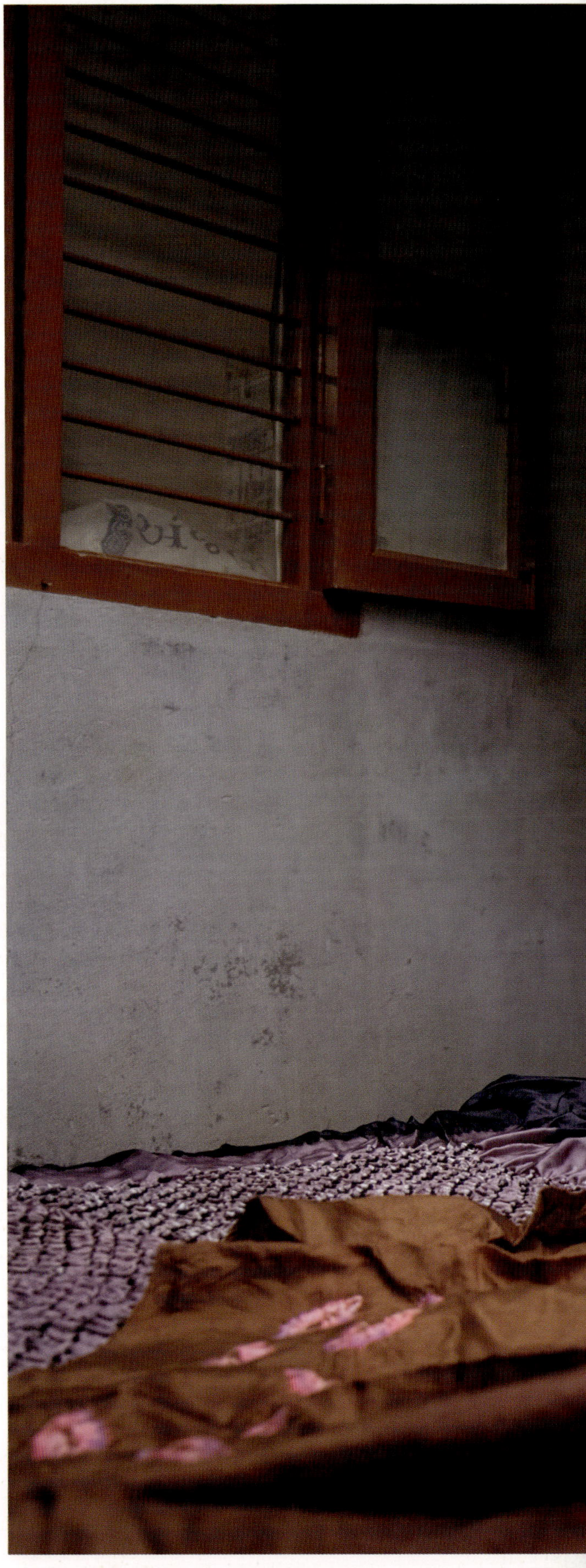

Bhuj, 2022. Alimamadbhai's grandson Saif ties bandhani now. He earned his engineering degree and now wants to study design at Somaiya Kala Vidya, where his grandfather was an advisor. People say that nature skips a generation. *Photo: Nevada Wier*

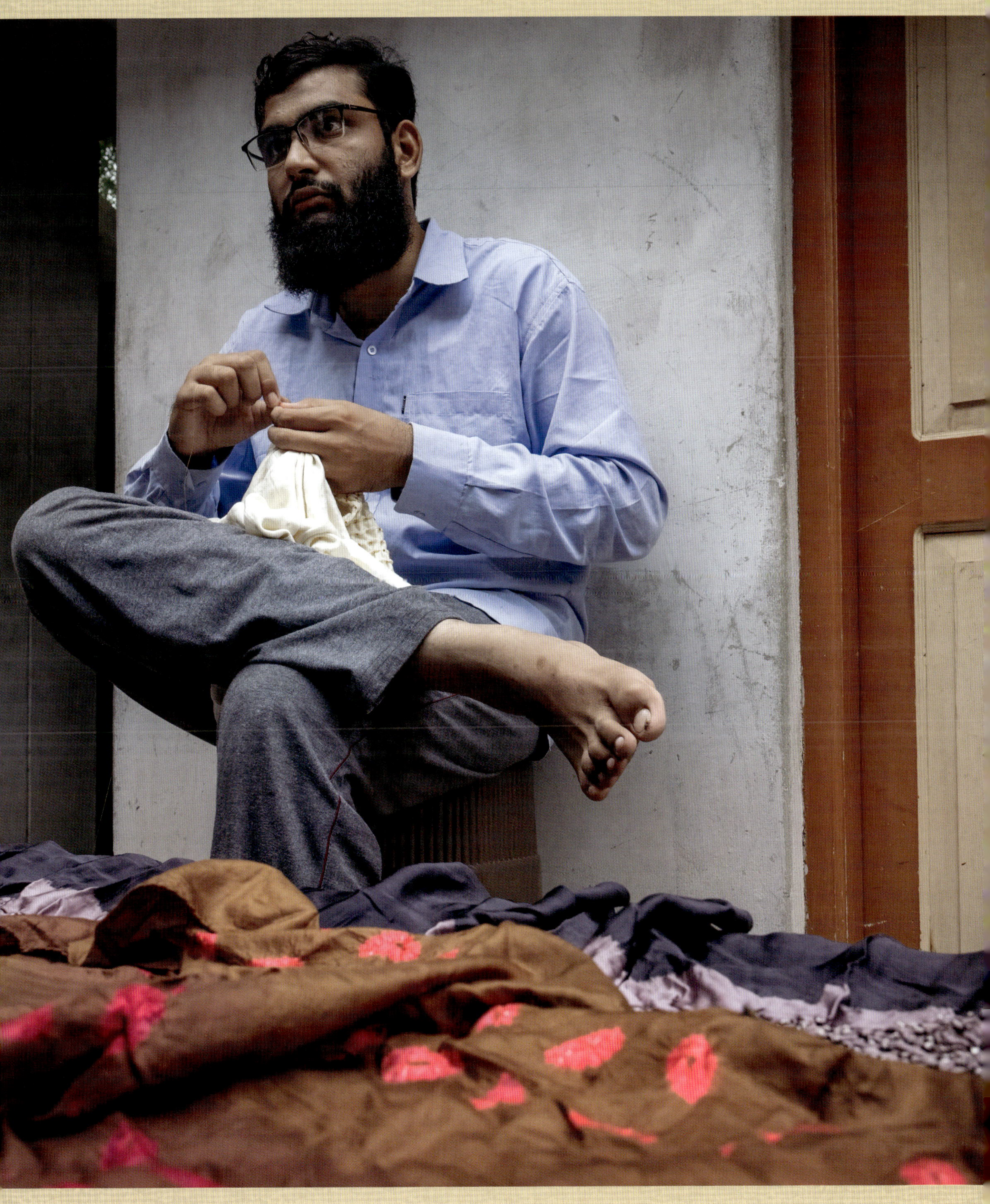

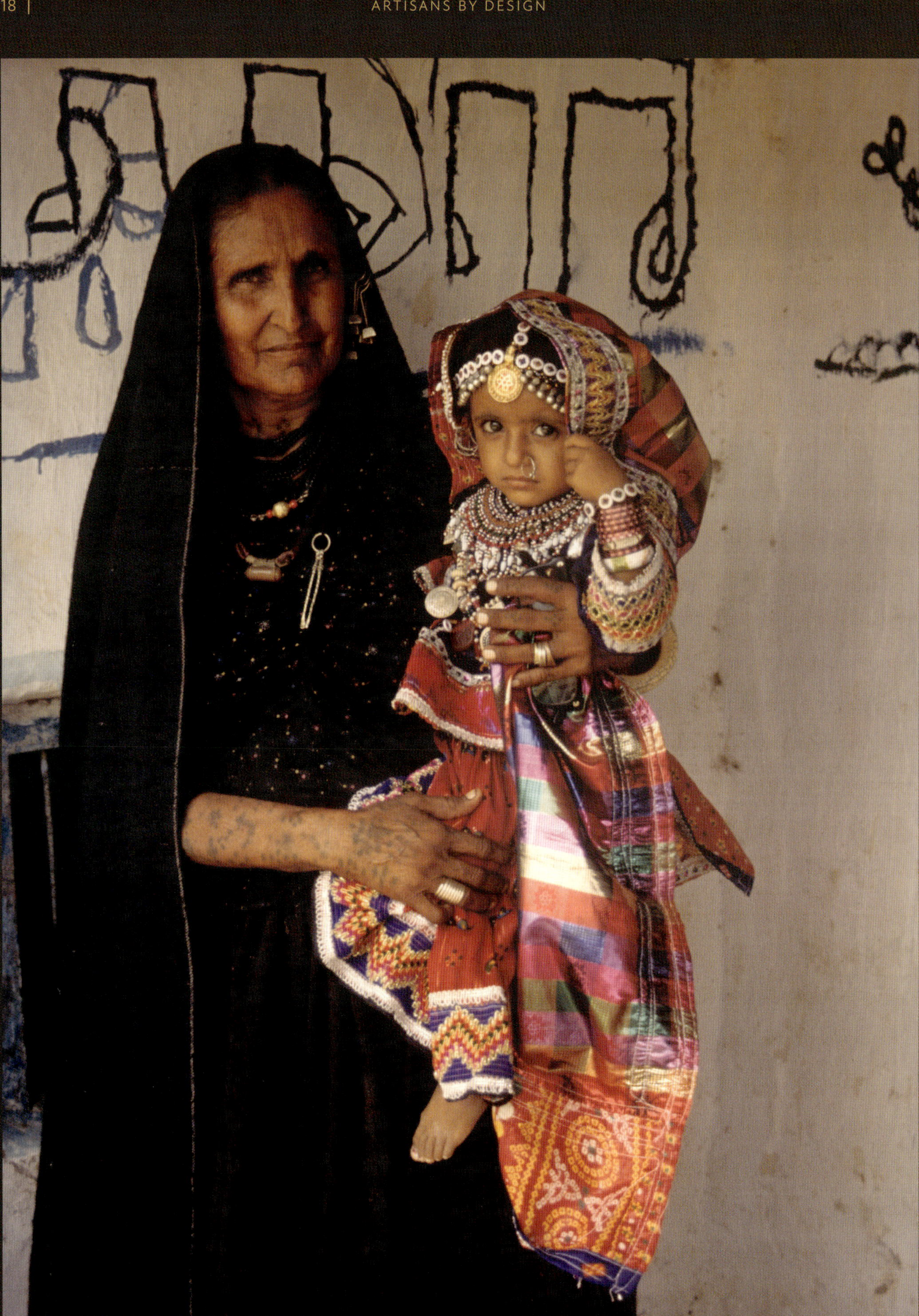

Chapter 3

EMBROIDERY AS CULTURE, COMMUNICATION: THE RESEARCH AND MUSEUM YEARS

1, 2, 3, 4, 5, 6, 7, 8, 9—nine different embroideries . . .
and all are Rabari.

~Harkhuben Bhojraj Rabari

When I was in fifth grade, Mrs. Helbig taught us batik. I took over my mother's kitchen, heating wax on the stove, painting on the table. I tried fabric printing, embroidery, tie-dye—any surface decoration I could find. The high school art department, kingdom of muralist Lou Vernon, was my haven of freedom and expression. Art was my passion, and when I began college, I intended to be an art student. I began by trying to convince the art department that textiles were art.

Within the first quarter of classes, I was accepted into a study abroad program in India. I thought I could learn advanced batik methods and find more-vibrant dyes there. Our group of seventeen students gathered for ten weeks of orientation. Since we would be based in Pune, we all learned Marathi. We studied Indian religion and culture and researched a topic of interest. I chose traditional art and pored over reference books.

We arrived in Pune in June 1970. I quickly realized that, for batik, I was in the wrong place. But there was art everywhere. I learned jewelry making from a hereditary goldsmith. Sitting with him and his nephew in a tiny workshop, I learned to forge by blowing the flame of a kerosene lamp through a brass tube, to make wires by pulling silver through graded holes, to hammer on an anvil—but so much more. Immersed in the community of artisans, I absorbed their comradery, their collaboration, and their knowledge. Most of all, I learned the heart of an artist. Vasant Rao would observe me struggling

Jhangi, 1993. A woman holds her granddaughter, who is lavished with embroidery and beaded ornaments for a wedding ceremony. *Photo: Judy Frater*

and say, "If the work does not come to you, leave it for some time. Go have a cup of tea and come back later." A poor man, when he finished an exquisite gold ring, he would take a moment to hold it up and appreciate it, then hand it to the customer.

When we had a break to travel, I persuaded two classmates to go to Gujarat and Rajasthan, because I had loved a film we saw on the textiles of this region. We pulled out the *Fodor's Guide to India* to plan. Kutch was a blank space on the map. It had only one road. "Let's go there!" I said.

My companions charmed an officer in the Bhuj District Headquarters into requisitioning a forest officer with jeep to take us around. We met Ahir artisans in Lakhond and Rabari artisans in Dhanetti. The austere women in black, with veils pulled over their faces, showed us vibrant, colorful textiles with dancing mirrored figures. I zeroed in on that; I would study the different ethnic communities and their embroidery styles.

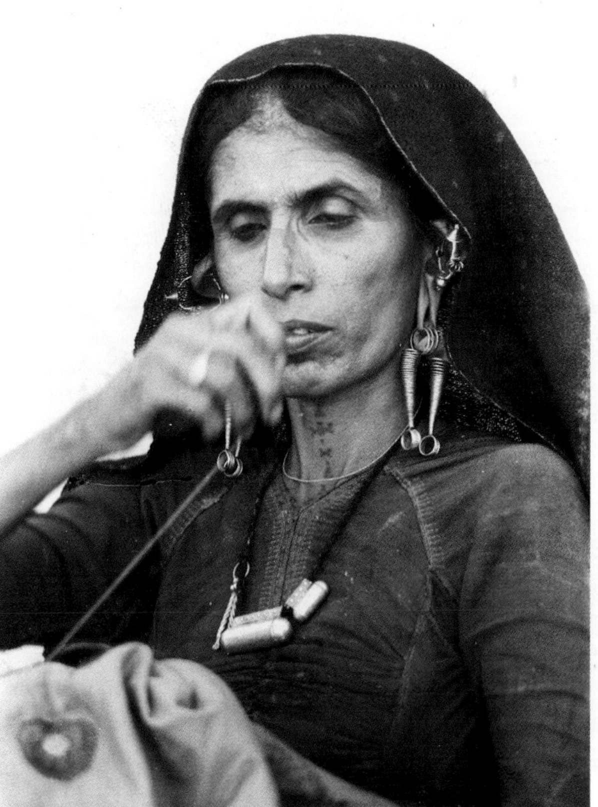

I made a few extra trips on my own, collected embroideries, talked to dealers mostly, and read the few books available at the time.

After six months, I went back to Wisconsin and dropped out of college. Sitting in classrooms reading books seemed irrelevant when there was a world from which to learn. Then a friend told me about a new program.

The year 1971 was a time of exploration in the education world. Lawrence University was looking for adventurous students to pilot a program in which the student designed and implemented his or her own course of studies. I proposed further language and research in India. I was accepted. I organized tutorials with Dr. William Stuart, a dynamic anthropology professor, who served as my advisor. I read beyond expectation; studied Marathi, Hindi, and tribal folklore; and returned to India to do fieldwork in 1972.

For six months, I lived with Kokni tribal people in Khandesh, learning about their sense of identity. But there were no textile crafts in Khandesh. My original questions about the expressive aspects of embroidery remained unanswered. After graduating, I proposed to study Rabari camel and sheep herders and create an exhibition of their textiles, to evoke their life in a way that viewers could grasp.

I received a grant and returned to Kutch from January to October 1974. Marathi was not useful here, so I searched for an interpreter. No one would send a brother, son, or husband with a twenty-three-year-old woman. No sister, daughter, or wife would travel with me either. So I picked up a *Teach Yourself Gujarati* book and plunged ahead. A friend took me to Bhujodi, at that time a distance by bus from Bhuj. He sought the headman, Khengarbhai, a shrewd man dealing in sheep wool on the side. Khengarbhai took me to his sister Jiviben, equally shrewd, who saw an opportunity. "I don't have a daughter here," she said. "You can live with me like a daughter." But when I returned, Jiviben was inexplicably gone, so Khengarbhai installed me in his home—for one night, he said.

Lachhuben Karna, his tough daughter-in-law, saw me as a burden and a threat. "There are no embroideries here," she said, fearing she might have to give or sell her precious work to me. It took weeks of patiently taking photos, recording songs, and playing with children before she felt safe enough to disclose her work. When I asked about the meaning of motifs, she brushed me off again. "They are

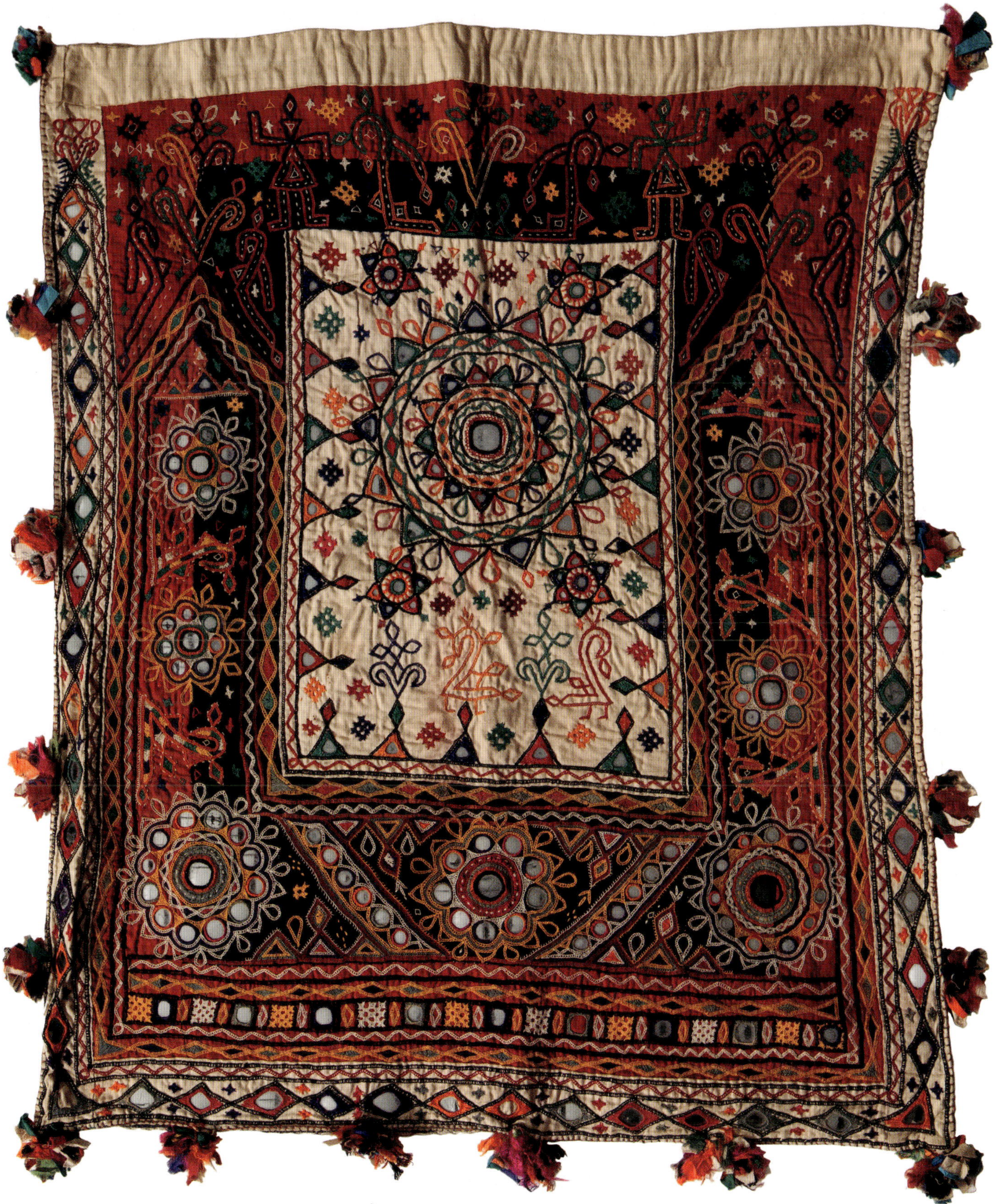

Opposite: Bhujodi, 1974. Lachhuben Karna Rabari, my first Rabari host, introduced me to the lifestyle and critical strategies of nomadic people. *Photo: Judy Frater*

Above: Kachhi Rabari *kothalo*, Nakhatrana taluka, ca. 1960. Cotton fabric and yarn, mirrors, Rabari embroidery. 30" x 34". Collection of the author. Nomadic Rabaris embroider a variety of bags to contain their belongings while they are traveling. The *kothalo*, which holds other embroidered dowry pieces, is closed with a string tied at the top. *Photo: Schiffer Publishing Ltd.*

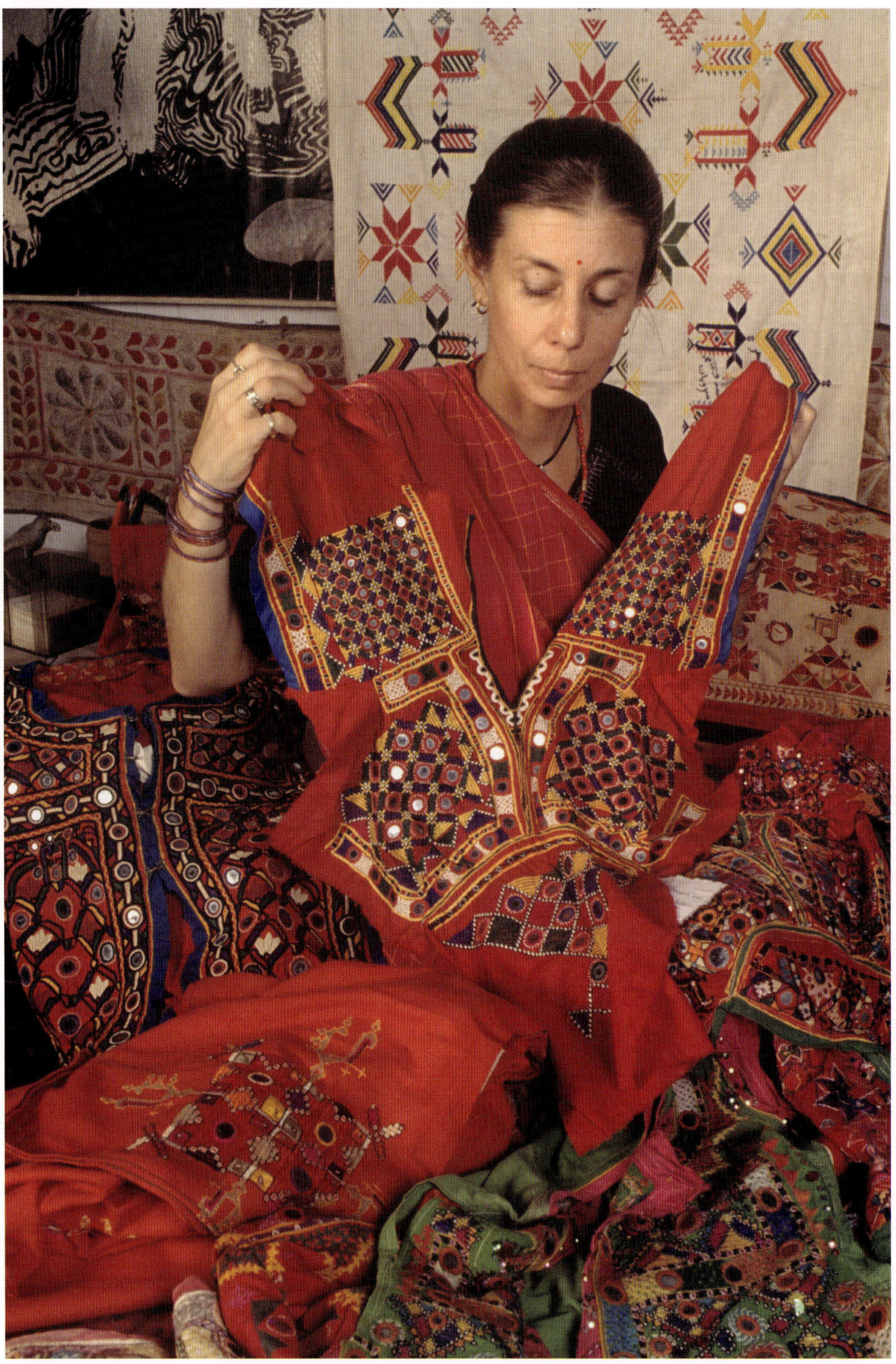

Delhi, 1991. On my Fulbright fellowship, I studied *suf*, *kharek*, and *pako* embroidery traditions from the Thar Parkar, Sindh Province, through immigrants who settled in Kutch after the 1971 Indo-Pak war. *Photo: Ravi Pasricha*

designs," she said. "Nothing more." More photos and tapes and trips to the bazaar with her daughter Rani. And slowly we built a rapport. I watched as she, Rani, and the next daughter, Devi, stitched directly onto fabric from their imagination. The needle was the pen; no need to draw before drawing. Their work did have meaning; it expressed their lives and community aesthetics. There were rules, and there was room for personal expression. Sometimes they discussed what would look good, which color would go where. Each motif, pictorial, or abstract had a name that referenced something in their world.

I traveled to Lachhuben's natal village Makhana, and to Sanosara, another village in which she had relations, and stayed for some time. I began to purchase embroideries, at first not in Bhujodi so as not to disturb relations. Lachhuben noted the parcels and asked to see what I had bought and how much I had paid. She decided this was an opportunity, and helped me make an inventory of what I should have in my exhibition. Khengarbhai knew a good deal and offered to help me have Rabari shoes made and to get some vessels and some of the cloths that had to be purchased—everything besides the embroidery. He took commission on all of it. When I realized that, I cried. But the Rabari world is tough. As Ramabhai told me years later, "If you wait for others before you eat, you may starve."

The family *barot* (genealogist) and elders filled me with legends and history. By October, I had ten months of context, and I could begin to read Rabari embroidery as a text, a story.

I went back to Wisconsin, installed the exhibition, and organized an exhibition tour with programs, hoping to give people a glimpse of a very different world and generate respect and value for the language of traditional craft. With the same goal, I published my first article in 1975 and did a master's degree, punctuated by two more trips to India.

I had postulated a theory of nomadic people adapting and maintaining aspects of identity and wanted to test it with other Rabari subgroups in Kutch, Gujarat, and Rajasthan. I wanted to see if I could trace Rabari migrations and articulate their history through the language of their embroideries and dress. I hoped to find something in common, a single mark of identity that would not change regardless of adaptations to local cultures over time.

In March 1983, I returned to India to spend a year and a quarter researching. Inevitably I collected embroideries, traditional garments, and jewelry. I understood that nothing can substitute for an object.

In each subgroup, dress and embroidery were different. Yet, within a region, one could easily discern Rabari people. What mattered was the coherence in each group, and that the embroidery told the stories and histories of the people who made and used them. I realized the personal quality of handwork. A textile gained another dimension because of the person who made it and the experience of finding and acquiring it. The simplest, humblest embroidery was the most valuable for me because of its history and value for the embroiderer.

I analyzed my experiences in a second master's degree. My conclusion was that Rabari identity is rooted in genealogy. As each subgroup migrated, they retained some elements and adapted others. It was the fact of retaining rather that what was retained that mattered.

I joined the Textile Museum, and soon after that I was awarded a Fulbright grant. It was an opportunity to fill gaps for an exhibition I was planning, and to continue my research. This time, I studied suf embroidery in Kutch because it seemed an anomaly. In fact, it is from the Thar Parkar desert of Sindh. So I learned about ethnic communities of regions spanning Sindh and Kutch, and *kharek* and *pako* as well as suf styles of embroidery. I was able to understand two categories of embroidery styles: regional and ethnic, reflecting different relationships between ethnic communities.

In one village of Thar Parkar immigrants, I found two very similar pako-embroidered bokanis. "Look!" I showed Harkorba. "The colors and patterns of both are nearly the same!"

"Yes," she rejoined. "I copied that one."

And with that I understood practically how a tradition works.

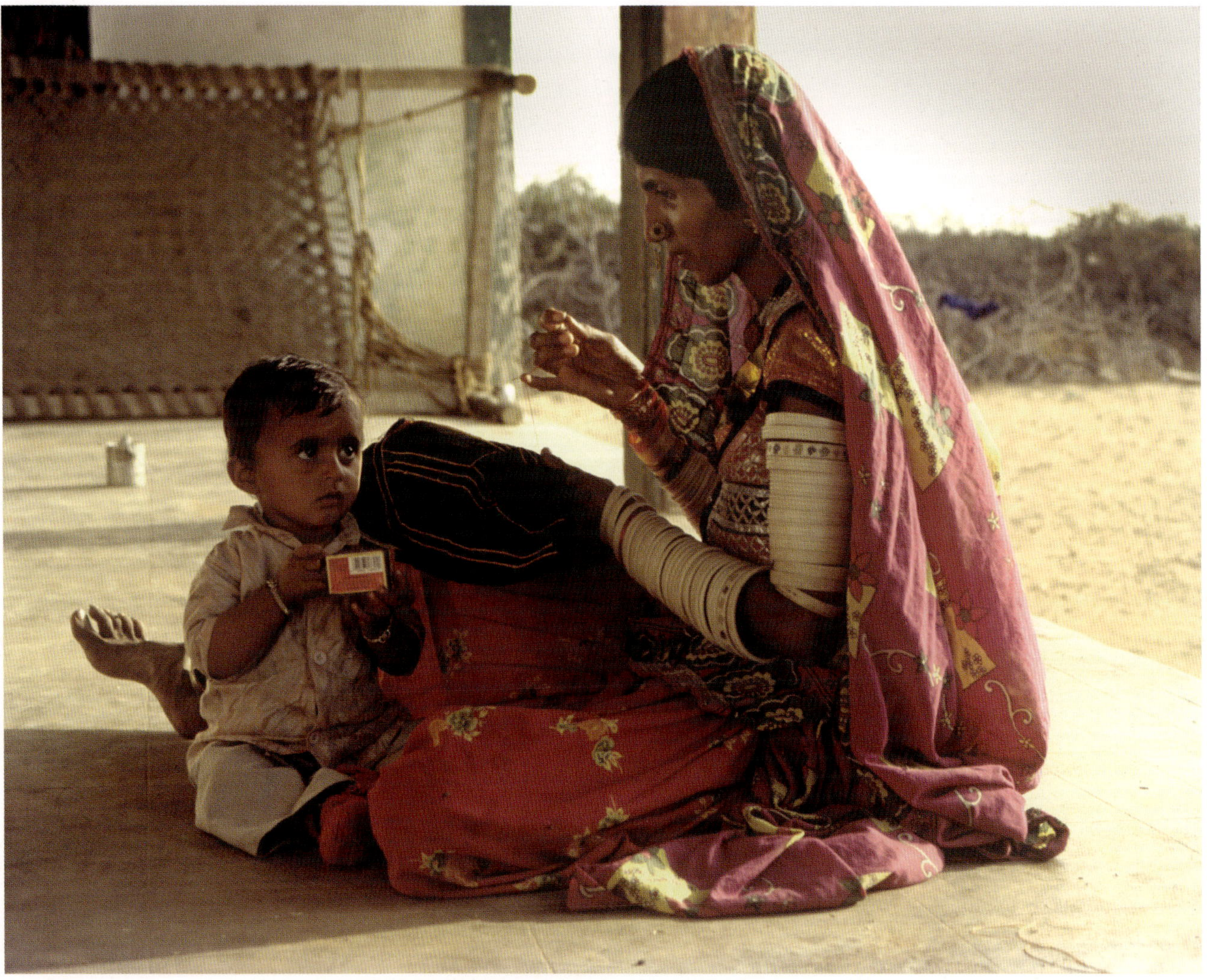

Staying in Kutch again, I resumed my connections with Rabaris too. By now, Lachhuben's children were grown and had children of their own. I had spent enough time and gained enough experience to observe the evolution of Kachhi Rabari work over more than the two decades I had spent researching in the context of their evolving world. I had experienced history.

I had read the stories of women, expressed within their culture and the layers of their identity.

Below: Moti Chher, 1991. A Sodha Rajput woman works on a pako embroidery. Regional embroidery styles, suf, kharek, and pako are practiced by many ethnic communities within a geographic area. *Photo: Judy Frater*

Right: Pragpur II, 1992. Maru Meghval women stitch suf and kharek embroidery, both styles counted on the warp and weft yarns of the fabric. Traditions evolve through study of other artisans' work. Dayaben Bhanani won the President's Award for craftsmanship with this example. *Photo: Judy Frater*

Following pages: Bhopani Vandh, 1994. Traditionally, Rabaris made their own bhunga, round one-room homes, from locally sourced mud and thatch. For a wedding, they covered interior walls with a set of elaborately embroidered hangings and beaded decorations. *Photo: Judy Frater*

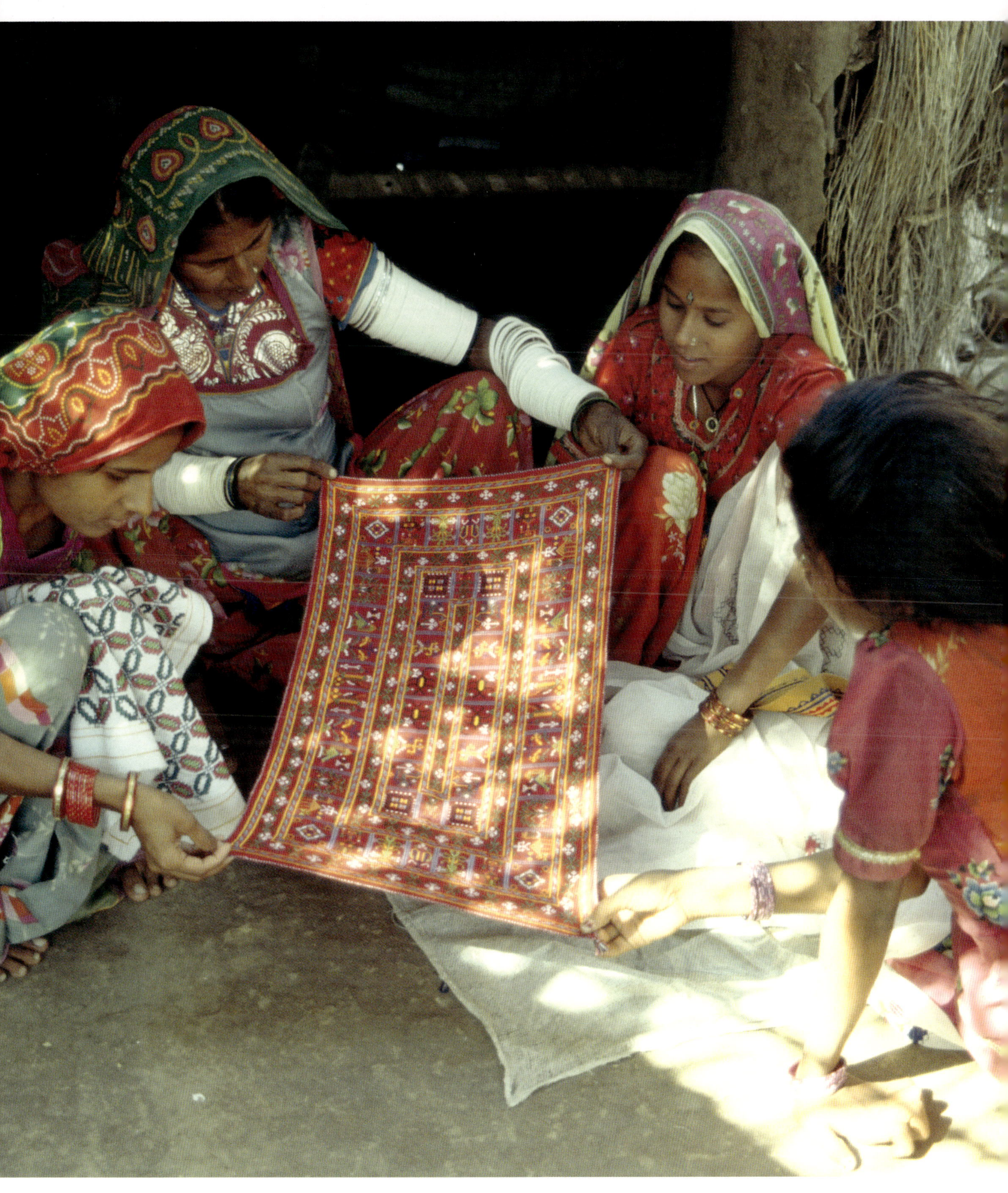

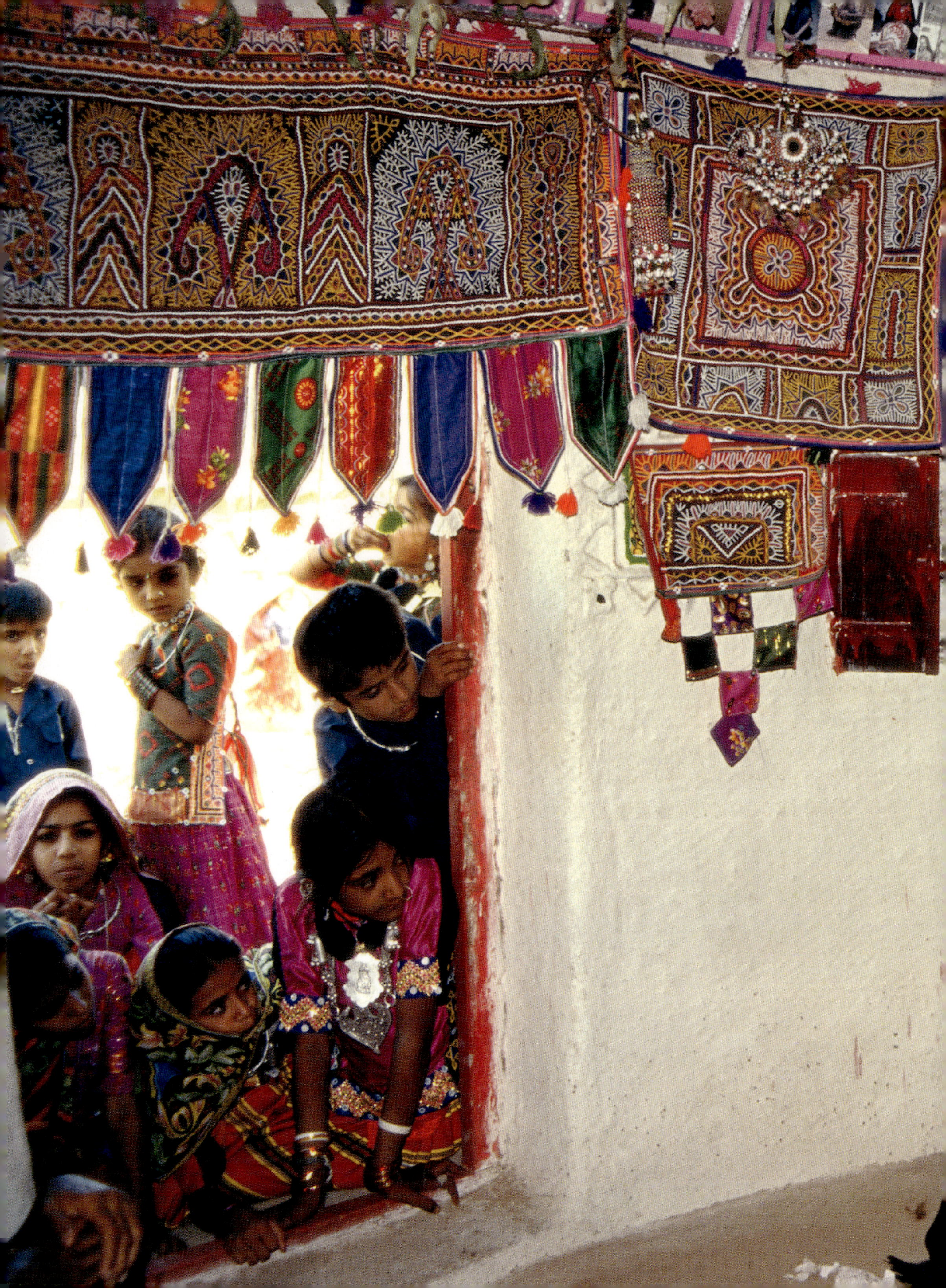

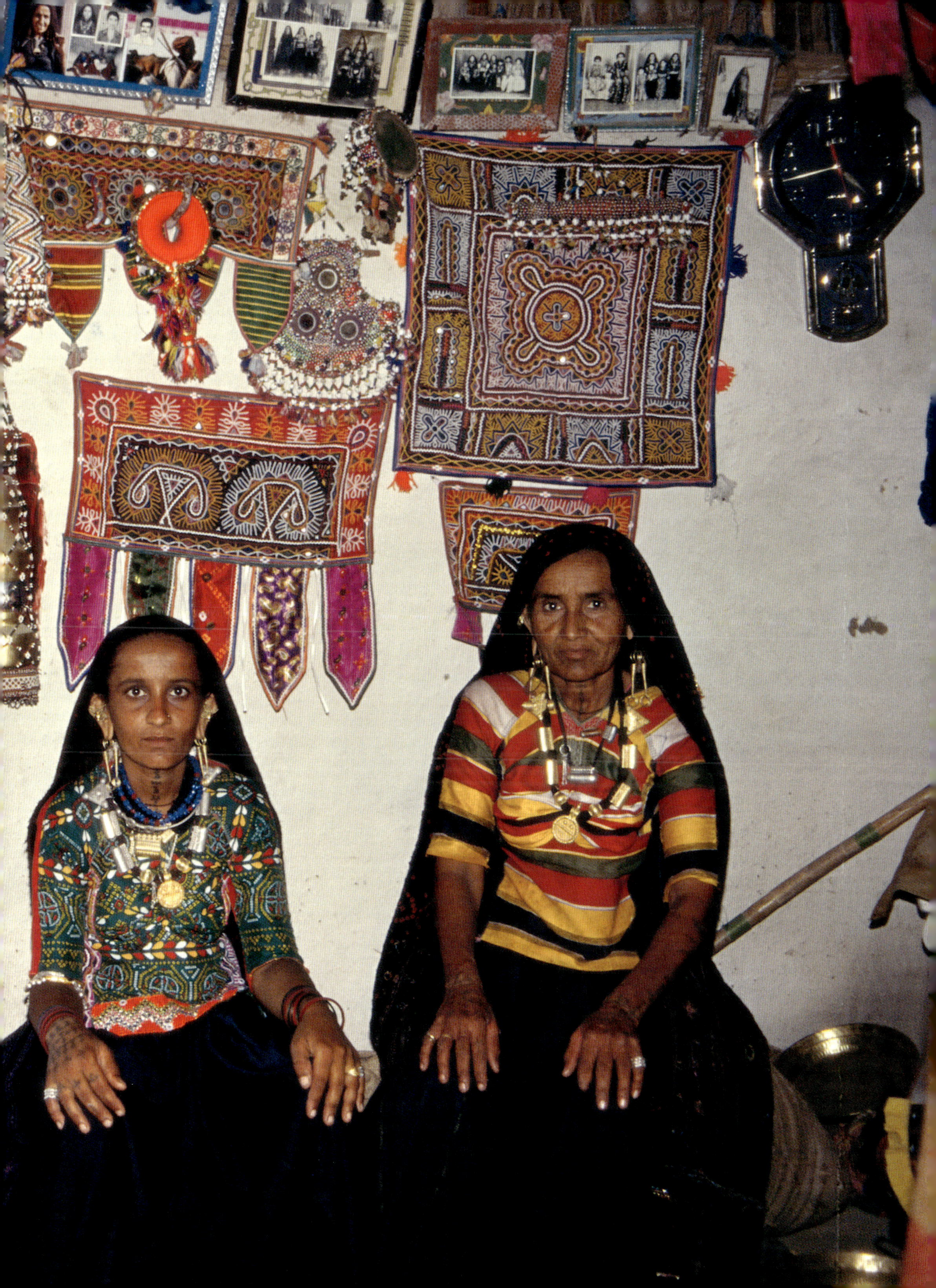

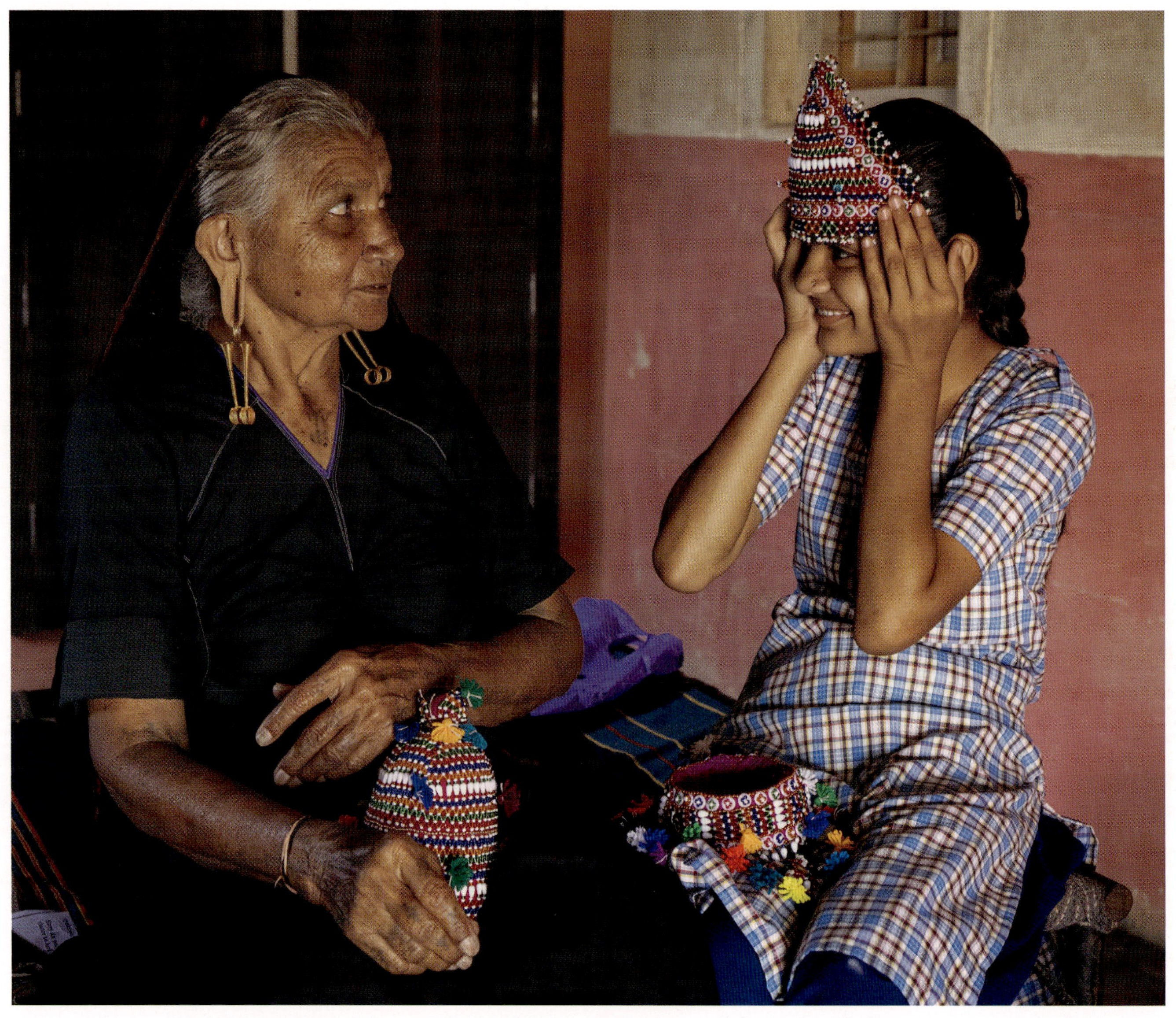

This is an art. You have to compose . . . or it won't look good. No matter how good your stitches are.

~Harkhuben Bhojraj Rabari

Above: Bhopani Vandh, 2022. Harkhuben and her granddaughter Sonu play with traditional beadwork. Sonu models a *mod*, a groom's wedding headdress. Grooms also carry beaded coconuts, and village women welcome the wedding-procession carrying pots on beaded *hindhoni*. *Photo: Nevada Wier*

Opposite: Nagor, 1996. Dhebaria Rabari women pack their belongings onto camels, ready to move to their next encampment. Dhebaria and Vagadia Rabari subgroups continue to migrate with herds of sheep and goats till today. *Photo: Judy Frater*

Chapter 4

HARKHUBEN BHOJRAJ RABARI: CURATOR OF RABARI TRADITION

Identity in India is layered. A person is a resident of a region, a member of an ethnic group, a member of a family, and an individual. In traditional societies, individual identity is subordinated by affiliation to community and family, nowhere more so than among pastoral nomads such as Rabaris. And in traditional societies, community affiliation is expressed by dress. Within a region, people quickly know community, marital status, and whether there is a festival or a time of mourning by the details of individuals' dress. Cultural heritage communicates.

For centuries, the nomadic Rabaris have moved with their herds and stitched with their skills and imagination.

"Where did embroidery come from?" Harkhuben Bhojraj Rabari rhetorically asks. She is a born performer and is basking in her opportunity to be recorded on film. "It was two hundred years ago . . .

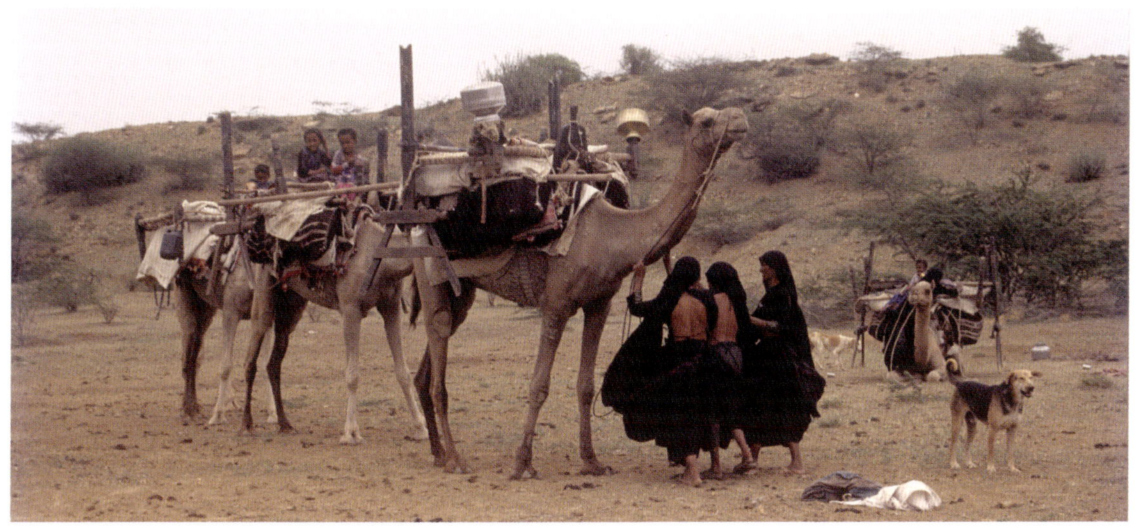

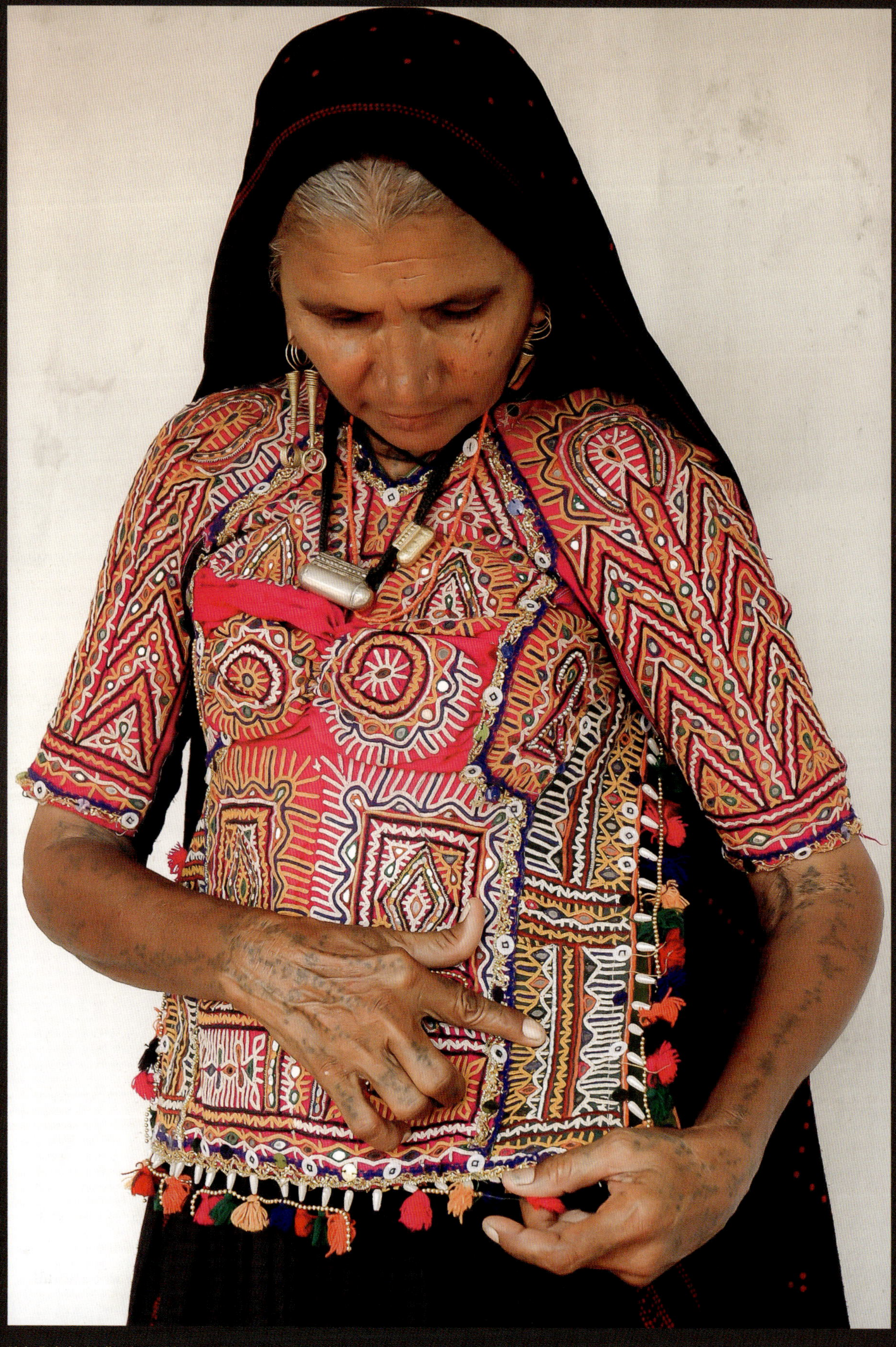

Kala Raksha Vidhyalaya, 2007. Harkhuben names the motifs of a *kanchali*, a traditional Kachhi Rabari festival blouse. *Photo: Judy Frater*

our subject was herding. There was no business as such. We drank milk and buttermilk. We took needles and embroidered. Someone intelligent must have come up with an idea . . ."

Harkhuben, a Kachhi Rabari, was born in 1947, the year of India's independence. She grew up in a family of camel herders in Sanosara and learned embroidery from her mother at the age of fifteen, when it was time to start working on her dowry.

She picks up an embroidered dowry bag. "For seven generations we have known this embroidery—seven generations! This *kothalo* is from seven generations ago. When we came to our in-laws' we brought our new clothes in it . . . *ludi, pachedo* . . . and this *kothali* is for *rotla*. We would make millet flat bread and keep it inside, to send with the daughter. We also embroidered a *gharanu* for wrapping *rotla*.

"We carried *rotla* when we traveled, when we were nomadic. We might have to stay overnight outside . . . we used to go by foot, or by camel or cart—there weren't vehicles then . . ."

Embroidery was never thought of in commercial terms. It was an essential part of social exchange. "We embroidered for ourselves, our friends, our relatives," Harkhuben says. "Besides that, we didn't embroider—never! There was never an idea of anything but for ourselves. It was like, I want to look good; if my embroidery is good, I will look good."

Tradition had rules developed by consensus. Women worked from a shared aesthetic, developed completely within the community. Harkhuben illustrates using the *kothalo*.

"First we do a *jharmar* border. We start with *kungari*, outline the top, then do a *buti* [freestanding motif, often floral], and that way we measure. Then we fill with mirrors in the middle. We do the center medallion first. Then, measuring with our hands, we set the mirrors for one corner. Then we measure and set mirrors for the next corner. Then we do the other side. After setting the mirrors, we embroider the center medallion and then the others.

"You have to measure first before stitching," she emphasizes. But Rabaris never drew motifs; they imagined them. "I work from my mind," Harkuben explains, "by estimation. No drawing, no printing, no measuring tape. By finger and hand—these are our measurements!"

Rabari women evaluated the design of embroidery independently of its technical quality. Composition was determined by the object. The *kothalo* would be closed by gathering and tying the top, for example, so women would not waste effort on embroidering much on the top. Color also had logic. "Color is what we consider first," Harkhuben says. She illustrates with a *kanchali* (blouse). "See, the body is pink. So we would make the sides purple or blue. Then we think of the embroidery. On the pink, first we do all of the black outline. Then we do the border, alternating yellow and white. Without a border it looks incomplete. The design has to stand out."

Many embroideries were made in sets, to be used together.

"When a daughter went to her in-laws' she needed six things," Harkhuben says. There were three *gupchi*s (envelope bags), a *kothalo* (dowry bag) a *kothali* (smaller bag), and a *gharanu* (food wrap). The *kothalo* was white, with black-and-red sides, and the little *gupchi* had a red center with black or white sides. They were related, color-wise, and unified by the embroiderer's hand, so it looked good.

"With a *toran* (doorway hanging) there were two *chakla* (square hangings), two small *toran*s, and two *latkaniya* (smaller hangings)—seven pieces. They would be embroidered with common motifs in each. This blouse is from my era, so with it we wore a *ludi* (veil) with *buti*s and a *pachedo* (skirt) with *chaini* (interlaced motifs)."

Harkhuben recalls her dowry of forty years ago with minute detail. "I made five *kanchali*, and all were different. I made an orange one with the going style—traditional. Then I embroidered a green one with four *nala* patterns and a border, a purple one with a half flower and teardrop-shaped mirrors, a black one with half flowers and mirrored flowers, and a maroon one. Each of them was different. It looked good. And otherwise, people would say she did only one embroidery. If they see the same old thing it's not interesting, but if it's new, they say, 'Oh, she brought something new!'

"But it has to fit. For example, for my dowry I made a *ludi* with a medallion with eight mirrors. Eight! I wore it to my in-laws' home in Vandh. When I saw the fashion was different there, that very night I cut out all of the mirrors and embroidered *kharakli* motifs instead!"

Harkhuben understands that tradition as evolving. "I'm old, and I wear what is of my time," she says. "And now it's come back! It's traditional and it's come back. First, we did running stitch. Then it evolved to chain, and it looked nice. At first, we did a simple chain stitch. Then a tighter one. Then, we did backstitching . . ." She organizes some collection pieces chronologically to illustrate.

"1, 2, 3, 4, 5, 6, 7, 8, 9—nine different embroideries . . . and all are Rabari.

"Now my daughter and my daughter-in-law will do something different.

"It's like this. Lakhi embroidered that border. Right? My daughter-in-law and daughter will see that and get an idea. That's how embroidery evolved—seeing and copying! We used to compete like that. Even today, it's like that. They will see that Lakhi has done something new and think, 'It looks good, and I'll do something better.'

"This is an art," Harkhuben says. "Art comes from the mind. You need intelligence above all. It's not a question of education. If one doesn't have a mind, they have nothing. If there wasn't art—if we didn't use intelligence and just embroidered, went on making chain stitch and mirrors—it wouldn't look good. There has to be balance. You have to think what goes where. If you do whatever, you have to take it out. You have to compose. If you have too much white or yellow, it won't look good. No matter how good your stitches are."

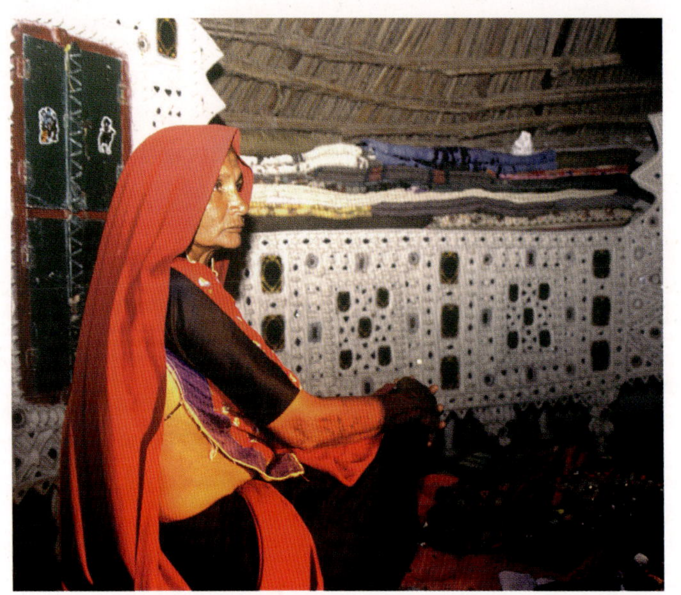

It is 2009. Harkhuben has embroidered commercially since the 1980s. She is skilled at mud relief work, beadwork, and appliqué as well as embroidery. Her arts have taken her to Delhi four times, Mumbai three times, Ahmedabad, and Bhopal. The earthquake that ravaged Kutch in 2001 spared the traditional round mud bhunga for which her village Bhopani Vandhi was famous. "As long as I'm alive, I will live in my bhungo," Harkhuben vowed.

But the onslaught of post-earthquake industry targeted the village squarely. Two 4,600-megawatt, coal-fed thermal power plants surround Vandh now, engulfing it in pollution. Nearly everyone in the village now earns from power-plant-related menial jobs. And Harkhuben bulldozed her *bhungo* in 2008 to build a cement house.

Working for wages, women have little time for embroidery. Time has come to consciousness, consuming the patience that embroidery requires.

"In the old days, embroidery needed a lot of effort," she reflects, "and there was art. In traditional work, we learned, understood, and did fine work, needing effort, intelligence, and precision. The intelligence of this work was its regularity. If the embroidery composition and technique are balanced, it looks good. In old times we had enthusiasm. We were into it because we didn't have to earn. Now there is inflation. Everything is getting expensive.

"As we thought only how to work quickly, the tradition was lost; embroidery became crude and without art. Now, we embroider for money. Now we don't starve. We can eat *double roti [leavened buns]* in restaurants. It wasn't like that before—we could never even get tea! Today people don't go hungry.

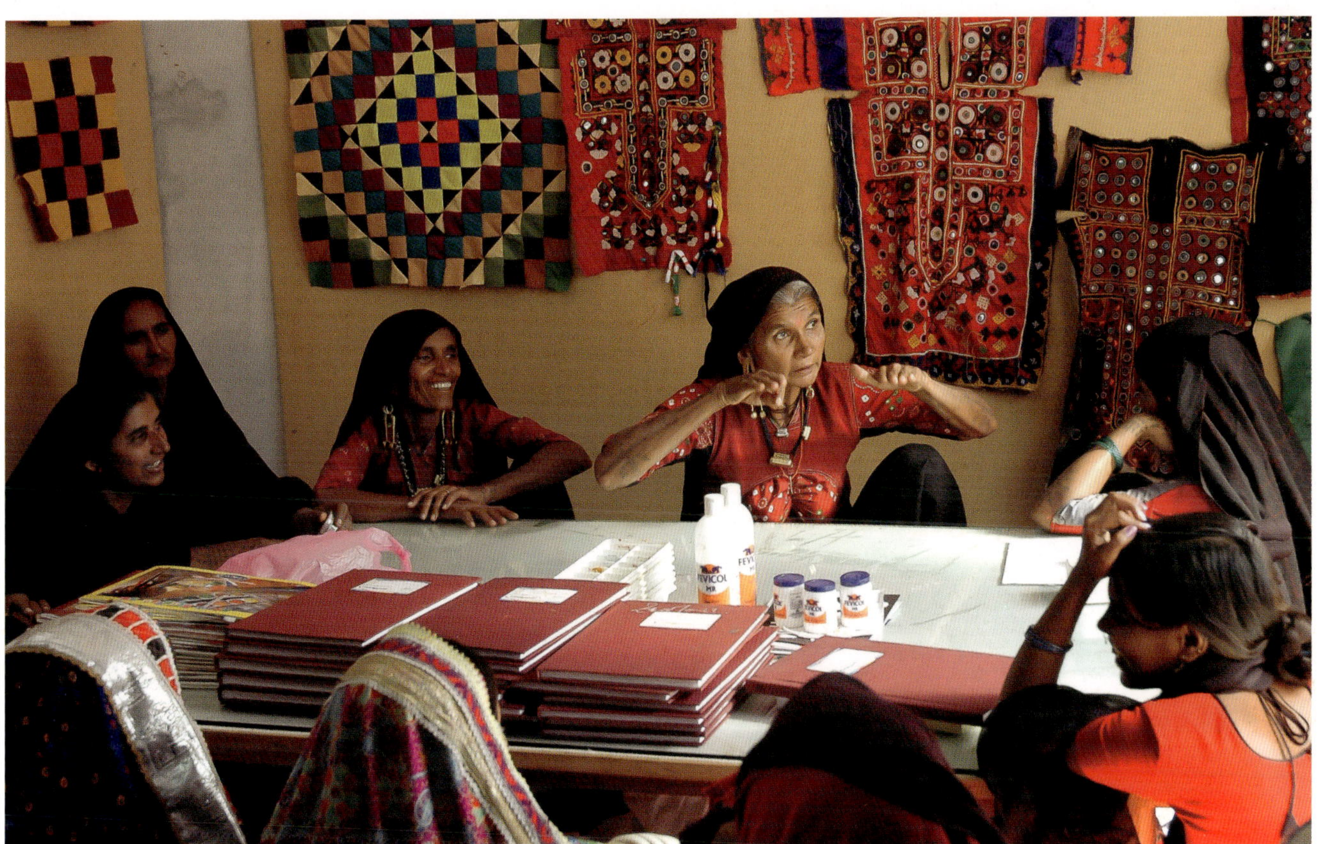

"For our own work now, we use only one color [of] cloth and one color [of] thread all the way through. We use machine embroidery and just add mirrors. It's fast!! There's no effort in this. Times have changed, embroidery has changed, and our subject has changed."

Fashion and design came into Rabari consciousness. The change was in the degree and pace of change. In 2007, Harkhubben took the yearlong design course at Kala Raksha Vidhyalaya and graduated with the award for best presentation.

"We learned to be inspired by themes and to mix our own style with new ideas," she said. "Now we can expect to meet the market needs. If we are confident and use our own intelligence, it will bring both us and Kala Raksha benefit.

"If we have art, we can learn design," she reflected. "Craftsmanship is the ability to do. An artisan is someone who can do everything, can design, do any work, compose. That's an artisan—we can do it all."

We look at work done by a young Rabari woman for her impending wedding. The fabric is bright royal blue, and the stitching white and tomato red. She had the outlining done in machine embroidery and left space for the hand-embroidered accents she planned. "First I outlined another pattern," she says. "But it didn't look good. I was going to do all *bavaliyo* [interlaced stitch], but it wouldn't have looked good, so I thought to mix *bavaliyo* with *bharat* [chain stitch and mirrors]. When it's done, both will be there. My inspiration was fashion. I saw a *chaniya-choli* in a bazaar with bright colors, and thought, 'Why not make our clothes in these colors?'"

Will this new work be recognized as Rabari? I ask.

Harkhuben answers without hesitation. "Yes. This is contemporary Rabari!"

Opposite: Bhopani Vandh, 2005. Harkhuben in her mud-and-thatch *bhungo*. She wears the maroon veil of a *Bhopi*, a woman shaman. The village is named for its prevalence of shamans. *Photo: Judy Frater*

Above: Kala Raksha Vidhyalaya, 2007. Early in the first class, Color: Sourcing from Heritage and Nature, Harkhuben entertains her classmates, including pako and suf embroiderers, with stories of Rabari embroidery traditions. *Photo: Judy Frater*

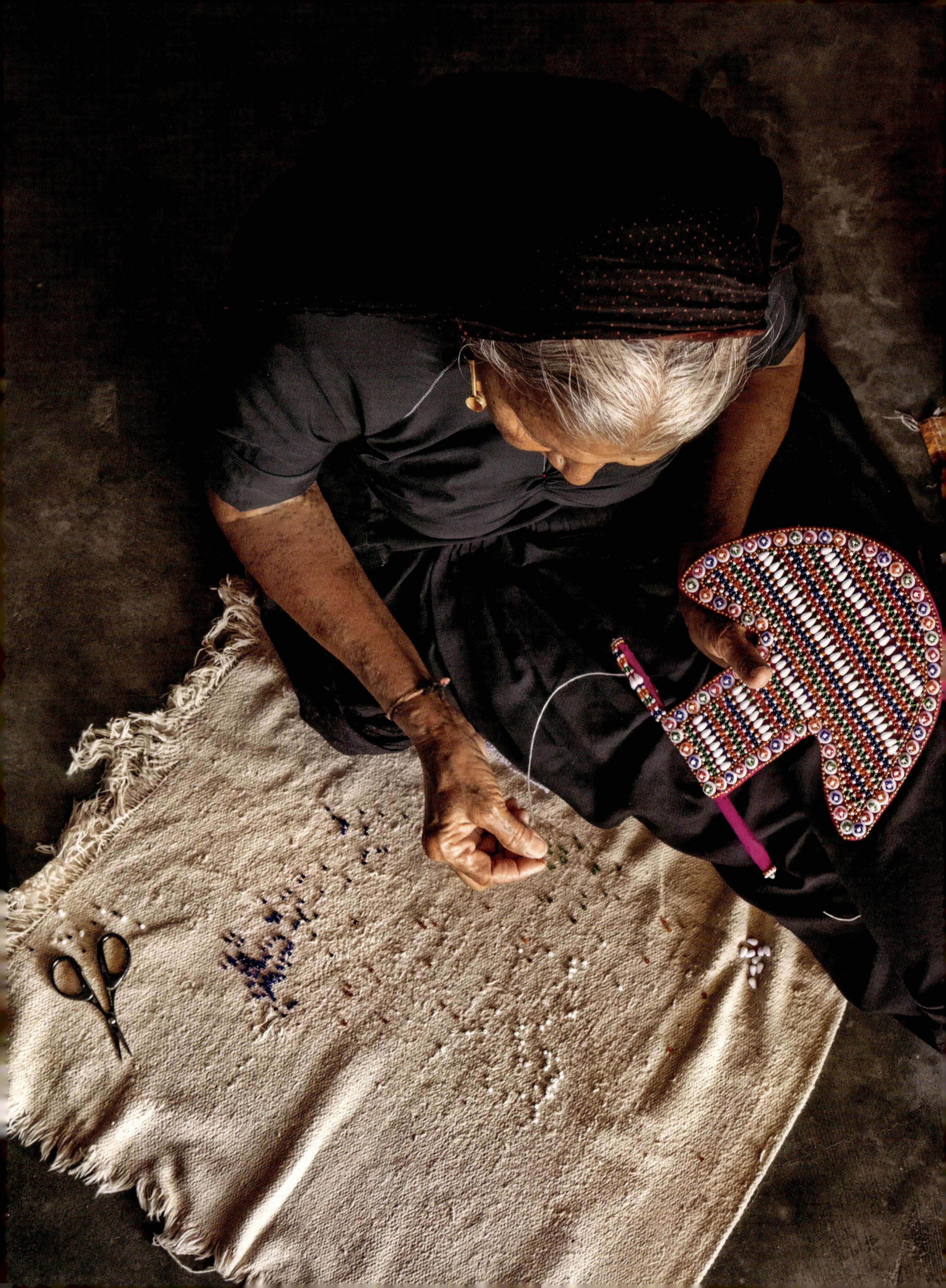

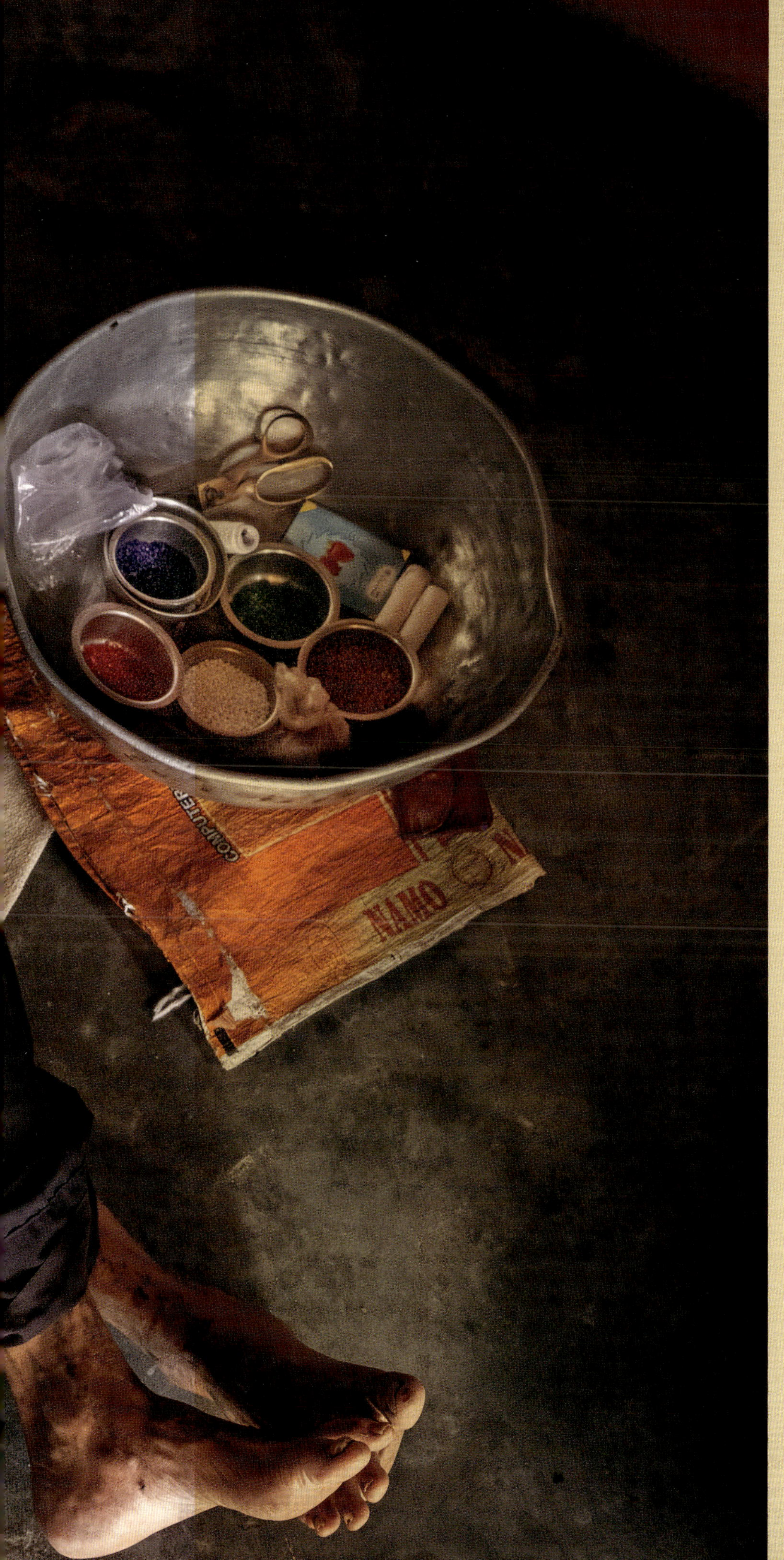

Harkhuben expertly beads a *vinjano*, a ceremonial hand fan. Bhopani Vandh, 2022. *Photo: Nevada Wier*

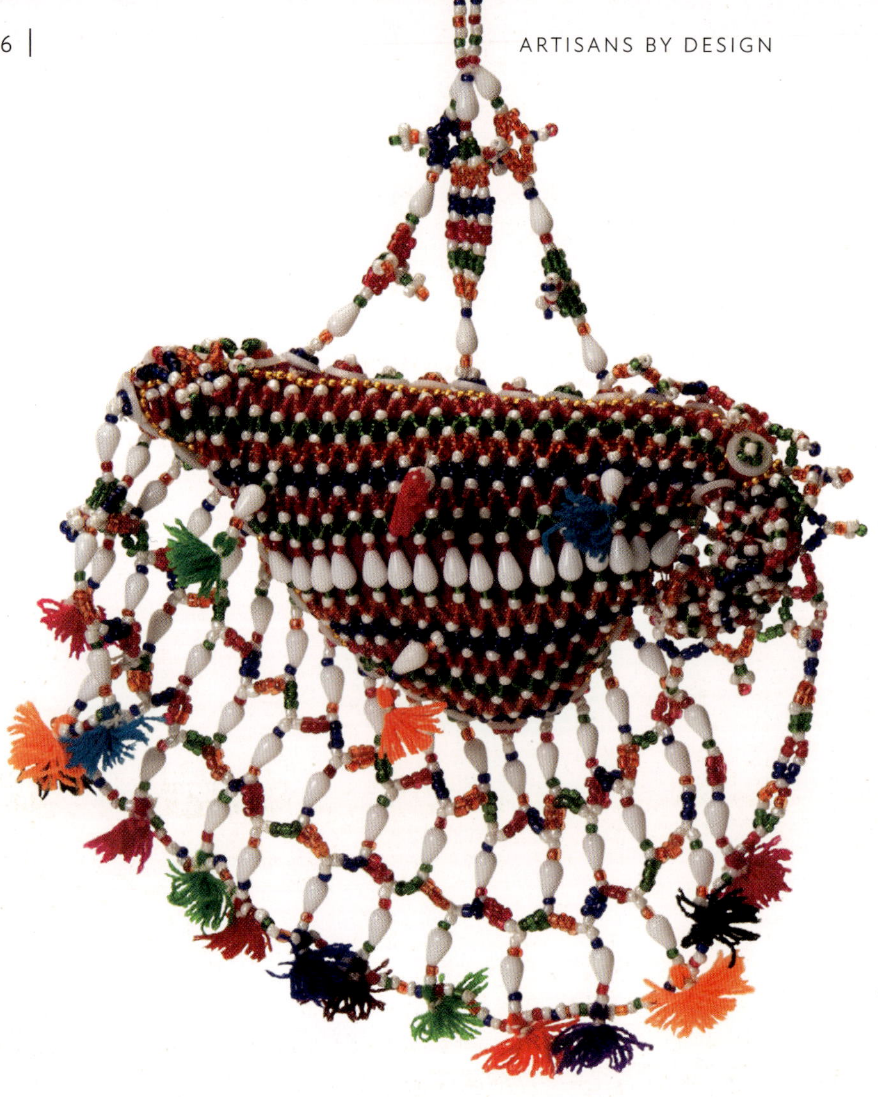

2022

Bhopani Vandh has survived COVID-19, a social earthquake, without a single fatality. Harkhuben has a steady microenterprise, making beadwork for her own community. Rabari women love beadwork as well as embroidery and still want it for their dowries and ceremonial occasions. But they don't have the time or patience to create handwork. Harkhuben knows their taste, so she can innovate appropriately, without any worry about whether her clients will like it. Sitting on the floor of her cement home, she is surrounded by glass beads and traditional beaded objects. There is a *mod* (groom's turban ornament), a *popat* (parrot), and a *hindhoni* (pot balancer), and now she is working on a *vinjhano* (fan). She dangles the *popat*, tantalizingly. "These are for an order," she says. "You taught us to always do new designs, so I made a parrot with a new shape and new plastic dangles."

Her granddaughter Sonu models the *hindhoni*. "This one is mine," she says. Love for things traditional endures. Sonu picks up the *vinjhano* in process. Harkhuben can't resist showing her how the beadwork is done. "I already know it," Sonu says. Indicating the order of colors, Harkhuben asks, "Where does the white go?" There is always more to learn—critical details. Innovation comes only after mastery.

▼ ▼ ▼

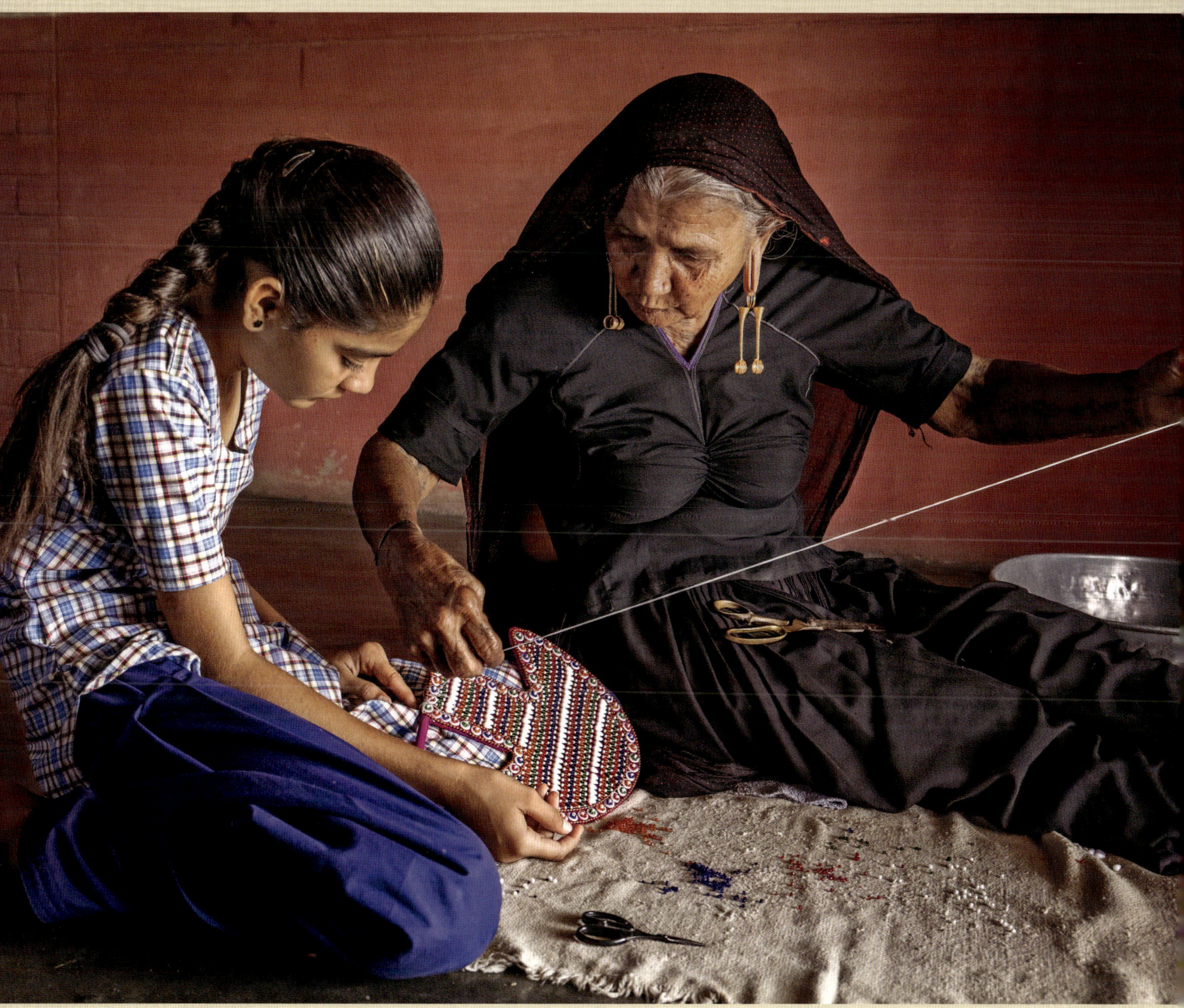

Opposite: Popat, by Harkhuben Bhojraj Rabari, 2022. Glass beads, synthetic cowries, acrylic tassels, and buttons over a cotton base. 7" x 11" plus hanging string. Kachhi Rabari artisans make a variety of beaded decorations. A beaded parrot hangs above a cradle to entertain and fascinate the baby. *Photo: Schiffer Publishing Ltd.*

Above: Bhopani Vandh, 2022. Harkhuben demonstrates proper beadwork to Sonu. Details matter. *Photo: Nevada Wier*

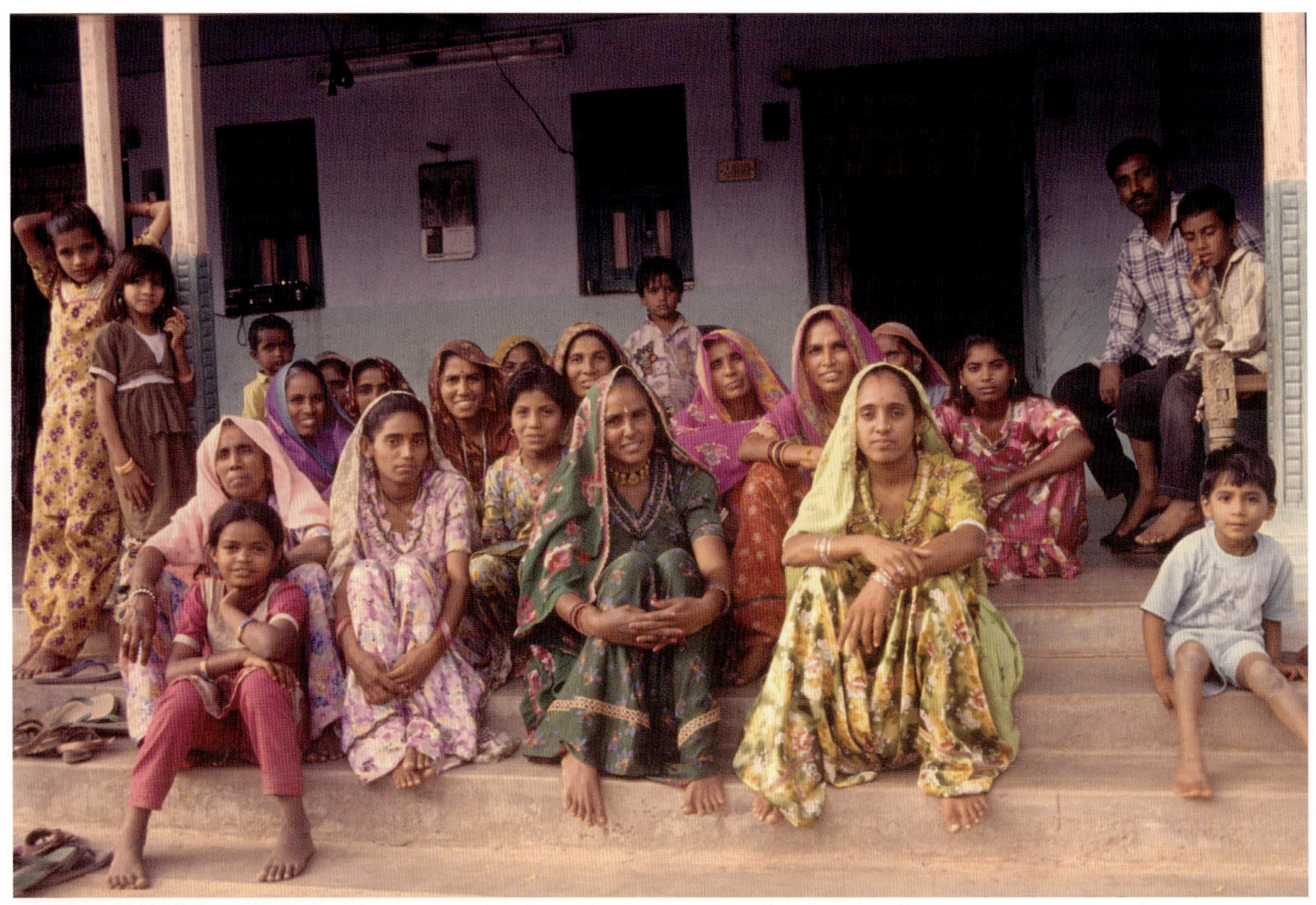

You don't even know our names.

~Babraben Moru Bhanani

Sumrasar Sheikh, 1994. Prakashbhai Bhanani (*far right*), his sister Dayaben (*lower row, right*), a group of twenty-five suf embroiders, and I began Kala Raksha Trust from Prakashbhai and Dayaben's home in 1993. *Photo: Judy Frater*

Chapter 5

FROM INCOME GENERATION TO CULTURAL EMPOWERMENT: THE KALA RAKSHA YEARS

"Why are you studying us? Why don't you *help* us?"

The question, boldly posed by Dayaben, a self-confident young suf embroiderer, startled me out of my documentation of suf embroidery and culture of Thar Parkari embroiderers. Dayaben was one of those embroiderers, and she popped off the page and made me see from her perspective.

Her family had brought her as an infant when they fled from Nagar Parkar, Pakistan, to India in 1972. They crossed the Rann of Kutch with their caravan of camels, carts, quilts, and prized embroideries, only to be confined to Indian government camps in Kutch until 1980. During that time, they struggled to make ends meet, selling most of the embroideries, men doing menial labor, women doing embroidery for equally menial wages. Dayaben's father, Ratilalbhai Bhanani, a teacher, initiated a school to teach Gujarati and basic reading and writing to camp members. The government was so impressed that it gave the school official standing.

The refugees were finally given citizenship in 1980 and plots of undesirable land in a few selected villages. The Bhananis are from a dalit[2] caste. They assessed the village to which they were allocated and decided to purchase their own land in Sumrasar Sheikh, a village that would be politically more comfortable for them.

By 1990, the family still needed more income than Ratilalbhai and his sons could earn, and Dayaben was still embroidering for minimal wages for a nongovernmental organization (NGO). She wanted more and saw me as someone able to provide better options.

I pondered Dayaben's question: Why *was* I studying the embroiderers?

The commercialization of craft had begun in the 1960s. Design was introduced as "intervention," and designers quickly stepped in to intervene. Embroidery had never been created for trade, and embroiderers were especially vulnerable to exploitation. In 1974, I watched the schoolteacher of Bhujodi open his briefcase and take out pieces of fabric for Rabari women to embroider. I was distressed by the commercial work. It had little basis in the rich traditions. Worse, designed by someone and given to embroiderers, it left no opportunity for creativity. It was simply labor work. Women made a clear distinction between commercial work, which they called *majuri kam*—the same term they used for construction work—and the traditional work they did for themselves.

Over the years, I had come to believe that there wasn't immediate danger of erosion of traditions; artisans did not like the commercial work they had to do to earn a livelihood, so those styles had not seeped into their own work. But it occurred to me that one day there may be no embroidery other than commercial work. So I was frantically documenting tradition before it was lost.

Dayaben made me realize that artisans now had to earn. I wondered, might there be another way to preserve a tradition while it was still living? Might artisans be able to earn while practicing their traditions? Could they have agency in commercial work?

I assessed my position from a new perspective. As a curator at the Textile Museum, I had some status and some connections. I knew a bit about suf embroidery and a bit less about the market. I contacted Aid to Artisans. They told me that the Ford Foundation had lots of money for projects. The woman I met at Ford Foundation laughed at that but said they did have some funds for women's income generation projects. However, they could not give funding to an individual; they could give only to an organization. Find a good one to work with was her advice, or start your own. I looked around and decided that Dastkar in Delhi and SHARE in Mumbai were good fits—Dastkar for the domestic market and SHARE for export. I thought it would be good to work with both organizations. They did not agree, so I chose Dastkar. A domestic market is within reach of artisans, and they could grow from the feedback they received.

Dastkar and I received a Ford Foundation grant and began the Dastkar Kutch Project. It would work with three of the communities I had studied on my Fulbright grant: Maru Meghvals in Sumrasar, Sodha Rajputs in western Kutch, and, of course, Rabaris. I formed a team to begin. Dayaben's brother Prakashbhai had been working with me as a research assistant. He understood and loved embroidery and wanted more value for artisans. Raniben, my Rabari friend in Bhuj, had helped me make embroidered clothes for myself and had connections to artisans. Both Prakashbhai and Raniben had also helped me collect some good examples of traditional work. For the Sodha Rajputs, Harkorba, who had helped with my research, would coordinate embroidery.

Laila Tyabji, chairperson of Dastkar, came to Kutch and launched the project by giving stitched kurtas to each group, with kits of matching threads. The coordinator of each group would supervise the work and collect it for Dastkar's next visit. Dastkar would sell it in their shop in Delhi. Soon after we inaugurated the project, I was due to return to the Textile Museum, so we hired an overall coordinator and set up a small office in Bhuj.

One of the main things I had learned during my Fulbright fellowship was the essence of tradition, why and how it exists. Access to excellent work ensured traditions. Yet, artisans could not often afford to be sentimental. They sold their art to dealers, tourists, and collectors like me to survive.

For the Ford grant, I made sure to include building a collection of traditional embroidery as a resource base for contemporary work. Ford generously offered me an individual grant to make the collection, so after eight months I returned to Kutch.

I went straight to Sumrasar to see how the project was going.

OK, they said. But from Prakashbhai's and Dayaben's faces, I knew it was not. Finally, they told me that they embroidered the kurtas and sent them off to Delhi and that that was all they knew.

They wanted to know more?

Yes, they emphatically said. Why can't we start our own organization?

In Sumrasar, they had a group of twenty-five or so suf embroiderers eager to earn. They had almost a year of experience working with Dastkar. Most important, they were motivated. So our suf group left the Dastkar Kutch Project and set up Kala Raksha Trust. Prakashbhai was the chief executive. I was the program coordinator. Full of adrenalin and hope, we began. The first thing I implemented was natural materials—no blended fabric and no rayon thread. I capitalized on the goodwill of people I knew with craft businesses and got orders.

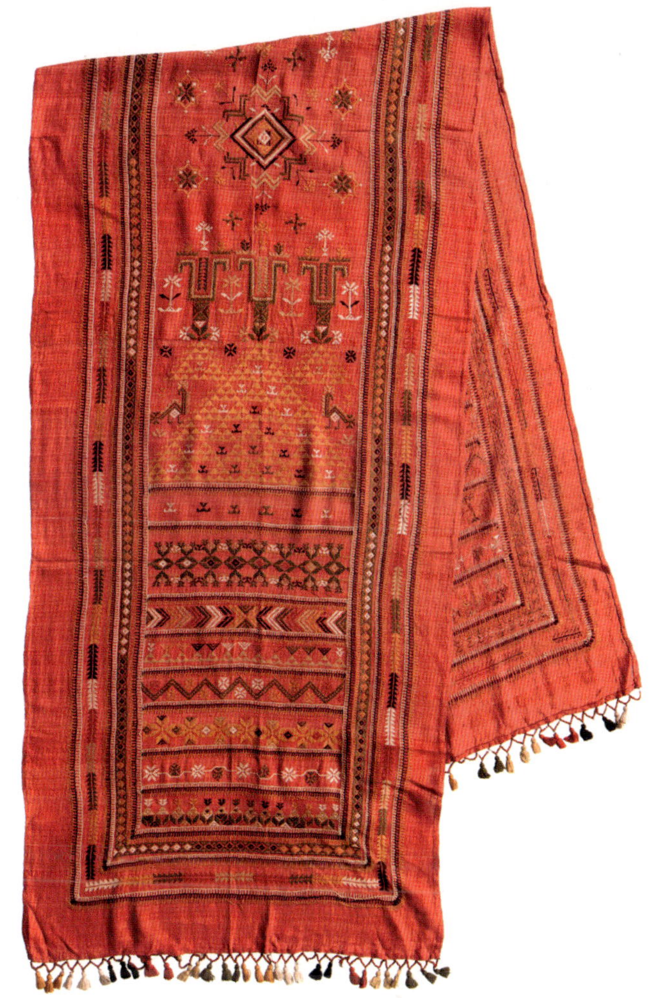

Scarf, 1994. Matka silk, cotton yarn, suf embroidered. Collection of the author. Suf embroiderers must work on plain-weave fabric. 22" x 82". Traditionally, they used cotton. I urged them to try matka silk. Finally, Babraben Moru agreed; the group applauded her results. This original sample was inspired by the sash at the Textile Museum that was used to illustrate the invitation to an exhibition I curated there in 1992. *Photo: Schiffer Publishing Ltd.*

I began with two simple principles: inspiration from tradition and engagement of artisan creativity. I made sample home furnishings and accessories derived from the growing textile collection, and asked artisans to embellish them as they wanted to. After several rounds of prototypes, we were having a discussion when Babraben soundly admonished me. "You don't even know our names!" she said. I realized that not only was each artisan's expression unique—personal recognition was of utmost importance.

The Kala Raksha years were a time of tremendous practical learning and growth. Together, we identified problems and tried to solve them. We connected to a local weaver for handloom fabric and a natural dyer for dyeing, creating a network that supported the local economy, remained within our control, and furthered our eco-friendly approach. I brought in a designer friend and her tailor to initiate a tailoring unit. I engaged elder women in making quilts for sale, using the block-printed fabrics of our natural dyer. Our membership and product range grew.

We had no salaries in the beginning. To support myself, I had been developing embroidered samples with the fashion designer Ritu Kumar. With the help of Lachhuben Raja, a Kachhi Rabari artisan who had embroidered garments for me, I formed a group of artisans in her village, Bhopani Vandh. Lachhuben gave me my first lesson in management. When I was exasperated by inconsistent quality, I asked her, can't you supervise the women?

"No," she said simply. Then she patiently explained: "You gave them the work. I can supervise only if I give the work." She also advised me that village artisans need regular work. She became my assistant. And when working with Kala Raksha and freelancing became too much, I convinced Kala Raksha trustees to take on the Rabari group, and Lachhuben became a salaried coordinator.

Meanwhile, through prolonged sheer persistence, I was able to procure a grant from the government office of the Development Commissioner Handicrafts to build a center for the organization. We purchased the plot of land at the edge of Sumrasar, hired an architect, and slowly constructed a center.

Prolonged persistence also enabled Kala Raksha to keep the textile collection I had built with the Ford grant, and I instituted using the collection as the basis for work to sell.

Prakashbhai and I decided to expand to garments. We engaged a National Institute of Design (NID) student to make simple, embroidery-friendly patterns. In 1996, we had our first solo exhibition at the Blind School in Delhi. It was an unprecedented success: RS 500,000 (Indian rupees, over $14,000 at the time) in four days! Kala Rakasha was on its way to becoming known in the Indian world of craft.

The following year, we added embroidery groups from Garasia Jat, Dhebaria Rabari, Mutava, and Sameja communities, further expanding membership and product range, and we built a website.

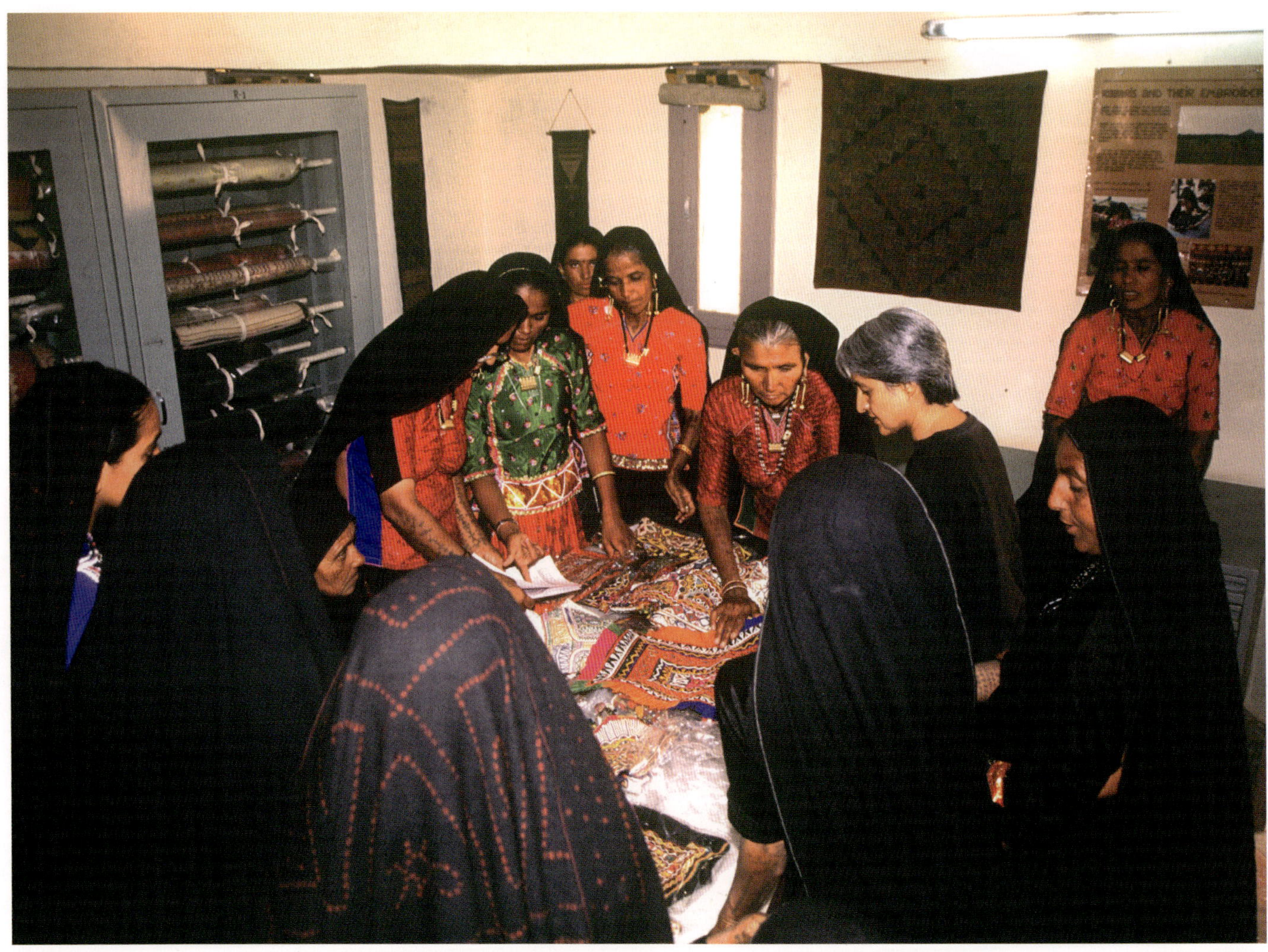

We began Kala Raksha in 1993 with only RS 43,000 ($1,000 at the time) and a lot of sincere, hard work. In 2003, we turned over RS 5,400,000 in sales—an increase of more than 100 times in nine years. In 2007, sales grossed over RS 10,000,000. Money was an important measure of success, and we motivated artisans by honoring the highest earners of each community each year on the Kala Raksha foundation day. But once everyone had achieved a level of security, I began to think of cultural as well as economic empowerment. All the embroiderers were from marginalized communities: Dalits, Muslims, and nomadic pastoralists. Their social disadvantage was thrown in our faces when more than once I tried to take them to a major hotel or designer shop. We were turned away at the door.

When I congratulated our watchman on his son passing tenth grade, he blankly answered, "Oh, did he?" After that, I turned to adult education as a means toward more comprehensive empowerment. If parents experienced education, they could support their children. I secured a grant from Tata Trusts to complete housing of the museum collection and begin an education program. Any material could be used for literacy, so I dovetailed the literacy program with a preventive-healthcare program to ensure relevance and further increase capacity.

Above: Kala Raksha, 2002. I established a museum of traditional textiles at Kala Raksha center as a resource base for embroidery artisan members. Every year we held workshops encouraging artisans to use the collections to develop new products. *Photo: Judy Frater*

Opposite: Kukadsar, 2001. I initiated education programs in each village of Kala Raksha artisans. We trained group leaders to teach basic literacy and numeracy to nurture agency among members. *Photo: Judy Frater*

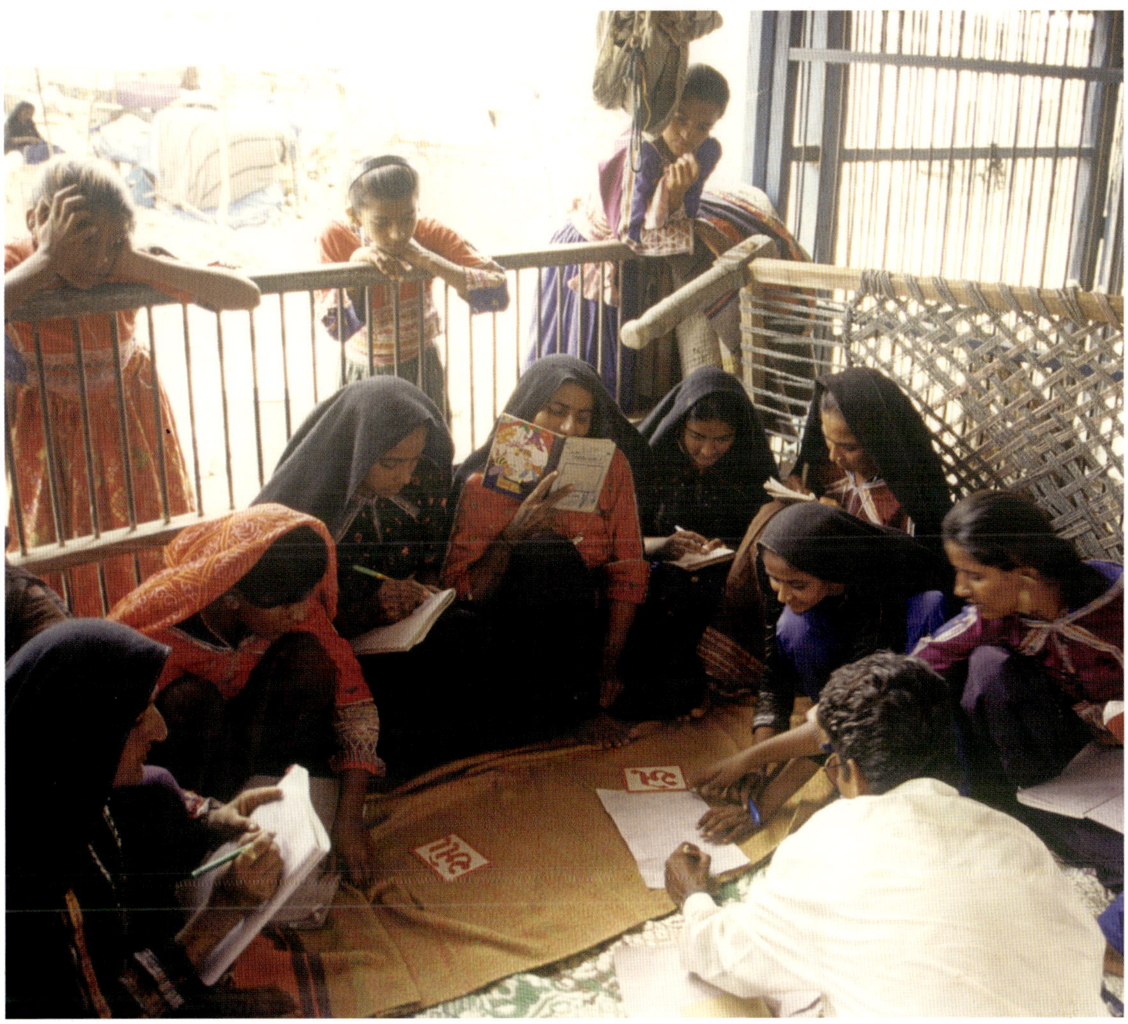

For artisans, most important to capacity was creative agency. Prakashbhai's mother, Raniben, made clear the importance of actively involving artisans in designing their own work. One day, she watched us sort through the patchwork she makes, with increasing agitation. When she saw her own piece go into the reject pile, she said, "Then you tell me what to do; I don't know." I realized how easily, even with the best intentions, we could actually *dis*empower artisans. Hariyaben, a creative suf embroiderer and one of the original Kala Raksha trustees, further guided me to understand the important connection between design and pricing. We began artisan design and pricing committees, in which she was an active member. Each year we called the Design Committee to work on the embroidery embellishment for a new collection. We pulled objects from the museum and had members choose sample garments, and then the group took inspiration from the museum objects and embroidered directly on the samples. When the collection was ready, the Pricing Committee determined the wages for each piece. I insisted that artisans always attended the pop-up sales that Kala Raksha held in urban metros, so that they could learn what customers liked. The staff also reported experiences to artisan groups after each show. The Design Committee honed their embroidered designs, and they almost always sold.

Meanwhile, artisans continued to create their traditional embroidery. Over the years, Lachhuben Raja shared with me the relationship between Rabari women and their embroidery. Working for wages, whether from commercial embroidery, construction, or domestic servant work, they had much less time for their own work. At the same time, requirements for embroidery for dowry were increasing. Rabari women responded by cleverly using time-savers such as machine embroidery and ready-made

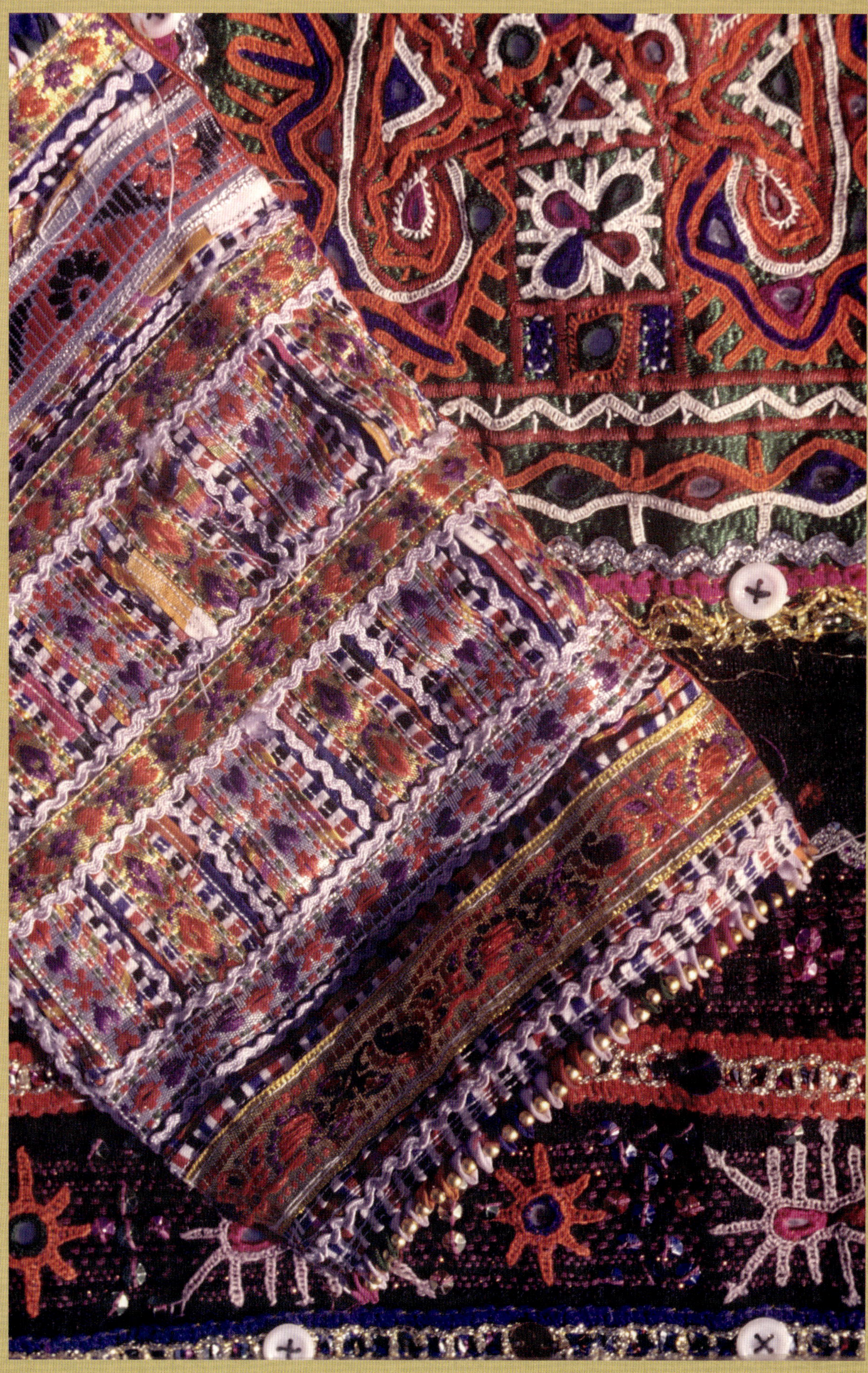

rick rack and ribbons; this enabled them to satisfy the aesthetic need while meeting the demands on their time. The need to minimize time spent embroidering allowed entry of new elements, which women chose according to their own vital sense of aesthetics—essentially, they followed a design brief.

Eliminating some of the tedium of handwork, Rabari women enabled their traditions to remain culturally and economically viable. They happily shifted the focus of creativity to design rather than execution.

Design as a separate entity was alien to preindustrial India, and its introduction began the separation of concept and execution, emphasizing the power differential between designer and maker. However cautiously, we periodically hosted design interns at Kala Raksha to help develop new work. They rarely studied the collections in our museum. I watched them struggle to push their own designs on artisans, and the artisans roll their eyes when the designers weren't looking. They should have a design school for artisans, I thought.

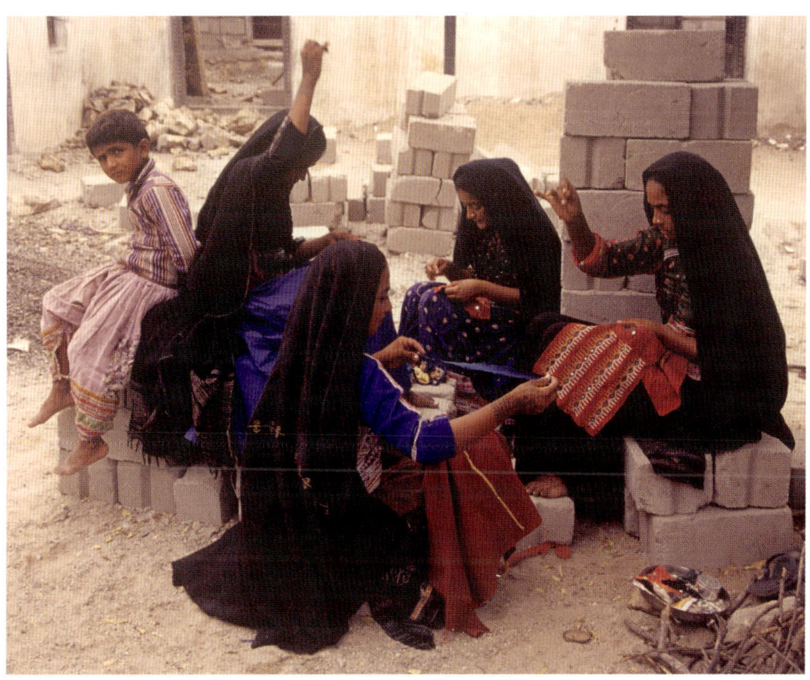

On January 26, 2001, an earthquake devastated Kutch. Twenty thousand people were killed. Miraculously, not one of Kala Raksha's staff or artisan members perished. But two villages in which we worked were leveled. The 70 percent annual growth we had enjoyed was also leveled. We gathered ourselves and, at a group coordinators' meeting, made a commitment to move forward.

The huge relief and rehabilitation activity was like a tidal wave. I was new to the internet but learned by plunging into fundraising. It seemed easy. Working day and night, I raised enough to rebuild 124 houses in one village and centers in three villages. Prakashbhai came up with the brilliant idea to begin a matching grant program to encourage women artisans to become actively involved in their own rehabilitation. From a generous grant from the American India Foundation and funds solicited from friends and well-wishers, we made 100 percent matching grants against embroidery wages. For one year, we matched every rupee a woman earned with an equal amount.

The project was successful beyond our imagination. Women worked not only more but also better. They told us that the project brought them a sense of stability in the face of anxiety. With reliable increased earnings, they took their work more seriously.

Opposite: Bhopani Vandh, 2000. In embroidery they made for themselves, Rabari women sought time-saving innovations. Among Dhebrias, whose hand embroidery was banned in 1995, women machine appliqued rick rack and trims (*left*). Kachhi women used a combination of machine zigzag and hand embroidery (*right*). *Photo: Judy Frater*

Above: Kukadsar, 2001. After an earthquake devastated Kutch, we initiated the Stone Soup project, in which Kala Raksha used funds raised for relief to pay matching grants to embroiderers for their work. *Photo: Judy Frater*

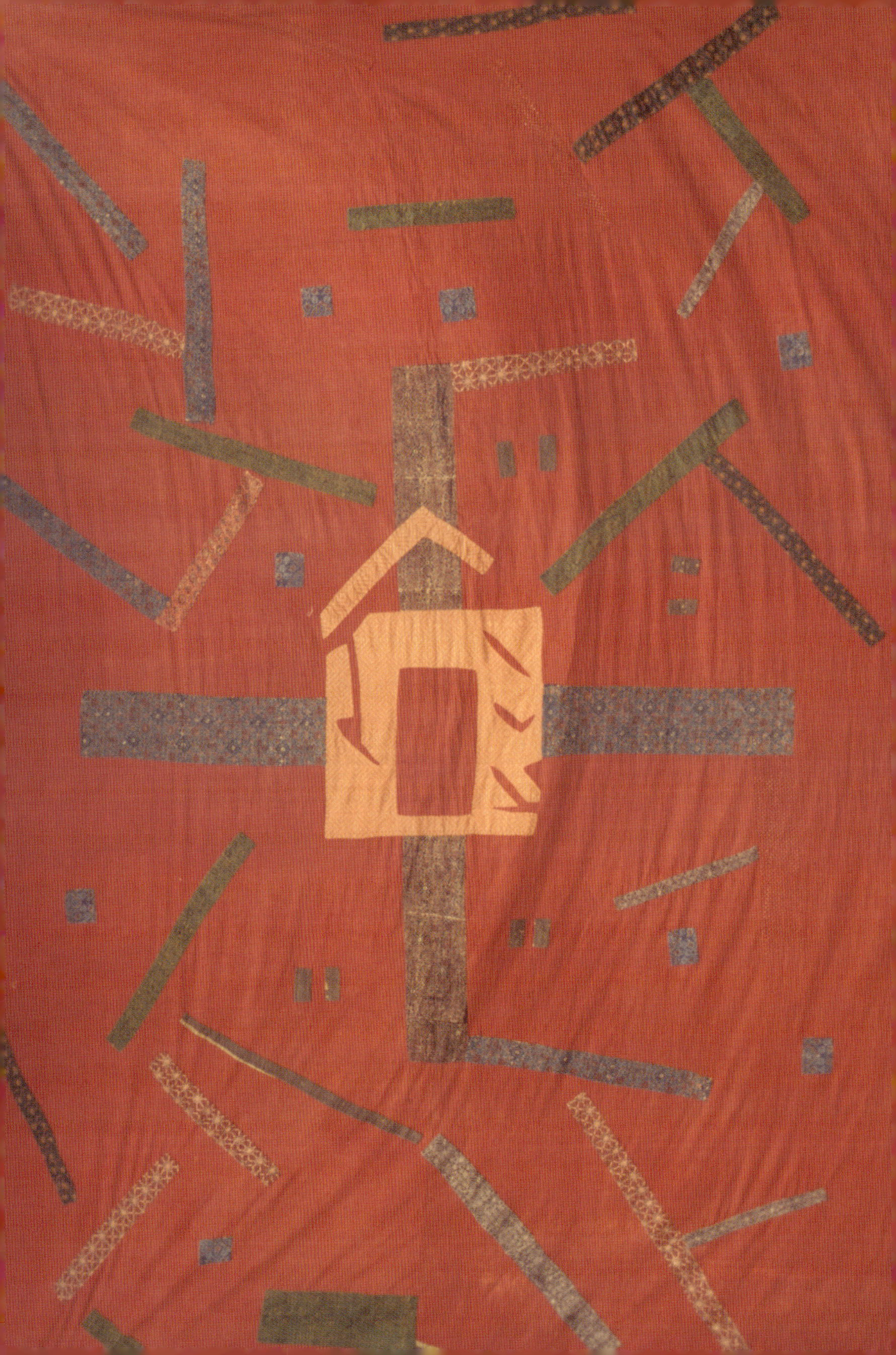

Asked how they used the funds, women answered that they repaired homes, bought the nutritious food we taught them about in the education classes, planted fields, sought timely medical attention, and paid off loans. One woman bought a goat. Why? Revolving! She exclaimed. She could earn by selling its milk. I realized that it was never that women did not know how to invest money; they did not have a reliable income. Earning more enabled women to dare to reach for what they want.

The earthquake also provided an opportunity to further explore creative capacity. We were invited to participate in *Resurgence*, a narrative art exhibition on the earthquake to be held in Manly, Australia. There is no narrative tradition in Kutch. At first, I did not feel that the project was appropriate. But when a second request for expressive art came, I asked Raniben Bhika, a patchwork artisan who had lost her home in the earthquake, if she could make a piece expressing her experience. Her work was so powerful that I realized that not only could women do narrative work, but also that we could not decide who was capable. We offered the opportunity to make a narrative piece on the earthquake to all of Kala Raksha's members. Scores of women took the challenge, and each one made a unique and evocative embroidered or appliquéd story. "It was the earthquake that made this possible," Fatmabai told me. "Otherwise, I could not have done work like this."

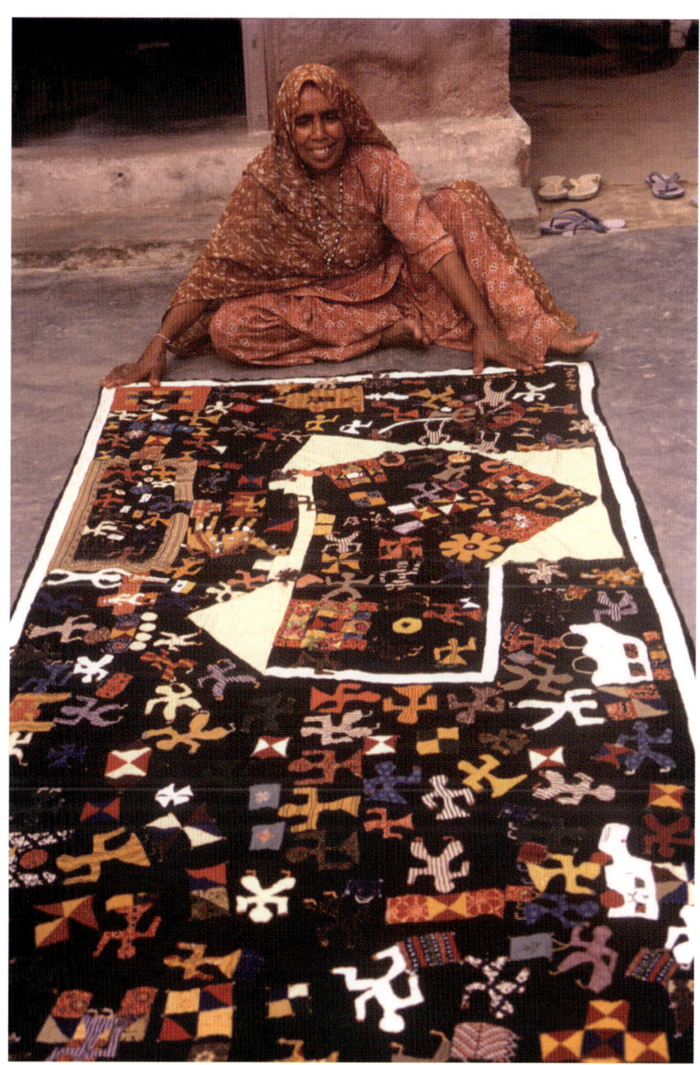

Raniben Ratilal, who had given up confidence when her patchwork cushion cover went into the reject pile, created an incredibly complex and vibrant work for the *Resurgence* project. She was able to extend beyond her capacity simply with encouragement and protected space to explore. And she was so transformed by the experience that afterward she initiated a second narrative work—the story of Kala Raksha, for our tenth anniversary. "The difference between his work and what I used to do," Raniben said, "is night and day. I'm not just sticking cloth on cloth. I'm thinking."

Opposite: *Earthquake*, by Raniben Bhika Rathod, 2001. Natural-dyed cotton, applique. Raniben, an expert patchwork artisan, lost her home in the 2001 earthquake. I asked her to depict her experience. The squares and rectangles that she used to make quilts flying in all directions were an epiphany of the untapped creativity of traditional artisans. *Photo: Judy Frater*

Above: Sumrasar Sheikh, 2003. Raniben Ratilal Bhanani, appliqué artisan, ran with the opportunity for narrative expression. She created a fabric mural depicting the story of Kala Raksha. *Photo: Judy Frater*

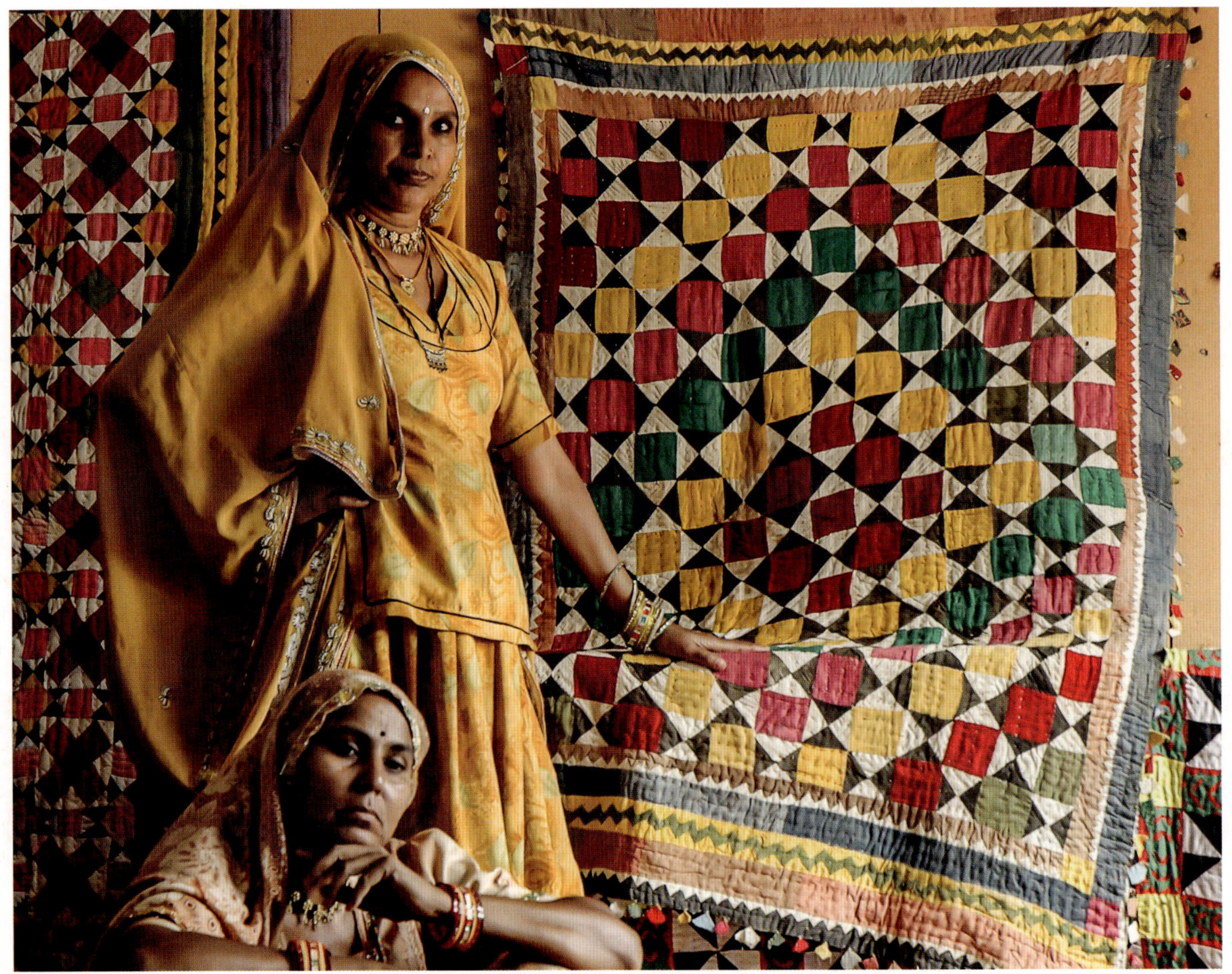

It's not that we had nothing to say.
We just did not have a way to say it.

~Hariyaben Uttam Bhanani

Kala Raksha Vidhyalya, 2009. Hariyaben and Champaben present their shared quilt tradition to the class during the fourth module of the design course: Concept, Communication, Projects. *Photo: Judy Frater*

Chapter 6

HARIYABEN UTTAM BHANANI: ELEGANT SAGE

Hariyaben was thirty-three when Kala Raksha was founded, and she was one of four artisan trustees. She was wise, sharp, and elegant as a queen. She dressed. Her ensembles were carefully chosen, the colors distinct and matching, and her veil over a bun high on her head was like a crown. At one of the early trustee meetings held at her home, an uncle who worked for another organization planted himself right in front of our group, obviously a spy. I thought of a culturally appropriate response, telling him that if he sat there, the women would have to cover their faces in the customary *laj* (respect) and would not be able to speak freely. He left. Hariyaben made tea for everyone but did not drink it herself and was uncharacteristically subdued. Later, she confronted me. "You insulted our uncle," she said. That was day one of her course, Complexity of Culture 101.

Hariyaben was born in Thar Patiya, Pakistan. Her father was a leatherworker, and he had a shop where he sold fabric and thread. She was eleven when the 1971 Indo-Pakistan War broke out. "We left Pakistan," she recalled, "and arrived at Bakhasar village in Rajasthan riding on camels. We had eight camels. And we stayed there seven years. We built small mud houses. We were refugees. The government provided us basic facilities and gave us some land for agriculture. I had a feeling that we should go back to Pakistan, but my father told us we would stay here. He said we could settle anywhere, but only in India.

"In 1977, I was married at the Jura Refugee Camp in Kutch. My father-in-law lived in the camp, so we stayed there until 1979. Then we got citizenship, seventeen families together purchased land in Sumrasar Sheikh village, and we settled there."

Hariyaben was not educated. There was no school in Bakhasar. She learned all kinds of stitching from her mother—the community traditions of suf and kharek embroidery, appliqué, and sewing. And during the years in the refugee camp, she sold her textiles to tour guides—for nothing, she later realized.

"We don't know where our work went," she said. "That's how pieces ended up in museums. It was old, real traditional work, with art. Our work was *hem-chandi*[3] to us originally. If we had it now, we could go from there."

In Sumrasar, Hariyaben did commercial embroidery for NGOs. Men of the community would bring the work and give them RS 30 per one-and-a-half-to-two-days' work.

When the Dastkar Kutch Project started there in 1991, it promised better wages. Though skeptical, she joined it. Within two years, I, Prakashbhai, Dayaben, and the group of twenty-five women in Sumrasar started Kala Raksha, and Hariyaben was a trustee. When Kala Raksha attended its first exhibition, in Chandigarh, she volunteered to go. It was a brave step. Women of her community did not venture outside their homes—even to the well for water or the bazaar for vegetables. Men negotiated with the outside world. She was afraid, and she was taunted. But she went. En route, she confided to me that Chandigarh was a dangerous place. Her husband worked with a Punjabi man, and he had told her this. We kept close together throughout the show and then went to see Nek Chand's outsider art masterpiece Rock Garden, a fantasy of mosaic figures made of recycled ceramics. She observed keenly and quietly. On return she exhaled. "See, I told you it was dangerous!" she said. "Did you see all of those *paliya*!"[4]

Hariyaben was an expert manager. She and her three daughters began to earn well doing suf embroidery for Kala Raksha. And she took her role as a trustee seriously. Soon after the Kala Raksha Trust began producing for domestic markets, she called me into the workshop. She had displayed three embroideries. "Are these all the same?" she asked. The pattern was the same, but the quality of the work varied. "Why, then, are the artisans all paid the same rate?" she wanted to know. This inaugurated an Artisan Pricing Committee, a group that determined the wages for all embroidery work, and a step for women to be responsible for their earning. Hariyaben remained an active member. "We have some agriculture land, but it fully depends on rain," she told a visitor. "Today, I am earning, and because of that, I was able to provide for my son's marriage."

When I set up a museum for Kala Raksha's textile collection, the first step was to decide what to display in the interpretation center; next, we replicated those pieces, since permanent display would harm the originals. Hariyaben, keenly interested in her traditions, advised in selection of objects and supervised the replication group. When it came time to dress the mannequins, we had an embroidered *kanchali-kurti* (backless blouse and vest) set from Hariyaben's Maru Meghval community, but there was no skirt to complement the outfit. "What shall we use for the skirt?" she asked.

Traditional, I answered.

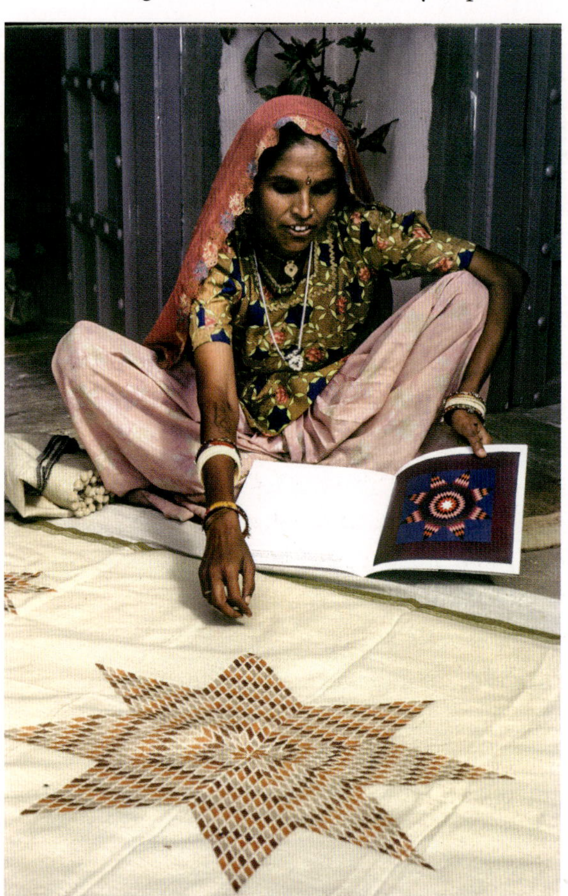

Left: Kala Raksha, 1994. Intrigued by a book on Amish quilts destined for the Kala Raksha Museum library, Hariyaben translated a quilt motif into a suf embroidery. The scale as well as the pattern are a world away from suf tradition. *Photo: Judy Frater*

Opposite: Sumrasar, 1999. Hariyaben taught her daughters and other village girls suf embroidery, as her mother had taught her. She wanted them to learn the language of traditional motifs as well as stitching techniques. *Photo: Judy Frater*

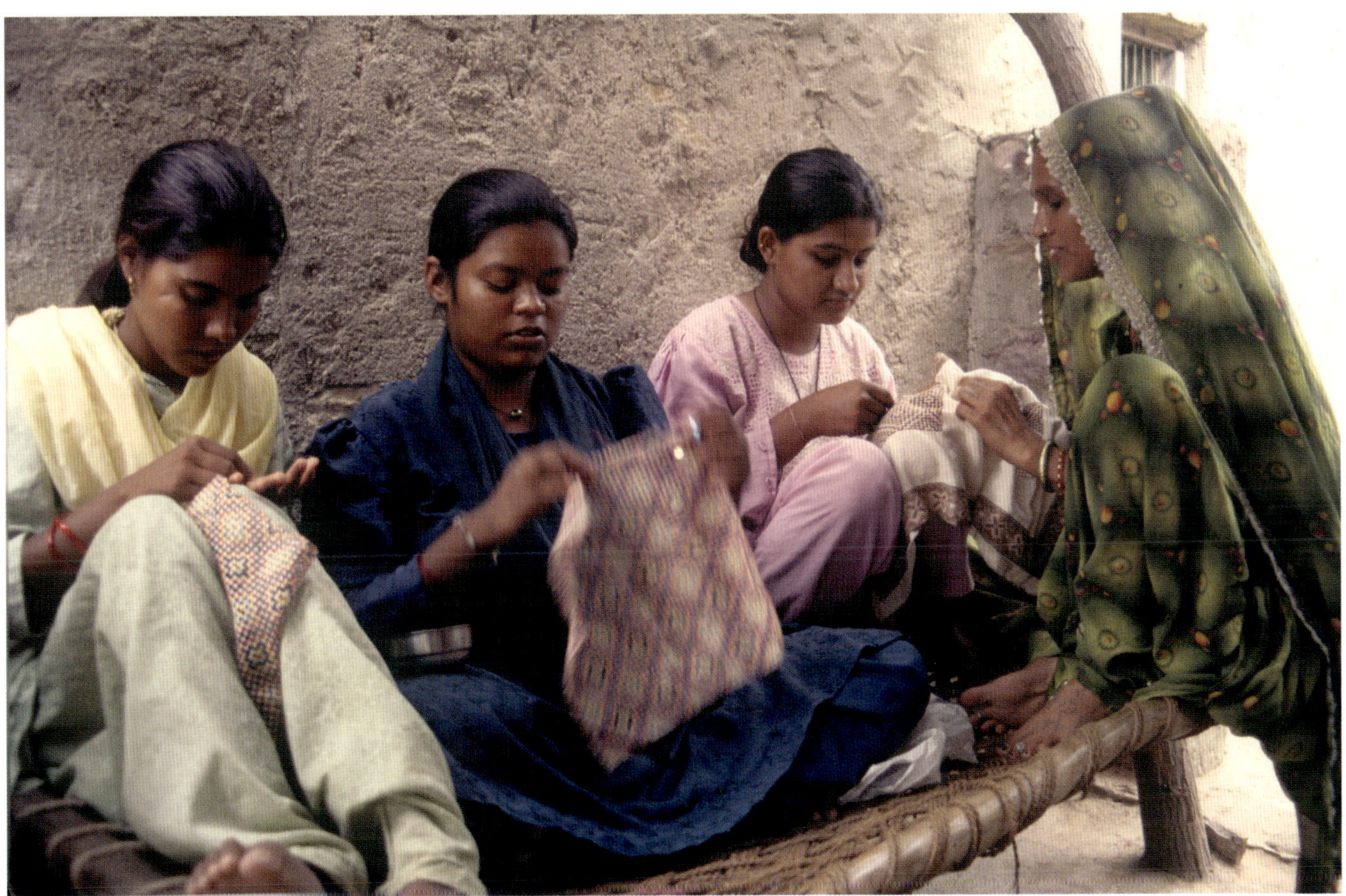

"But *which* tradition?" she wanted to know. Tradition, she understood, was not static but ongoing.

Working on the exhibition for some time, she observed, "This exhibition idea of yours is not new. We already have it. Every time a woman is married, she displays her dowry for her village—and then her husband's—to see. That is the idea of an exhibition."

I added a library to the museum for inspiration. Hariyaben understood resources before we even cataloged the books. One morning she brought a very unusual suf shawl that she had just embroidered. It had a huge, complex medallion in the center. Where did you get that idea? I asked her. "From those books you had piled in the office," she said. Over the years, she used the museum and library collections to develop many more popular designs.

In addition to being a quick study, Hariyaben was a perfecting teacher. She taught many young women to make uncompromisingly beautiful suf embroidery. Reflecting on the Kala Raksha collections, she remarked, "Old work wasn't fine, but it was exemplary. There were many motifs and colors in a piece. Today's girls know fine suf technique but not traditional motifs. We must teach them our art so they know. We need it for our homes, and it expresses our identity when we go out."

Sometime during the Kala Raksha years, Hariyaben began to wear the *kanchali kurti* that the community had shunned in the 1980s. She pulled out traditional silver bangles, *poptiyo* and *gajaro*, and, with her conscious attitude, made tradition a new fashion. But this was more than a fashion statement. The community had abandoned their dress because it proclaimed their Dalit social status, and they wanted to assimilate in Kutch as higher status. A community leader, Hariyaben was stating, "This is who we are, and we are proud of our identity."

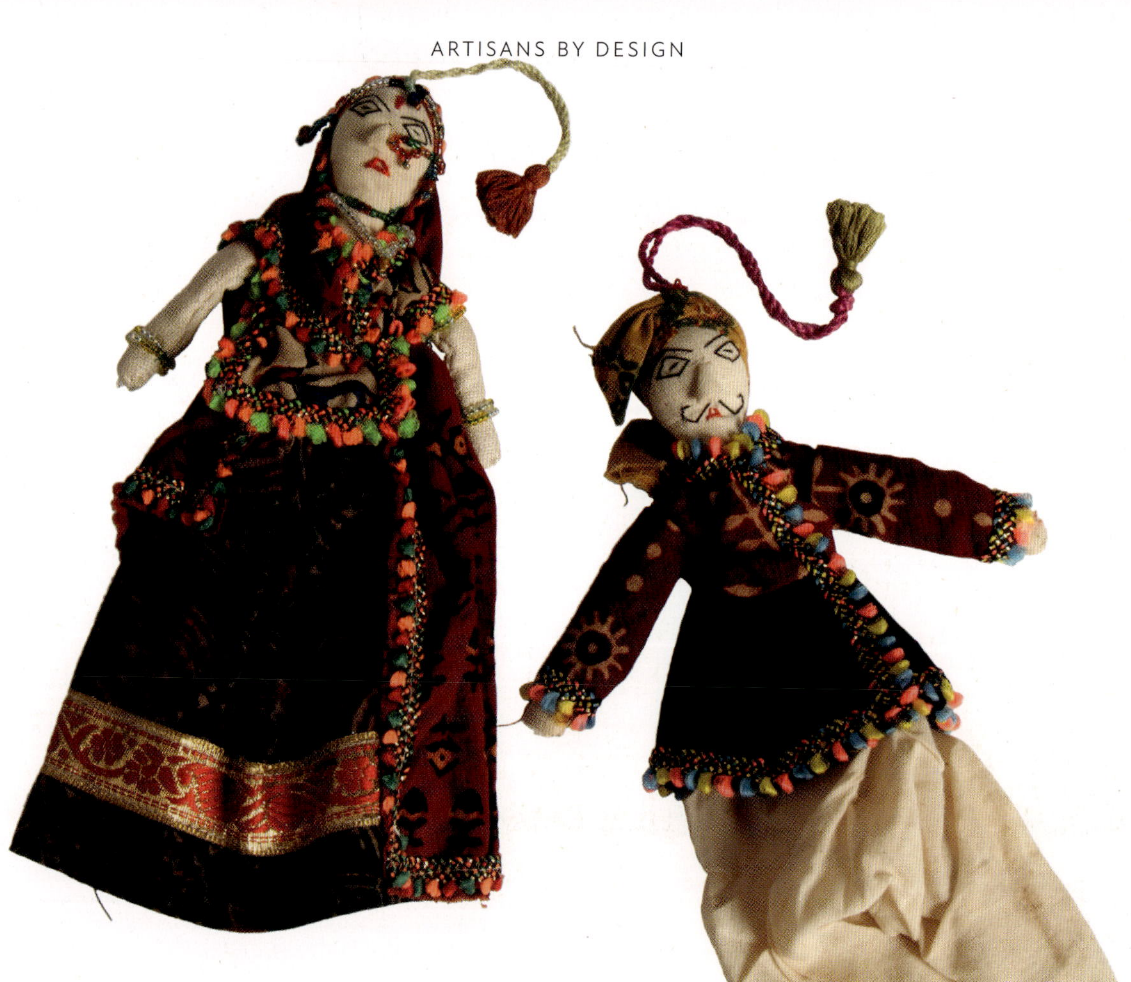

Maru Meghval couple, by Hariyaben Uttam Bhanani, 2015. Cotton fabric, beads, ribbons and braid, embroidery. 5.5" x 8" each. Hariyaben crafted culturally accurate dolls by upcycling scraps from Kala Raksha production. *Photo: Schiffer Publishing Ltd.*

By the earthquake of 2001, Hariyaben was forty-one, and she found it hard to see the warps and wefts to count suf embroidery. She turned to appliqué and patchwork, with equal creativity. Disturbed by the wastage of embroidered fabric in the finishing process, she scooped up scraps from the Kala Raksha cutting-room floor and went home to invent charming stuffed toys. She fashioned camels, elephants, and culturally correct dolls that became bestsellers and the basis for beginning an upcycling program.

When Kala Raksha began the narrative appliqué project, she found a wonderful medium for her imagination. "It's not that we had nothing to say," she quipped. "We just did not have a way to say it." She did an elaborate piece on the first Rann Festival held in Kutch, depicting me, Prakashbhai, the Collector, and herself in sharply observed detail. And there near the center was the unmistakable chief minister at the time, Narendra Modi. She depicted the Mandvi palace Vijay Vilas, a political meeting, scenes of nature, and Gandhi. She did calligraphy in appliqué and illustrated Kutchi proverbs with tongue-in-cheek humor.

Kala Raksha received an order for 15,000 narrative appliqué works. Although we had never used production methods, I decided we would have to use cardboard templates. We had a workshop, and Hariyaben was to teach Rabari and *paako* artisans how to cut out the figures. They laid the template to the side and cut freehand, looking at it. I tried to intervene. Hariyaben said, simply, "We don't do it that way." And so, Kala Raksha did all 15,000 as unique works of art.

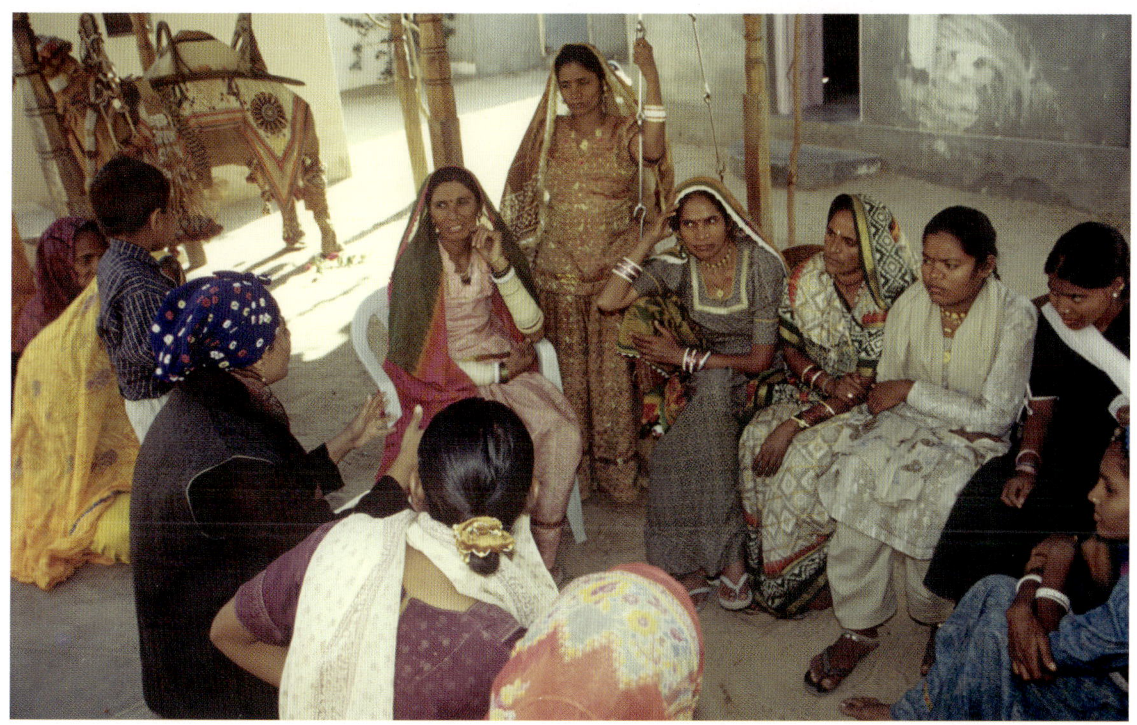

Above: Kala Raksha, 2003. Before embarking on my Ashoka Fellowship to develop a design school for artisans, I met with Kala Raksha embroiderers to hear what they wanted to learn. As always, Hariyaben zeroed in on the objective. *Photo: Judy Frater*

Below: Kala Raksha Vidhyalaya, 2009. Hariyaben and her class listen intently as a staff member of Fabindia discusses products during the Market Orientation module of the design course. *Photo: Judy Frater*

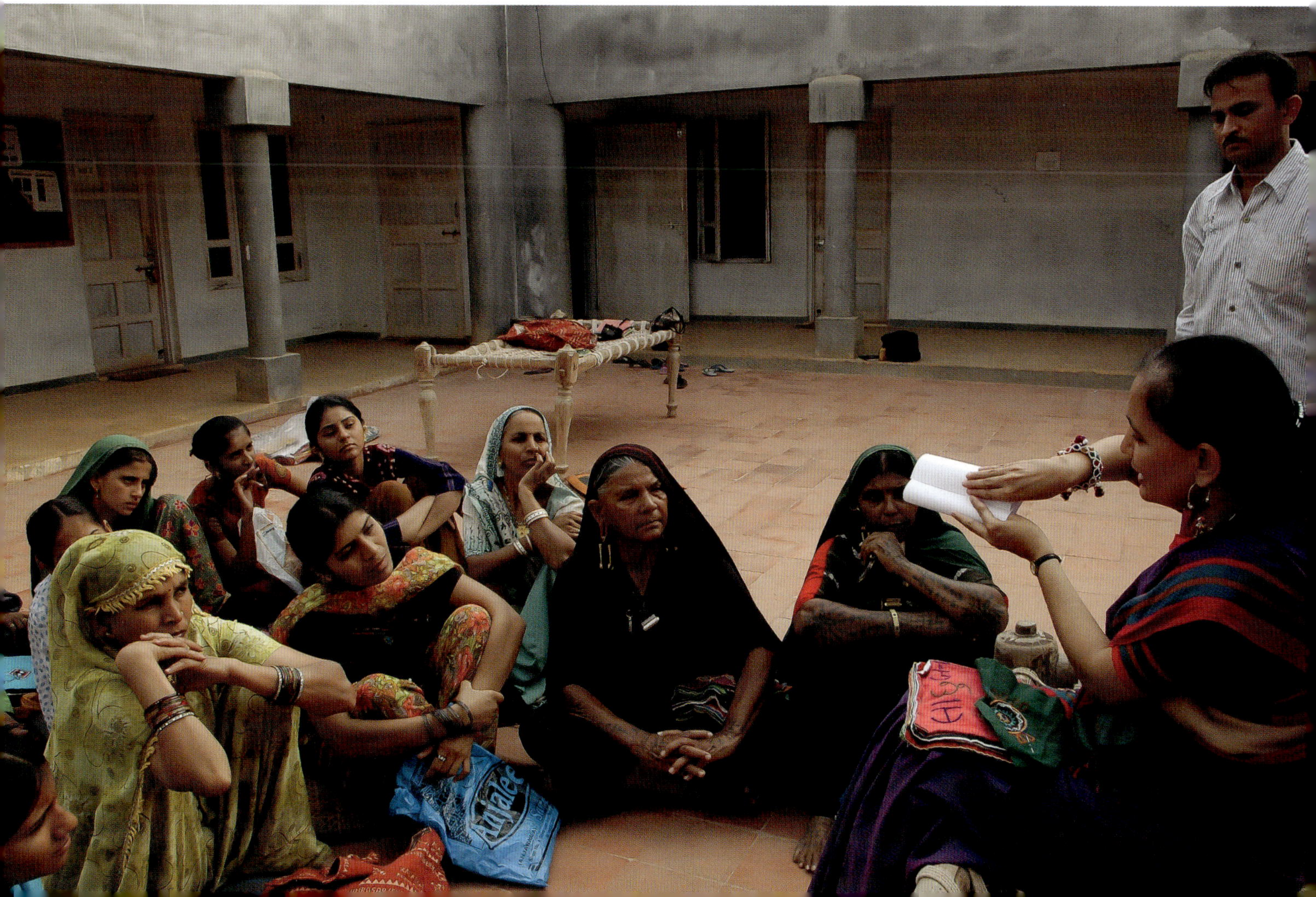

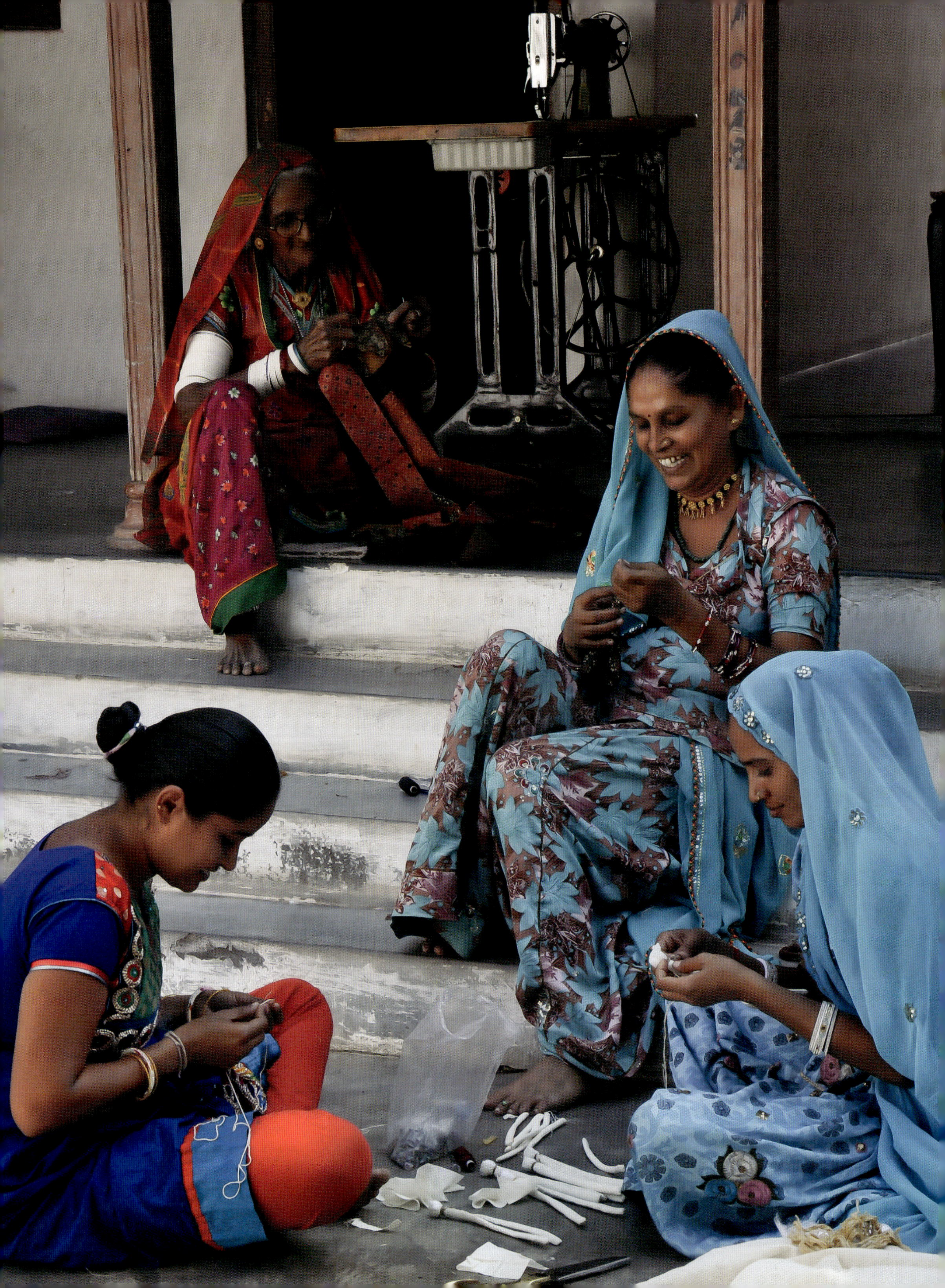

In the turbulence of post-earthquake work, my idea of a design school for artisans emerged. As I related my dream of women studying together to a group of embroiderers and appliqué artists in Sumrasar, Hariyaben listened. When it was her turn to speak, she drawled, with perhaps a tinge of tongue in cheek, "I think that, well, maybe we don't know so many designs, so they can teach us. But if we learn a bit, then we may get the desire to not depend on anyone but use our own creativity and make our own new designs."

She observed the school, Kala Raksha Vidhyalaya, for three years and in 2009 took the course. People in Sumrasar taunted her. "What will you learn there?" they asked.

"At first I was homesick," she recalled. "But I learned that we have to go out to learn. I didn't know about warm/cool colors or mixing. I got colors from water; that's how much capacity a person can have. I learned that nothing is bad; we just don't know how to use it. We can put the light color next to the dark to make it look good. I know how to use lines, movement, and rhythm. I learned to look. I learned to try. In Ahmedabad, we saw how homes and shops are arranged. I learned about customers' tastes. I saw, so I learned. We couldn't have known this at home. In class, we learn from each other because everyone likes different things. The main thing is that we can talk about our work, so now we can take orders. Finally, if our name doesn't come, there is no meaning—crafts will deteriorate. I am able to think in a different way because of my design education."

Hariyaben represented Kala Raksha artisans at the launch of the Artisan Design label in Delhi in 2011 and served as a design intern to create one-of-a kind art to wear in 2012. Through her continued efforts, she was able to increase her income from hundreds of rupees a month to thousands. Significantly, she asked for RS 500 a day to teach a workshop—unprecedented among women artisans. Designers who worked with artisans at that time took RS 75,000 per month.

In 2013, when she participated in *Co-Creation Squared*, a fashion event in Mumbai, she saw her cocreators, male artisan designers, turning brisk sales with their new designs. She calculated her assets and quietly decided she could begin her own independent business. The next year, the newly established Somaiya Kala Vidya began a Business and Management for Artisans (BMA) graduate course. Hariyaben quickly signed up. She wanted to stand on her own feet. "I didn't want to waste what I had learned," she said. She knew the risk. She knew her strengths: her art, her experience, and a corps of artisans she could tap. She characterized opportunity as a computer screen with an English letter "A" on it, and she was determined to work on her limitations.

"Women have an obstacle in mobility," she observed, "but we can use our strength to confront it. To do business, we need raw materials, money, some knowledge, and clients." Hariyaben managed to go out to Ajrakhpur, the village of her 2013 cocreator Irfanbhai, to source fabric for her collection of quilts based on the date palm.

She knew she was not well. She detected a lump behind her breastbone. I went with her to hospitals in Bhuj and then Ahmedabad, trying unsuccessfully to get a clear diagnosis. It was hard to get a biopsy, and painful. She got fed up and decided to trust in God and take herbal medicine. But she was determined to study. Despite not being literate, Hariyaben did well in the BMA course. She made a masterpiece quilt collection. But when she wanted to produce it for a pop-up sale, she did not give samples for women to copy. She got four women to sit at her house all day, and they worked as they could, trying to interpret the theme.

Sumrasar Sheikh, 2014. Hariyaben engages her daughter Varsha (*left*) and women from her community to fashion dolls for sale in her upcoming BMA course exhibition. She thought in terms of creation, not production. *Photo: Judy Frater*

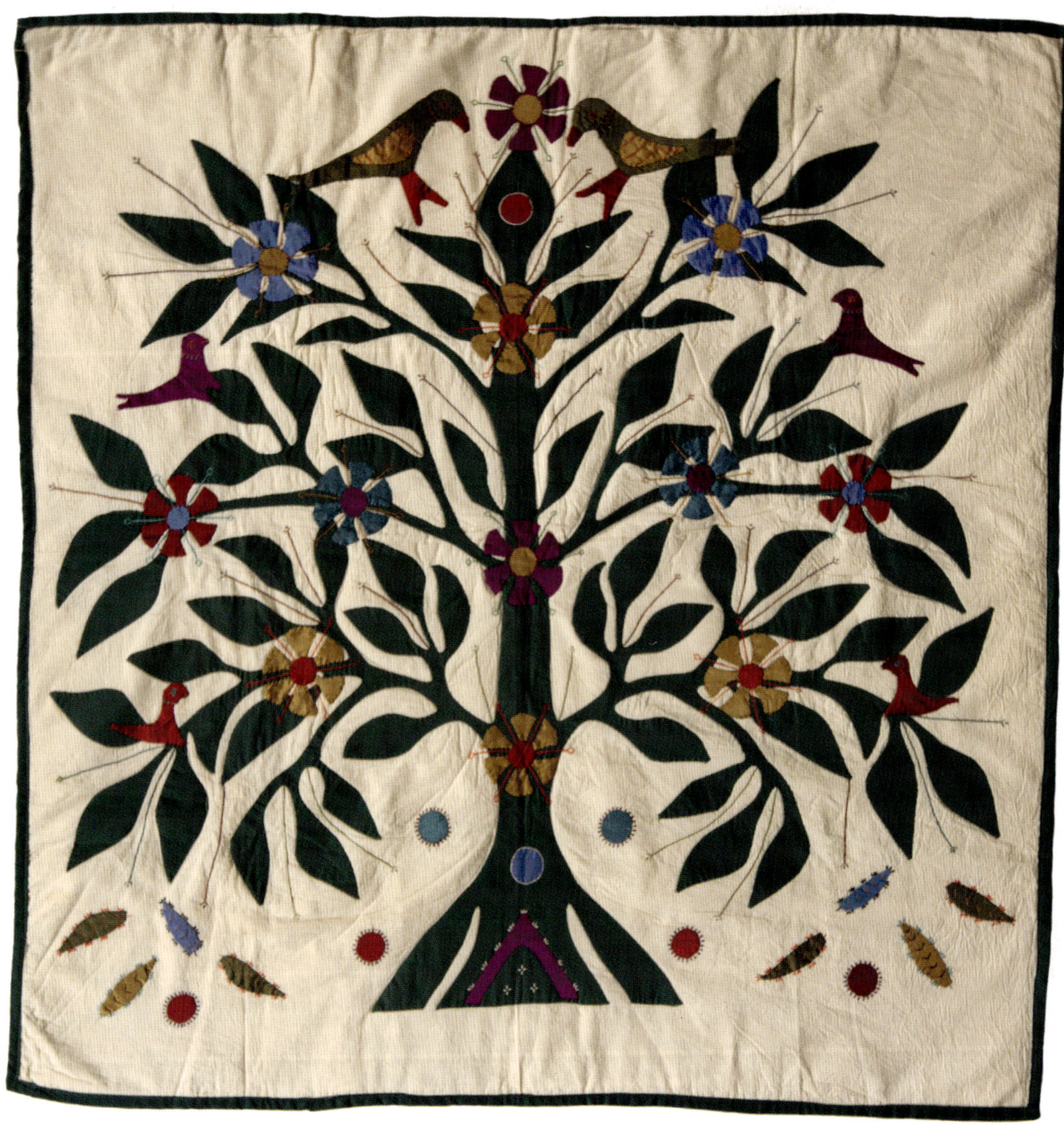

Above: *Tree of Life*, by Hariyaben Uttam Bhanani, 2015. Cotton with cotton and silk appliqué and embroidery. 40" x 40". Collection of the family. When she did not have the keen eyesight needed to count threads for suf embroidery, Hariyaben turned to patchwork and appliqué, creating curvilinear forms and lyrical figures not possible in suf. Her tree is filled with birds, life, and joy. She used her signature circles and silk fabric accents. *Photo: Schiffer Publishing Ltd.*

Opposite: Hariyaben designed her logo in her BMA class. The motif is derived from traditional patchwork. Kaam Bole means "the work speaks."

Oh, no! I thought. She hasn't understood the concept of production!

But Hariyaben was encouraging the other artisans to create! For her, *this* was the work of a designer. "Good design is not told by words and explanation," she said. "It speaks itself." She named her brand Kaam Bole, "the work speaks."

In the analysis course following the pop-up sale of the BMA students' collections, she reflected, "The learning of all the previous classes came to use in this final class. The session helped me to identify my own mistakes in accounting. I hesitated about sales so made less than I planned. The five-year planning exercise enabled me to think of BIG numbers!"

Hariyaben began her business within her restrictions and enlisted her daughter and son to help. I met her a few days before she passed away. She knew she did not have much time left. She was always beautiful, always dignified. Her nails were painted, and she was dressed in pink. She asked her daughter to bring her the dolls they had made. Carefully, she selected the right one and gave it to me.

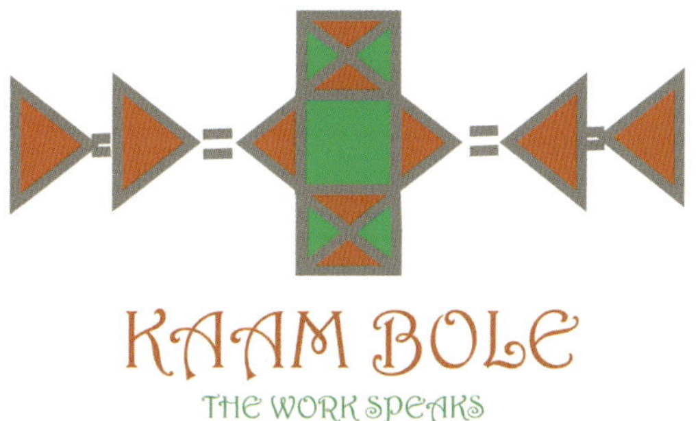

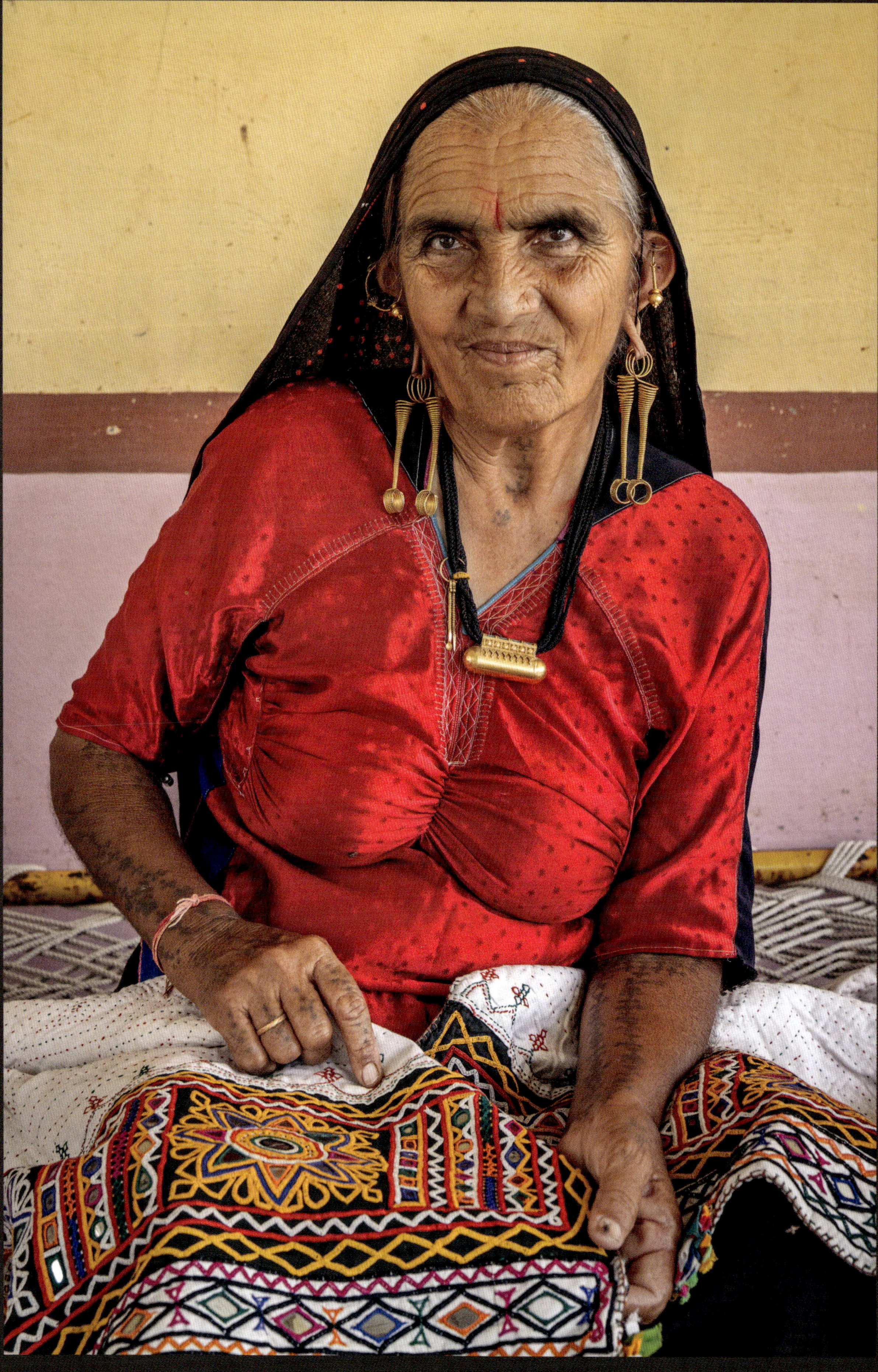

Chapter 7

LACHHUBEN RAJA RABARI: ELOQUENT EARTH MOTHER

You have to use your own creativity to keep on making new things.

~Lachhuben Raja Rabari

In 1993, Bhopani Vandh is the end of the world. Soft-brown, round *bhunga* with thatched roofs that sweep gracefully almost to the ground cluster in the afternoon sun like magical mushrooms in the white, treeless landscape. The Gulf of Kutch is just beyond the horizon. Lachhuben Raja is comfortably commanding a meeting of Rabari embroiderers in her bhungo., which inside is a palace sculpted with wildly imaginative mirror-studded relief work. The women are tough, but she knows them all intimately. Everyone in the village is related—the men through a common ancestor, the women through marriage.

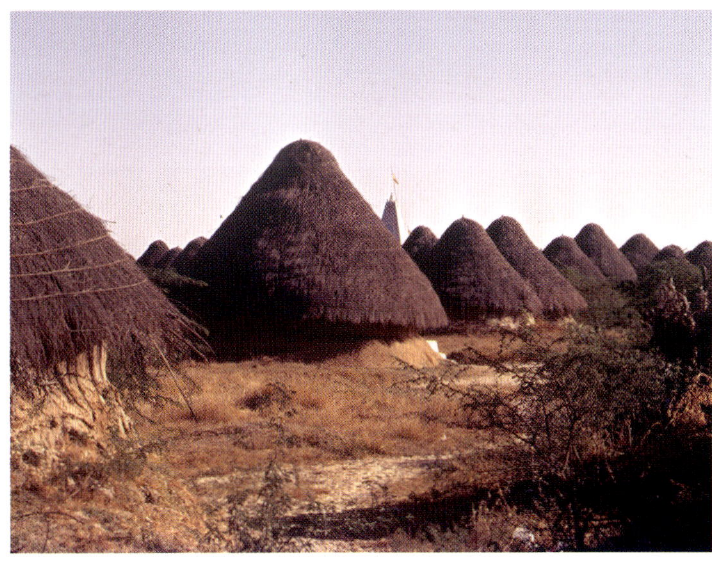

Opposite: Bhopani Vandh, 2022. Lachhuben shows a *kothalo*, a dowry bag that she embroidered for her *judio* (dowry) in the style of stitching, colors, and motifs that were in fashion then. She sold the rest of her *judio*. This is the only piece remaining. *Photo: Nevada Wier*

Above: Bhopani Vandh, 1994. Traditionally camel herders, Rabaris spent much of the year migrating, stopping in campsites called *vandh*. Generations ago, a family of bhopas, or shamans, built mud-and-thatch bhunga and settled—a permanent *vandh*. The family's goddess prohibited cement homes until the early 1990s. *Photo: Judy Frater*

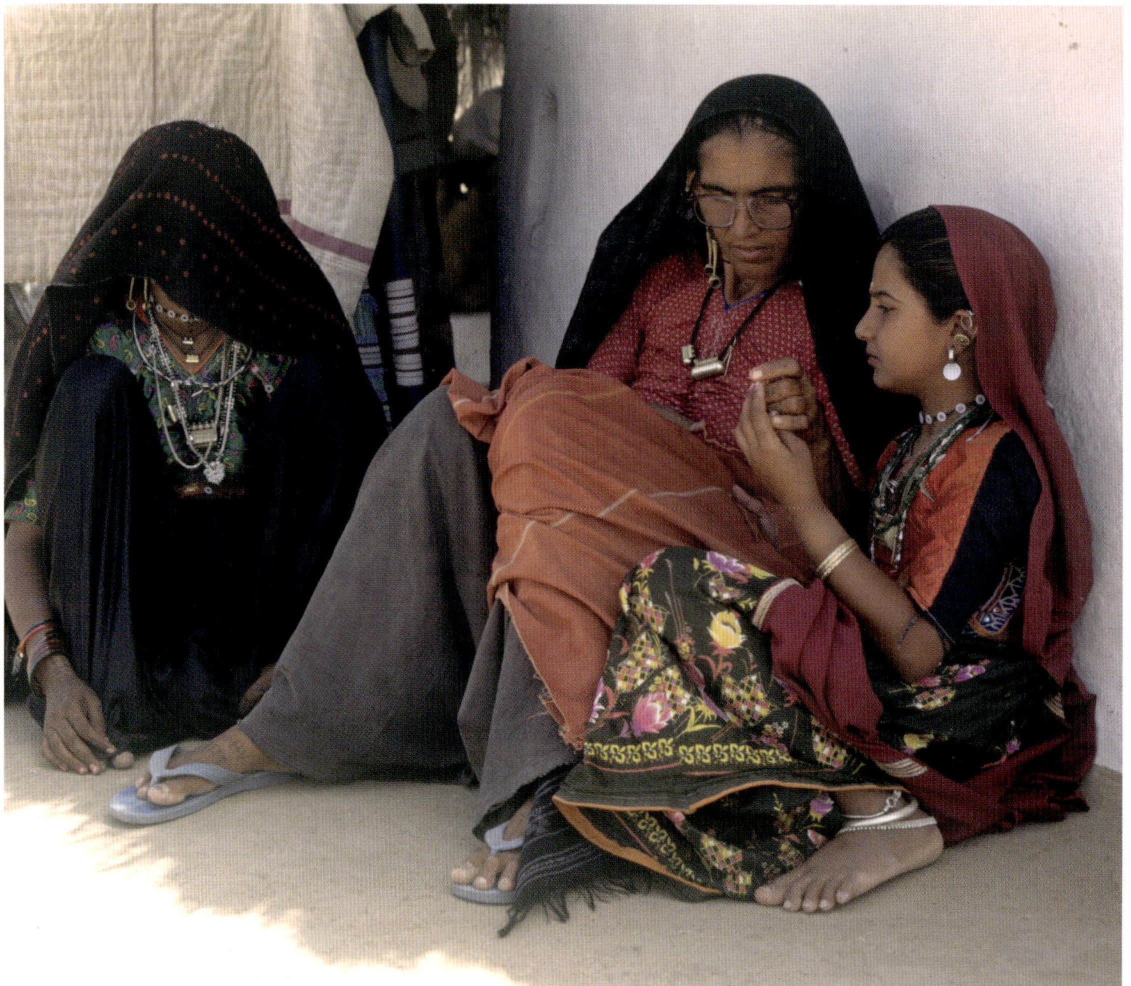

She spreads the colored thread on the fabric. None of the colors is traditional Rabari. "The pink will be the yellow," she explains. "And the green will be the white." They all immediately get it. This is code for how Rabaris use color.

She is the supervisor, and the artisans will do consistently good work. They would not think of fooling each other.

For years after her marriage, Lachhuben didn't have even a bhungo.. She lived with her in-laws. But for much of the year, she moved by foot with her husband, Rajabhai, and their herd of camels, traveling as far as southern Gujarat. They camped in the open without so much as a tent. "It was a hard life," she recalled. "Sometimes we didn't have oil for cooking or soap for washing. Then we could not afford this life anymore, and we came back to the village and started to earn a bit."

It was for the wedding of a relative that she and Rajabhai finally built one bhungo..To begin to settle, they gave up camels for cows. But the herd all died from eating the poisonous *gandho baval* (*Prosopis juliflora*) that now grows unchecked in this salty desert land. After that, Rajabhai utilized his ingenuity to find other ways to earn a living: machine embroidery, a flour mill, and finally work as a coordinator for Kala Raksha.

Above: Bhopani Vandh, 1997. Lachhuben teaches her younger daughter, Ramiben, embroidery in the way her mother taught her. *Photo: Judy Frater*

Opposite: Bhopani Vandh, 1996. On the Holi celebration after the birth of her first son, a Kachhi Rabari woman presents the bulk of her *judio*, or dowry, to her in-laws. Women of the village come to review the offering, a peer jury. *Photo: Judy Frater*

Lachhuben grew up in Viyar. By the early 1970s, many Kachhi Rabaris of western Kutch had already stopped migrating more than a day's distance. She stayed in the village but did not go to school. Instead, she and her friends sat together and stitched as if in a class, intent on learning the elements that comprise the unique Rabari embroidery style.

Embroidery was essential. The girls would need to embellish their own festive garments, gifts for family members, and their own dowries—an ever-growing list of embroideries. And it was a way of expressing one's abilities. The dowry would be carefully appraised for its creativity.

Lachhuben recalled how her mother taught her—first the characteristic tight, square chain stitch, then mirrors, round first, then shapes. At this point, her mother took over. Since she knew the traditional patterns, she did the outlining and Lachhuben filled in. She worked on geometric borders in specific repeats of zigzags and mirrored shapes, and bold portrayals of parrots, trees, and other familiar aspects of Rabari life. She mastered the characteristic color patterning: yellow alternating with white, accents of a succession of bright colors. Then, she learned outlining. "That is really the key," she said, "the foundation of embroidery." Finally, she learned the repertoire of accent stitches that decorate traditional Rabari work. The combination of stitch, color, pattern, and motif defines Rabari style.

The first actual piece that Lachhuben made was a *gupchi*. After that, she made a few *kanchadiyo* (girls' blouses). "By that time, a girl feels like making her own garments for ceremonies," Lachhuben observed, "and she is on her way." She became known as a skilled artisan, working in the same conventional way as her peers. Excellence was doing the expected well and adding one's own innovations.

She listed the pieces she made, her own festival clothing: twenty or so *kanchali* (backless blouses), two *paheranu* (wrapped skirts), a *ghagharo* (gathered skirt for the wedding ceremony), and a *ludi* (woolen veil) as dowry pieces to be brought at the time of marriage.

The bulk of the dowry was brought after the birth of the first son, so she had some time to finish it after marriage. She made a five-piece *toran* set to decorate the doorway of the home. The dowry required a series of embroidered bags: a *gupchi* (envelope bag), a *batuvo* (purse), and four *kothalo* and *kothali* (large and small sacks to carry the dowry pieces and later used as duvet covers for quilts at home).

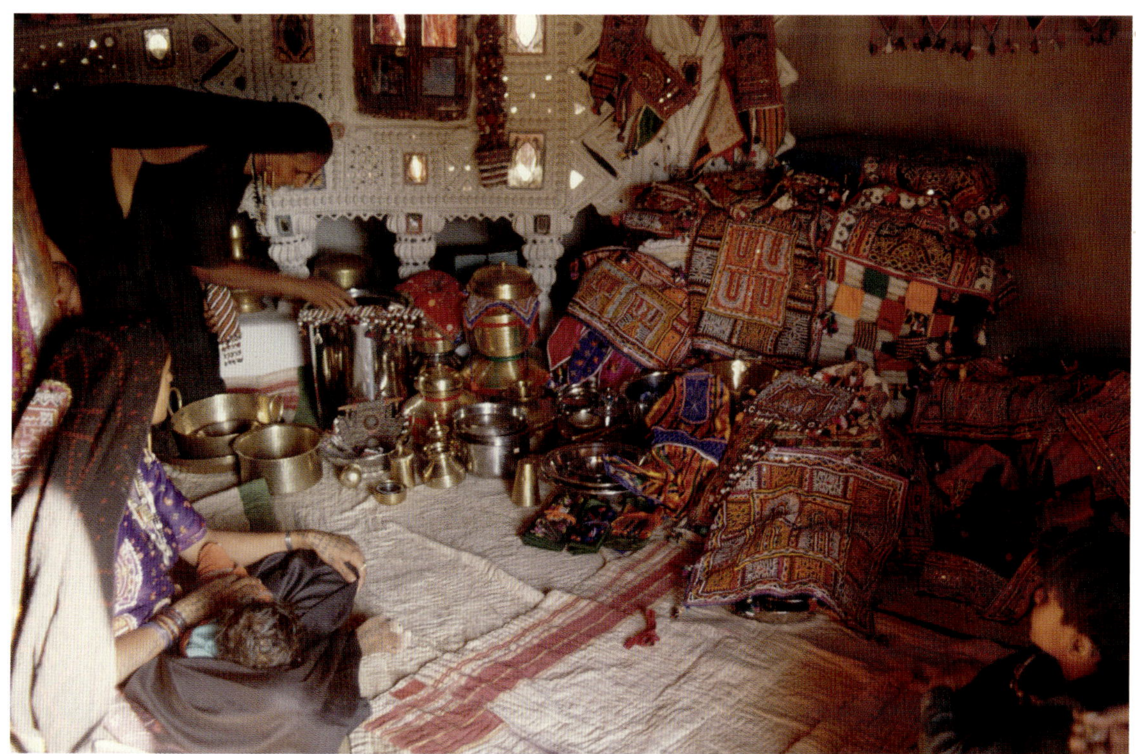

By Lachhuben's time, some of the sacks were replaced by a *theli* (shopping bag), and two *oshikun* (pillows). On the Holi after the birth of Vanka, her son, Lachhuben displayed the glittering wealth she had created—her *judio*—at her parents' home in Viyar, and then at her in-laws' home in Bhopani Vandh. Women of both villages scrutinized and discussed her work, critiquing it and getting ideas for their own embroidery.

By the early 1980s, after the herd of cattle had perished and before Rajabhai tapped into his entrepreneurial side, income became critical. Rajabhai went to Muskat to earn as a laborer. Lachhuben, like other Rabari women, traded her embroideries for vessels and sold them for cash. "I traded Rami's blouse for a *hail* (set of metal pots)," she confessed. She sold a *bokani* to a Rabari dealer. Much later, she traced the life of the *bokani* with amusement when she discovered it as the frontispiece in *Threads of Identity*. It was bought by Lachhuben Karna's daughter Rani, who sold it to me as her own.

The need to supplement meager earnings from the sale of milk and wool loosened restrictions for women. At the same time, embroidery became fashionable in the domestic market. Kachhi Rabari women began to seek embroidery job work. At first, they did embroidery for shopkeepers. But they had to go out of the village to pick up the commissioned pieces. A woman could not go alone, so two women from Vandh would pick up enough work for a group. For six months they did this "labor embroidery"—whatever was given to them. But neither artisans nor customer was satisfied. They sought another client, but she criticized their work. A third customer quoted a price and, when the work was delivered, paid a fraction of that.

By the early 1990s, the women of Vandh were frustrated and jaded. Fortunately, Rabaris have fewer social restrictions than many traditional embroiderers, so they had earning options. They could do agricultural labor in neighbors' fields, dig ditches for drought relief, or even do construction work, and they found this manual labor often more lucrative than "labor embroidery."

However they chose to earn, women worked. The impact was that they had little time to embroider for themselves or their own families. They were forced to apportion their limited time for multiple tasks. Calculating their efforts, Kachhi women creatively innovated on their tradition—they had professional tailors machine-embroider blouses, skirts, torans, and bags in traditional patterns, and they hand-embroidered details. Rajabhai returned to Kutch, saw an opportunity, and learned machine embroidery.

Lachhuben watched the changes. "Our village is 570 years old," she said. "All of the people are from one family. We are devout believers, and so we are called Bhopa Rabaris. Our mother goddess forbade us to have cement houses, electricity, kerosene, or gas. We never sold milk or our sheep, goats, or female camels. Then, around 1991, the goddess gave us permission, and we started to do these things."

She had a special concern for the attrition of handwork. So she agreed to work on the samples I gave her for Ritu Kumar. The patterns were not printed onto the fabric; they could use their art and make patterns they liked. She became a supervisor—and an advisor. "The women need constant work," she told me. "If you give once and don't come back for a long time, they won't be waiting for you."

"When you started a group, I earned much better," she recalled. "For a year, it was just a little work. Then you started Kala Raksha, and we got a lot of work. Rajabhai became a coordinator, and I became a supervisor. We started several new groups for Kala Raksha."

Then there were two trains running: embroidery for earning a living, and their own traditions. People always asked how the commercial work affected the tradition. The answer was always the same: not at all. "Except," Lachhuben exclaimed, "that we now wear less embroidery!!"

"What we do for ourselves is a separate entity, with our own standards," she said in an interview in 2005. "It is art; it was always art. We did not embroider for a market. There was no question of time or money. An artist is one who works for her own pleasure, not for money. And our work always had as much imagination as stitching."

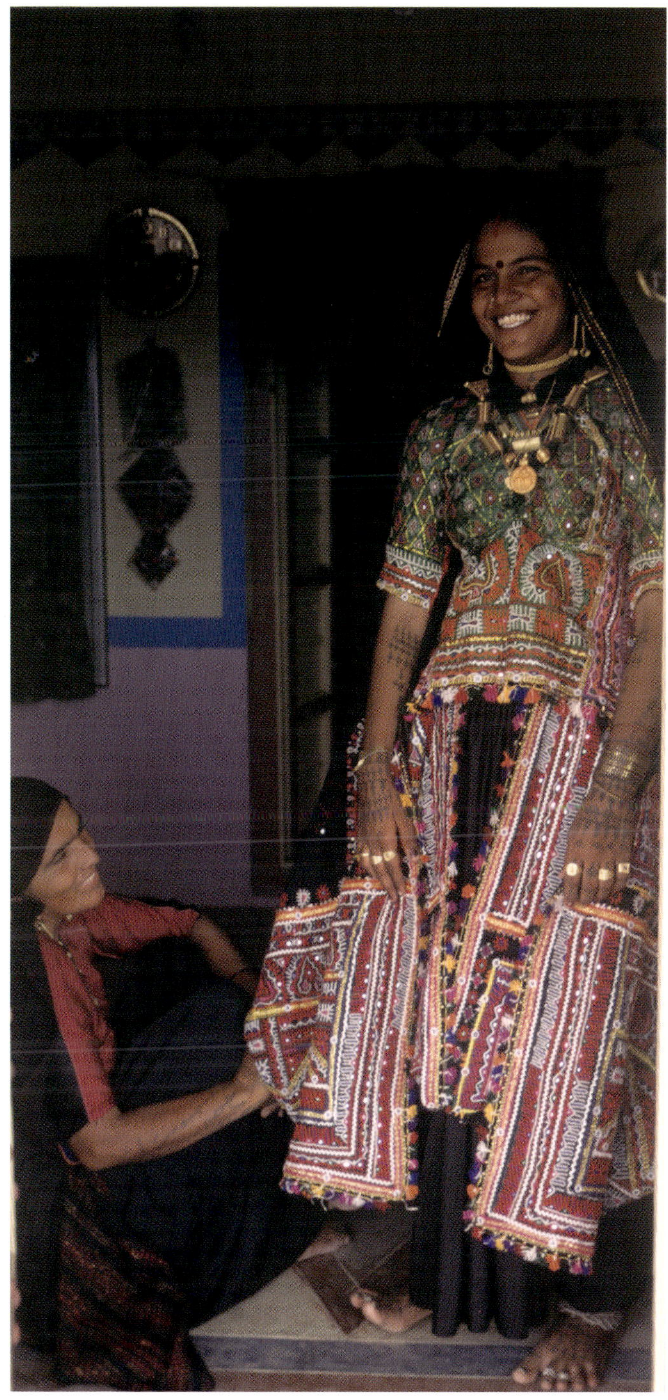

Bhopani Vandh, 2002. Lachhuben's elder daughter, Monghiben, models the *ludi* she embroidered for her wedding. The fully embroidered border, stitched on a separate synthetic fabric and attached to the woolen veil, was a major innovation and became instant fashion in Vandh. *Photo: Judy Frater*

With young women working and enjoying exposure, the entire concept of embroidery changed. "Now embroidery is the realm of the young," Lachhuben continued. "Girls used to wear the fabrics their elders brought them. Now, they are independent; they get their own. They do what they like. Colors are changed. If someone has the courage to make something new, and others follow, it becomes a fashion trend.

"There is still a relationship between artisan and art," she concluded. "It is the same, but it has changed. Now, we are using more sewing-machine work, and that has enabled girls to be more creative. When the art is in machine work, girls who are artists want to be behind the wheel!"

The list of dowry pieces was no longer compulsory, and many pieces were no longer done. "Women don't want to do them," Lachhuben reflected. In fact, she disclosed, girls now did dowry under duress, in fear of in-laws. Doing commercial work put a new spin on this. When women didn't bring much embroidery in their dowry, they were chided: "You spent all your time earning for your parents and didn't think of your in-laws!"

"I liked working as a child, when there were no worries or pressures," Lachhuben said. "I remember I made a *toran* just as I liked, while wandering with the herds. I did not sell it, and I will never sell it."

Kala Raksha collaborated with the embroiderers in the group in design, quality control, and pricing. This turned out to be more demanding than any of Lachhuben's previous attempts at earning through embroidering. "What we do for Kala Raksha is different," she said. "It is not just filling in printed patterns like most commercial work. It requires thinking, effort, and there is satisfaction in it. But time and money are involved too.

"We learned to increase our earnings," she elaborated. "I went to Delhi, Mumbai, Ahmedabad, Hyderabad, Chennai many times over the years. I went to America four times and Australia twice. I taught embroidery. People didn't know about our life, so I could explain it to them. The value of our personal work increased. Even the value of commercial work increased. Finally, Rabaris became valued."

Lachhuben would seem successful and empowered. In 2002, she and Rajabhai completed a spacious cement house. As it was under construction, she mused wondrously that in her life she could not have dreamed they would ever have a house. But she saw success as beyond increased income. "If we get the fruit of our work," she said, "if people praise, desire, or even copy it, this creates status, and success."

Thinking further, she added, "If you work for sale, you eventually learn responsibility." She felt the weight of responsibility in keeping track of materials and in mediating between community and the Kala Raksha Trust. She was extremely responsible in her role as coordinator for Vandh village. Over two decades she created new designs, monitored quality control, and communicated these to her group. The Rabari women of Vandh are not educated, she noted, so she had to convey the needs of the organization, while keeping in the forefront the viewpoint of the community.

Yet, the market part confounded her. In 2005, she confided that from the first design workshop we conducted at Kala Raksha, she got so nervous she couldn't eat or sleep. She was anxious about any new work or design. In her own work that never happens, she reflected. "I can make new things for myself, but it doesn't make me anxious."

The new market is the unknown. Nomadic, Rabaris traditionally lived in an uncertain world. But the parameters of that world were well known. Information gathering was their skill for survival. This new market is a true unknown.

I asked Lachhuben how we can maintain quality in handwork and be cost effective. "It is THE question," she acknowledged. "It takes time and effort. And education is necessary. But," she added, "it is too hard to learn."

In 2006, Lachhuben attended the pilot class of Kala Raksha Vidhyalaya.

"We learned products," she reflected. "It is important to know the context of the piece. For example, if it is a runner, from far we see the edges; from close we see the top. Even if we don't know the names, we can say where the piece is used and how. We also learned sampling, and many finishes. This is a very important and practical step."

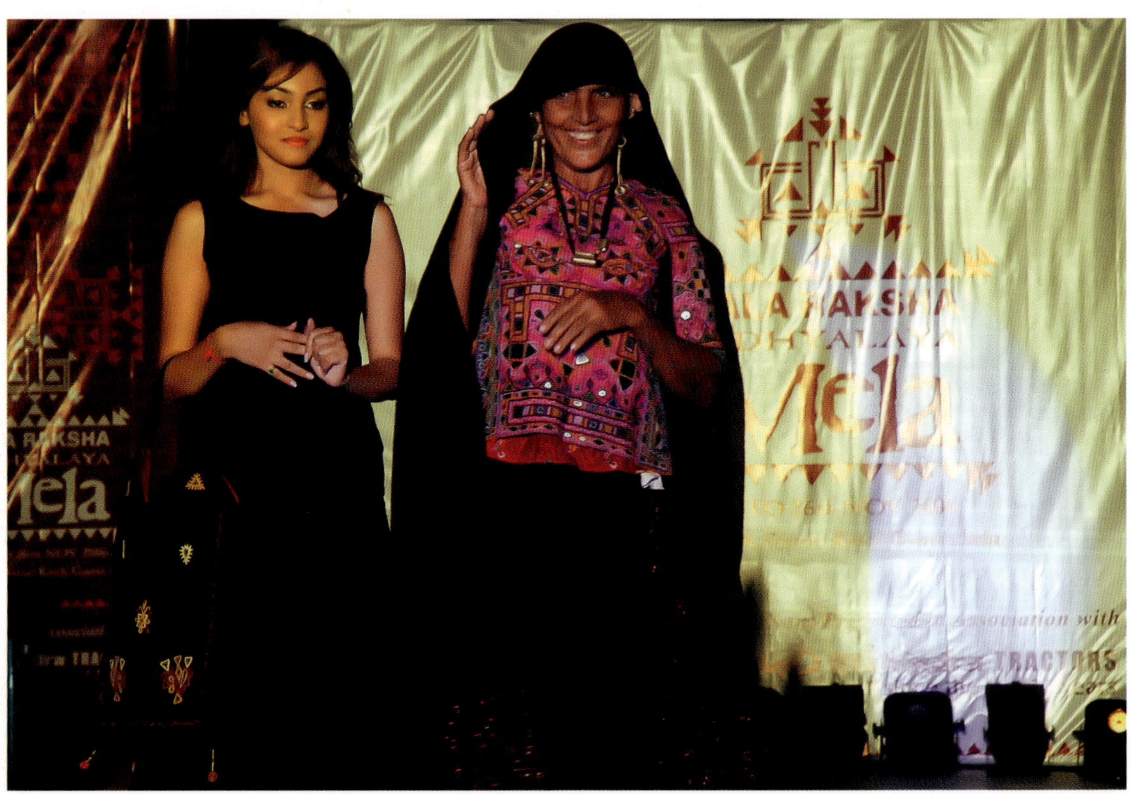

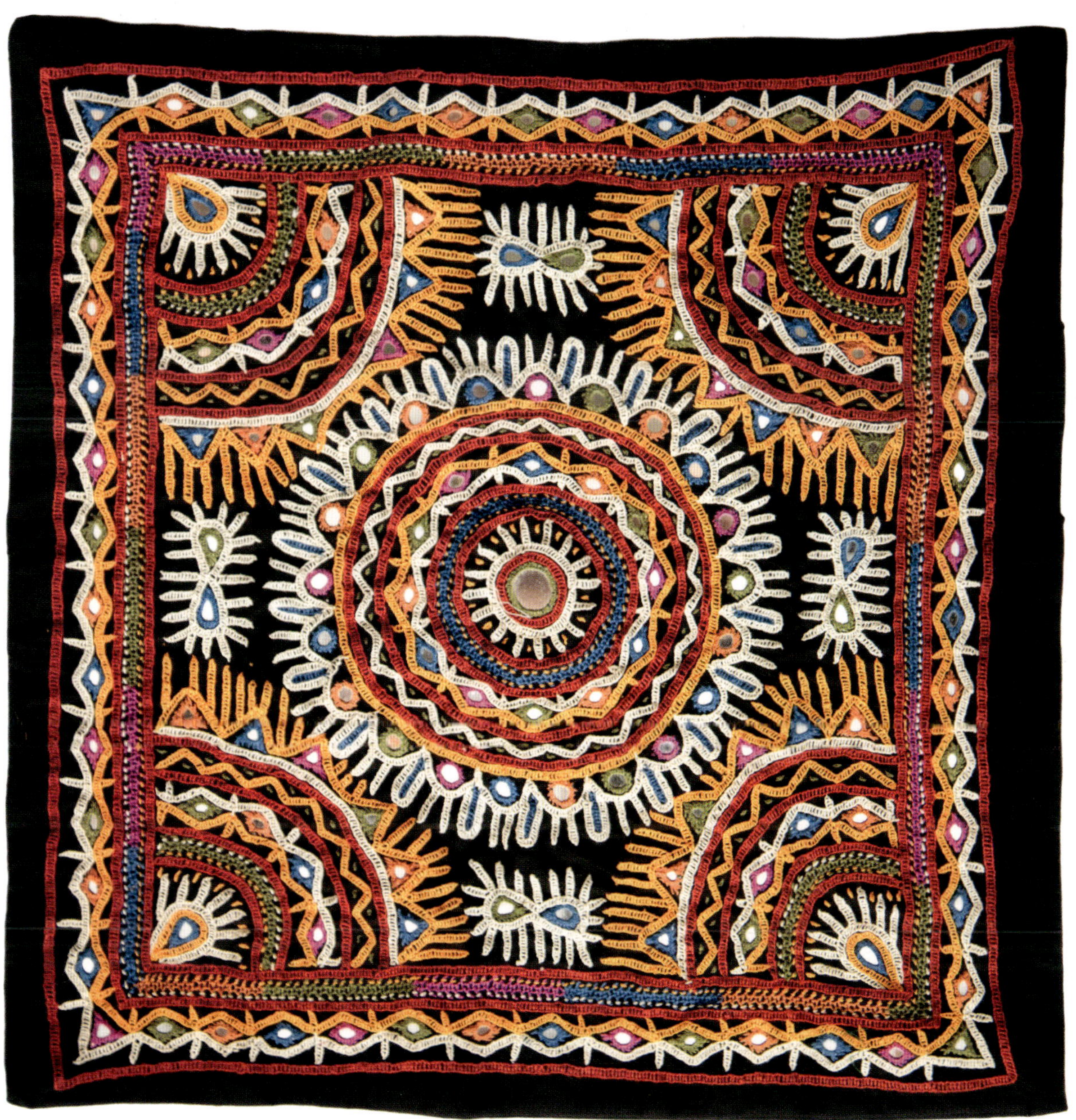

Lachhuben graduated from KRV with the award for Most Marketable Collection. The main thing she took away was this: "By thinking, each person makes something new. We learned to create new from tradition. After studying at KRV, I feel that I have stepped into a world where I myself make new designs as per the demand. You can't just think about one order or client or organization. You have to use your own creativity to keep on making new things."

Opposite: Kala Raksha Vidhyalaya, 2006. Lachhuben walked the fashion show ramp with her collection at the first KRV Convocation Mela. Practicing the customary *laj*, she covered her face on the side toward where men of the village sat. *Photo: Ketan Pomal, L.M. Studio*

Above: *Chaklo*, by Lachhuben Raja Rabari, 2022. Cotton fabric, cotton thread, mirrors, Rabari embroidery. 15" x 15". Lachhuben created a wall hanging with the joy of the Rabari style of her era. She used traditional colors and mirrors. Everyone does round, she says; she used five "designs" (mirror shapes)—all Rabari. *Photo: Schiffer Publishing Ltd.*

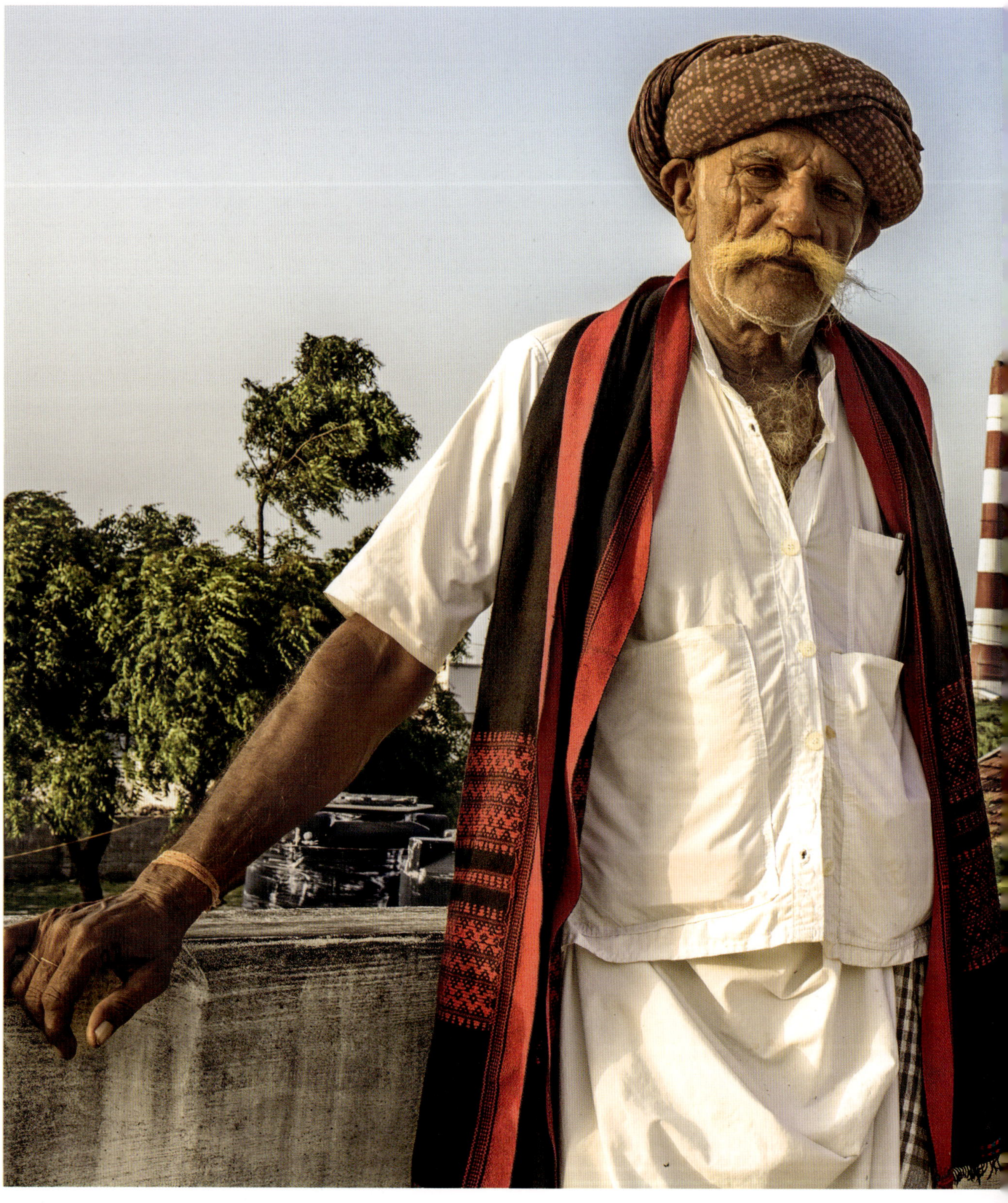

She was a mentor at Kala Raksha Vidhyalaya. She spoke at the 2007 KRV Convocation and participated in workshops to develop new products. But Lachhuben never considered starting her own independent work. In reality, it is still a far reach even for a feisty Rabari woman to imagine herself dealing directly with new markets. And it is an important part of Rabari culture not to stand out from the group too much, particularly in economic terms.

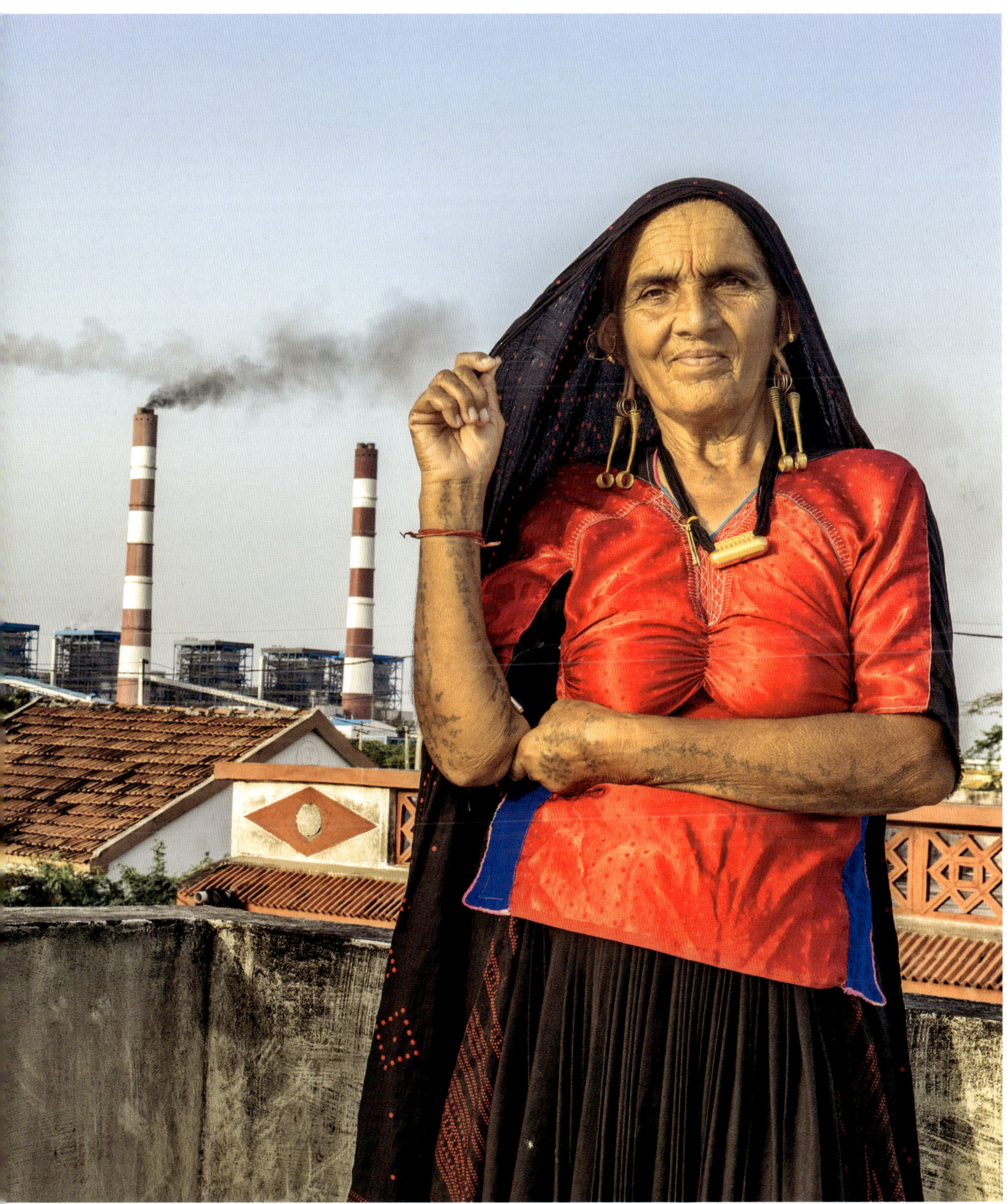

Bhopani Vandh, 2022. Lachhuben and Rajabhai pose on the roof of the cement home they built since working with Kala Raksha. The village is all cement homes now. Chimneys of Adani Power, one of two plants that flank the village, spew smoke from burning coal behind them. *Photo: Nevada Wier*

About the time Lachhuben was graduating from KRV, the Indian government began to establish an "Ultra Mega" coal-fed thermal power plant in her village. Soon after, Adani Power began an adjoining one of equal size. Today the village is sandwiched between these giants.

In 2011, Lachhuben created a narrative piece on the situation. Explaining it, she said, "Kutch was always a dry and poor area. Now we have money. Companies have come to our village. We used to be able to walk anywhere without fear. We never had to lock our homes, and we had no walls. We were free. Now we earn money from the companies, but we are afraid to go anywhere because everywhere we look, there are strangers—laborers not from Kutch. The companies are making power. There is a lot of coal and pollution. I know there is going to be trouble, but we don't know what. We may fall ill. We don't know what will happen to us in the future."

By 2019, after resisting for years, Lachhuben began to earn daily wages from one of the plants, like all of the other women from the original Kala Raksha group. Few women have patience for embroidery. And even with her salary at Kala Raksha plus embroidery wages, she couldn't make as much as she did sweeping in the company a few times a day. "There is a lot of cheap embroidery around," she said. "If I charge more for my work, it won't sell.

"My granddaughter Rani won't embroider," she continued. "She will study. Maybe she'll get a job. How could she do embroidery too? She is wondering how she will prepare a dowry, but she has no time."

2022

But in three years, the world was upended, again. Rani did finish her bachelor's degree. And she did land a job, as a constable with the local police force. And before she could begin, COVID-19 raged through Kutch. Confined to her home in Vandh, she used the two-year break to learn embroidery, and she got into it—exactly the way Lachhuben described a new artist: you learn it and feel like doing it.

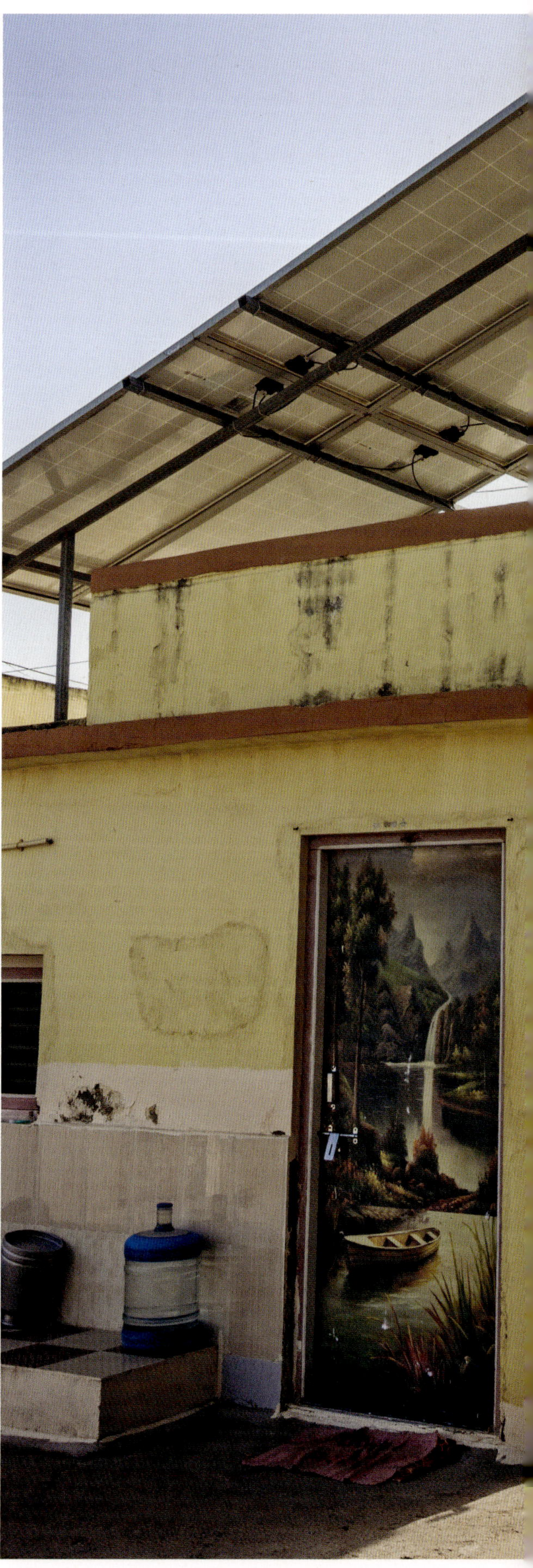

Right: Bhopani Vandh, 2022. Despite dangerous proximity to Asia's two largest coal-fed thermal power plants, the Vandh community pays high rates for electricity that is unreliable. Practical and forward thinking, Lachhuben and Rajabhai's son Vankabhai installed solar panels above the kitchen. *Photo: Nevada Wie*

Following pages: Bhopani Vandh, 2022. Lachhuben's granddaughter Raniben presents the embroidery she created during the pandemic lockdown—her *judio*, which she will bring to her in-laws' home when she marries. The style is currently in fashion among her peers. *Photo: Nevada Wier*

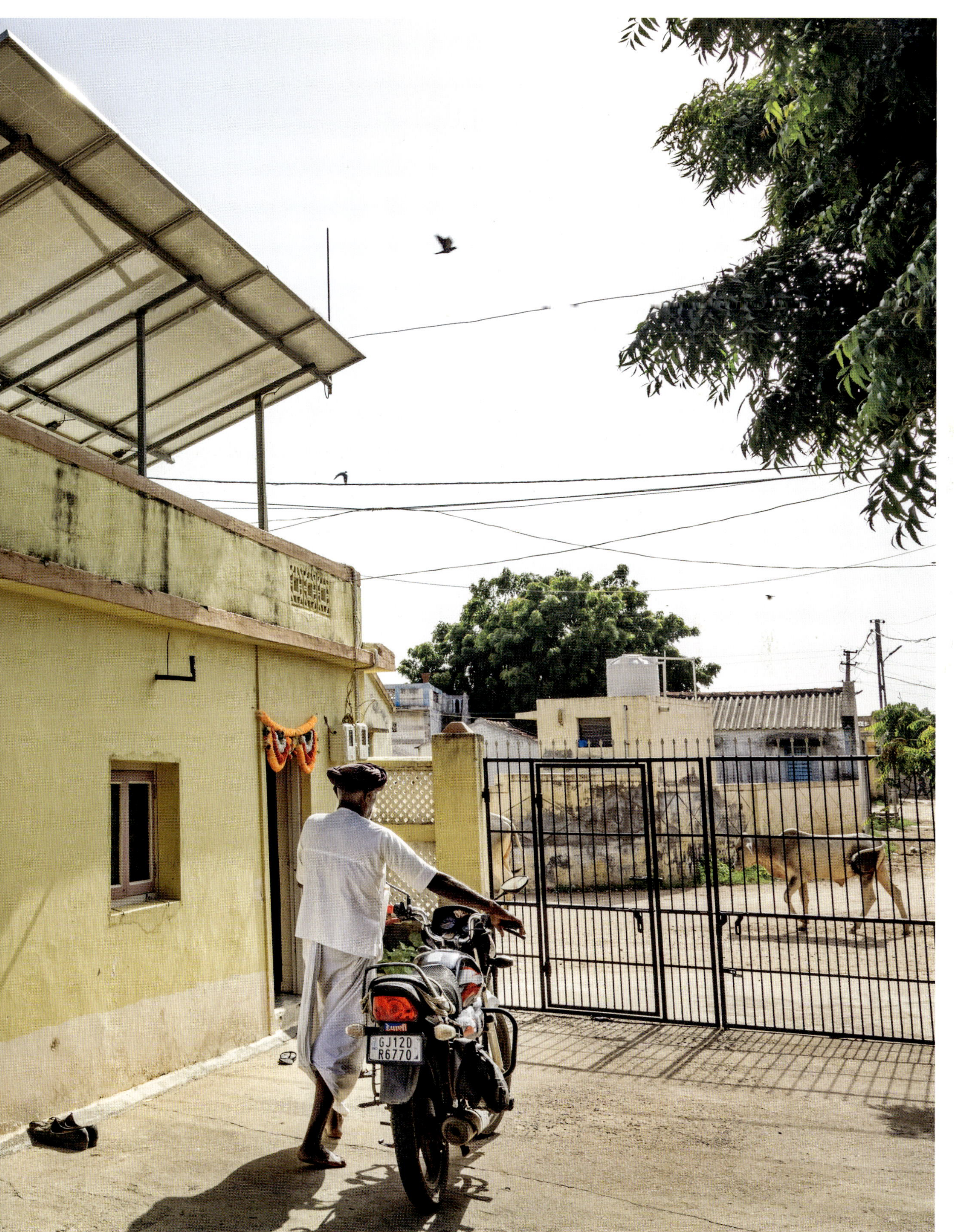
GJ12D
R6770

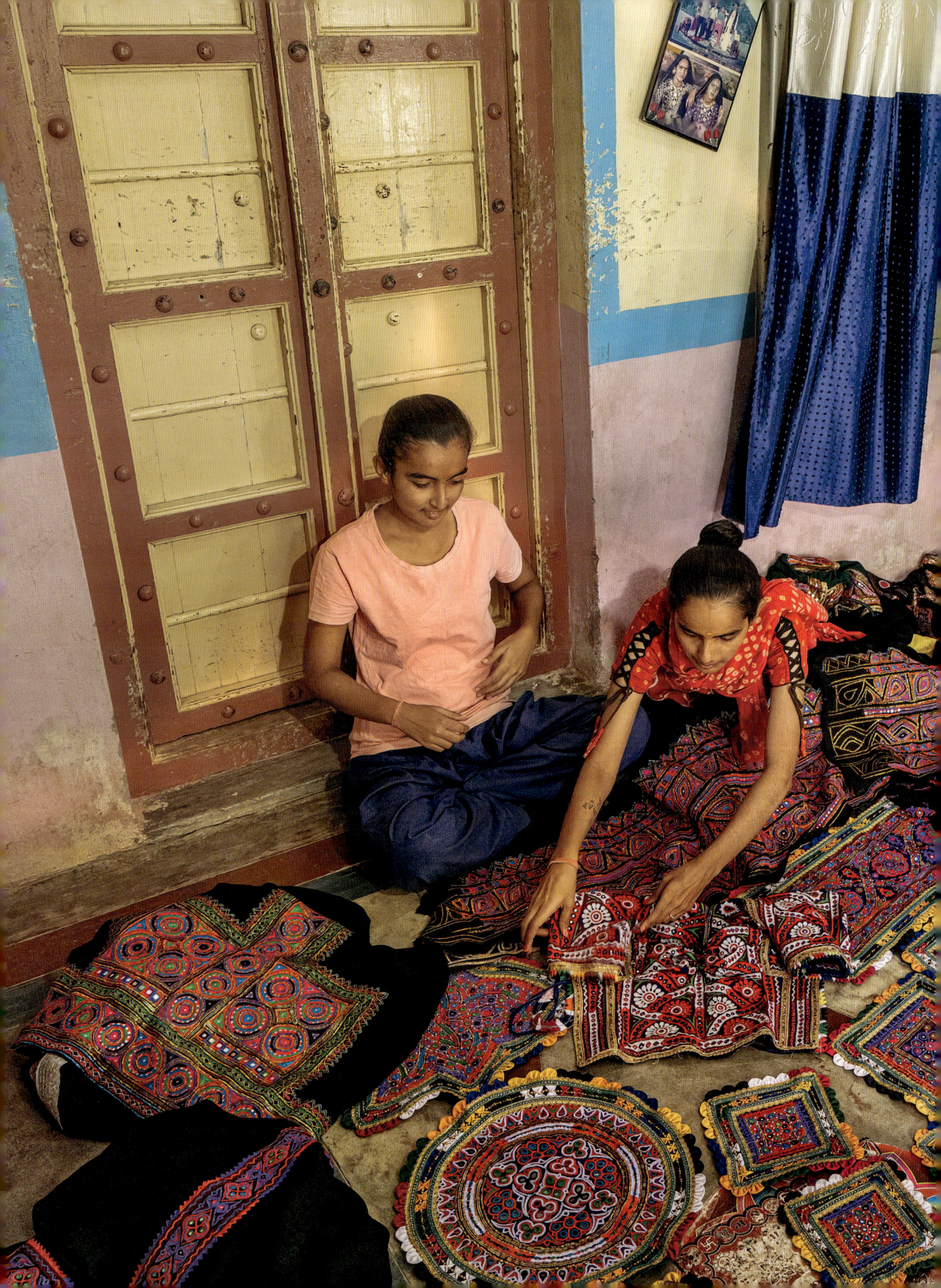

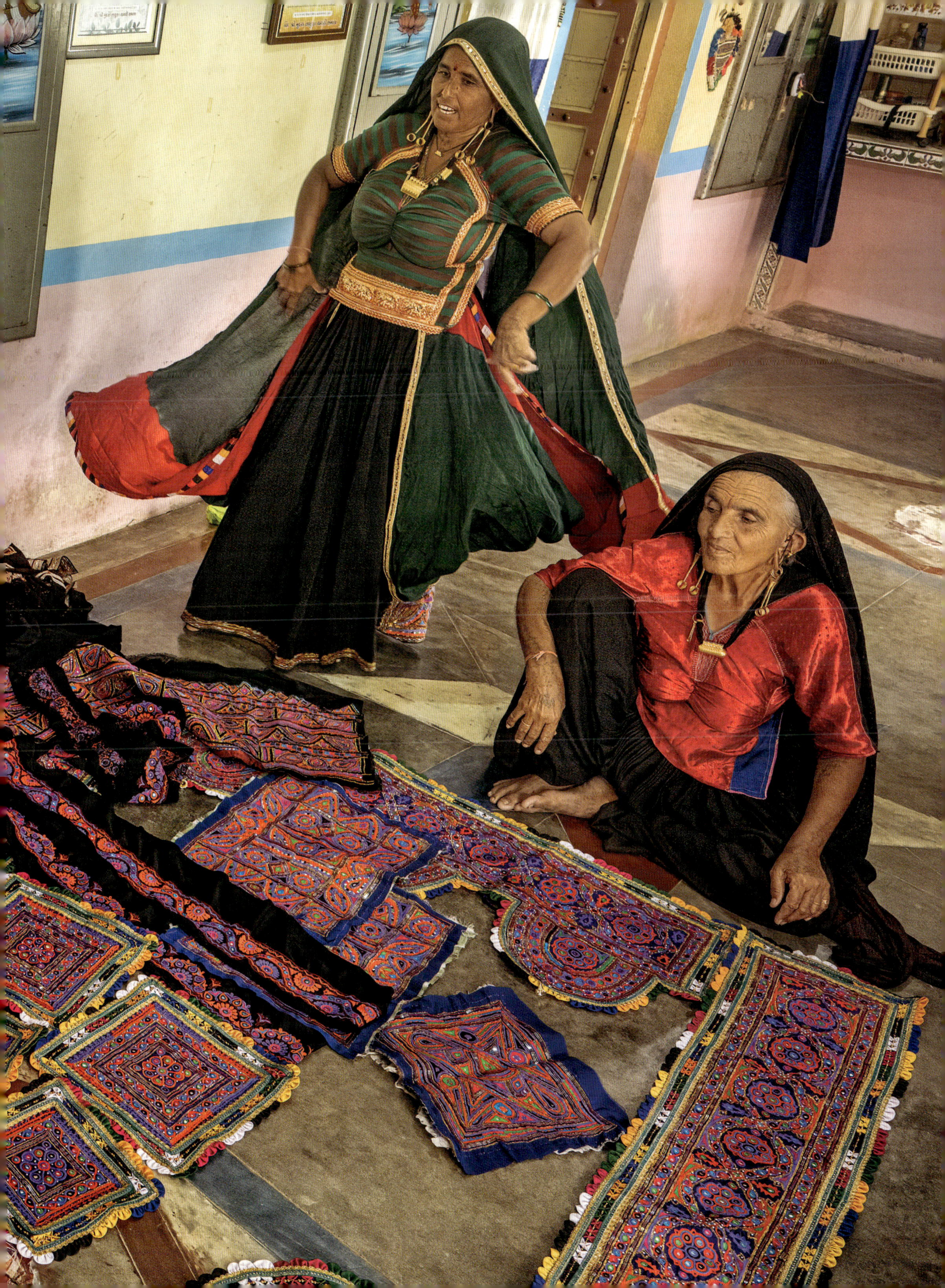

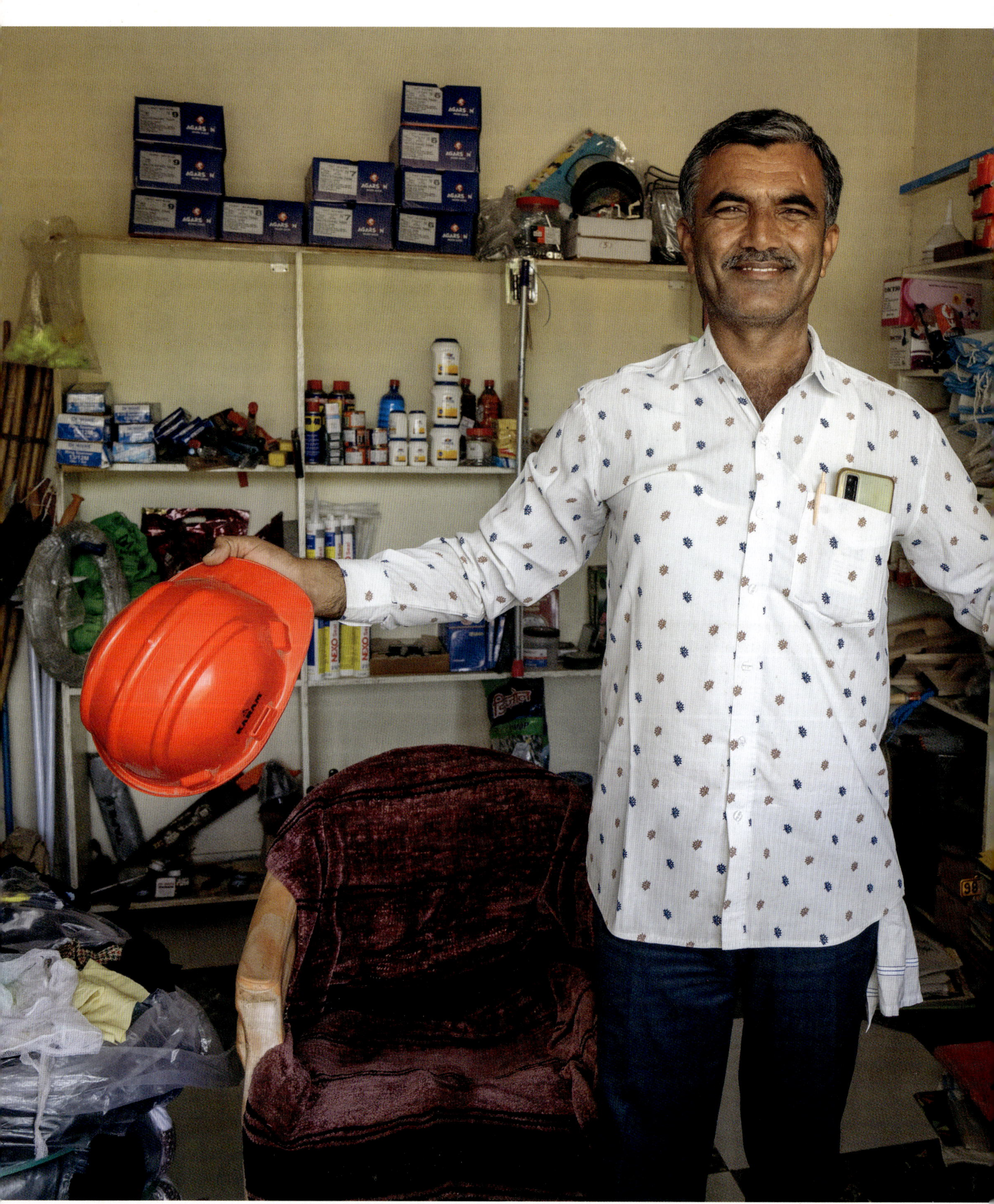

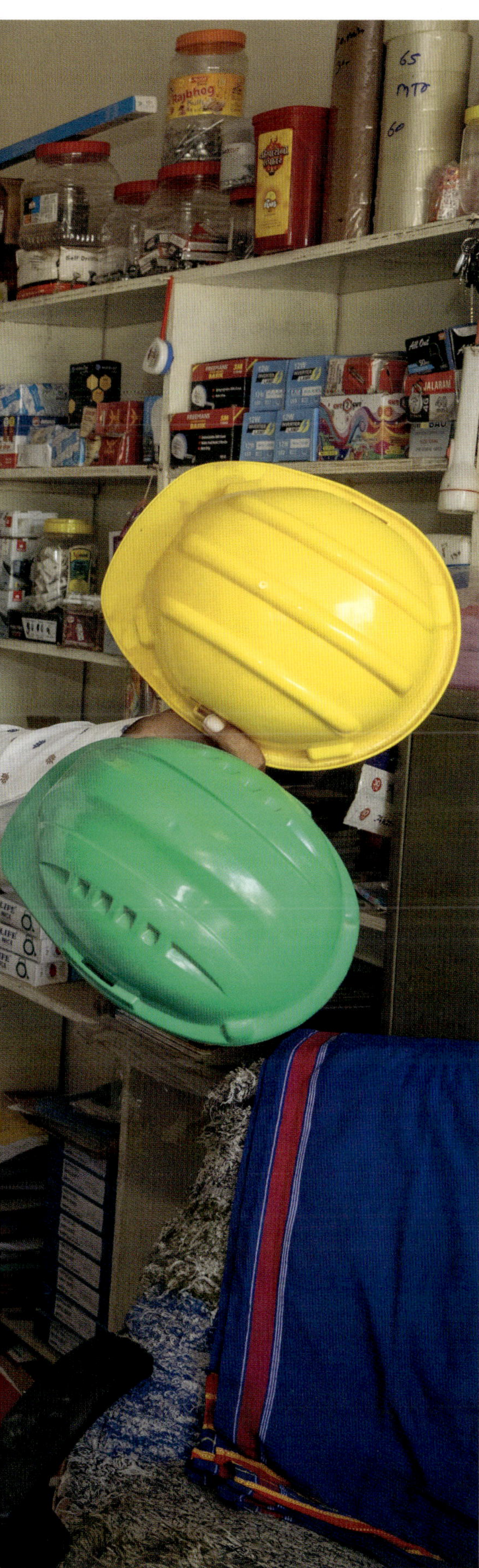

Rani pulls an unending array of embroidery from the cupboard. There is a new-styled *toran*, revived *barsang* (doorway decoration)—without the leaves! All of it is embroidered in Ahir style, the fashion now, in blue and magenta, some pieces with machine zigzag, some all by hand, some with *zari* metallic thread. Only three pieces don't go; they have bright-orange stitching in the middle. Those aren't in the collection, she says; they were done before. It IS a collection—for her dowry. She's engaged, and her in-laws wanted the marriage this year. But Rani said no. She wants to take up her job.

Lakhiben, her mother, gets out a few pieces of her own. Rani pushes them out of the way, obsolete. The fashion now is good chain stitch, mirrors, and some revived *bavaliyun* and *kungari* (interlaced techniques).

"But they change the names!" Lachhuben exclaims. Now, *bavaliyun* is called *chamkudi*. And *kungari* is called *dungar*!

Lachhuben says her son Vankabhai told her to stop working at the company. It was tiring her out, and the family doesn't need her income now. They have a shop selling what the companies need—helmets for each level of worker—like the army, color coded. Fuel, boots, whatever they need. Gotcha. And Vankabhai has put in solar panels—the ultimate irony, sandwiched between two coal-fed thermal power plants, using solar energy.

Rabaris adapt once again. Their *bhunga* are gone, they no longer wander, and they embroider in Ahir style. But they are ever Rabari.

Bhopani Vandh, 2022. Today, most of the village depends on the power plants for one livelihood or another. Like his father before him, Vankabhai saw an opportunity; he started a shop selling products that power-plant workers need. *Photo: Nevada Wier*

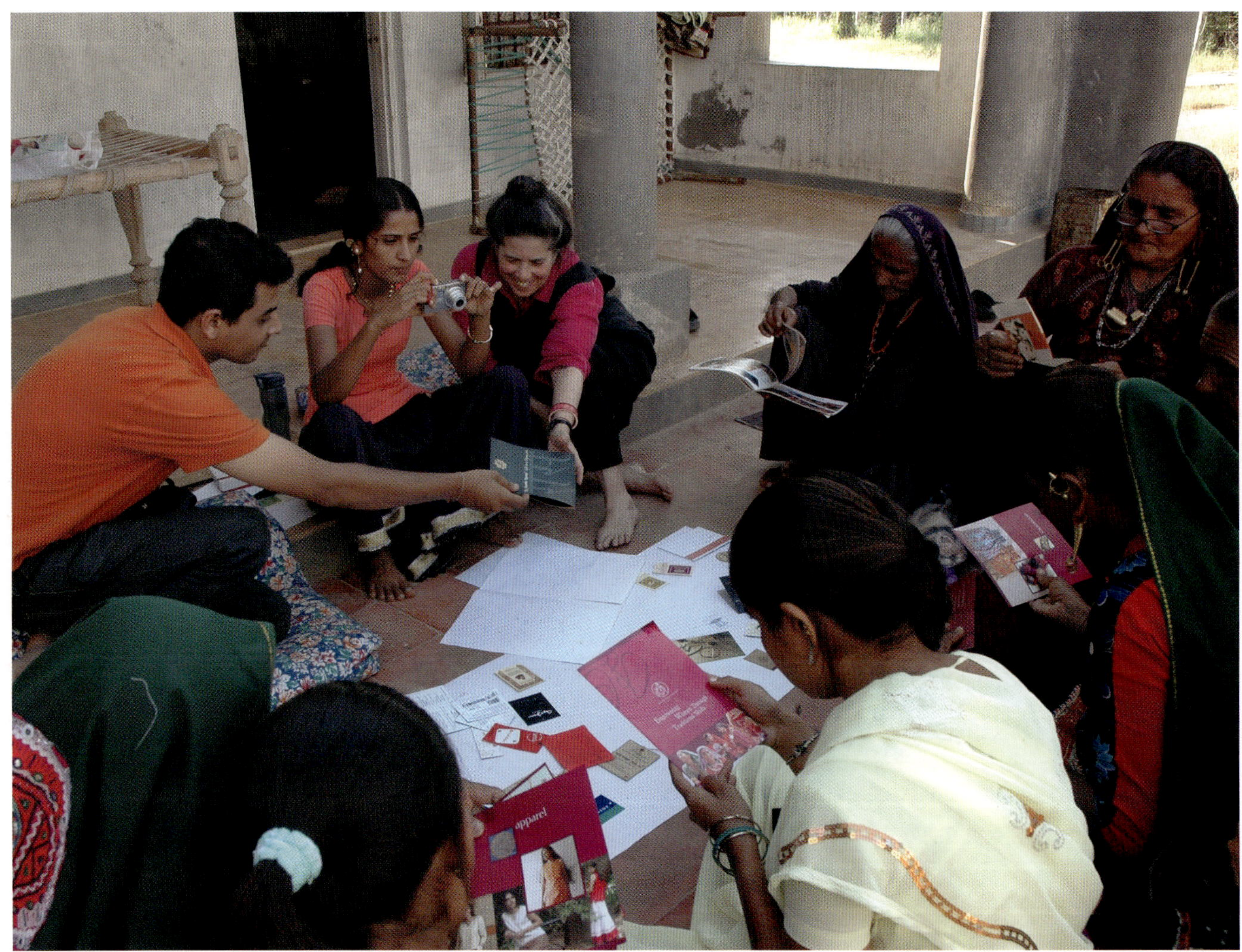

Don't teach us embroidery! Embroidery is what we do.
Teach us something useful.

~Bhagvatiben Laxman Bhanani

Above: Kala Raksha Vidhyalaya, 2008. Jan Baker cotaught Merchandising, Presentation, with Lokesh Ghai in 2008. In this final module, students make logos and learn to present their collections verbally and through display and promotional materials. Graduates from previous classes mentor and document each module. *Photo: Judy Frater*

Following pages: Kala Raksha Vidhyalaya, 2008. The studios, dormitories, and exhibition hall of the KRV campus were designed and built by Hemen Sanghvi, an architect committed to vernacular techniques and materials salvaged from historical structures. An avid gardener, he also planted morning glories. The campus was overseen by Lakhmirbhai, a Rabari from Vandh. *Photo: Judy Frater*

Chapter 8

ARTISANS DESIGN: THE KALA RAKSHA VIDHYALAYA YEARS

It was freezing cold at dawn. We were sleeping in an open field, afraid to be in the village, burrowed under blankets and quilts. My body was stiff from shivering night after night. A reporter pushed a mic to my face and asked, "What do you hope will emerge from this earthquake?"

"A design school for artisans," popped out of my mouth.

Uh oh, I thought. Now I will have to do it.

The aftermath of the 2001 earthquake was like floating in space. The familiar became treacherous; anything was possible. Running from that deep anxiety, striving to create stability, I met a world of agencies converged in Kutch. Pradeep Kashyap, cofounder of American India Foundation, saw the potential for social change in my idea and nominated me for an Ashoka Fellowship. With a mentor from the organization, I worked to imagine it in practical terms—with timeline and budget. In 2003, Ashoka granted me a fellowship. It gave me support and a sense of responsibility. It solidified my mission.

Artisans were struggling to reach new markets, and the swelling wave of commercialization and "design intervention" was turning them into laborers in their own traditions. The alternatives they saw were to go on producing the same designs or to make haphazard innovations and sell them at cheap prices in the many craft bazaars. Or they could do job work for middlemen—designers, merchants, or master artisans. Top-down intervention diffused the essence and strength of traditions. At a Dastkar exhibition when I congratulated a weaver that his son had joined him in weaving, he said, "Yes, well, he didn't pass tenth grade; what else could he do?"

Women embroiderers were innovating on traditional objects in the Kala Raksha museum. But real change requires sustained input. I believed that a program in design education could both strengthen the capacity of rural artisans and revitalize traditions in terms of new markets.

The Ashoka Fellowship opened doors. I visited design schools in the US and India. It seemed that much of a design course was devoted to developing a medium to which design could be applied. The students of the course I envisioned already had traditions: highly developed skiils, knowledge, and a

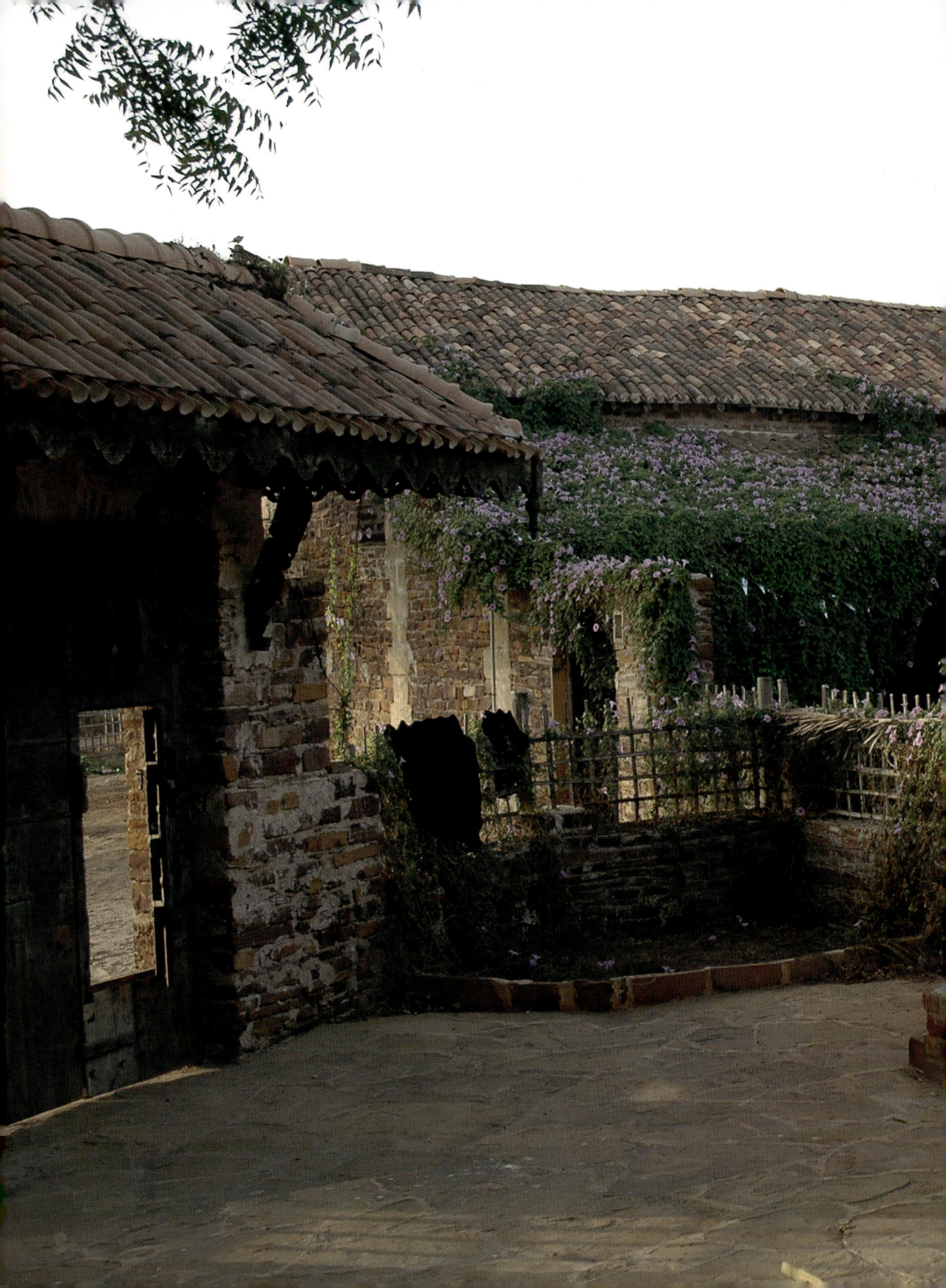

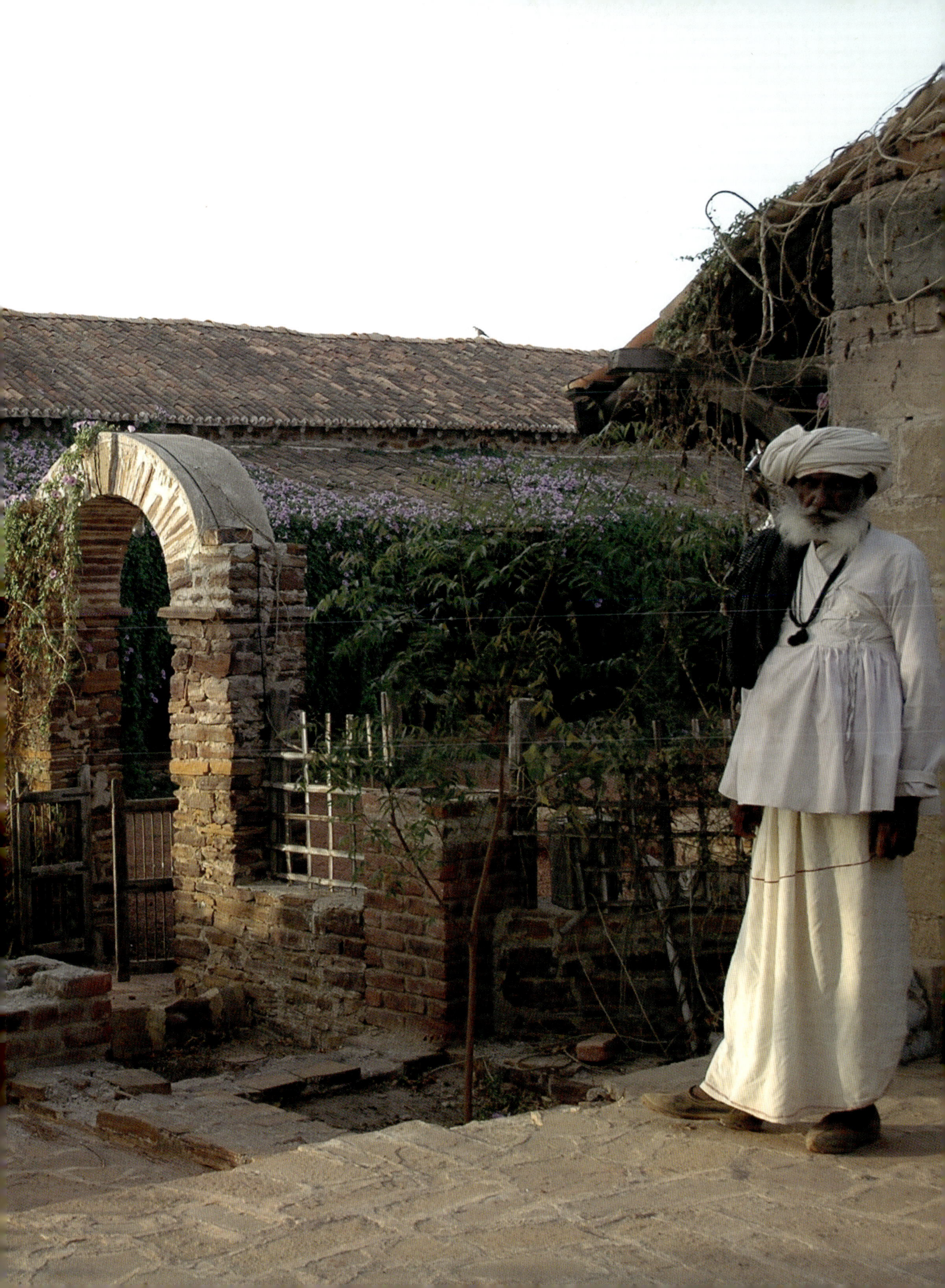

distinct sense of aesthetics, so their course could be shorter. In September 2004, I brought together people with experience I needed to develop a curriculum. We brainstormed for two days at the Rhode Island School of Design (RISD). At the end of the second day, Jan Baker, faculty at RISD, sat quietly with me and showed me her practical, tried-and-true way of working new things out. We wrote key ideas onto 3 × 5 recipe cards and moved them around on the table until we had a structure that made sense. I began with that model, and it remains the backbone of the core course.

I wanted to create protected time and space in which artisans could disengage from the demands of their lives, find inspiration from nature and their traditions, explore, and reflect. But it had to be possible for them to take the course. I decided to structure it as two-week residential modules scheduled around ritual and livelihood timings. I decided to have visiting faculty. This way, students would experience a range of views and methods, and the institute could secure excellent educators. The visiting faculty would create their own syllabi based on the curriculum, ensuring their preparation and engagement in the course. Between courses, artisan students would return to their homes and do homework projects that reinforced their understanding and contributed to their ongoing work. Over a year, artisans would learn practically, using vernacular language, how to develop a design collection. The course would end with a professional jury and a public exhibition and fashion show.

Because design as an entity is alien to traditional culture, Indian design institutes follow a largely Western curriculum. I wanted to ensure that whatever I did would strengthen and not erode traditions. At this point I realized that I needed to include men weavers, printers, and dyers of Kutch. I also needed artisan community support.

I asked Kala Raksha women embroiderers if they wanted to learn. They were excited. "But don't teach us embroidery!" said Bhagvatiben. All the workshops conducted for artisans do just that: teach them craft skills. "Embroidery is what we do," she explained. "Teach us something useful."

I went to Ismailbhai Khatri, a leader in the traditional block-printing community, and presented my proposal to him and his sons in their new home in Ajrakhpur. It was one of the most difficult presentations I have ever made—a completely new idea, out of the blue. I faltered, anxious, blushing, listening to them listen to me. Ismailbhai was skeptical. He rolled the idea around in his mind. Then he sternly said "We know what goes on at NID. If anything like that happens in your school, we'll shut the doors." So we would hold men's and women's classes separately.

Even after village reconstruction and matching grants, Kala Raksha had funds that I had raised for earthquake rehabilitation. We purchased 8 acres of idyllic land shaded by date palms, neem, and liyar trees outside Bhopani Vandh (known by outsiders as Tunda Vandh), Lachhuben and Rajabbhai's camel-herding Rabari village on the Gulf of Kutch; we hired an architect and built the first building—a guest house for faculty. During this time, I reconnected with architect Hemen Sanghvi, who was restoring earthquake-damaged properties of the Maharao of Kutch. He was dedicated to authentic traditional technology, and his aesthetics were exquisite. I asked him to build craft studios on our campus. Using antique wood and stone elements, recycled *desi* tiles, stone, lime mortar, and almost no cement, he created studios and then dormitories. The completely green buildings seemed as if they had been there for decades. Most importantly, they embodied the concept that tradition is the foundation of innovation, providing an appropriate context.

I established an advisory board of senior textile artists: Ismail Mohmed Khatri, Alimamad Isha Khatri, Umar Faruk Khatri, Gulam Husen Khatri, Shamji Vishramji Siju, and Lalji Khengar Vankar. I presented my ideas to them and added their feedback. We made only two prerequisites for admission: students must be traditional artisans, and they must know their craft. There were no restrictions on age or formal education. I trusted that the advisors would be fair to their communities; they nominated the first men students, for the most part their family members. Rabari embroiderers from

Bhopani Vandh were the first women students. I wanted the village to know what we were doing, and the women would not have to stay overnight.

I cobbled together a budget for a year. And then suddenly I felt like I was standing at the edge of an abyss. What was I doing? I had no experience in making a school! I couldn't bring those artisan students here and dupe them! But there was no going back now. I took a deep breath and plunged in.

To the rhythm of ongoing construction, we held a workshop for sensitizing the first visiting faculty, and then in 2005, Kala Raksha Vidhyalaya quietly opened its doors for course 1: Color, Basic Design, Sourcing from Nature and Heritage.

The men students arrived from their villages carrying their clothing and tools. They ranged in age from seventeen to thirty-two. Some did job work for other businesses or NGOs; a few had their own family businesses. Many had limited direct contact with clients, and some had never traveled outside Kutch. Most could read and write in Gujarati. They did not know what to expect. "I had no clue we'd actually learn designing. I thought a designer would tell me what to do, and I'd do it," Khimjibhai, a weaver, said.

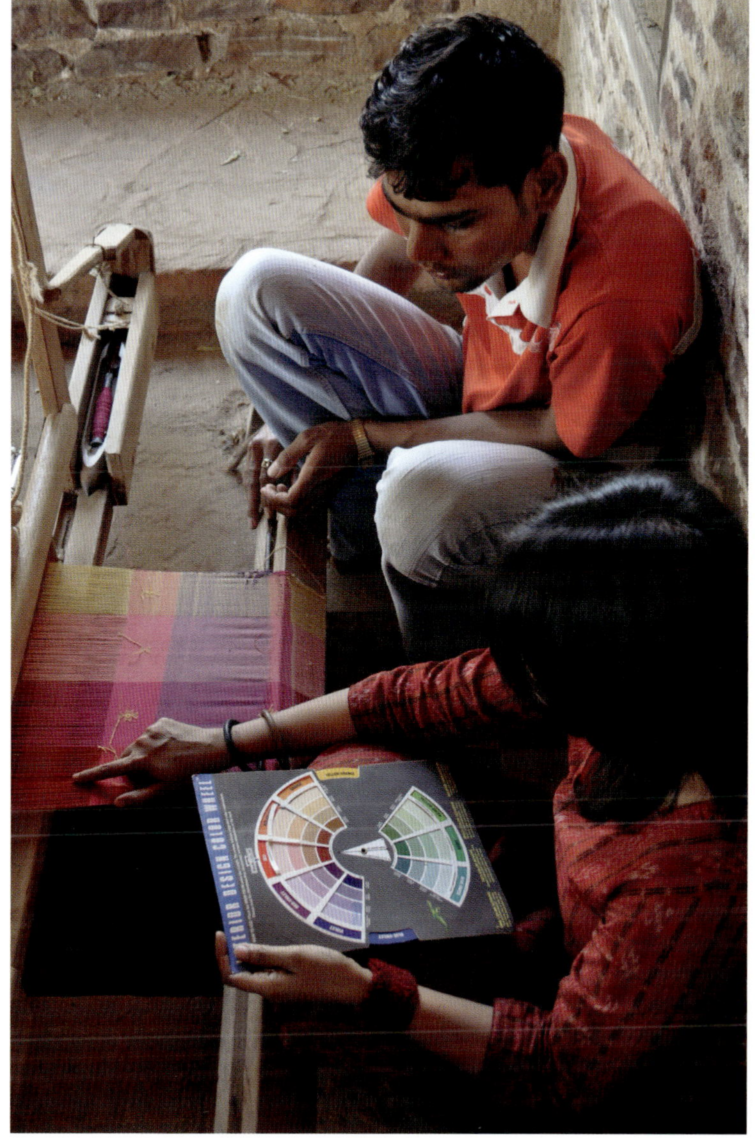

Kala Raksha Vidhyalaya, 2010. Color theory is taught on the loom, in dye studios, and with embroidery thread. Quickly applying theory to craft practices ensures relevance, and students absorb and retain material. *Photo: Judy Frater*

They resisted much of the theoretical teaching. Azizbhai, a bandhani artist, told me, "I'm here only because my father respects you." But for sampling they plunged joyfully into the looms, printing tables, and dye baths of our studios. They explored design principles, layout, and proportion through their crafts. Clearly, they thought in their media.

And they learned. "The first time I made color, I did it randomly," Khimjibhai observed. "But by the last time, I learned *how* to mix and kept records so that I could repeat it."

"I hadn't used a pen for four years," Maganbhai exclaimed. "I had never seen the sea! I enjoyed the freedom, the fun, the support of team members. The first few days were hard . . . but I never imagined such a school!"

"We went to the beach for fun," Junaidbhai added, "but had our eyes opened. Now, I will always see in a new way."

The women students' understanding of their tradition was not primarily professional, but innovation was an integral part of embroidery. So these students brought with them experience with the design process and a direct link between design and creation, but limited commercial exposure and almost no formal education. They were quicker and harsher in their judgment. Course 1 had no relevance to their art, they said. When they were asked to translate paper concepts to embroidery, one woman observed, "Of course the embroidery is going to look like bad drawing!" After a few days, they went home crying. I followed them and convinced them to trust us for the two weeks.

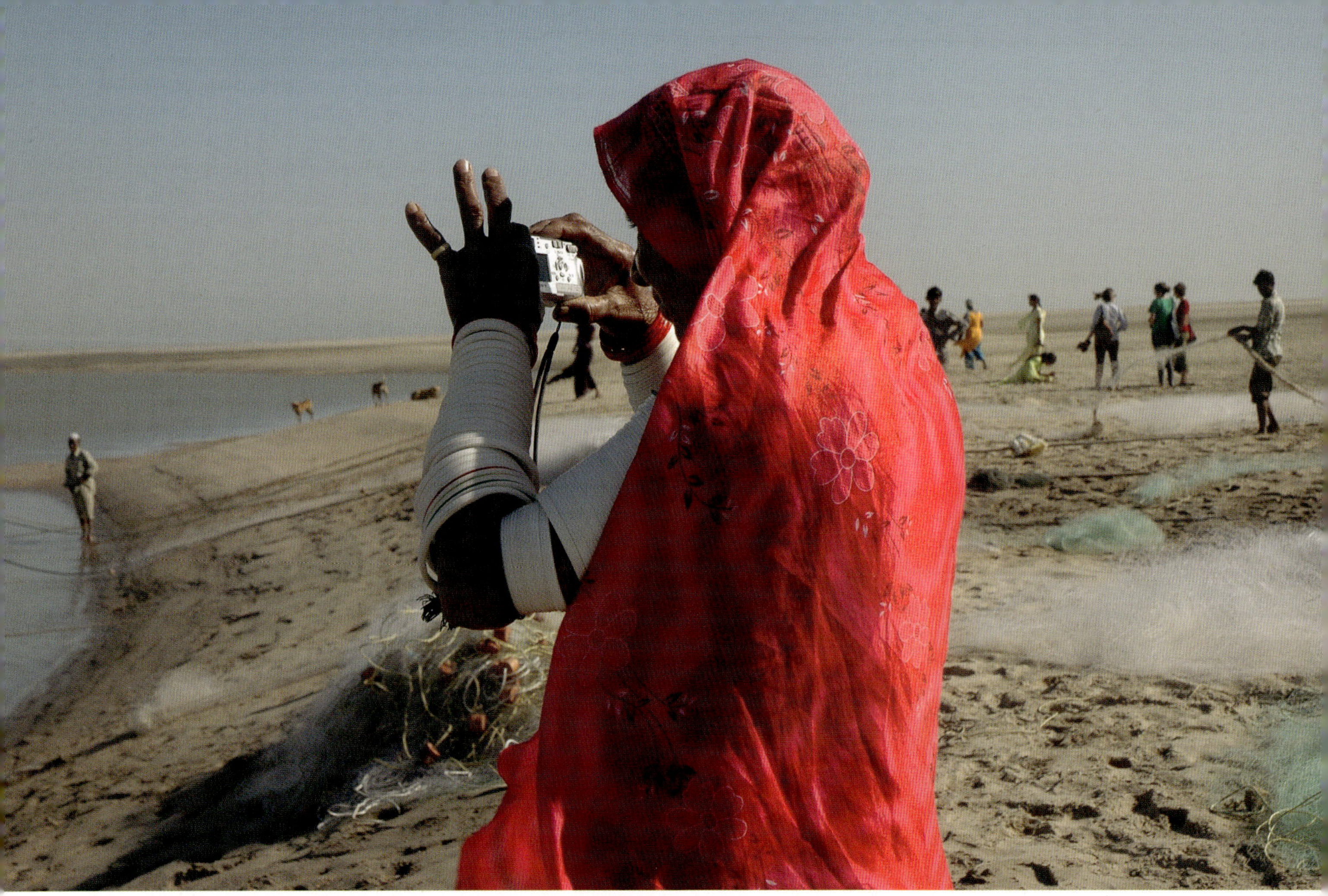

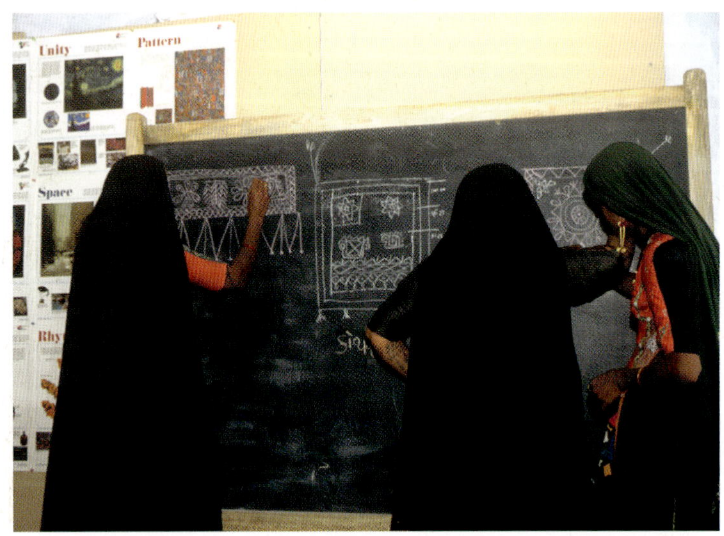

By the third course, we had settled enough logistics that I could begin to focus on learning, incorporating and strengthening traditional methods of design, and articulating course content in terms of known cultural concepts.

The men told us that when they worked in groups, they felt constrained because it forced them to think too abstractly. When they developed concepts individually, they could ponder the problem through their own media, and this was exciting. I realized the need to change the balance of plan and experiment. As Azizbhai said, "Writing, seeing, and doing are all different. These should be done in proportion . . ."

Top: Kala Raksha Vidhyalaya, 2008. Nature is the endless resource. Field trips are an essential part of modules. Students learn to observe, document, and draw inspiration from their environment. *Photo: Judy Frater*

Bottom: Kala Raksha Vidhyalaya, 2006. Rabari women embroider directly on the fabric. In the first year of the design course, they found drawing intimidating until a teacher told them to use the chalk like a needle. *Photo: Judy Frater*

Opposite: Kala Raksha Vidhyalaya, 2008. Senior artisan advisors teach students about their traditions, a foundation that builds respect for tradition and helps students recognize that heritage textiles used the basics of design. *Photo: Judy Frater*

A key factor for all students was beginning with what they know. For women students, the course material had to be modified and presented differently. When women were simply asked to draw in the way that they would embroider, they delighted in extending their vocabulary, within the Rabari style. "Drawing and embroidery used to be two different things!" Jilliben exclaimed. "Now they are one." When a teacher asked women to make sense of a pile of colored embroidery yarns and they all discussed it, they loved learning color. "Of course, we used color before," they said. "But we didn't know *how*." Then they taught us all their own concepts of organization: high and low contrast. "*Apna vishay chhe*!" they proclaimed. This is our subject.

Artisan students learned to see and appreciate their traditions in the context of a new design language. They realized what they already knew. They moved from "Just tell us what to do" to the excitement of trying new ideas, the satisfaction of good design, and the confidence in the ability to do it again.

Devalben, a Rabari embroiderer, exclaimed, "I never knew I could use my own ideas! I just embroidered. But when I did a windmill motif, I discovered my ability. I see the potential of embroidery now. I have dreams!"

"I went only to fourth grade," Deviben, the youngest woman student, related, "but now I feel educated. I learned how to talk, how to write . . . I was able to correct what one mentor wrote on the blackboard! Now, we can correct each other because we have reached a level of education."

But Ramiben, a thoughtful student, had one doubt. "We have to exercise our minds. The experience gives us pride in ourselves. Though, sometimes I wonder: these motifs look Rabari but they are not. So, are they OK?"

Khimjibhai, a weaver, responded, "In innovating we must keep the traditional, retain the identity of being a Kutchi weaving. Otherwise, we make something that anyone anywhere can do."

This is the crux of design for traditional artisans. As long as the students and the teachers are sensitive to personal and community identity, education remains dynamic and relevant.

Aditi Prakash, a visiting faculty member, reflected, "Being a teacher helped me look at each craftsperson as an individual, to help them to build their potential. And I realized the difference between vocational training and education. In training, you are dictating. In education, you are encouraging people to think."

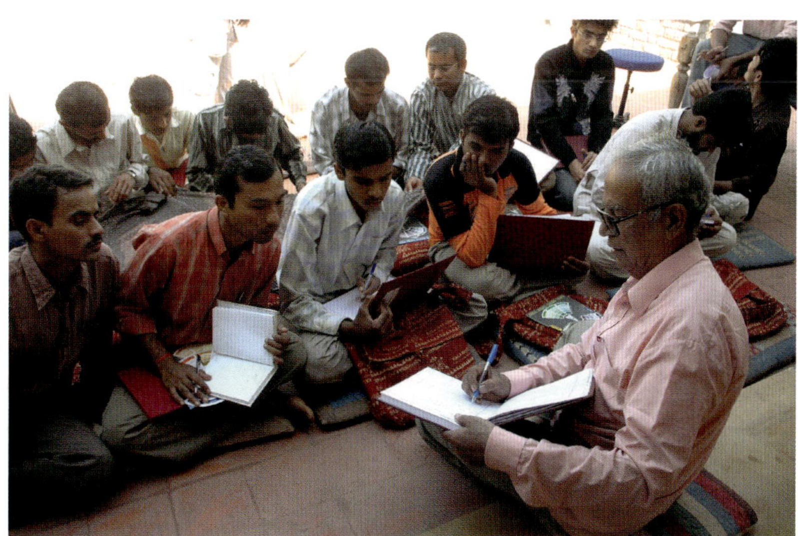

Jan Baker had the opportunity to teach in the program she helped create. In 2008, she wrote: "Following my teaching experience at KRV, I visited several craftsmen. Those who had attended KRV continued the vital traditions of their families but implementing fresh new designs. Those who had not taken the course were just repeating their same designs as usual. It was visibly apparent that a well-thought-out curriculum brought outstanding results. It made me proud to be a part of an extraordinary process. This was one of my most rewarding teaching experiences (in the thirty years of my design teaching career!)."

After each year, I reflected, contemplated, and fine-tuned the curriculum. The first course needed more time, so I separated it into two courses. To emphasize and strengthen the focus on traditional identity, I engaged our advisors in guiding students to discover, articulate, and utilize existing systems

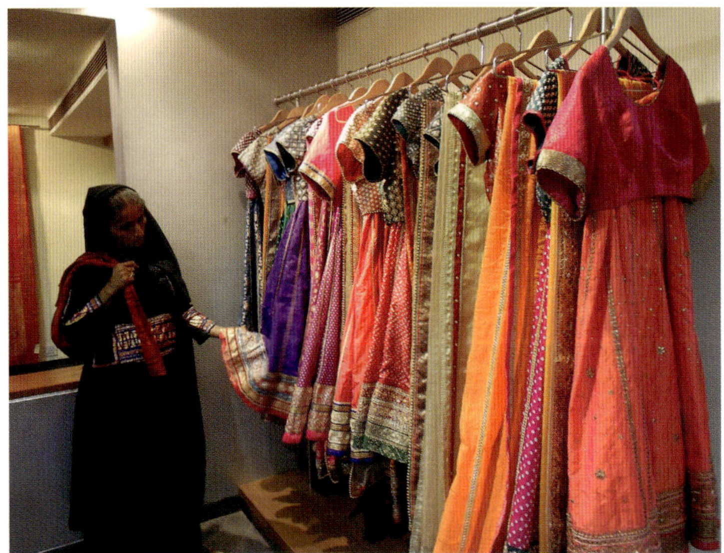

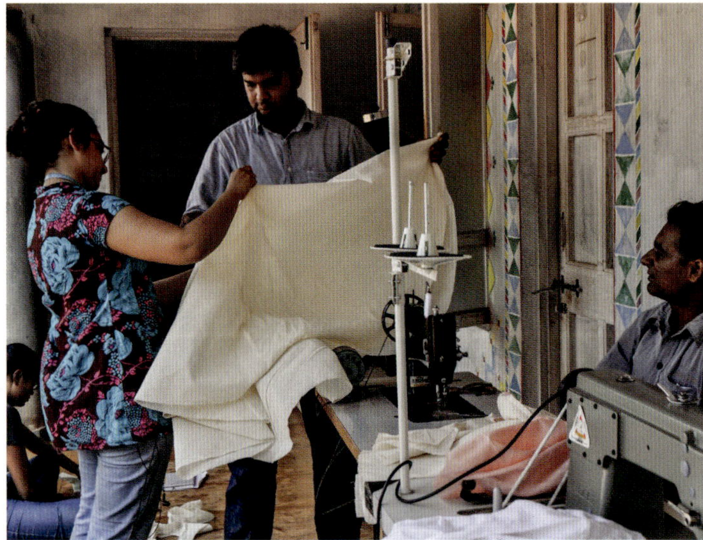

of knowledge and innovation. Each year, during course 1, they spent a day showing traditional textiles and discussing both aesthetics and culture. The students also spent a day examining textiles in the Kala Raksha textile museum.

After learning what they can vary in their traditions, in course 3, Market Orientation, students learned why they had to innovate. Using a centerpiece field trip to Ahmedabad to visit a range of shops, the course introduced them to discerning and targeting different clients and to analytical thinking. Then, at a direct-sale opportunity for graduates at an international school, Azizbhai came bursting out of the director's bathroom. "A shower curtain!" he exclaimed. "It's a new product!" I realized the importance of knowing the end user. Thinking of the house-and-garden tours we love in the US, I added visits to individuals' homes in Ahmedabad. The personal element made a critical difference. Students effortlessly and enthusiastically differentiated homework for people they had met. Craft remains personal; at its best, it is interaction between creator and client.

In course 4, Concept, Communication, Projects, students learned to organize their innovations around a theme. From the first year, we used international trend forecasts, donated by a friend who was an ace trend forecaster. Using trends, however, is both controversial and difficult. I continued to revise how to use trends most effectively. The effective point is that artisans learn to use professionally developed color stories that extend beyond the familiar. But they must relate to the stories to create successfully. I added field trips to engage artisans to reinterpret concepts and to exemplify the value of primary over secondary sources of inspiration.

The fifth course began as "Finishing," learning to add value with minimal cost to increase appeal and income. But when the first-year final jury complained that all the women's collections were Kala Raksha products, I revised the course to Finishing and Collection Development. The dilemma remained. The artisan students were essentially textile designers. Teaching them adequate product design within the yearlong course was not practical. I initiated a codesign program with urban design students. This enabled KRV students to develop products and also provided guided experience in working collaboratively with product designers. I made one caveat: the KRV students would engage the urban students

Top, left: Ahmedabad, 2011. In the Market Orientation module, students travel to Ahmedabad to study shops that feature handcraft and homes of craft consumers and begin to connect with modern markets. *Photo: course mentor*

Top, right: Kala Raksha Vidhyalaya, 2013. As a sustainable solution to enabling students who are essentially textile designers to make products, I introduced a codesign element. In the fifth module—Finishing and Collection Development—design students from urban institutions worked in teams with KRV students. *Photo: Judy Frater*

and ultimately be responsible for the products developed. This changed the usual dynamic and resulted in an eye-opening and respect-building experience.

The final course was Merchandising, Presentation. Students created logos, brand identities, and portfolios and practiced display and verbal presentation to maximize the value of their work. Village people don't often share their experiences at home, so the first year I invited the elders of Bhopani Vandh to hear the women students' presentations. Though the women had to present with their faces covered, a Rabari custom, the elders were duly impressed. From the second year, I instituted a family jury prior to the final professional jury. This became a beloved activity of the course, which I secretly feel is the real jury, because families view the innovations in terms of traditions. Though nervous, students welcomed the opportunity to share what they learned in a more formal, professional way than would be possible at home. Families swelled with pride at these presentations, and this also helped extend the impact of design education to the community.

Directing Kala Raksha Vidhyalaya for eight years, I experienced the transformative power of education. I learned that everyone loves to be creative, and everyone loves to learn. Our youngest student, Halimabai Jat (age thirteen), reflected, "I didn't know how to talk. Now I can express myself." In the same class, our oldest-ever graduate—Jivaben (age eighty), said, "I learned I can learn. I learned day by day, and as long as I live, I will learn."

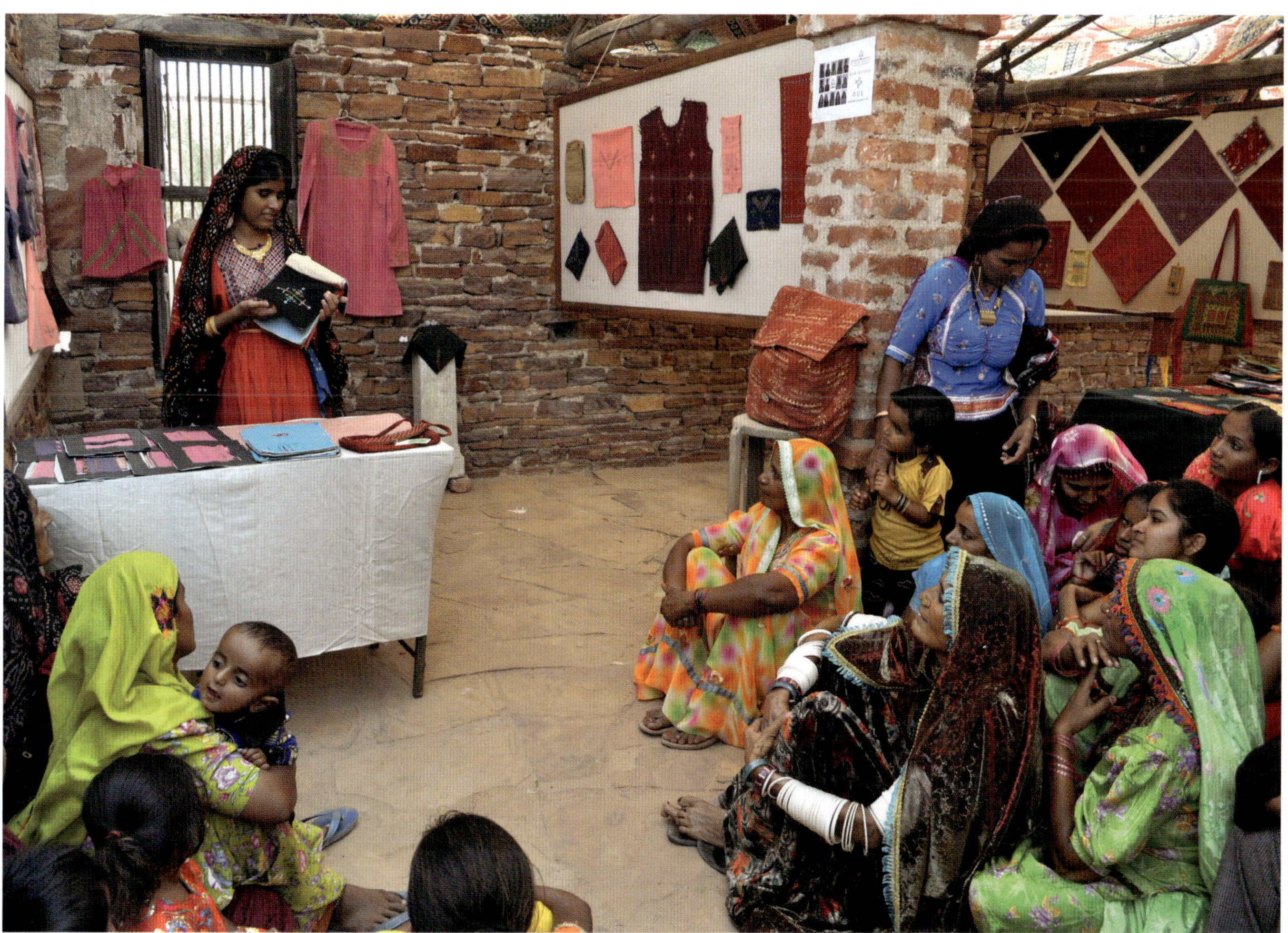

Kala Raksha Vidhyalaya, 2009. Family members attend a dress rehearsal before the final professional jury. This prepares the students and allows families to share the experience of the year of design education and glimpse a professional side of loved ones. *Photo: Judy Frater*

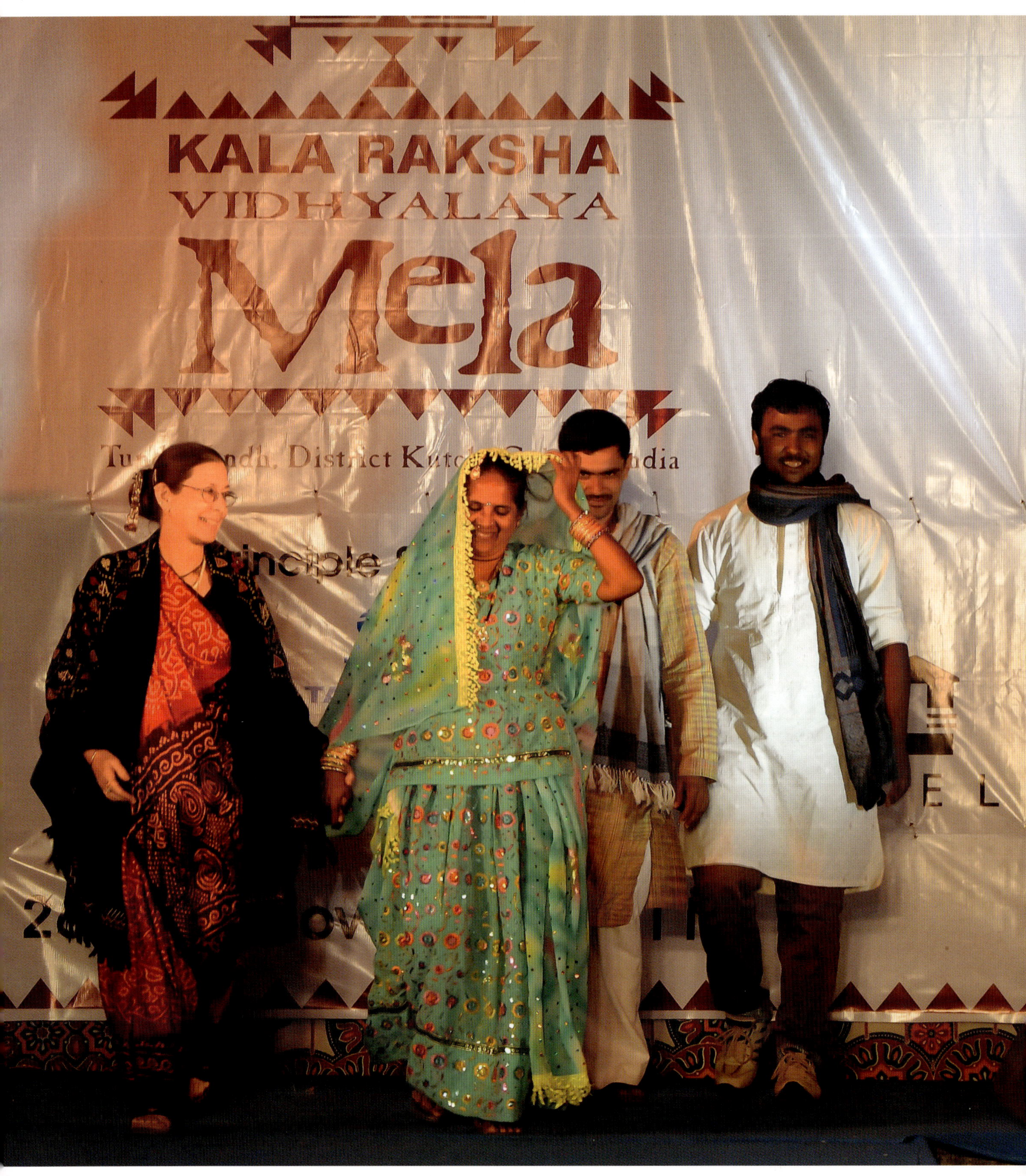

Kala Raksha Vidhyalaya, 2011. The yearlong course ends with a convocation that features eminent guests and a fashion show that compels thousands of visitors to view handcraft as contemporary fashion. The year 2011 was the only time I walked the ramp—to fill in for the special guest, who had fallen asleep! *Photo: Ketan Pomal L.M. Studio*

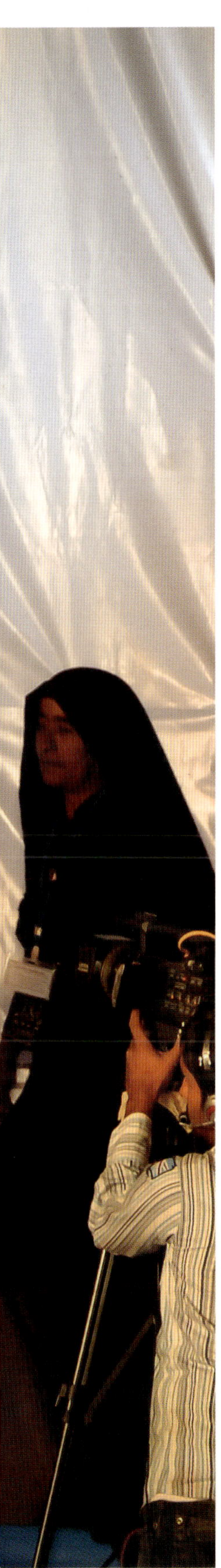

The design education year ended with a gala two-day convocation including the final professional jury, a fashion show, presentation of certificates and awards, and a night of traditional music and dance. Graduate artisan designers walked the bright lights of the fashion show ramp with their collections, to enthusiastic cheers. Though in everyday life they wore the latest local fashions, for the convocation most students wore their traditional dress, a decision they collectively made and perpetuated as an expression of pride in their identity.

Graduates have connected to new markets, increased incomes, and won awards. The word on the ground is that anyone who has taken the course has built a bigger house and workshop. In 2009, I was awarded the Sir Misha Black Medal for Distinguished Services to Design Education.

For me, success is realizing potential. Each year, while we stressed knowing and maintaining key aspects of traditions, individuals emerged. They transformed from representatives of a genre to artists, each with their own interpretation of a shared tradition, like butterflies from cocoons, like birds freed from cages. The creativity of the individual is infinite. Among 124 graduates of Kala Raksha Vidhyalaya, there were virtually no duplications, and I always sat quietly in awe thinking what if they had not had the chance?

"Through this course I came to love my traditional art," avowed Oveshbhai.

Bhagvatiben, addressing a group of development professionals at UNDP Delhi, introduced herself, "My name is Bhagvati. I am from Sumrasar, and I am a designer."

Damyantiben related, "Now we can go ourselves to choose the fabric, the thread. And we make our own designs. And now the design is in my name—Damyanti's design. When anyone else makes this design, my name comes. It makes me happy."

The final test of success is time. Women graduates surmounted obstacles to attend the course. To abide by social conventions, young women brought elders with them. And they often had to bear taunting by other women of their village. Intentional but challenging was the fact that all but one of the women graduates were members of Kala Raksha. After graduating, they went back to production for the organization. They did not work on printed patterns, but their ability to use the creativity they had tapped in the course was very limited. Trying to integrate the education program and the income generation program, I instituted women's design internships, in which graduates created samples for Kala Raksha's new collections. The women valued these opportunities to use what they had learned and honed their design skills. They created dynamic, fresh new work. Still, designing on contract limited their engagement with the work. Few considered the possibility of working independently.

For the men graduates, diversified styles drove expansion of the market. As Dahyalalbhai noted, "My income has increased ten times, while the longtime major producer, for whom I used to work, has not suffered at all. It is win-win!"

The Vidhyalaya brought Kala Raksha increased visibility and mixed reviews. One person said we should leave craft alone. Another said it's all well and good to teach artisans design, but who is going to do my work? Those supporting the endeavor said the school was blurring the line between artisans and designers. For me, that was always an artificial line.

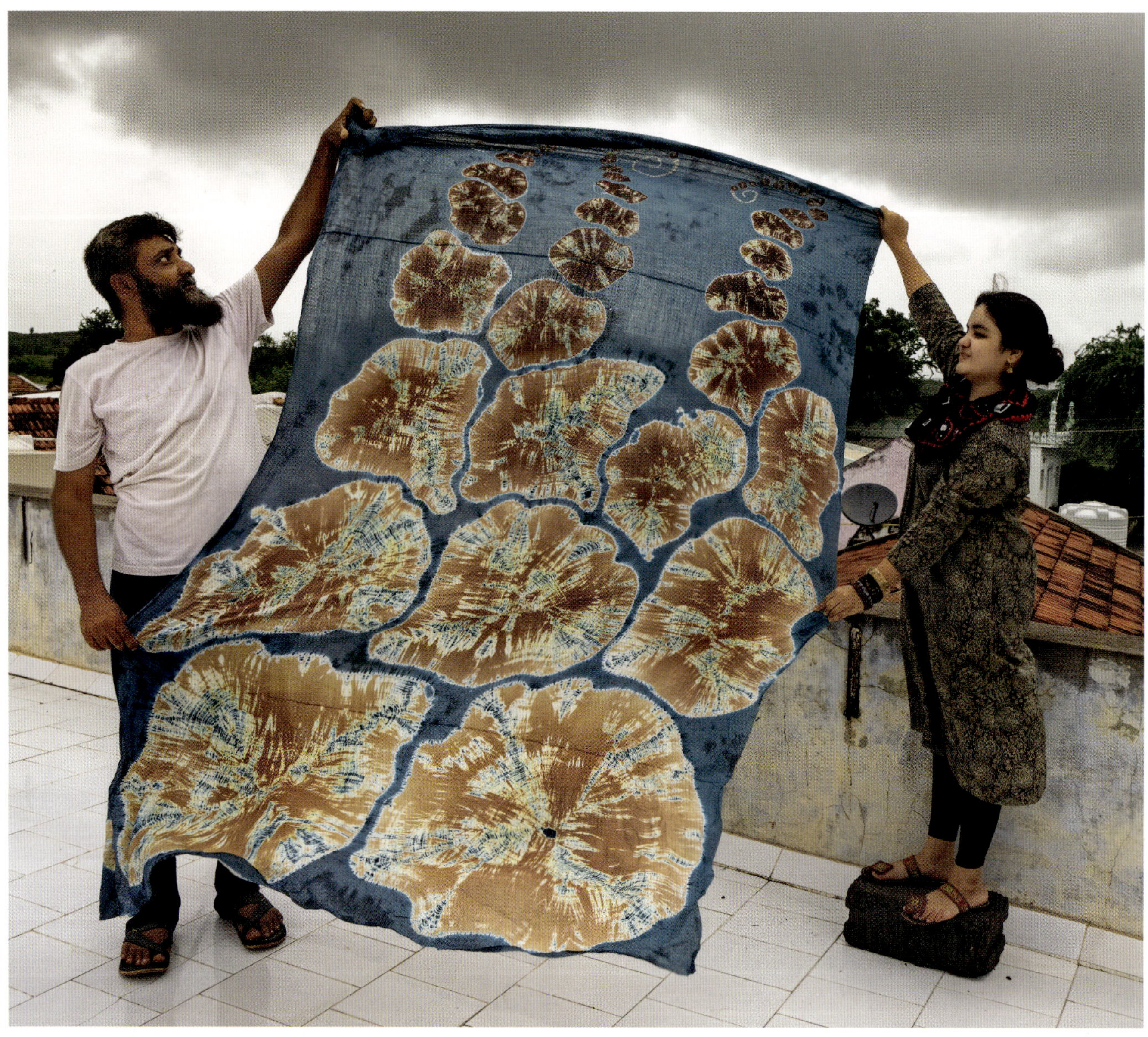

This course is like a ladu [sweet] for a hungry man, a well for the thirsty! We knew everything else. This is what we needed!

~Azizbhai Alimamad Khatri

Above: Bhadli, 2022. Azizbhai and Tainabanu display an art bandhani that Azizbhai made on climate change. He envisioned the earth as a cross section of wood because deforestation causes destruction. Glaciers melt and the earth shrinks, drowning. *Photo: Nevada Wier*

Opposite: Kachhi Rabari *ludi*, 1994. Wool, hand woven, bandhani, embroidered. 46" x 122". Collection of the author. Rabari women traditionally cover their heads with a woolen veil, the creation of a network of local artisans. Patterns and colors indicate details of social status. *Photo: Schiffer Publishing Ltd.*

Chapter 9

ABDULAZIZBHAI ALIMAMAD KHATRI: FROM SKEPTIC TO ADVOCATE

AbdulAziz is crouched on the ground, staring at a colony of ants.

What are you doing? I ask.

"Getting an inspiration," he answers.

Azizbhai was once the headstrong and sometimes wayward son. His father, Umarbhai Faruk, dyed woolen bandhani shawls for Kala Raksha, always punctual and expecting equally punctual payment. Azizbhai sometimes came with him to deliver the order. He could never sit still for very long, perpetually driven to activity.

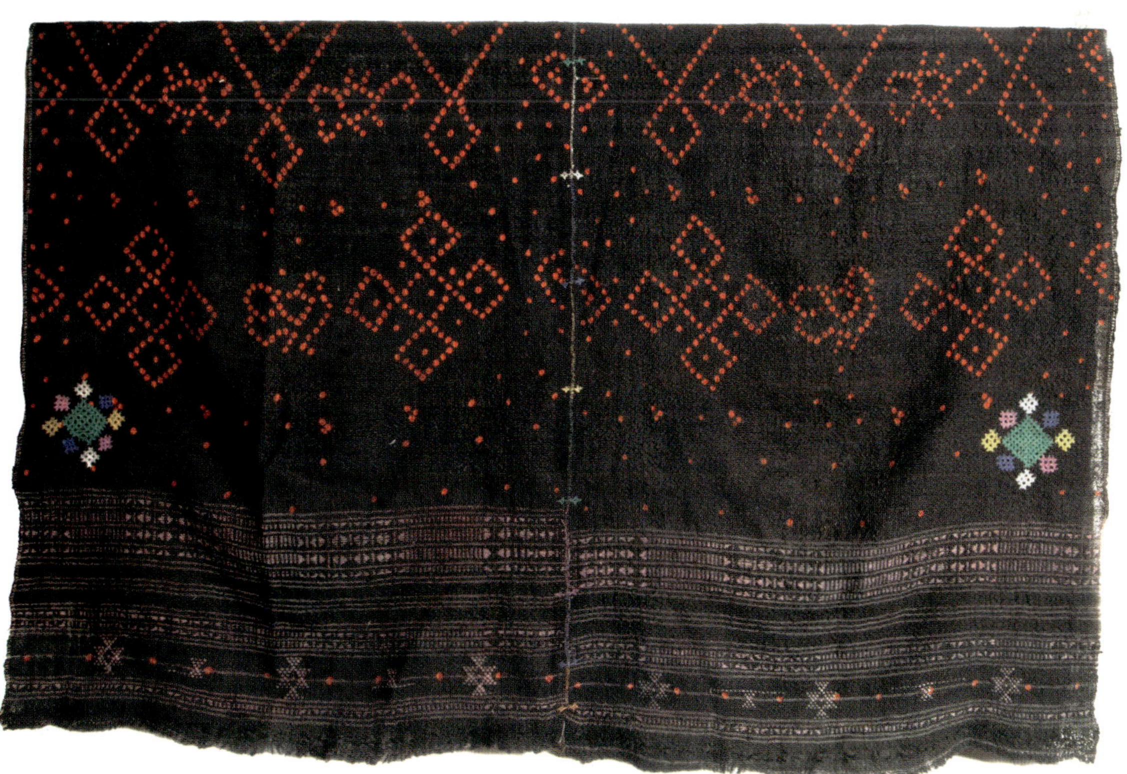

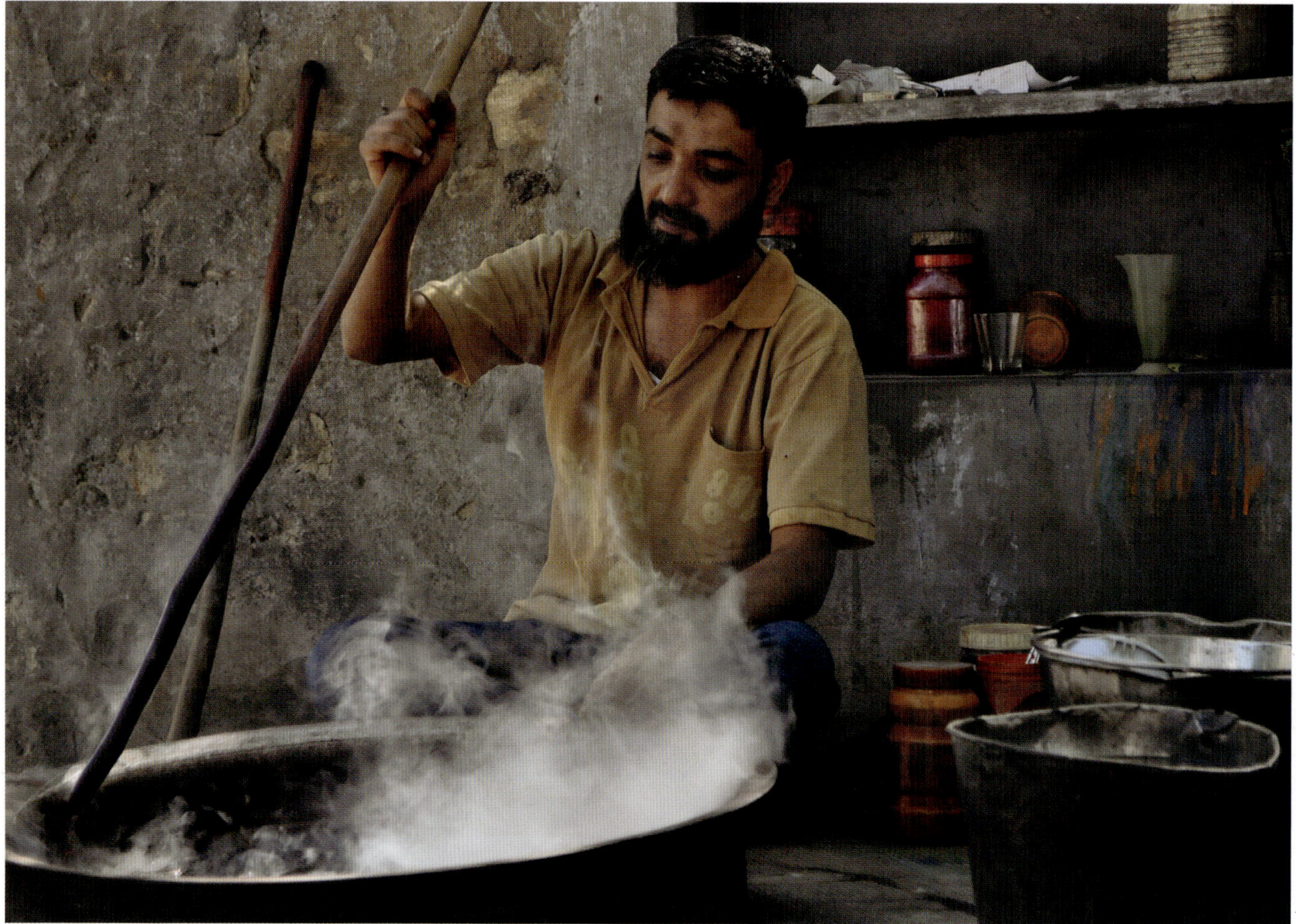

Traditionally, Umarbhai and his forefathers tied and dyed *ludi*, the woolen veils of Rabari women. Ahirs, Bharvads, and Meghvals also wore woolen bandhani veils. Each had specific colors and patterns for different ages and occasions. Umarbhai says the Khatris gave all of those designs—here, this is your traditional dress. But historically, Azizbhai's family in Bhadli village worked closely with Rabaris and weavers. Rabari women hand-spun the wool of their sheep and gave it to weavers. The weavers passed on the woven, undyed veils to the Khatris, who dyed them black with bandhani resist dotted patterns and returned them to the Rabari women. The system was as much personal as it was professional. Umarbhai and his father and grandfather before him would carry the veils to a village and sit for the day in the home of a Rabari woman he had made his "sister," distributing them.

Over time, Rabari women began to prefer softer, lighter acrylic for their veils, and then cotton and polyester printed with bandhani patterns. Fortunately, production of shawls for urban markets simultaneously developed in Kutch. Umarbhai shifted to job work for large-scale weavers and NGOs such as Kala Raksha. Azizbhai's mother tied a special shawl for competition and won the President's National Award for craftsmanship in 1993—the first award for bandhani work on wool. Azizbhai learned traditional patterns from her and his grandmother, and dyeing techniques from his father.

Motivated to learn more, he received a scholarship from the All India Handicrafts Board in 1998 to study natural dyeing in Dhamadka. In 2003, he also studied at ATIRA (Ahmedabad Textile Industries Research Association), where he learned about water treatment, water conservation, environmental concerns, and types of dyes. Azizbhai's proficiency with dyeing and color matching became known and desired among weavers, NGOs, and companies.

In 2005, Umarbhai became a member of the newly formed Kala Raksha Vidhyalaya Advisory Council. "We need students who can catch the education and who can teach the teachers," the advisors advised. "In the pilots, everyone must succeed—students, teachers, and Kala Raksha. We will need to have an exemplary class!" At first, they thought of upper age limits—not more than thirty years old. But later, they decided that a minimum age was more important. By fifteen—no, eighteen—a person has learned the skills and knowledge of his tradition. After a lot of discussion, they all agreed that educational qualification was not a critical criterion. The advisors nominated the pilot-year students. Umarbhai nominated Azizbhai. He was twenty-seven.

"I had been experimenting for a long time," he recalled. "I didn't know what we were going to do there. Neither did my father, but he sent me because of Judyben." Azizbhai had hardly lived away from home. And this place was a village! The dormitory and studios were made of stone and lime mortar—no plaster on the walls. The floors were plastered with cow dung. The doors and windows were old-fashioned wood. The metal lights made him feel like he was in an operating theater. And dust filtered through the mud-tiled roofs. "I worked hard to get away from this stuff," he muttered.

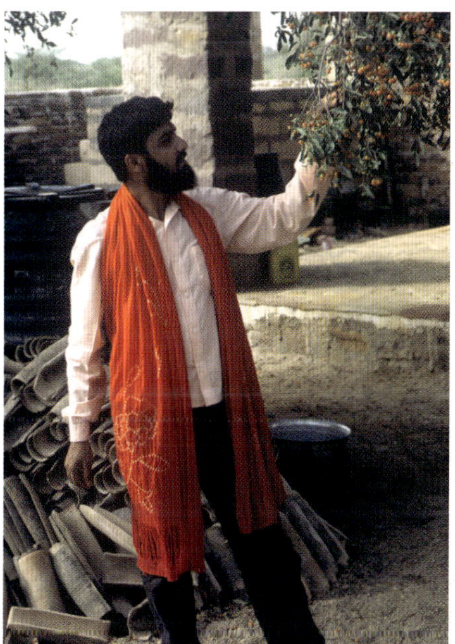

And the food was bad, he pronounced.

In what way?

Just bad.

Can't fix it without specific complaints.

. . . Too much oil.

OK. Anything else?

. . . Too much turmeric.

OK. Done.

But it was not his mother's and wife's cooking; that was the problem.

Anyway, the purpose of Kala Raksha Vidhyalaya was to learn design. But Azizbhai wasn't convinced of that either. What was the point of all of this drawing and painting? And it was hard to have people tell you what to do all day long. He found comradery in his classmates, however. The eleven weavers, printers, and bandhani artisans participating in this experiment had fun with it. As Junaidbhai Ismail said, "At home there are Mummy, Papa, aunties, and uncles . . . here it's just us and we can be FREEEEEEE!"

The class was wild and naughty, testing boundaries. Azizbhai could mock and mimic anyone mercilessly. But he freed his imagination in the making. In the first class, he took the theme Yellow Garden and made a technically challenging door curtain. He used as many bandhani techniques as he knew. To make a range of colors, he had to dye the fabric several times and then discharge it to make a yellow background. To achieve the width of the doorway, he cleverly created a meandering hand-stitched seam in keeping with the garden theme. After the Market Orientation class, he made a wild children's quilt and, after meeting my nineteen-year-old niece visiting from the USA, decided to create bandhani T-shirts. "This course is like a *ladu* [sweet] for a hungry man!" he declared. "A well for the thirsty. We knew everything else. This is what we needed!"

In the Concept Development course, Azizbhai chose the theme "Eden" and made *dupattas* with simple, dramatic placements and luminous colors to evoke a luscious garden. The teacher who was to coteach Concept dropped out suddenly but came to teach the following course, Finishing, instead. We

Opposite: Bhadli, 2010. Azizbhai dyes in his old outdoor workshop. Years ago, he recalls, they had to wait two years to save up RS 7,000 to repair the dyeing hearth. *Photo: Judy Frater*

Above: Kala Raksha Vidhyalaya, 2006. During his year of design education, Azizbhai shows a scarf from his first theme, Eden. *Photo: Judy Frater*

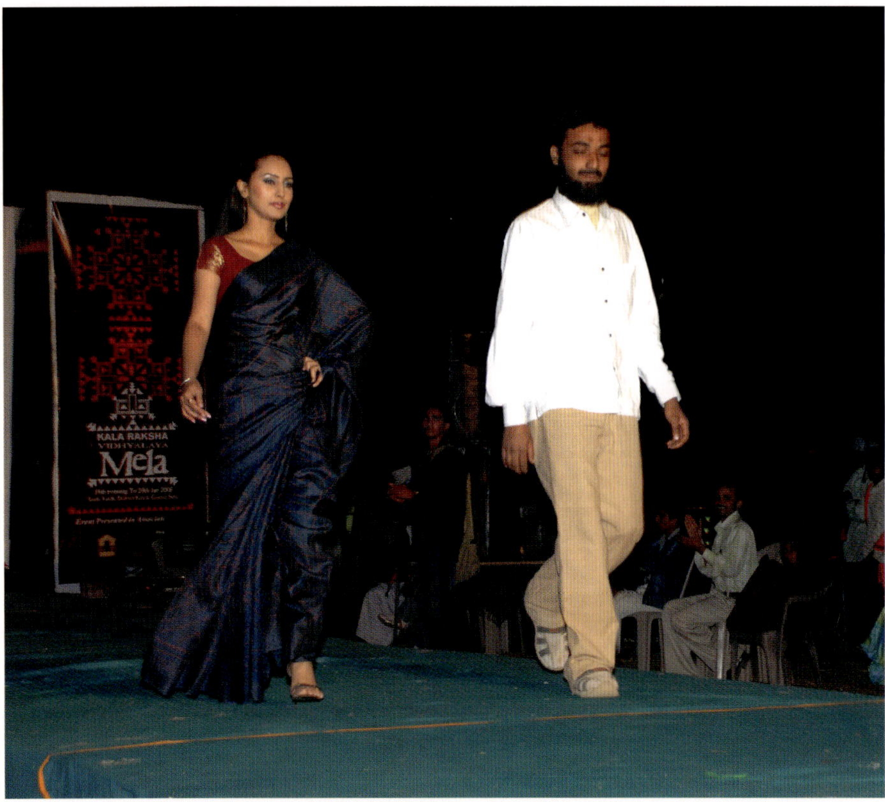

Left: Kala Raksha Vidhyalaya, 2007. Alumni created new work to present in subsequent convocation fashion shows. Azizbhai's second collection was inspired by tradition. The tassar silk sari is an innovation on the traditional woolen *ludi. Photo: Ketan Pomal, L.M. Studio*

Opposite: Santa Fe, New Mexico, 2015. Azizbhai shows a potential customer his bandhani scarves at the International Folk Art Market. *Photo: Judy Frater*

had just received our first magic box of trend forecasts from LA Colors, and she could not resist doing concepts all over again. This time, Azizbhai chose "Safari Chic." He could not grasp this subtle Western concept, however, and interpreted it literally. His final collection was an eclectic aggregation of pieces decorated with simplified jungle motifs. Imaginative and humorous, it drew sharp reproach in his final jury. "Where is your tradition?!" jury members shouted.

This stinging critique hit Azizbhai like a slap. He went home and thought and pulled all that he had learned that year together. He studied the *ludi*s that his ancestors made and adeptly transformed them into scarves. "The jury was as useful as one whole class," he said.

It took some time to digest the experience of a different kind of education. On reflection, Azizbhai decided he had learned a lot. "We were afraid to take risks in our craft," he said. "When I came to Kala Raksha Vidhyalaya, I thought we will starve if I follow these ideas. After the Market Orientation course, I reworked our pricing. I added in all the things I had missed: overhead, etc. And with the higher prices I lost some customers!

"After the course and the fashion show, my father, brother, and other people laughed at me. They said this is a waste of time. We all thought that traditional was correct, real craftsmanship. But when I made my second ludi collection, someone bought the whole thing. So Umarbhai was convinced. And others started appreciating me."

On the different inputs from each faculty, he said, "One thing I learned was that everyone has his own ideas, so in the end, I have to trust my own judgment."

And after the graduates held a pop-up sale at the New Delhi American Embassy School, he mused, "In just one trip to Delhi, I learned so much! I learned the importance of exposure and English language. Now my dream is to go abroad for a year, to learn design, international culture, and English."

The course gave Azizbhai a license and direction for his creativity and opened his eyes to possibilities. But he still needed support. "I couldn't get beyond ongoing work," he said. "So, in 2008, I convinced my brother Suleman to attend the design course." After that, the Bhadli brothers worked together. "There was no tassar silk bandhani then," they recall. "We did the first bandhani on tassar. The color didn't come out well. We experimented and had success. Our new bandhani went well in the market. We did [high] quality. In 2010 we got a nineteen-lakh order. We had 'Eid,' and we started from that."

They took the family from job work woolen shawls to their own thriving business of silk stoles and saris for high-end urban and international markets.

"We can create fifty designs out of a single object," Azizbhai said, "Five will sell immediately, and the other forty-five will sell in the near future." The Victoria and Albert Museum, London, acquired two of his bandhanis and showed them in the contemporary-design section of their exhibition *The Fabric of India*.

In 2015, Azizbhai came to the US. He attended the International Folk Art Market | Santa Fe (IFAM); taught workshops in San Francisco, LA, and New York; and fulfilled a dream. He attended IFAM in 2016, 2017, 2018, and 2019 as well. He and Sulemanbhai created the brand Ababil, named for the miraculous swallows mentioned in the Qur'an for protecting the Ka'ba in Mecca, and they are now known in the design craft world. Azizbhai participated in Lakme Fashion Week in 2017 and has worked with international designers Nor Black Nor White and Donna Karan.

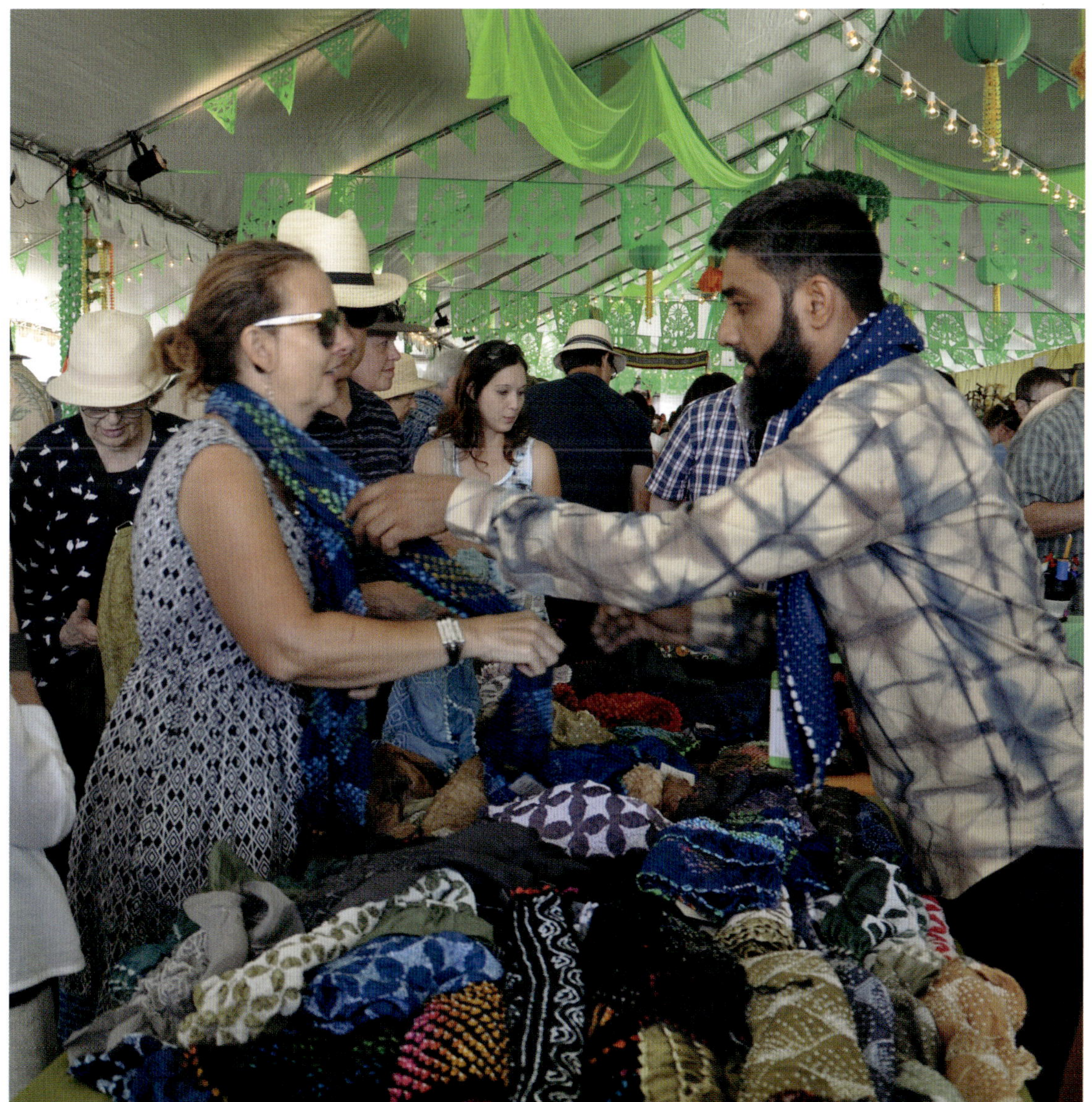

Following pages: Bhadli, 2022. Azizbhai and his daughter Tainabanu, both design graduates, critique one of her collection pieces. *Photo: Nevada Wier*

In 2018, Azizbhai sent his daughter Tainabanu to Somaiya Kala Vidya. At eighteen, she was as talented and headstrong as her father. Azizbhai had great expectations for her. When she went home to create the collection she had designed on the theme "Gamdai" (Of the Village), he called to wage a forty-five-minute tirade. Her designs looked like what was available in the local market! he shouted. We did not know how to teach design!

Tainabanu's collection won the jury award for Best Collection, and she walked the fashion show ramp with poise and confidence beside Gautam Vazirani, fashion curator for Lakme Fashion week. I asked Azizbhai what he thought of her collection now that it was done.

"It was good," he said, pleased. "She already got an order for five hundred pieces."

2022

Azizbhai and Sulemanbhai have built a state-of-the-art workshop in Bhadli. Designed like a *haveli*, it has three stories and a spacious room for each step of bandhani, inviting creative work. They have also built a grand house in Bhuj, where the joint family now lives.

Tragically, Umarbhai succumbed to COVID-19 in September 2020. Azizbhai refused to work for some time, understanding that he couldn't know what the world would be like following the upheaval of the pandemic.

Slowly, life normalized. Azizbhai began to implement another dream that he has had for five years. Two years were spent gathering Kutchi indigo seeds. He bought land in Bhadli and built a farmhouse, simple and appealing, including a sparrow apartment that he designed and built. Along the bumpy dirt road to the farm, he brings a huge bag of dog biscuits and feeds each skinny feral dog on the way. The land is planted with local indigo now. Azizbhai's vision is totally local indigo. He'll use lime from a local quarry just over the hills and *gud* from sugar cane that he'll also plant. "I don't lie or misrepresent," he says. "And when I do it, I do it fully.

"When wool was replaced by acrylic, we lost the shawl market and went back to doing bandhani for Rabaris," he reflects. "We had to borrow money for tickets to travel. When I took the design course, we had to struggle to manage."

Sulemanbhai says they could never have imagined the workshop they built. Showing me his son Mohamed's shiny new MG, he recalls, "When we started, we had to save up to buy Azizbhai a second-hand scooter for RS 5,000. And it didn't always work. But the satisfaction in that purchase was greater than buying this car."

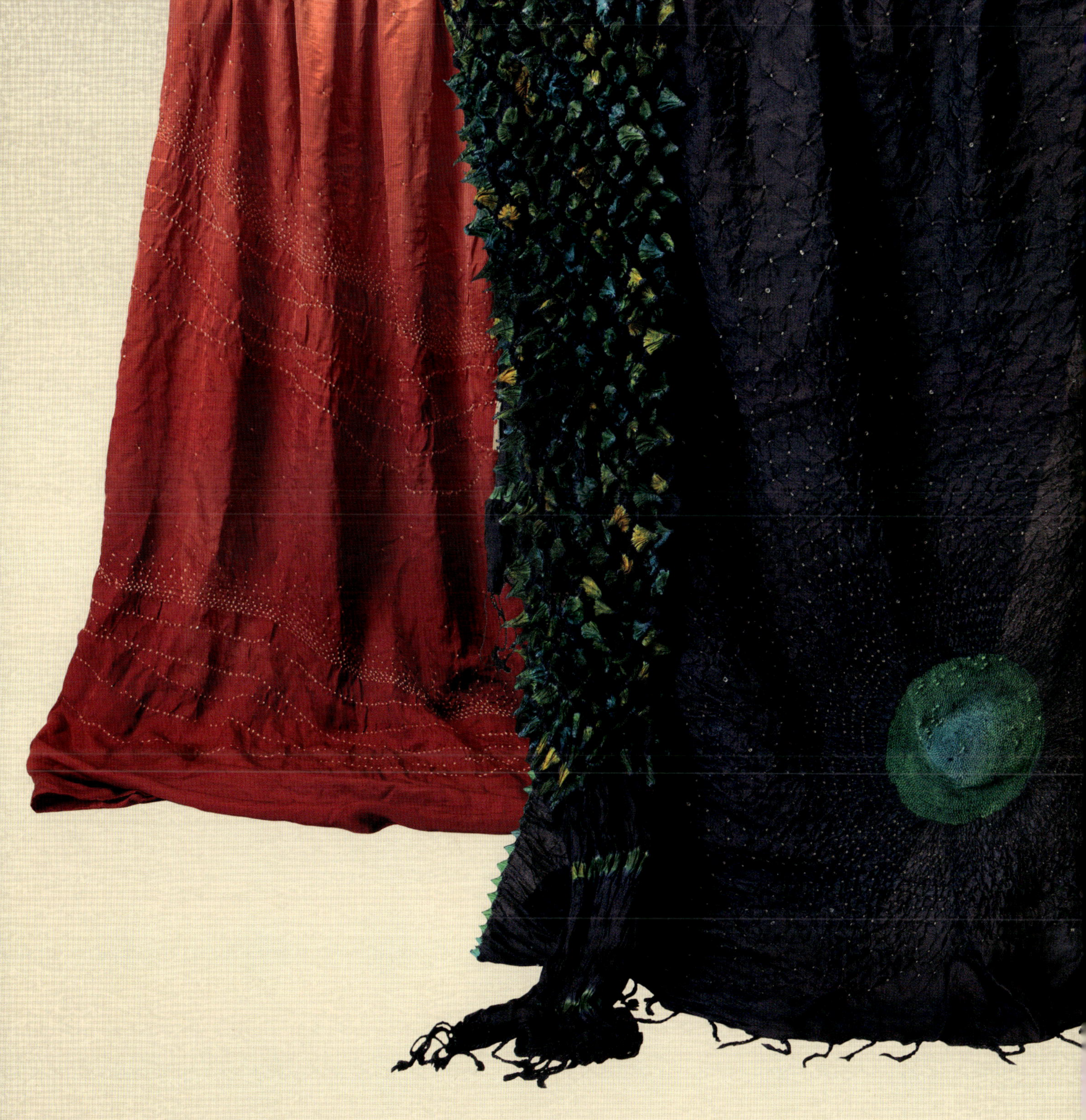

Above, left: *Pink Sea*, by Tainabanu Aziz Khatri 2021. Silk, natural dye, bandhani. 44" x 101". Tainabanu's design is inspired the textures left on sand by waves of the sea. Her style is distinctly different from her father's. *Photo: Schiffer Publishing Ltd.*

Above, right: *Center, Multi-kanda*, by Azizbhai Alimamad Khatri 2021. Silk, azo-free acid dye, bandhani. 22" x 50". Onion layers inspired this design. The multicolored, enormous dots were Azizbhai's innovation. *Far right, Kutch Monsoon*, by Azizbhai Alimamad Khatri 2021. Silk, azo-free acid dye, bandhani. 24" x 74". The design is inspired by insects swarming lights. The dense bharti dots was also Azizbhai's innovation. *Photo: Schiffer Publishing Ltd.*

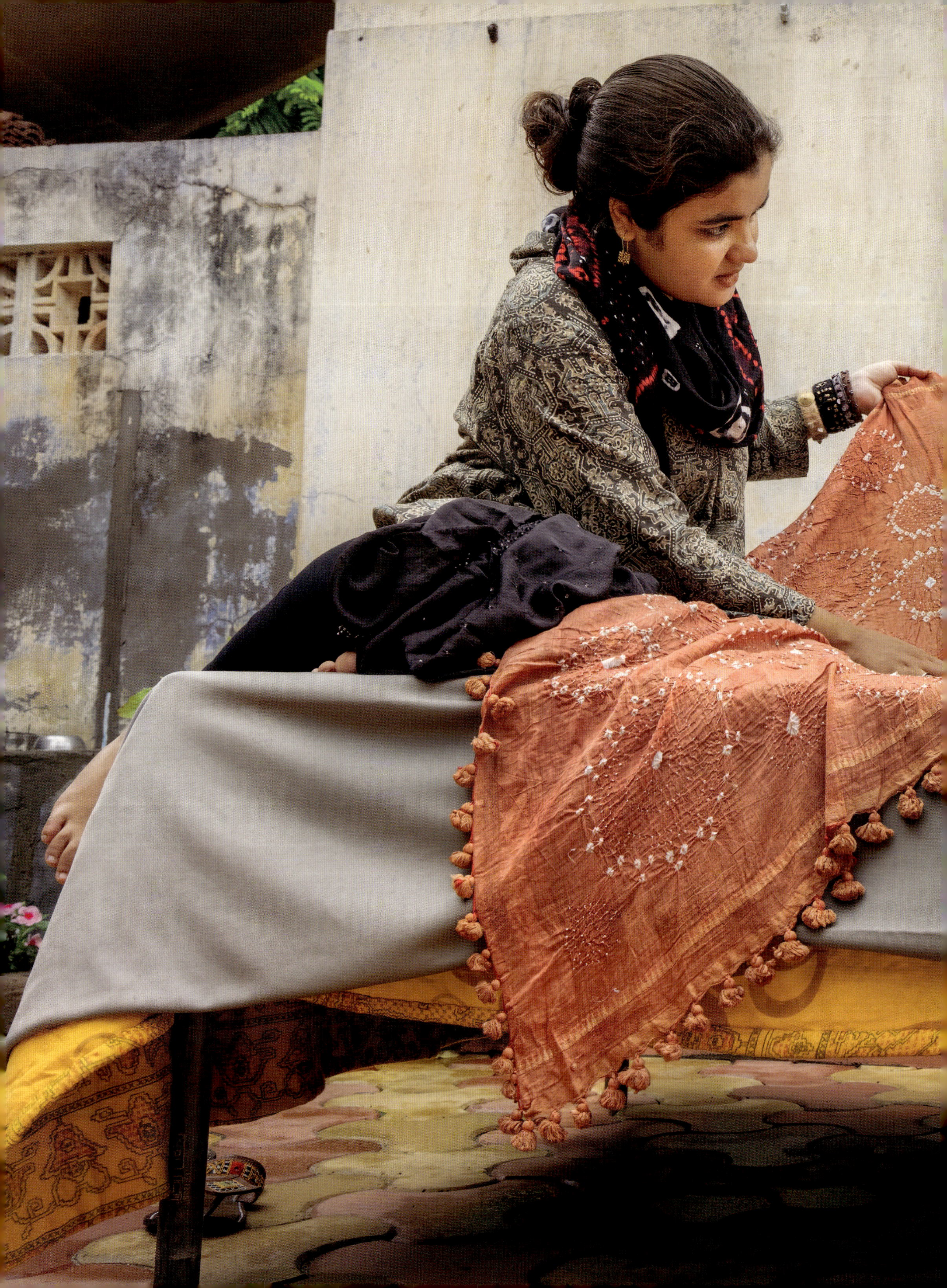

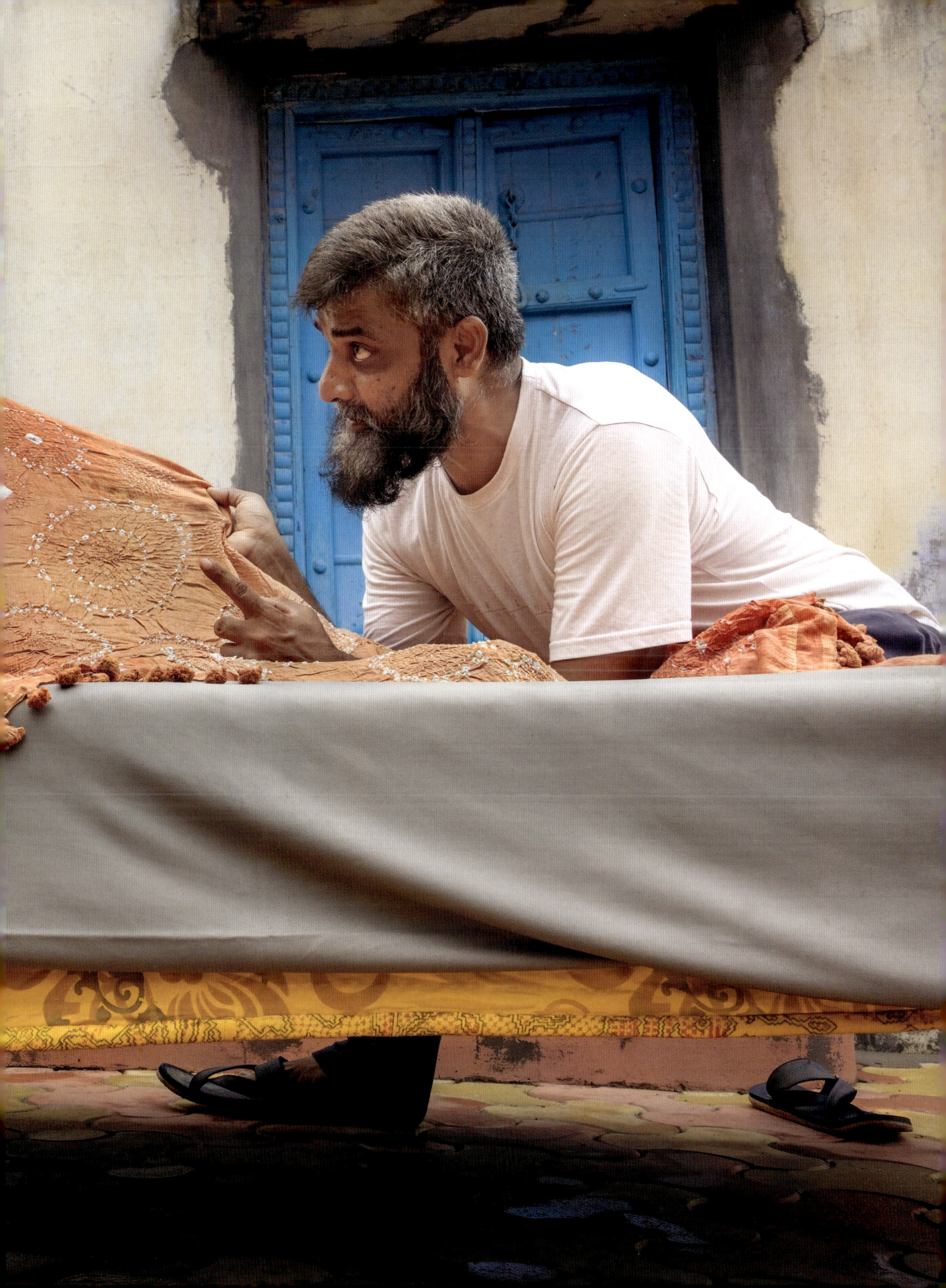

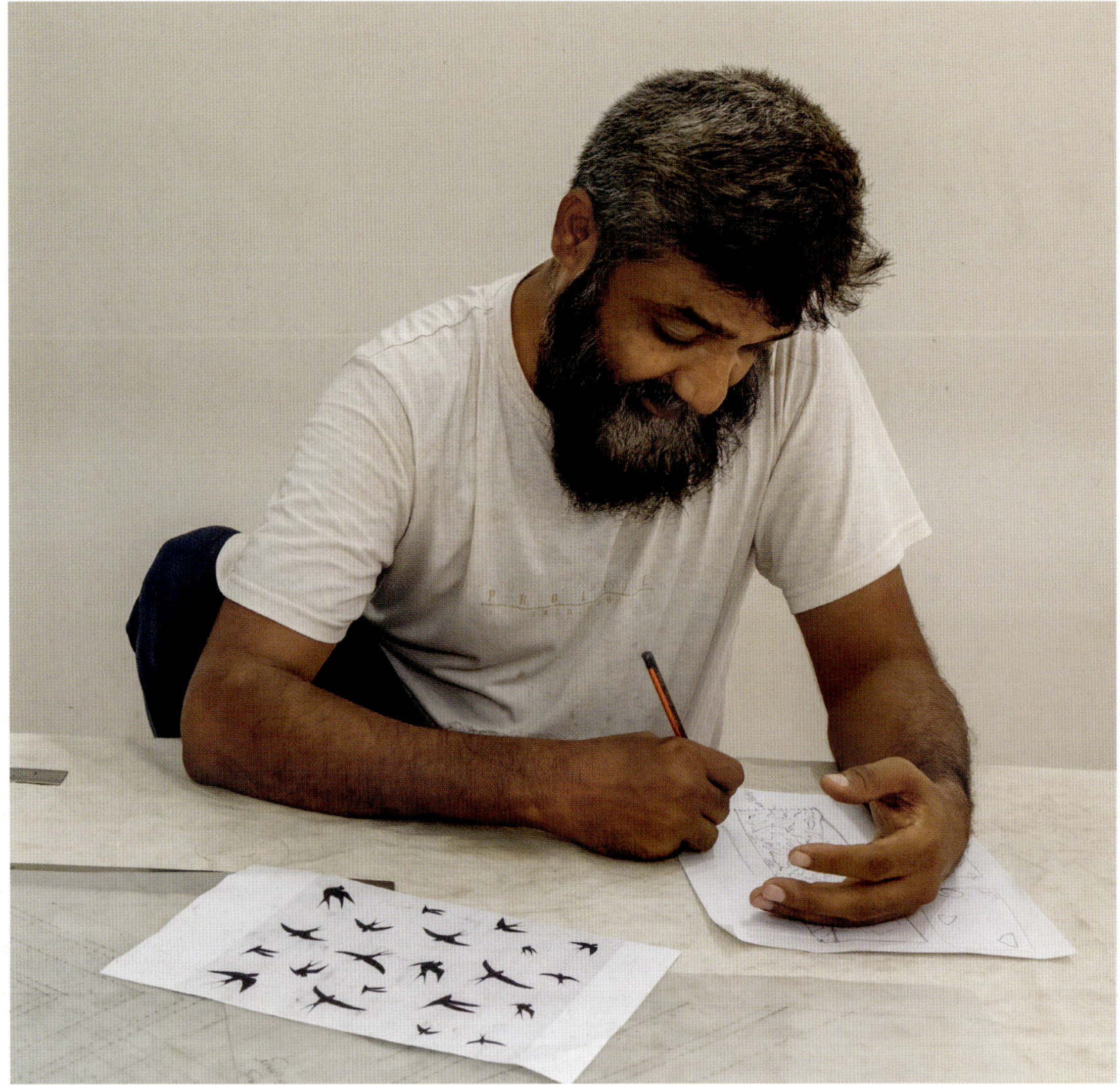

Bhadli, 2022. Azizbhai works on a design for a client. She wanted a repeat of his logo Ababil. Instead, he's making the swifts all different; when she wears the sari, it will look like a flock flying. Ababil is his brand because the swift is an artisan, fast and with magical powers. *Photo: Nevada Wier*

Sitting in the workshop office, Azizbhai can show what the domestic market wants—regular, symmetrical, bright—and what foreigners want—asymmetry with balance, subtle colors. It's a headache, he says. International customers come and you spend a whole day explaining, and they buy RS 15,000. An Indian buyer says, I know bandhani—just show me the goods—and buys in *lakhs*.

Yet, he has to create. He says that when he has an idea, it compels him; he works through the night, wrestling with it. And his taste is more like that of the foreigners. His dream is for Sulemanbhai and Mohamedbhai to handle the domestic market. He and Tainabanu will create new designs.

"When we learned design, we learned inspiration," Azizbhai says. "There has to be a story behind a design. Birds we call Mascati latora come to Kutch in the winter to eat berries, and they fly from the bushes together in thousands. We made a design from that. Artisans have gotten help from the government and NGOs. But when their thinking changes, they can stand on their own feet. When artisans learn design, they can do what others cannot, and they can earn as much as designers do."

And here is our shared dream.

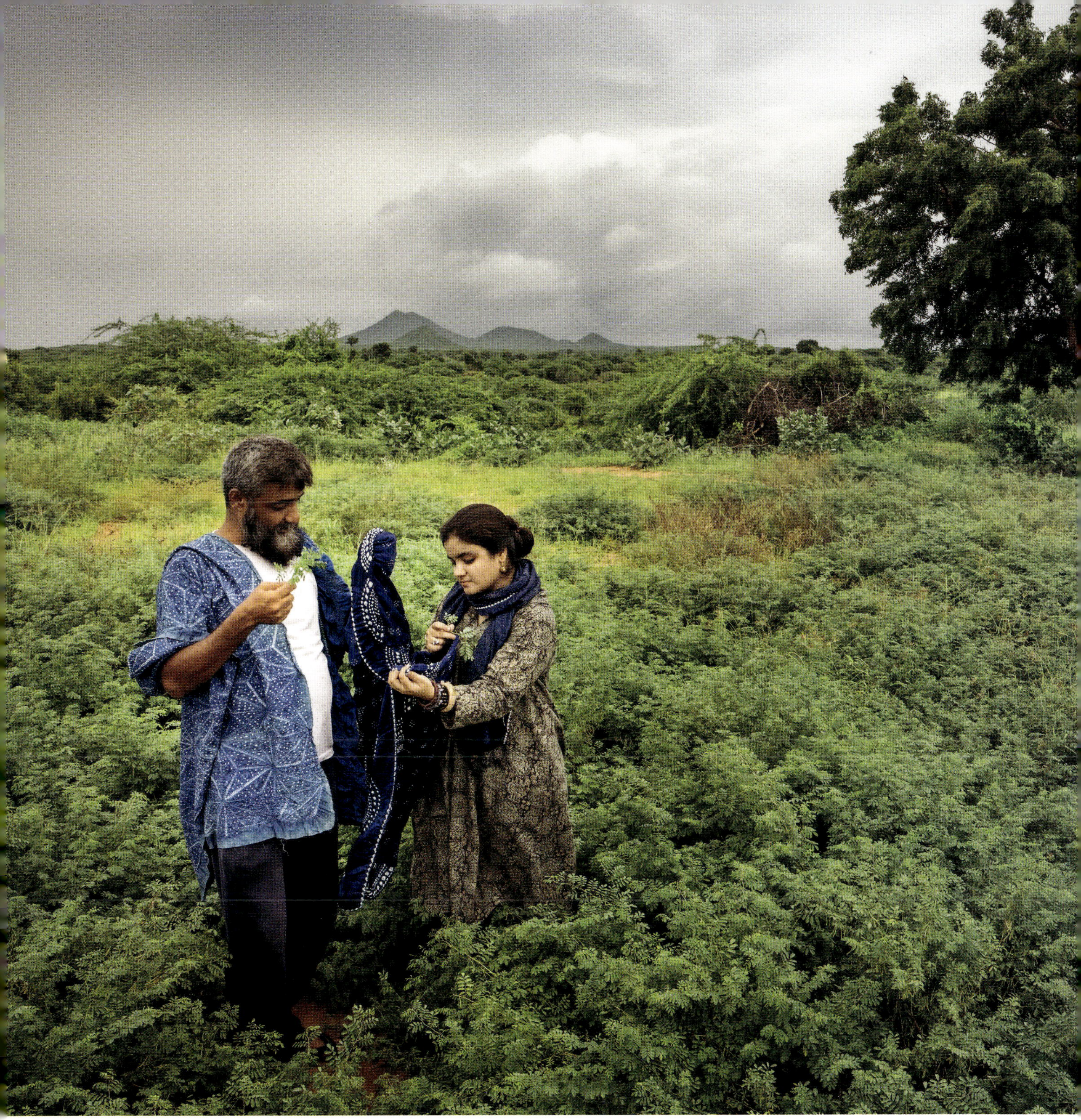

Above: Bhadli, 2022. Azizbhai and Tainabanu in their field of dreams: Kutchi indigo. To process completely local indigo, they will use lime from a quarry in the hills beyond. *Photo: Nevada Wier*

Right: Azizbhai designed his logo before going to the International Folk Art Market in 2015. Ababil is a swift, a bird legendarily revered in Islam.

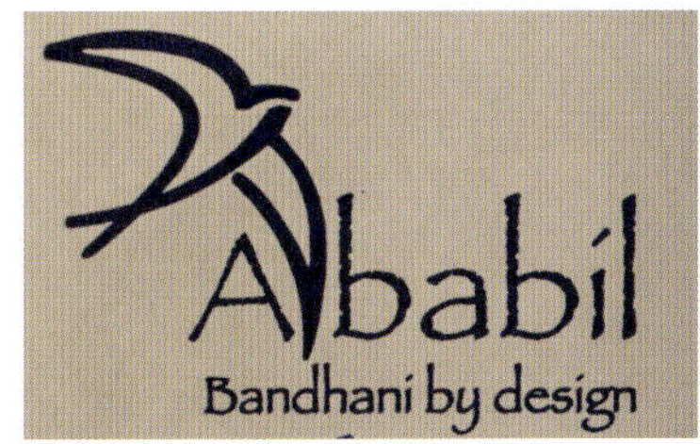

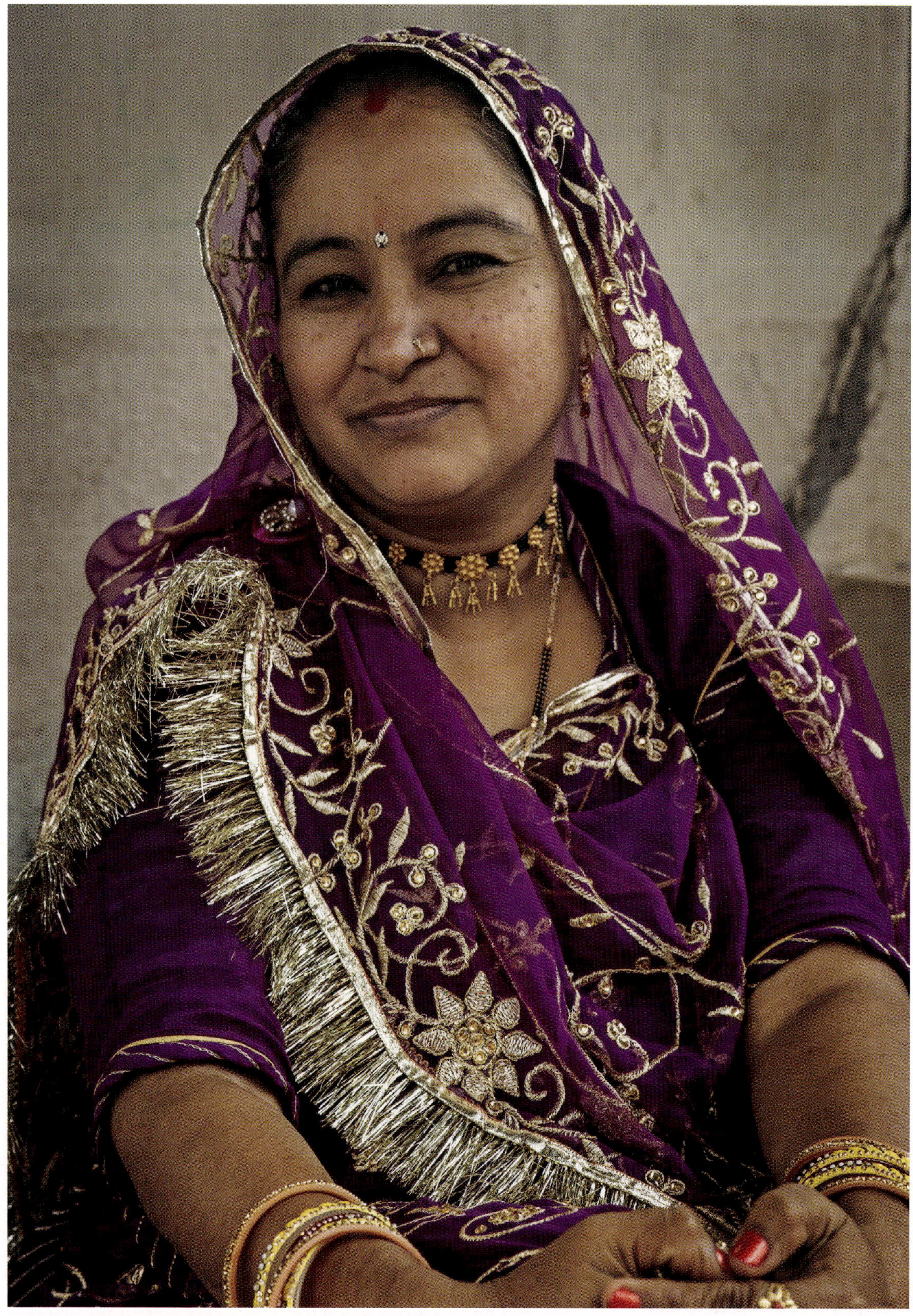

Above: Sumrasar Sheikh, 2022. Varshaben wears the traditional *kanchali-kurti ghagharo* (backless blouse, vest, skirt, and veil) of her community. Married, she prioritizes family and home but hopes to find time for creating embroidery. *Photo: Nevada Wier*

Opposite: Sumrasar, 2012. Varshaben embroiders during her KRV internship. The internships were intended to provide opportunities for graduates to use their education so that Kala Raksha could benefit with new designs, and interns could earn better rates than for production embroidery. *Photo: Judy Frater*

Chapter 10

VARSHABEN UTTAM BHANANI: JUDICIOUSLY COURAGEOUS

After I did the course, my work became known by my name.

~Varshaben Uttam Bhanani

2019

Varshaben shoots me a WhatsApp album of nine images. She is sitting in a beautiful peach sari with gold lace borders, laden with gold necklaces, hair ornaments and rings, and white and red bangles that pile halfway to her elbows.

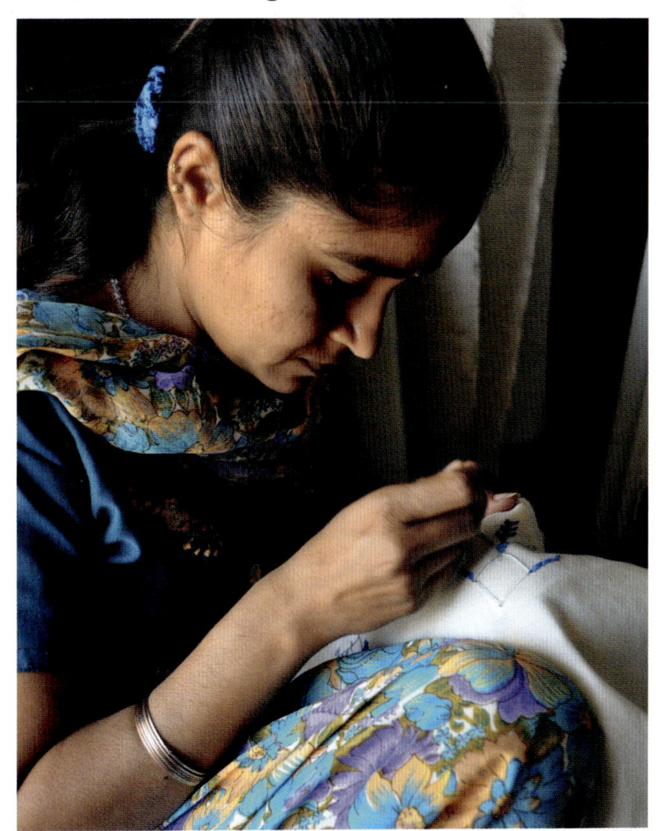

She is standing in a beautiful pale-pink kanchali-kurti ghagharo and veil, with the same gold ornaments and bangles. There is the traditional aarti lamp the community makes from wheat flour dough, with the head of Krishna at the top. There is a treasury of suf-embroidered pillows, bags, elaborate tassels, and framed wall hangings all coordinated in harmonious monochromatic colors. There is Varshaben veiled and the groom in a suit and tie, wearing a necklace of pearls and carrying a dagger in his hand. It's an invitation. She has returned to Sumrasar after her marriage four days ago. She is twenty-nine; it is a late marriage by traditional standards.

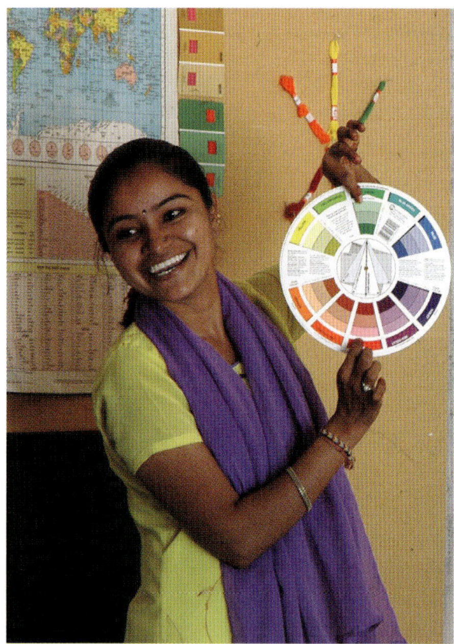

Kala Raksha Vidhyalaya, 2008. Varshaben explains the color wheel in her final presentation of the first course module, Color: Sourcing from Heritage and Nature. *Photo: Judy Frater*

Varshaben was born in Sumrasar Sheikh, to parents who migrated from Nagar Parkar, Pakistan, in 1972. She attended school to the seventh grade and considered further education, but there were no other girls who would accompany her the 27 kilometers to Bhuj for classes. She had a pension for embroidery. She learned suf from her mother when she was in the fifth grade and would come home at recess to stitch with her two elder sisters, who worked with Kala Raksha. Varshaben began working with Kala Raksha too, and through the organization, she attended exhibitions in Delhi, Mumbai, and Ahmedabad and a design workshop taught by a National Institute of Fashion Technology intern.

Like most girls in her community, for her own work she was inspired by looking at dowry collections. Before a wedding, brides-to-be would display their handwork for all the women of the village to review. Brides who married into Sumrasar would show their dowries after marriage in the same way. These were social occasions, but the main point was to critique the artisan's creativity. Varshaben grew up fully understanding the distinction between copying and inspiration. No one thought of copying, because they all knew everyone else's work well, and only unique work brought praise. She learned directly and always did her own designs. She saw new designs in her mind, she said.

In 2008, when she was eighteen, Varshaben studied design at Kala Raksha Vidhyalaya. "Suf embroidery is my art, and my heritage," she said. She elaborated that the importance of embroidery is social and cultural—and it satisfies the need to decorate. "But people like our embroidery because it is hand art. If designs keep evolving, suf work will increase. And a suf artisan has only a short time to create, as the art requires keen eyesight." She wanted to make the most of her time. Asked what her dreams were, she retorted, "Of course I have dreams, but I am not going to reveal them to anyone." She did say that she hoped to learn tailoring and computer skills as well as design.

It was only the second class for suf embroiderers. The pilot year had only Rabari women students. The year before, three suf embroiderers from Sumrasar and one elder appliqué artisan cum chaperone had taken the course. Varshaben and her three classmates from Sumrasar brought a chaperone too. But after the first course, Gomtiben decided she did not need to work so hard. "I live in a green garden," she said. "I have everything I want." So she dropped out. I was sure the girls would follow, and in fact two did drop out for reasons of sociopolitical pressure. I lost hope for Varshaben and her friend Damyantiben. They would have to leave too. But Varshaben, in her calm, cool, steady-as-a-rock manner, said no, they came because they *wanted* to take the course. There was no question of their dropping out. We managed by escorting them to and from Sumrasar.

Still, it was not an easy year for them. They loved learning. But there was constant taunting from women in Sumrasar. KRV was 95 kilometers from Sumrasar, well out of surveillance range. "Why do you have to go *there*?" they would ask. "What do you *do* there? Are you starving for work?"

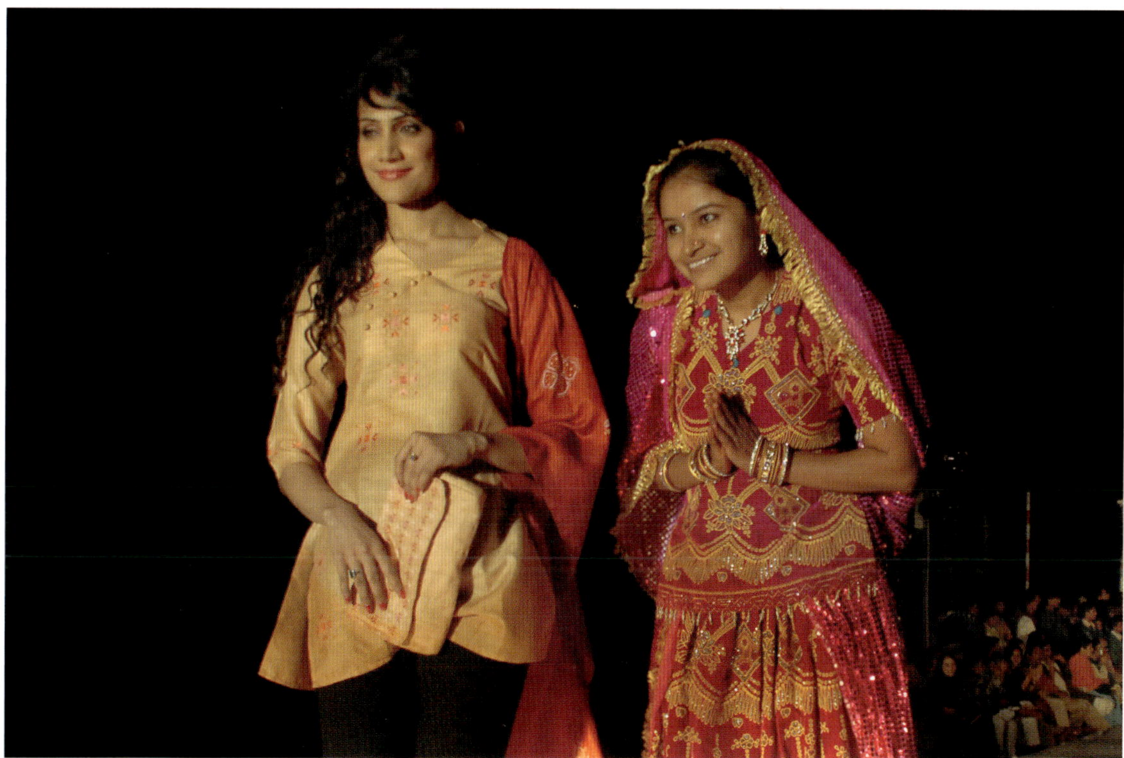

What they did was explore, in their art and as individuals. In the first few classes at the end of the day, Varshaben and the other girls would joyfully race around the spacious campus, with no one to reprimand them. They played. "We can't do this at home," Varshaben said.

In the Color class, they went to the Vandh beach. It was a revelation of colors. "I had never seen it like that before!" she marveled. "Now, I am thinking that we learned about contrast, complementary, primary, and secondary colors, but how do we name all of the others?"

Always years wiser than her age, Varshaben took on the role of mentor as well as student in the first class. The visiting faculty were two American art teachers. She grasped the concepts quickly and helped translate them to the other students. Varshaben explained warm and cool colors by citing the sun and moon, one faculty member wrote in her report. She helped students who could not write. She was fascinated with monochromatic color combinations despite their low contrast. This prompted a discussion in which the students noted that they all prefer contrast but considered that other people and markets may prefer something other than their own preferences.

"When I went back after the first class," Varshaben recalled, "everyone—even boys—was curious about what I had learned. When I told them, they were impressed. They said, you have better facilities than we get in school. I told them this *IS* a school—a school for US!"

Over the year, she observed the ways that faculty taught, and gained the confidence to critique them too. "One faculty member yelled at us for not knowing how to take pictures," she remembered. "But if he had explained, we could have done it."

Opposite: *Thelo*, by Varshaben Uttam Bhanani, 2015. Cotton with rayon thread, kharek embroidery. 14" x 14" plus 28" strap. Collection of the family. Like suf, kharek embroidery style is also counted on warp and weft yarns. It was practiced in Nagar Parkar, from where Varshaben's family migrated. More labor intensive too, kharek is precious and stitched for personal use more than for sale. Varshaben embroidered this bag for her dowry but decided not to include it. She kept it for herself. *Photo: Schiffer Publishing Ltd.*

Kala Raksha Vidhyalaya, 2008. Varshaben takes a bow on the fashion show ramp at her graduation, with a model wearing three pieces from her Garden collection. *Photo: Ketan Pomal, L.M. Studio*

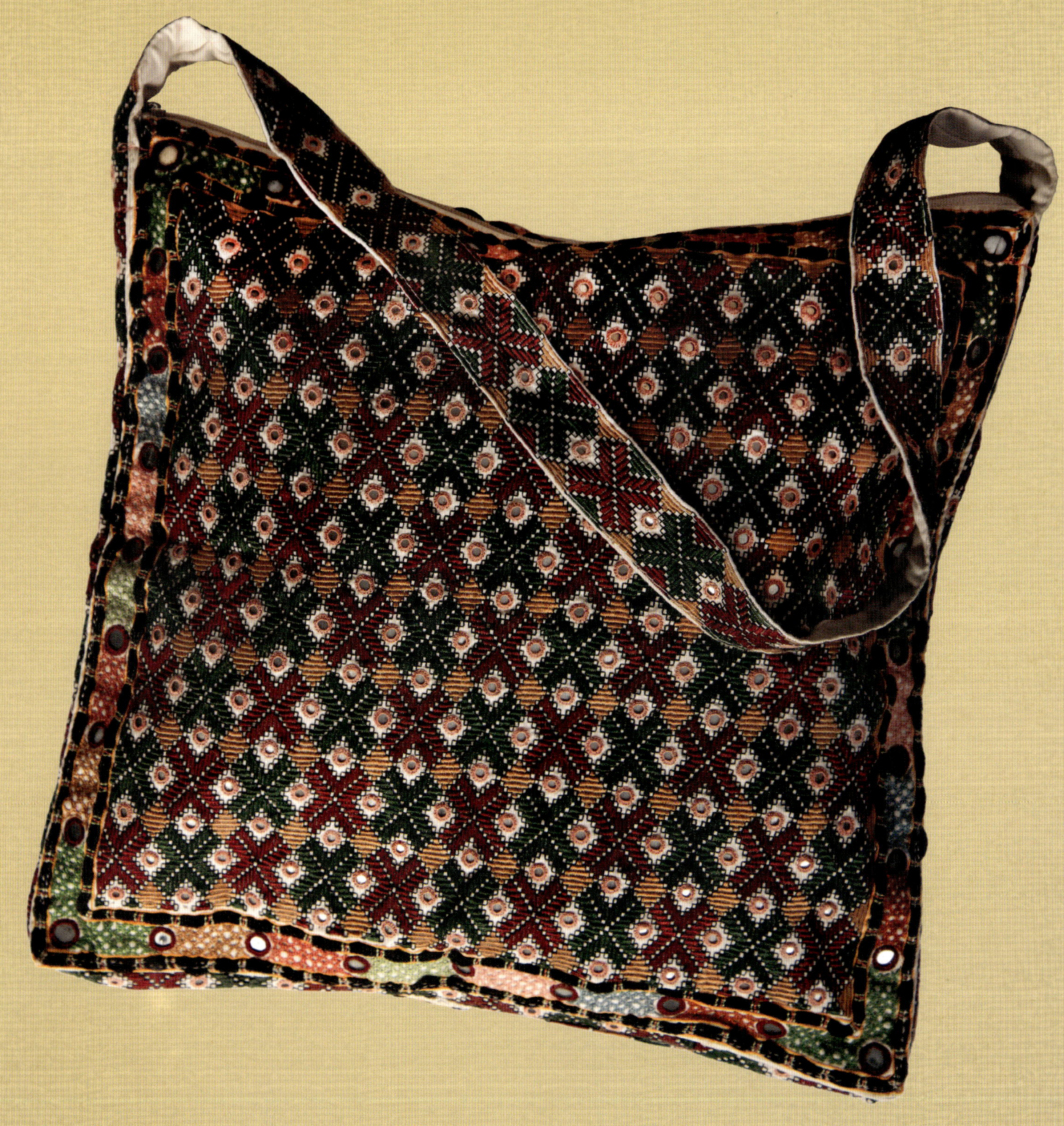

She enjoyed the experience of visiting shops and homes in Ahmedabad. In her childhood, women were severely secluded. They did not even bring water from the well or vegetables from the market. Men interacted with the world beyond the home. "I can't even go to my uncle's shop in Sumrasar," she mused. "But here I am visiting Ahmedabad!" She speculated that an artisan would pay close attention to customer reaction because it was her subject. We could take this into our own innovation, she concluded. And she enjoyed the homework for this class. "We are happy to create for someone we know," she explained.

For her final collection, she chose the theme "Flower Garden." "This was the first time I ever thought about theme," she said. "I had to think how to make flowers using suf." She delved into the garden. By the end of the course, she was seeing flowers in her mind. "In preparing my portfolio," she recalled, "I used the colors of my theme and the same motifs and showed how the embroidery is done. I practiced for the jury with my eyes closed. At the presentation I was so nervous, but then I thought that the teachers have taught me, so I will explain what I have learned. The success of effort is sweet."

Varshaben graduated with the award for Most Promising Artisan. She was a mentor for the classes of 2010 and 2011, which was an opportunity to review what she had learned. "In the first class, everyone says, 'We're uneducated,'" she noted. "But by the end, no one says that. They all say we are educated.

"We need to have courage and confidence to grow. The difference in education is this: when Damyantiben and I came to KRV, we were just two girls. We worried what people would say, but we put it aside. And that way we two went ahead. We learned a lot, and now we are given embroidery work first. We also learned to price our own work."

I believed that Varshaben had more to offer than first dibs on work. In 2009, I established an internship in which KRV graduates developed new product samples for Kala Raksha. Varshaben was an intern from October 2010 to March 2011. She embroidered jackets with a sea theme, a tradition theme, and an extraordinarily sophisticated white-on-white Rann theme. She embroidered shawl and scarf samples and a lyrical linen purse that is still selling at Kala Raksha. She created more art-to-wear jackets in 2012 and a personal logo for a show done by the embroidery artist Alice Kettle. Varshaben named her logo "Sushobhan/Decoration" because she said that's what makes us each unique.

"Earlier we just embroidered as work," she reflected. "There was no recognition. Even at Kala Raksha, people knew it was an artisan's work but didn't know the artisan's name. Gradually, I realized that I could grow. I wished that people would ask whose work this is, and discover it is Varshaben's work. After I did the course, my work became known by my name."

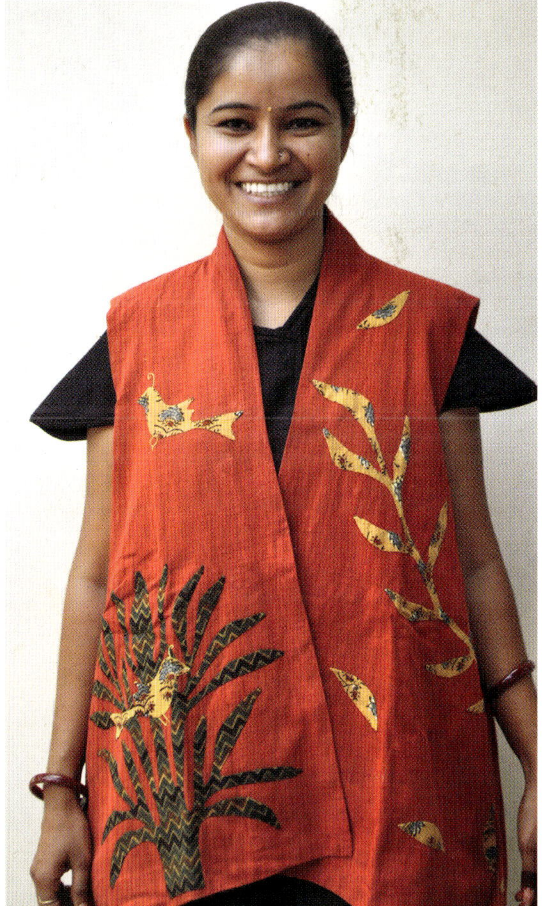

Above: Sumrasar Sheikh, 2012. Varshaben models an art-to-wear jacket appliquéd by her mother, Hariyaben, who was also a KRV intern. *Photo: Judy Frater*

Opposite: Thelo, by Varshaben Uttam Bhanani, 2015. Cotton with rayon thread, kharek embroidery. 14" x 14" plus 28" strap. Collection of the family. Like suf, kharek embroidery style is also counted on warp and weft yarns. It was practiced in Nagar Parkar, from where Varshaben's family migrated. More labor intensive too, kharek is precious and stitched for personal use more than for sale. Varshaben embroidered this bag for her dowry but decided not to include it. She kept it for herself. *Photo: Schiffer Publishing Ltd.*

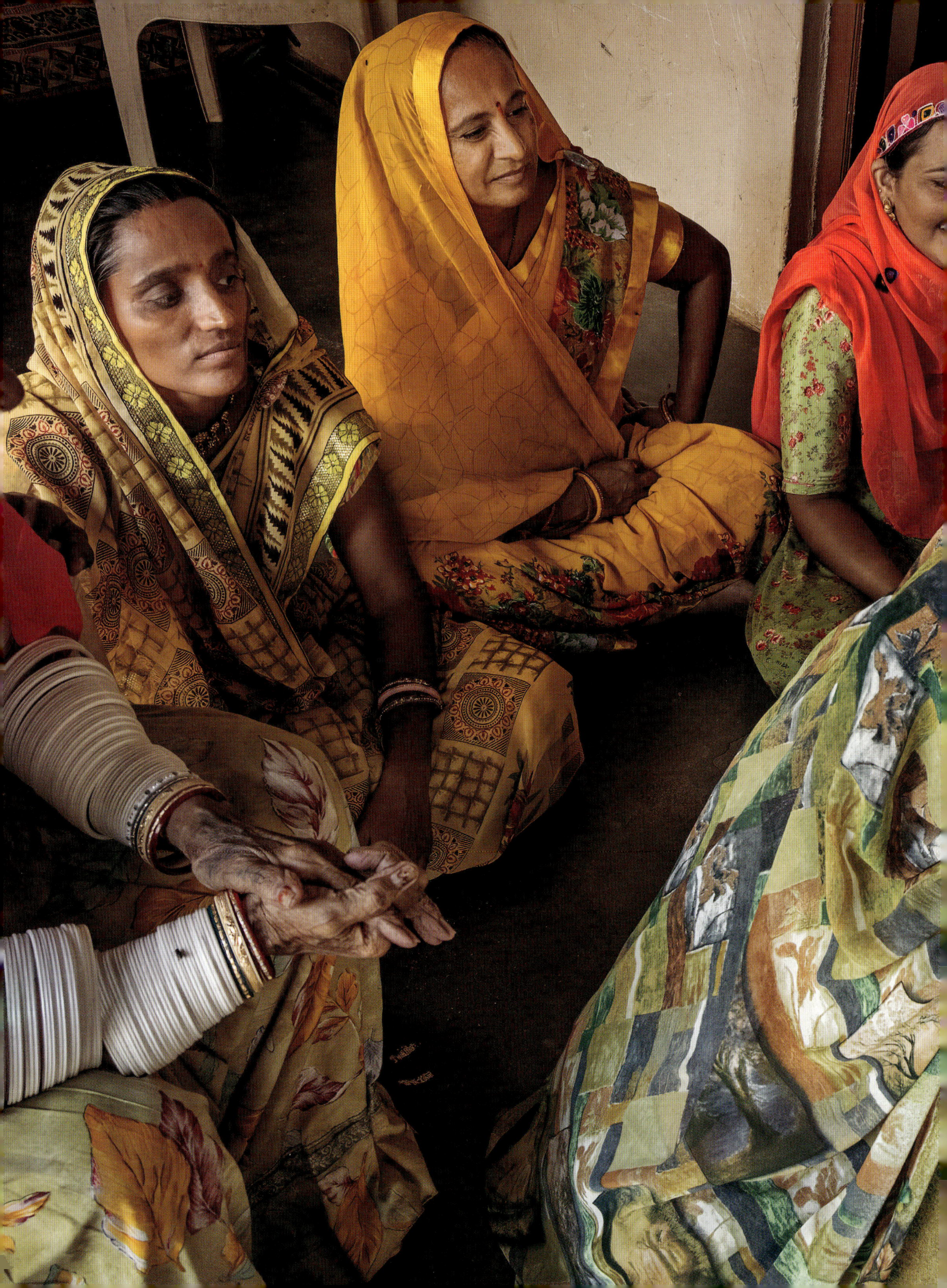

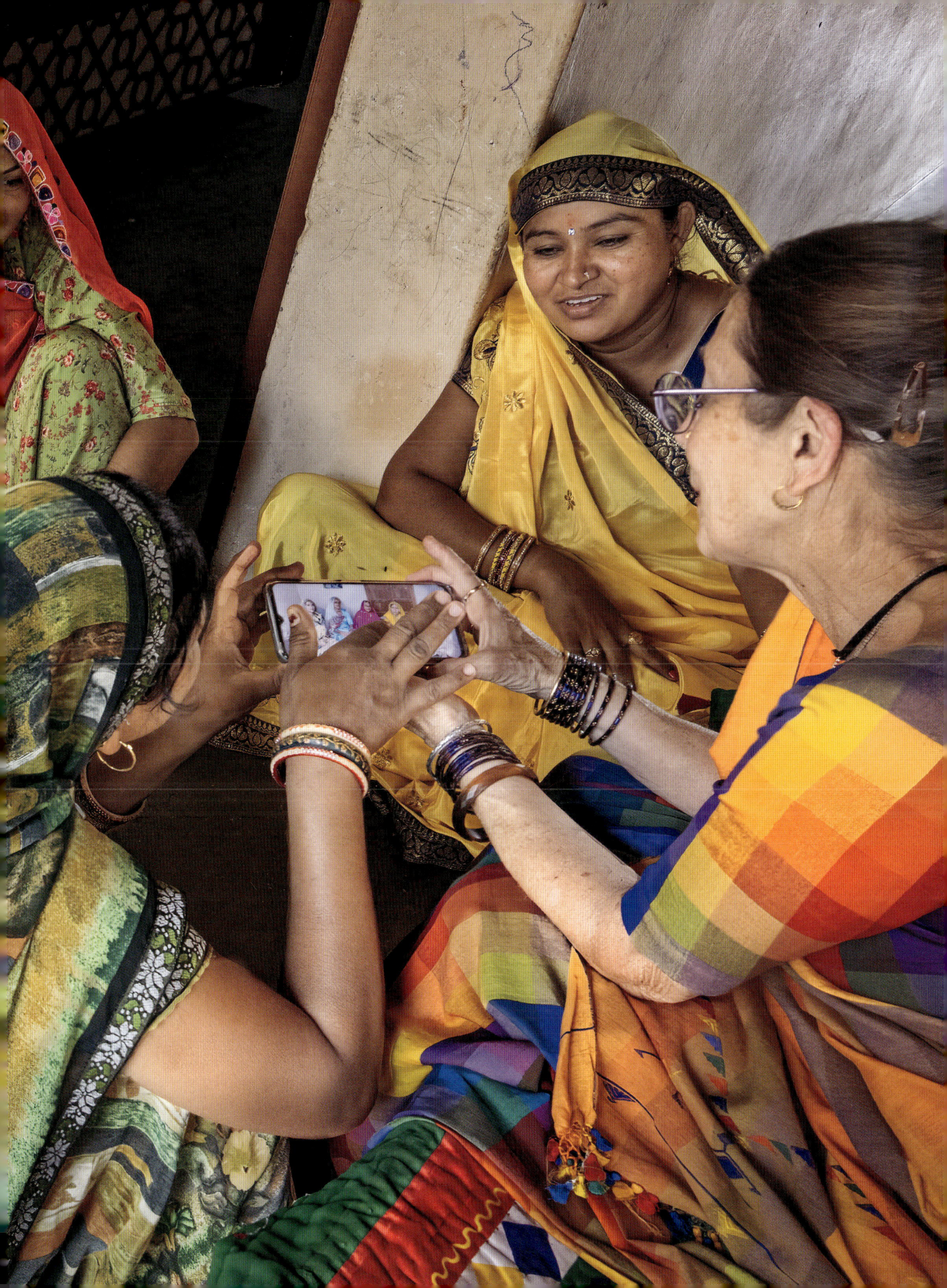

In 2013, Varshaben participated in Co-Creation Squared, a project in which embroidery design graduates embroidered garments by fashion designer Anju Modi, and weaver, printer, and bandhani design graduates paired with them to complete the ensembles. It was the first time that men and women graduates worked together. Varshaben paired with Dahyabhai Kudecha, a weaver designer and KRV faculty member. The collection was remarkable. It was presented in a fashion show at Good Earth in Mumbai and then sold at Artisans Gallery. None of the young suf embroiderers, including Varshaben, were allowed to attend the event. The men of their community decided that. The elder women who did go to Mumbai observed that sales were much higher among the design graduates who were there to present their work.

The next year, I left Kala Raksha to launch Somaiya Kala Vidya. Varshaben began to embroider her own work for direct sale. She could not think of going to pop-up exhibition sales, since she would not be able to travel on her own and, in any case, could not create in volume. But she sold to visitors who came to Sumrasar and to some shops and designers with whom she had made connections.

Accepting Varshaben's invitation, I arrive in Sumrasar. She is sitting in a little crowd of women relatives, beaming her million-dollar smile. She is wearing another peach sari with green accents and all the jewelry. Everyone is happily sharing news and discussing community affairs. Varshaben's younger brother was married just a few days before she was, and his wife is among the group, drawing her veil over her face whenever a man is around. She spreads an impressive array of embroidered pillows, bags, ornaments, and some patchwork quilts for everyone to examine. The work is fine, but the patterns and colors are not remarkable. In the pile are a toran and a bag her mother had embroidered. She shows these and says, "This is what they used to think looked good."

Varshaben always sees the big picture, in depth. She quietly critiques her sister-in-law's dowry and tells me what's behind the choices in recent engagements of some design graduates, the politics and powers at play.

I ask her if she will keep embroidering now that she is married. Her in-laws are in Tharad, and she will live there now and have to do as they wish. She wants to, she says. And her elder brother Ranjitbhai said he would support her. They want to keep Hariyaben's business going. It's not till now that she remembers her mother. Tears quietly roll down her cheeks.

Previous pages: Sumrasar Sheikh, 2022. Varshaben, her family and friends from her natal village, and I catch up after a long absence. Sisterhood is a foundation of village life. Mobile technology is now an everyday element. *Photo: Nevada Wier*

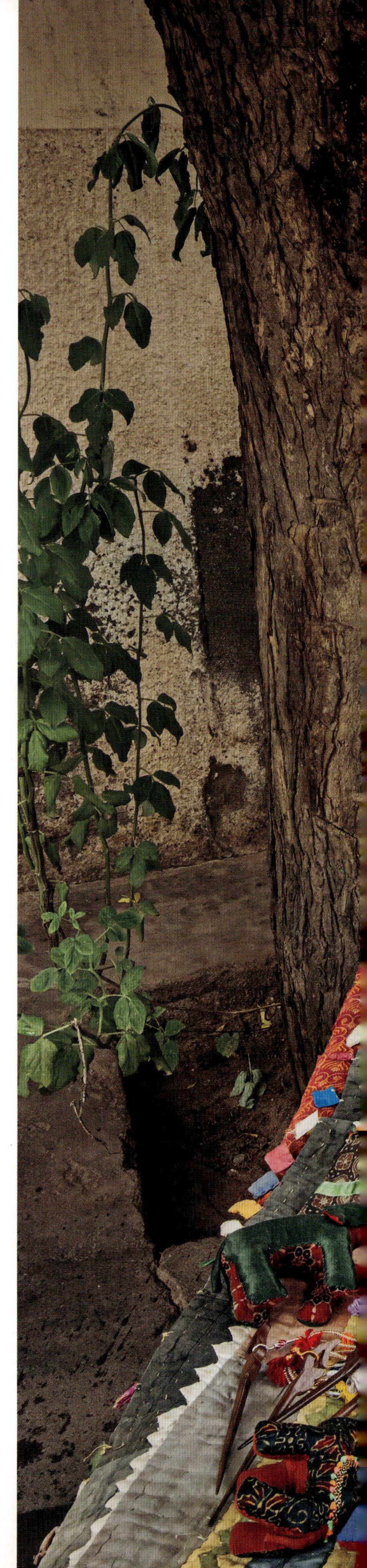

Right: Sumrasar Sheikh, 2022. Varshaben displays dolls designed by her mother. The dolls are traditional. Hariyaben's innovations are now owned by the community too. *Photo: Nevada Wier*

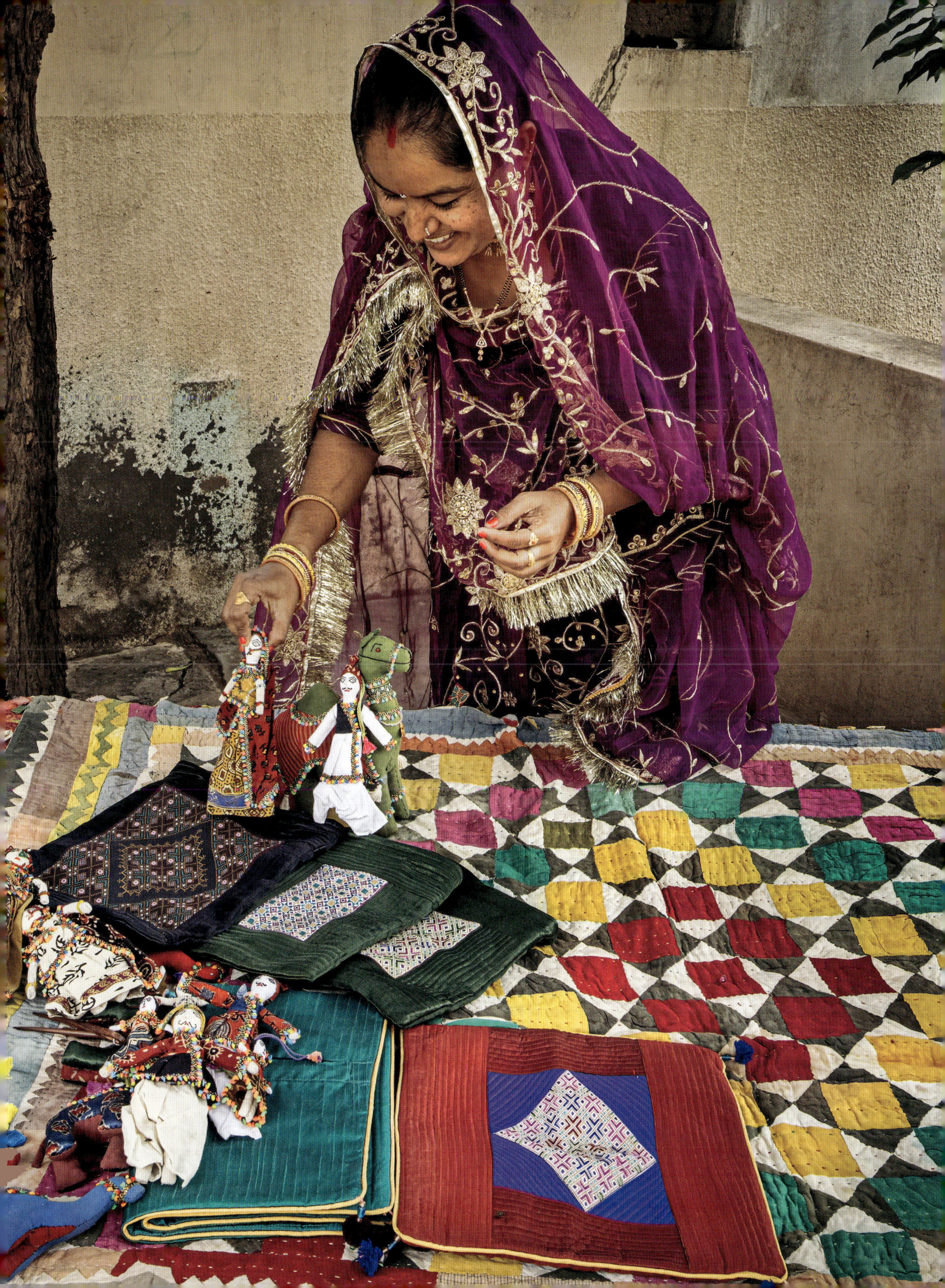

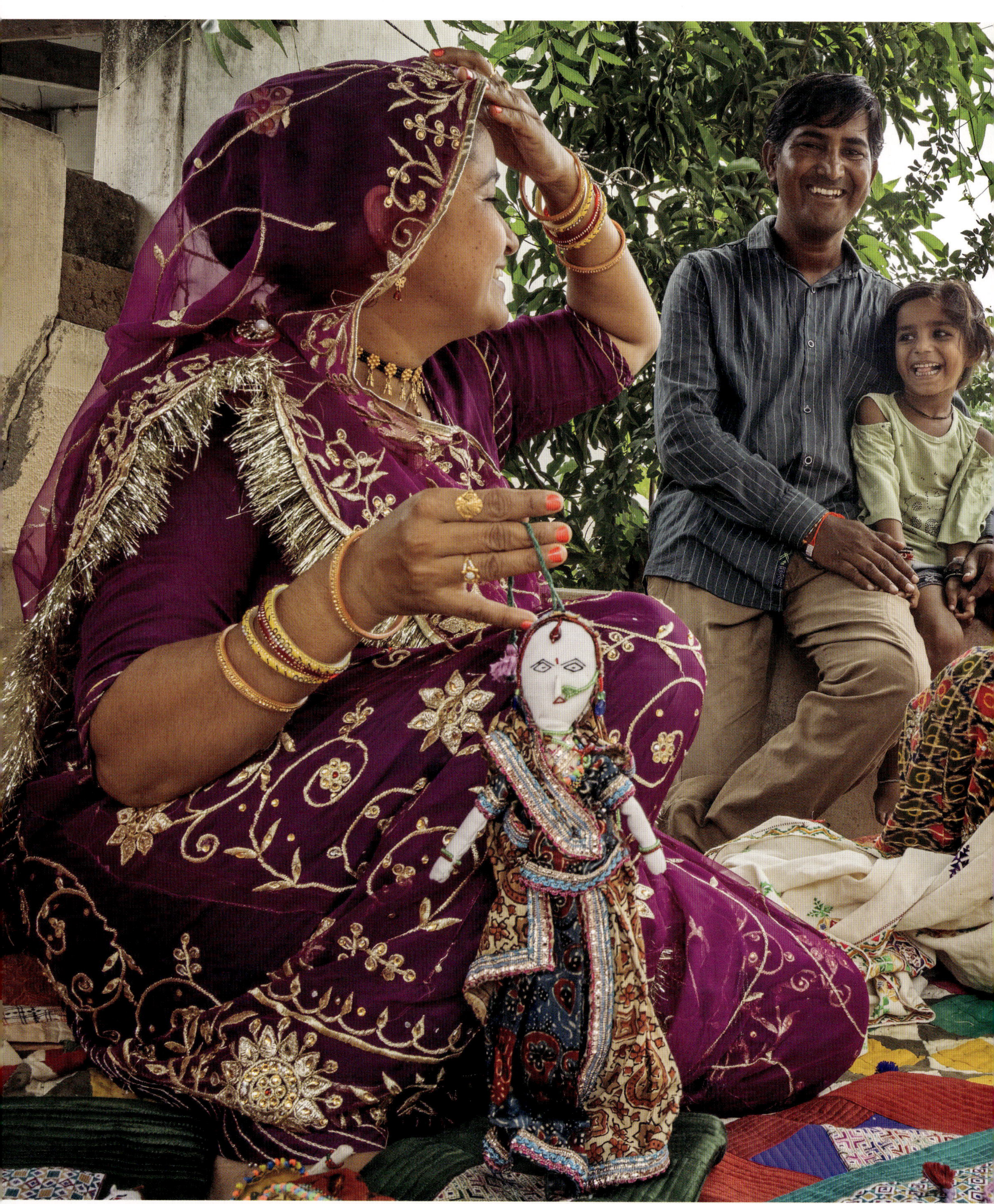

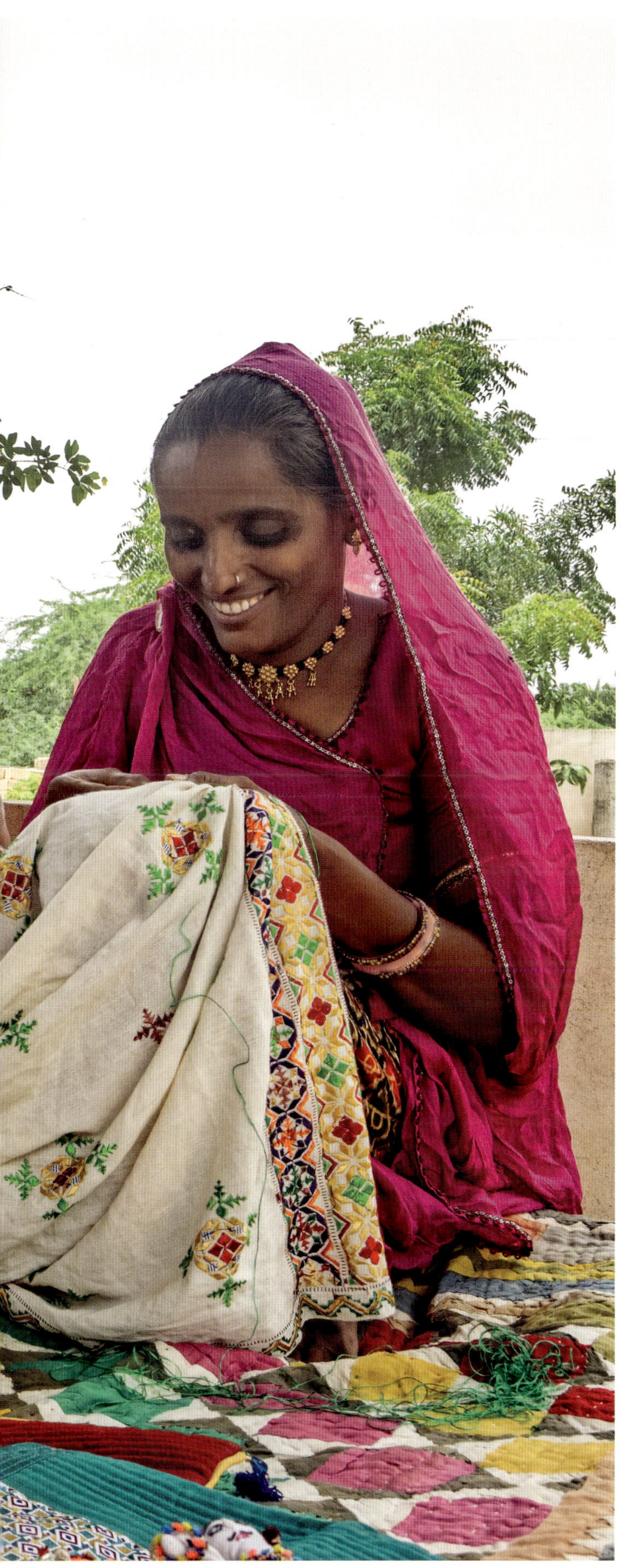

2022

Varshaben is visiting Sumrasar again, shining as always, with a beautiful one-and-a-half-year-old son. And in a few minutes, a small group of women design graduates come, and we have a meeting. These are the women who now do Kala Raksha work only occasionally. They are starting to create their own work. "You taught us!" they say.

Ranjitbhai is farming now, and with his wife, Geetaben, he is starting his own embroidery business. He does exhibitions, gets invitations, finds marketers—and marketers find him. Varshaben hopes that she will soon be able to get back to embroidery. She has a great desire, she says. She and Ranjitbhai will do it together. Their collection includes Hariyaben's toys and dolls. The product returns to the rightful owner. And they are selling under Hariyaben's brand, "Kaam Bole."

"We learned a lot in the course," Varshaben says. "We want to move ahead. After all, *majuri* [labor work] is *majuri*. One's own work is one's own work."

Sumrasar Sheikh, 2022. Varshaben's brother Ranjitbhai and his wife, Geetaben, are carrying Hariyaben's brand Kaam Bole forward. Their daughter, Pari, who some say is Hariyaben incarnate, was born just two months after Hariyaben passed. *Photo: Nevada Wier*

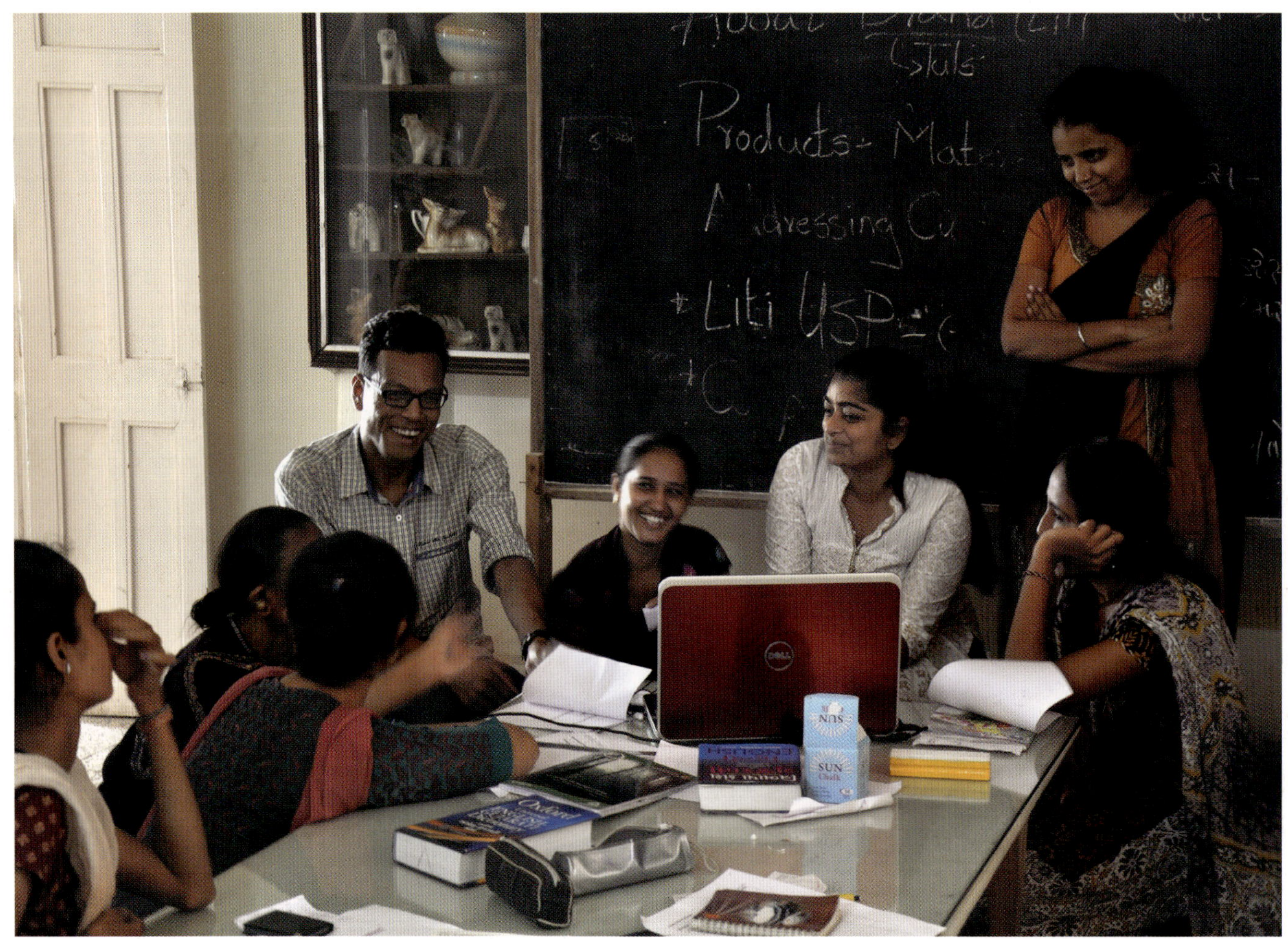

We earn by selling to brands. But they sell our work under their own labels. We artisan designers should make our own brands—and draft our own terms and conditions.

~Irfanbhai Anwar Khatri

Somaiya Kala Vidya, 2014. For the first year of the new location, we held the pilot Business and Management for Artisans course. A graduate course, it was open only to design graduates. Like the design course, it was modular residential, and men's and women's classes were held separately. *Photo: Judy Frater*

Chapter 11

FURTHER INNOVATIONS, RECOGNIZING OWNERSHIP, BUILDING COMMUNITY: THE SOMAIYA KALA VIDYA YEARS

Like Fatima of the Sufi tale (see the Appendix, page 287), I was once again washed ashore on a foreign land . . . a little yard in a little town; a group of artisans filled with anxious anticipation; a staff of four loyal, capable, focused colleagues; two creative faculty members; and a trustee I hardly knew. We lit the ceremonial lamp; I exhaled and plunged into a course in business and management—a subject about which I knew little.

Amid the exhilarating success of Kala Raksha Vidhyalaya, there were tragedies. Within the first year of classes, the government of India had, unbelievably, selected the Vidhyalaya's very spot to build Asia's largest coal-fed thermal power plant—and a plant of equal size sprang up adjacent to it. We were a tiny doughnut hole inside 9,200 megawatts of air, sound, and social pollution. At the end of the sixth year of the school, my colleague Prakashbhai was diagnosed with fourth-stage cancer.

At the juncture of Prakashbhai passing, after completion of the eighth course, I took stock. I had to raise the entire budget for the program every year; that consumed all of my creative resources. The program had reached its limitation in the situation of Kala Raksha Vidhyalaya. I needed support. The K. J. Somaiya Trust, which had over fifty years of experience operating educational institutes, had approached me with interest in working together. I decided to invest my energy and experience in building the program to an institute. With sadness, trepidation, and hope, I resigned from Kala Raksha and joined the K. J. Somaiya Gujarat Trust.

A program is not circumscribed by its premises. I brought with me the curriculum I had developed as my Ashoka Fellowship, the faculty I had trained, the advisors with whom I had worked, the community of Kutch artisans whose trust I had built, many supporters, and more than eight years of experience. But the move entailed a fundamental change. At Kala Raksha I was a trustee, making decisions for the organization and being responsible for their impact. At the K. J. Somaiya Gujarat Trust, I was an employee. I was unprepared for how demotivating a reprimand from a boss could be, and how

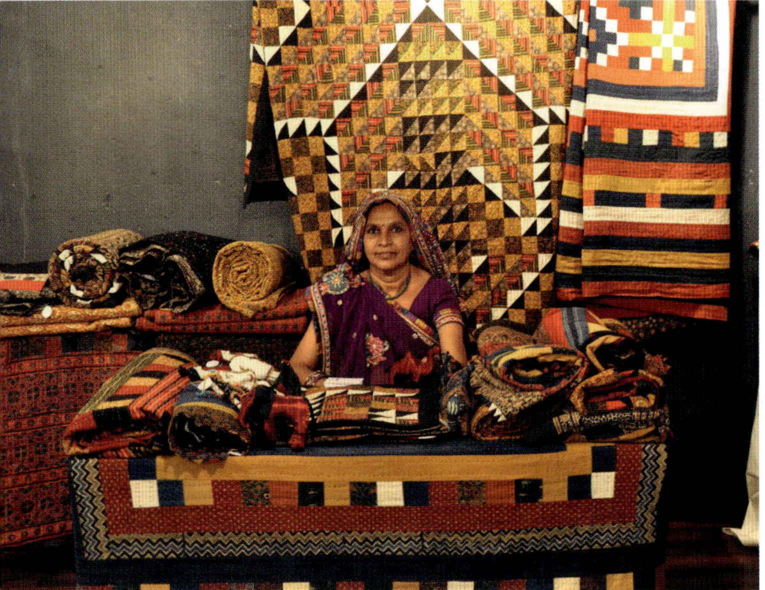

Mumbai, 2014. Hariyaben displays her quilt collection at the BMA pop-up exhibition. Presentation is a critical element of design and business. *Photo: Judy Frater*

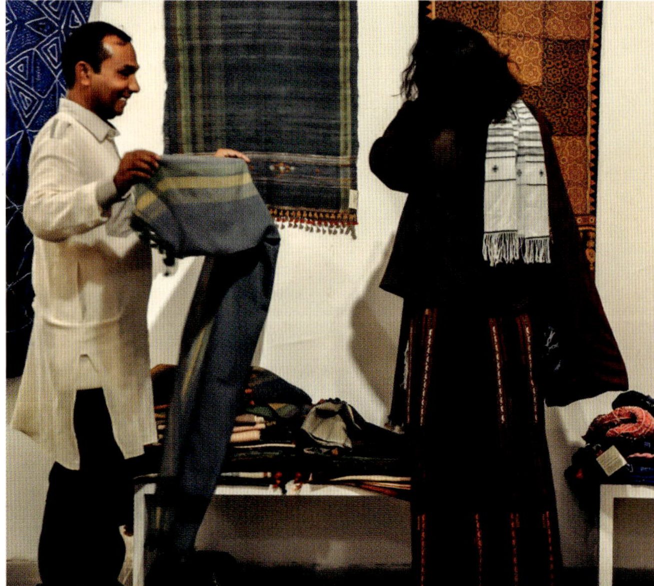

Delhi, 2016. Puroshottambhai shows shawls from his BMA exhibition. The students researched and selected the venue, promoted the show, displayed their work, and sold to customers. *Photo: Judy Frater*

frustrating it would be to have others claim my intellectual property. But this was a boon in disguise. Empathy with creative people in constraint shaped the programs I developed during the next six years.

Establishing Somaiya Kala Vidya was an opportunity to reassess and reinvent the education program. At the same time, I wanted to ensure that the momentum of all that we had achieved was not lost, and that we nurtured the growing community of artisan designers. We were contained in a temporary, scaled-down premises in Adipur, a town 50 kilometers east of Bhuj. We did not have craft studios, only three rooms for students and faculty to stay in, a small makeshift classroom, and a wonderful garden.

I put on my creativity cap. By now, an industrial trend had begun—corporates needing to spend a percentage of profits on corporate social responsibility were grabbing the craft handle and getting artisans to work for them. Other organizations and individuals were monitoring our program and also engaging artisan design graduates to do their work. While this was flattering and easy for artisan designers, it obviated the capacity they had developed. And in all cases, the sale of work for others would glorify the organizations and leave the artisans nameless.

The goal of education for artisans was for artisans to become independent and recognized, which would ensure continued innovation, robust artisans, and vibrant traditions. Did graduates have what they needed to make good decisions?

While most artisan design graduates could develop remarkably good new designs, not all of them could successfully get to markets that would appreciate them. Numerous obstacles thwarted realizing capacity. Many, I felt, could be mitigated by a better understanding of business. Graduates themselves noted that they needed to know business. Through the Ashoka network, I solicited expertise. A business consultant, with the support of the Institute for Rural Management Anand (IRMA), my staff, and I developed a curriculum for teaching business and management to artisan design graduates. We used the modular format, visiting faculty, and one-year limit of the design course. I wanted to call this course the MBA—Management and Business for Artisans—but was told the acronym was already taken. So I dubbed it the BMA—Business and Management for Artisans.

I invited the graduates to date and presented the course proposal. Many were enthusiastic, but in the end, only five men signed up. I handpicked seven of the seventy-one women graduates, those whom I thought could consider establishing their own businesses. Then I searched for faculty. I listed craft businesses I thought were successful. The list was soberingly short. As always, I leaned on friends and well-wishers. The first big surprise was that many business teachers flatly refused the honorarium we offered. No design teacher had ever flinched—and at SKV, we had raised the honorarium by 40 percent! The learning curve for all of us was steep that first year.

The BMA course was truly a graduate course. The students, all familiar, worked more comfortably and much harder than before. The course culminated in a real-time exhibition that students would conceive and produce, while balancing the design and production of new collections. They were intensely engaged. The dramatic contrast between this and the design course was ownership. Students would directly reap the benefits—or shortcomings—of their work. It would be sold with their own brand tags. During the exhibition preparation time, an intern from IRMA interviewed the BMA students. They told him that recognition was as important to them as increased income.

The exhibition was a great success. Ownership translated to enthusiasm, and customers delightedly responded. The final postexhibition module, Analysis, was also a revelation. Hariyaben was sure that one of her quilts was stolen. The entire team of students, faculty, and staff went into a tailspin for most of the two weeks, only to learn that her suspicion was based on expectation of more income than she had received. The unforgettable lesson was that guesswork does not work in business.

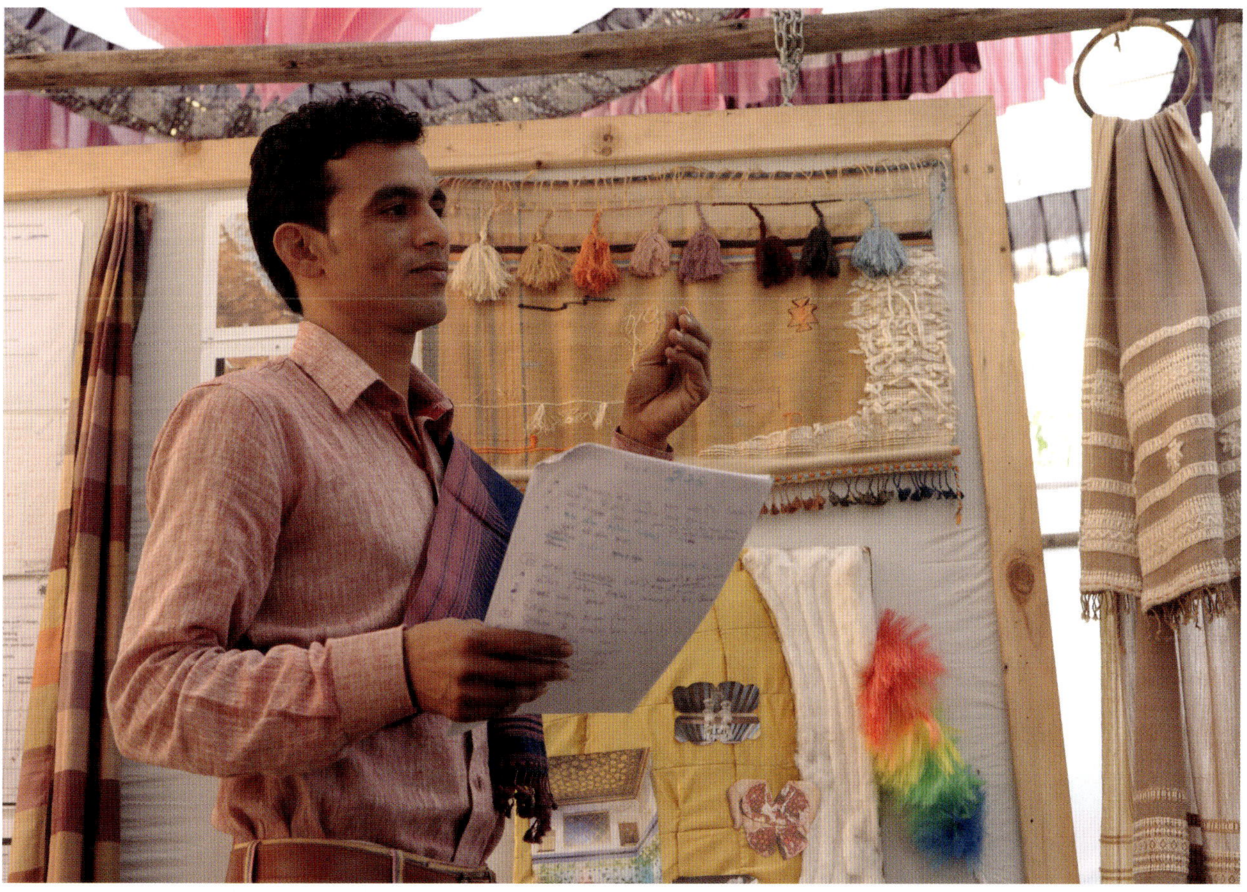

Somaiya Kala Vidya, 2016. Rajeshbhai presents his year of Business and Management for Artisans to the final jury. The course entails developing business strategies, creating a new collection, producing a pop-up exhibition, and analyzing the entire year. *Photo: Ketan Pomal, L.M. Studio*

While we were teaching artisans to brand themselves, I was also working overtime to create a name and identity for the new institute. We needed support from outside as well as from the artisan community. In the craft world, the Somaiya name was unknown, though I personally had developed some repute. Despite struggles with the administration for recognition, I leveraged my name when I could to distinguish this new entity. Within the year, I developed a logo, a website, and a Facebook page. We put out a newsletter and an annual calendar and advertised our exhibition. SKV began to have a presence.

We were set to run year two of the BMA when some politics in the local community forced the prospective students to drop out. The BMA course was scheduled from April through January, so that artisans with existing businesses would be able to finish domestic-sale peak season, concentrate on classes, and launch new collections the following season. The design courses had been scheduled from January to November so that the convocation held in Kutch would be during tourist season.

It was April 2015. We needed to maintain momentum. Though I had wanted to wait until we had the campus with craft studios that was already designed, I made a quick decision to hold the first SKV design course. We had done a bandhani and dye workshop in the backyard of the premises. We covered this far-from-ideal space and would make it do.

The venue was already booked for the BMA exhibition in December. This sparked another innovation. I added the BMA learnings: an exhibition added an important, real element—we would include an exhibition in the design course. Students would experience ownership, market feedback, and analysis of the experience afterward. I restructured the course so that jury feedback could be implemented in

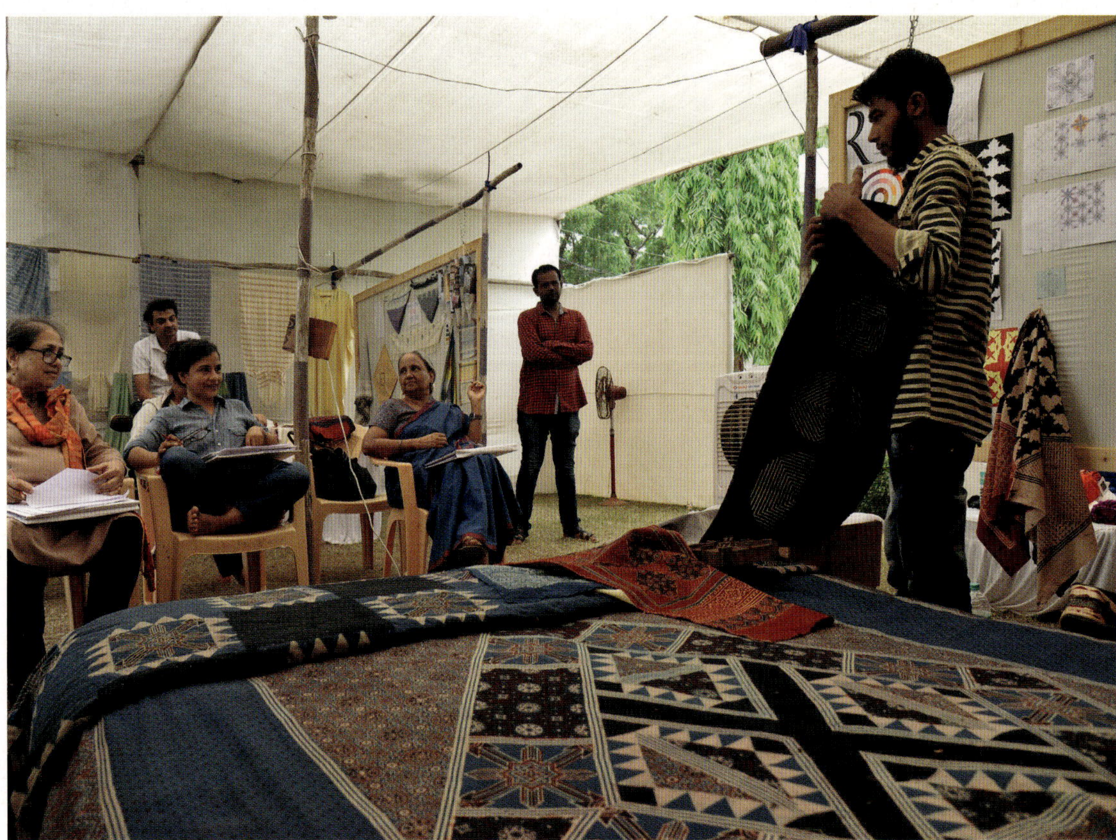

Above: Somaiya Kala Vidya, 2016. Mustakbhai presents his year of Design Education for Artisans to the final jury. Students learn elements and principles of design, market orientation, concept and collection development, and presentation. Incorporating jury feedback, they revise their collection samples and produce collections for a pop-up exhibition. *Photo: Ketan Pomal, L.M. Studio*

Opposite: Bhujodi, 2019. The most popular part of the annual convocation is a fashion show of graduate collections. Before SKV had a campus, we hosted the event in Bhujodi with support of the alumni. Achla Sachdev and team choreographed exceptionally joyous shows for equally enthusiastic audiences. *Photo: Ketan Pomal, L.M. Studio*

collections to ensure the best sales possible. I added an orientation workshop so that students would become familiar with each other and preview a kind of education that was new for them, and we could maximize the time in course 1.

Working around constraints was a key learning experience for me at Somaiya Kala Vidya. I learned from artisan students. They were cheerfully accommodating to the limited space. They were there to learn. They came with hopes and dreams—not to be superstars, but to be successful in their own terms.

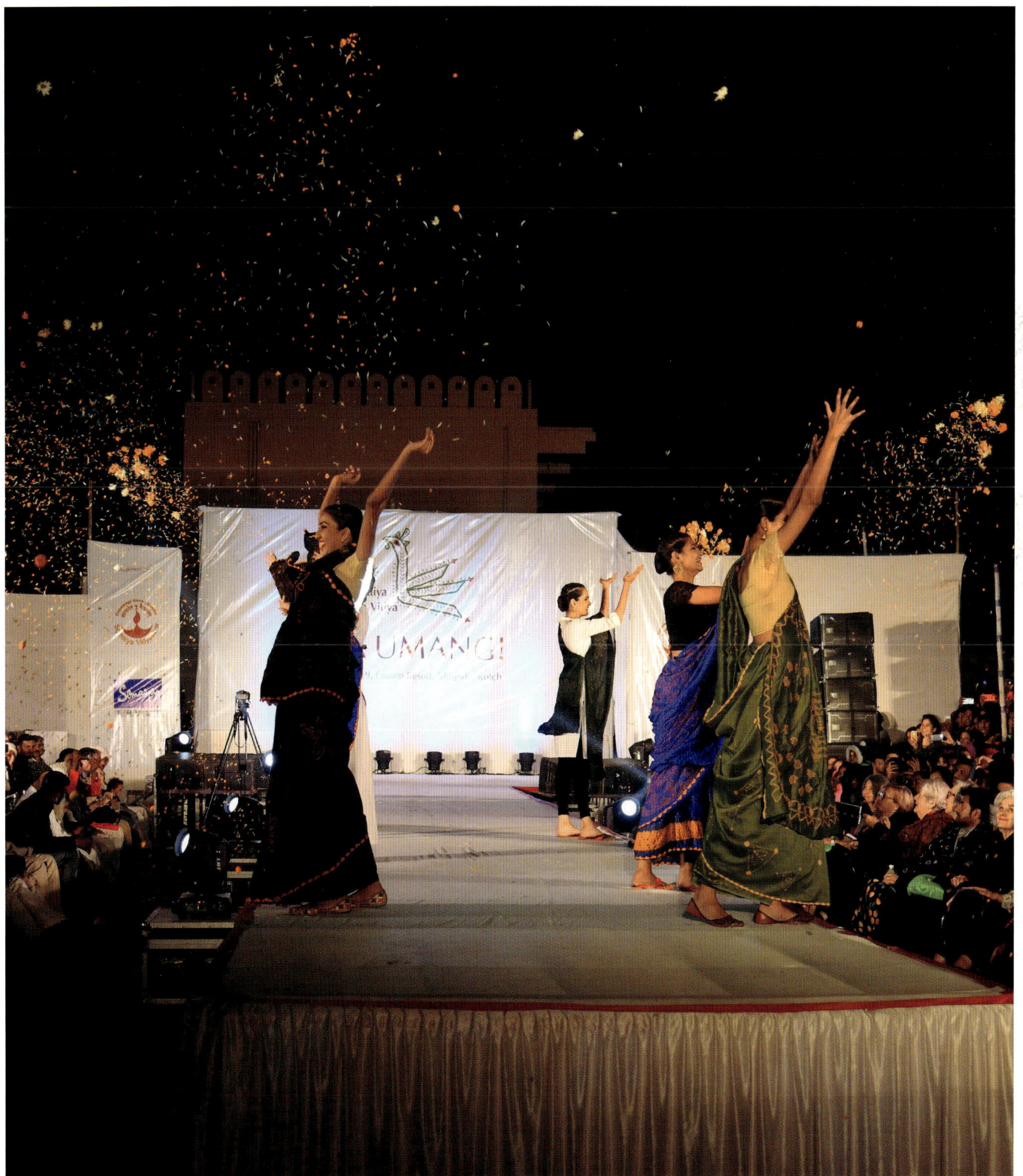

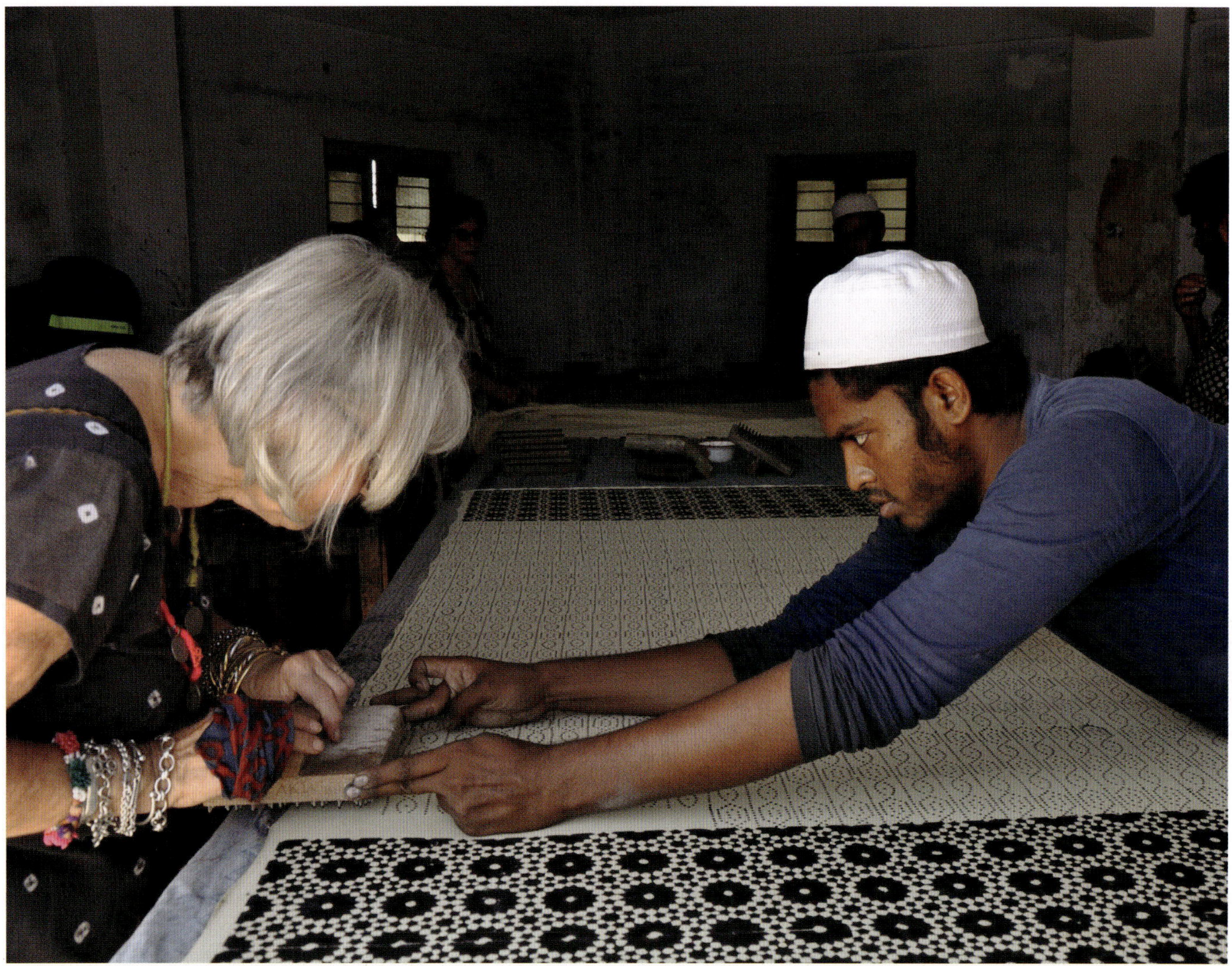

In our new incarnation, we worked together. Because of having limited space, I decided to hold the convocation with a fashion show in Bhujodi village, where the majority of weaver graduates live. They enjoyed partnership in the event and happily took responsibility for making it a great success. I held workshops for visitors in Ajrakhpur, where the majority of block print graduates live. Sharing spaces, we built a community of artisan designers.

The biggest sacrifice of the restructuring was the loss of women students. At Kala Raksha Vidhyalaya, we had a captive audience of the organization's membership: women income-generation participants. At Somaiya Kala Vidya, artisans who wanted to become independent applied. After the 2014 BMA course, we did not have a quorum of women applicants until 2018. Significantly, of those women there were three bandhani artisans and one weaver. Not one embroidery artisan applied. Sadly, by then traditional embroidery—made by artisans for themselves and their families—was all but gone. Women did not have the time or patience for embroidery; it was no longer culturally relevant. Women of embroidering communities could not envision embroidery as a livelihood. Existing wages were at the

Above: Ajrakhpur, 2018. Khalilbhai teaches Ajrakh techniques. Graduates organized workshops that SKV offered to visitors in their own studios. *Photo: Judy Frater*

Opposite: Somaiya Kala Vidya, 2017. Senior artisans Alimamad Isha Khatri, Dr. Ismail Mohmed Khatri, Umar Faruk Khatri, Shamji Vishramji Siju, and Gulam Husen Umar Khatri were advisors. They guided me in developing the program from its inception, selecting students, and teaching them about their craft traditions. *Photo: Lakhabhai P. Rabari*

bottom of the scale. Even at Kala Raksha, where women set their own wages, in the context of the market they dared not ask as much as Rabari women paid each other to create embroidery for their dowries and festival wear. Women did not want to embroider, and our course was for artisans who wanted to advance their traditions.

As artisan communities observed consistent success of graduates, applicants for the design course increased year by year. As with graduate courses, the BMA had a more limited appeal. We ran a second BMA in 2016. We honed the curriculum and implementation. Creating a second collection, with a deadline and minimal guidance, the students extended themselves. They chose a venue that was a risk. They worked as a team and produced one of the most beautiful—and successful—exhibitions I have seen.

The curricula I had developed were expressly for teaching traditional artisans. I presumed that traditional artisans were steeped in a comprehensive body of knowledge that comprised a tradition—not only skills but an aesthetic with a long, complex history. Over the years, I observed a striking drop in knowledge. Younger artisans who had been formally educated and those who had worked as laborers no longer knew the aesthetic aspects of their traditions. I tried to adjust the course to include research and more discussions of what comprised tradition. I brought in our advisors and more-knowledgeable alumni for support.

Always touching base with the origins of craft for guidance, I realized that in many ways, the education program was reimagining traditional systems in an appropriate contemporary form. Master artisan advisors teach students about traditions, as children once learned from elders; teaching weavers, printers, and dyers together in classes revitalizes the interdependence of weavers and dyers in creating

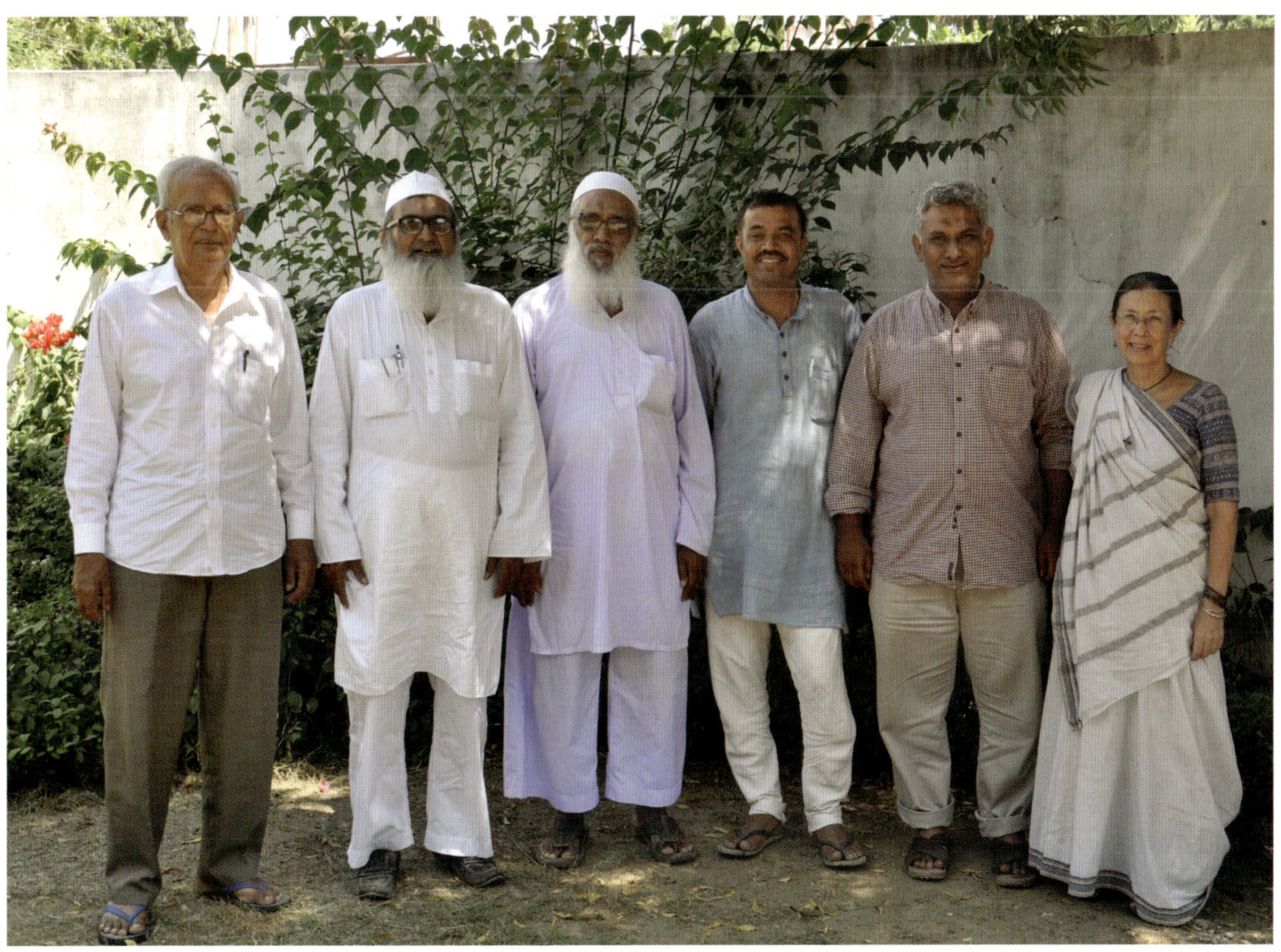

traditional textiles; and enabling direct interface between artisan designers and urban markets reinvents the system of direct contact with hereditary clients.

Scale is the backbeat of India today. Firmly in the industrial mindset, contemporary India believes that scale is an essential indication of success. Because culture is integral to craft, I did not envision expansion in terms of building a bigger monolithic institute, but rather in terms of taking what we learned to other regions and adapting the principles in locally appropriate ways. Serendipitously, as Somaiya Kala Vidya was being formed, I was called to Karnataka to participate in a think tank to envision Bagalkot as a model district. My part was to consider the local tradition of Ilkal sari weaving.

Weaving needs to be considered by a weaver, so I invited Jentibhai, a weaver design graduate, to accompany me. First thing, we set out to meet the weavers. In contrast to in Kutch, weaving in Bagalkot and much of southern India is produced in a "master artisan" system. The term is euphemistic. Businessmen with capital employ weavers as laborers, generously loaning them money when they need it. At the wages they earn, the weavers will never repay these loans, resulting in a neat locked-in arrangement. After seeing several workshops, Jentibhai suggested to a weaver that he might change the color schemes they were all using.

"These are the colors we use," he replied.

"OK," Jentibhai said. "What about altering the layout?"

"This is the layout we use," the weaver answered.

"OK! So, what about making dupattas or stoles?"

"Don't do that either" was the final word.

"What's wrong with these weavers?" Jentibhai asked.

"I don't know," I answered. "What do you think we should do?"

"Let's invite them to Kutch!" he offered.

And that is how we began our Outreach program. With effort, we identified five weavers who were willing to venture from Chamundeshwari Handloom Weavers' Cooperative Society in Kamatgi village, and they made the journey to Kutch. Three weaver design graduates were the venturers from Kutch. They showed the Kamatgi weavers their work and talked about innovation. During the workshop, a tour group serendipitously arrived. In half an hour, they purchased nearly RS 200,000 of contemporary work. The Kamatgi weavers were sold on the project.

Teams comprising Bhujodi and Kamatgi weavers worked quickly and, within eight months, codesigned new Ilkal saris, stoles, and dupattas for an exhibition in Mumbai. The Kamatgi weavers had hardly left Karnataka and were anxious about visiting this metro city. For the second time, they were amazed—this time to see their own saris selling at prices they could not have imagined.

At the end of the show, I asked what they had learned.

"Green does not sell," answered Dasrathbhai.

OK, I rejoined. Would you like to take a color class?

They eagerly agreed. I tailored the design curriculum to their situation, spreading the course over two years with an exhibition each year. I did some research on Iklal traditions, and we held the courses in Kamatgi. Fortunately, I found Kannada-speaking designer faculty. Our Kutch weaver mentors cotaught. Both Kamatgi and Kutch participants made new collections for each show so that everyone benefited.

The Bhujodi-to-Bagalkot project had ups and downs. The Kamatgi weavers quickly became confident and creative. The collections were imaginative and well received. The participants nearly doubled. They made their own shirts from the cotton they now wove, a sure sign of ownership and pride. In a region in which weaving is so despised that families will not marry their daughters to a family in which

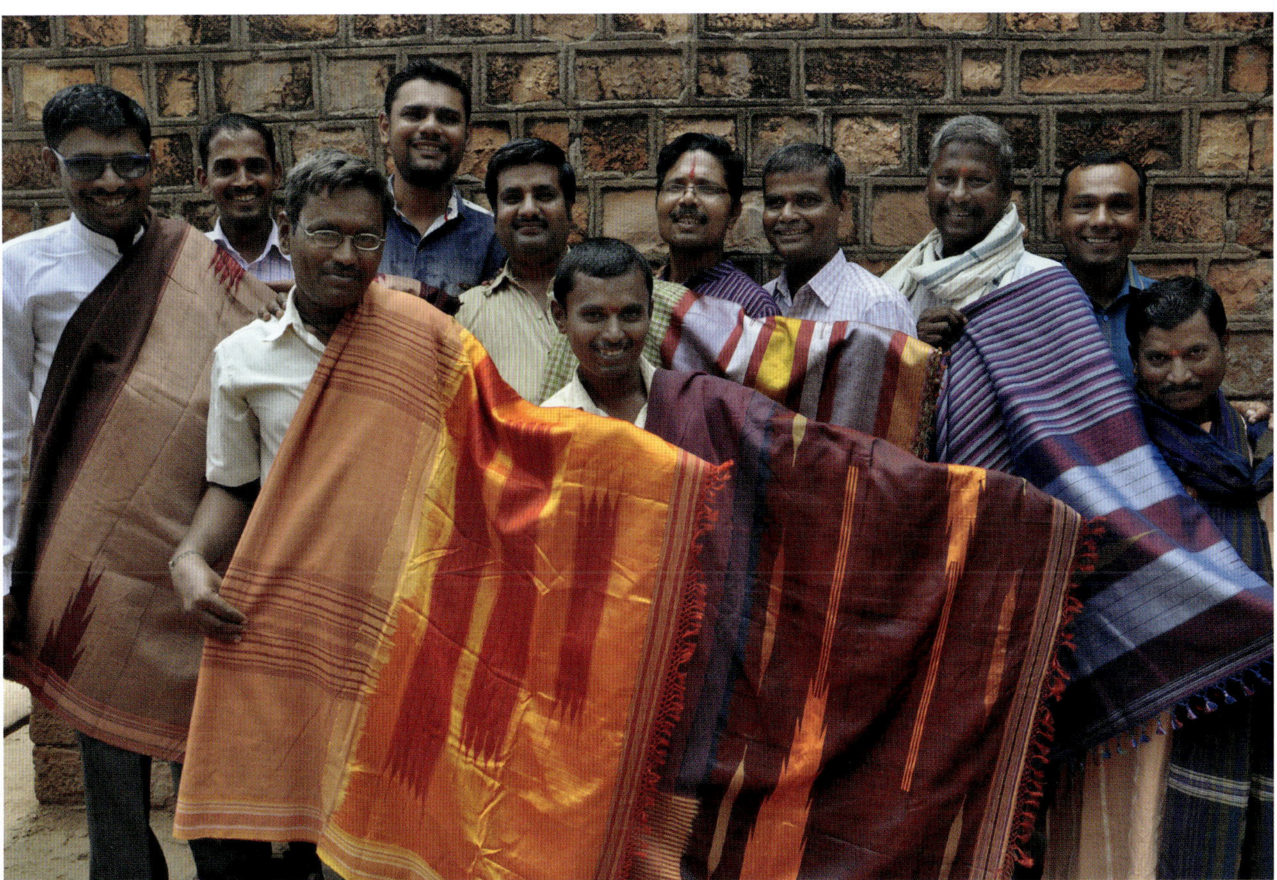

Kamatgi, 2017. The Bhujodi-to-Bagalkot team. Kutch weaver designers collaborated with Ikal sari weavers to teach innovation in tradition. The Bagalkot weavers gained enthusiasm and confidence and developed striking new renditions. We changed the Kutch team every few years to provide exposure and experience to more graduates. *Photo: Judy Frater*

there is a loom, they said, "We want to weave." But the business, management, and marketing side of the project eluded them, limitations that were hard to overcome. However, the weavers attended the SKV convocation in 2018 and 2019 and confidently waved to the crowd from the fashion show ramp. And after six years of our struggle to convince them to retain *kondi*, the unique warp-joining feature of Ilkal saris, they told us they had invented a streamlined *kondi*!

We did a second Outreach project with chikan embroiderers in Lucknow. Then I cowrote a grant with Dr. Kathryn Rudy that enabled us to explore where else in the world we might teach design to artisans. We visited Oaxaca, Mexico; Kathmandu, Nepal; and Tilonia and Kumaon in India.

Subsequently, we conducted a third Outreach project with weavers of Avani in Kumaon. In all three projects, the partners magically grew in confidence and creativity, and the Kutch mentors learned through teaching. All the work was fresh and alive.

Feasibility is the bottom line. I am certain that artisans everywhere can learn design with brilliant results, and that this is key to sustaining traditions. But in my research and experiences, I have learned that building a program requires time, support, and an environment with several key factors:

- a craft tradition within living memory
- diversity of craft in the region
- an appealing story
- accessibility to domestic and tourist markets
- a local organization that shares value for tradition and creative capacity

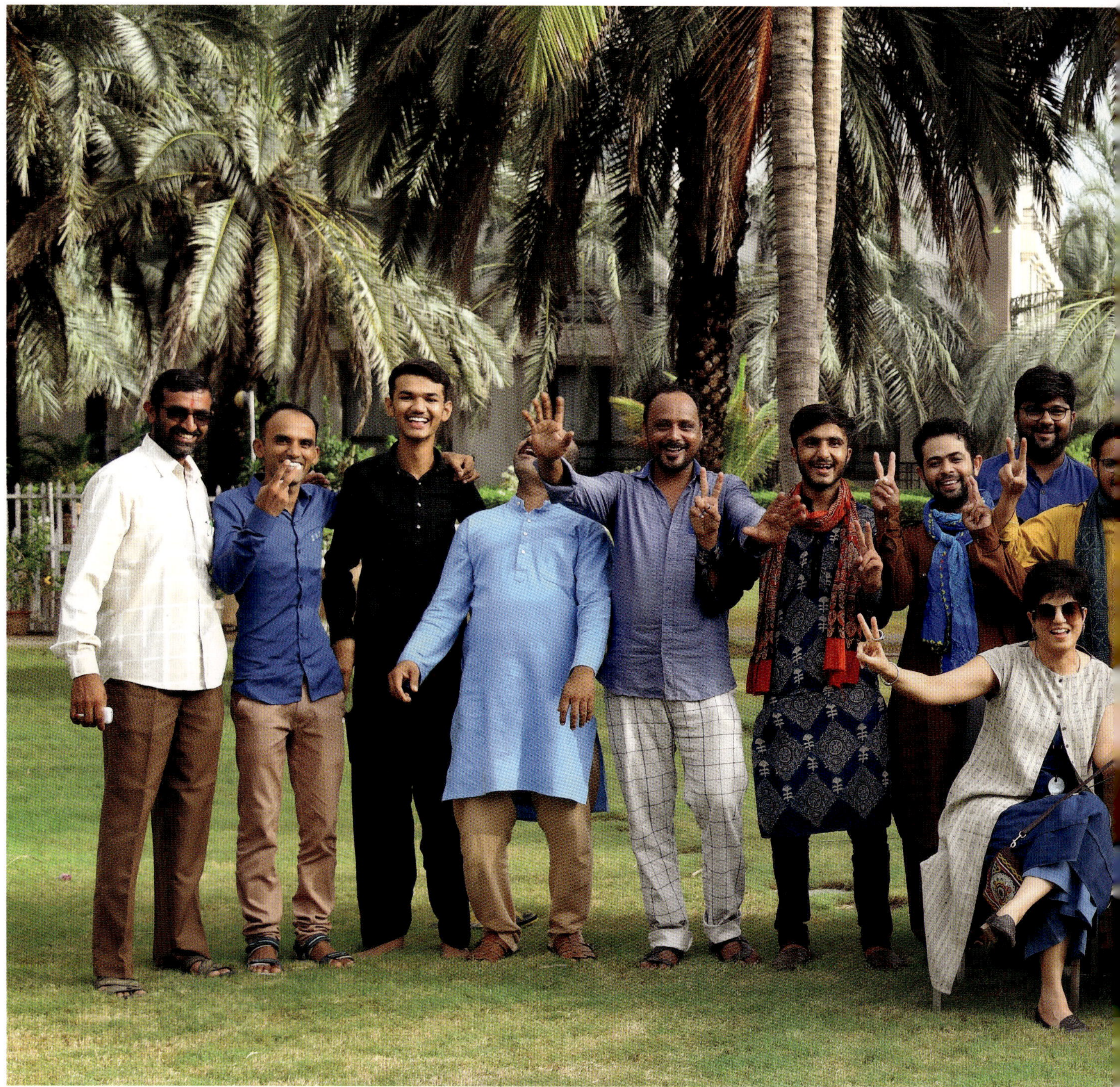

Fortunately, those factors coalesced in Kutch. Incorporating experiences from the BMA and outreach programs and from codesign programs that I developed, I was able to enrich and strengthen the core design course. At the end of the fourteenth year of design education, I commissioned an impact assessment. Graduates candidly shared experiences that were remarkably cohesive.

The course addressed their situation and perceived needs, they said. It increased their awareness and appreciation of shared traditions and gave them confidence to explore unique interpretations. It helped connect them to markets directly, without intermediaries. We are known as individuals now, and our work is valued, they said. The course provided them with ownership of their work, and it resulted in understanding community as well as personal worth. Graduates were able to define values and success for themselves.

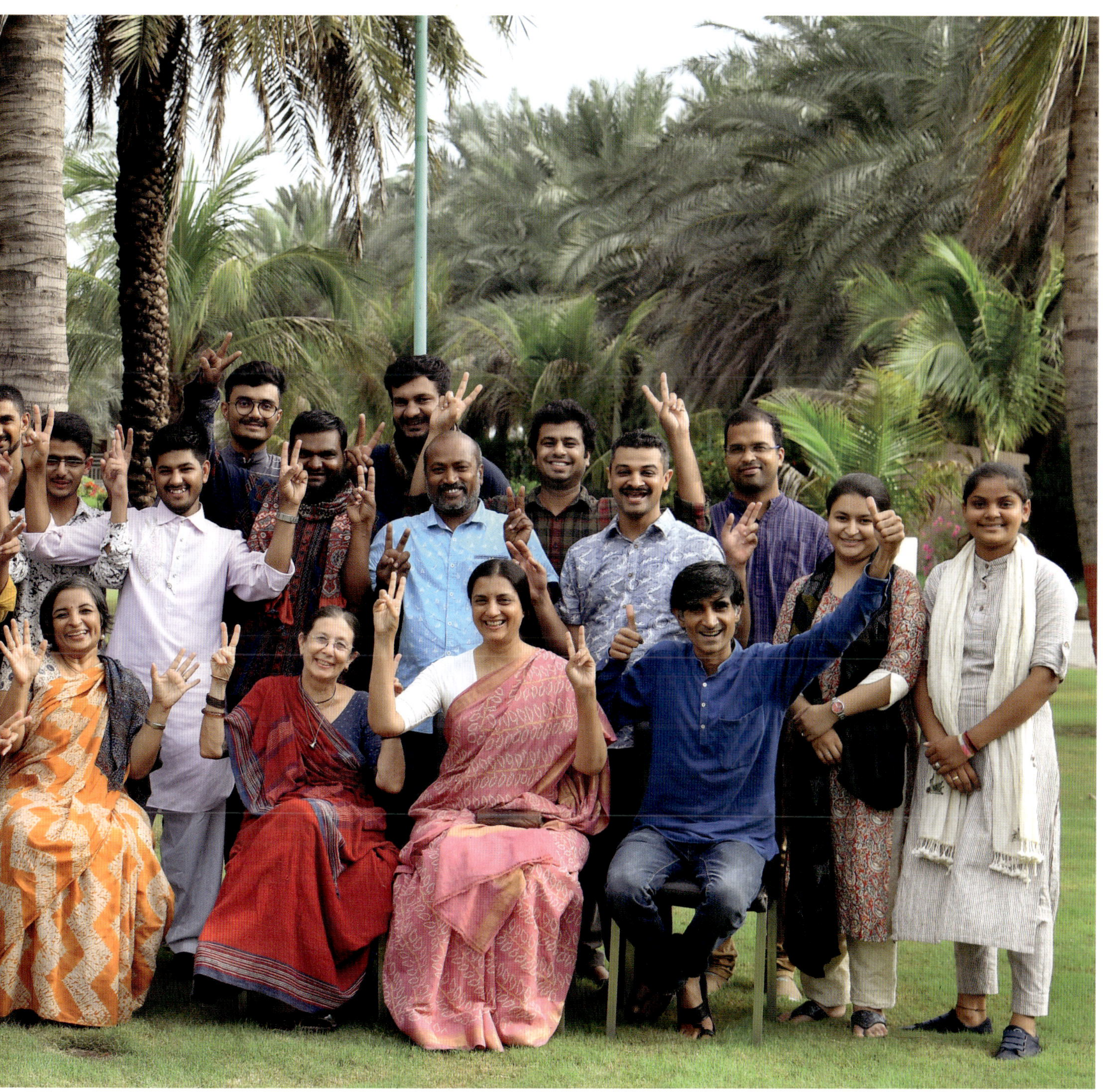

The course taught design as a means to innovate. There may not be many Chanels or Sabyasachis in the world, but there are many designers. And for artisan designers, being able to create—not becoming Sabyasachi—was the goal.

Sharma Resorts, 2019. For the final jury, I invited designers, educators, and market professionals so that students received feedback from different perspectives, and made sure that the mood was collegial, supportive, and exploring. For students, the jury was as useful as a two-week session. *Photo: Ketan Pomal, L.M. Studio*

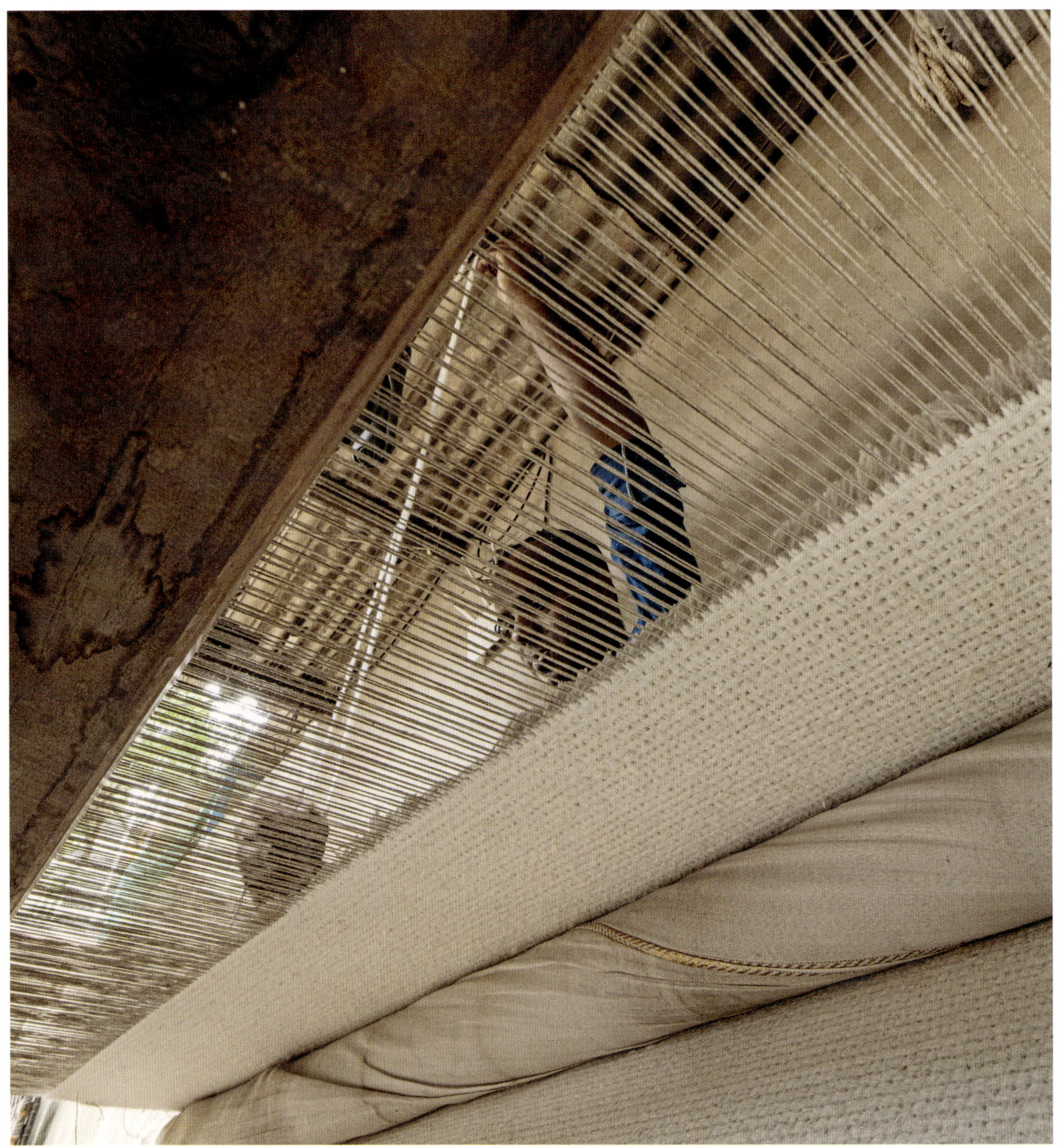

Risks are necessary. You have to face your own struggle.

~Prakashbhai Naran Siju

Bhujodi, 2022. Prakashbhai works on a pile weave carpet for his longtime Finnish client, with whom he is now a partner.
Photo: Nevada Wier

Chapter 12

PRAKASHBHAI NARAN SIJU: BUILDING A TRADITION

2020

I am zoom-recording Prakashbhai's evaluation of a codesign project with artisans in Oaxaca, Mexico.

"I did three or four codesign projects with UW Madison design students," he says. "They did not know weaving, so we had to explain what is possible. In the Oaxaca project, I worked with another weaver, so we easily understood each other. We discussed weaving, culture, craft, and nature and chose culture as our theme. My partner wanted us to make the same thing, but I suggested that we each use our own ideas to make something unique. I created a wall hanging using traditional motifs to depict dance in both cultures. I learned a lot about Oaxaca without going there, and I am still thinking about bringing designs from the project into new work."

We continue to talk, and Prakashbhai tells me that they have finally been able to employ two new carpet weavers. And his longtime Finnish buyer has asked him to supervise weavers in Rajasthan. She is paying him to teach and manage. The weavers' work has improved. And now she has made him part of the design team and pays him royalties on his designs.

So, in turn he felt he could ask if she would help him build a workshop. If the artisans can work in his village, he reasons, he can supervise more efficiently and save time and expense in traveling. She agreed.

What a wonderful new take on the mutual respect and appreciation in the traditional client-artisan relationship!

Prakashbhai is of the seventh generation in a weaver's family. They are one of the very few families in Bhujodi who make flat-weave carpets. In 1965, the designer Prabhaben Shah gave the whole village orders for new products derived from tradition. Prakashbhai's father got an order for a carpet and thought it would be good to have a specialization. For twenty years, he wove job work for a master weaver, making the same "Bharvadi" design. "There wasn't much money, no recognition, no joy," Prakashbhai said. So he decided to take a course in electrical training. He learned weaving simultaneously by observation, and one day when his father had gone out, he finished three carpets on the loom. Then he thought, this is our heritage—a gift and a responsibility. In 2008, he took the design course at

KRV. He felt that few weavers made carpets because they could not access a range of markets, he said. He believed that by making exclusive products, he could capture high-end and export markets. "I have a dream to establish my own carpet-weaving studio and teach this art to others," he avowed.

The course was far better than his expectation. "My observation power increased," he said. "I now understand the use of drawing. The education at KRV gave me an opportunity to sharpen my creative skills." One of the youngest students of a large and boisterous class, Prakashbhai was very shy. "I was afraid," he recalled. "We had to do presentations. That gave me experience, and I learned to open up." For his theme "Abstract Art," he wove carpets with traditional motifs that were enormous or cut in half. He graduated with the award for Most Promising Artisan.

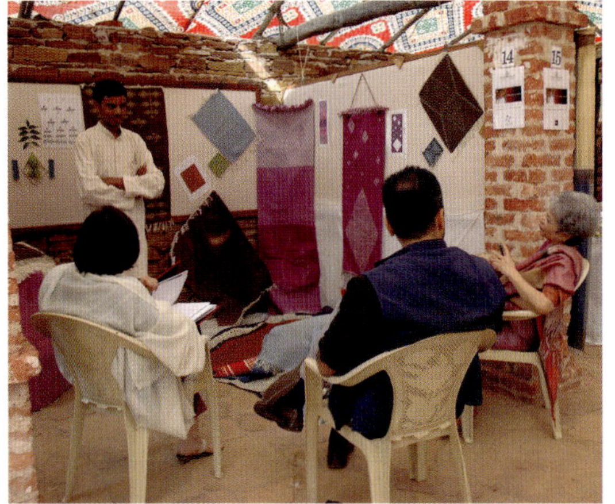

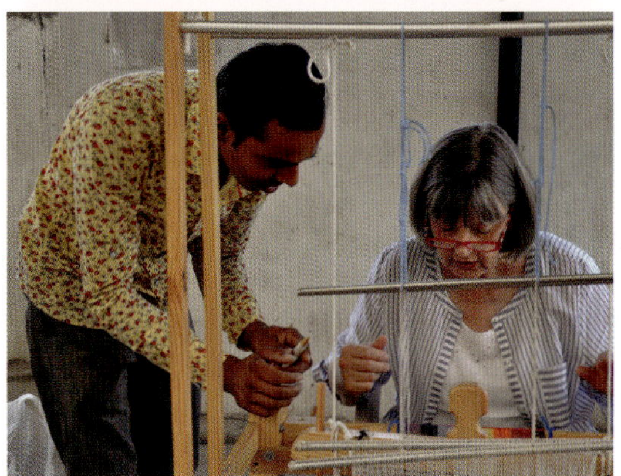

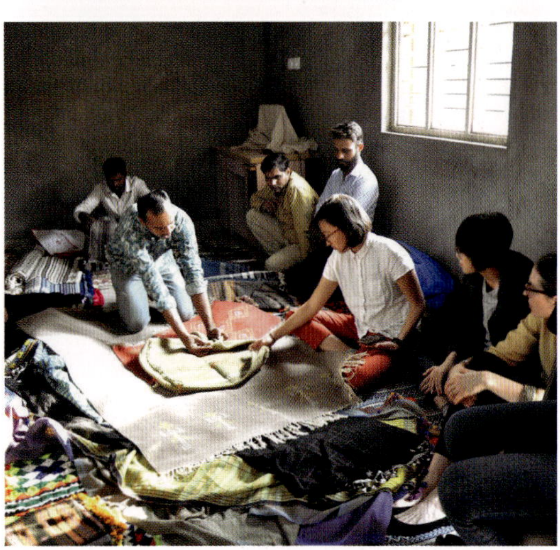

Although the learning experience at KRV was valuable to Prakashbhai, the collection he wove was not. "We had to invest time and materials for the course," he remembered. "And when I came back from class, I had to maintain ongoing work as well as do homework." In 2008, the design program did not include marketing support. "There were no exhibitions or projects like codesign, workshops, Open Studio Tours. All of that started with SKV. So I didn't have a further connection with KRV."

After he graduated, an NGO gave his family an order from a Finnish client, and they wove a limited series of patterns in quantity for six or seven years, occasionally supplementing these with their own work. But weavers in Kutch prefer to work in familial relationships, so they decided to omit the intermediary and to work with the client directly. "There is a big difference in communicating directly," Prakashbhai said. "The client guided us with what they wanted: double-ply wool, a different reed, and it improved the quality." They also learned to source materials at better rates. "We made a good connection in Bikaner, a major wool market," Prakashbhai related. "So they let us buy less than their usual minimum."

When we established Somaiya Kala Vidya, I prioritized building an alumni community. Prakashbhai attended meetings and liked them. I held the first SKV convocation, for BMA graduates, in a modest ceremony at Somaiya Bhavan in Mumbai. But when we ran the design course in the second year, I was in a dilemma. We had created a popular convocation event at KRV, including a fashion show and an evening of folk music and dance. Our temporary campus in Adipur was just a guesthouse with a little garden. I held a meeting of our SKV advisors and the weaver graduates of Bhujodi and asked if they would host the 2015 convocation in the village. Prakashbhai came forward at that point. I had not fully recognized

Top: Kala Raksha Vidhyalaya, 2008. Prakashbhai presents his carpet collection to the jury. His colors and patterns were major departures from the carpets his father wove. *Photo: Ketan Pomal, L.M. Studio*

Center: Somaiya Kala Vidya, 2016. Prakashbhai teaches basic weaving on the sampling looms that students use during course sessions. He has actively participated in SKV programs. *Photo: Judy Frater*

Bottom: Bhujodi, 2020. Prakashbhai explains his carpet designs in an Open Studio Tour. At the end of each tour, all graduates of the village are invited to show their work in a pop-up exhibition. *Photo: Judy Frater*

him until then. He was young, and he was an outlier because he wove carpets. Now he took a leadership role in organizing a team. They decided who would be responsible for leveling the ground; who would coordinate with the tent people, the sound and light crews, the caterers, and security; and who would distribute invitations and hang up posters.

I relied on Prakashbhai; he delivered and reconnected to the education program. The next year, he participated in the first codesign program with UW Madison. "My partner gave me a round shape, so I tried using interlocking and a hand-thrown shuttle, our traditional technique," he assessed. "It took fifteen days and would probably be five times more expensive than a regular carpet." But it gave him ideas. He participated in the codesign program in 2018, creating another new range of carpets. "There is a big difference between this work and the earlier carpets," he noted.

Over the years, Prakashbhai learned English and studied natural dyeing in depth. "I ruined a lot of materials," he admitted, laughing. But he became an expert. He experimented methodically and labeled his samples in detail. He began to teach workshops at SKV, and when I introduced Open Studio Tours, he helped organize. Artisan graduates were not active in communication. Prakashbhai helped me herd cats. He initiated when no one else spoke up. He insisted that those who were interested participated.

Looking back, he reflected on the value of design education for his community. "After taking the course, my vision changed," he said. "I learned what our tradition was, and realized its value. For our first homework we had to learn about our traditional motifs. As a group, we sat with our elders and asked them the history and meaning. Graduates have brands, and different concepts. Before, if there was an exhibition, all the weavers there would have the same designs, the same color combinations, so there was competition. Now, each has his own specialty.

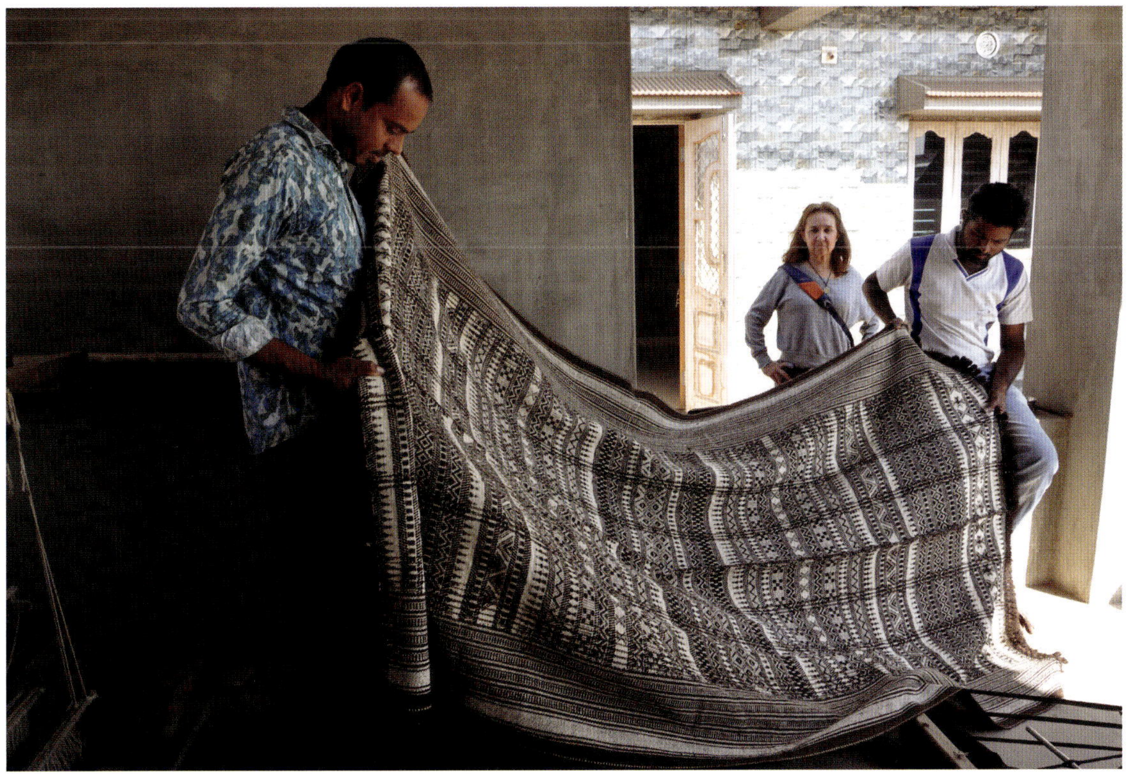

Above: Bhujodi, 2020. Prakashbhai and Pachanbhai show a *dhablo*, the blanket that their ancestors wove for Rabari herders, in an Open Studio Tour. The *dhablo* is a foundation for contemporary innovation. *Photo: Judy Frater*

Following pages: Bhujodi, 2022. Prakashbhai took a workshop on natural dyeing and then experimented. Today, he is recognized as an expert. *Photo: Nevada Wier*

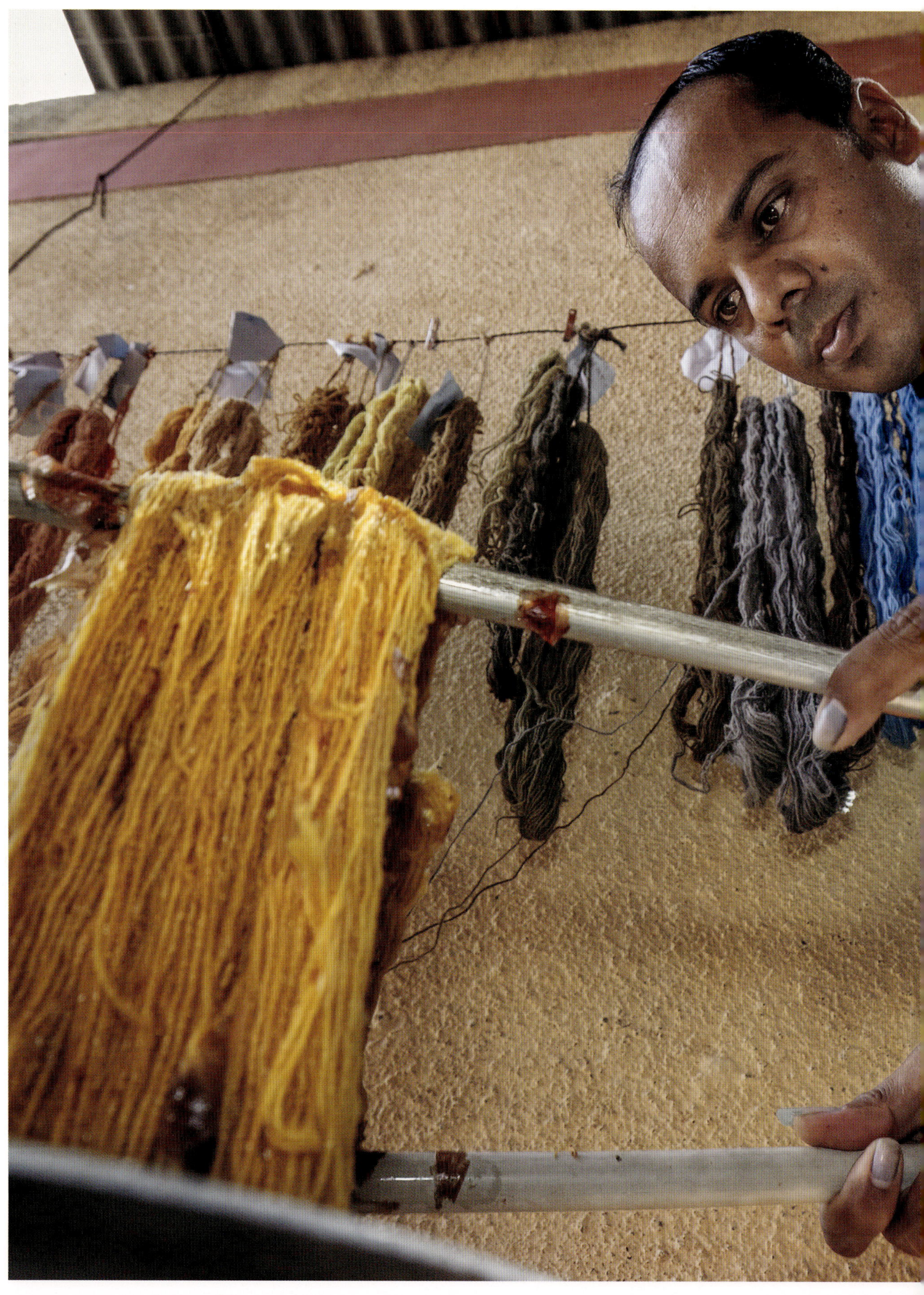

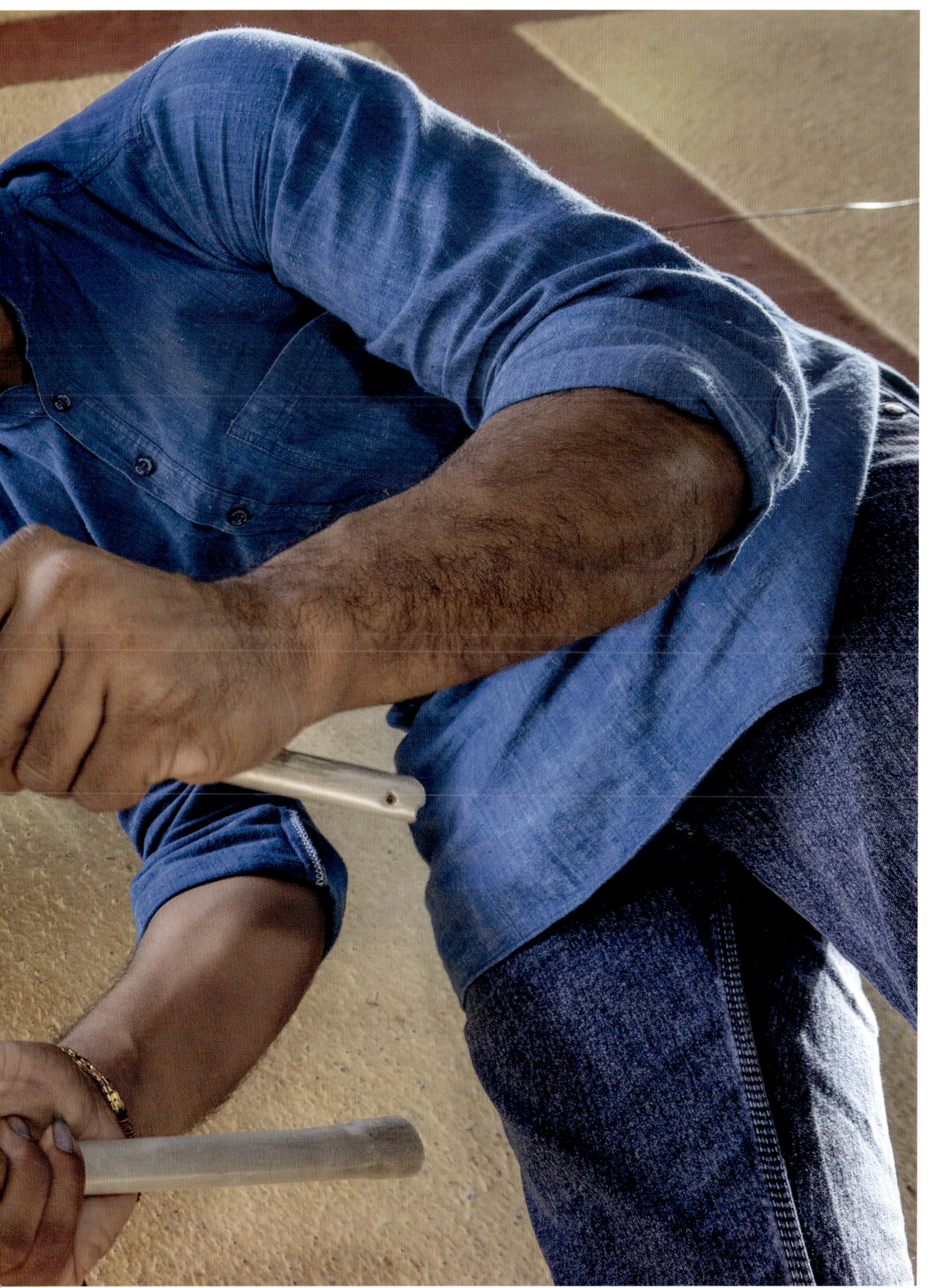

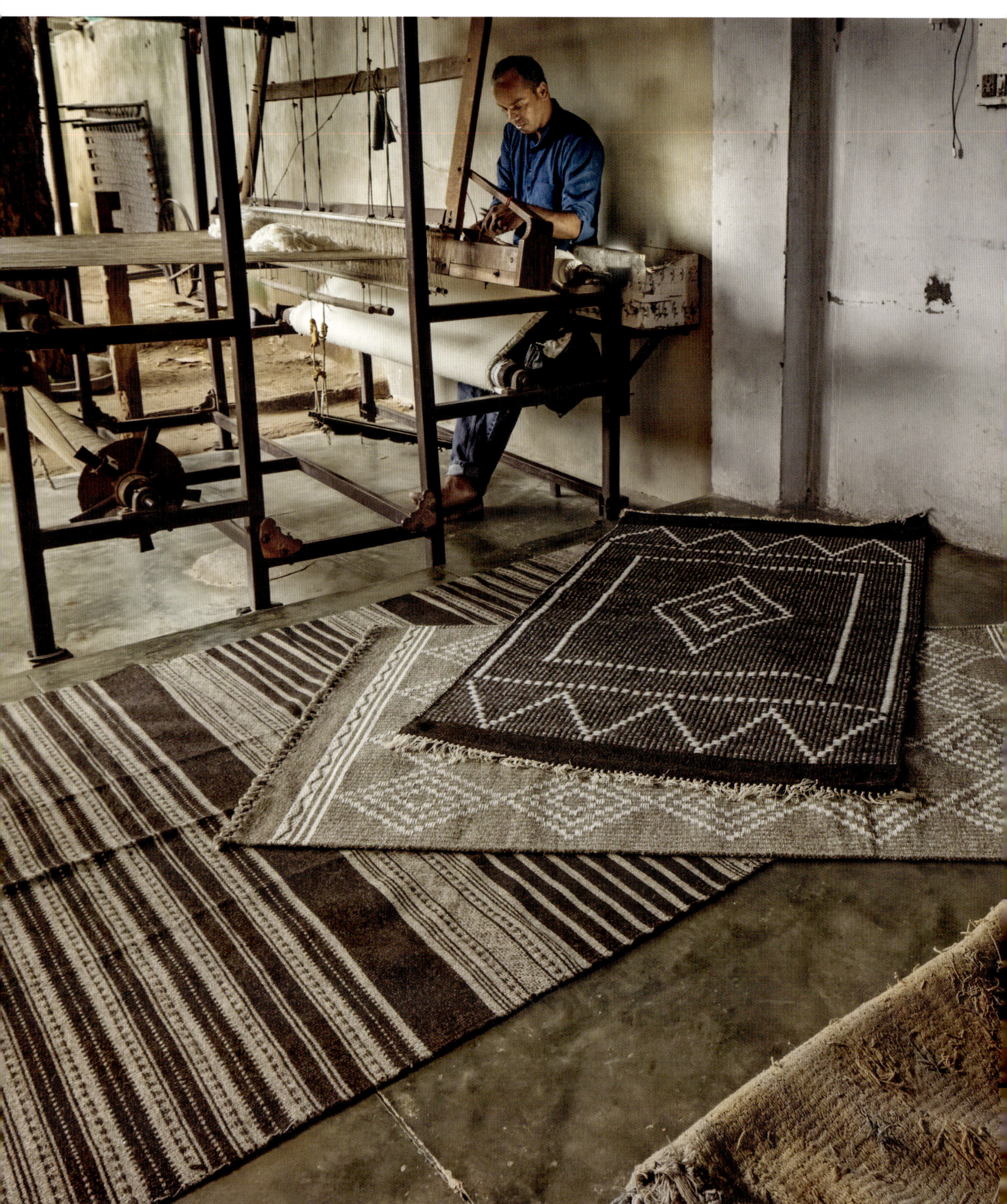

"Those who take the course get new direction," he continued. "So, more people come. Seeing the graduates, weavers have come back from working in industries to weave. They have begun to join craft."

His brother Prashantbhai is an example. In 2013, an NGO sent him to a course for weavers that was far away from Kutch. He could not fit in and returned home. In 2018, Prashantbhai graduated from Somaiya Kala Vidya with the jury Special Mention award, and he is now weaving with his family.

Prakashbhai felt that the real value of the course was in teaching innovation within traditions. "Designers try to take us beyond tradition," he said. "We refuse. We can change materials but not lose our identity. If this institute was not here, the level of craft might be different."

But Prakashbhai's desire to develop his tradition remained unfulfilled. He wanted people to know that carpet weaving is also a craft in Kutch. Production limitation was a major constraint. Original carpet weavers grew old and retired. "Carpet weaving is technically more difficult," Prakashbhai explained, "and we can't speed it up to cover extra time. My father trained fifteen to twenty artisans in carpet weaving. But they couldn't maintain the quality, and we bore a loss. Ever since then, we work within our limits. One client said she would send workers from UP so that I could scale up. I refused. We don't want that kind of factory setup. Ours is a family craft. If we outsource, it won't be craft. At the least, we keep the work in the community."

With little time to make stock, the family rarely left Kutch to sell in pop-up exhibitions. They relied on social media and visitors to Bhujodi for orders. But that opportunity, too, diminished with the development of the Rann Festival. "There is a different level of tourist now," Prakashbhai noted. "People come for entertainment, not to learn about Kutch. Today, there are many shops in Bhujodi selling all kinds of stuff, and Bhujodi's specialty of over half a century is being lost.

"I'm not sure if we can make a group or an organization," he concluded. "When you don't know the market, you are afraid. But risks are necessary. You have to face your own struggle. I want to try to teach weavers."

2022

Prakashbhai is glowing. He worked virtually with me as a cofaculty member of my residency at UW Madison this year, supervising the team of weaver designers in Kutch as well as creating an imaginative new collection with a student partner. He gave invaluable feedback on the course. "After doing codesign," he observes, "we work differently with all designers. I don't just execute designs; I critique and give my opinions." And now he is a graduate advisor at SKV.

He used the COVID-19 lockdown as an opportunity. With limited raw materials, he created using additional workmanship that would earn more value when markets reopened. And he worked to enhance online presentation skills

Bhujodi, 2022. Traditionally, Kutch weavers used a pit loom. Carpet weaving requires tighter tension and beating than do blankets or shawls, so when frame looms were introduced to Kutch, the family adopted them. Prakashbhai's recent collection, inspired by *ludi*, Rabari veils, is woven with natural undyed sheep wool. *Photo: Nevada Wier*

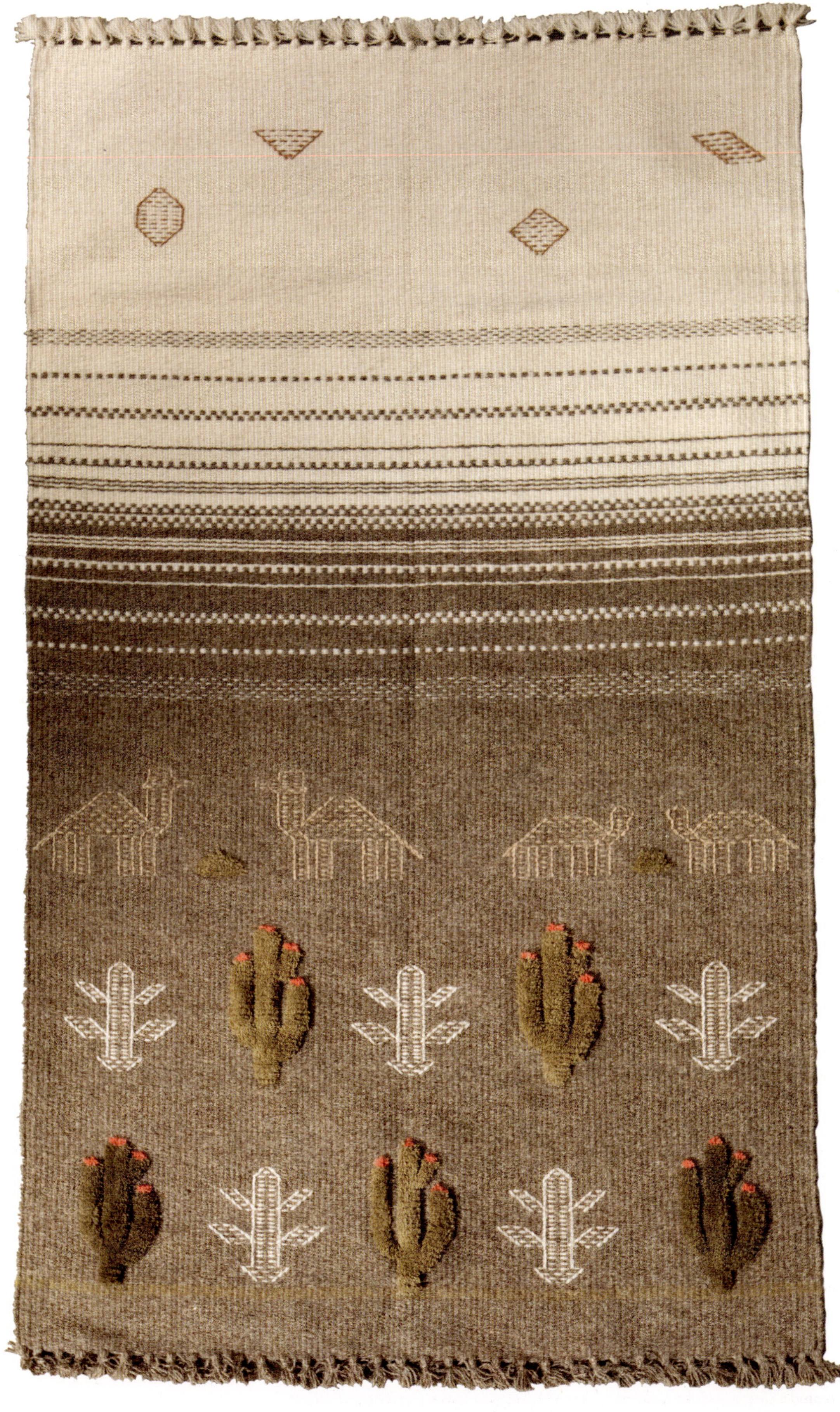

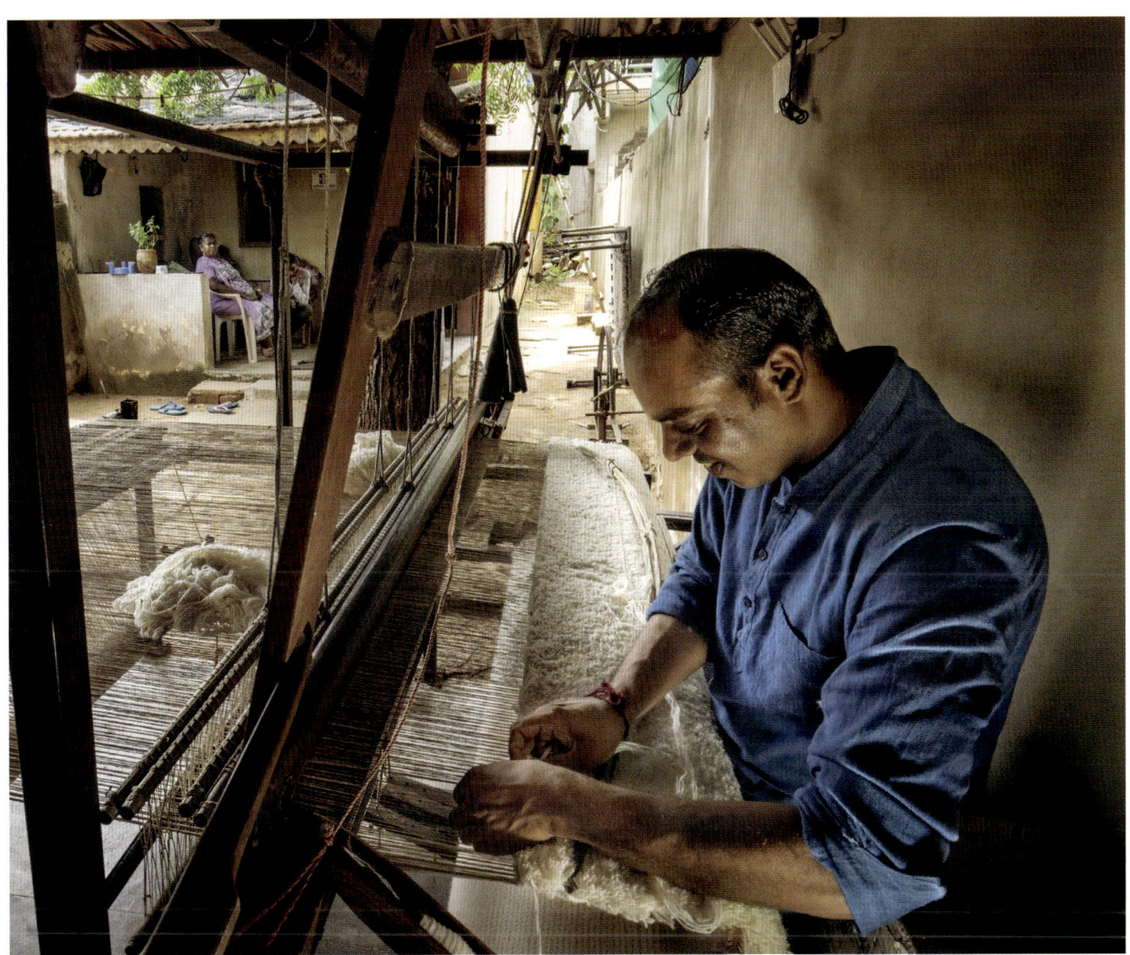

to become known in the market. He shows us his natural wool carpets, a collection developed with inspiration from the traditional Rabari *ludi*.

And on the suggestion of his Finnish partner, he learned pile weaving by watching YouTube and has given it a wonderfully creative twist in two new samples.

Nevada asks him if he has thought of applying to the International Folk Art Market. He demurs. Some day . . . With that, she jumps onto a cot and photographs the collection. In two days, Prakashbhai and I write up the application.

He is juried into IFAM 2023.

Left: *Desert Carpet*, by Prakashbhai Naran Siju, 2022. Cotton warp, natural and natural-dyed wool weft, extra weft, and pile yarns. 36" x 60". Because pile weaving is not traditional, Prakashbhai could use it in a unique way, inserting it for emphasis like a 3-D version of traditional extra-weft patterning. Here, he has created an ode to the desert environment of Kutch. *Photo: Schiffer Publishing Ltd.*

Above: Bhujodi, 2022. Pile-weaving technique is not traditional to Kutch. Prakashbhai and his brother Prashantbhai, also a design graduate, learned it by watching YouTube videos and have created their own innovations. *Photo: Nevada Wier*

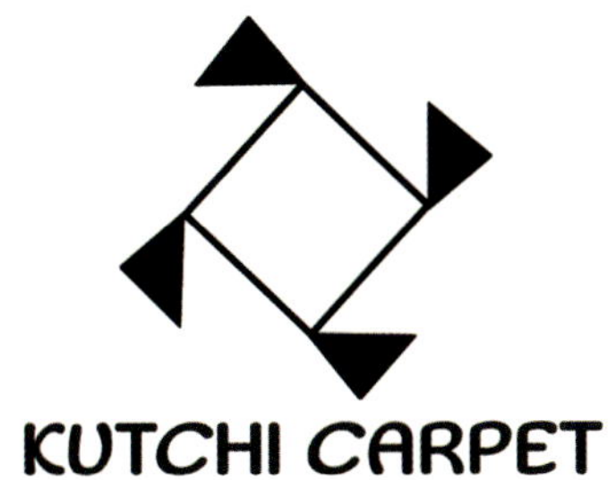

Right: *Creating logos was introduced in Prakashbhai's class in 2008. Prakashbhai created a simple, stylized motif and named his brand Subtle, a play on shuttle. Later, he changed his brand to Kutchi Carpet to distinguish his work.*

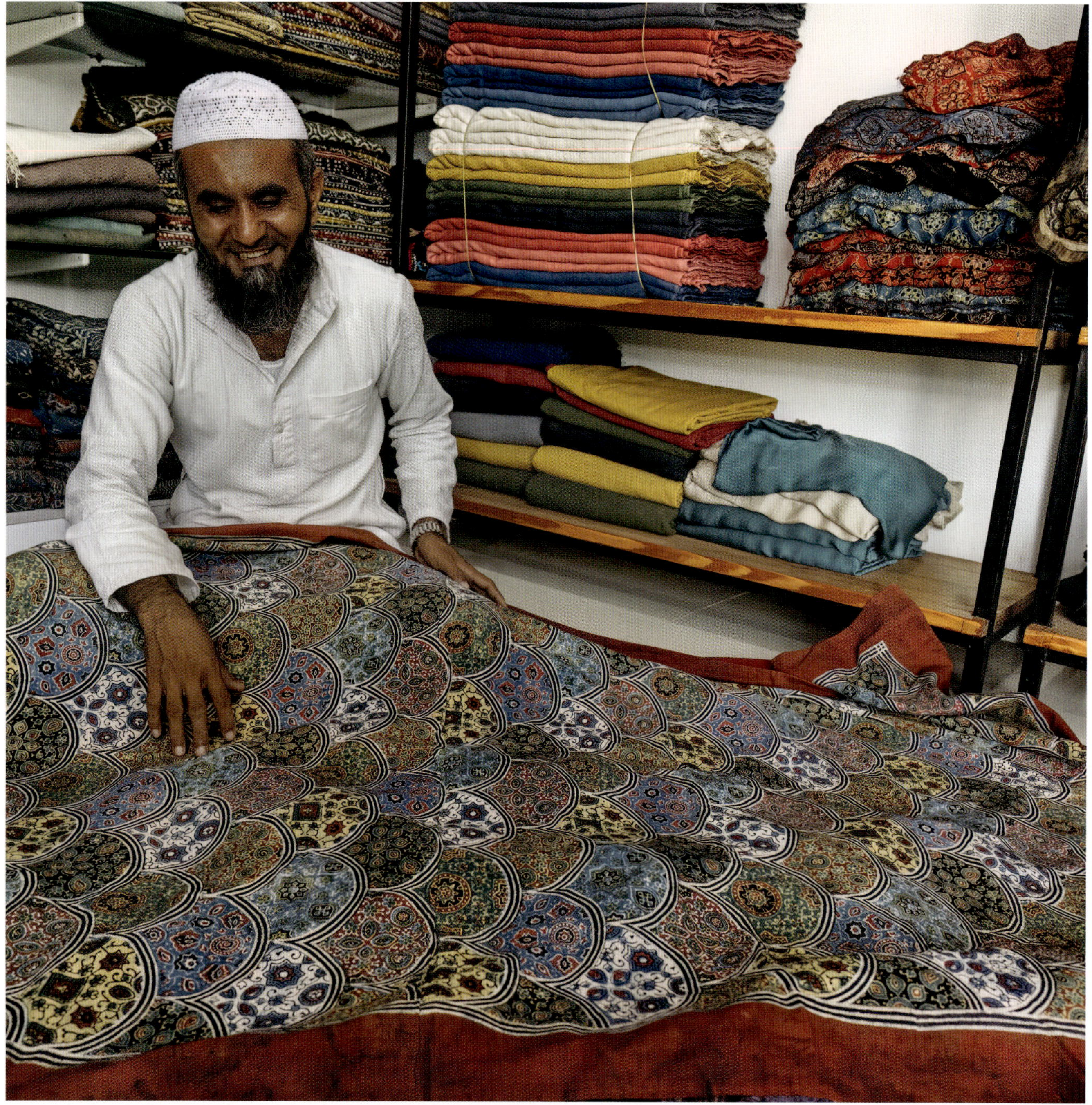

The World is my client!

~Irfanbhai Anwar Khatri

Ajrakhpur, 2022. Irfanbhai created a color masterpiece following his year at KRV. It took two months. He had to number the masks so that he could register each set. He'll never sell this piece. He's innovated many times on it, but this one was his soul, his art. *Photo: Nevada Wier*

Chapter 13

IRFANBHAI ANWAR KHATRI: THE MASTERMIND

2019

The big workshop is only two years old, but constant hard use has made it seem like it's been here forever. Nine or ten men are chatting, joking with each other as they print fabric on four huge tables and four smaller ones, pounding rhythm to the chirping sparrows who echo their continual movement. Continual, casual, and congenial is the atmosphere of big production in Ajrakhpur.

Vinodbhai is having trouble with *mashru* yardage. The resist paste of the *rekh* outline has shrunk the fabric, and now the *datlo* filling block won't register correctly. The team drops their work and huddles around the table. Salimbhai, a printer who is acting foreman, tries his hand at correcting the problem. More discussion. And then Irfanbhai comes through the doorway. Assessing the scene in a glance, he goes over to the table, rolls up his sleeve, and takes the block. The master begins the design and finishes. Irfanbhai hasn't printed for production for at least a decade. But he did print for a decade straight, he grins. His registration skills will never leave him.

Irfanbhai's family was from Vagad, eastern Kutch, and printed *sadla*, engineered partially stitched garments that fall between a sari and a veil, for Kanbi Patel agriculturists. They moved to Dhamadka and began to print Ajrakh and other textiles for the Muslim pastoralists of the Banni grasslands. Irfanbhai learned block printing when he was fifteen. For most of his childhood, it was a family business; family members printed and dyed. They made five or six pieces and took them to the villages of their clients to trade and sometimes sell.

I asked how in barter they ensured that the trade was of equal value.

"We didn't," he answered. It was not about money but seeing that everyone got what they needed.

Irfanbhai would go with his father to trade, and because he was interested, he learned what people wanted, as well as hand skills. Slowly, the community began to work for urban markets and to hire workers for expanded production.

In 2001, Dhamadka was flattened by a massive earthquake. The community came together to build a new village closer to Bhuj and named it Ajrakhpur. Irfanbhai's family was among the first to move to the new village. In Dhamadka, artisans sat at a small, low table to print. In 2004, Irfanbhai's father was

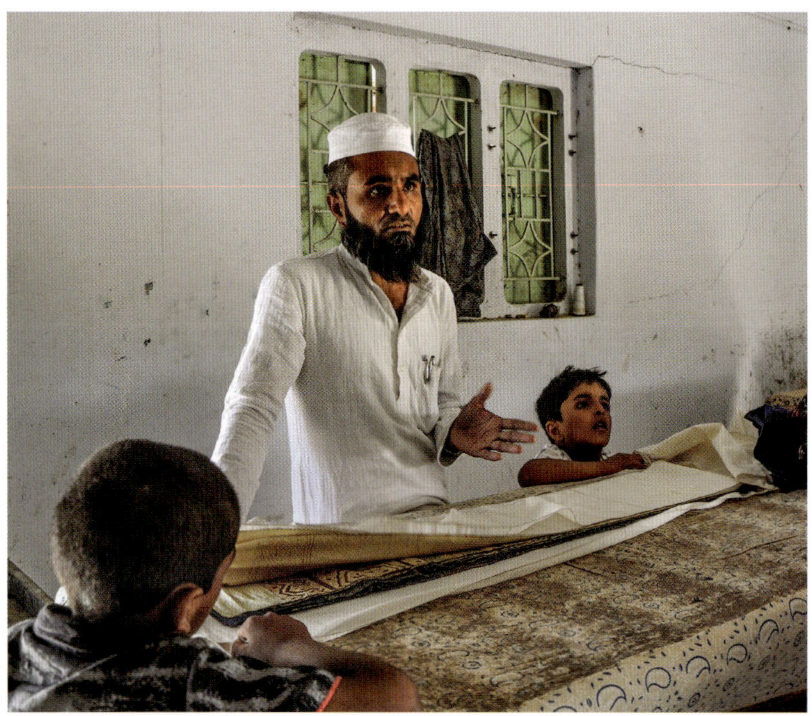

Ajrakhpur, 2019. As Irfanbhai teaches international visitors about Ajrakh, his son listens—a contemporary version of how he learned about Ajrakh from his father. *Photo: Judy Frater*

the first to make a higher, longer table for production. But he never had the chance to use it. He passed away suddenly and was the first person to be buried in Ajrakhpur.

At twenty-two, the second eldest of six brothers, Irfanbhai had to assume responsibility for running the home and the printing business. He went to pop-up exhibitions all over India. He worked with designers who sourced Ajrakh. Exposure made him eager to develop his work. He learned computer skills and produced a CD catalog of his Ajrakh collections.

In 2005, when I launched the pilot design course at Kala Raksha Vidhyalaya, Irfanbhai was nominated as a student. Although he was shy and quiet, the other students recognized his clear and mature thinking and made him president of the class. When he began the course, Irfanbhai said, "My dream is to receive a national award for my work and to visit many other countries."

From the first course, he began to think out of the box. Taking the *gulmohar* (flame tree) as inspiration, he simplified versions of traditional blocks and enlarged them to create new forms. "I liked making color to music," he said. "I liked observation at the beach. I learned I can get inspired by anything. And I made my first block for homework." In his written feedback, he wrote, "The review process gives practice in talking. I understood a bit about how the teachers critique, but we need to learn more about criteria."

After the trip to Ahmedabad for the Market Orientation class, Irfanbhai made two natural-dye collections: sturdy cotton bags for a local person, and shiny *mashru* bags for a Delhi resident. The fabric, colors, and shapes reflected different lifestyles. He was the first Ajrakh printer to try *mashru*, a satin rayon and cotton fabric. It brought a new look to the traditional cloth, and he immediately received an order for his innovation.

Working out the curriculum, teaching methods, and faculty in the pilot year, we ended up doing

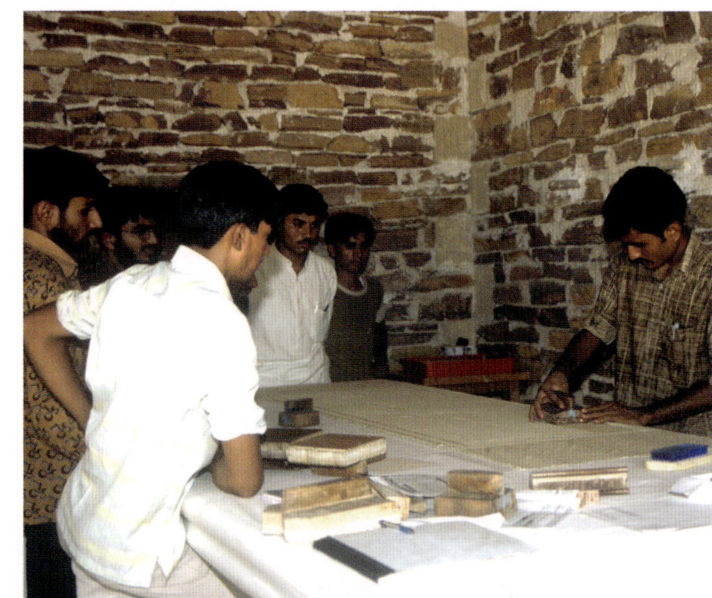

Kala Raksha Vidhyalaya, 2006. Even as a pilot student at KRV, Irfanbhai's printing drew the attention of his classmates. *Photo: Judy Frater*

concept development twice. For the first iteration, Irfanbhai took rhythm as a principle and worked out his concept in the studio. "Sketching is good," he said. "Sampling is important. You forget unless you apply."

His teacher wrote, "Irfan is a keen observer. When he was unable to get perspective sketching right, he got the camera and took pictures of perspective. He experiments, and his strength is thorough understanding of printing. He hesitated to do layouts, but once he moved to the printing table and started trying out combinations, he got creative. He transcended a symmetrical layout and got a rich look with fewer blocks. Overall, his performance was fantastic."

For his final concept, he took the theme "Tropical Tango." Combining his success with *mashru* fabric and the dramatic palette of the theme, he made a collection of bags and ties. When he displayed his collection for the jury and the public, sales were as good as critique. The jury gave him the award for Most Marketable Collection.

"At first I thought this course was hard," he reflected. "When I did the practical part, I understood what to think about. The teachers here don't think about time. They work with us until we understand, teaching us into the night. . . . I learned the relationship between paper concepts and actual work; I learned to develop themes. And especially, I learned how to make a collection."

Asked what he would remember most, he thoughtfully replied, "There are symmetrical designs and asymmetrical designs. And there is balance. In symmetrical patterns, which we usually do in block printing, balance is inherent. But for an asymmetrical pattern you have to make sure to create balance."

After graduating, Irfanbhai continued to explore and grow. In 2007, he participated in a show in the UK, initiating his dream to travel. "This gave me an experience of new cultures and thinking," he said. "I also had opportunities to teach international visitors Ajrakh techniques. I found that craft is a means of cross-cultural communication. I began to source inspiration and communicate through the internet."

He created a collection of patterns inspired by screens at the Taj Mahal that went viral in the community, an achromatic series and new ranges of natural colors, bold zoomed-in patterns, and new ways of combining block print with *bandhani*. He sourced new fabrics and collaborated with a batik artist. He got the first iPhone in Ajrakhpur and made a website. When he adopted *sunnah*, the orthodox white clothes, beard, and cap, it juxtaposed sharply with his active imagination and expertise in information technology. We traveled together to Mumbai in 2016. Landing at the Bandra railway station, we were engulfed by taxi drivers vying to see who could cheat us the most. Expressionless, Irfanbhai reached for his phone. Are you calculating the cost for the ride? I asked. "No," he answered. "I'm calling Ola [an Indian rideshare company]." Then he helped me set up the app on my phone.

Irfanbhai's family of six brothers grew their business riding the wave of popularity of block prints and natural dyes. They saw the opportunity and went for it.

"Ajrakh has been passed through generations," Irfanbhai said. "Today, the challenge is to maintain the essence of this tradition while keeping it contemporary. In-depth experiencing of new cultures will enhance my ability to create for new markets." He traveled to Indonesia, Nepal, Tajikistan, Dubai, Ukraine, Kazakhstan, and China to attend conferences and conduct workshops. He did not entertain any obstacles or constraints. He just fielded invitations, purchased tickets, and got on planes. And if appropriate, he took a daughter with him. Exposure linked with financial success honed and validated his aesthetics. When I eagerly took him to the newly opened Hermes shop in Mumbai, he looked at the intricate scarves. "Nice," he said. "Screen print." Then his gaze wandered to the leather bags. He examined one, including the price tag. "Do you have this in a larger size?" he asked.

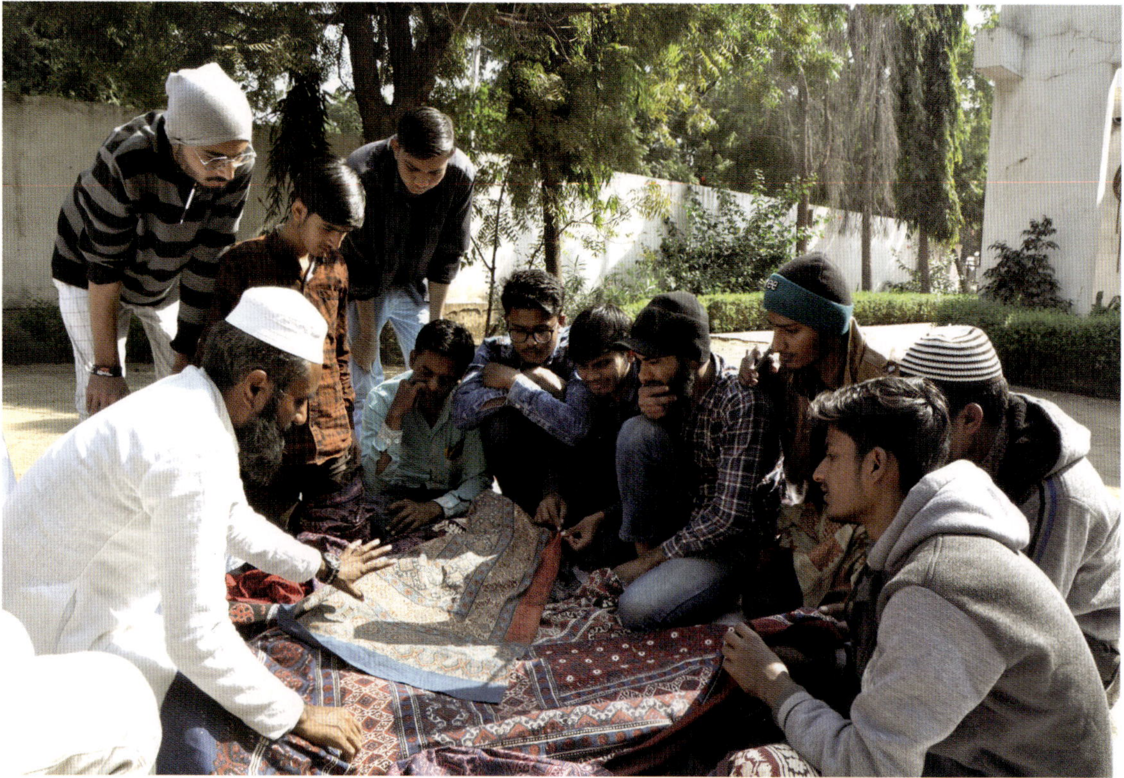

Somaiya Kala Vidya, 2020. Every year, senior artisan advisors teach new students about their craft traditions. A young elder, Irfanbhai is a member of the SKV Governing Council and now a graduate advisor. In 2020, he also taught this segment. *Photo: Judy Frater*

Irfanbhai was one of a few artisans of the next generation who knew their traditions deeply. He used his knowledge with wisdom and piety to gain respect—not just locally but internationally. He created his own world and simply followed his integrity. In 2014, when I left Kala Raksha to begin Somaiya Kala Vidya, he was the one graduate I asked to be a member of the Governing Council. He advised me in the transition and in building the institute. He observed, considered, and then spoke. He helped strengthen the alumni association and helped develop workshops into a three-week Craft Traditions course. He was instrumental in starting Open Studio Tours in Ajrakhpur and envisioned creating a major event that would draw people to Kutch. It should become a go-to event, he said.

After a decade of design education, I organized a seminar in Delhi to share experiences of graduates and craft leaders. When Irfanbhai was given the mic, he said, "Before the design education that started in 2006, the market for our products was limited. We went to bulk customers; they selected some designs and gave us an order that lasted a month. After that, we had to create something new and then look for another customer. The design course brought many changes in our ways of working and made creating new designs easy. Then, we didn't have to go to the market looking for new customers; they came looking for us. Many of us now work with established brands and earn decent profits. But the brands sell our products under their own labels. I think we artisan designers should make our own brands. In addition, when we work with these brands, they have terms and conditions to which we have to agree. I feel artisan designers should draft our own terms and conditions to which brands must agree." The entire seminar spontaneously applauded.

Following up, I suggested to Irfanbhai that he brand his own work. Not a paper tag, but something integral to the work. He got up and shuffled off for some other work, as is his habit. In a moment, he returned with a small wood block with the initials IK, and a scarf in which it was printed in a corner. No gloating, no smirk; he's a step ahead, just a fact.

Right: Jungle scarves, by Irfan Anwar Khatri, 2020. Satin silk, hand block printed with natural dyes. 21" x 74" and 34" x 96". Irfanbhai did codesign with a partner in Oaxaca and the inspiration of animal prints. "Ajrakh is based on symmetrical Islamic patterns," he said. "Animal patterns are asymmetrical. But often the filling blocks of our patterns are asymmetrical. I experimented by overlapping filling blocks, and I got the look." *Photo: Schiffer Publishing Ltd.*

Following pages: Ajrakhpur, 2022. At left is an innovation on the masterpiece, simplified by using fewer colors. Irfanbhai was a virtual cofaculty member in my 2022 Residency at UW Madison. With a student, he codesigned the black scarf. *Photo: Nevada Wier*

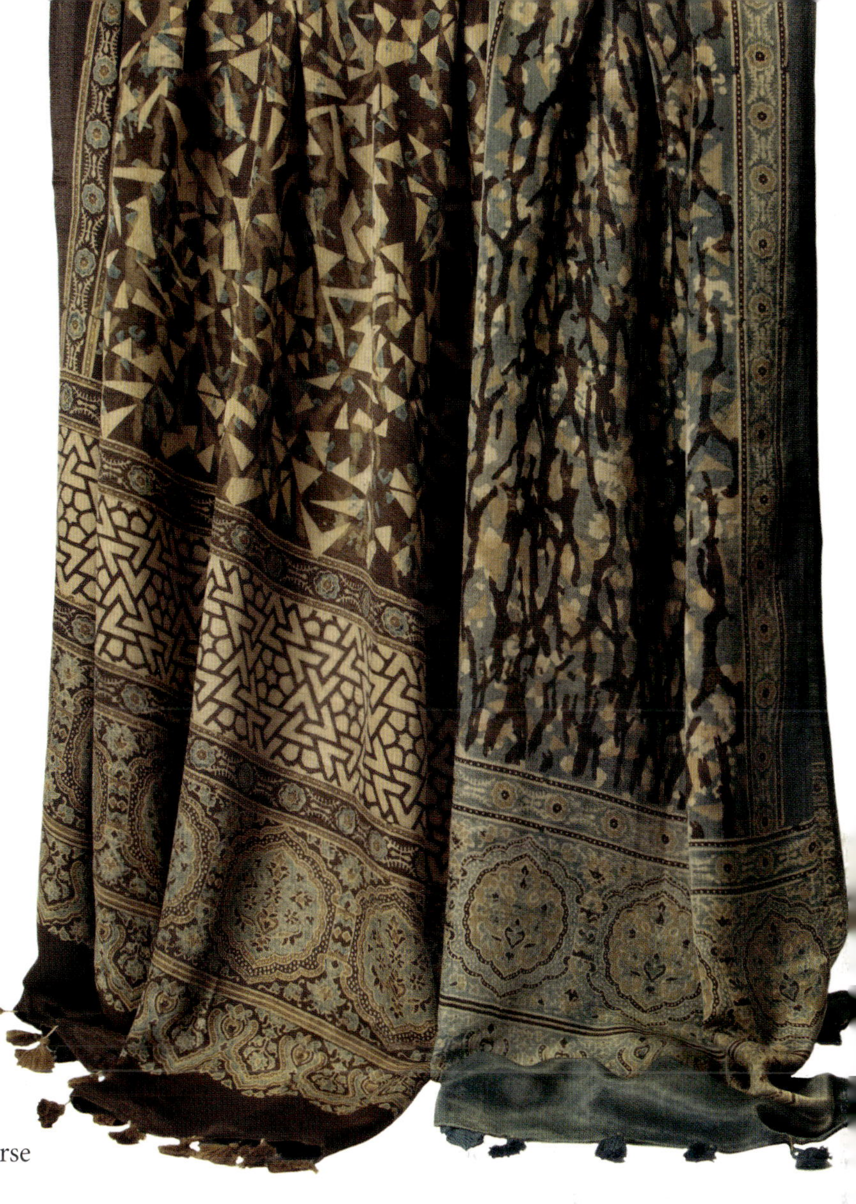

By 2019, Ajrakhpur's community of 150 families was producing an estimated 70,000 meters of printed fabric per month. Irfanbhai and his brothers divided the family business but continued to share resources and together produced about 12,000 meters a month. Two brothers made a screen print workshop with mind-boggling tables 40 meters long. "When customers want cheap, the only recourse is big production," they said.

Recently a new issue emerged: competition. Irfanbhai explained its complexity. "The ancestral designs of craft traditions belong to the Khatri community," he said. "Artisans who take the design course make their own designs, as they must in the new fashion world. But there is no advantage to new designs if an artisan can't keep them secret. In the market, designs are known by artisans' names. If a copier takes the design to the market first, it is known as his. Whoever makes something new must benefit first and earn from new designs." Always practical, he concluded, "Copying *will* happen. It's inevitable. And then it becomes 'tradition.'" His Taj *jali* series is now owned by all Khatris.

Irfanbhai's own production was 1,000 meters a month, less than the brothers' average. "Our traditional prints have multicolored patterns and printing on both sides of the fabric," he said. "I enjoy pushing the limits of my tradition, but that work cannot be produced in quantity." He told students of the Ajrakh Craft Traditions course that he made new designs from his own interest. But he thought of production, and he kept an eye on business. He was not sure how many clients there were for high-value products.

Then he brought out two masterpieces that he printed himself, as a gift for a *pir saheb* who was visiting from Allahabad. Both were the traditional double-side print, perfectly rendered, one with the conventional center of overall patterning, and one with an intricate Islamic pattern in the center.

And which did the *pir saheb* choose?

He smiled. An engineered one. This was the original system of exchange. Irfanbhai made masterpieces for someone he respected and knew would cherish them. They shared an understanding of valuation.

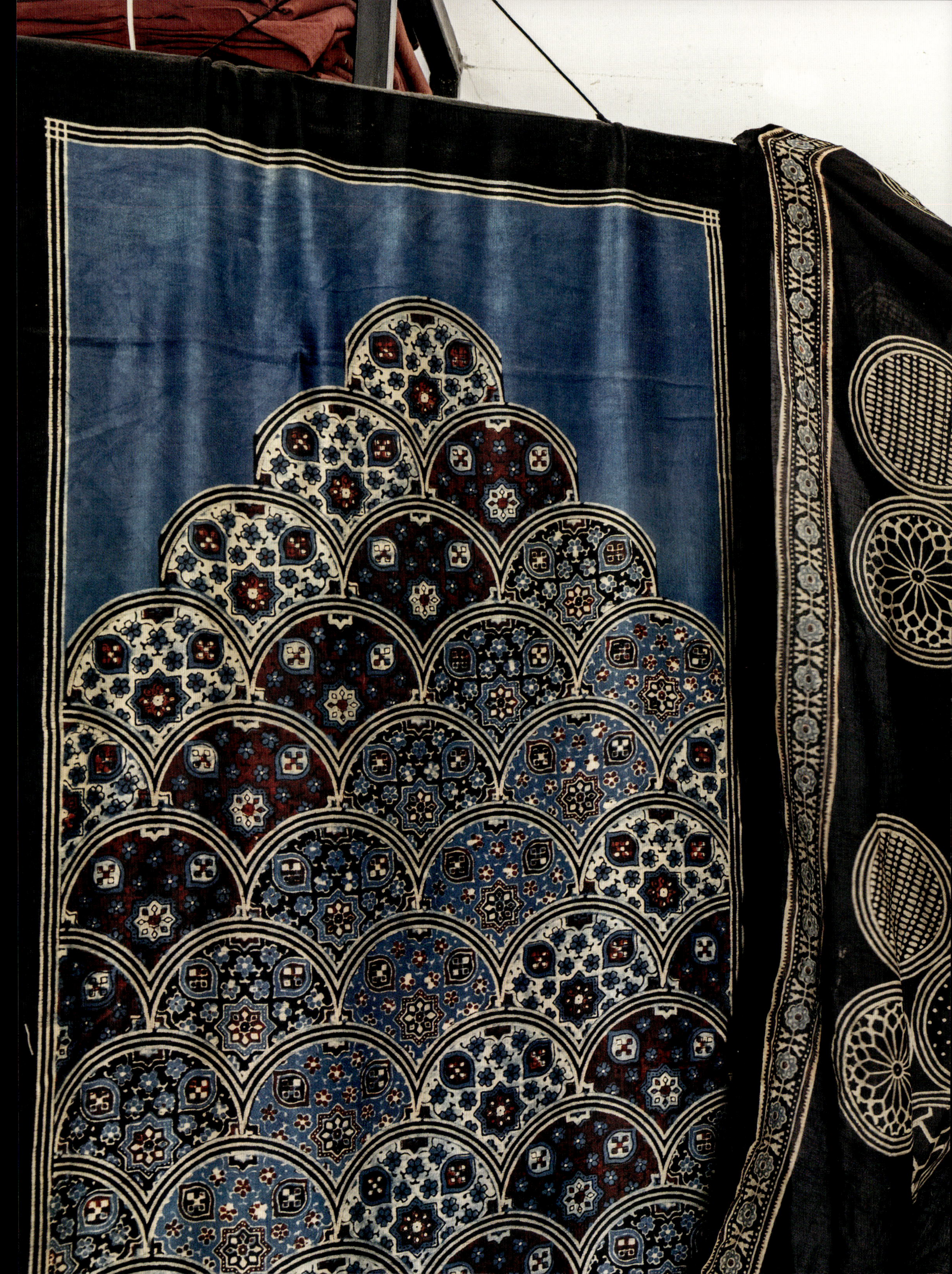

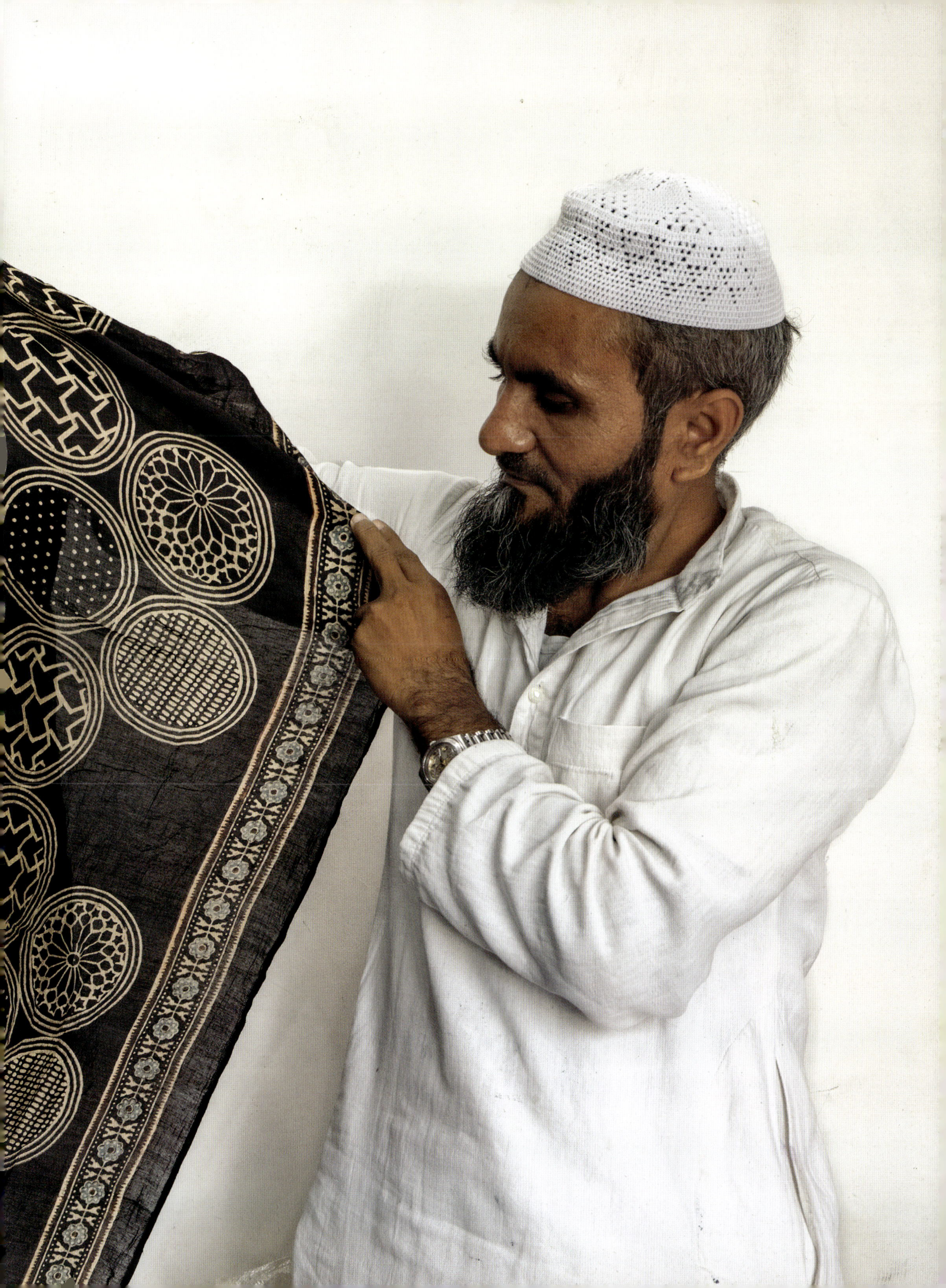

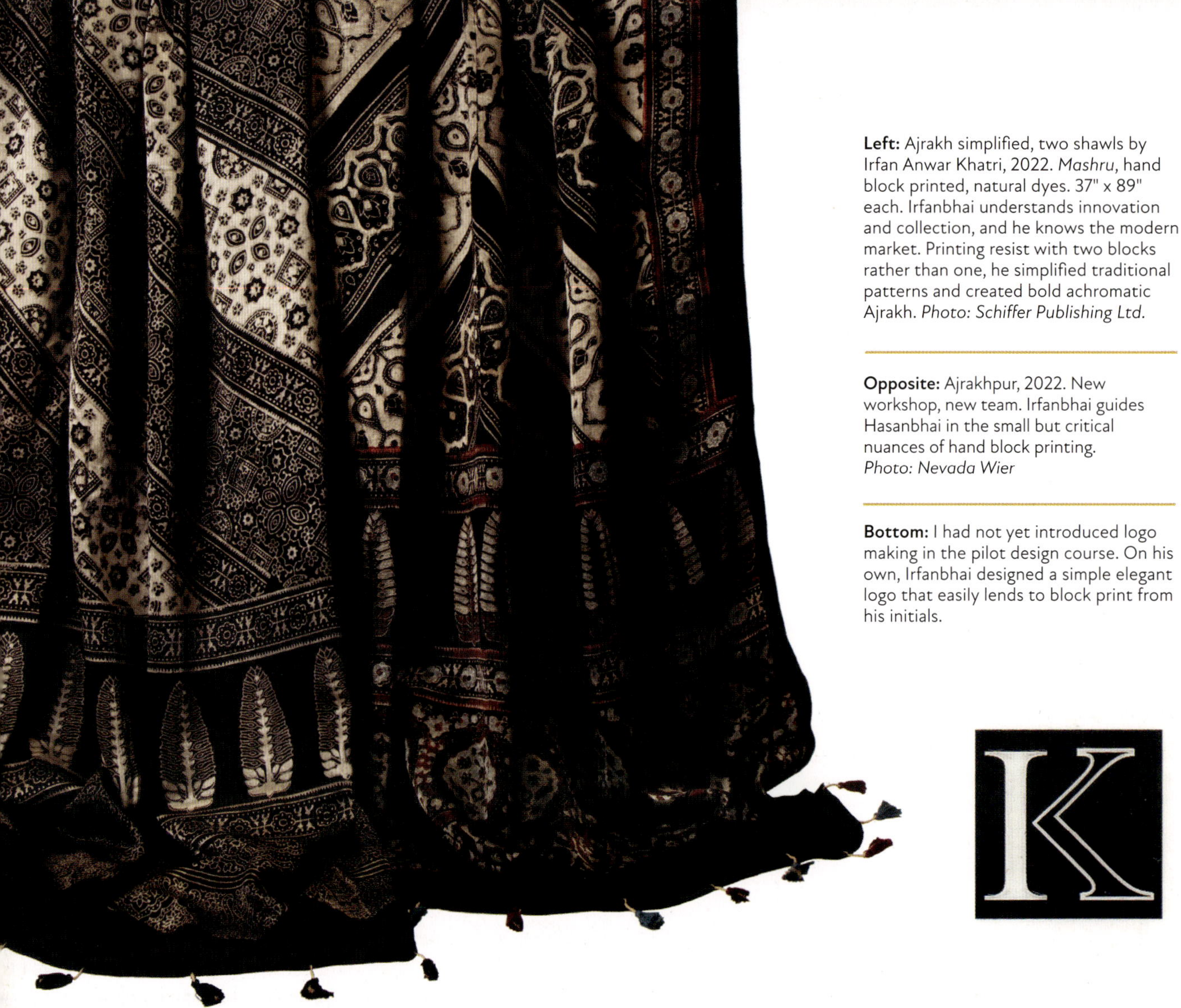

Left: Ajrakh simplified, two shawls by Irfan Anwar Khatri, 2022. *Mashru,* hand block printed, natural dyes. 37" x 89" each. Irfanbhai understands innovation and collection, and he knows the modern market. Printing resist with two blocks rather than one, he simplified traditional patterns and created bold achromatic Ajrakh. *Photo: Schiffer Publishing Ltd.*

Opposite: Ajrakhpur, 2022. New workshop, new team. Irfanbhai guides Hasanbhai in the small but critical nuances of hand block printing. *Photo: Nevada Wier*

Bottom: I had not yet introduced logo making in the pilot design course. On his own, Irfanbhai designed a simple elegant logo that easily lends to block print from his initials.

2022

During COVID-19 lockdown, Irfanbhai built his own workshop. They couldn't go out, but work could not stop. It's smaller than the big new workshop his brothers had shared, just two long tables and two short. He's starting over, so he had to think about what he intended and how he could do it. For the market, he had to produce in scale, and he had to hire new workers to do it. "There is a dearth of workers," he says. "They often are not remunerated fairly, so they leave one workshop and join another. We must treat our workers fairly to retain them." He trained a small team: Hasan and Majid, neither Khatri, and a man from UP, all new to Ajrakh. They will work loyally with him, and then perhaps they'll move on, start their own workshops with blessings. Everyone wants to be recognized.

They pin down a *mashru* piece. Irfanbhai tells Hasan the plan, and he prints resist ends and borders, but Irfanbhai isn't satisfied. He doesn't complain. He picks up the block and continues. The idea is to print the ends with three colors—traditional Ajrakh, and in the body both the *rekh* and *datla* will be resist—a simple innovation that opens the pattern to be a bold black and white—a contemporary rendition of tradition.

Does it sell?

He laughs. Yes. Irfanbhai understands his clients; his work always sells.

Now his staff is watching him, learning. He prints effortlessly. Ajrakh is his life.

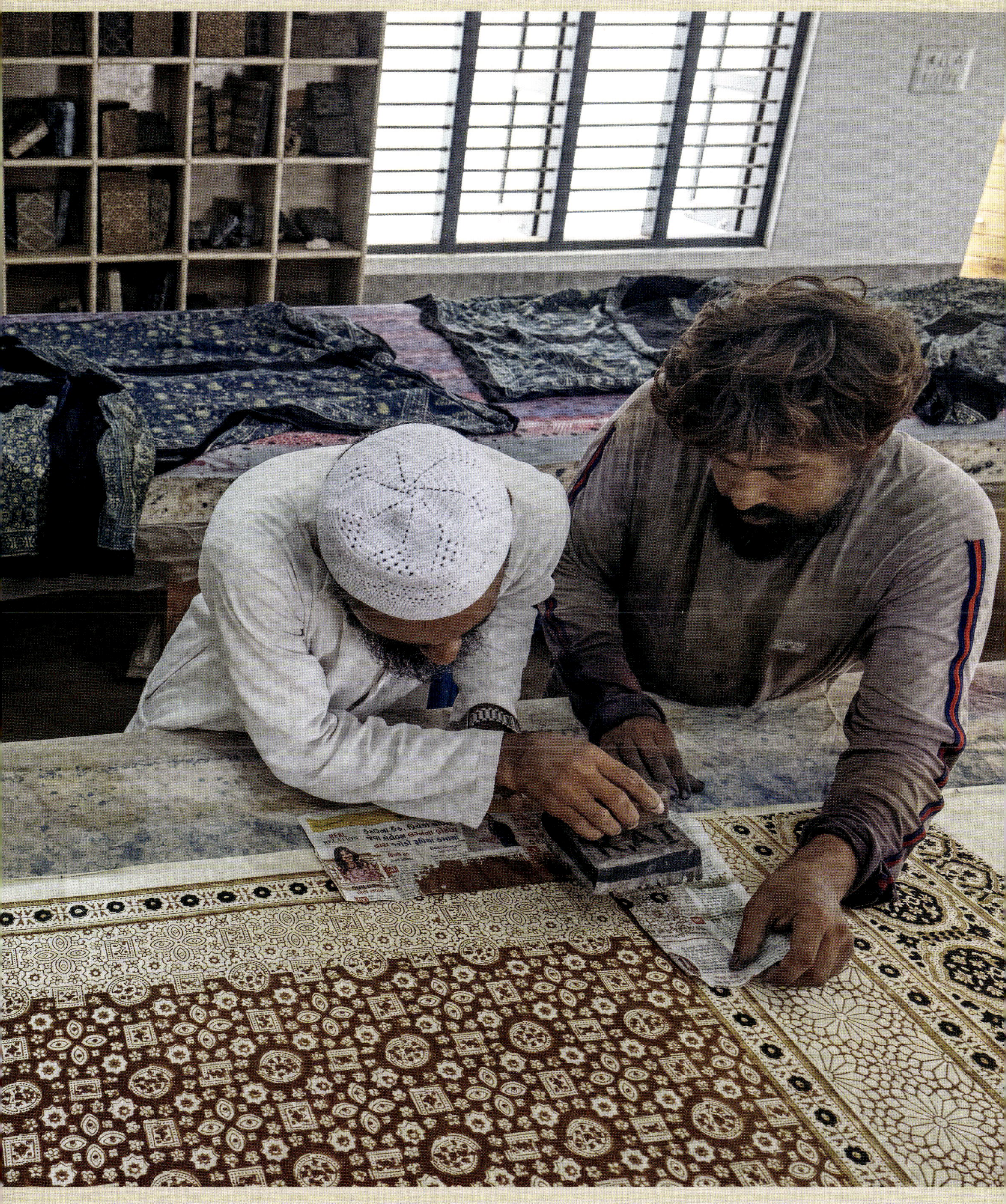

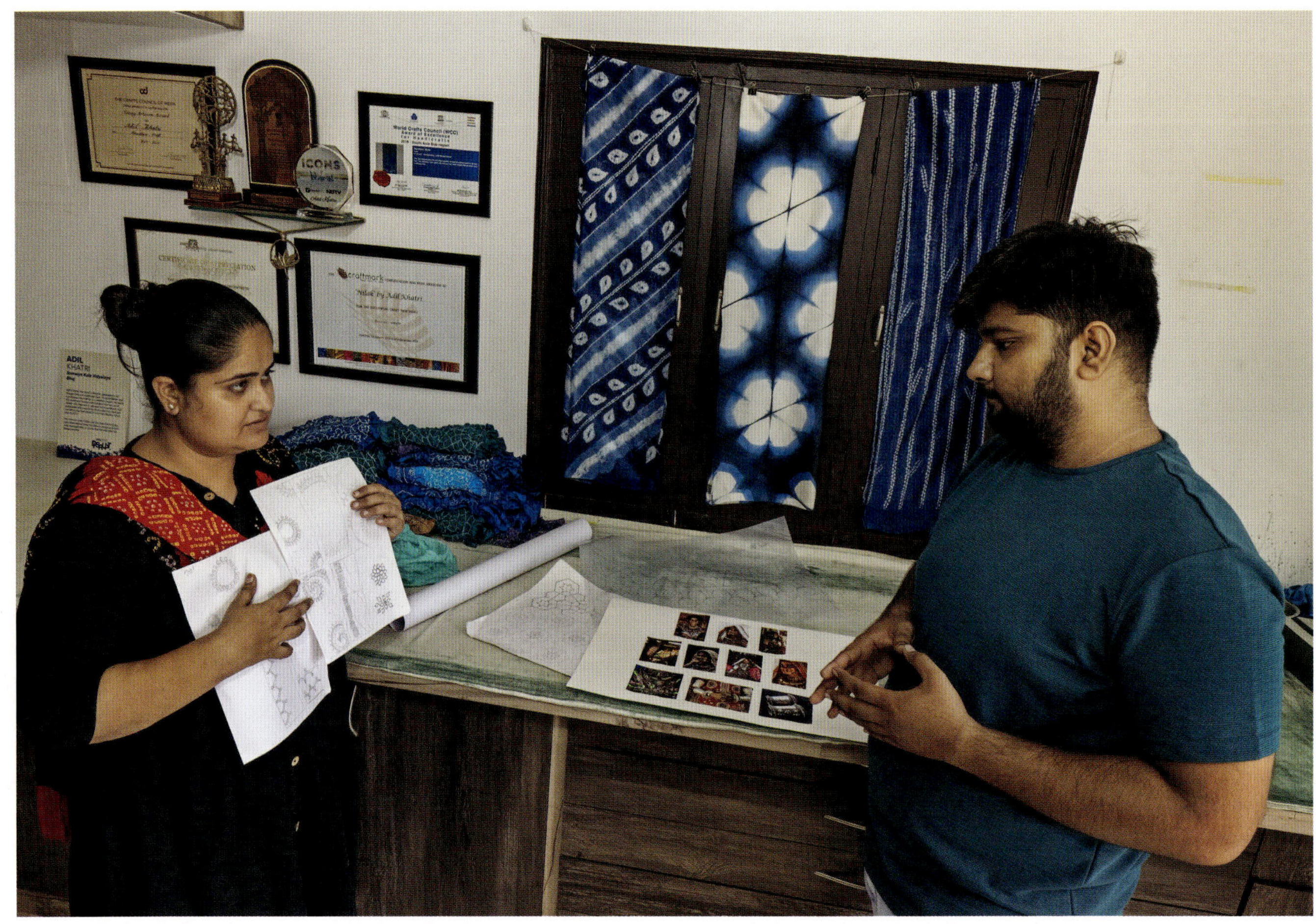

When we think we know nothing, that is the beginning of education.

~Zakiyaben AdilKhatri

Now I think anything can be done in bandhani.

~Adilbhai Mustak Khatri

Bhuj, 2022. Having worked in codesign, Adilbhai and Zakiyaben are better able to work together. They always critique each other's designs. *Photo: Nevada Wier*

Chapter 14

ZAKIYABEN ADIL AND ADILBHAI MUSTAK KHATRI: KINDRED EXPLORERS

I'm having my morning tea when the phone rings. "Ma'am, I need to talk to you," Zakiyaben says. Uh oh. Must be some trouble in the women's BMA class. I tell her to come over.

But when I open the door, Zakiyaben is beaming next to Adilbhai. "Ma'am, we're in a relationship," she says.

Zakiyaben and Adilbhai, both Khatri artisans, took the design course in 2013—in separate classes as per the culturally appropriate mandate of the program. I observed both classes, monitoring each student's progress. Zakiyaben's father's family did batik. They were known in Mundra for being orthodox and close knit. Until 2005, the sixty-six family members lived together. Zakiyaben's father, the youngest brother, was the one less conventional. He treated boys and girls equally and supported Zakiyaben's education. She excelled in everything. But design was her passion. She learned batik by watching and did wax brush painting in the workshop when the artisans weren't around. When she was deemed mature, her father made her a batik studio at home. She also tied bandhani for income and had her own bank account.

Zakiyaben's cousin Shakilbhai took the design course in 2009. "I saw the fashion show and thought how women are doing the work and men are getting the credit," she said. She thought about going to other design schools after twelfth grade but finally opted for KRV because it was practical: near home, taught in Gujarati and Hindi, and reasonable in cost. "Artisans will decide the future of our traditions," she said. "I want to take the tradition forward, make something that is both traditional and never been made before. I want to start my own company. Bairaj, a traditional batik motif, will be my company name. It means 'rule of women.' The logo will have bangles and a stick."

After the first course, she said, "My vision and understanding have changed. From sketching I learned to see shades of colors. In nature I saw how to make harmony from contrast." After the second course, she observed, "If we use principles, there are many ways to make traditional designs new. Now I will see rhythm, movement, balance everywhere."

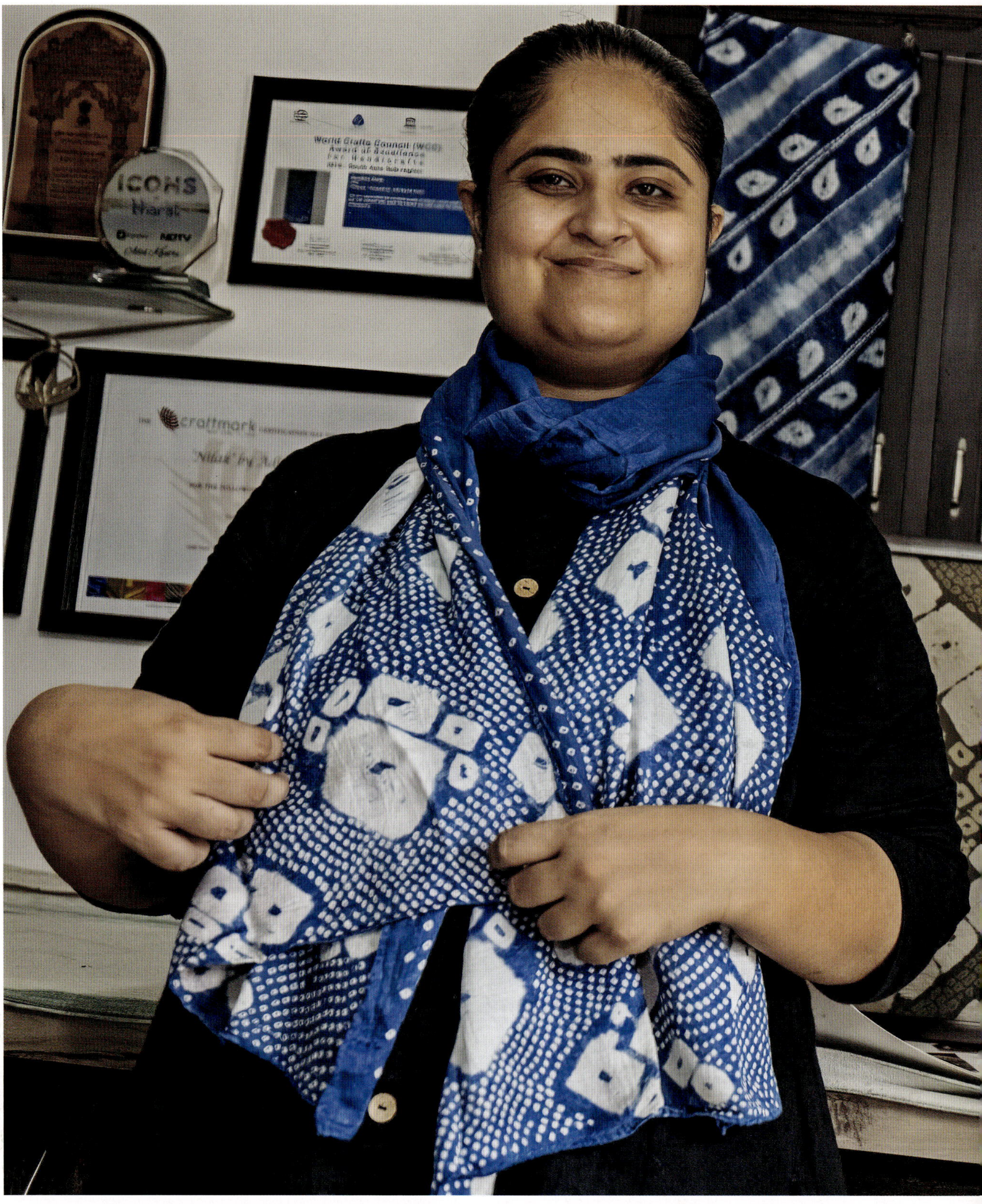

In the fourth course, after visiting a potter's village, Zakiyaben redefined a trend forecast as "The Magic of Mud." Working within her own technical limitations, she had decided that bandhani was more feasible for her than batik, and experimented with varying sizes of bandhani dots for homework assignments. She applied her experiments to inspiration from the shapes and textures of pots and designed a collection of garments from traditional to Western to suit the modern working woman's needs.

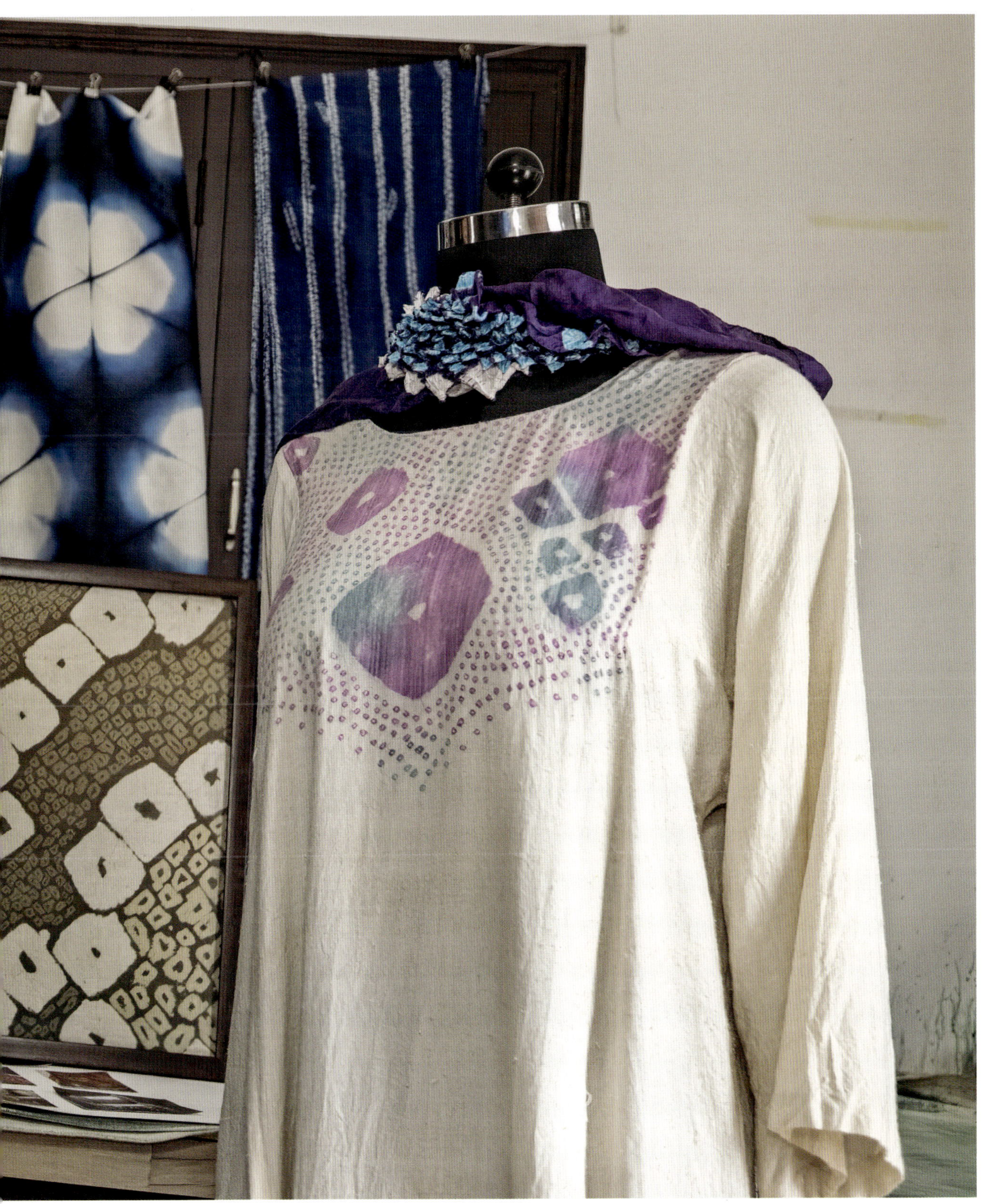

Bhuj, 2022. From her design course in 2013, Zakiyaben has explored variation of scale and texture in bandhani. Today she is researching traditional garment construction of Kutch. *Photo: Nevada Wier*

During the course, Zakiyaben's father suddenly passed away. He had been her champion, her source of confidence and strength. She went home to be with her mother, sister, and extended family. But she decided to finish the course. She knew her father would have wanted her to. She graduated with awards for Best Collection, Most Marketable Collection, and Best Student. "When we think we know nothing, that is the beginning of education," she said. "Challenge takes you ahead. KRV gave me a chance. I was the first woman bandhani artist to take the course, and I learned much from my Rabari classmates. They are experienced, and free in expressing their ideas."

Meanwhile, in the men's course, Adilbhai was charting a parallel course.

Although his family members were dyers by tradition, his grandfather was a professor and his father had a government job. His mother tied bandhani for income, and his uncle had a bandhani business. After twelfth grade, Adilbhai decided to learn bandhani from his uncle and quickly wanted to take the craft in new directions. He took the KRV course to increase his understanding and knowledge of bandhani.

Summing up the first course, he said, "Whatever work we do needs effort and perfection. We learned all color variations in two weeks! The tint, shade, and chroma exercises were fun. I got the desire to do something new."

After the second course, he said, "When we use principles consciously, we can do something. In nature I observed that everything is harmony. And nature is the basis of everything." He made a wonderful fresh piece textured with large and small dots and shibori-stitched resist for homework, for which Fabindia later gave him an order.

The visiting faculty for course 3 wrote, "Adil is eager to learn and open to feedback. He understands that he is inexperienced, so he asks questions. He works conscientiously and has good analytical and perception skills."

Adilbhai reinterpreted his trend forecast theme as "Dream City." He explored fantasy and pushed as many boundaries of bandhani as he could. "Traditional work can't be used every day," he explained. "I want to make new things for new uses." He became so immersed in his theme that he dreamed his theme board. "In sampling I realized how much rests on the material. Fabric affects color," he said.

For his collection, he created airy resort wear garments highly textured with his large and small bandhani dots and shibori. "I chose a theme where I could bring in new concepts and experiment," he said. "I looked for minimum stitching and maximum texture. I lost mental limitations. Now I think anything can be done in bandhani." He graduated with awards for Best Collection, Best Presentation, and Best Student.

These two are perfect for each other, I thought. But as a cultural outsider, I could not say anything. Communities had their own intricate methods for deciding matches.

The next year, we formed Somaiya Kala Vidya, and I began the Business and Management for Artisans course. Adilbhai quickly signed up for the men's course. He wanted to explore new options in design and felt that business was an essential link. Though he did pose the question, in a pilot course, would the students be getting full-quality education. Zakiyaben was among the artisan graduates that I selected as suited for the women's course. She was clear from the start that she would continue. "Design is not enough," she said. "You also need business." She had considered doing a BBA but decided that the SKV BMA was better because it was focused on craft.

After the first women's class, the visiting faculty member wrote, "Zakiyaben is keen to include technology in her work and already has a working knowledge of computers and English. She leads by example and is empathetic. Yet, her current social barriers stand in her way. She has so much potential, I want to see her shine bright."

Zakiyaben assessed her own situation: her strengths were English, presentation skills, and exclusive collections; her weakness was lack of knowledge about natural dyes; her opportunities were marketing connections through SKV and contacts she had made; and her threats were the many artisans and shops in Kutch who sold bandhani.

Adilbhai's self-analysis was that his strengths were design education, skills in developing new textures, experience with natural dye, and product exploration; his weaknesses were that he works alone, has a small workshop, and has few customers; his opportunities and threats were one—social media. Immediately, he hired a helper.

Zakiyaben developed a collection with her own theme: monuments of Lakhpat. It gave her the opportunity to travel to western Kutch and see the ancient town firsthand. She conservatively chose to make scarves, dupattas, and a few *abha*, traditional women's tunics. She used soft neutral colors and her characteristic large and small dots, along with fresh networks of fine dots.

Adilbhai developed a collection with the theme of storm. He used bold contrasting cool colors and dramatic textures. Conservatively, he also chose to make scarves, dupattas and a few *abha*.

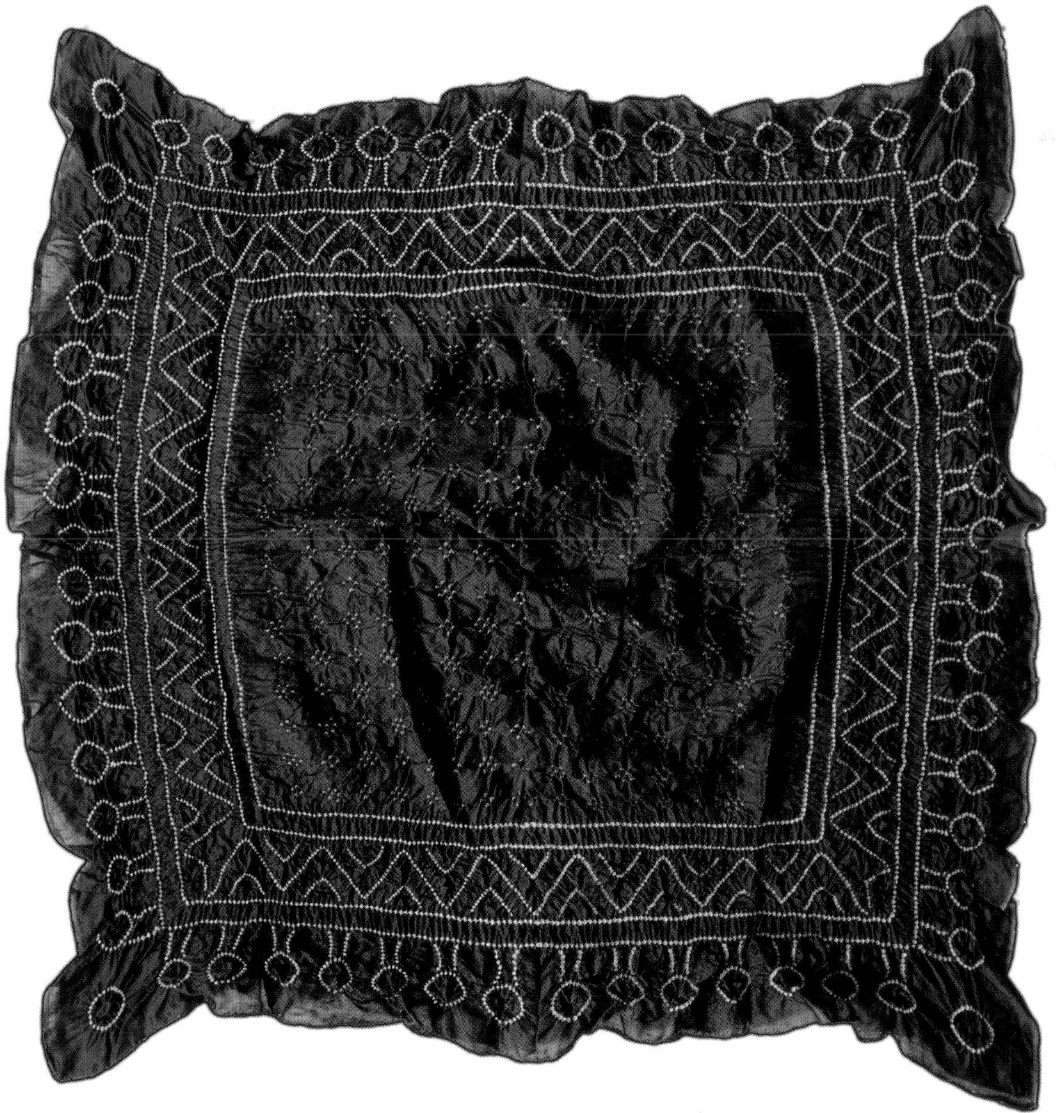

Above: Jharmar, square scarf by Zakiya Adil Khatri, 2022. Silk, bandhani, beads. 38" x 38". Fascinated by traditional jewelry of Kutch, Zakiyaben translated metal forms into two-dimensional motifs to create an innovation on the traditional jharmar border, which is inspired by a necklace. The use of red as well as white dots is technically demanding. Zakiyaben finished the scarf with tiny glass beads that echo bandhani dots. *Photo: Schiffer Publishing Ltd.*

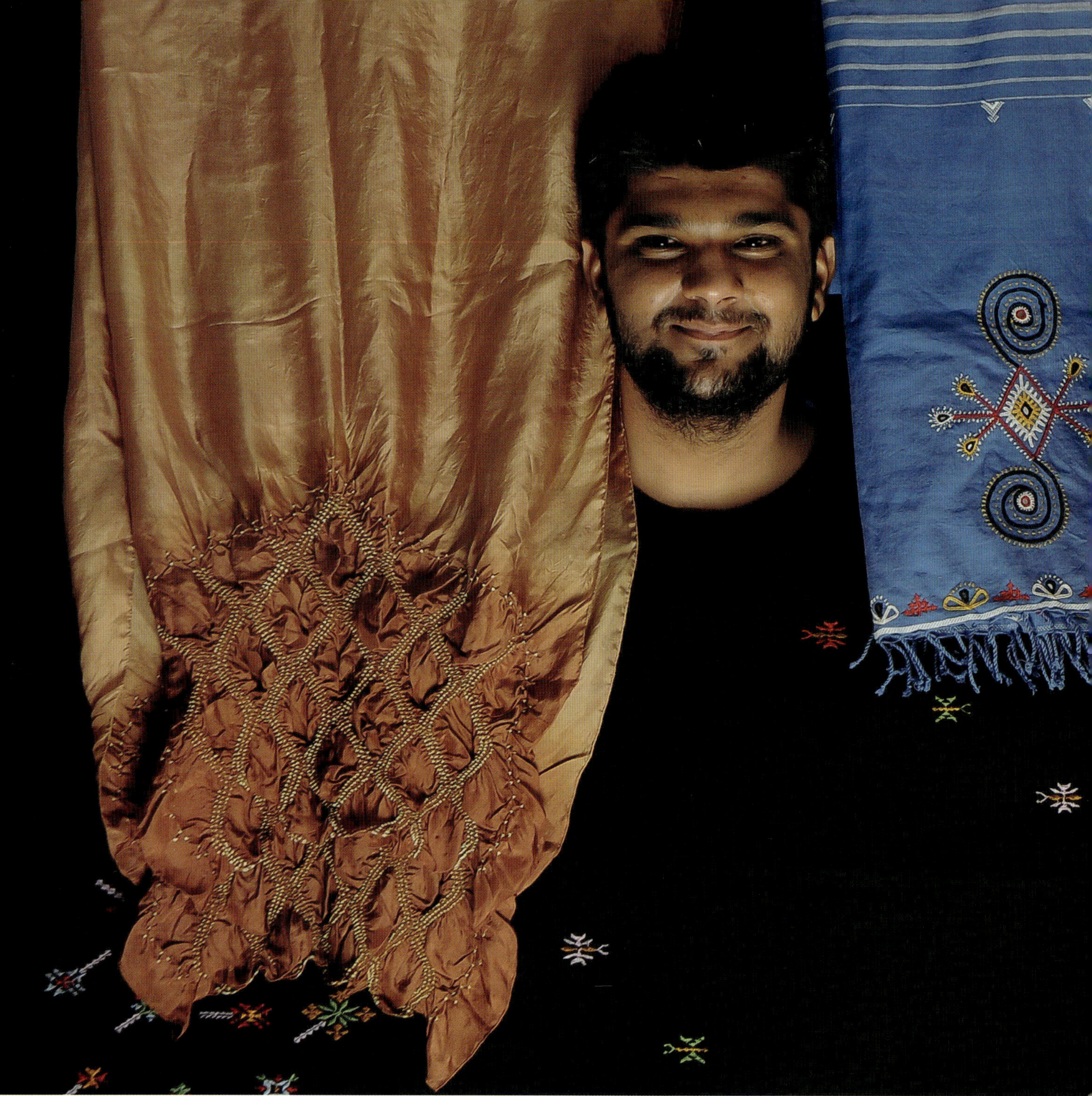

The first time the men and women students got together was to plan their exhibition in Mumbai. Brainstorming, they named it Craft Re-Defined. Adilbhai, an avid photographer, took charge of styling the photography for the invitation. He called from the photo studio in a panic; he knew the photo wasn't right. I and an intern just happened to be near the studio. I asked if we should we come.

"Yes!" he answered and sent out for *dabeli* (vegetarian sloppy Joes) and strong chai.

A team of students were in the studio on the job. We brainstormed, verbally, visually. Adilbhai really wanted an image of scarves of each artisan pouring out of a trunk. But it was static, silent, and a bit of a cliché. We tried several suggestions. Zakiyaben was the one to realize that while it was important to them to include each craft, if not each artisan, it wasn't working visually. She suddenly understood editing at a deep, useful level.

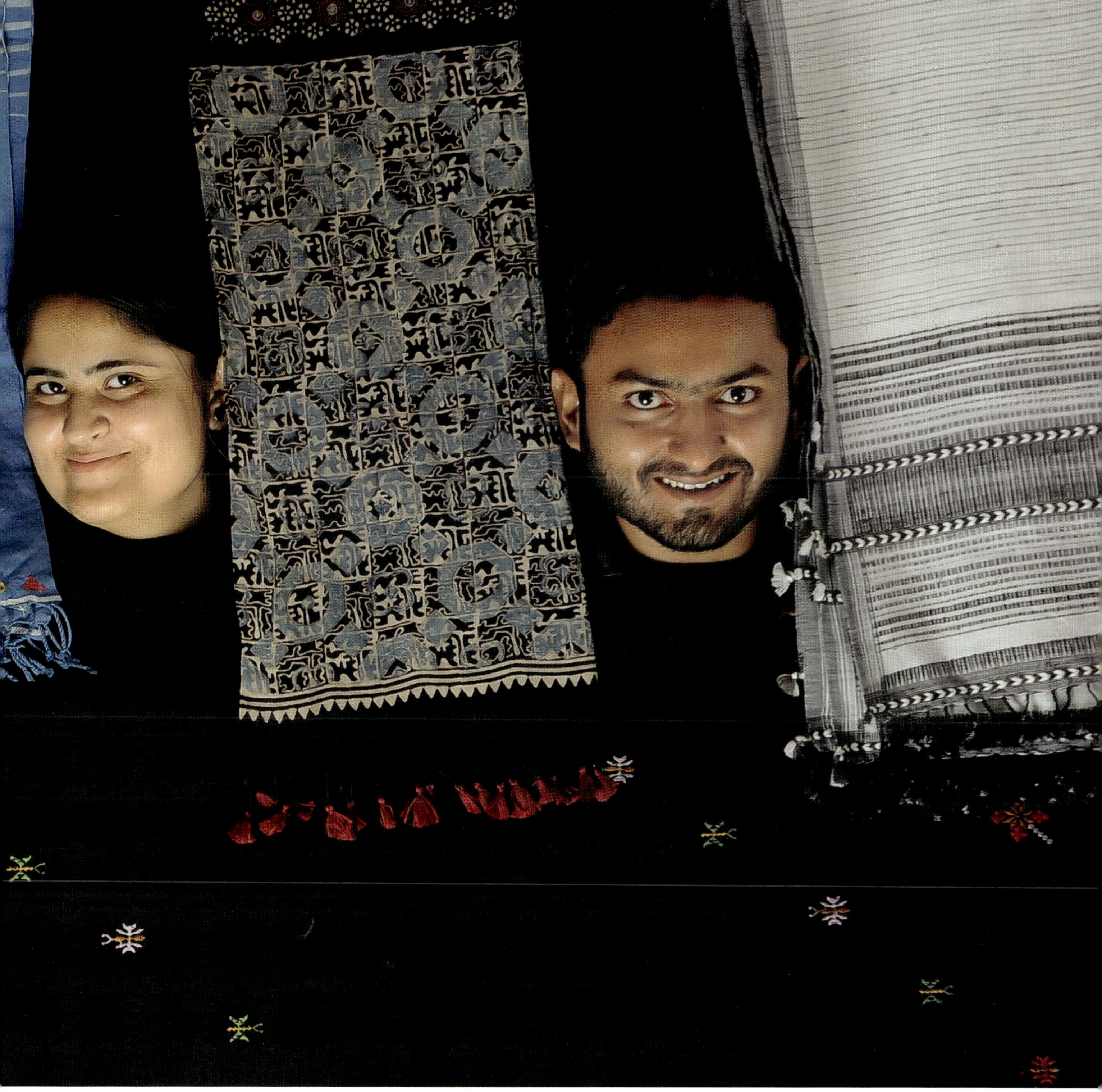

The intern suggested putting the artisans in the photo with their faces covered—the unknown artisan. But that was exactly what we were redefining! The faceless worker, the hands without a head . . . then he had a flash—what if we had a row of scarves with the artisans' faces peeking out? Artisan designers in the picture! Everyone had fun, and we all knew it was the perfect, engaging invitation.

The exhibition was a success. Everyone sold under their own brands. Zakiyaben's Bairaj sold over 65 percent of the stock. In the final Analysis course, she thought deeply. "It's not just the color, but the tone," she observed. "And the expensive pieces sold first as the designs and the materials were new."

Bhuj, 2014. Craft Re-Defined. The students of the first BMA course named their pop-up exhibition Craft Re-Defined. The invitation showed artisans' faces with their collections, a crucial innovation in the world of craft in India. *Photo: Ketan Pomal, L.M. Studio*

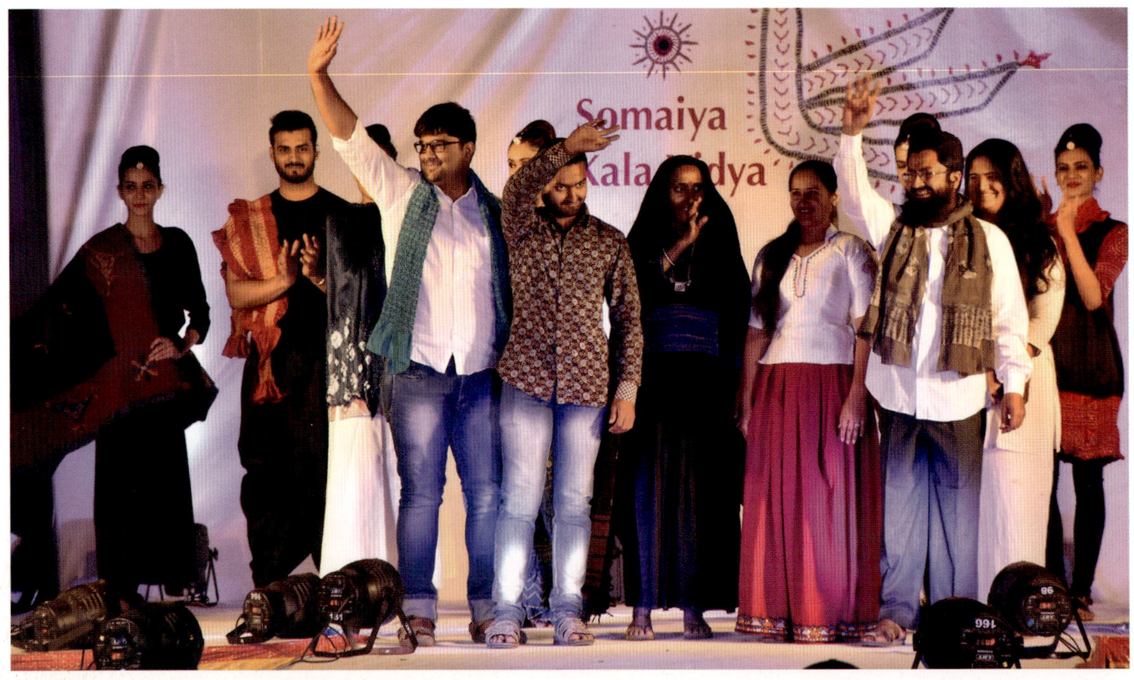

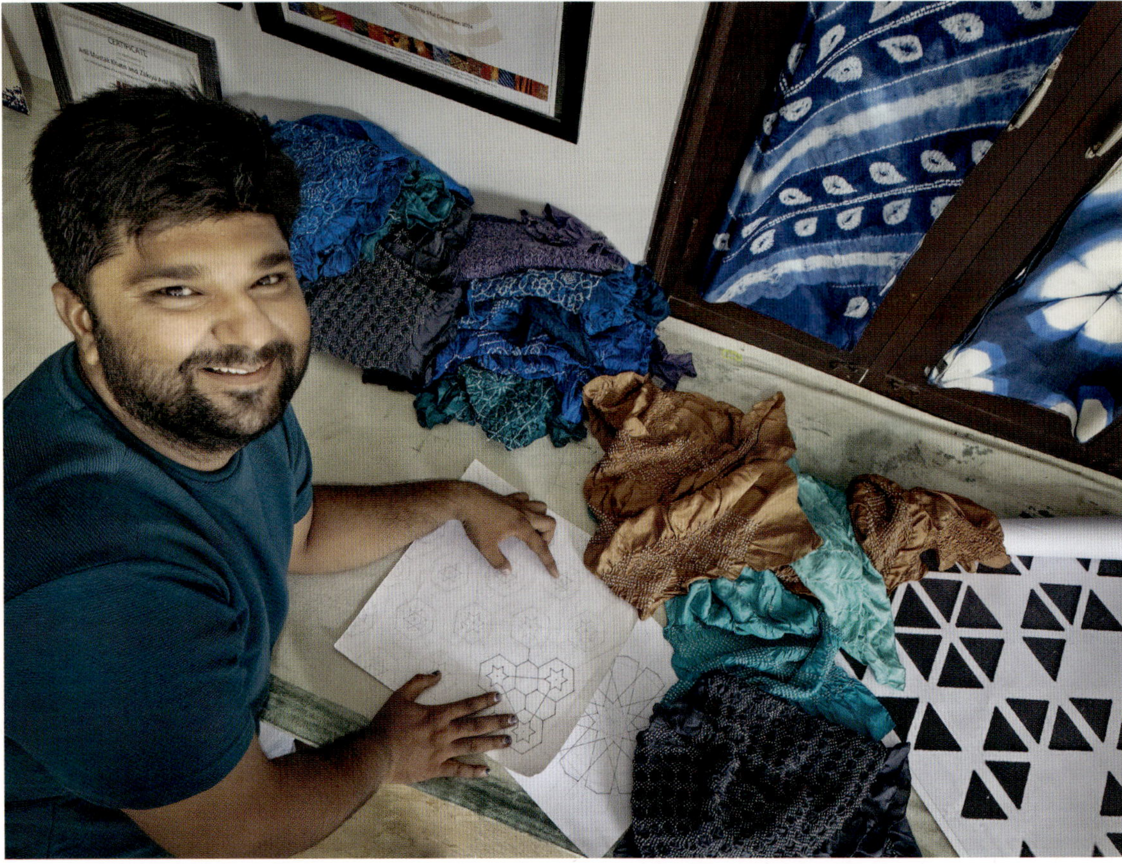

Above: Bhujodi, 2015. The first Somaiya Kala Vidya convocation in Kutch featured a fashion show that included the 2014 BMA collections. Adilbhai and Zakiyaben walked the ramp again, with their classmates. Photo: *Ketan Pomal, L.M. Studio*

Below: Bhuj, 2022. Adilbhai has a fascination with Islamic geometry and finds endless inspiration in tessellations. *Photo: Nevada Wier*

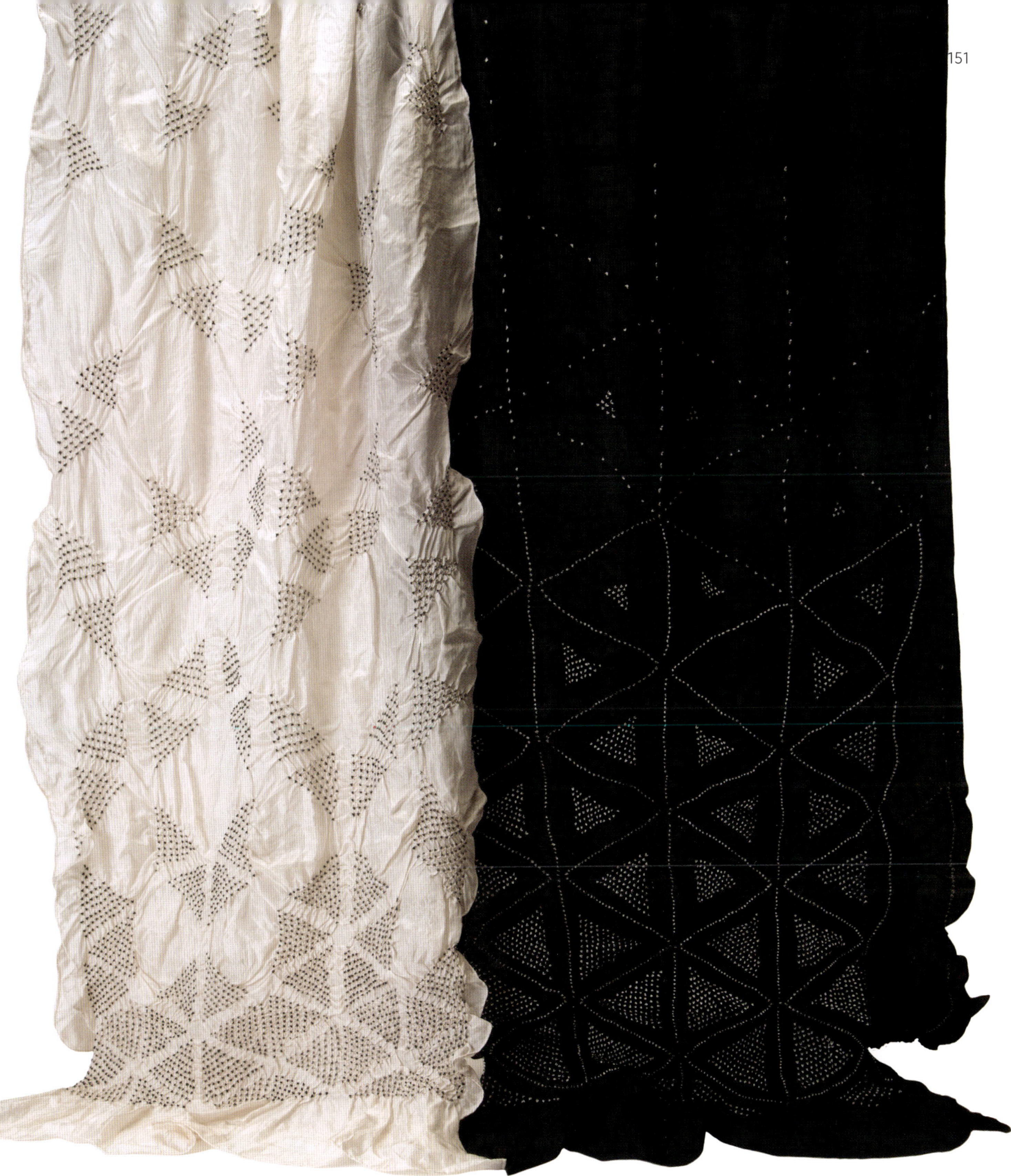

Top: Chiaroscuro, two scarves by Adil Mustak Khatri, 2022. Silk, bandhani. 22" x 82" each. Using *bharti* filling technique, a simple triangle motif, and the principle of negative and positive space, Adilbhai created two contemporary masterpieces of bandhani that displayed together add another level of negative-positive contrast. *Photo: Schiffer Publishing Ltd.*

Adilbhai's brand Nilak sold 52 percent of the stock. "Applying what I learned in class brought success," he said.

Each BMA student finally made a five-year business plan. Zakiyaben planned to work with women. "I feel excited to work after envisioning my five-year goal," she said. "Risk is necessary. I will aim for RS 200,000 of product and a profit of RS 25,000 per exhibition." On further reflection, she added, "Through this course we understood the limitations of a design course. Many women are equipped only to work for others. I realized the importance of ownership, and I passed it to the women tiers I work with. I showed them my designs before giving them work, and the finished products after I had dyed them. They were keen to know what sold. I got more respect in the community after doing the course."

Adilbhai envisioned that Nilak would be a global brand famous for its unique designs. Immediately he would explore natural dyes and focus on domestic exhibitions and online shops. His long-term plan was to explore stitched garments, participate in international exhibitions and workshops, and collaborate with other designers. "Risk leads to profit," he said. "We learned to prioritize and plan for the long term. I realized that in business it is important to be honest, ethical, and do good-quality work."

Zakiyaben and Adilbhai found each other. They were engaged before the BMA was over and married in November 2016.

Zakiyaben moved easily into Adilbhai's welcoming, casual, and comfortable family. They started a joint business, keeping both of their labels—one on either side of their recycled-paper-bag packaging. They began an ever-evolving collection inspired by Islamic architecture—with a tongue-in-cheek piece inspired by the wealthy Ambani family mansion in Mumbai for good measure. They sold their work to young contemporary designers and established businesses. Their work became technically excellent and refreshingly contemporary. Kutch has hundreds of bandhani artists, and bandhani is ever present in a range of markets. In that scenario, their collections are original and memorable.

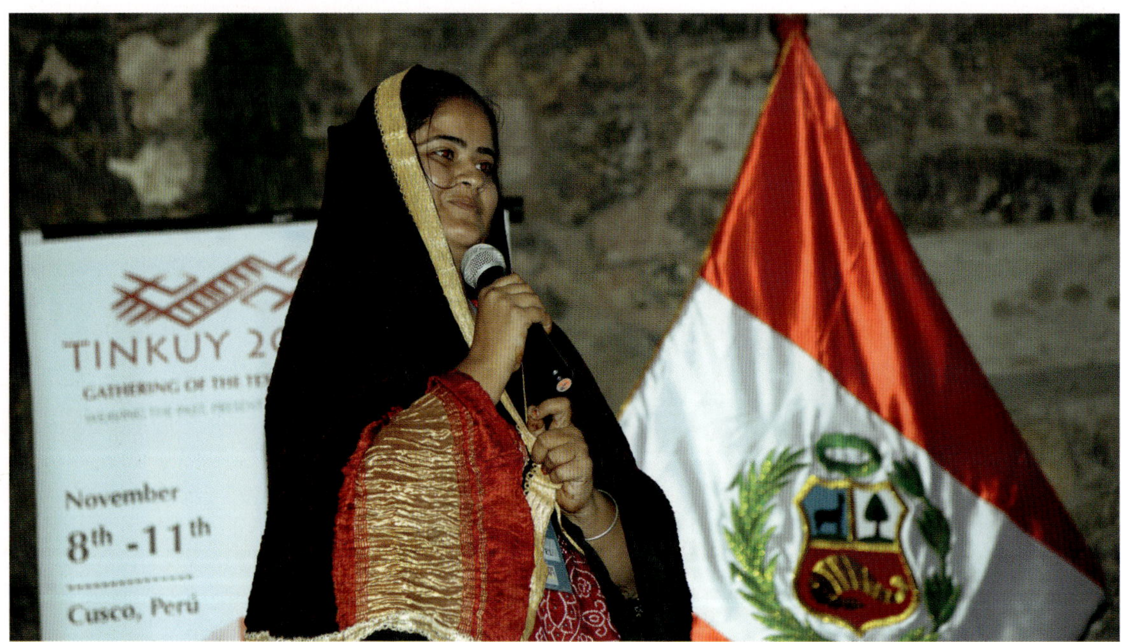

Above: Cusco, Peru, 2017. Zakiyaben was a keynote speaker at the 2017 Tinkuy, a meeting of international textile artisans. Wearing her wedding abho (tunic) and chandrokhani veil, she spoke on empowerment of women. *Photo: Carol Ventura*

Opposite: Teotitlán, Oaxaca, Mexico, 2022. After participating in a codesign program, Adilbhai journeyed to Oaxaca to meet his partners, Rina and Miguel. They exchanged gifts of their work, with love. *Photo: Judy Frater*

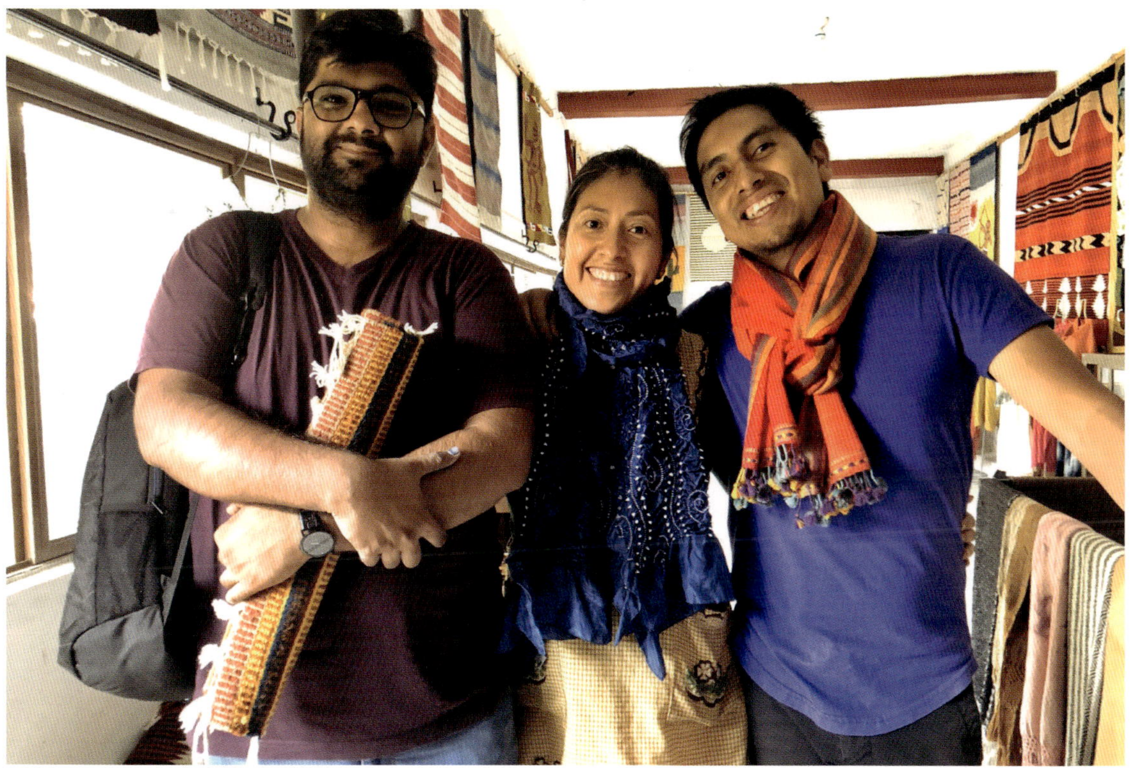

Adilbhai was the youngest bandhani artist ever to win the Gujarat State Award for Excellence in craft. He spoke at Kala Umang!, the convocation for the SKV Design class of 2015, urging graduates to take the business course. Zakiyaben spoke at Kala Umang! the following year. "There are a few seats empty here," she said. "I hope to see them filled with women graduates next year!"

In November 2017, I went with Zakiyaben to Tinkuy, an international gathering of weavers and textile artisans in Cusco, Peru. The seminar topic was empowerment of women, and Zakiyaben addressed women from the Andes, Mesoamerica, Asia, and the US. "Education is everything," she said, and the audience applauded.

She participated in a codesign project, working long distance with a student partner from the University of Wisconsin–Madison, and in April 2018 she visited UW Madison to teach workshops in bandhani and participate in live codesign. At a public talk, she elaborated on her experiences. "The first thing to keep in mind is that women in India face great obstacles," she said. "Even getting suppliers of raw material to take me seriously is difficult. In India a woman can be successful only if her father—and later her husband—support her. Artisans think practically, in terms of their technique and in terms of marketability—as they know it. They limit themselves, so codesign helps get beyond that, to new levels."

She inspired other women artisans, and, in 2018, three women bandhani artisans and the first woman weaver took the design course.

Adilbhai also realized his dream of recognition. In 2018, he won the Crafts Council of India Kamala Award for Young Artisans—an award created for him to honor his exceptional creativity—and the coveted World Crafts Council Seal of Excellence. He went on to receive the first All India Artisan and Craft Workers Welfare Association award for Next Gen Entrepreneur and was selected as an "Icon of India."

In 2019, Adilbhai participated in a codesign project with artisans from Oaxaca. He realized that his partners had different interpretations of the theme they chose, water. "I learned ways of thinking,"

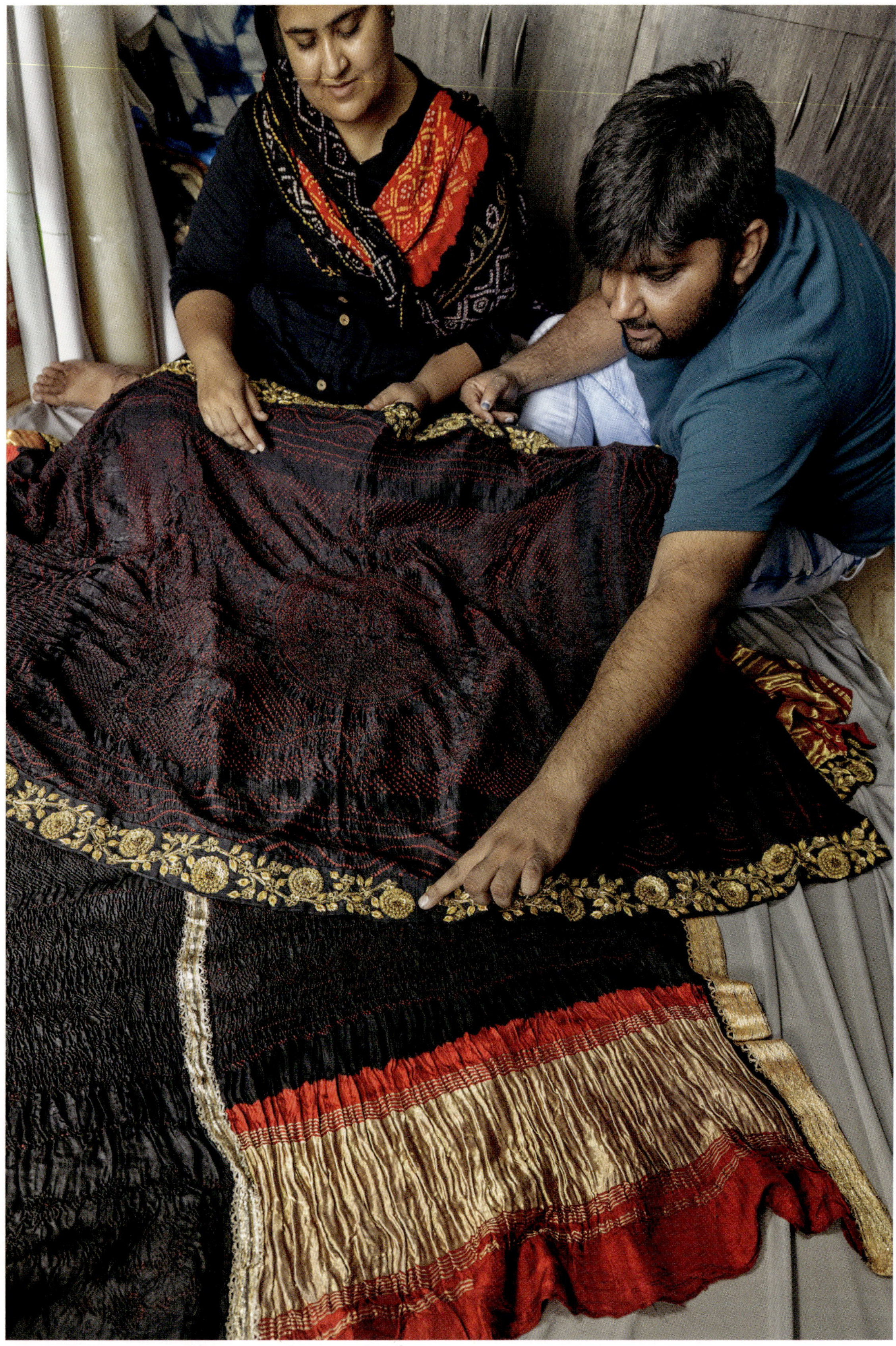

Bhuj, 2022. Adilbhai and Zakiyaben examine vintage *chandrokhanis* in their collection with new eyes each time. The bandhani and the design were extraordinary; work and design were intertwined. Nothing approaches traditional work now. But it can inspire contemporary design. *Photo: Nevada Wier*

he said. "Rina and Miguel were very open. They didn't think we are going to produce a collection, so we do this and that. They did whatever naturally came to their minds. This kind of collaboration lets artisans go beyond their limitations."

I asked if he would now produce the collection he had made. He flatly said no.

No?

"This is work for a market that understands and appreciates design," he said.

The market to which Adilbhai and Zakiyaben have access is pop-up exhibitions and shops operated by craft organizations in India. They feel that for these venues, people expect what is already in the market. So they always take traditional designs in red and black, and whatever is currently already in fashion. They have questions about marketing bandhani. "Should craft be mass produced?" Adilbhai earnestly asked. "I mean, if the same design is replicated in 2,000 pieces or 3,000 meters, is it going in the right direction? And when we make a new design, should we protect it or show it to the world?"

Zakiyaben said, "The bottom line is that artisans have to survive. Otherwise, craft will stop. Because of design education, graduates enjoy their craft and earn well. Customers try to bargain artisans down. But if you have your own design, they have to buy it from you, and you can ask the price."

Adilbhai and Zakiyaben were juried into the International Folk Art Market | Santa Fe in 2020 and again in 2022. They had two opportunities to experience a higher-end clientele, and for the second show Adilbhai sent some of his water collection, blue bandhani with patterns of drops and waves. Their work was appreciated, and they earned more than they can in India. Sadly, due to COVID-19, they were not able to attend.

But in 2022, Adilbhai traveled to Oaxaca to conduct bandhani workshops, share his codesign experiences, and meet partners Rina and Miguel. Opportunities to explore international markets, virtually and personally, were important for both Adilbhai and Zakiyaben in establishing identities, and in enhancing their understanding of the value of bandhani.

They care deeply about their tradition. Both Adilbhai and Zakiyaben were cofaculty in my UW Madison 2022 residency and taught students about history and culture as well as technique. They have slowly invested in a collection of exquisite antique bandhanis for inspiration. Zakiyaben wants to know why she has never seen a bandhani old enough to be naturally dyed. She says her grandmother told her that traditionally, women were buried with their *chandrokhanis*. "I think that traditions were not made to last forever," she says. "They were personal, not meant for sale or museums."

As long as Adilbhai and Zakiyaben consider, question, and search for answers, traditions are alive.

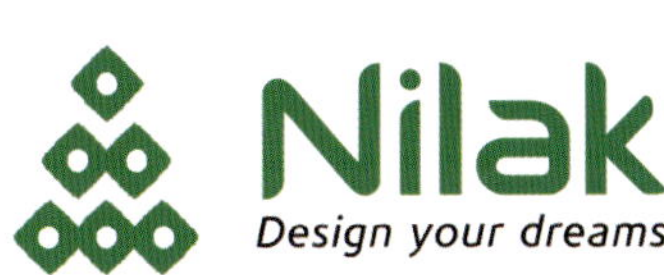

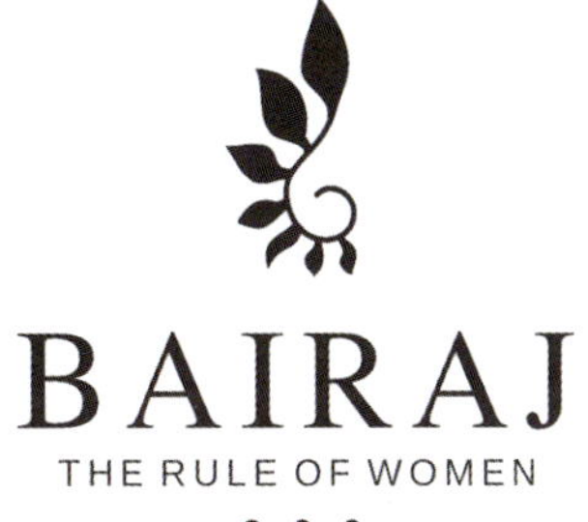

Above, left: Adilbhai designed his logo in his design course and refined it in his BMA course. Nilak is the fugitive green dye applied to bandhani for accent. Green also refers to Adilbhai's commitment to sustainability.

Above, right: Zakiyaben knew the name of her brand before beginning the design course. She created the logo and refined it in her BMA course. Bairaj, a traditional batik motif, means the rule of women. She capitalized the A to remember her father, Ayubbhai.

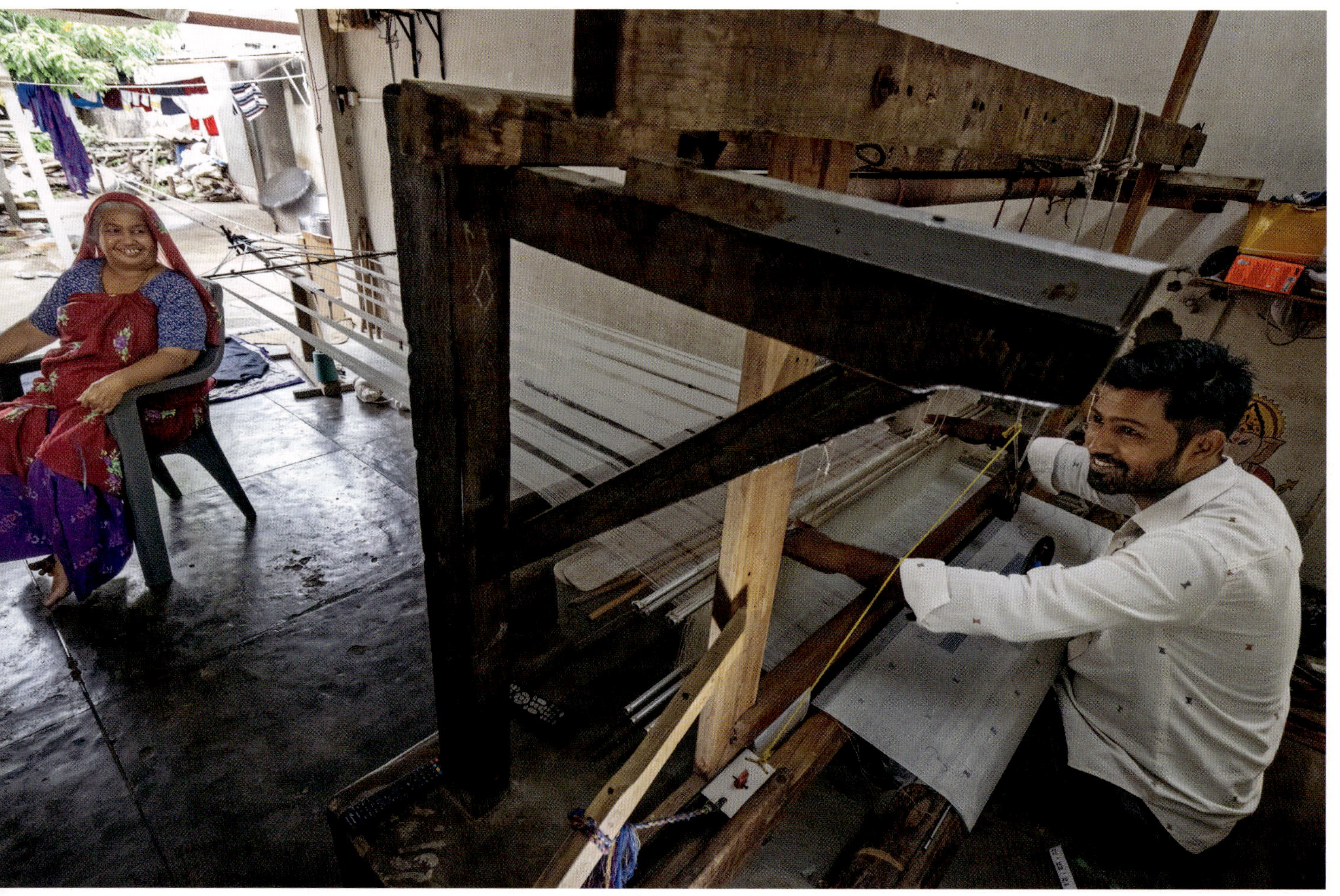

Don't make craft cheap, because if you do, you will be working for money and not from the heart—and that is the strength of craft.

~Pachanbhai Premji Siju

Above: Bhujodi, 2022. Pachanbhai's grandfather was a renowned weaver. Through education, he and his brothers found a way to bring respect to their weaving heritage. *Photo: Nevada Wier*

Chapter 15

PACHANBHAI PREMJI SIJU: GIVING BACK

2019

Pachanbhai is sitting on the floor, encircled by visitors from the USA. He exuberantly shows his scarves and shawls, subtle rainbows of colors, patterns, and textures, each one more delightful than the last. His enthusiasm has vanquished all barriers of language and culture.

"I have woven all my life," he says. "What I have done with my weaving is what is important."

Pachanbhai's grandfather was a renowned weaver and a founder of the Bhujodi weavers' cooperative society. His father, Premjibhai, was a master weaver who made carpets and shawls. But Premjibhai told his sons not to continue weaving. Do anything else, he said; there is no future in this. In 2000, when Pachanbhai was in ninth grade, Premjibhai suddenly passed away, and the family was plunged into financial crisis. Pachanbhai's eldest brother, Damjibhai, wove job work for a master weaver in the village. His second brother, Puroshottambhai, heeding his father, worked with a company in Bhuj, making designs for embroidery artisans for a modest salary. Pachanbhai had learned weaving from his father and elder brothers. So to help support the family, he left school and, like Damjibhai, started weaving for a master weaver. But he wasn't satisfied with the wages. After three years, he took a job as a cleaner on the night shift at a mineral-mining company just outside his village. He worked with dedication and commitment and, within six months, was promoted to field operator. However, the pollution of the factory affected his health. So he quit the job and returned to weaving.

In the meantime, Puroshottambhai had decided he wanted to earn from his own tradition and restore his grandfather's name. He took the design course at Kala Raksha Vidhyalaya and was struggling to set up a business. Damjibhai left job work to join him. And Pachanbhai made three. The brothers live together with their families and their mother. When they started their own business, everyone contributed to weaving. For the most part, Damjibhai and Pachanbhai managed production, Puroshottambhai did the outside work—banking and marketing, and the women did warping, bobbin winding, and finishing.

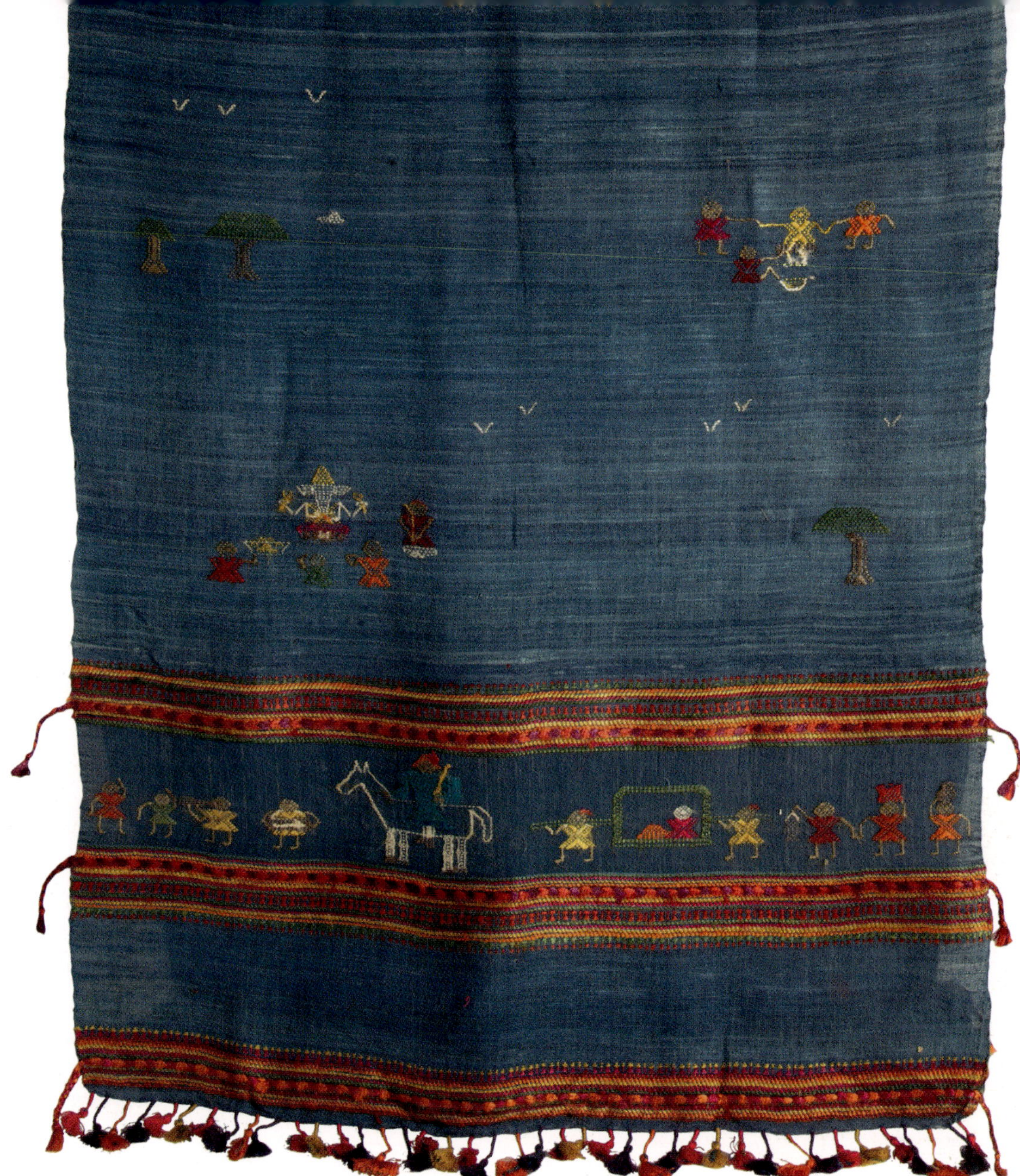

Pachanbhai had nine years of experience in weaving. But his world was very small. He had never traveled outside Kutch. Despite eight years of school, he was not comfortably literate. When visitors would come, if Puroshottambhai and Damjibhai were out, he would shoo them away, saying, "No one is home."

Puroshottambhai knew his brother had potential, so when we began Somaiya Kala Vidya he sent Pachanbhai for the first design course in 2015. Pachanbhai came with the resistance of someone coerced. The class of eleven men was crammed into two rooms of the guesthouse, with an equally tight classroom where they drew and painted on two low tables. They had to weave in the garden and print and dye in the makeshift backyard studio. They made it work.

After the first course, Color, Pachanbhai said, "I know weaving, but I didn't know color. I could not get the way Puroshottambhai knew color. Now I get it. I learned how to talk in front of people, to talk about my work." He reveled in design education when he understood that it did not depend on reading and writing. "I understood that this was a course for me," he said. After the fourth course, Concept, Communication, Projects, he reflected, "Before, I thought design was a fixed notion. Now I am able to play! We can use principles to improve each layout. I learned to think of the effect of warp and weft. I learned to abstract."

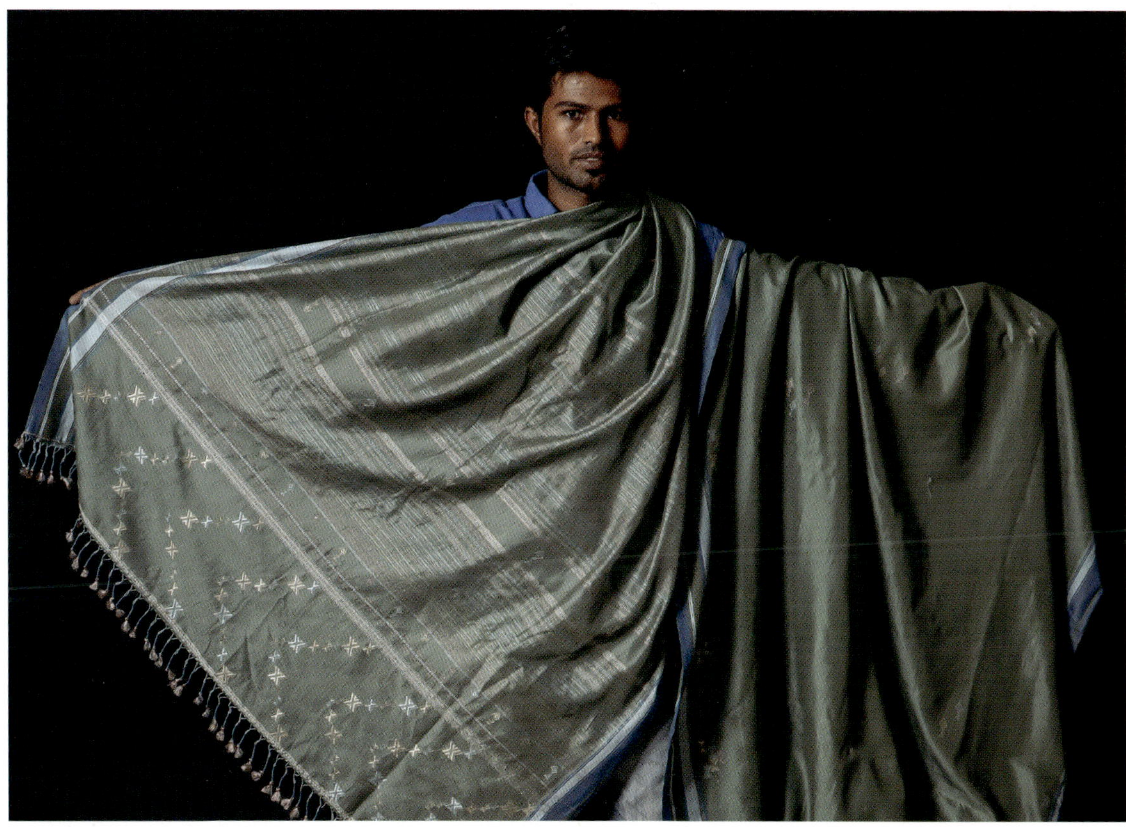

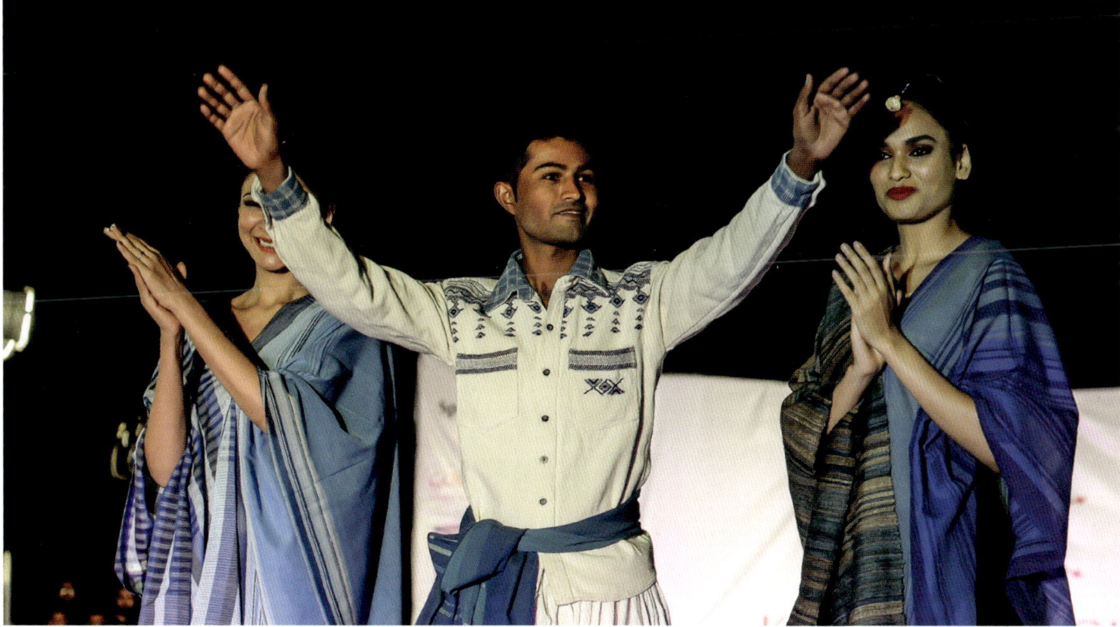

Opposite: *The Story of a Marriage*, shawl by Pachanbhai Premji Siju, 2022. Cotton warp, tassar silk weft, hand-woven with hand-inserted tassar silk extra wefts. 22" x 86". Weddings among weavers of Kutch are elaborate, including days of ceremony. The bride and groom are readied in their homes. The groom comes in procession. Shawls tied together, bride and groom circle a sacred fire. Then everyone dances and feasts. *Photo: Schiffer Publishing Ltd.*

Top: Somaiya Kala Vidya, 2015. Saris are not traditional dress for village Kutch. For his design course, Pachanbhai wove a sari for the first time. He had to restructure his loom as well as design for the larger format. *Photo: Ketan Pomal, L.M. Studio*

Above: Bhujodi, 2015. Pachanbhai realized what he had achieved in a year of design education. In his graduating SKV fashion show, held in his village, he proudly wore the loose trousers traditional to his community with the shirt his brothers wove for him with their Three Threads logo. *Photo: Ketan Pomal, L.M. Studio*

Kutch weavers traditionally wove woolen blankets. In the 1960s, they began to weave lighter woolen and then acrylic shawls. This expanded into cotton scarves and dupattas. Pachanbhai wanted to weave a sari for his course collection. Now Puroshottambhai discouraged him. It wasn't practical. They would have to alter the loom and find fine yarns. But Pachanbhai was determined. After renovating the loom and sourcing yarns, he had time to weave only one sari. It was exquisite, moss green with fine patterns and sheen, and for the first time in the village, Pachanbhai introduced bamboo yarn for softness and drape.

Good design comes from a depth of thought, he said. "Weaving is more than livelihood. It is art, a means of achieving respect from the society, and a thread that links me and my brothers." In the final Presentation module, he designed a brand and logo Three Threads, symbolizing warp, weft, and extra weft and the three brothers. Excited, he WhatsApped an image of his design to his brothers. They surprised him by weaving the logo and making the fabric into a shirt for his birthday. SKV got him a cake. It was the first time in his life that he celebrated his birthday.

Pachanbhai graduated with the award for Most Marketable Collection, and the renowned fashion designer Ritu Kumar, a member of his jury, purchased some of his collection for a fashion show for Rajasthan Heritage week.

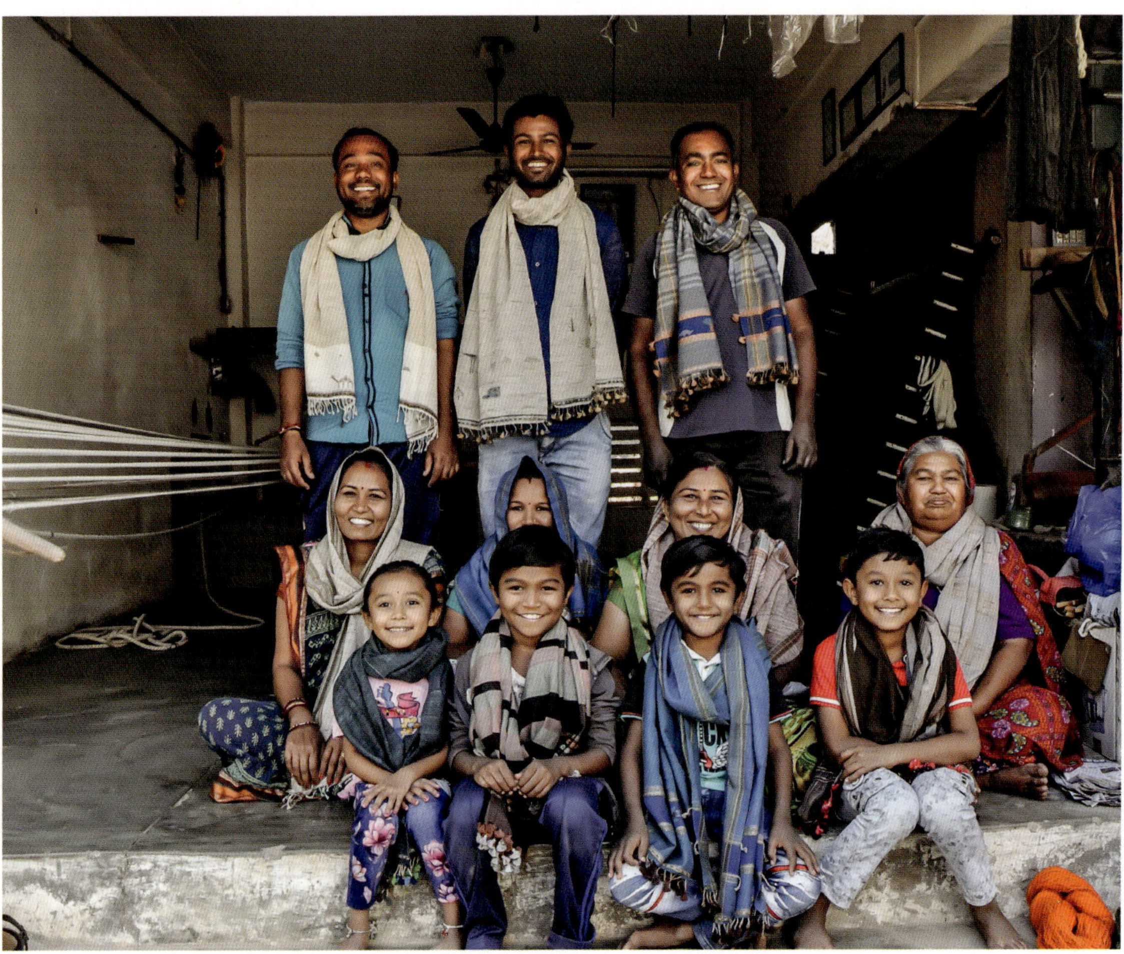

Above: Bhujodi, 2019. Family support is essential for success. Pachanbhai and his elder brothers Puroshottambhai (*left*) and Damjibhai (*right*) work remarkably harmoniously under their brand Three Threads. But there are really more threads: their wives, their mother, and all of their children. *Photo: Judy Frater*

Opposite: Avani Kumaon, 2018. SKV conducted an Outreach program with Avani in which Kutch design graduates shared their experiences innovating within tradition. Collaborating with women weavers, Pachanbhai had his first experience teaching what he had learned, and for the first time the women planned and designed their own work. *Photo: LOkesh Ghai*

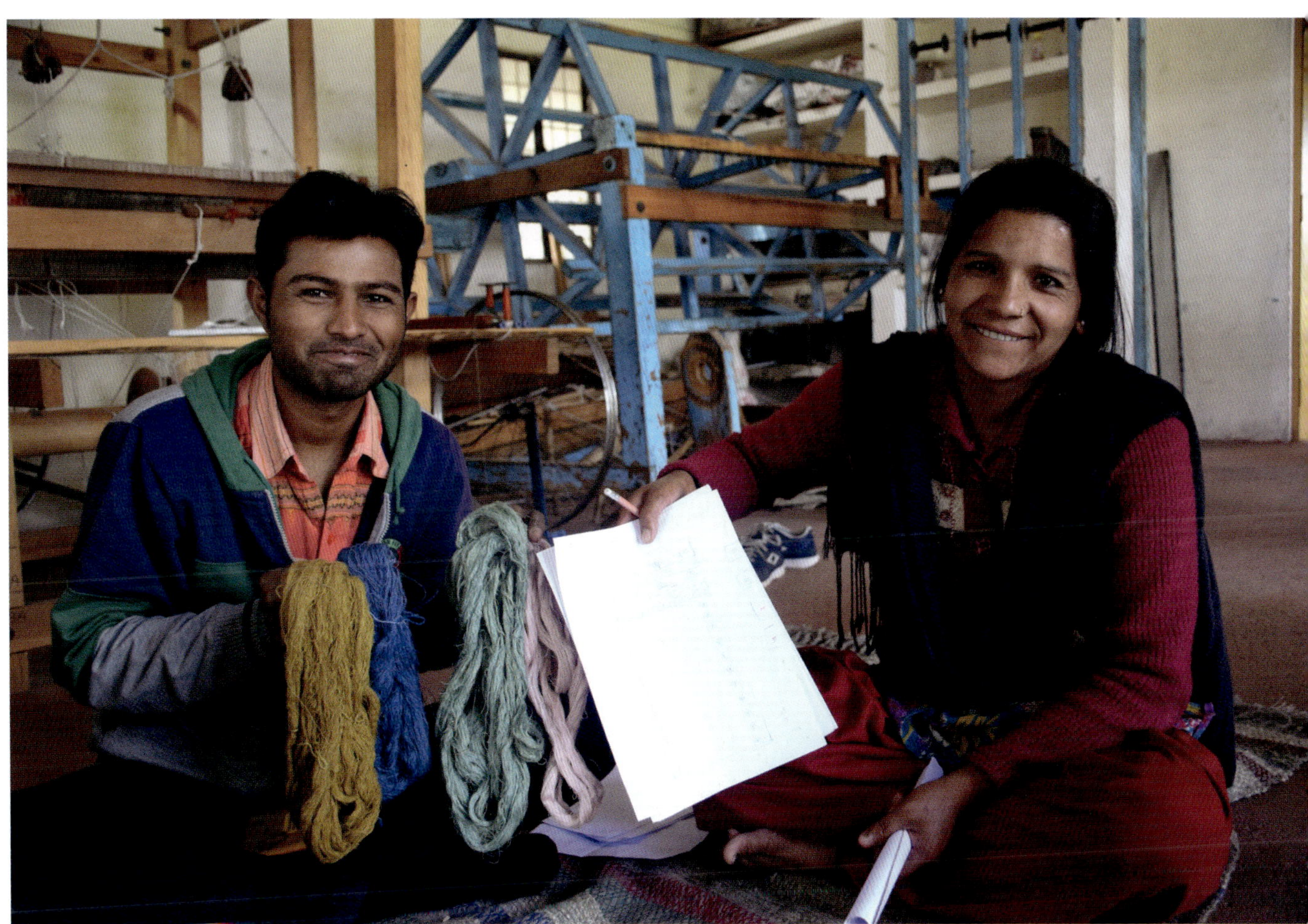

Reversing roles, the next year Pachanbhai urged Puroshottambhai to take the Business and Management for Artisans course. He did, and he developed a stellar collection as well as a solid business plan. The students designed and produced their own exhibition, a memorably excellent show. The first day, a customer wanted a discount on one of Puroshottambhai's saris. She said it was her birthday. Conflicted, Puroshottambhai finally refused. She bought it for full price. "In KRV we learned design; we could create designs with our eyes closed," he said. "But I also learned confidence, and a desire to progress. I wanted people to know me from my work, so I took the SKV BMA course.

"After my BMA, we began to work differently," he continued. "We stopped doing job work. In the beginning we went to four or five exhibitions a year. Once we got clients, we reduced that. Exhibitions are risky. Three good ones are good. We didn't use to do this kind of planning. Our theory is different now. We want ten customers, not a hundred. But they should return to us because our work is good."

Together, the brothers grew Three Threads to a bit beyond the family's capacity. They successfully negotiated terms with India's best-known craft companies and received steady bread-and-butter orders. They worked with boutiques and showcased their work in pop-up exhibitions. They employed four additional weavers.

In 2016, Pachanbhai participated in SKV's first codesign project with the University of Wisconsin. Using the phone app WhatsApp, enlisting help from his nephew to overcome the barriers of literacy and language, and with photos, videos, and video calls, he corresponded with an American design student. They developed his course collection, "Treasures of the Sea," to new levels and created a collection of scarves.

When an opportunity to mentor women weavers in an Outreach project came up in 2018, Pachanbhai quickly volunteered. He and the SKV team took the long, arduous journey into the hills of Kumaon. "The women would not talk to us," he related. So to break the ice, he asked them to take the team to their villages to explore tradition. Pachanbhai enjoyed talking to the elders and learned that the women had previously had bad experiences with teachers, so when they heard the SKV team was coming, they were afraid.

Armed with some background on the region, the women, and weaving traditions, he began. "We had to teach," he said. This was his first experience. "At first it was hard. We had to really get a grasp on what we knew about design. But the women understood, because we taught in their language—not just Hindi, but the language of craft."

Pachanbhai realized that teaching was about encouraging creativity and building confidence. One woman said she couldn't work because she had been possessed by black magic, he recalled. He convinced her that just working anyway was the best remedy. The women were skeptical about making so much extra effort. "When they come to the jury and the exhibition, they will know," he predicted. "I used to want only easy work. Now that I am independent, I like challenging designs."

The most gratifying experience was when one woman cried because she felt she didn't know anything. She felt limited because she did only plain weave.

Pachanbhai walked her to the shop. "What do you see here?" he asked.

Plain weave, for the high-end market.

"So is it not a design?"

Still dubious, she said she wasn't educated; she couldn't read or write.

That came up again and again; the women had been convinced of their insurmountable obstacles. With a huge grin, he laughed. "I can't read either!" he said. "So it's no excuse."

Upon return, within just three weeks Pachanbhai designed and wove two splendid saris inspired by his experience. He had never been to the mountains before. His inspiration was a pine cone. But he had learned much more. He created a whole collection of one-of-a-kind saris. The warp was common, but in each one he made unique weft and extra-weft patterns, all evoking the pine cone. In the project exhibition, he priced his saris at double the price of other saris. And he had the highest sales every day—a huge learning experience for everyone.

In 2019, Pachanbhai's opportunity was a codesign project with artisans in Oaxaca, Mexico. "My first codesign experience was with a student, and there was a big gap," he said. "Here, we are all artisans. I knew that a theme enables clear vision. So my first priority was deciding a theme." His partner Moises lived in a mountain village and shared beautiful images of hills and clouds. Pachanbhai began with clouds. "Then we must think of a story," he continued. "I thought, many times we see abstract things in the sky. I am a weaver, so I see our traditional motifs. Others will see things related to their work. From this story we could share our worlds. So we chose the theme Story of Clouds.

"When you collaborate," he concluded, "it is a different kind of enjoyment, because there is effort and enthusiasm from both sides. It is win-win."

Having missed out on formal education, Pachanbhai wanted to make sure that his children would have the best education possible. He enrolled his elder son at an English medium school. But observing, the brothers realized that English medium education was not that much better, and meanwhile, the children were not learning Gujarati. Weavers speak Kutchi, a scriptless language, and learn the state language at school. So Pachanbhai sent his younger son to a Gujarati medium school.

On a quiet evening, I watched the family children enthusiastically playing marbles together. "They are playing," he pointed out, "because we don't let them have phones." He understood the importance

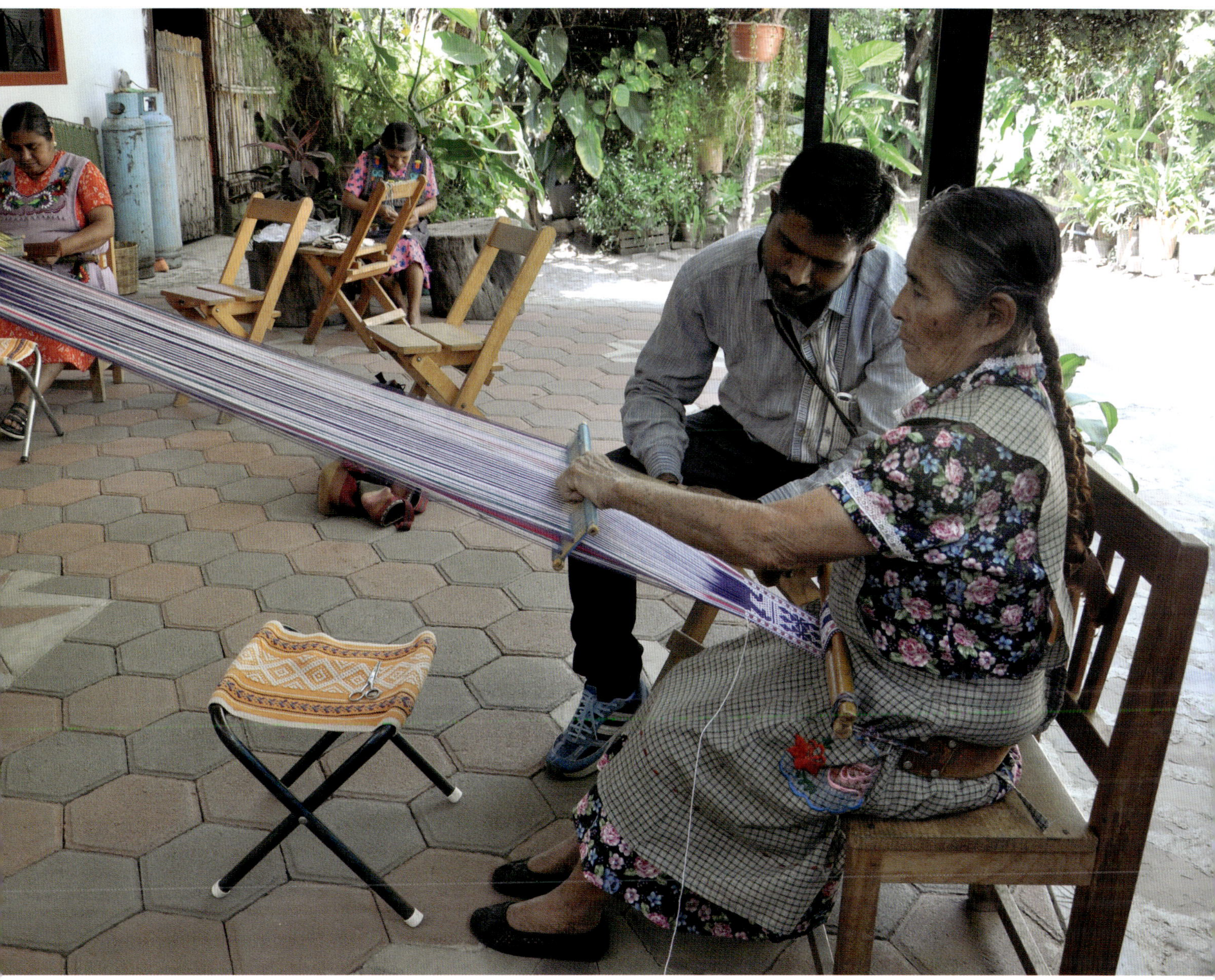

Santo Tomás Jalieza, 2022. Pachanbhai met traditional backstrap weavers in Santo Tomas Jalieza, Oaxaca, studying their technique and getting ideas. Later, he taught his extra-weft techniques to weavers in San Pedro Cajonos, his codesign partner's mountain village. *Photo: Judy Frater*

of observation, connection, experience. Phones would come later. He wanted their grounding to be in the real, material world.

After experiencing the toxicity of pollution, Pachanbhai became mindful of the environment. Studying at Somaiya Kala Vidya deepened his concern. In his personal time, he slowly and intricately wove extra-weft-patterned stories of man and nature, rural life and industrialization, and climate change. When he began the design course, he said his dream was to participate in the International Folk Art Market | Santa Fe. For 2020, he applied with his climate change collection.

The last question in the application was, Why should IFAM give you financial aid? Most artisans respond with their limited resources. Pachanbhai thought a few minutes. Then he smiled confidently and said, "Because my work is excellent!

"If I am selected," he elaborated, "it will be an inspiration for other small-scale artisans. And I would be grateful to share my message about the environment with an international audience."

He was selected but could not get a visa to attend. He sent his collection and studied the sales report. People appreciated his stories, he felt, and they preferred indigo to neutral colors. So the next year he applied with his Oaxaca "Story of Clouds" collection. He included the ponchos from his Oaxaca experience. And on his tag, he put a QR code linking to a monsoon song that he had used for inspiration. He wove just a few more pieces than had sold the previous year, and his collection sold out. Again, he could not get a visa to attend the event.

But in 2022, Pachanbhai and Adilbhai were able to visit Oaxaca to teach workshops and share their codesign experiences, and Pachanbhai visited his partner Moises in his mountain village. Using his cross-cultural teaching experiences, he joyfully connected with his Mexican students. Quickly, he found Gujarati to Spanish on a phone app translator and added an important step—listening to the app's version of what he said and finding a way to rephrase when there were errors. He managed to convey his philosophies and humor along with weaving technicalities.

"I enjoyed seeing my partners' weaving," he said. "They put on a new warp for each piece, which gives them freedom, and they are very enthusiastic about doing something new. Today, we weave for the market and put on a warp for ten to twenty pieces. I learned that we could do one at a time; to do something new, we should have this patience."

These observations segued into a discussion on scale. Pachanbhai is not interested in weaving in bulk. But the question is, how to grow? And how to remain an artist? Does the artist have to end up supervising others less talented? Pachanbhai said the answer is to focus on how much you need. And to give others ownership. If your colleagues are responsible, he said, they will focus on work rather than thinking about what they're doing after work or what they're having for dinner. Supervising in the usual sense, he said, doesn't result in good quality.

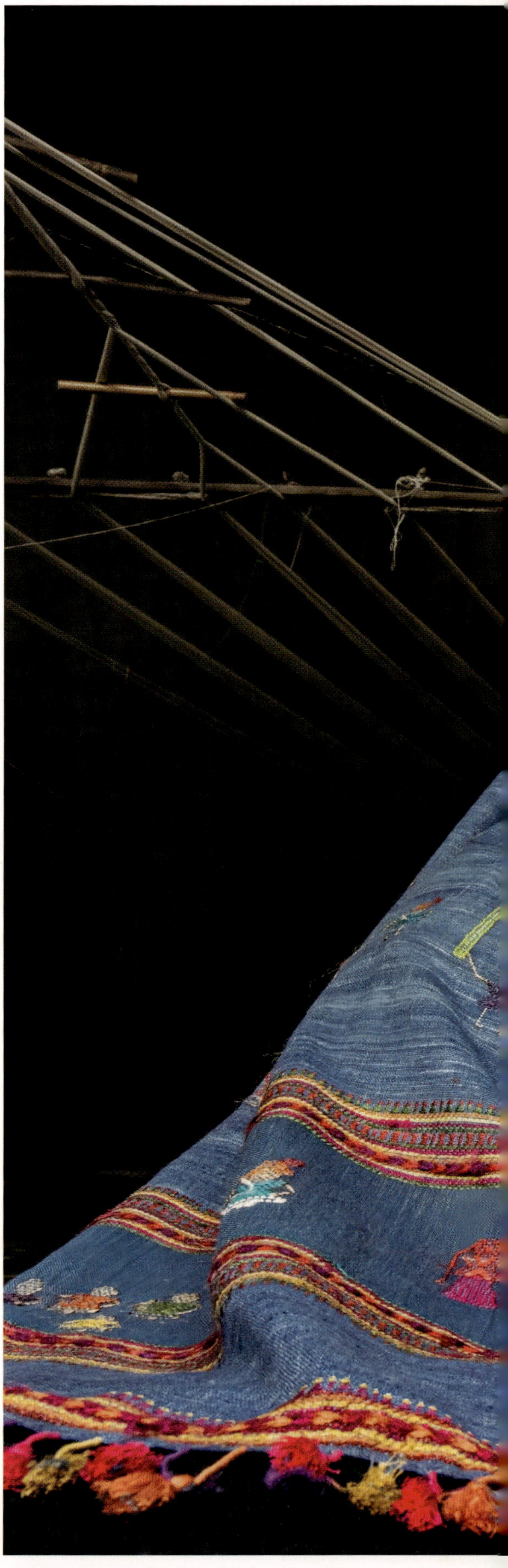

Bhujodi, 2022. Pachanbhai shows a video of highlights of his nephew's engagement. The scarf that he wove for this book illustrates the film, he points out. He wears it with the memories of many ceremonies past. *Photo: Nevada Wier*

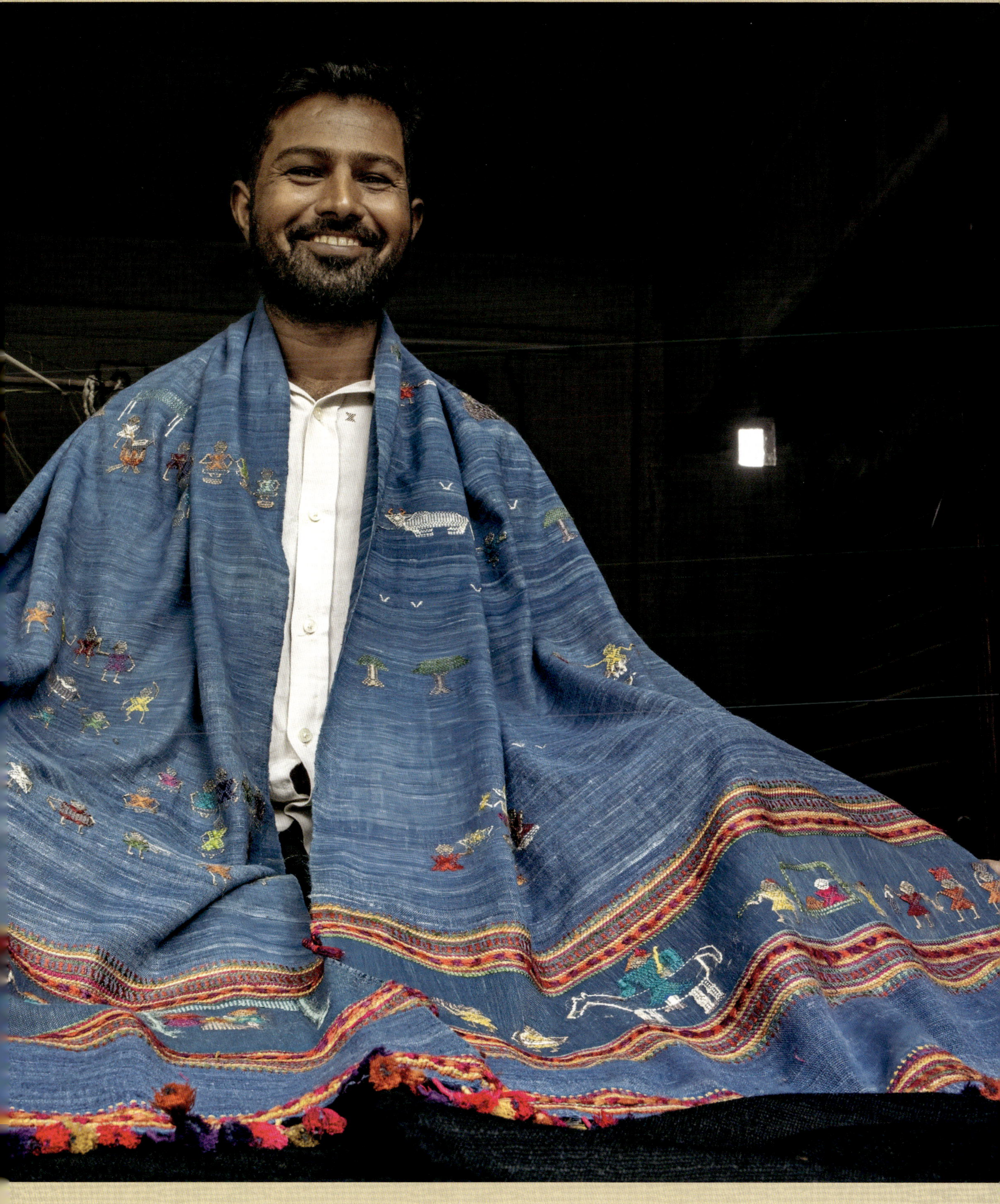

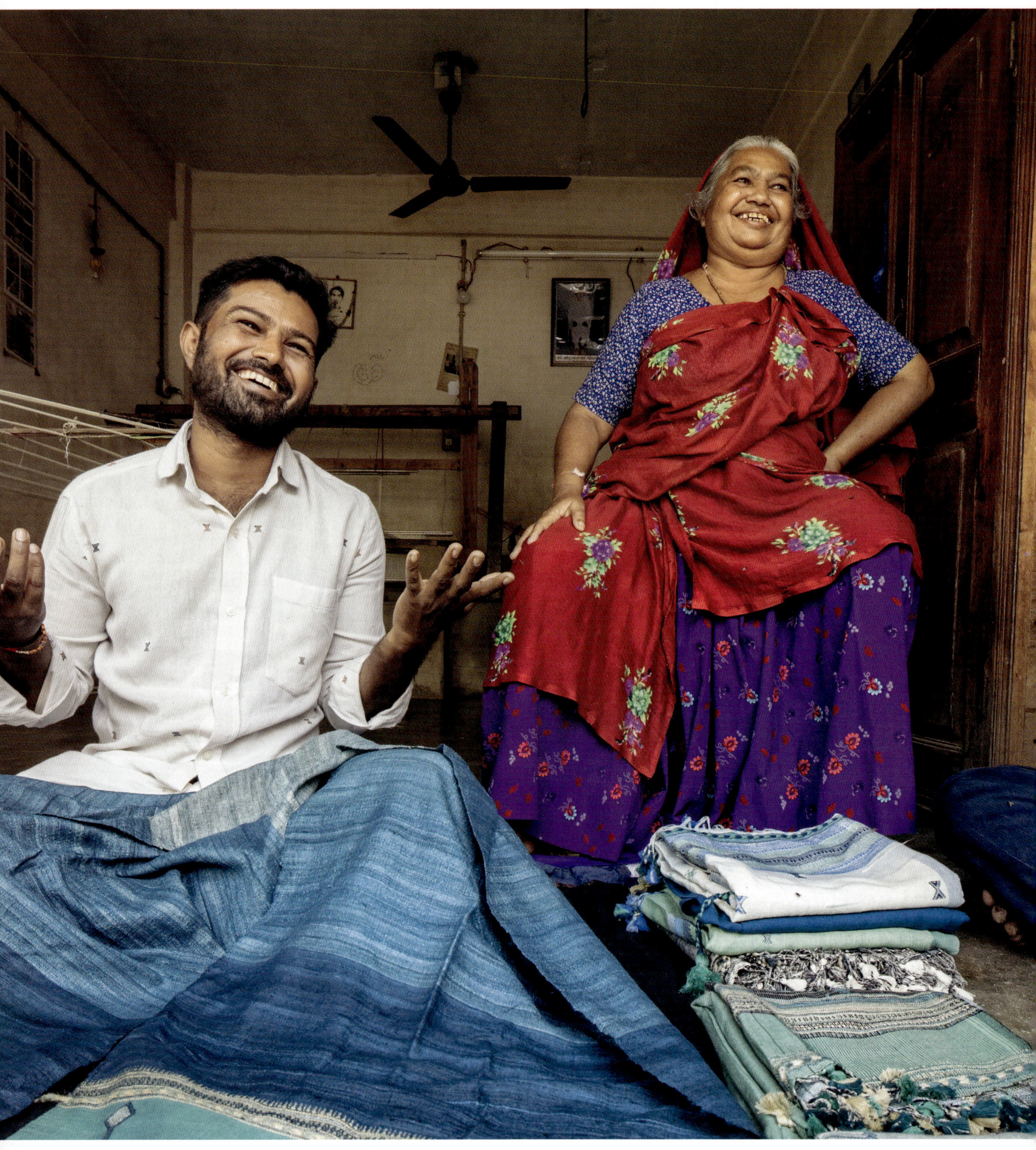

Above: Bhujodi, 2022. Living together, joint family members intimately share work and social life. The community is an extension of family, where relatives and friends are hard to distinguish. *Photo: Nevada Wier*

Right: Pachanbhai designed his logo during his design course. Three Threads refers to the warp, weft, and extra-weft yarns of weaving, and to the three brothers.

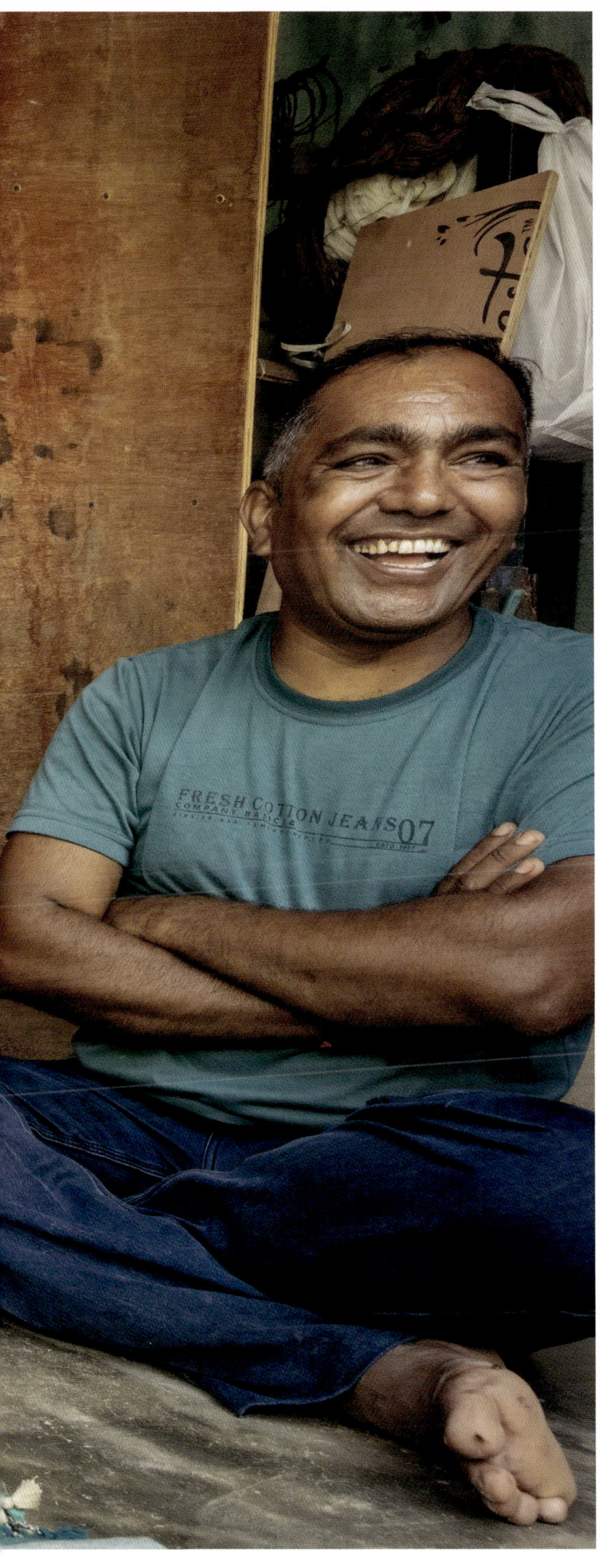

2022

Pachanbhai, Damjibhai, and Puroshottambhai work as a team. We decide everything together, they say—Three Threads. You have to have courage—and support! No one checks on anyone. We each do our own work and trust each other.

"If God gives you a gift, you should use it," Pachanbhai says. "You must know your strengths and not experiment with them. And you should not make craft cheap, because if you do, you will be working for money and not from the heart—and that is the strength of craft."

Three Threads has achieved success and recognition. But it comes with a price. Within the close quarters of the weavers' society, every move has a repercussion. Many who have not enjoyed design and BMA education see craft today as a zero-sum game. Pachanbhai's mother has insight from experience. "This is not new," she tells him. "It has been there from the beginning."

Pachanbhai respects his mother's wisdom. And he weaves the gems of her heartwarming philosophy into his next collection.

"My work should have a story, culture, and our heritage woven into it," he says.

The ponchos, shawls, and scarves, richly colored and textured, are juried into the 2023 International Folk Art Market. And Pachanbhai gets a visa at the eleventh hour and has the chance to see their success in the US.

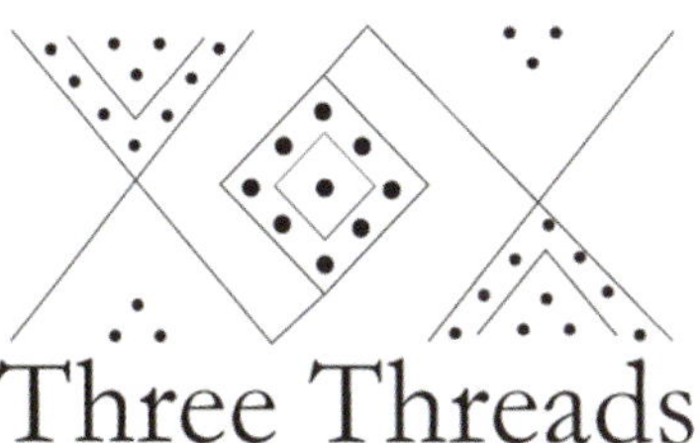

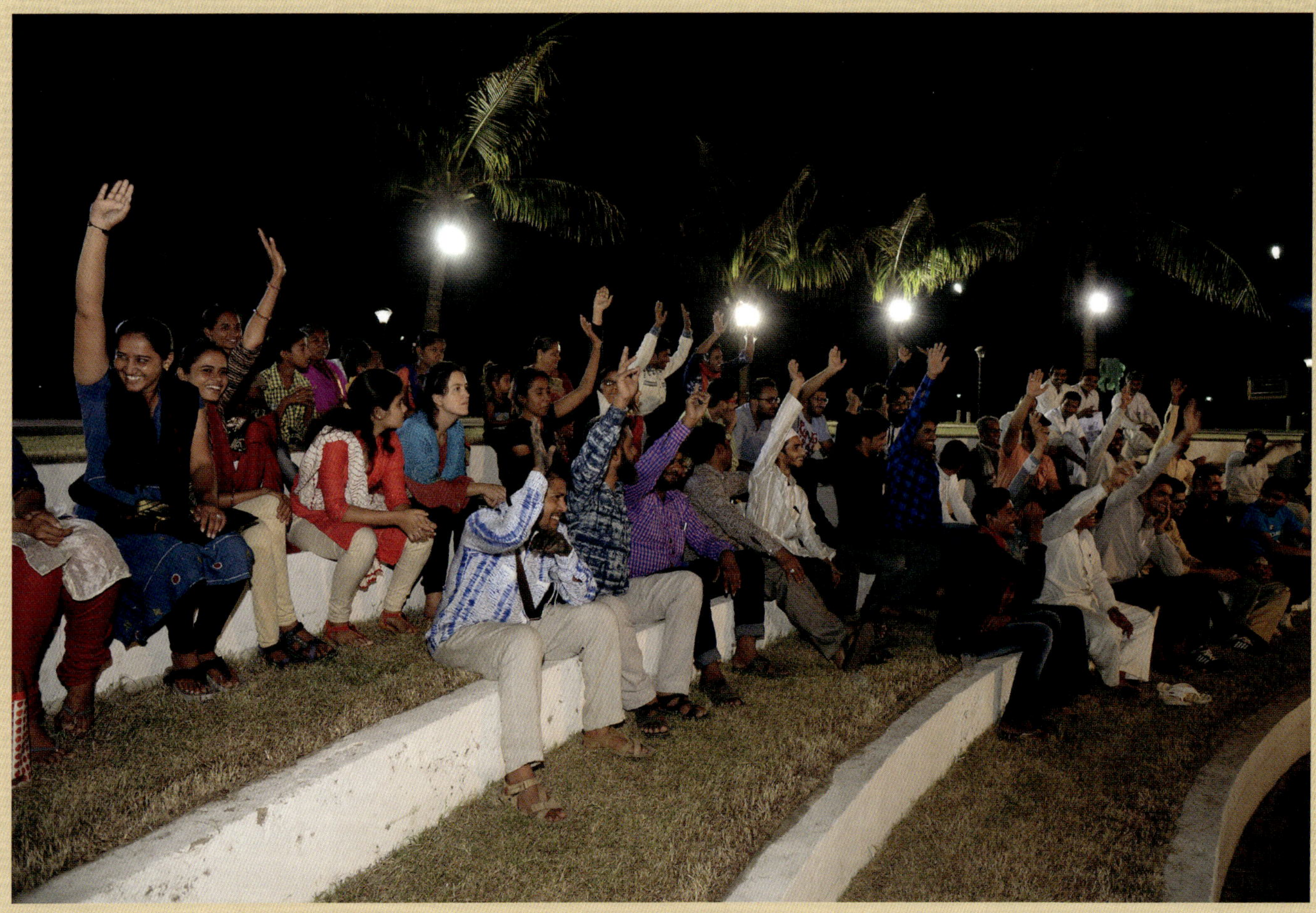

What about artisans' desires?

~Dahyalalbhai Kudecha

Sharma Resorts, 2015. At the first seminar for the artisan designer community in the outdoor amphitheater of Sharma Resorts, a jury member asked who promised to teach their children their craft traditions. *Photo: Ketan Pomal, L.M. Studio*

Chapter 16

PERSISTENT ISSUES: REVISITING THE IDEAL OF THE ARTISAN DESIGNER

The artisan designer community filled the amphitheater under tall coconut palms in the cool autumn evening. Facing them on the stage was the 2015 jury, including the renowned fashion designer Ritu Kumar; Anuradha Kumra, of Fabindia; Dr. Reena Bhatia, of Maharaja Sayajirao University of Baroda; and Gita Ram, of Crafts Council of India. After the tenth class of education for artisans, they were discussing how to take their work from "handicraft" to design craft.

Although they did not get many answers from the experts, the artisan designers identified the questions:

Dahyalalbhai Kudecha, *weaver*—"We always talk about customers' demands. What about artisans' desires? Do we ever think what artisans actually want?"

Adilbhai Khatri, *bandhani artist*—"Should craft be mass produced?"

Khalidbhai Usman Khatri, *Ajrakh artist*—"I have a huge order for one of my products, but I have limited production capacity. Should I take the order?"

Azizbhai Khatri, *bandhani artist*—"How can we solve the problem of design copying? Screen printers are printing bandhani designs in huge quantities. How can we make designs that can't be copied?"

Soyabbhai Khatri, *Ajrakh artist*—"All design and BMA graduates have created our brands. But how can we promote ourselves in the market?"

Laxmiben Parmar, *suf embroidery artist*—"I created new motifs, explained my concept and my work. But customers advised me to stick to tradition. What exactly does 'The Market' want?"

LOkesh Ghai, *faculty*—"How can artisan designers and urban designers work together?"

After a decade of education for artisans and building an artisan designer community, after creating extraordinary innovations within traditions, artisan designers still struggled with persistent issues.

The most challenging is the deep-rooted, insidious conception of who artisans are. Government schemes give handloom weavers work in terms of plain white bedsheets for the Indian Railways and yardage for school uniforms and hold workshops to teach them weaving; designers and well-meaning NGOs give them orders for yardage for garments for which the designers and organizations will command high prices and earn a name. Again and again, artisans are portrayed in images of hands without a head. The perception of artisans as skilled workers is so pervasive that it occludes other realities.

The widely perceived solution of "helping" poor artisans earn more is product oriented rather than artisan oriented and implies reinforcing a mutually accepted social hierarchy. Frustrated by a project for weavers in which a stated goal was to "create the iPad of weaving," I brought the project team to Kutch to hear what weaver design graduates actually wanted.

"Who here considers himself successful?" I asked the group.

All hands shot up.

"OK. So, what is success?" I asked.

Success is achieving goals, they answered. It is decision-making power and targeting your market. Success is using your creativity, having your own concepts and identity, and being able to articulate them. Success is having a voice and being able to take responsibility. "You must value your own work," Puroshottambhai said. "Otherwise, your customer won't."

Strikingly, not one artisan spoke of success in terms of money (and certainly not in terms of product).

"Money was an early goal," Dahyabhai said. "Now I want to be my own person."

I asked if their goals had changed because of design and business education.

Prakashbhai laughed. "Before the course, we had no goals!" he said.

Visibility and valuation of the artisan as a creative individual rather than a worker have been intrinsic goals of my work. I have invited people prominent in the craft and design worlds as jury members and chief guests at convocations and included artist presentations for customers in pop-up exhibitions to provide experiences of artisans creating and presenting their work. The 2015 seminar and one in Delhi in 2016 provided public opportunities for artisan designers to articulate their views to similar audiences of people concerned with handcraft.

The question about the role of urban designers identified another area in which exposure and experience were needed. Urban designers were here to stay, and many wanted to work with craft. Codesign seemed like an appropriate solution. I had included codesign in the Collection Development module, bringing design students from urban institutes to work with artisan design students—with the enforced caveat that the artisan designers were engaging the urban design students to help them, and not the more common reverse. The urban students almost always concluded that their appreciation of artisan designers had multiplied.

In the original BMA curriculum, the grand finale was a high-level internship, another opportunity for codesign. For the BMA class of 2014, I carefully matched each graduate with a sensitive, creative, and successful designer. Not one partnership materialized. Artisan designers and designers each had reasons for the failure—different and similar. Listening to both sides, I realized that the barrier was the same mutually perceived power imbalance—real or imagined. Designers assume that artisans can't think creatively, and artisans assume that they cannot dialogue with designers. "We don't like to work with designers," one artisan designer declared. "They tell us what to do." Another shared that he worked with one designer only after he demanded that she stay at his home and observe the family weaving for three days.

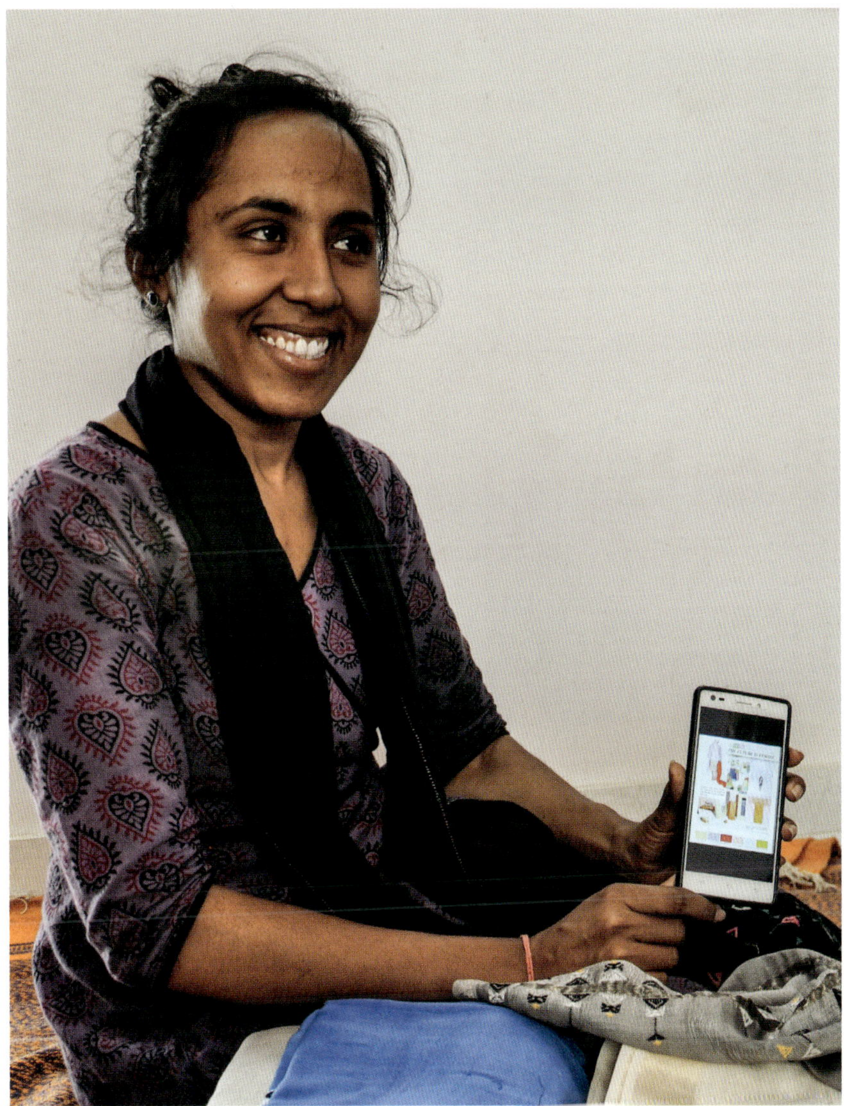

Faradi, 2017. Codesign had been part of the design curriculum since 2008. In 2016, I initiated a virtual international codesign program with University of Wisconsin–Madison design students. Artisan design graduates quickly learned to use WhatsApp to share ideas. The distance actually mitigated persistent issues of social hierarchy. *Photo: Judy Frater*

So in 2016, when a proposal to create a program of long-distance collaboration came from the University of Wisconsin–Madison, I welcomed the opportunity to develop a genuine, equitable method of codesign. A key point of the program was to work as equals, in addition to making fresh designs. The artisan designers met challenges of language, culture, and time zone differences to collaborate with American students they had not met. Most interesting, it seemed that the distance and electronic communication had an equalizing effect on the usual power imbalance.

Domestic codesign experiments reiterated the challenges. In a project with an Indian institute, despite the absence of language barriers, artisan designers felt discounted. The problem was another level of communication. When there is a power differential, the socially more powerful partner can easily justify an illusion of a partner's engagement. A faculty member of another Indian institute spent a year developing relationships with artisan designers. Finally, when he clicked with one, the artisan designer exclaimed, "This is real codesign! We are working as an equal team."

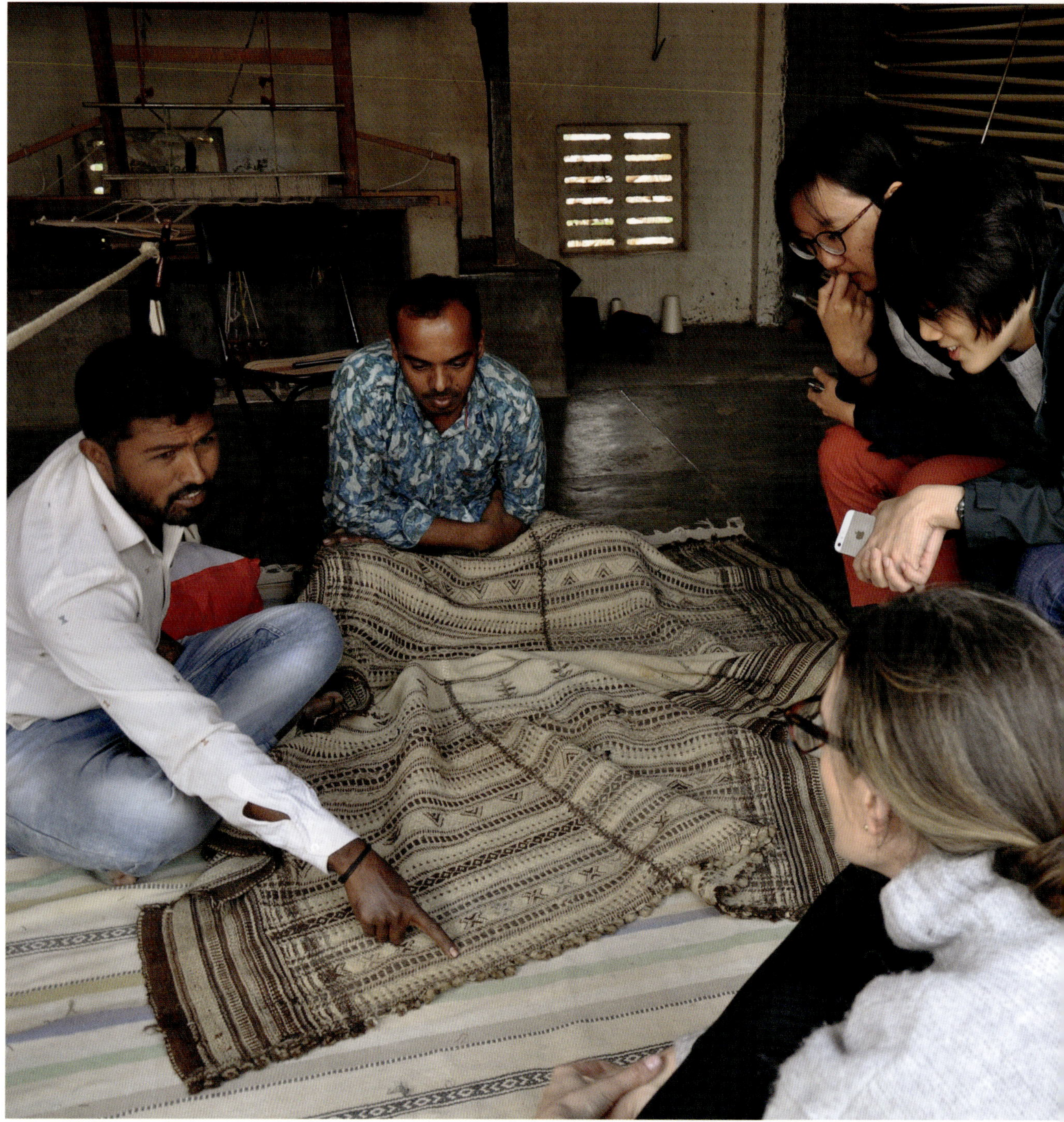

Other persistent issues ensue from the perception of craft as manufacturing. There is tremendous pressure from many directions for artisans to scale up. The pressure manifests desire without understanding or valuing craft. The demand for volumes of weaving, printing, bandhani, and embroidery is mind boggling. Dr. Ismailbhai Khatri, senior Ajrakh artist and advisor, returning from a seminar on indigo, summarized, "They want natural indigo, lots of it, and at cheap prices. How is that possible?" A reputed designer noted that today it is difficult to differentiate between handloom and power loom fabrics, and the customer wants them at the same price. The question then is "Why handcraft?" If the answer is "Because I like it" or "Craft should be democratized," that is not enough. Craft is made by artisans, and the quality of their lives in addition to income will determine the sustainability of craft traditions.

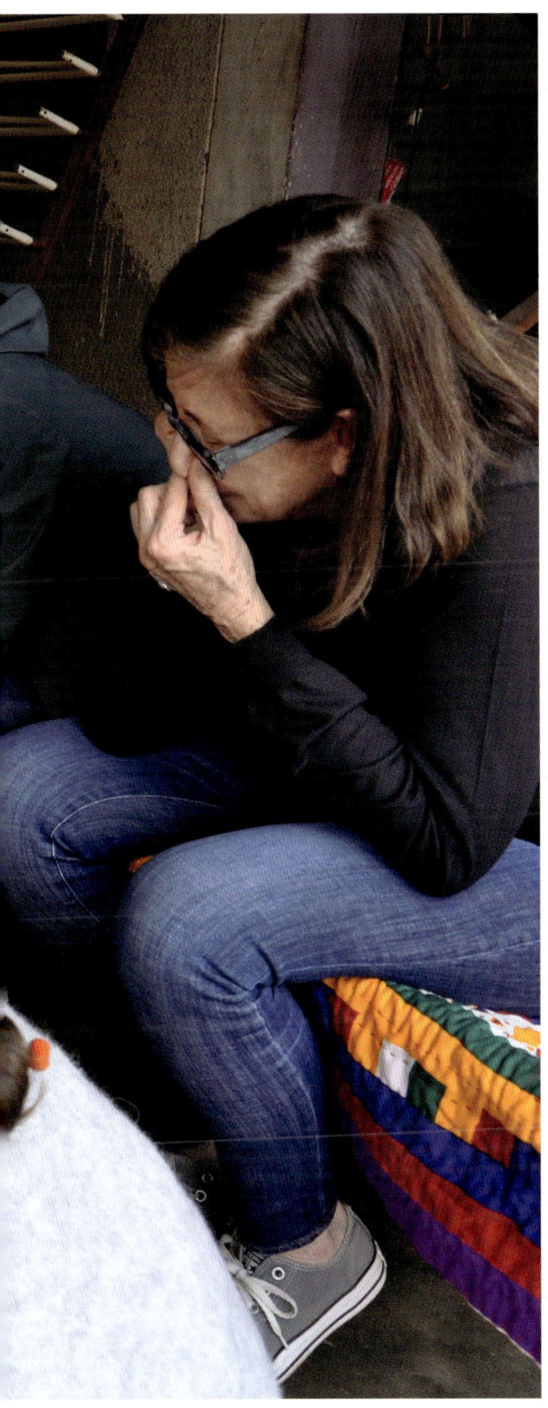

Bhujodi, 2020. Kutch enjoys robust tourist traffic. However, most tours visit the few well-known artisans. I launched Open Studio Tours to provide design graduates with experience of direct connection with craft aficionados, and to provide a fresh experience to visitors. *Photo: Judy Frater*

Scaling up generates additional issues. Artisans who can produce in scale have attained wealth and recognition, and to meet increasing demands they employ artisans who don't have the means to produce as their workers. Traditionally, members of artisan communities were of more or less equal status. When economically stronger individuals become "master artisans," they gain higher social as well as economic status, and the perception of the artisan as worker reemerges in a new, socially threatening form.

And with increasing competition as artisans enter a world of scale and design, copying becomes an inevitable issue. By 2020, 181 artisans had graduated in design, and sixteen had graduated from the BMA program. Among them, I had seen no duplication in final collection work. And yet, in the market, copies of their work abounded, for the most part made by artisans who were not graduates.

As artisans became artisan designers, they articulated the persistent issues of their world. I believed they would have to formulate the answers as well, so I began to organize more seminars. Along with the 2017 jury, we held a seminar titled "Coping with Copying." Artisan designers and jury members had innumerable experiences with copying. But what to do?

We have to distinguish between traditional designs, which belong to the community, and those created by graduates of the design course, the artisan designers concluded—and between copying and taking inspiration. They all agreed that they had no interest in copying but acknowledged that they had to take full advantage of their hard work. You will be copied, they said, and you have to move on. But they agreed to shun companies and designers who copied or asked them to copy.

With the 2018 jury we held a seminar, "Who Are the Workers?," to discuss the more sensitive and difficult issue of scale. A group of alumni produced a skit on the topic, in which they equated the levels of artisans with grass, deer, and lions—a cyclic food chain in which the bigger eats the smaller. They said, we will teach beginners who will then become artisans, then designers, and then master artisans. But everyone knew it was not so simple.

Zuberbhai, bandhani artisan designer, articulated the issue from another perspective: "How does someone who has been working for someone come forward?"

The group discussed paying workers fairly and agreed they must teach their children to ensure that their traditions continue. But the fact remains that no one wants to be a worker. The artisans who come to learn design dream of having their own business. Jabbarbhai Habib Khatri, class of 2019, was a job work printer for five years. "How long can you print yardage?" he asked. "I have never made a product, never made a corner." He got a large printing table and decided to take the design course.

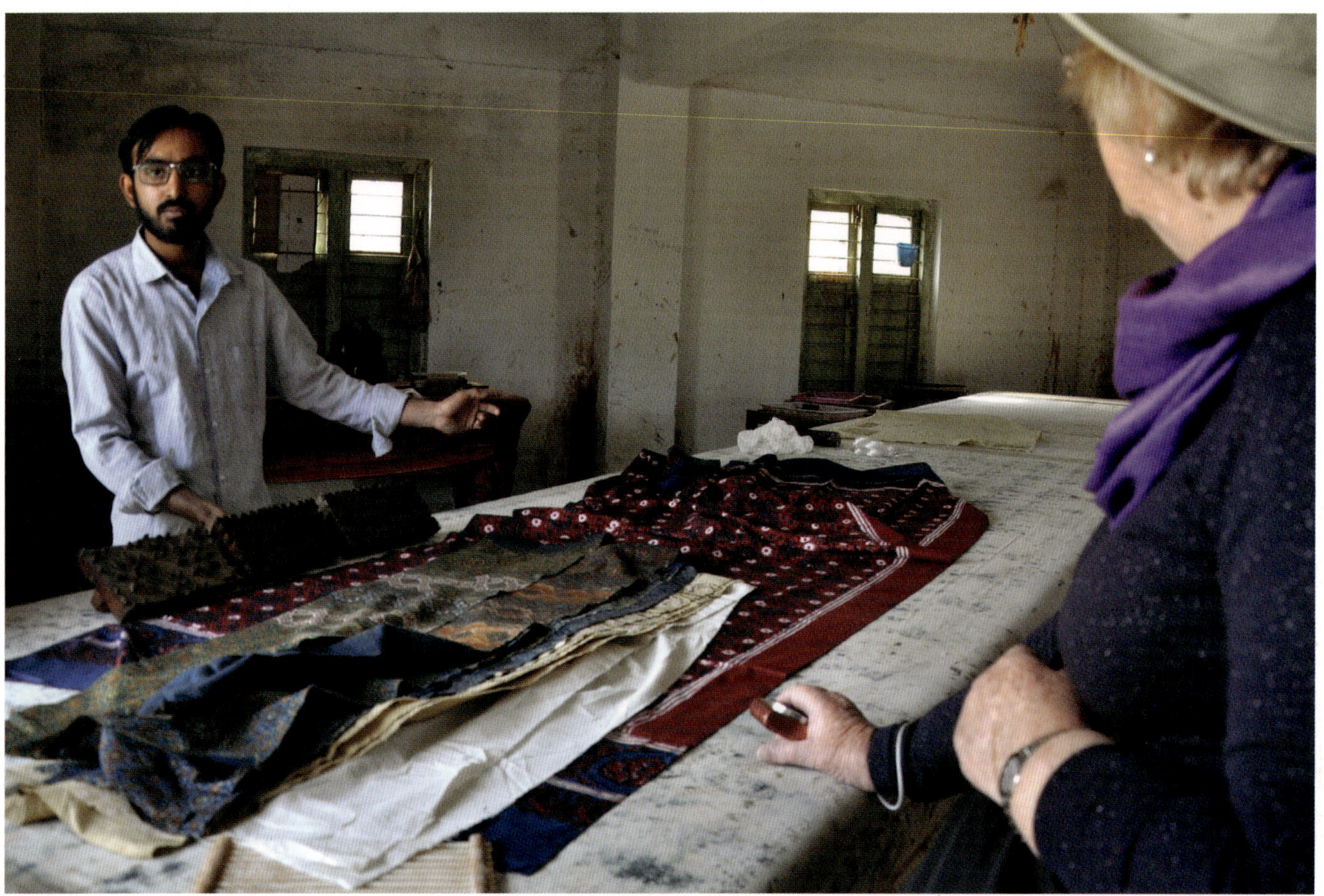

For the small emerging artisan designer who wants to work creatively, visibility and recognition are challenges. Kutch fortunately enjoys substantial tourism; markets come to artisans' doorsteps. But, as in most tourist places, visitors and new clients contact the same few economically stronger artisans who have been able to develop business networks.

For years, I had conducted workshops with artisans to generate value for craft traditions. In 2016 I began to think of the open studio tours organized by groups of artists in the US and Europe, and in 2017 I launched an experiment in Bhujodi and Ajrakhpur, villages where many weavers and Ajrakh printer design graduates live.

It was a mutually beneficial idea: visitors would interact with artists and take home more than a product—a special behind-the-scenes experience. Less known artisan designers would have direct contact with potential clients. And as the dates were planned, artisans would not be annoyed by interruptions but be ready to welcome visitors. The design graduates decided to designate three hosts for each tour, and that there would be no sales till the end, when everyone would display together in a small exhibition.

After the first season, it was clear that there were even more benefits. The artisan designers had risen to internally manage the tours. They realized that interaction with guests provides opportunity to overcome barriers of inhibitions. They had begun to consider the visitor's experience. "Open Studio Tours are a human exchange, not just a commercial one," Pavanbhai declared.

As 2019 drew to a close, the class of artisans entering the design world was asked to name the most important part of their work. They all said the craftsmanship—the tying in bandhani, the printing in Ajrakh, and the weaving in weaving—the part that "master artisans" are no longer doing! For their upcoming final show, they set conservative goals. They didn't have helpers, they said. Until now they had themselves been workers. Other workers were already working elsewhere. So they planned to make their own collections.

I became anxious. Would that be enough work? Are ten saris and thirty stoles enough to justify the expense of attending an outstation show? And then I caught myself. The concept of the artisan designer is exactly that—doing it oneself. The artisan designer is an artist, not a producer.

The students held their exhibition in Ahmedabad and pronounced it a success, and they began to plan developing their practices in earnest.

Finally, there is the conundrum of "The Market." How to connect to a market that appreciates handcraft, how to break in, how to know what that market wants? *Market Forces* was the next seminar that I planned but never conducted. I wanted to hear from artisan designers about how they defined their relationship to "The Market" that they know, and to ask them how they imagined the ideal market for new designs.

And then came COVID-19. Artisan designers assessed the situation and thought creatively. They used lockdown time to build new workshops, create new designs, make more-intricate and more-valuable work, and learn to navigate online and reach out to worlds beyond.

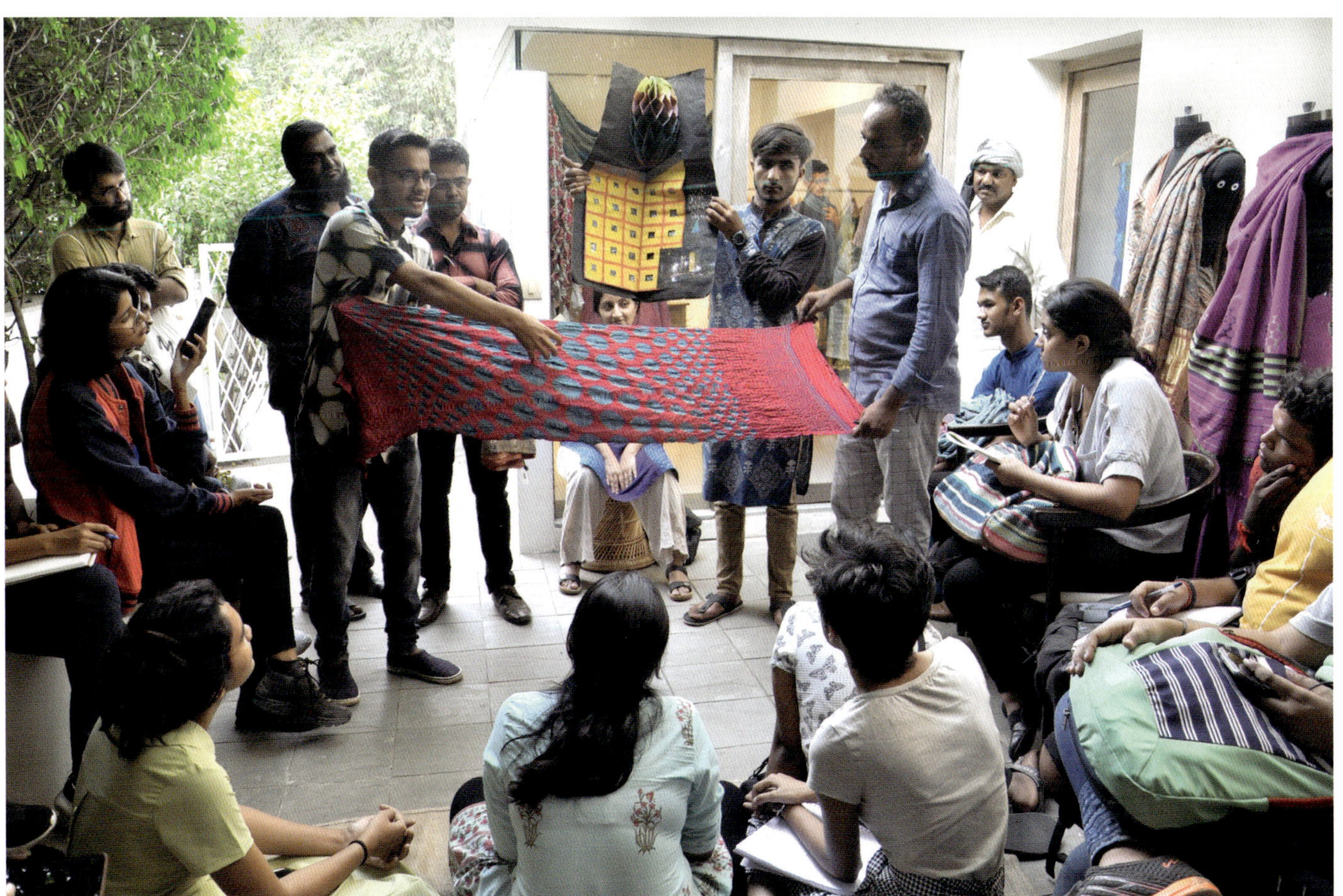

Opposite: Ajrakhpur, 2018. An added benefit from Open Studio Tours was the opportunity for artisan designer groups to share experiences, manage, and optimize the events. *Photo: Judy Frater*

Above: Ahmedabad, 2019. Within a year, artisan students learn to effectively present their work. Articulation enhances value, so I included daily public presentations during the pop-up exhibitions that culminated the course. Customers and students mutually benefited. *Photo: Judy Frater*

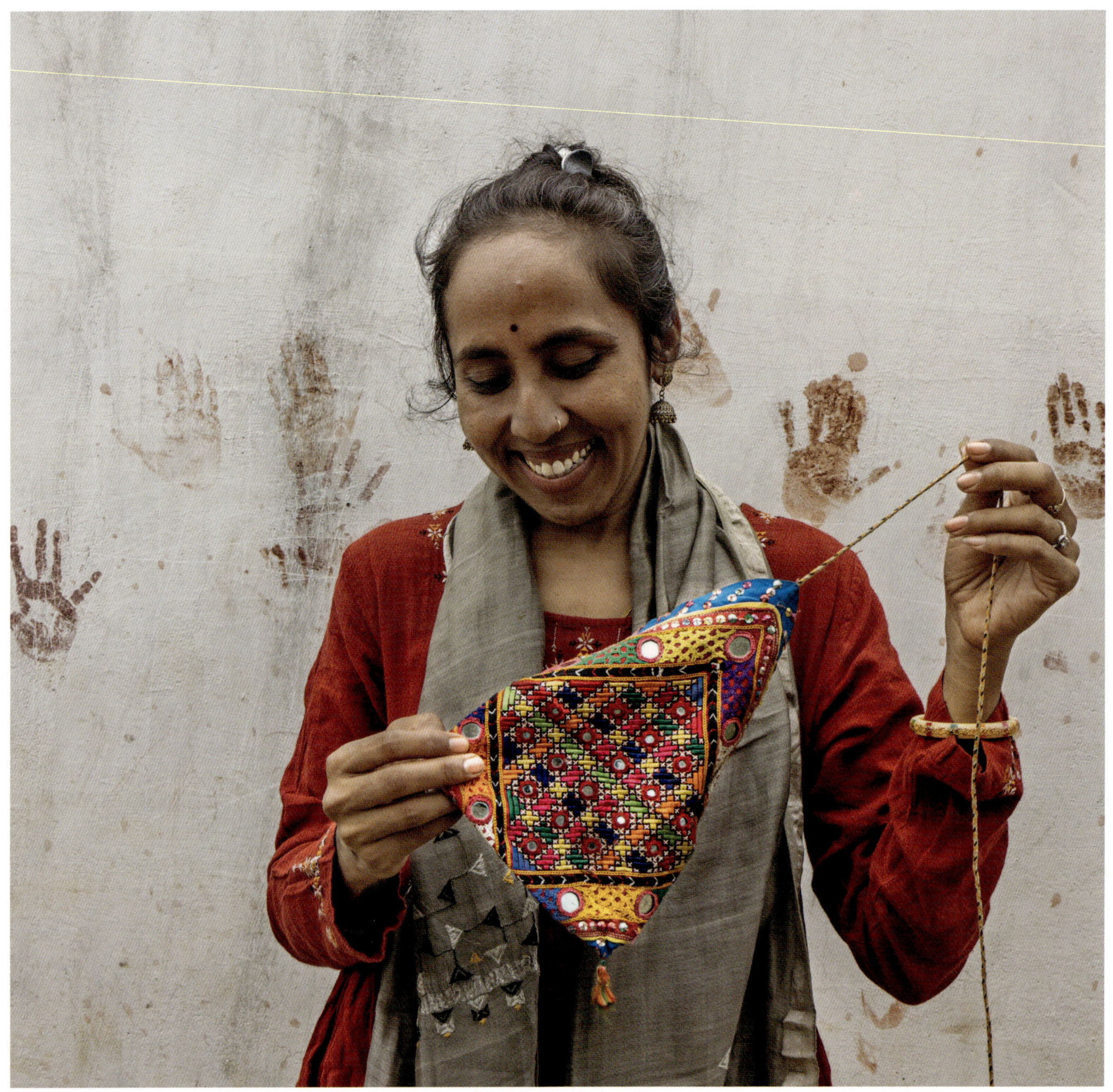

We had learned the language of design, we were doing work, but we didn't know about business. We learned that in the BMA course.

~Tulsiben Purshottam Puvar

Above: Faradi, 2022. Tradition is the inspiration to which artisan designers always return. The *bagchi*, a bag presented to the groom, was embroidered by Tulsiben's mother in kharek style. Tulsiben embroidered her scarf in contemporary suf style in a UW Madison codesign project. *Photo: Nevada Wier*

Opposite: Sharma Resorts, 2018. Quiet and reticent, Tulsiben gained confidence through regular presentations in design and BMA classes. *Photo: Ketan Pomal, L.M. Studio*

Chapter 17

TULSIBEN PURSHOTTAM PUVAR: CHALLENGING LIMITATIONS

Listening to the discussion about retaining workers in large-scale production, and wondering how small-scale artisans can grow, the seminar moderator wants to talk about cooperation. He says, "There are three embroiderers who work together; they can share their experiences with you."

Tulsiben takes the mic. "Before that, I want to ask a question to all our advisors and our artisan designers," she says. "Everybody keeps saying that artisans should succeed and become artisan designers and start their own businesses. If everybody becomes an artisan designer, who will do the production?"

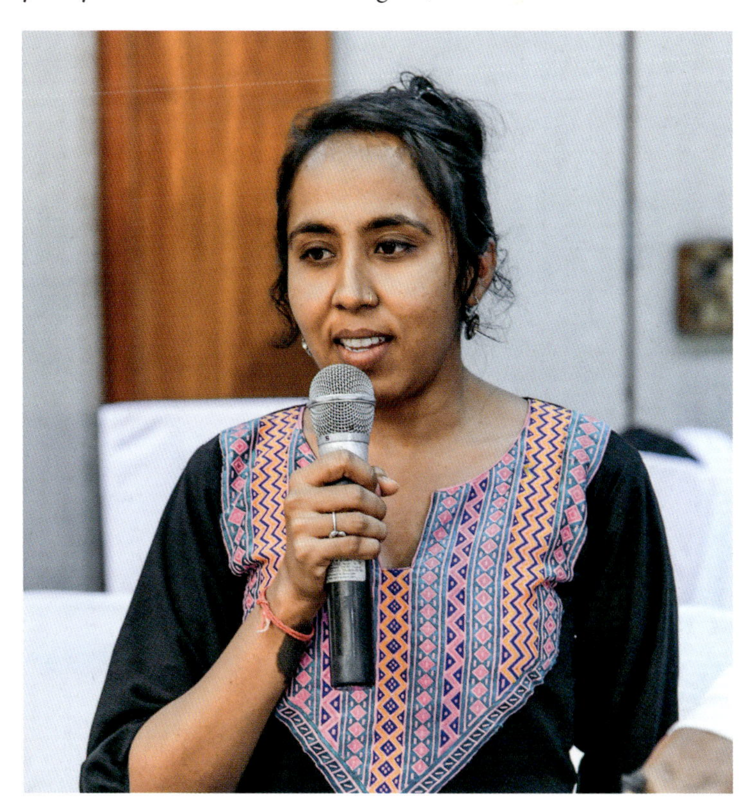

A jury panelist responds, "I don't feel that in any society everyone is capable of designing, so it will never happen that there are only designers and nobody to work."

Tulsiben is not entertaining that. "If we share our experience with other artisans," she says, "they will also want to learn and participate on a deeper level."

This is the wisdom of an artisan who has been there, who has learned, grown, and taught others.

Tulsiben's family emigrated from Sindh in 1972 and finally settled in Faradi, a village in southern Kutch, where she was born. Her father used to cut diamonds in Surat. Today he is a truck driver on the route from Bhuj to Morbi. Her mother does housework and embroidery for home use. The third of four siblings, Tulsiben studied through the seventh grade. She enjoyed

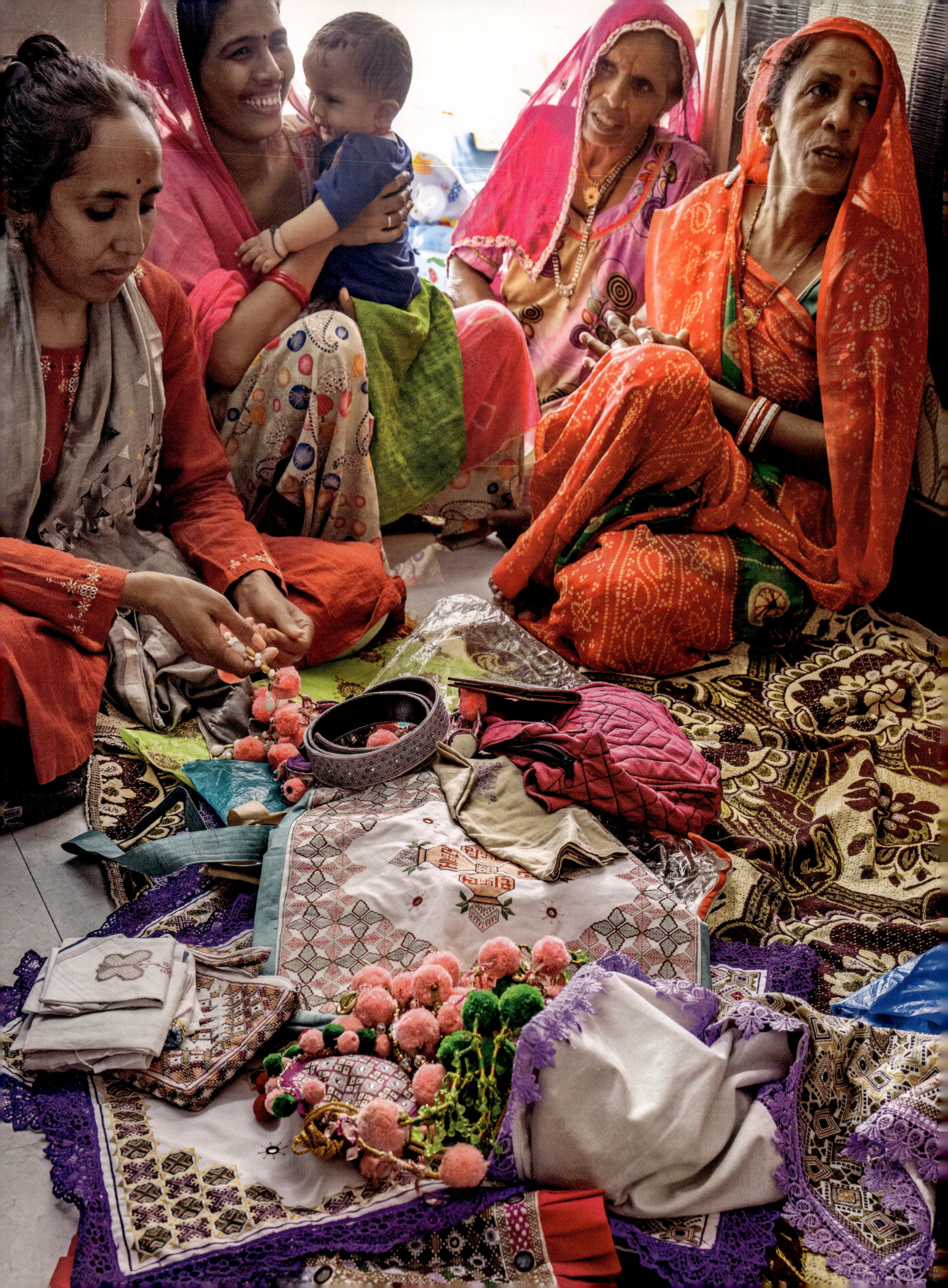

Opposite: Faradi, 2022. Women of Tulsiben's family review a recent dowry: bags, cushion covers, handkerchiefs, and a belt for the groom embroidered in the current fashions of suf and kharek embroidery. Peer review drove innovation in embroidery traditions. Originally, embroidery was personal, never for sale. *Photo: Nevada Wier*

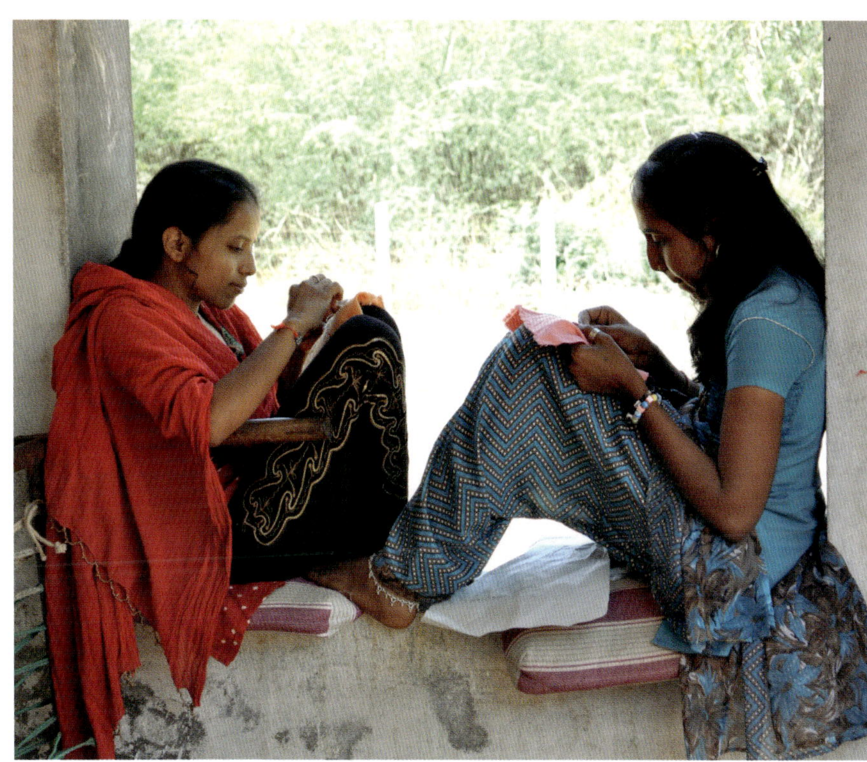

Right: Kala Raksha Vidhyalaya, 2011. Cousins and friends, Laxmiben and Tulsiben worked together through the design and BMA courses. There was never a question of copying ideas. Personal innovation was an essential part of women's traditional embroidery. *Photo: Judy Frater*

school, was at the top of her class, and won prizes. But there was no eighth grade in the village school, and girls did not leave the village. Tulsiben left school and learned suf embroidery from the women in her family. She embroidered for wages for several years, contributing to her family's earnings.

"When we embroidered, we were in the limits of the NGO," she recalled. "They gave us work and we did it. We had no name, and we didn't get the value for our work. Still, we did it because we didn't have any other work."

She had relatives in Sumrasar and knew about Kala Raksha and the Vidhyalaya. She saw the KRV fashion show twice. "We thought it was great that artisan graduates were making their own designs and walking the fashion show ramp," she continued. "We had never done anything like that and thought we should go. But we didn't know what it was; we thought they must give designs. We didn't know it would be so professional, with NID faculty. Later we realized that—and also the value of our embroidery."

Tulsiben and her cousin Laxmiben decided to take the design course. "There were two of us from Faradi," she said. "The local faculty member, Harishbhai, was my uncle, and everyone knew Judyben. So the community didn't stop us."

We made it possible by picking up the two girls at the beginning of each course and dropping them off at home at the end. Tulsiben's expectations were limited and practical. She hoped to receive appreciation, and to learn to make good designs. And she dreamed of taking embroidery forward—without forgetting tradition.

Tulsiben and Laxmiben had worked together in Faradi. For their KRV admission interview, they brought one shawl between them. It was for an NGO, and they had embroidered more than the budget they were given, thinking they would earn more. The NGO didn't want to pay what they asked, so they were stuck with it. Throughout the course, the cousins were inseparable. They bickered constantly. Laxmiben was fast, impulsive, and outspoken. Tulsiben was calm, cool, and circumspect. But the bickering was superficial, Tulsiben assured, "It's our way of relating."

Tulsiben loved returning to learning. "Drawing makes you see," she said. "It's difficult till you get it. Then it's easy. I never knew there were so many colors in nature. Before the class, we used only symmetry. After learning, we thought of doing other layouts, like starting from a corner. You can use composition to fill a piece with less work. We also changed traditional color and used only warm or gray-scale colors. We made changes like this."

In traditional societies, embroidery is a woman's space to be an individual and express creativity. For her final collection, Tulsiben chose the trend forecast theme "Manifesto." It was far beyond the experience of a girl from a small village in Kutch. But she looked at the visuals and connected to aspects of painting. On an inspiration visit to a potters' village, she studied women's traditional painting on pots and renamed her theme "The Art of a Traditional Line." For her collection, she embroidered pink, black, and turquoise garments with fine, minimal suf work, intelligently placed. "Theme helps us focus," she said. "We followed a method: theme, inspiration, and principles. I learned from every step." She graduated with awards for Most Marketable Collection and Best Student.

The next year, Tulsiben and Laxmiben encouraged six more girls from Faradi to take the course. Among them, another of Tulsiben's cousins, Taraben, was the youngest. Shy and determined, she graduated with the award for Best Presentation. At the end of that year, Laxmiben's father came to me in desperation. Laxmiben does not want to get married, he told me. She says she is going to join Brahma Kumaris (a spiritual movement that advocates celibacy). What shall I do?

I told him that whatever he did, he must not force her.

"Why don't you take her?" he said.

So I hired Laxmiben as a local faculty member. A year later, when I left Kala Raksha to form Somaiya Kala Vidya, Laxmiben came with me.

I began the institute with a pilot course in Business and Management for Artisans. For the women's cohort, I knew it would not work to ask for volunteers. I handpicked students, thinking carefully about who would really want to have her own business. Laxmiben, as faculty, was a pilot student. Tulsiben and Taraben were among the six other women.

"Between the design course and the BMA," Tulsiben related, "we did only occasional work. We had learned the language of design, we were doing work, but we didn't know about business. The Market Orientation session didn't teach us how to get clients or go to exhibitions. We learned that in the BMA course."

After the first BMA module, Business Strategy / Understanding Markets, the visiting faculty member wrote, "It is a pleasure to have Tulsiben in the class. She has a positive attitude, tries to understand every task, and then works on it. She actively participates in discussions and activities and helps her classmates. She has understood most of the concepts and now needs to apply them."

Since the goal of this course was clearly independence, each student would plan and implement their own collection and source their own raw materials.

For women, the course could have been subtitled "Soul Searching, Confronting your Demons, Getting Ready." Women are acutely aware of their limitations. While the question for men was how to grow their business, for the women it was how to start. How to circumvent all the real and imagined obstacles? How to procure raw materials, contact the market? In the fourth course, we realized that Tulsiben and Taraben had never attended an exhibition on their own.

Tulsiben, Laxmiben, and Taraben decided to work on a common theme, "The Life of Butterflies." They chose the concept because butterflies are colorful and light and can travel anywhere. It worked with their delicate suf embroidery.

They watched YouTube clips of caterpillars wholeheartedly enveloping themselves in their chrysalises. Then the caterpillars struggled magnificently to emerge, wet and exhausted, dry their wings . . . and fly. Did the artisan designers realize the metaphor they had chosen?

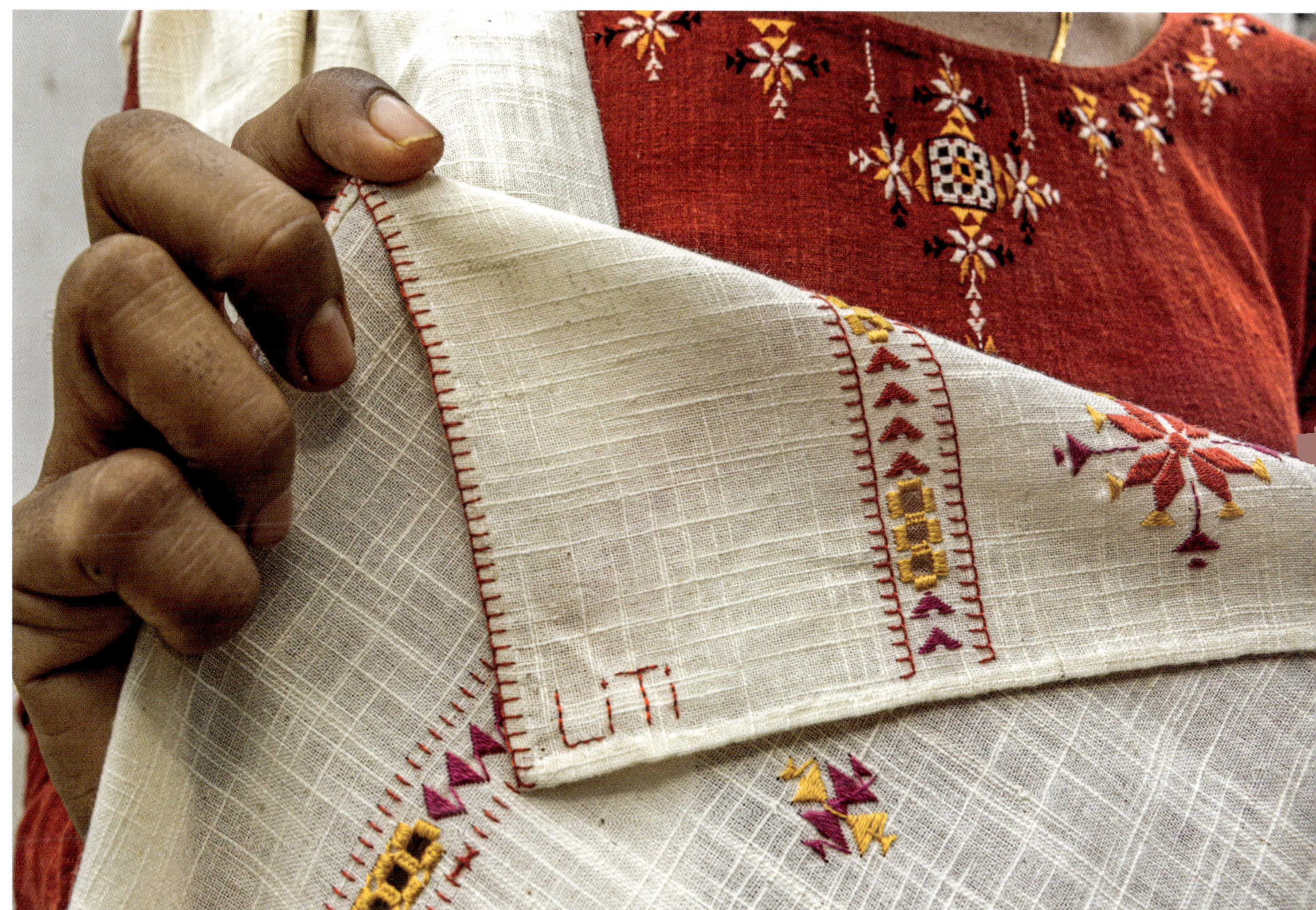

Faradi, 2022. Liti (Line) is Tulsiben's brand. She signs each of her products in embroidery. Paper hang tags are thrown away. Tulsiben's brand remains. *Photo: Nevada Wier*

Tulsiben sourced Chanderi saris. The cotton-silk fabric is gossamer. No one had attempted to embroider suf, which is counted on warps and wefts, on a fabric so fine. She made whimsical renditions of caterpillars and butterflies on the sari borders and ends. The work was extremely painstaking and exquisite.

She liked SKV advisor Dr. Ismailbhai's practical advice: always have a few new products. Design, she felt, was the key to competition.

Finally, each student created an individual brand. Tulsiben created the brand Liti (Line), a continuation of her design course experience. Together, the students planned and implemented a pop-up exhibition of their collections. Tulsiben sold over 48 percent of her stock.

After the final module, Analysis / Maximizing Business Performance, Tulsiben reflected, "Business means we must know what customers want and work accordingly. We learned how to do our own exhibition, how we can reach customers. We got the fruits of our efforts, so we enjoyed this course. I had never thought about my future! I enjoyed thinking about where I want to be in five years." She decided that she wanted to enhance suf tradition with new, good-quality materials and design. She wanted to increase investment and earnings and have an annual profit of RS 30,000.

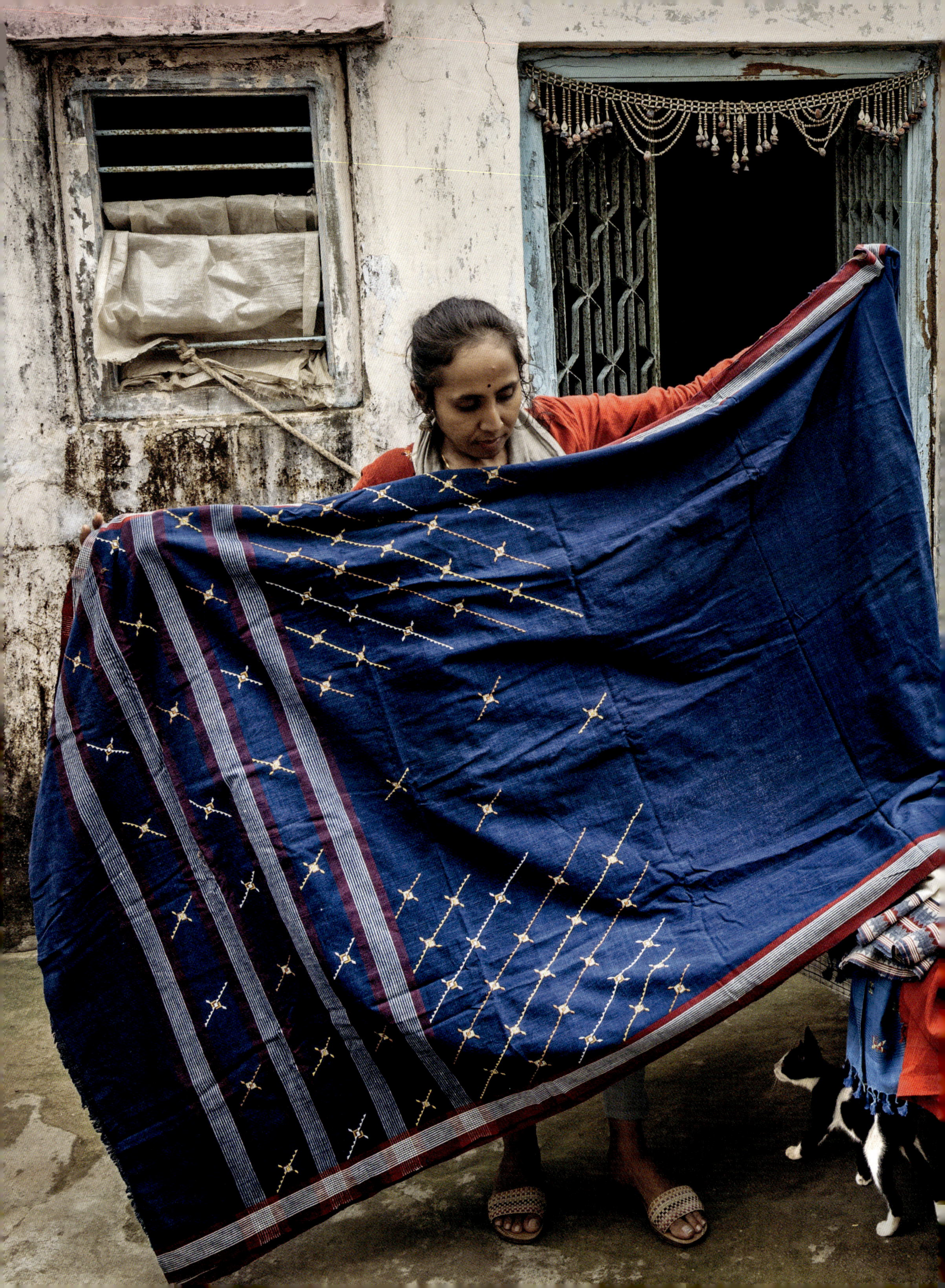

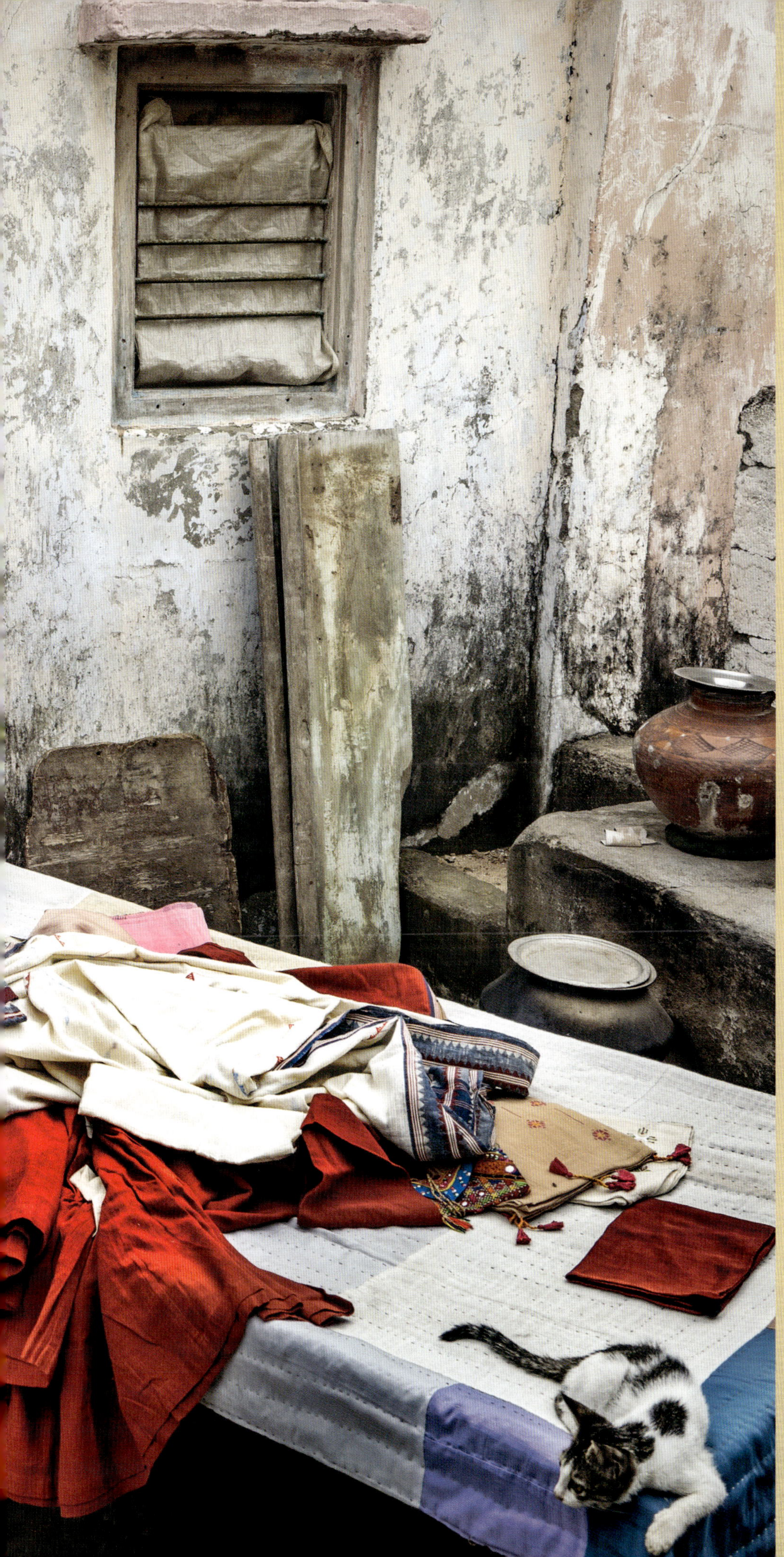

Faradi, 2022. Unusual among women of her community, Tulsiben started her own embroidery business. She works on projects; she embroidered this indigo sari for Lakme Fashion week in 2017. *Photo: Nevada Wier*

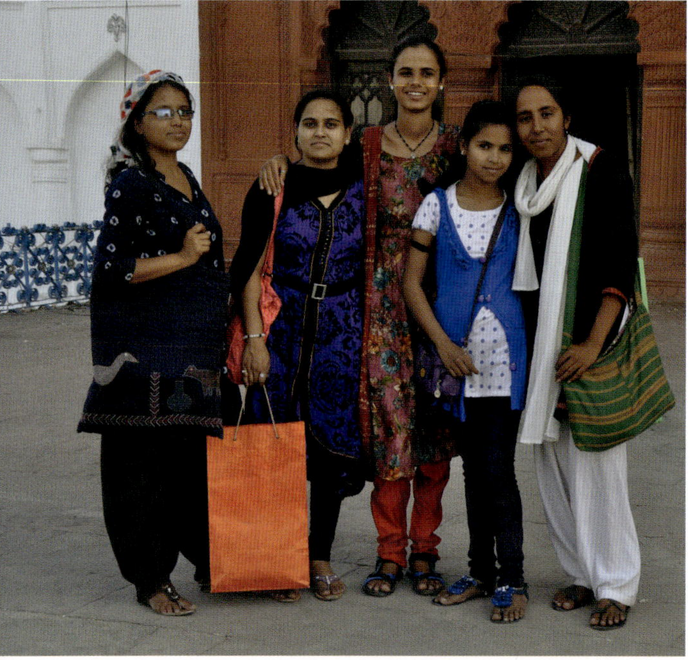

Left: Lucknow, 2015. Suf embroidery partners Laxmiben, Taraben, and Tulsiben took chikan embroiderers Khushboo and Manisha to explore historic Lucknow. Drawing inspiration from Rumi Darwaza, the Imambara, and textile collections, they designed and created fresh embroidery for contemporary garments. *Photo: Judy Frater*

Opposite: Somaiya Kala Vidya, 2019. Codesign is one of Tulsiben's favorite creative methods. Collaborating with Magdalena and Susana in Oaxaca, she designed and created a collection of huipils embroidered with motifs inspired by coral reefs. Taraben models a huipil in process. *Photo: Judy Frater*

Working together in the BMA, the three women decided that teamwork was their future. They started a joint business but kept their separate brands. Determined, they found clients through online shops, through Facebook and Instagram accounts, and sometimes through visitors. Unlike men graduates, they did not attempt pop-up sale exhibitions.

"We have limitations, so we can't do exhibitions," Tulsiben explained. "Embroidery is time consuming, so we do limited production. We don't have capital, so we purchase outright, just two to four saris, or a few meters of fabric, what we need."

In 2015, I launched a second Outreach program with chikan embroiderers of Lucknow. Tulsiben, Laxmiben, and Taraben were the mentor team. As with the Bhujodi-to-Bagalkot program, they would work one on one with chikan embroiderers to demonstrate the benefits of innovation in traditions, and this in turn would expand their own capacity. Both groups would show their work in a pop-up exhibition and earn through the sale of their products.

Chikan had been commercial for so long that the embroidery was only wage labor for women. People had lost interest in its history and meaning. The suf artisans immediately connected to the first group of embroiderers they met. The women were embroidering the characteristic white-on-white textured work, following patterns printed in bluing. They had never seen the finished products on which they worked, or even their work once the guidelines were washed off. Had they ever thought of doing their own patterns?

"Of course!"

Had they ever thought of doing their own work?

Immediately a woman asked, "But where would I sell it?"

"They didn't have enough savings," Tulsiben understood. "Or the right situation. The businesses and NGOs think, if the artisans are independent, then who will do our work?"

Searching for partners, we were told clearly that women have to obey their fathers, their brothers, and their husbands. So in the end, Khushboo and Manisha, two courageous cousins, were our Lucknow team. Tulsiben, Laxmiben, and Taraben fell in love with them.

"We taught whatever we had learned," Tulsiben said. "We took them to see the architecture of their city, showed how to take inspiration. We taught them to draw motifs, make layouts, make new products, and to think of customers." By the end of the first workshop, Tulsiben, Laxmiben, and Taraben were filled with their own ideas for the embroidery duets.

Over three years, the women worked together, creating new collections. Inspired by the drawn work of chikan, the suf team revived the abandoned drawn work of suf tradition. They worked on natural-dyed handloom fabrics—Chanderi, Maheshwari, and Malkha—to create the most innovative

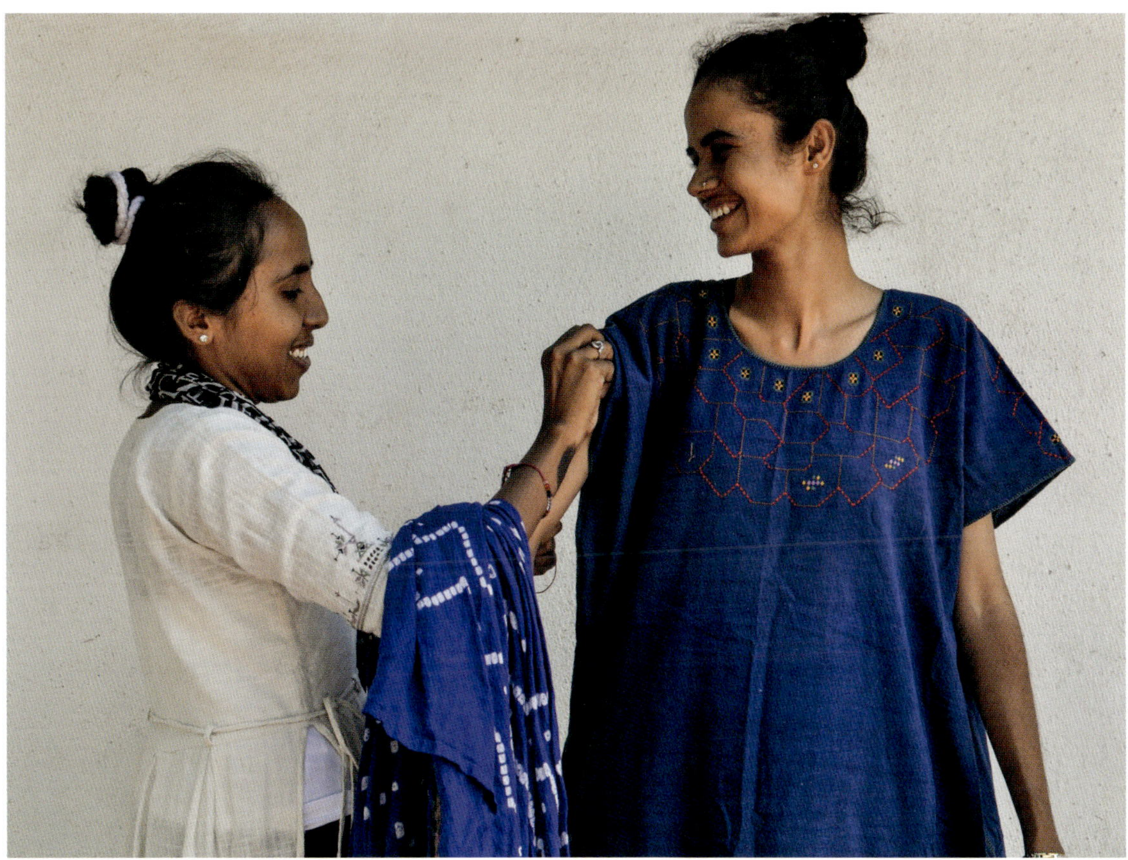

and beautiful suf work I had ever seen. Khushboo and Manisha created inspired hand-drawn motifs on the same fabrics. But in the end, their families overpowered them so that they could not develop their own business.

Participating in exhibitions, Tulsiben, Laxmiben, and Taraben began to slowly learn how to value their work. "In the first exhibition, we sold 50 percent of our stock," Tulsiben recalled. "But when we took out the expenses, there wasn't that much profit, maybe RS 5,000–10,000." In a joint exhibition with the Kumaon project, she observed how well Pachanbhai's expensive saris sold. "People aren't so price sensitive," she said. But they have to like the product. We can price according to design."

In 2016, I began a codesign program with the University of Wisconsin–Madison. Artisan design graduates paired with American students to codesign long distance, by using WhatsApp. In a sharp turn of events, Laxmiben was married that year. She continued her job as a faculty member and her business; that was the contingency on which she agreed to the marriage. But with additional responsibilities, she could not participate in the program.

Tulsiben and Taraben were happy for a new opportunity. They each communicated with three different partners over three years, each time creating a completely fresh collection. It was here that Tulsiben finally emerged as a star. In this work, she could be truly independent. It was appropriate to innovate, and working electronically was much less stressful than anything before. Without leaving the comfort of her home, Tulsiben focused on inspiration and expression and easily allowed her own brilliance. Not only was her work wonderfully fresh, but Tulsiben also excelled in communication. She listened, responded, and kept the conversation going. And she used a translation app on her phone—with cross-checks to ensure accuracy—to make it work. "One actual advantage of codesign," she said, "is that our partners don't know about our technique. So we need to translate, combine, and find a balance."

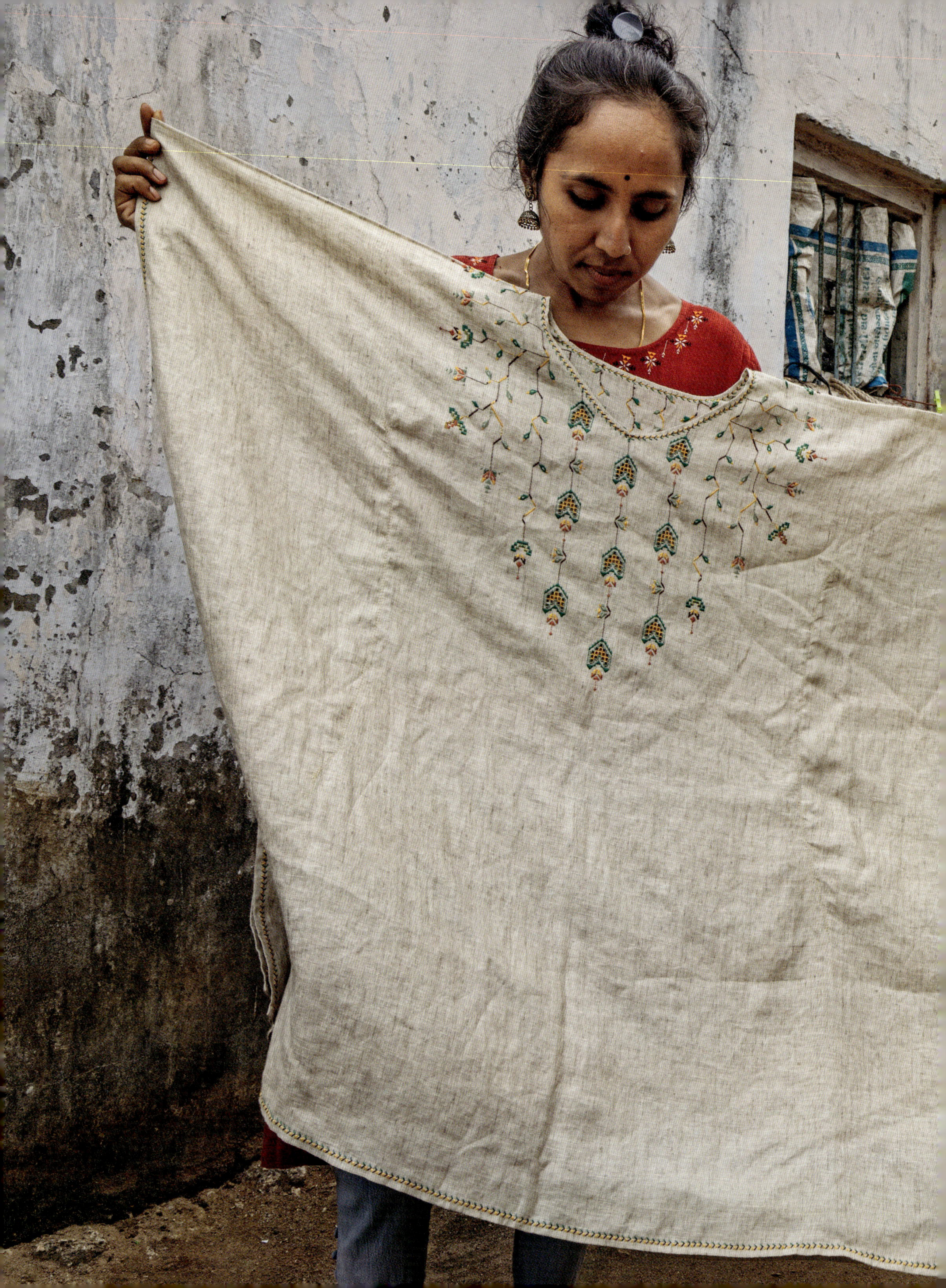

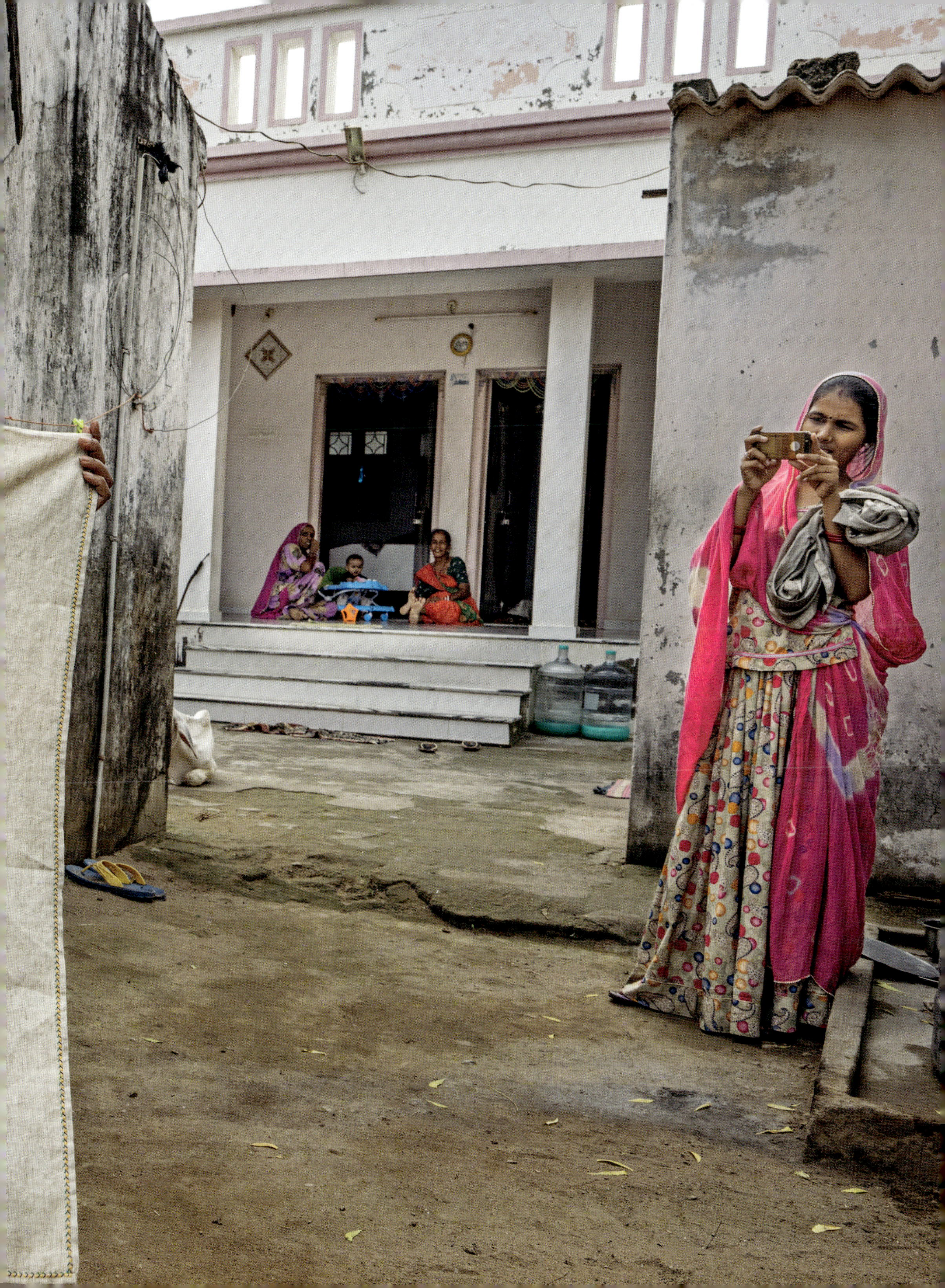

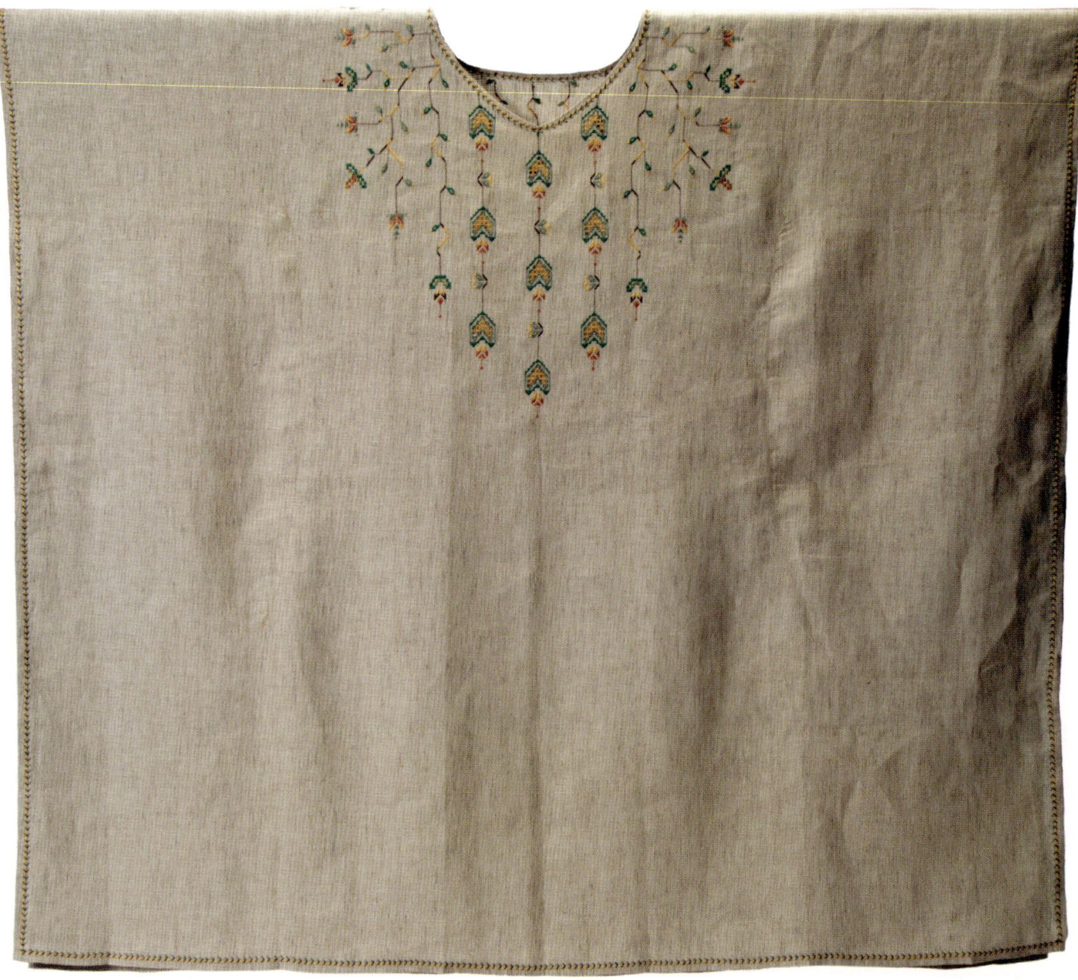

Previous pages: Faradi, 2022. For this book, Tulsiben decided to embroider a linen kaftan; she could stitch the garment as well as embellish it. Her sister-in-law snaps a photo. These days, artisan designers amply document their work. *Photo: Nevada Wier*

Above: *Texture of Leaves Kaftan*, by Tulsiben Puroshottam Puvar, 2022. Linen, cotton yarn, suf embroidered. 35" x 40". Tulsiben sourced trend forecasts and liked spring/summer 2022 Junglelines. She used the texture of leaves as her inspiration and created new suf motifs, including the delicate drawn work that she and her partners had revived. *Photo: Schiffer Publishing Ltd.*

The culmination of the codesign program was a project with artisans in Oaxaca, Mexico. With her partners Magdalena and Susana, Tulsiben created a collection inspired by coral reefs, where she again reinvented fine and delicate suf embroidery.

"The drawn work that we have in suf embroidery worked well in expressing a coral reef," Tulsiben said. "Inspired by my partners, I also made new motifs and used their finishing techniques. From the start, I have enjoyed codesign. Sharing opinions and ideas, you learn how partners think and can make something new. And artisans understand each other, so I liked this project even more. As artisans, my partners work within limitations, so they knew what was possible. Most of all, I enjoyed learning about their culture. Embroidery is culture."

The first time that Tulsiben gave a presentation in the design course, she fainted. Laxmiben revived her, and she simply continued. In 2017, she walked the ramp at Lakme Fashion Week in Mumbai as a designer in her own right. And she gave a speech on her experiences as an artisan designer to the full house of the SKV convocation.

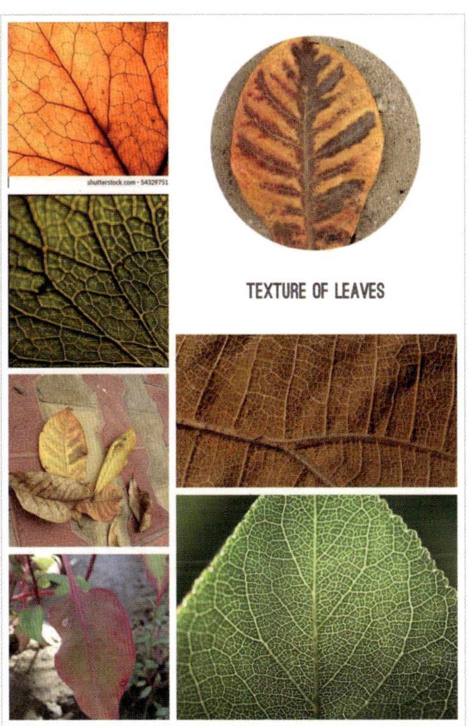

In 2018, when Laxmiben took maternity leave, Tulsiben and Taraben stepped in as faculty for the women's course. Tulsiben proved to be a wise, capable, and responsible teacher. She delighted in participating in each woman's creativity unfolding and enjoyed the opportunity to learn bandhani and weaving.

Eager to express and achieve, Tulsiben had come a long way, gently, carefully pushing the boundaries of her traditional culture, but always within propriety. She and Taraben traveled without a male escort to SKV and with nonfamily SKV staff to Lucknow, Mumbai, Delhi, and Chennai. But at the age of twenty-six, she worried about her future. Would she be able to embroider after marriage? She once answered the question with the exclamation "I don't want to get married!"

But she did marry in 2020, and she weathered the pandemic, embroidering masks with scorpion motifs and participating in one more codesign project with UW Madison students, this time in a residency that I taught.

2022

Tulsiben loves the process of design. She loves to think of themes, and she loves embroidery. Visiting her parents' home, she displays embroidered memories of projects past. Her work has slowly, quietly progressed in sophistication.

She never learned to cook, she laughs. Her mother and sister-in-law handled that, and now her mother-in-law is still strong and vital. Her father-in-law passed away, and Tulsiben's husband is the only son. She says her mother-in-law wants her to do her own embroidery. She used to run a group, so she understands. And they need the money. So Tulsiben's way is cleared. She is looking for a project, something to strive for. She's preparing intelligently to launch, and she will do her own creation.

"No one knew us before," she says. "We didn't know anything but embroidery. We didn't even have traditional pieces with us or know about old techniques. We learned about that in our courses. Before those six design classes, I was going to leave my tradition. I had studied only to seventh grade. I thought what is embroidery that we should put so much into it? But then I found a new path in my art. I did so much. I gained confidence. I can tell everyone that I am a BMA graduate, and I am doing my own business. We are recognized now, and our art is recognized and valued. That's why we are doing our own work. Artisans are leaving their art. In the same way, maybe someone can be inspired by me and not leave their art."

Top: Tulsiben created this theme board as inspiration for her kaftan.

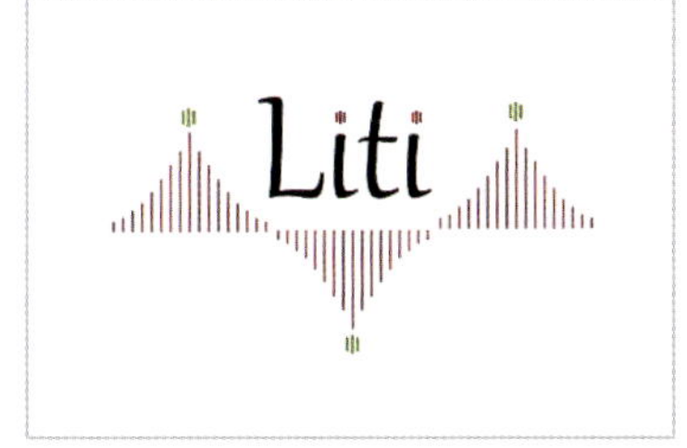

Right: Tulsiben derived her logo Liti, which means line, the beginning of suf embroidery, from her design class collection. She refined it during her BMA course.

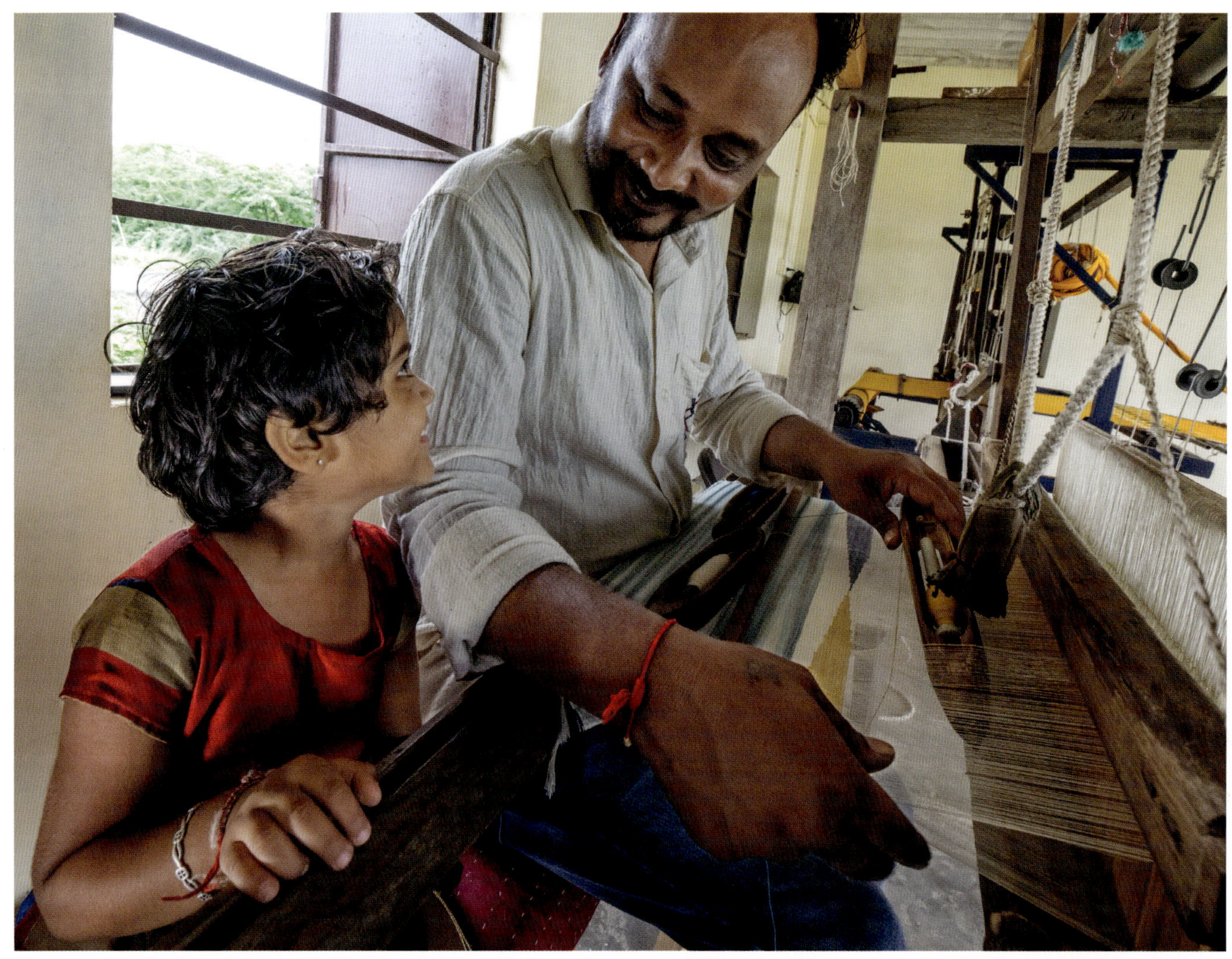

I don't only want to personally advance;
I want weaving to come ahead.

~Bharatbhai Vershi Jepar

Mota Varnora, 2022. Bharatbhai's daughter is learning weaving by osmosis. It's not learning, but knowing. Traditionally in Kutch, women did not weave, but today girls are breaking that barrier. *Photo: Nevada Wier*

Chapter 18

BHARATBHAI VERSHI JEPAR: STARTING UP

2022

Varnora is a tiny village of under a thousand weavers and Rabaris. Located 12 miles northeast of Bhujodi, it is well under the radar of the tourism that the larger weavers' village enjoys. It's a place you deliberately visit. Bharatbhai lives in a large open house, with a spacious workshop next door, four looms flooded with natural light. From zero to this! He built it after taking the design course in 2019, he says. He is the only practicing weaver in his family, but he has hired artisans. He was getting orders from the Instagram account he started. Then came COVID-19.

At fourteen, while he was still in school, Bharatbhai suddenly lost his father. He dropped out of school. Although his family had left their weaving tradition for two generations, Varnora was home to the first national award-winning weaver and famous for woolen *dhabla* blankets. Bharatbhai became interested in weaving and decided to learn from others in the village. He fitted a loom in his house and started to work for a medium-scale weaver. There was no electricity in Varnora then. He worked by lantern light and began to experiment with his own designs. His employer encouraged him to make the designs for him.

After the 2001 earthquake, the demand for weaving declined. Bharatbhai was also interested in painting and music. He sought work painting the village temple, where he further experimented with mixing colors and making textures with a sponge and comb. His brother picked up their father's real estate work. The family also started farming. But Bharatbhai realized that farming wasn't his work. "Weaving is my heritage," he said. He returned to weaving, working for another established weaver of Varnora. After hours, he wove his own designs with wool donated as earthquake relief. His employer saw one shawl with intricate patterning and gave him RS 25,000 for it—a month's earnings at the time. A good weaver can weave four or five shawls in a day. Before the earthquake, job work weavers earned RS 10 per shawl; after the earthquake, they got up to RS 15.

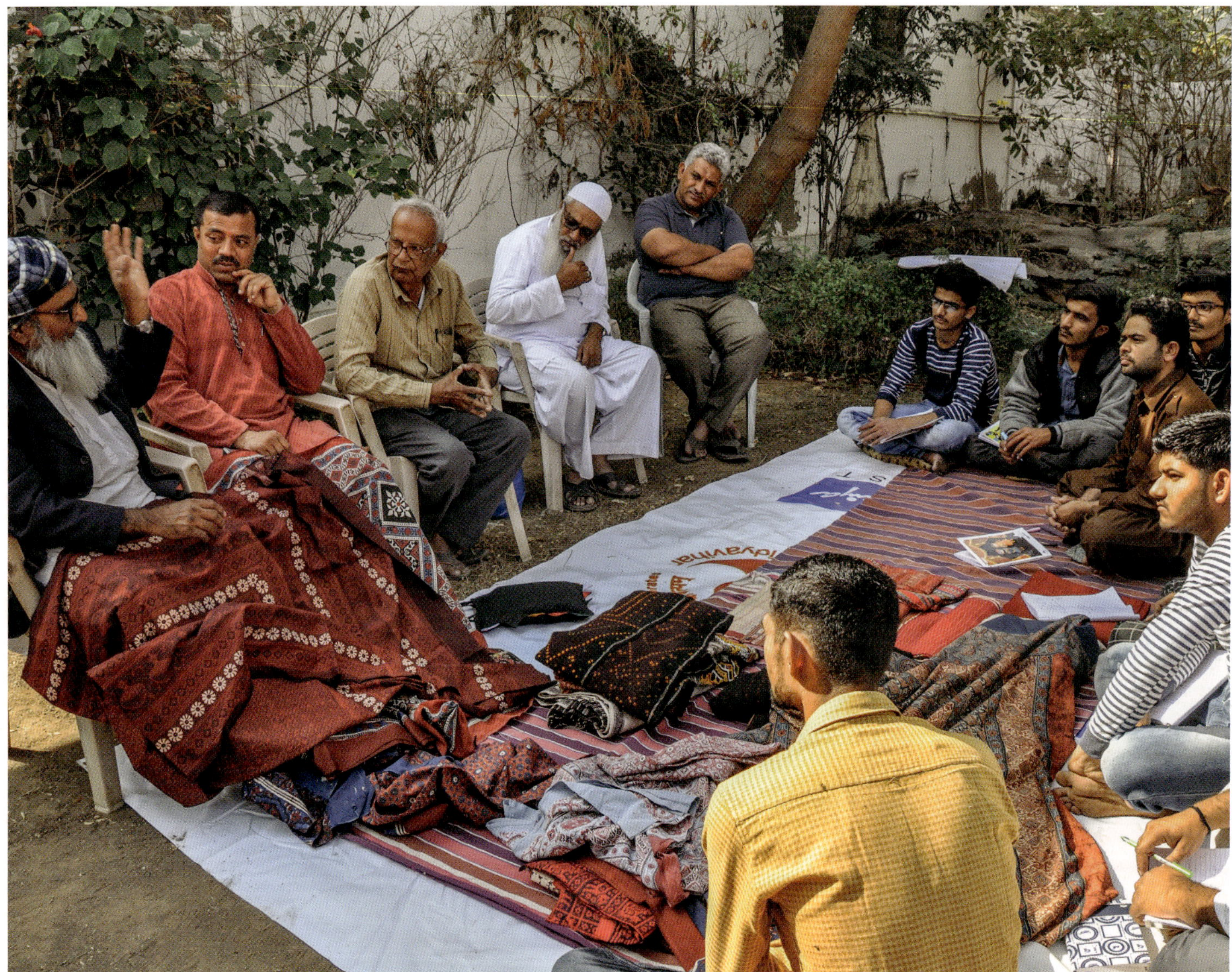

Bharatbhai's responsibilities had increased after the earthquake, and he was working to support his family. Without access to better urban markets, he began to sell his own work in the bazaar of the Rann Festival, a state government initiative to bring tourists to Kutch in the wake of the earthquake. Although he knew the venue devalued craft, he depended on it for five years. His brother encouraged him to do his own work rather than job work, and when Bharatbhai learned of SKV, he supported him in enrolling in the design course.

Bharatbhai wanted to gain access to new materials and learn yarn dyeing. In the first session of the course, he was fascinated to hear master artisan advisors narrate their traditions. When Dr. Ismailbhai explained how a Malir depicted the lifestyle of the herders for whom it was made, he exclaimed, "I have never heard such stories about our weaving!" He grasped the value of a theme. Everything he learned was useful, he said. He also learned costing and the role of the market.

When he took the course, Bharatbhai was thirty-six. There was another classmate from Varnora who was forty. In the world of Kutch artisans, they were both approaching aged. Bharatbhai did not consider his classmate a rival but a colleague. He gently supported him, and they worked together. "If he wove a piece for homework with the same technique as mine, I made sure to weave a different design," he said.

For his final collection, Bharatbhai chose trees as his inspiration. "I learned I can get an idea from anything," he said. "All trees have different barks. I see that now." He looked for tones of brown and textures. To develop the concept, he created an installation in the garden, pasting dried leaves on the trunk of a large tree in patterns punctuated with bright-pink bougainvillea leaves. He honed the concept and created a theme board, not flat but creatively shaped into a 3-D cylinder. With effort, he named his collection, beginning with "Tree Trunk" and finally arriving at "Lord of the Forest." Then, with considerable encouragement, he wove saris for the first time, as well as shawls and scarves. He had to modify his loom to accommodate the wider fabric. He developed a sophisticated style, balancing skill and restraint. "If a piece needs no ornamentation, don't do it," he said. But, he clarified, he did not advocate artisans weaving plain yardage. "There is no recognition of the weaver in plain yardage," he stated.

The final jury saw potential in Bharatbhai's work. His compositions with dynamic diagonals were brilliant, they wrote, and could reach a mature market segment. But he needed to focus on variety, and to choose material that would give returns for design. He had not managed his costs well, but he was clearly learning. They presented him with the award for Most Promising Artisan.

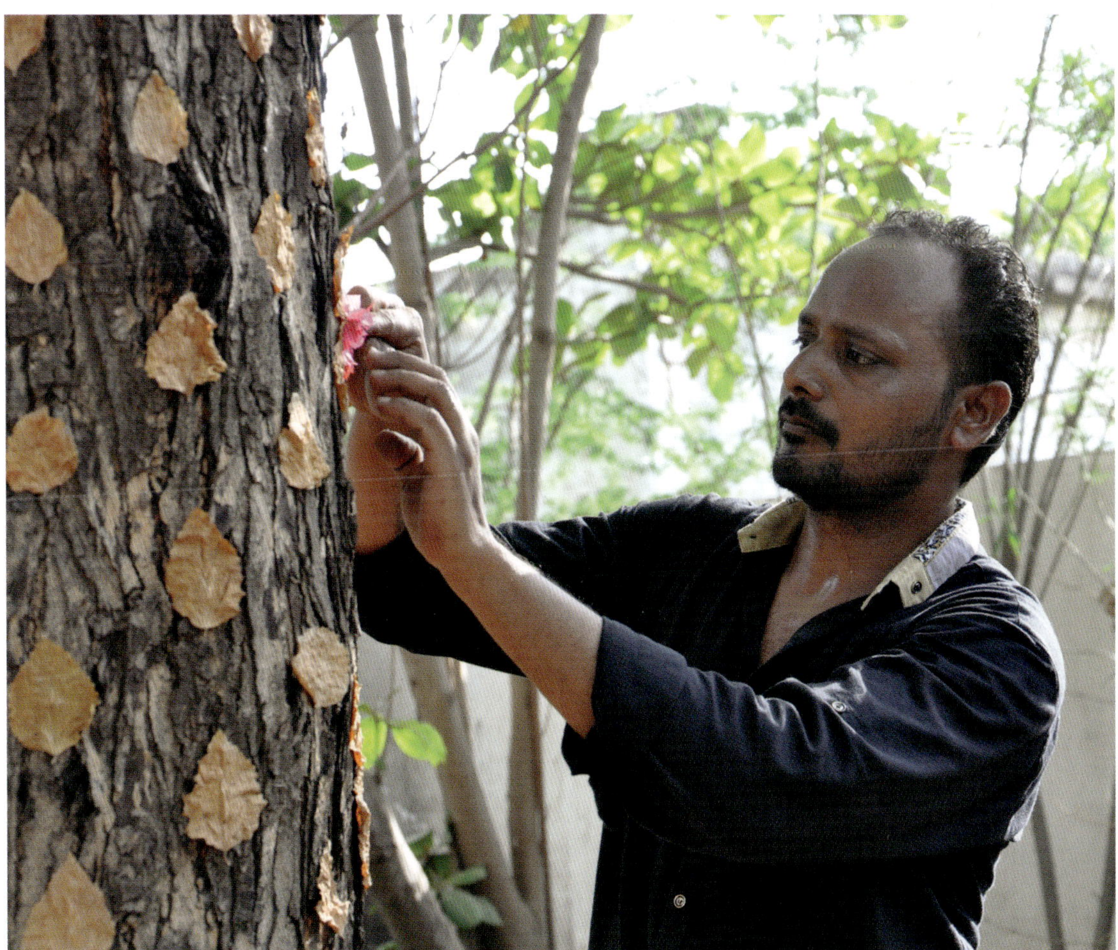

Opposite: Somaiya Kala Vidya, 2019. In the Advisors session, Ismailbhai interprets the motifs of a block-printed Malir. *Phuladi* represents the wind of the desert; *ladvo* is the Jat pastoralist's thatch mat home, rolled during migration. And the "ace" design was originally a mud pot, used as a float while fording a stream. *Photo: Judy Frater*

Above: Somaiya Kala Vidya, 2019. To delve into concepts on a holistic, experiential level, students create installations on campus. Bharatbhai chose the theme, trees. Intrigued by tree bark, he added dried leaves and bougainvillea to a tree in the garden to create patterns of texture and color. *Photo: Judy Frater*

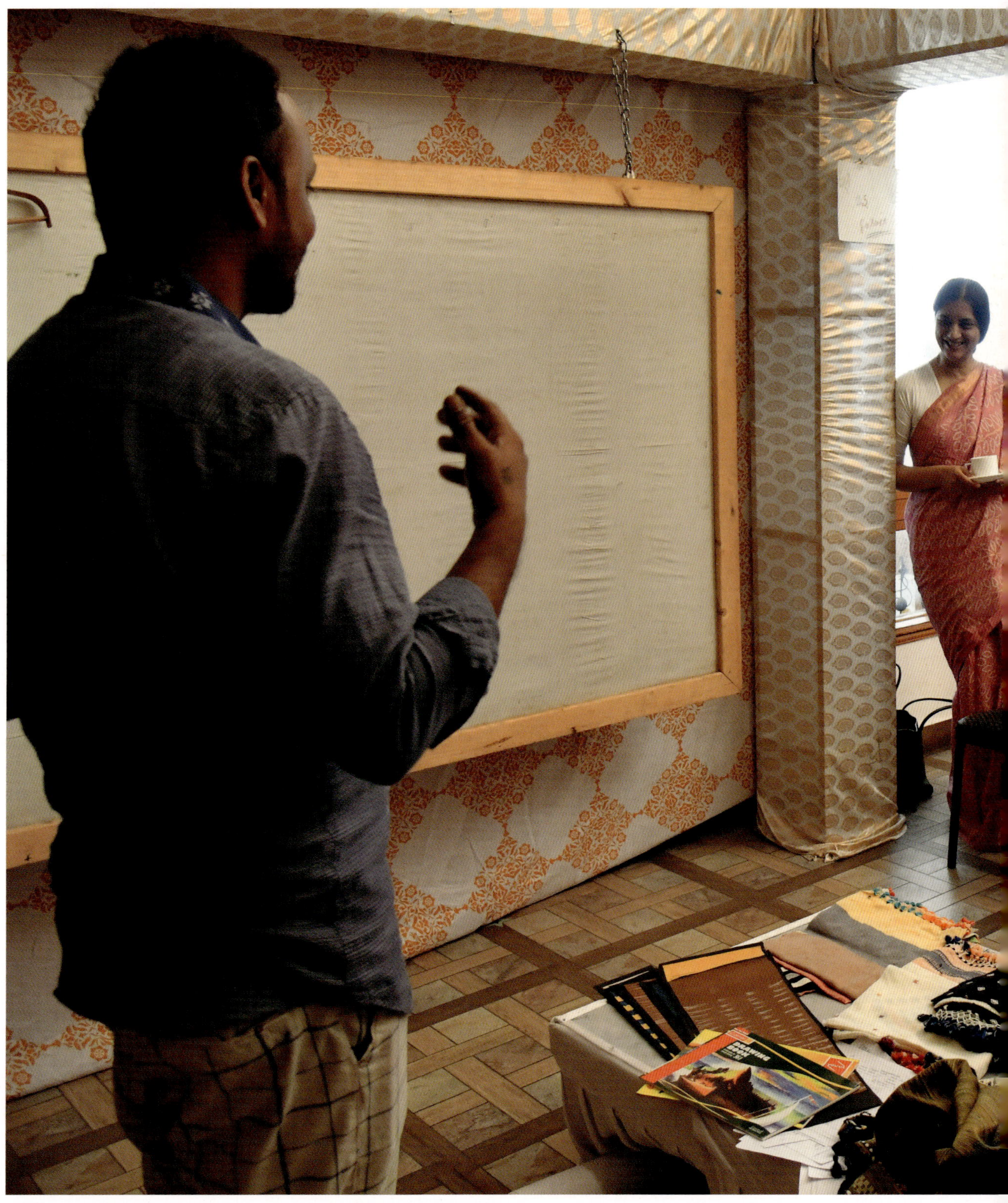

The encouragement gave Bharatbhai the confidence he needed. Talented, he had not found validation. Recognition gave him courage to venture. He wanted to promote his new brand, Thread View, through social media. However, he did not want only to personally advance. "I want weaving to come ahead," he said.

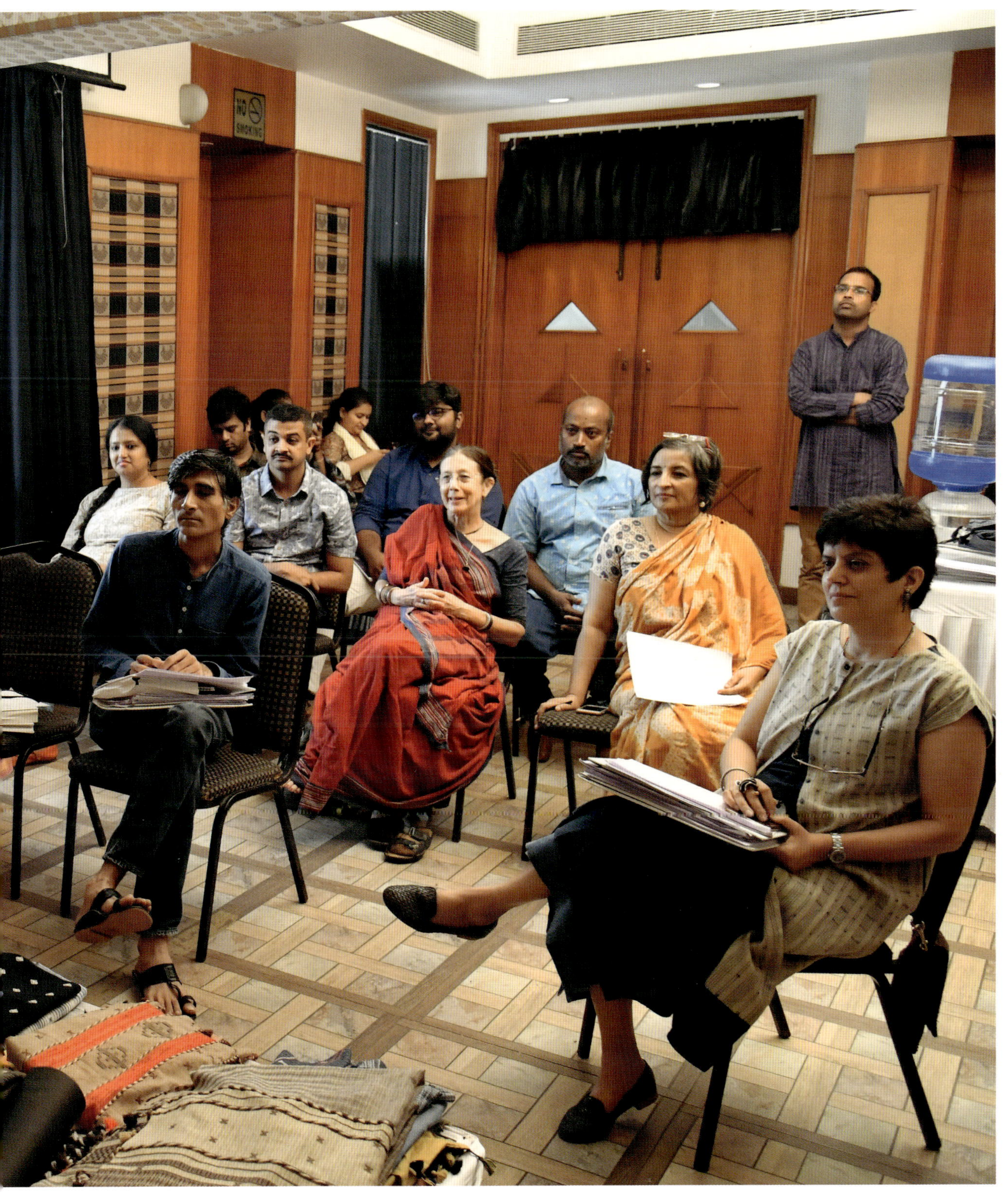

Sharma Resorts, 2019. Bharatbhai presents his year of design education to the final jury. The jury is a review process for students as well as jury members, and a chance to comprehend a year's learning. *Photo: Ketan Pomal, L.M. Studio*

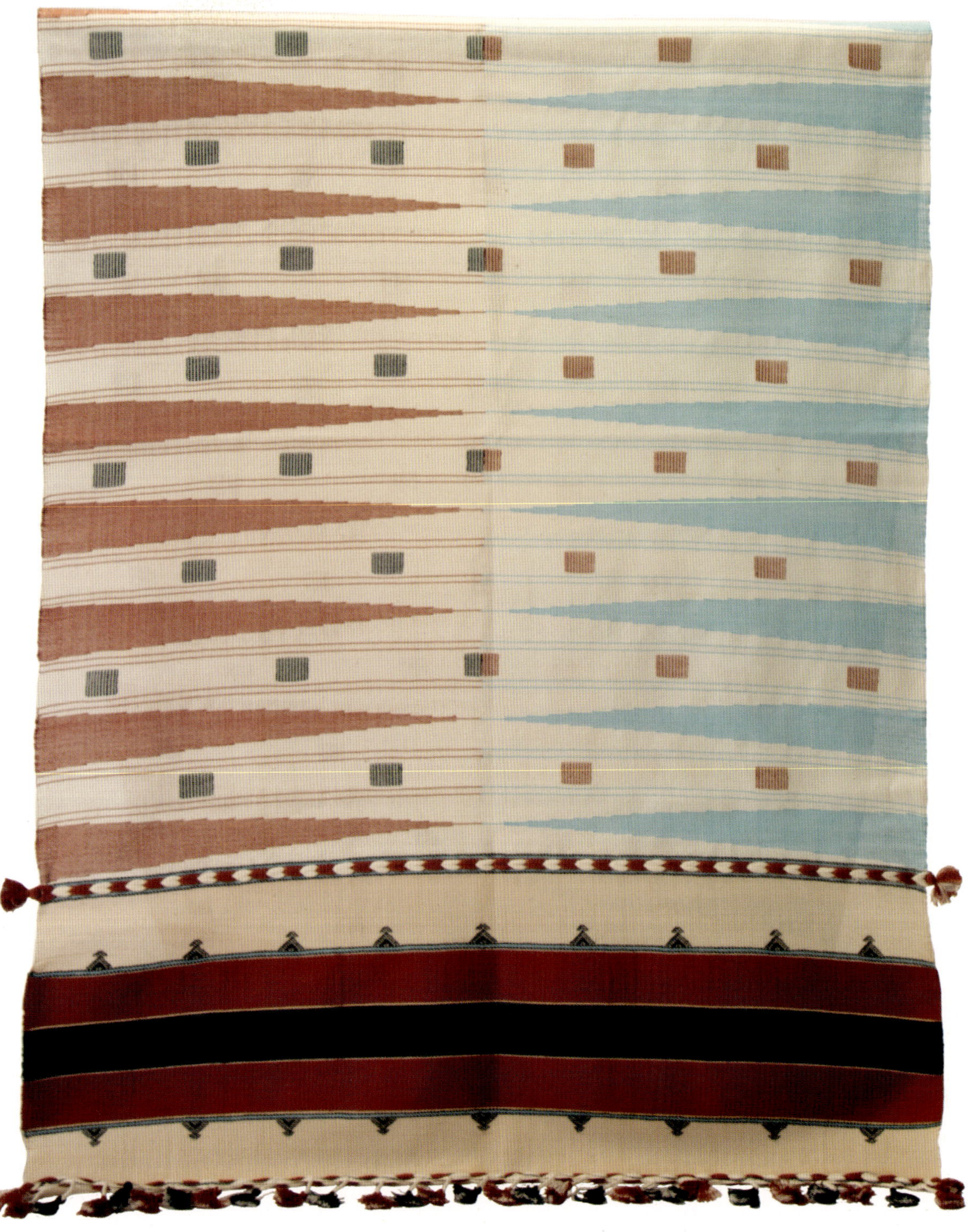

Above: Sachi Kor, 2022, scarf by Bharat Vershi Jepar, 2022. Cotton yarn, hand-woven with interlocking. 24" x 78". The traditional *dhablo* blanket of Kutch was woven with interlocked motifs along one side. In a codesign project with UW Madison students, Bharatbhai took a technical challenge: weaving interlocked motifs on both sides by using three shuttles. *Photo: Schiffer Publishing Ltd.*

Opposite: Mota Varnora, 2022. After the first sample, creating is easier. Bharatbhai has incorporated three-shuttle weaving in new designs. The challenge now is finding people who understand and appreciate the technical virtuosity. *Photo: Nevada Wier*

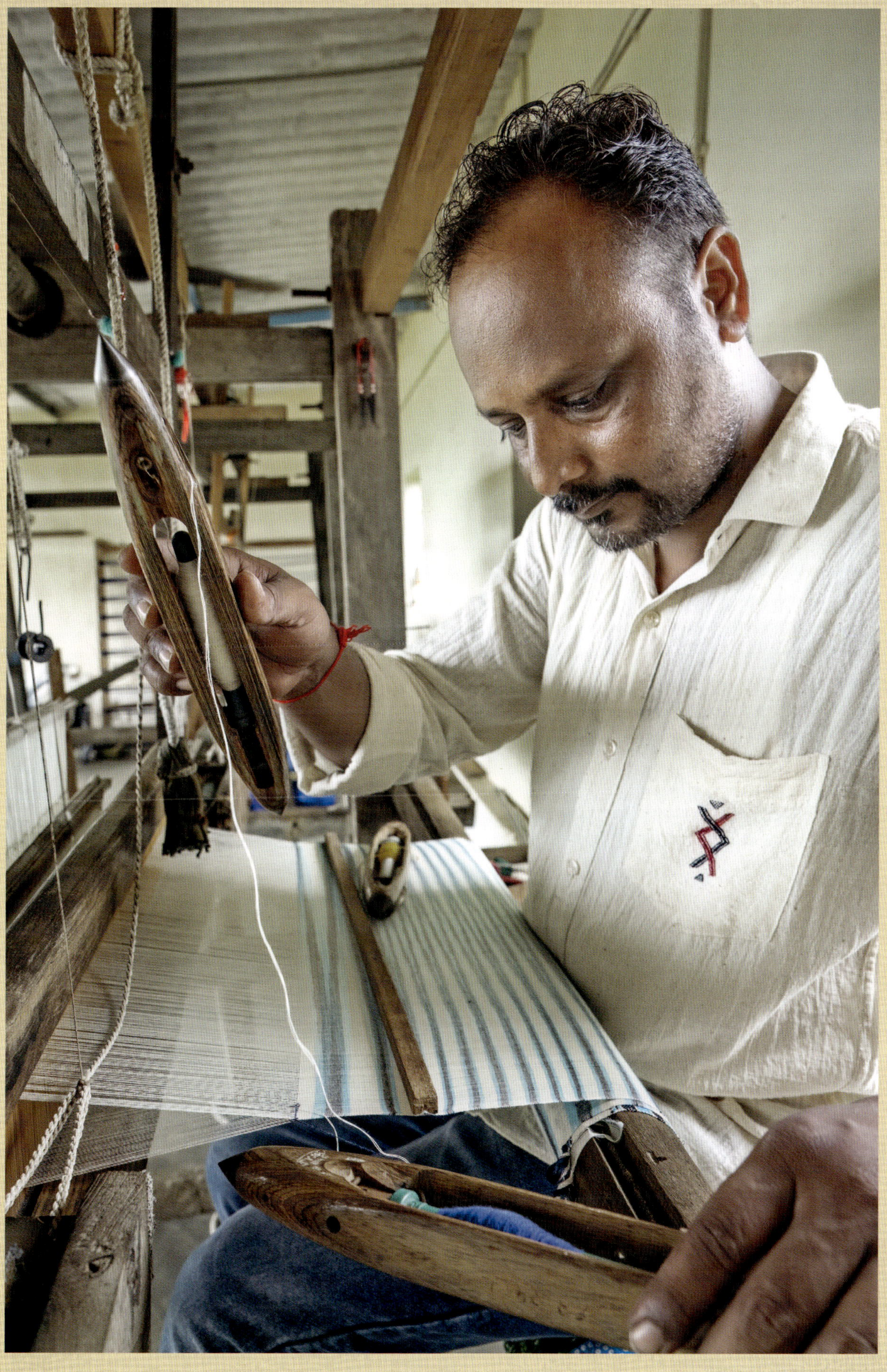

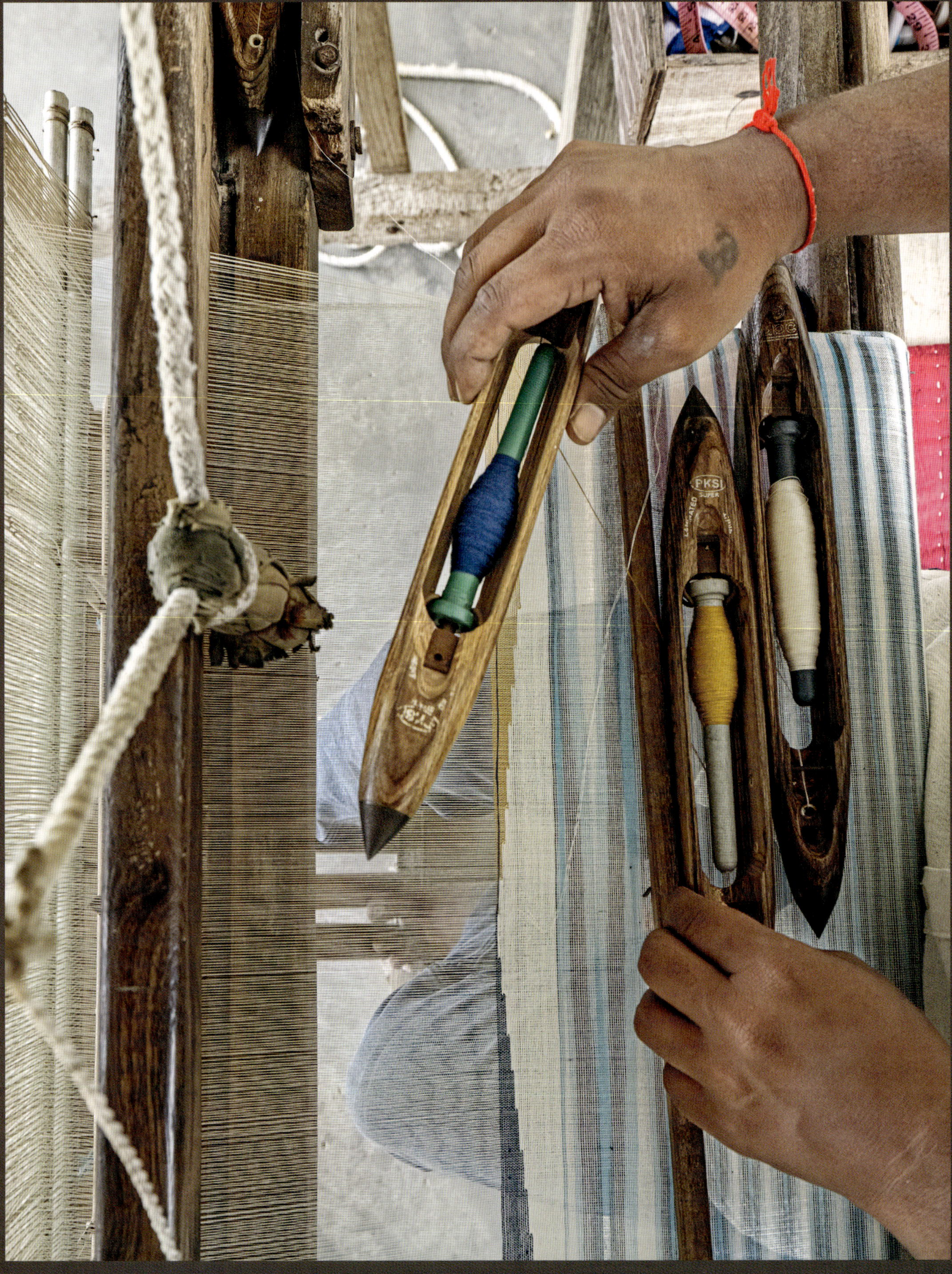
PKSI
SUPER

His biggest challenge was connecting to better markets. He worked at Instagram. He had an excellent eye for photography and painstakingly used a translate app. He got good orders and inquiries from NIFT students and then students from other institutes.

During the COVID-19 lockdown, when he had only enough yarn to last a few days, he wrote on Instagram, and he thought about how to work creatively. He was watching Lord Buddha's story with his son on his mobile phone at night. So he wove the face of Lord Buddha.

As COVID-19 began to subside, Bharatbhai participated in a codesign project with University of Wisconsin students in a residency that I taught. For inspiration, his partner chose a mid-twentieth-century bedspread woven with thick unspun elements. Impatient with the time that it takes to build a collaborative relationship, she submitted layouts in which Bharatbhai did not participate. Nonetheless, he managed to weave two fresh samples. One boldly used thick elements, when the trends in Kutch are finer and finer. The other was an extraordinary scarf woven with tapestry weave. "I used our traditional *sachi kor* interlocking technique," he said. "I had done it before, but only from one side. This scarf has interlocking from both sides. When I first tried this technique, using three hand-thrown shuttles, it was difficult. But in this codesign project, I succeeded in doing something I had wanted to try. In future products I hope to gain more value.

"It's hard for an artisan to break into new markets," Bharatbhai says. "The good exhibitions have their set favorite participants." He tried unsuccessfully to contact organizers when he participated in the SKV Dastkar exhibition in Delhi. It will take three to four years, he estimates.

Local weavers undercut. They don't know about indirect costs, he says, and they sell online at discounted rates. It is difficult to sell at a fair price. And now, large corporates are driving a nail in the coffin. "They employ artisans as workers in their industrialized craft enterprises," Bharatbhai relates. "It's hard to find artisans to work for me." But he will give it a try. When one corporate asked when he'll come and work for them, he responded, "When my own business doesn't take off." Now, he is invested in making a name for himself. He has the confidence and skills.

There are five design graduate weavers in Varnora. Four are thinking of working together, he says. It takes courage as well as contacts to work in isolation in an interior village. The other three graduates weave job work for the corporate, earning RS 500 a day. When there is a gap, they weave something of their own. Bharatbhai says he tries to help them.

I encourage them to make Varnora a destination. If they can work together, with just a little support, the entire community's weaving can come ahead. In December 2023, a group I lead comes to Varnora for an Open Studio Tour, and the design graduates host them with gusto.

Opposite: Mota Varnora, 2022. Each color has a separate bobbin, which is inserted into the shuttle. Because patterns are created by interlocking yarns, shuttles must be thrown by hand rather than the fly shuttle method, and weaving is slower and more painstaking. *Photo: Nevada Wier*

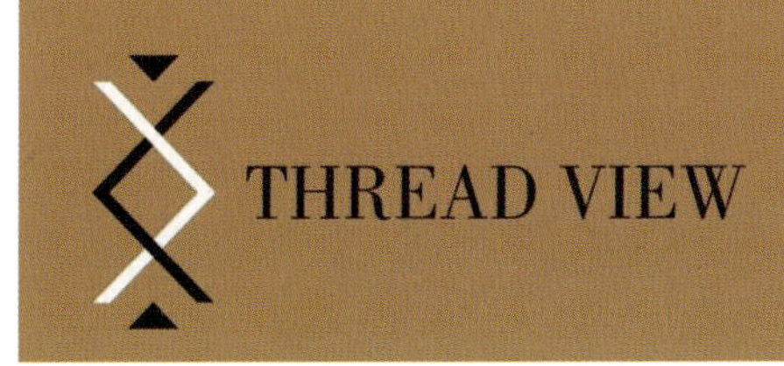

Right: In design class, Bharatbhai designed his logo, Thread View, making sure it related to weaving. He wove it in the shirt he wears.

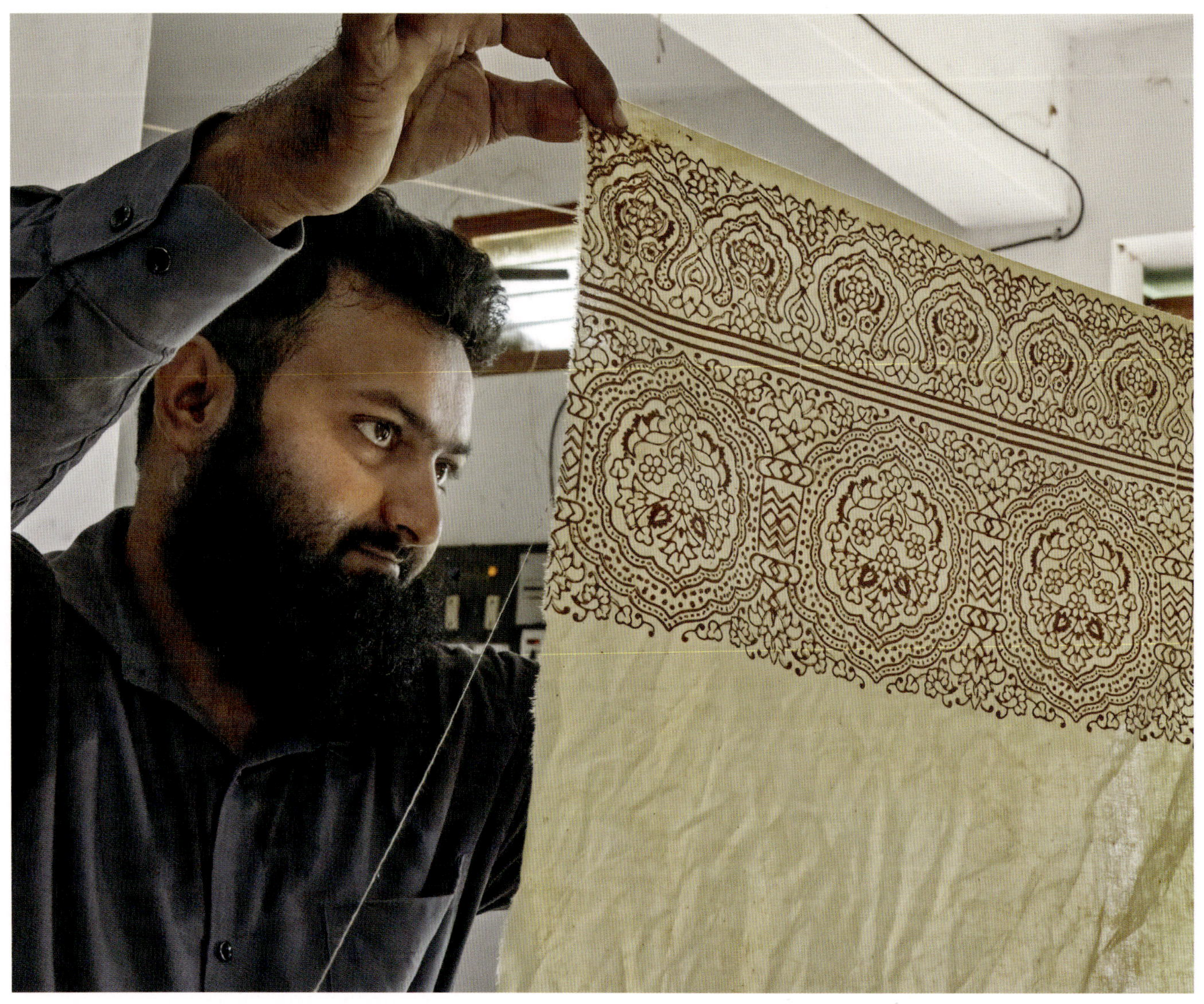

An artisan should work with concentration and passion.

~Soyabbhai AKT Khatri

Ajrakhpur, 2022. Soyabbhai prints a double-side Ajrakh sample. It's like exercise for him. He intently critiques his own work. The registration is out a bit here on the rekh, but perfect on the gachchh. He likes perfect. *Photo: Nevada Wier*

Chapter 19

SOYABBHAI AKT KHATRI: PASSION AND PROGRESSION

2019

Soyabbhai Whatsapps me four images: a glass door with a screen of Ajrakh print and big color-blocked checks, an interior with glass cabinets and a big executive swivel chair (still covered in plastic), a sleek desk with an air conditioner above it, and himself in the chair at the desk, with laptop computer and pink, purple, and blue lights glowing above. He's come a very long way.

It was incremental. His mother shows me the progression. The one-room house that everyone in Ajrakphur got when the village was built after the 2001 earthquake was expanded to two rooms; it's now a storeroom for hand-block-printed products. After some time, they were able to build a bigger house with tile floors, built-in wooden cabinets, and showcases, where Soyabbhai's cricket trophies are proudly displayed. Outside they planted a garden with one of each fruit tree they could find: mulberry, fig, orange, guava, pomegranate, *jambu*, and coconut. When Soyabbhai was engaged, they added two rooms above. And now he has a three-year-old son, and they have a spacious shop next door.

The workshop in the work section of the village has a similar tale. It began as the standard given to each family, not big enough for a long table. When Soyabbhai was taking the design course, in anticipation they expanded it to accommodate a long table. And during his Business and Management for Artisans course, they built a substantial workshop behind it, with three long tables and three small tables. They segregate the work, his father explains. The small tables are for yardage for local customers. The work is fast and cheap; they don't need to pin the fabric, and they print in part with pigment rather than natural dye. For more-valuable work—saris, dupattas, and stoles of their own designs and those of higher-end clients—they use the long tables. The fabric is silk or cotton/silk, and today often modal. They pin the products carefully to ensure straight, clear printing. Workers are paid differentially according to the work. There are no fans over the tables, since that would make the resist and mordant dry too quickly. But for guests they have a fan and some plastic chairs in one corner, he points out.

Soyabbhai's family is originally from Dhamadka, where his grandfather Tarmohamadbhai created Ajrakh for Maldari pastoralists. He worked for RS 2 per day in 1960. He had nine children, of which Soyabbhai's father, Abdul Karimbhai, was the fifth. After the earthquake of 2001, the family moved to Ajrakhpur. Soyabbhai's father originally worked exclusively with natural dyes and made yardage for garments, salvar-kamiz-dupatta suits, and bedsheets for sale in all domestic cities within India.

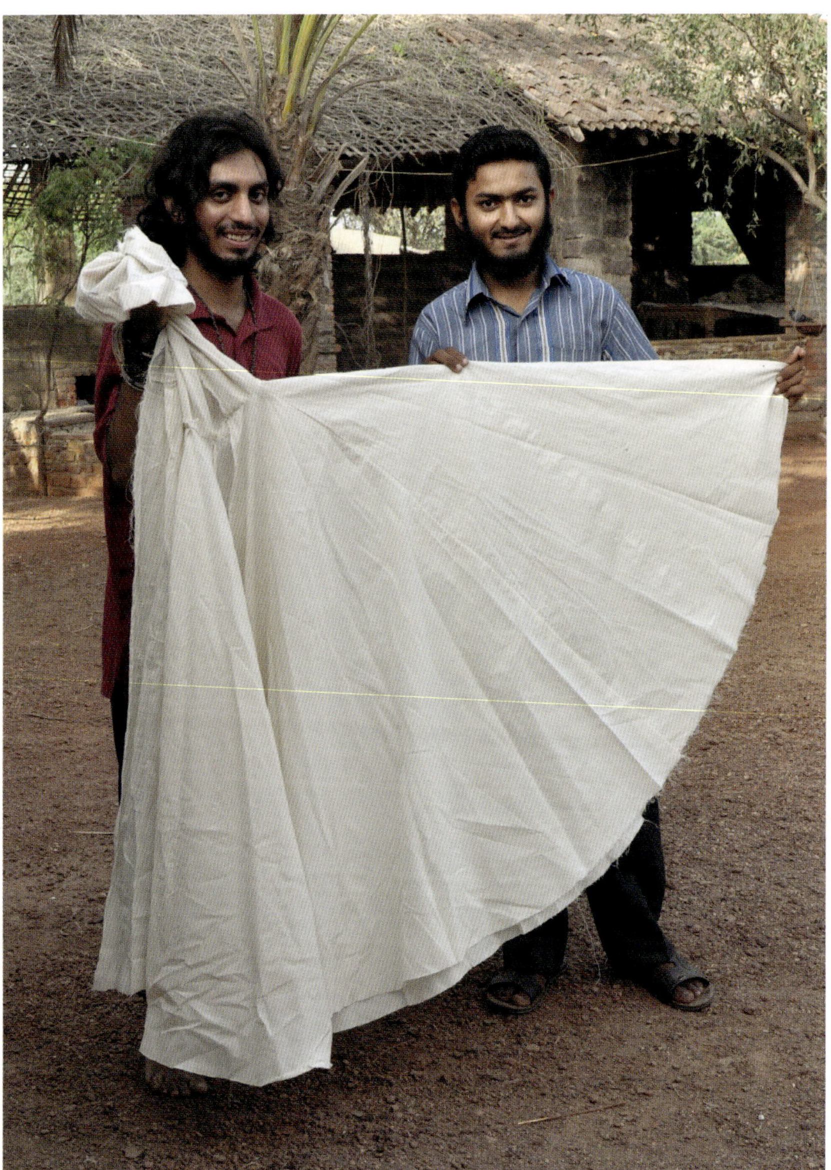

Kala Raksha Vidhyalaya, 2012. Codesigning in the Finishing / Collection Development module, Soyabbhai and Prateek spent time closely working together. They appreciated each other's strengths and became partners. *Photo: Judy Frater*

Soyabbhai started work as an *upperlo*, a washing boy, and then graduated to printing. His father says they watch workers and advance them when appropriate. They have to have ambition, he says. Soyabbhai is the only son in a family with six sisters. After printing for three years and observing design graduates in Ajrakhpur, in 2012 he decided to take the course.

His craft was very important to him, he said, and he was proud that his family used natural dyes. "These do not destroy or harm man or the environment," he noted. "People don't know how to differentiate between synthetic- and natural-dyed products, so it's important to educate buyers."

Meanwhile, he began with educating himself. He hoped to win the Best Collection Award at KRV and dreamed of taking his work to the international market. Soyabbhai learned first how to see. In morning sketching sessions, he drew the trees and leaves of the campus. "I kept a leaf I drew," he said. "I saw how as it dried, the color changed, and the texture emerged. That is the specialty of nature." He was full of enthusiasm and questions, determined to extract as much information as possible from each teacher. "Is there gravity in air?" he asked in the Basic Design course.

"In each class, the previous class was useful," he observed. "When I began to make motifs, I began to understand. Now I want to learn my own history." From the start, he was interested in the market. "A good artisan should be able to understand the market as well as materials and dyes," he said. On the field trip to Ahmedabad, he was impressed with Asal. The concept of a shop with only natural things was new. But he learned the most at Fabindia. "They showed us display, quality, and rejections," he said.

For his collection, Soyabbhai adapted the international trend forecast Safari Chic, renaming it "Jungle ma Mangal" (Splendor in the Jungle). He worked with Pearl Academy student Prateek to develop the collection pieces.

His teacher for the module wrote, "For Soyab, 'chic' meant 'style,' which he equated with newness. I explained that 'style' is not a synonym for new. He was very conscientious, putting a lot of thought in his work and layouts. Prateek similarly started out too literal, thinking of products to wear on safari. I explained that 'Safari chic' was simply the theme, not the category of products. Soyab wanted to make jackets for women and men; Prateek thought of cleaner, closer silhouettes. Soyab liked them."

Soyabbhai reworked his motifs and Prateek reworked the garments, coming up with a wonderful, flamboyant, asymmetric dress as the centerpiece. They clicked and codesigned garments that won them the award Soyabbhai had hoped for: Best Collection. Prateek said he fell in love with Ajrakh. Soyabbhai won the Faculty Award for Best Student as well. He understood that the experience of design education was more than learning principles and methods. "We will remember each other forever," he said.

After graduating, Soyabbhai demonstrated remarkable enthusiasm in developing new designs. He took a workshop in natural dyeing at MS University, Baroda, and through KRV taught workshops in block printing and natural dyeing to international visitors. "Teaching is harder than learning!" he quipped. He developed new techniques to evoke Jackson Pollock's paintings, which he had seen in class, and these were a hit with the visitors.

He had plenty of inspiration and a good collection but didn't know how to make a business. When I launched the pilot BMA course in 2014, he signed up. "Design isn't enough," he stated. "We also need a market." He wanted to increase his business and learn English. He wanted to sell via the internet.

In the first BMA module, Business Strategy / Understanding Markets, he did a SWOT analysis and decided that his strengths were his education in natural colors and design, his weakness was lack of workspace and workers, his opportunities were the course and upcoming events, and his threat was competition and copying. At the time, the family's sales were 70 percent wholesale, 15 percent retail, 5 percent exhibitions, and 10 percent online. Calculating his strengths and limitations, he decided to concentrate on smaller orders and direct customer sales. He wanted to market his brand, Real Handicrafts. Already active on social media, during the BMA course he took the big step of building a website. During the first module, he got an order from a boutique online craft shop.

The second module was Operations and Production Management. He followed the material intently. "He is very reflective and had an example from his work-related experience for every concept," his teacher wrote. "His active social network and positive attitude are great assets. He could scale his operation up fast. He could manage a workforce of 50 persons even now."

Thinking about the key problem that he had identified—inability to process orders—catalyzed Soyabbhai to build a bigger workshop. After the course, he found new suppliers and got more workers by asking what problems they had and offering them services in addition to better pay. "I could not organize my work," he said. "I learned planning in detail, ethics, service, negotiation. And practical application after theory made it easy to understand."

For his BMA collection, Soyabbhai took inspiration from Van Gogh. Fascinated by the film *Lust for Life*, which he saw in class, he immersed himself in Van Gogh's work. He created a large sunflower block and blocks to evoke Van Gogh brushstrokes. He overlapped existing blocks to make texture. He used his strengths in color range and hand painting. His mentor pushed him. "'Do more, do more,' he says!" Soyabbhai cried. "Does he think I have nothing else to do?!" But the results were fresh, bold, and exciting, and the last pieces were the best. His collection enjoyed the highest sales in the Mumbai exhibition.

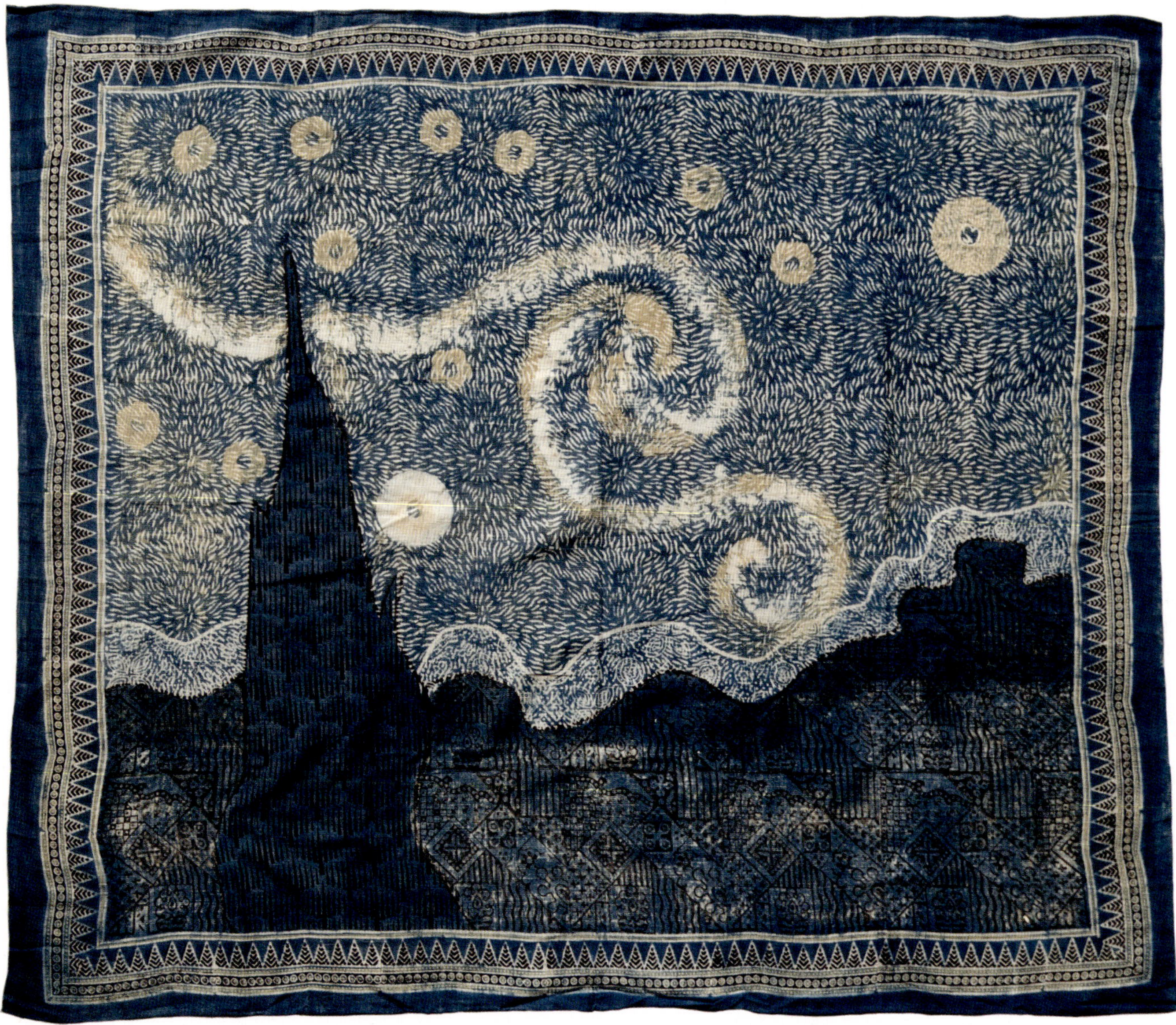

After the final module, Analysis / Maximizing Business Performance, he said, "I have done many exhibitions. But I never analyzed sales. I found that most of my sale was my newest work. I learned that I need to have color ways, and that shiny sells in Mumbai. Now I have information for developing my business. I will focus on the global market, and an eco-conscious niche. Business is like a bike trip," he concluded. "You have to be ready, check in the middle, have a backup plan, and manage speed."

He graduated with a special jury award for Most Entrepreneurial Artisan.

The last part of the course was to be an internship with a successful designer. I paired Soyabbhai with a young designer who works with artisans to create consciously eco-friendly, cutting-edge fashion. Though she was pregnant and working on her fashion week collection, she agreed to the project.

But Soyabbhai told her that he was too busy to work with her now.

I asked him what he was busy with. He gave me a list of orders and said he was working on a new collection with his partner.

Hold it; who is your partner? I asked.

It turned out to be Prateek!

Opposite: *Starry Night in Ajrakhpur*, wall hanging by Soyab AKT Khatri, 2022. Handloom cotton, hand block printed and painted, natural dye. 37" x 44". Charmed by Van Gogh, Soyabbhai created blocks inspired by the artist's painting style. Using new and traditional blocks, and his own brushstrokes, he evoked Van Gogh's famed *Starry Night*. *Photo: Schiffer Publishing Ltd.*

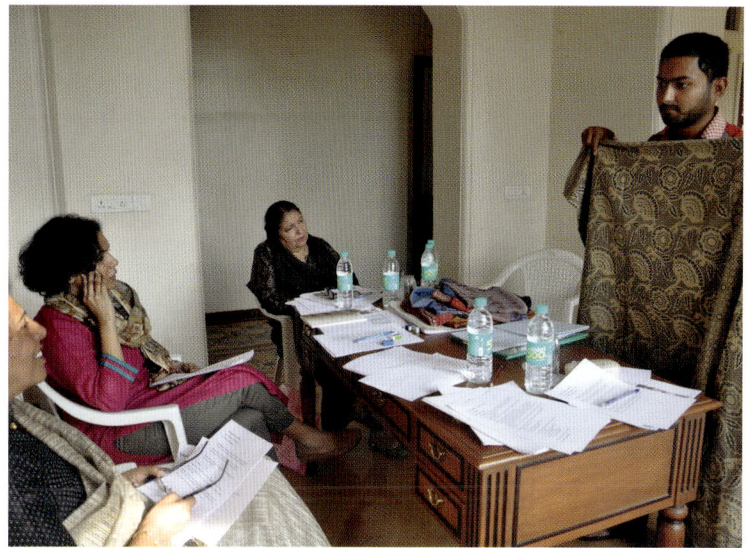

Right: Mumbai, 2014. Soyabbhai presents fabric printed with the sunflower block he made for his Van Gogh collection to his BMA jury. Impressed, they created a special award for him: Most Entrepreneurial Student. *Photo: Judy Frater*

Below: Ajrakhpur, 2015. Soyabbhai began teaching workshops through KRV. Organized and skilled, he made workshops a specialty. He enjoys sharing his tradition; he knows it brings value. Here he wears a shirt made of his natural-dyed "Jackson Pollak" fabric. *Photo: Judy Frater*

I probed further. What did he and his proposed mentor discuss?

"She said, 'It looks like you are inspired by artists. Is there anyone else you would like to draw on?'" he told me. "I said, 'Andy Goldsworthy.' She said, 'Hmm, I don't know.'" The conversation apparently ended there. She was a famous designer. Soyabbhai could not challenge her, question her, or imagine defending or discussing his ideas.

Prateek, on the other hand, was a student. Soyabbhai had already worked with him in person, in the structured, equalized situation of our design class. He felt comfortable with him and could consider him a partner. In the class situation he felt accountable to him. The relationship needs trust, a common wavelength, he explained.

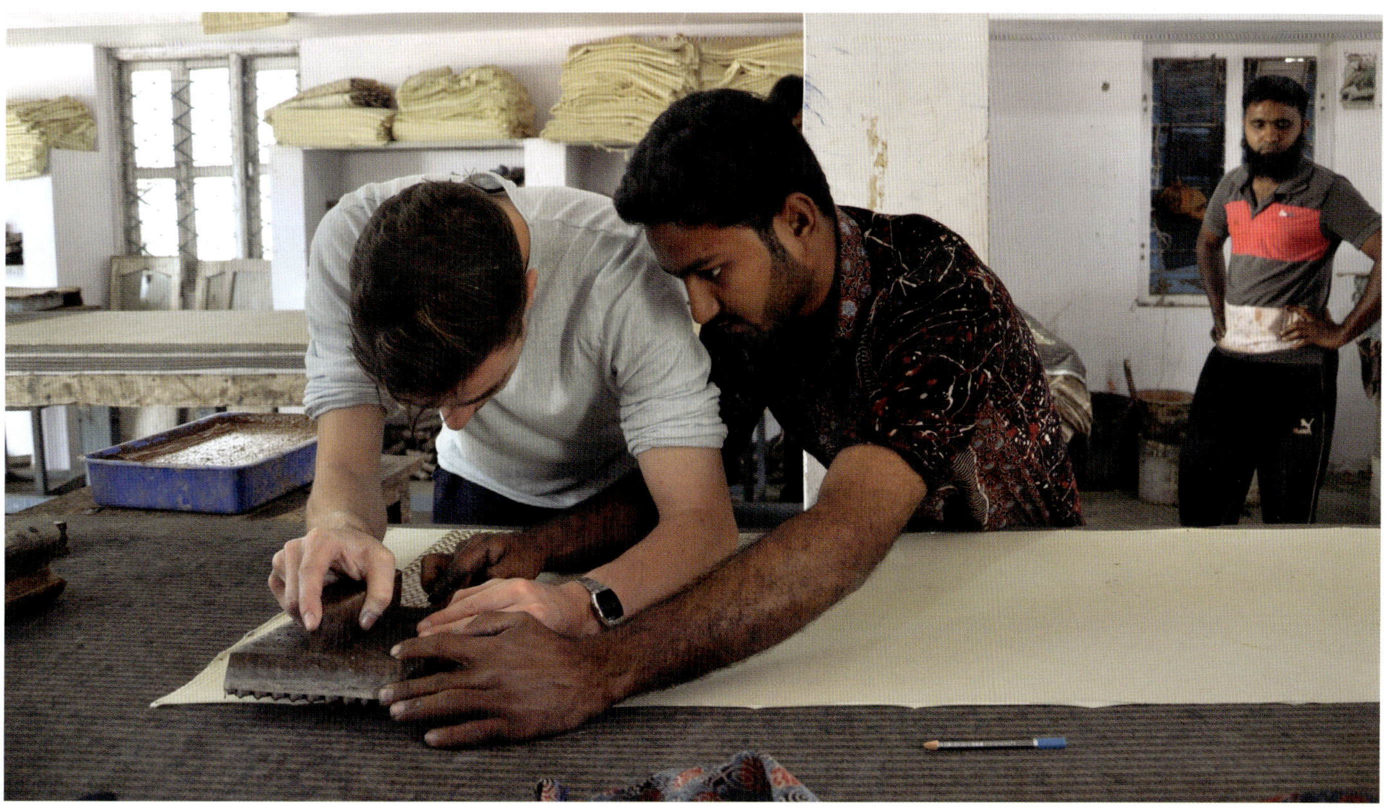

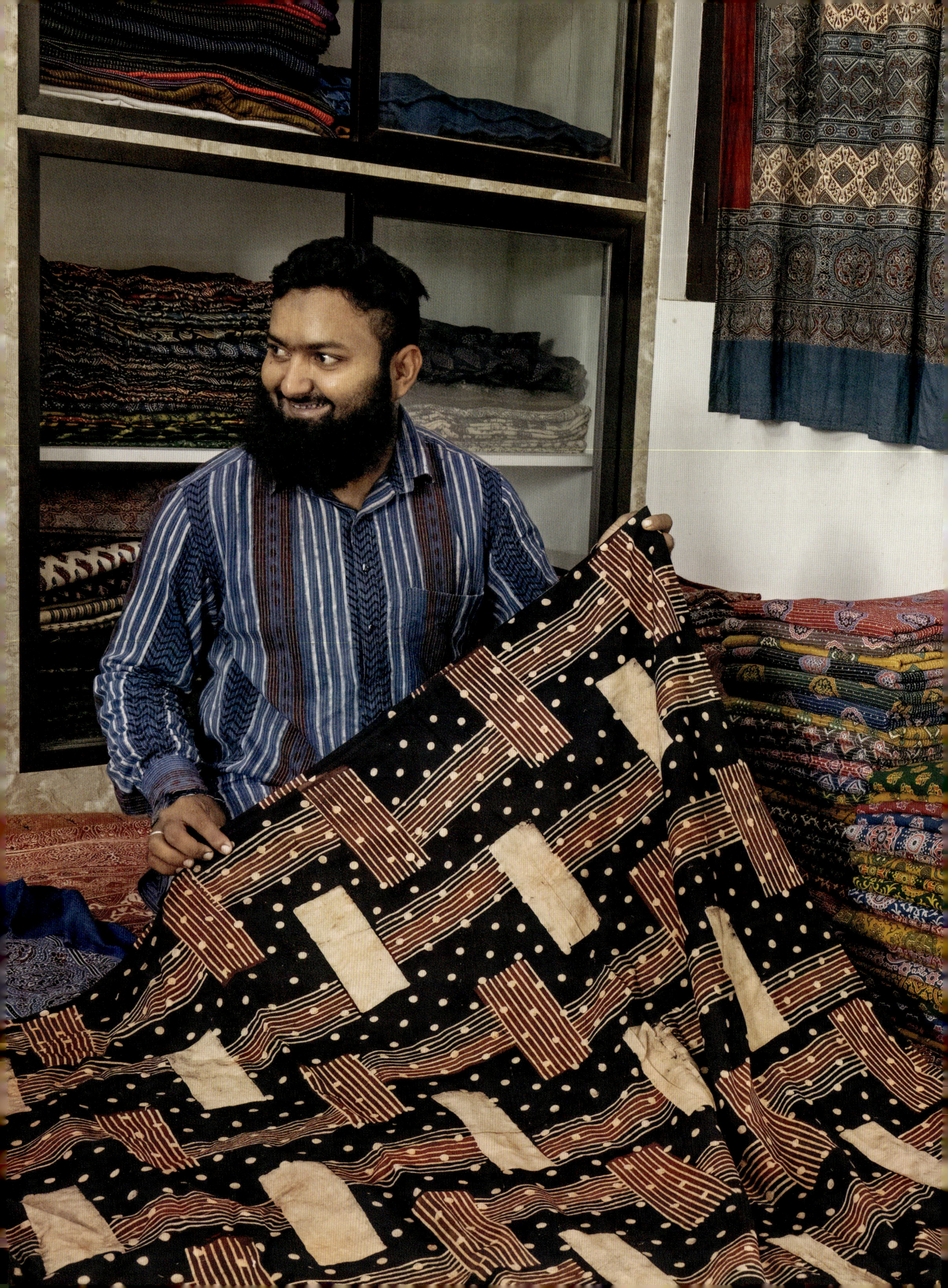

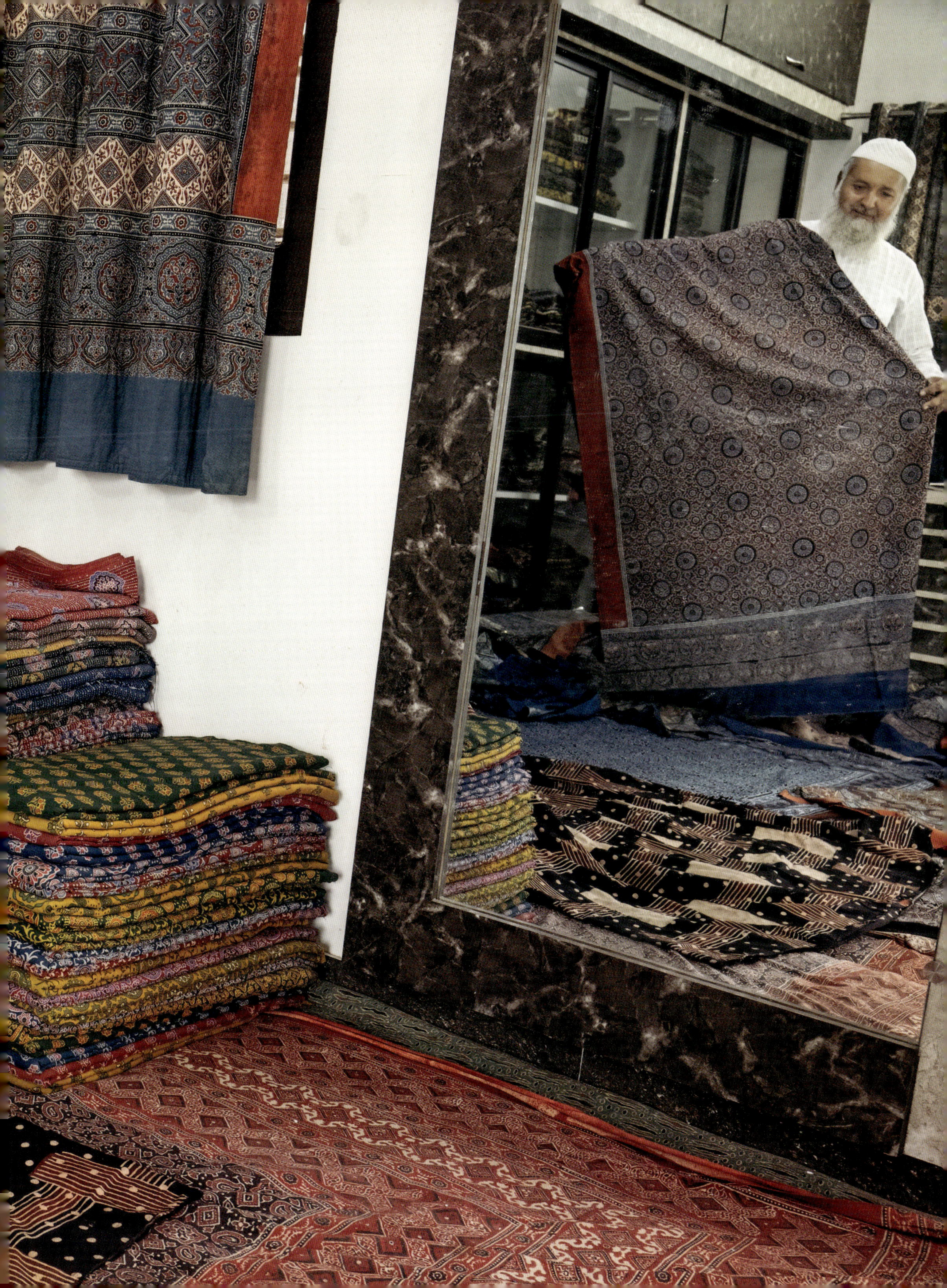

Previous pages: Ajrakhpur, 2022. Soyabbhai and his father, Abdul Karimbhai, show their respective work: a simplified contemporary print and half of a two-part traditional Ajrakh. Both take more time than the pace that production demands. *Photo: Nevada Wier*

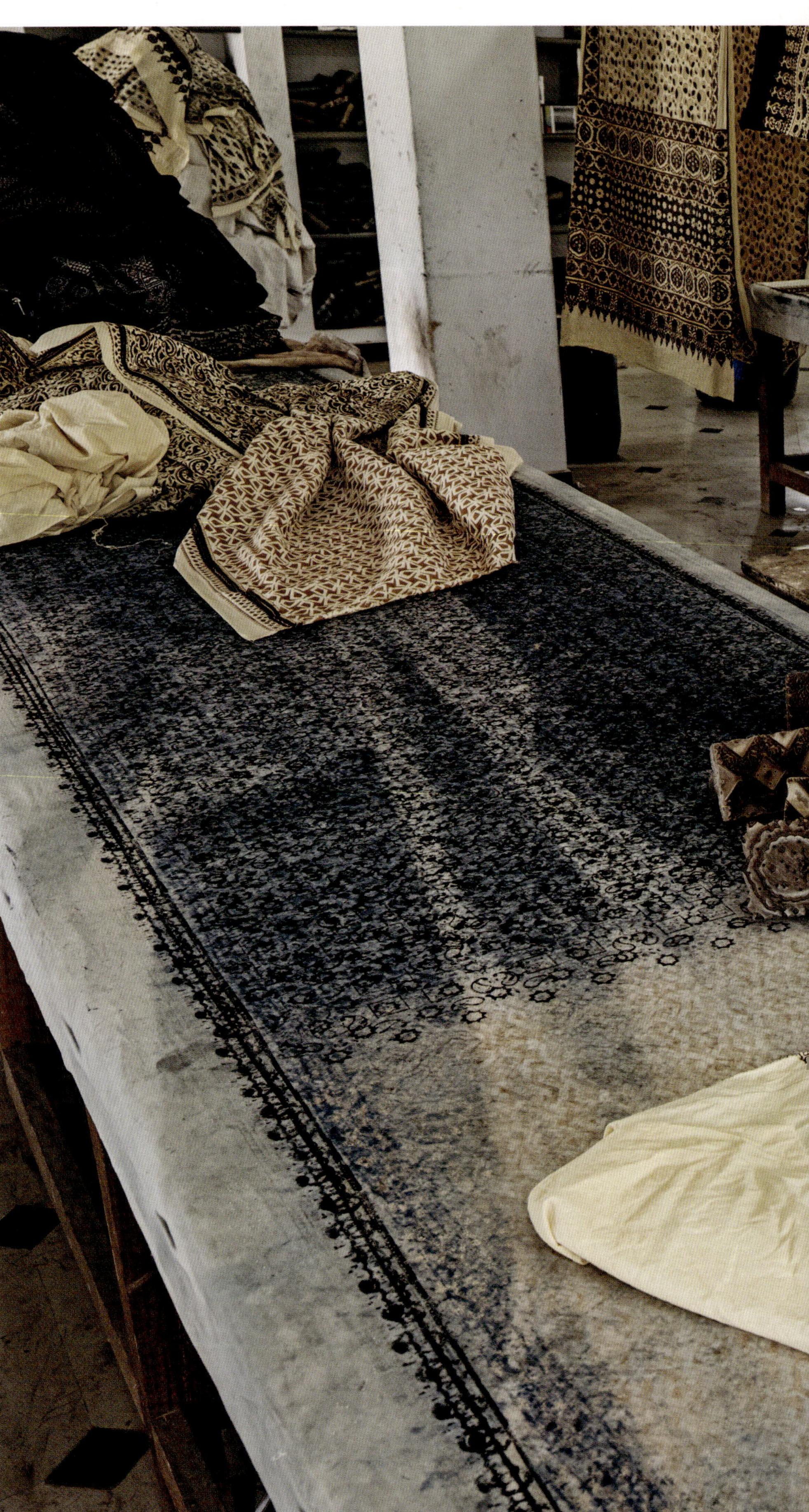

Right: Ajrakhpur, 2022. Though Soyabbhai is an expert printer and he enjoys printing, he creates only special work these days. Supervising and marketing consume most of his time. *Photo: Nevada Wier*

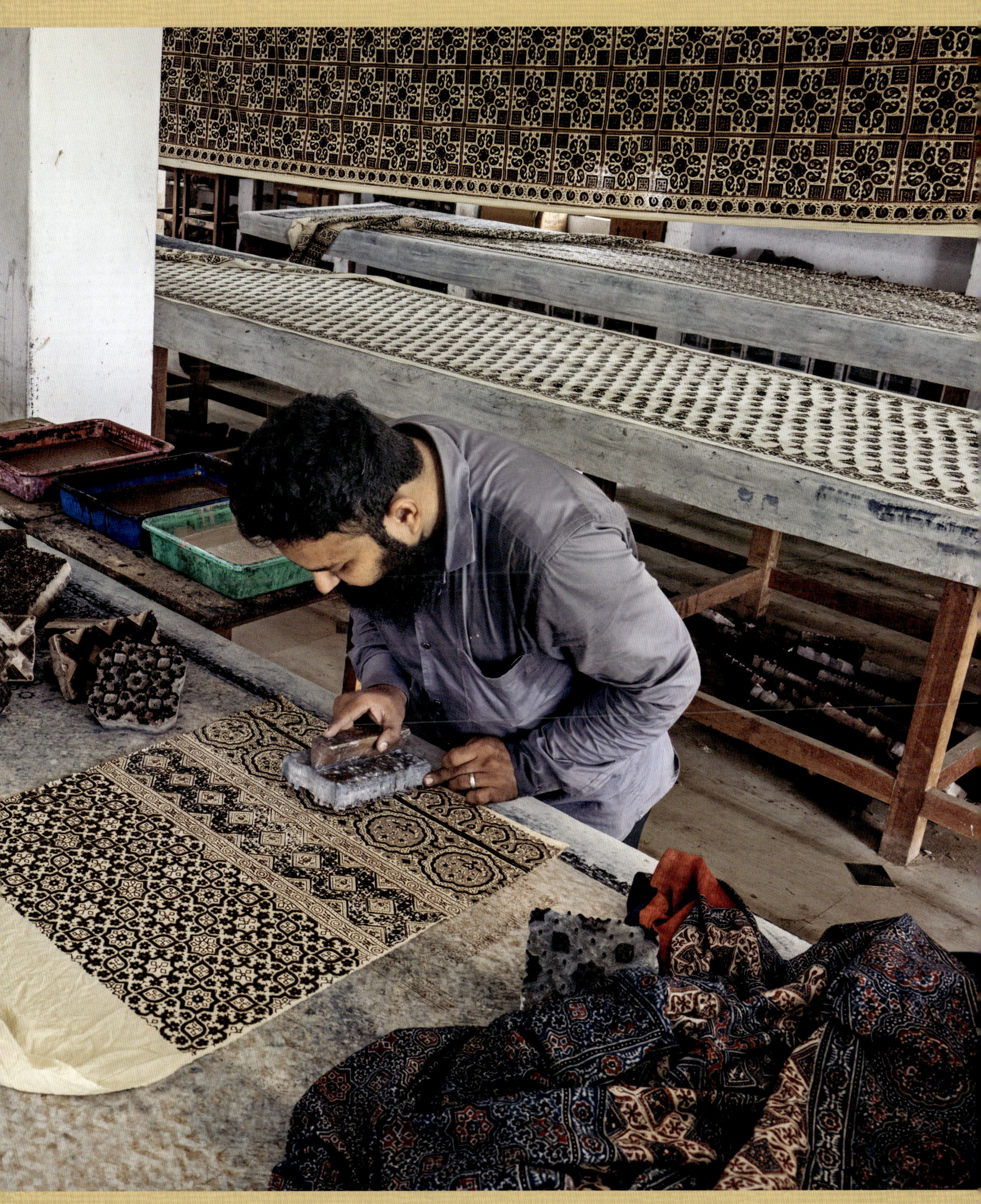

Soyabbhai subsequently participated in two codesign projects, and in the second he finally designed a collection inspired by Andy Goldsworthy. The garments that he and his partner created had the stamp of Soyabbhai's uninhibited style and recalled favorite Goldsworthy installations; for anyone familiar with his work, they brought an immediate smile.

Though Soyabbhai had articulated his goal as "Real Handicrafts will be a brand which will provide new design, and authentic and exclusive products to a global market," he still did not know exactly how to begin. "How can we promote our brands in the market?" he asked. "Exhibition organizers do not know us." To the answer, "Be patient and enjoy the process," he persisted. "I have been working with e-commerce sites and I have my own website. But I still feel that I have not been able to promote my brand," he said.

Open Studio Tours gave him an opportunity for some visibility. At a season-end review, he suggested that work presented in the tours should be fresh designs only. "Regular work is cheap," he remarked. "It makes the new work seem expensive. We must work together and be consistent."

"An artisan should work with concentration and passion," Soyabbhai said when he began his education. With faith and hard work, he and his father gained steady orders and built a state-of-the-art shop. They made sure there was something for everyone: modal saris for the local market, silk scarves for higher-end clients. Soyabbhai included the location on his website, Facebook page, and Instagram accounts, and customers began to find them via Google maps. Three months after the shop WhatsApp, Soyabbhai sent two more images: in the first, his father stood holding an oversized key in front of a shiny new Hyundai SUV. In the second, Soyabbhai held the key.

2022

Soyabbhai's shop has a huge hand-painted sign now. Handwork lasts longer, and you can see it from the road, he says. During the COVID-19 lockdown, he worked on social media and building a website with online sales capability. Once couriers started working again, he had a lot of sales. People got to know him, and now they come to the shop. His father made traditional Ajrakhs—bedsheets and *be-pota*, pairs of printed fabrics decoratively hand-stitched together. They all sold. Only two single Ajrakhs and a couple of *be-pota* still to be stitched are left. He also made the Ajrakh curtains that I had suggested—and of course, everyone wants them.

They have so many orders for the domestic market that they can't make more Ajrakhs now. Ajrakh takes more time to print, with the corners and composition. Yardage is faster.

Who prints the Ajrakhs? I ask.

Mixed, they say. Sometimes they do the *rekh* outline and give it to workers. Sometimes they print, but mostly only special pieces. Soyabbhai has only one of his contemporary prints. They also take more time than yardage and saris, so he doesn't get to creating new designs.

Be careful what you wish for? In the seminar "Who Are the Workers?," Ajrakh artisan designers agreed that artisans want something more than job work, but once you are set, you don't have to do your own work. There is a progression.

Above: Ajrakhpur, 2022. Good block printing, like any craft, requires concentration, precision, and enthusiasm. *Photo: Nevada Wier*

Opposite: Soyabbhai designed his logo Real Handicrafts by thinking of Ajrakh and his commitment to integrity.

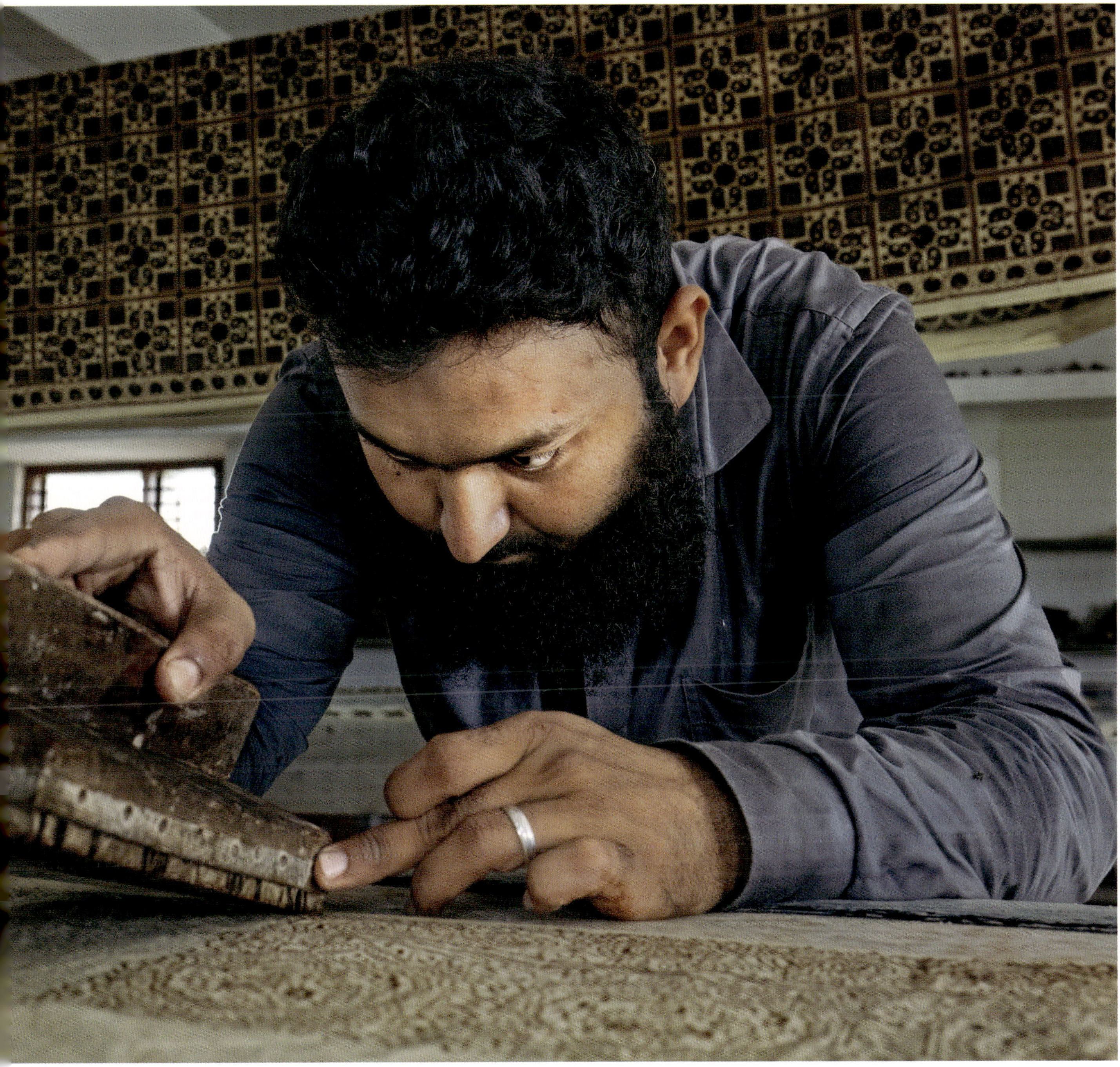

Soyabbhai does have one more special piece: the one he made for my book—an interpretation of Van Gogh's *Starry Night*. He used handloom fabric for it, he says. And natural dyes, of course. He shows how he used his Van Gogh brushstroke blocks in different ways, overlapping with a traditional Ajrakh pattern, and how he selected contemporary blocks to create the effects he wanted. He hand-painted the swirls in the sky. He pauses for a rare moment to enjoy his passion.

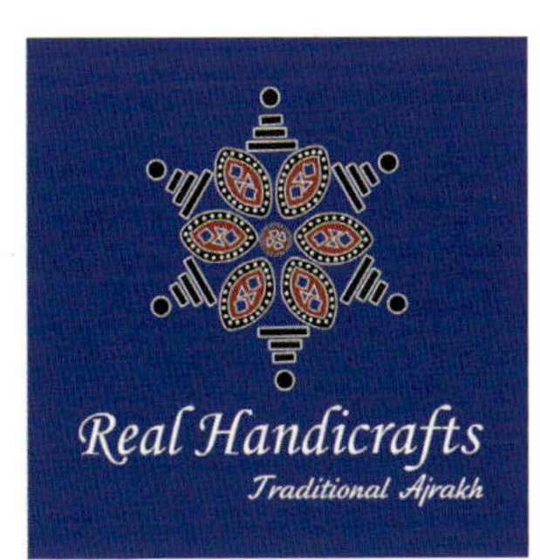

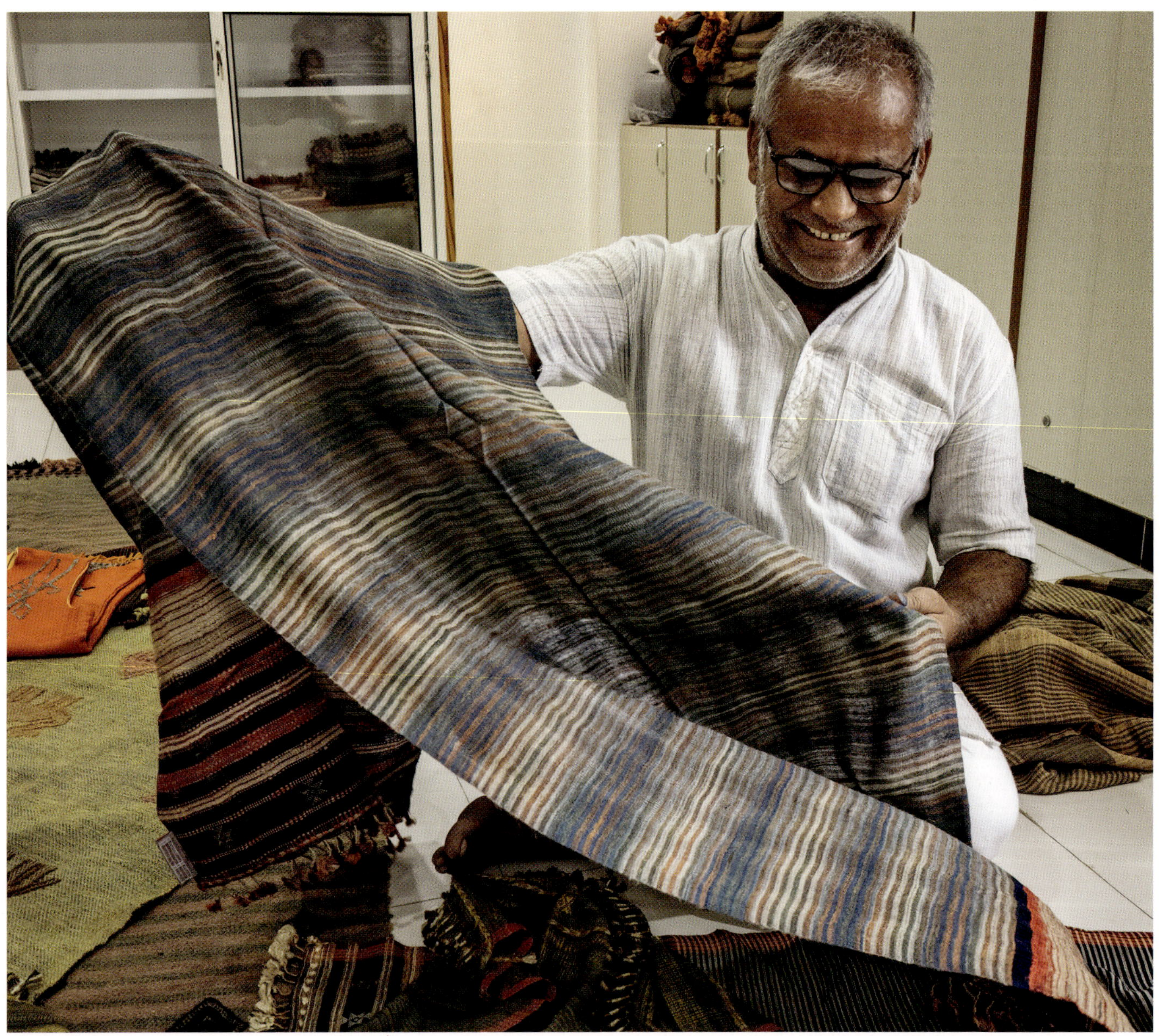

If I had taken the business course without learning design, I would have become a trader.

~Dahyalalbhai Atmaram Kudecha

Bhujodi, 2022. Light, soft, and subtle. Dahyabhai's natural-dyed scarves, in endless delicious variations, have been hits with the international and domestic markets. *Photo: Nevada Wier*

Chapter 20

DAHYALALBHAI ATMARAM KUDECHA: BALANCING ACT

People were raving. "I've never seen anything like this before!" they exclaimed. "This weaving is amazing . . . fantastic . . . gorgeous!" "Best in the show!" The accolades were pouring in. Curiously, there was in fact traditional weaving from Kutch just across the walkway. The exciting thing was that the visitors were instead focusing on Dahyabhai's *innovation* on the tradition. Design really worked! Fortuitously, the Santa Fe actress Ali MacGraw came into Dahyabhai's booth Saturday morning and was the first and most enthusiastic fan. She modeled his innovative rhythm checks for the next two days and directed customers to where they could get a scarf too . . . and that's showbiz.

At the end of the two and a half whirlwind days of the International Folk Art Market | Santa Fe, we sat quietly and tallied the sales. They were more than double what Dahyabhai averaged in a year. It was not all profit, of course. He had to extend his capacity beyond his family and hire two weavers. And he had maxed his cash credit account to purchase raw materials. But clearly, he was in the best financial situation of his life so far.

"The experience took me beyond my imagination," he said. "I learned about artisans of the world, and customers of the USA. I learned what people like, and the importance of tradition. People are attracted to our customs. I realized in a real way that we need to retain our identity and present our culture."

That was 2014, Dahyabhai's first experience of the International Folk Art Market. Two years later, he arrived in Santa Fe to find his image smiling way larger than life on a banner at the folk art market. By most measures, he had arrived—and certainly, he had come a very long way.

Dahyalal Kudecha is a traditional weaver from Kutch. His grandfather wove. His father gave up the tradition to work in a salt mine to earn more money, but when he needed medical treatment, the family migrated to Bhujodi, a weaving village, and Dahyabhai experienced his traditional art. He decided to learn weaving. He learned initial techniques from his brother-in-law and continued to learn by experimentation.

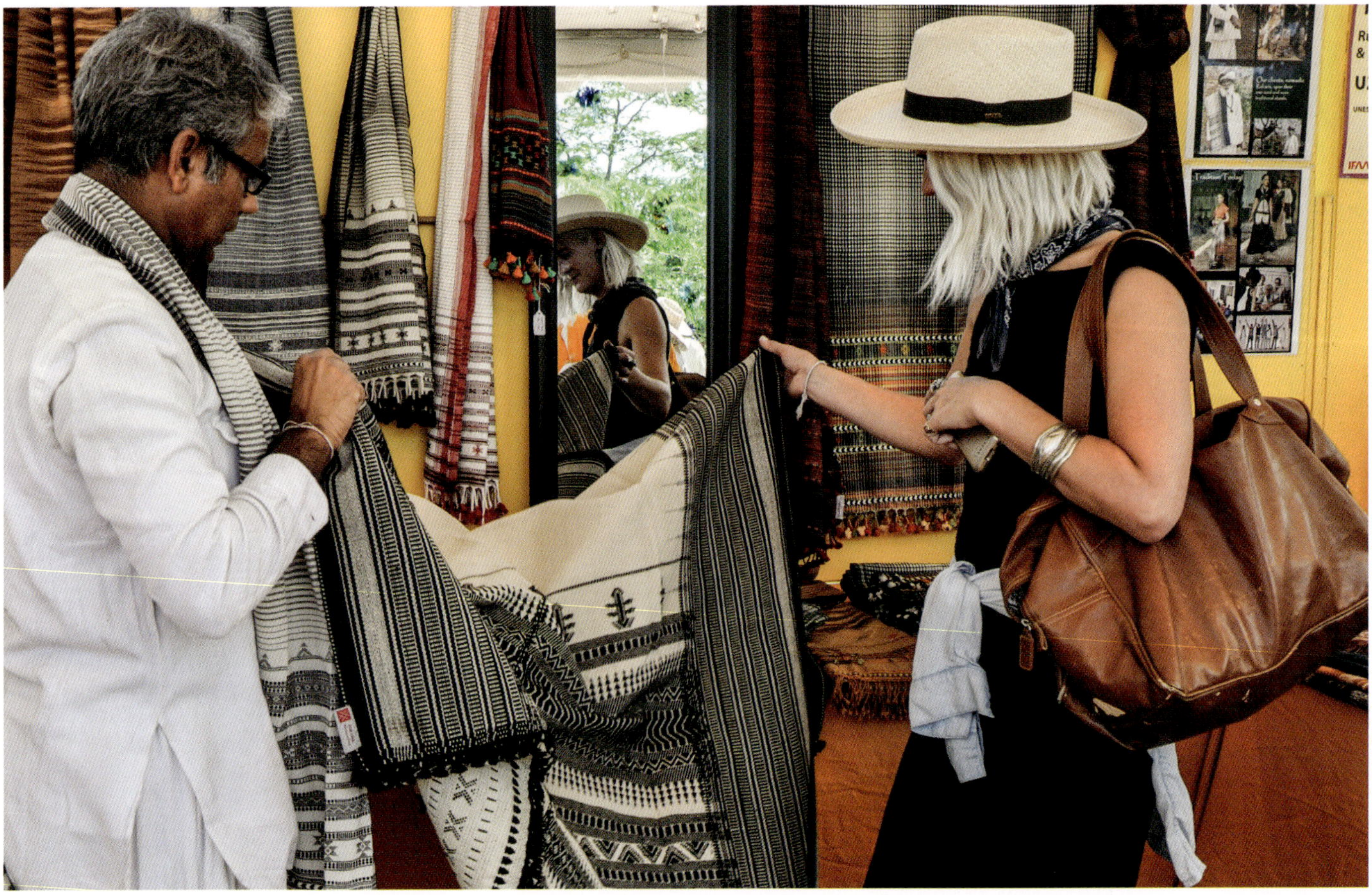

Above: Santa Fe, New Mexico, 2014. In his first International Folk Art Market, Dahyabhai had the foresight to bring a few *dhabla* along with his collection. He knew the traditional blankets would help explain his work. He realized that buyers liked the original. *Photo: Judy Frater*

Below: Kala Raksha Vidhyalaya, 2008. As Dahyalalbhai was sketching a pipal tree sapling, the visiting faculty member challenged him to weave it into a sample. When he achieved the innovation, he felt it was a creative breakthrough. *Photo: Judy Frater*

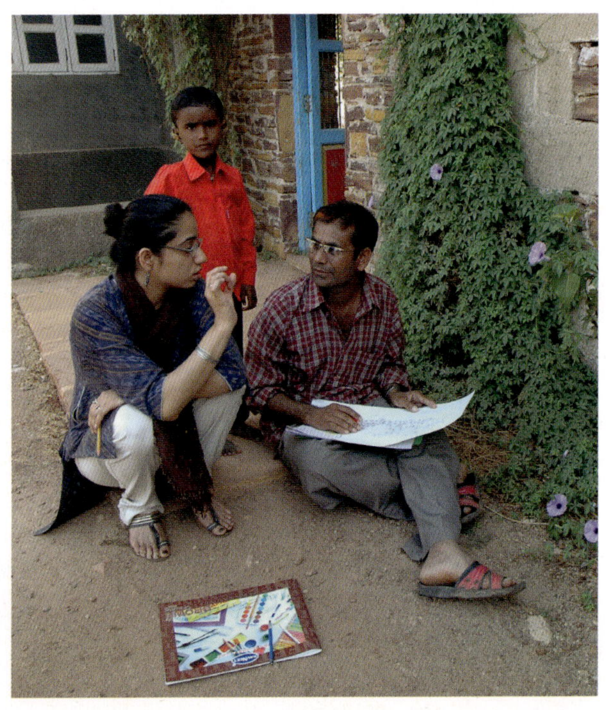

He worked under a master weaver for over twenty-five years. "I did job work," he recalled. "He gave me the yarn. I only earned on workmanship. Sometimes, I sampled new work. But I didn't feel it was my design. He had the name. I just worked." But he always had two dreams: higher education for his sons, and to become an independent artist. In 2006, he came to the first convocation of Kala Raksha Vidhyalaya to demonstrate weaving. It inspired him, he said. And in 2008, he decided to take the design course at KRV. His employer encouraged him. But it was a year's commitment, and his economic situation wasn't good. He taught his wife weaving so that they wouldn't lose their income. She wove while he was in class, and he worked fourteen hours a day in order to make ends meet.

Into the first module, he quipped, "Nothing is impossible in weaving!" By the second module, he said, "Design is the key to our art. At KRV, I learned to make motifs through inspiration from nature. Now I look at nature very differently. I feel magical when I can translate a natural form into my work. And I learned that I can make something traditional new just by size, proportion, or placement."

At the close of the course, he reflected, "My confidence grew after education. The fears I had about the survival of our craft in the industrial marketplace are gone."

Dahyabhai began to take creative risks. He began his own business. But he struggled financially, with two sons in college. I asked him to come as a mentor in the 2009 course, and when I saw that he was a natural teacher, I asked him to join KRV as a salaried core faculty member the following year.

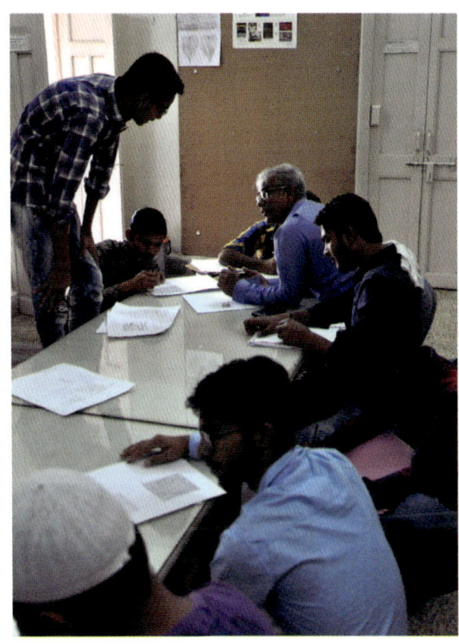

Teaching, he honed an understanding of design and a deep love for his tradition, both of which he seamlessly weaves into his work. Somewhere along the line, Dahyabhai added a third dream to his list: he wanted to participate in an international exhibition. "Our weaving traditions united the culture and tradition of different ethnic communities," he said. "We lived among other people and knew their history, customs, and tastes, and we made products for them accordingly. Immersion in another culture will expose me to the markets we strive to reach."

At the end of 2013, I brought Dahyabhai to Cusco, Peru for the Center for Traditional Textiles of Cusco international conference Tinkuy. It was his first time out of India, and he loved meeting weavers from the Andes and sharing his work. He had his rhythm check scarves with him and more. He became known, but more importantly, he gained exposure, which he could apply in design innovation.

Above: Somaiya Kala Vidya, 2017. As a local faculty member, Dahyabhai taught design with visiting faculty for eight years spanning Kala Raksha and Somaiya Kala Vidya—over one hundred students, he estimates. *Photo: Judy Frater*

Below: Cusco, Peru, 2013. Dahyabhai attended Tinkuy, a gathering of weavers from the Andes and beyond in Peru. It was his first travel outside India, and the Andean weavers equally enjoyed meeting a weaver from Kutch. *Photo: Judy Frater*

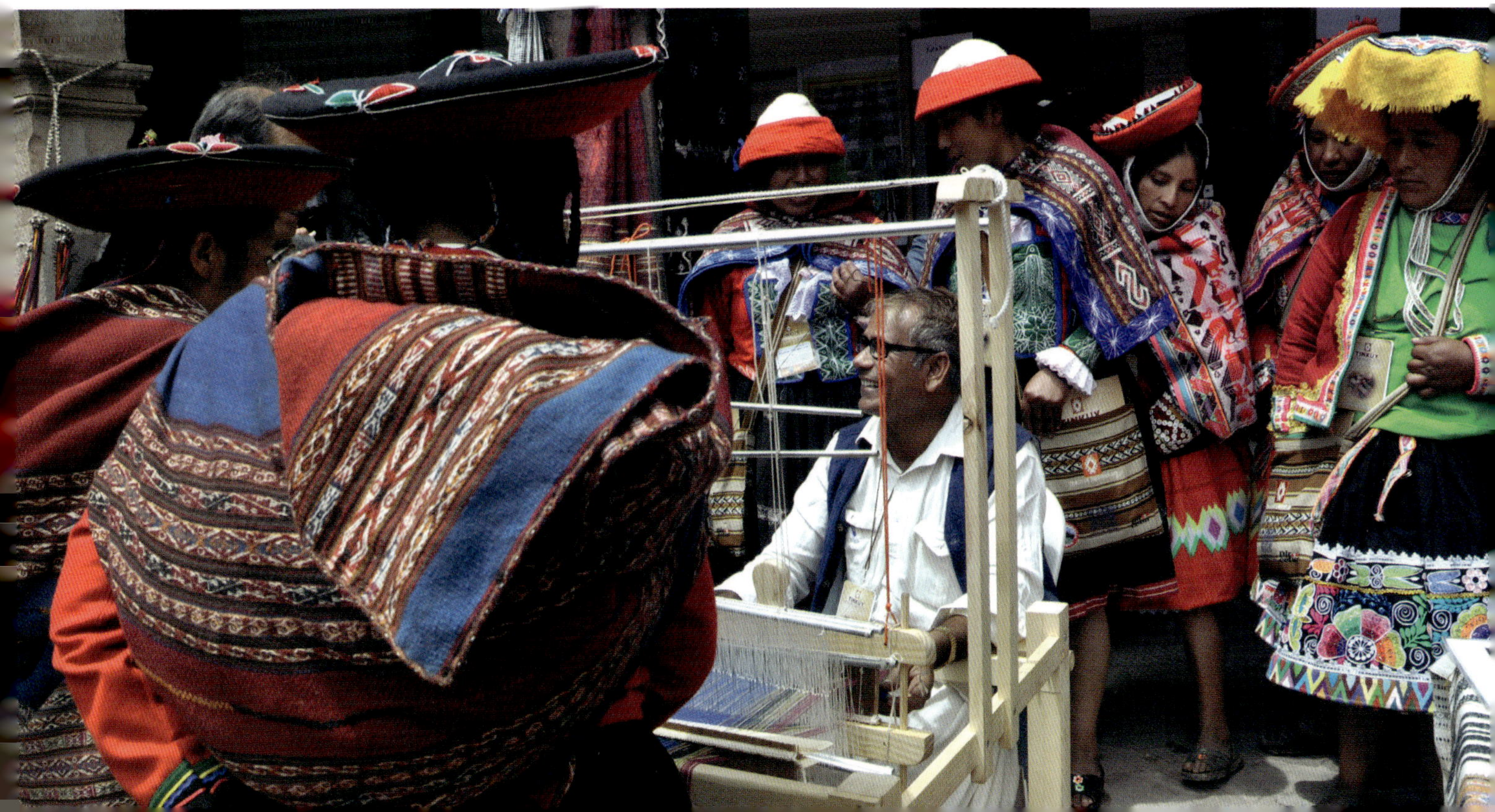

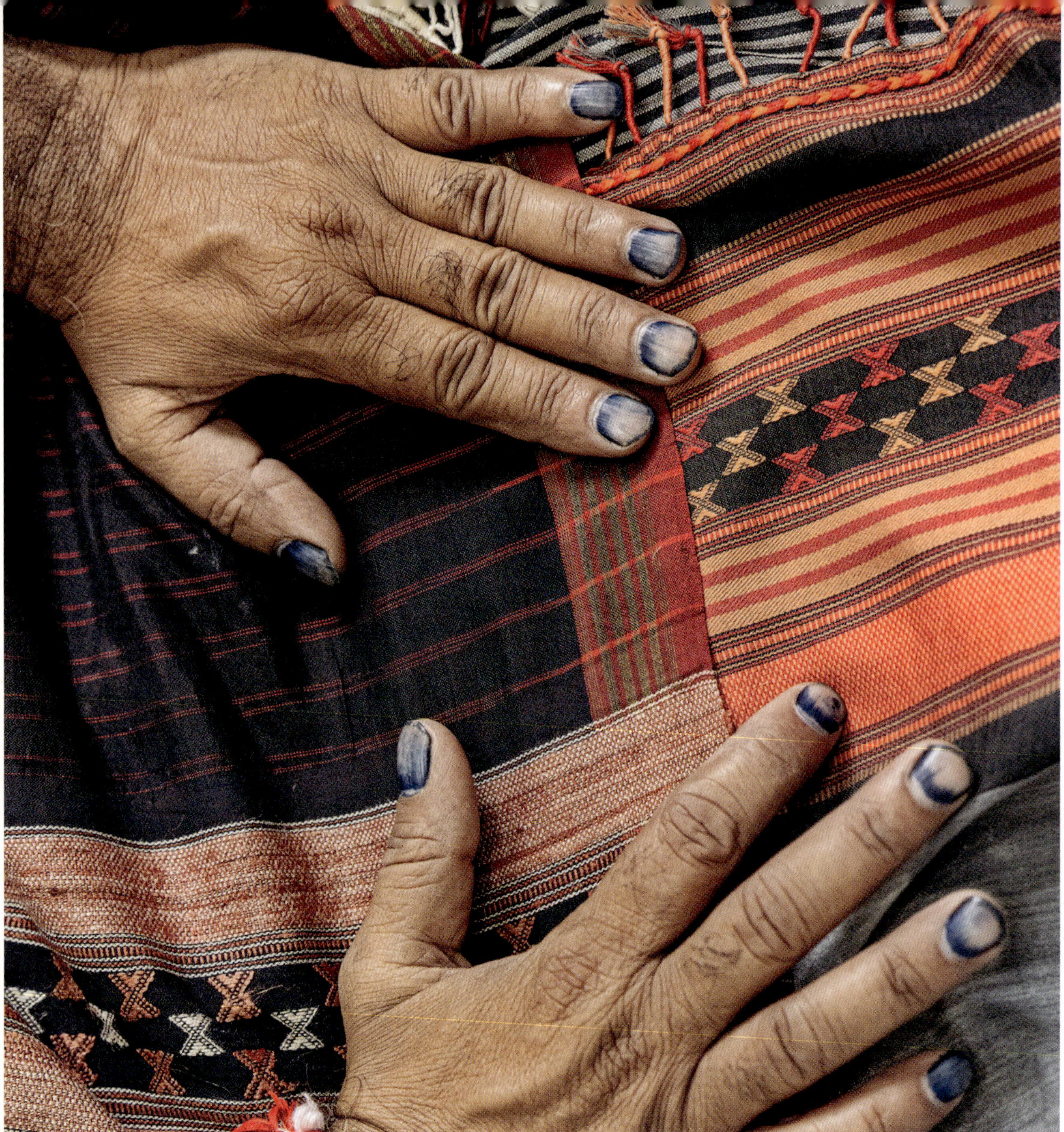

When we began Somaiya Kala Vidya, Dahyabhai joined as a faculty member. He began by taking the pilot Business and Management for Artisans course as a faculty member in training. Upon completing the course, he reflected, "To grow a business, we need to balance risk with return. Risk management really helped me make a business plan. In this course, I learned the value of time and planning, and to think more of satisfying the customer. I learned that you have to set goals and keep tracking performance. I learned to focus on growth—and to work with a pencil.

"I think my business is 60 percent new design and 40 percent business know-how," he continued. "If I had taken this course without learning design, I would have become a trader."

Dahyabhai's weaving took on a sophistication of texture and color. He learned natural dyeing. He tried ikat yarn dyeing. He added a variety of high-quality yarns—fine cotton, soft wool, different types of tassar and eri silk. He learned where to source fibers and had the confidence to invest. He thought about the market. "Sometimes if there is a lot of work in the piece, for example, we do simpler finishing," he said. "We look at color, how to bring it out if necessary. Customers see these details. We keep costing in mind. We learned that in class too—costing and editing." He experimented with reeds to create new textures—but never with essential aspects of his tradition. He practiced what he taught; he created a distinctive rich style, clearly Kutchi, and clearly Dahyabhai.

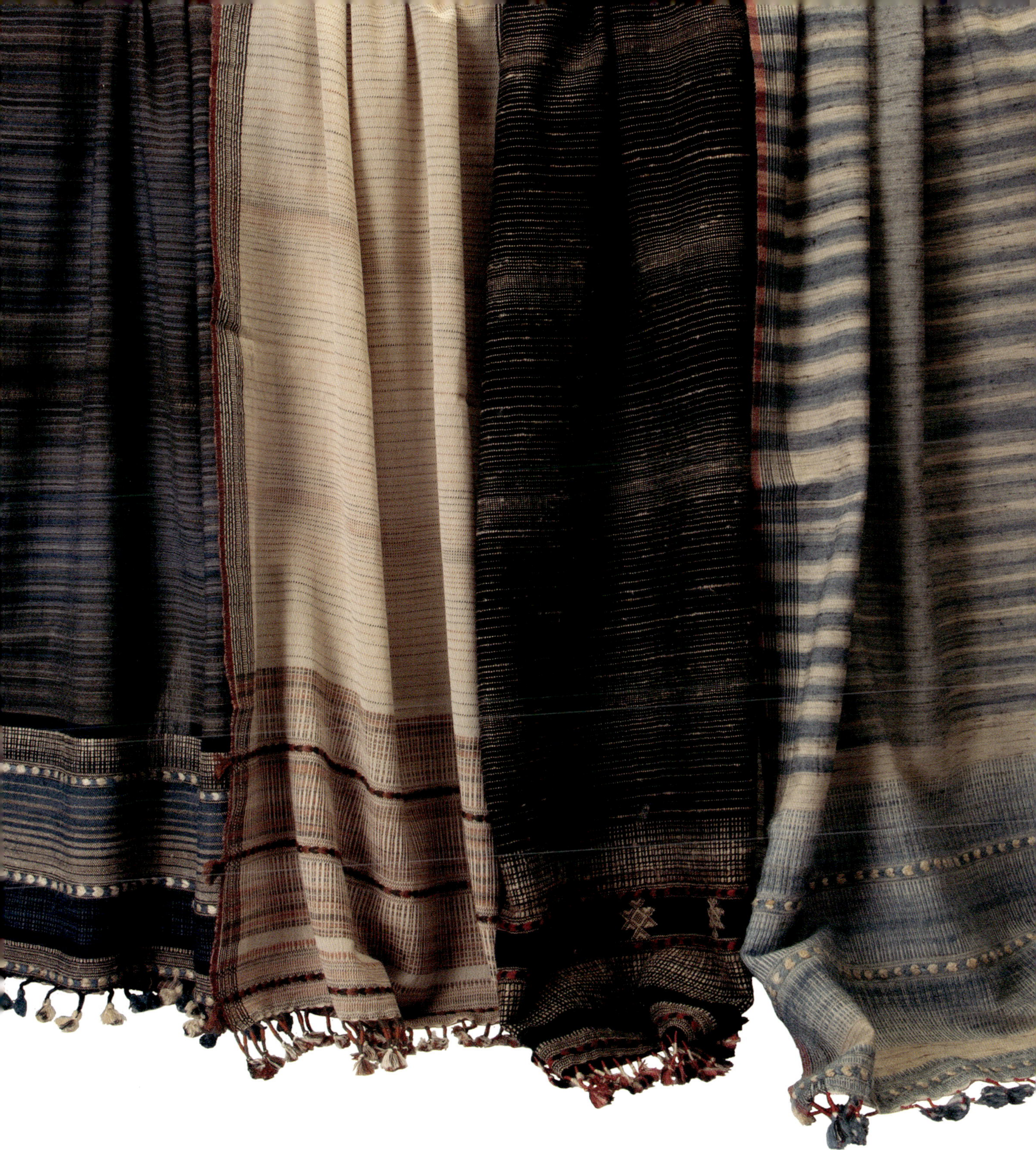

Opposite: Bhujodi, 2022. Traditionally, weavers of Bhujodi worked with undyed natural black, white, and gray local sheep wool. Dahyabhai and his son Dilipbhai, also a design graduate, have perfected natural-dyeing their own yarns, broadening their range of color and texture exponentially. *Photo: Nevada Wier*

Above: Autumn Mist, scarves by Dahyalal Atmaram Kudecha, 2022. Cotton warp, wool and silk wefts and extra wefts, natural dyes, hand woven. 23" x 78" each. Dahyabhai perfected selection of yarns, natural dyeing, and subtle variations in weaving technique through teaching design and direct contact with good markets. *Photo: Schiffer Publishing Ltd.*

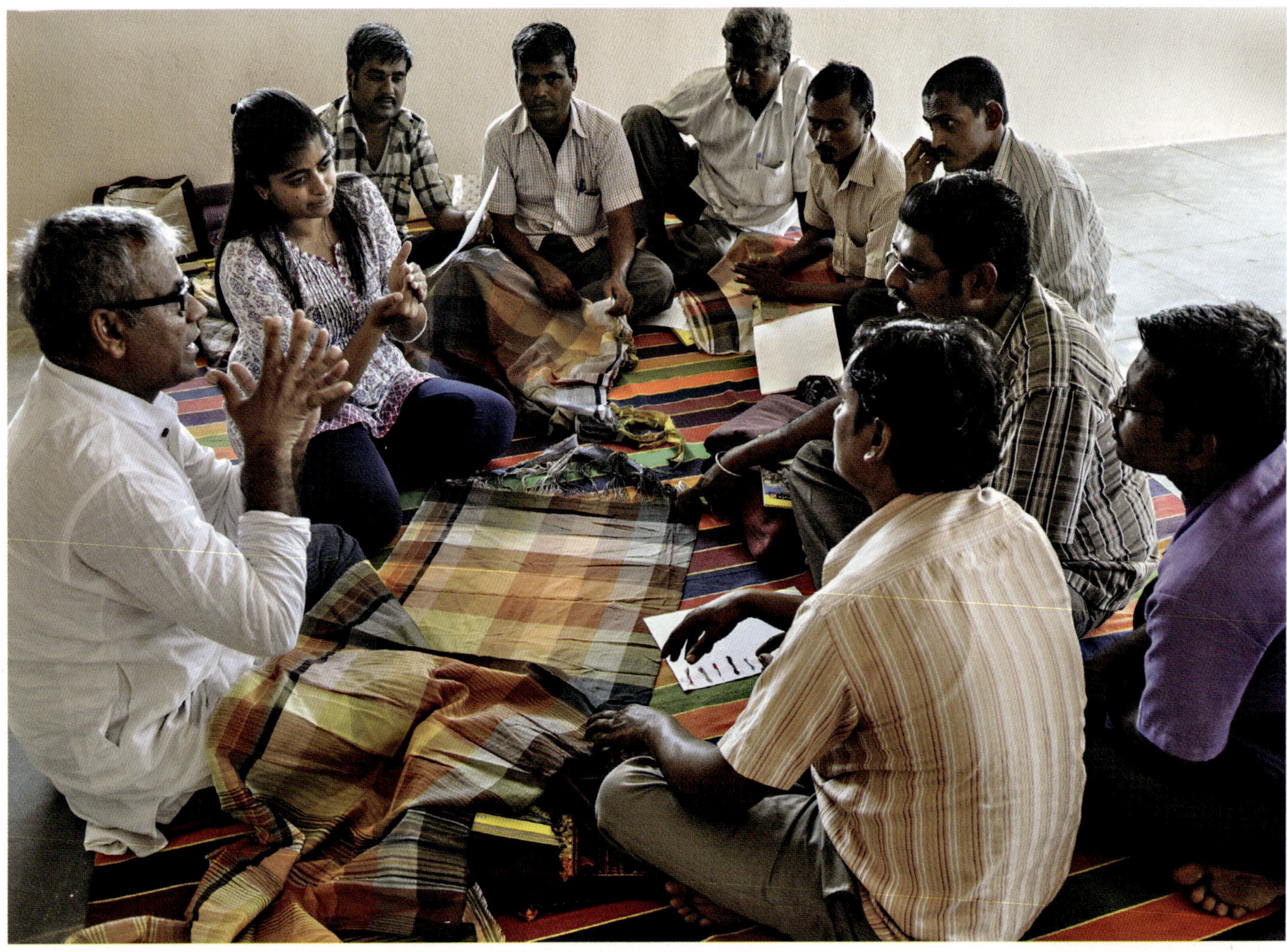

Above: Kamatgi, 2015. In the first Outreach program, Bhujodi to Bagalkot, Dahyabhai was a key member of the team, codesigning with Bagalkot weavers and then coteaching design in condensed modules tailored for their needs. *Photo: Judy Frater*

Opposite: Mumbai, 2017. In 2017, SKV was invited to participate in Lakme Fashion Week. We featured seven design graduate collections. It was the first time the event had recognized artisans as designers. Dahyabhai showed a collection of saris inspired by fog. *Photo: Lakme Fashion Week*

Early in his career at Somaiya Kala Vidya, Dahyabhai had another opportunity for cross-cultural codesign. In 2014, he was instrumental in developing the artisan-to-artisan Outreach program in Bagalkot, Karnataka. "In the beginning the weavers weren't willing to believe that their saris would sell for 4,000 rupees," he recalls. "Until they did the exhibition in Mumbai, they couldn't imagine that their work would be appreciated that well. But when they sold their products themselves, the joy they felt was priceless. I am fortunate that I could be part of this initiative to help fellow artisans.

"It is the responsibility of an artisan, really, because an artisan understands and trusts another artisan more," he continued. "There were barriers in the beginning—language and expectations. In the color class, they thought we would teach them how to dye yarn. We had to explain that first we had to teach them color theory. I realized that before teaching anything, we must address their way of thinking. What do they want to do? What are we planning to teach? Whatever we plan to do, we must share it with our students."

Dahyabhai grew from a job worker to entrepreneur. "I enjoy my freedom as a weaver," he said. "In the design course, I realized that the traditional artisan was independent. He was designer, maker, and marketer. There was no hierarchy and no boss. He was free. In this situation, an artisan can flourish. I want to continue to live like this. We have to nurture our creative capacity, or the capacity of the artisan and the craft stagnates. If we can do this, we can retain our value. Craft and life are not separated. We don't just come up with a design in so many hours. It comes to us while doing something else. We weave and design together. When an artisan works at home, he participates in family life, and traditional culture is sustained and embedded in craft."

When asked about the importance of scaling up, Dahyabhai flatly stated that he did not believe in scale. "If we work in large scale," he explained, "it is no longer craft. Growth is not always measured in numbers. You could have twenty looms and make a profit. But you could also make a profit with one. You have to see the relationship between quality and quantity. If you want quality, you can't do quantity."

But as his business grew, he needed production beyond what his family could do, and he hired weavers in the way that he had been hired by a master weaver. He gained insights. Addressing this in the SKV seminar "Who Are the Workers?," he said, "We always talk about customers' demands. What about artisans' desires? It is a question of priority. In my view, we must prioritize artisans, because if artisans aren't happy, we will not have good-quality products and we will not be able to participate in the market."

Through learning, teaching, and becoming independent, Dahyabhai's understanding of success also evolved. "It's not about just money," he explained. "Money can't buy everything. Because of design education, Kutch artisans understand that. In the first class we bring senior artisans to talk about tradition. In one day, we learn what we will think about for the rest of our life."

Dahyabhai's rhythm check shawl was featured in the Victoria and Albert Museum's exhibition *The Fabric of India*. His collection inspired by fog was shown in Lakme Fashion Week, Mumbai. He received the Crafts Council of India Kamala Award for Contribution to Craft and Community, and the International Folk Art Market Award for Living Traditions. He became a leader and spokesperson for craft and artisans, in Kutch, in India, and internationally. I asked him what he saw as key problems in craft today. He noted that markets for craft are falling because customers ask for cheaper goods—and artisans comply. "Shortcuts and undercuts lead to the death of traditions," he said. He also felt that a key mistake that artisans make is risk aversion. "You have to go out to experience," he said. "Taking risks is less risky when you have experience."

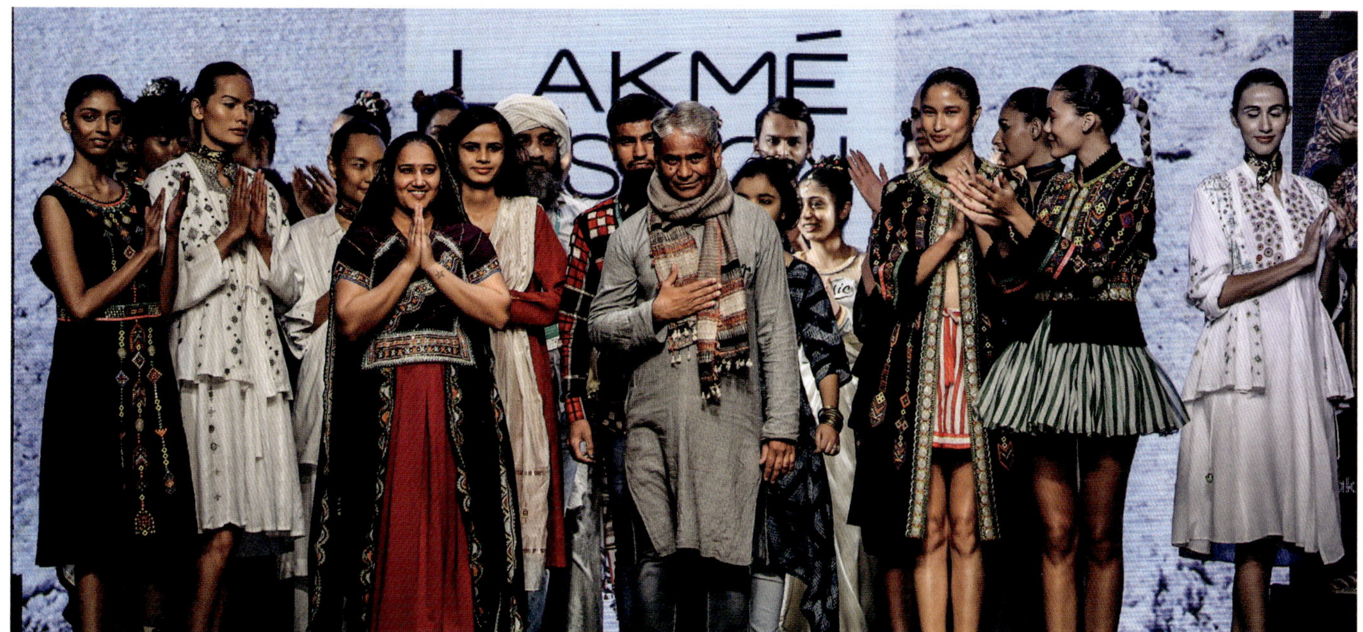

Above all, he felt that artisans need a platform. "We can learn how to create design," he noted, "but we need to be able to showcase those designs. It's only when artisans have a chance to present that they can explain to customers and interest them. If people ask why my new design is expensive, I have an opportunity to explain what I have done. And it is largely because of my experience in the USA that my status here has improved. Many times in India, people think that since I have been abroad, my products must be superior.

"Education gave me an opportunity to dream, and to fulfill my dreams," he concluded. "I am proud that my success has set an example for young people to continue or return to weaving. I asked my younger son, Dilip, to study further, and he said, 'What will I do after graduation? I will probably do a job where only my office staff will know me, and however much I work I will get a limited salary. If I am a weaver, the whole world will know me, and I can earn as much as I work.' This is how our society has benefited."

Dilipbhai took the design course in 2017 and began to work with his father in their brand "Forline." The following year, Dahyabhai left teaching to focus on his business. "As long as I was a faculty person, I had opportunities to teach and learn," he said. "But I couldn't maximize the benefits of my innovations."

2022

Today, Dahyabhai is surely successful in his own terms. He has balanced education, mindfulness, recognizing and capturing opportunities, planning, working hard, and being himself. But he has to manage his success. In the close quarters of the village, an individual's gain is viewed by others as a threat. "Dayabhai gained the most benefit of design education," a man who did not take the course resentfully says. Dahyabhai consciously nurtures community relations to mitigate his celebrity. "It's win-win," he points out. "Since my education, my income has increased remarkably. But the master weaver for whom I once worked has not lost a thing."

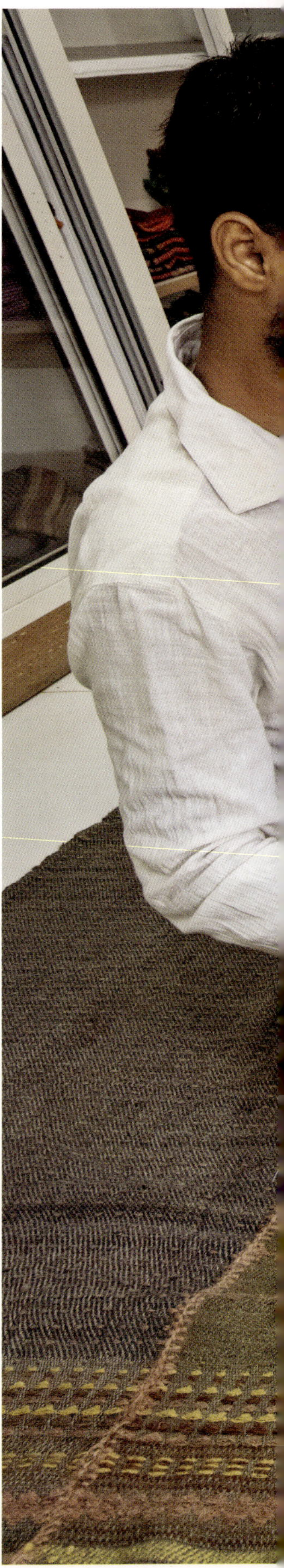

Far right: Bhujodi, 2022. Both Dahyabhai and Dilipbhai have participated in codesign projects. Now they are planning an in-house codesigned collection: Dahyabhai's checks and Dilipbhai's colors, blended by dyeing. It's a benefit of learning by teaching. *Photo: Nevada Wier*

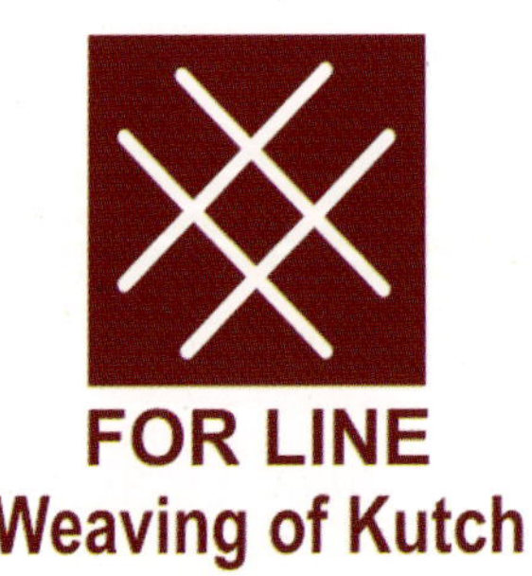

Right: Dayabhai designed his logo Forline during his design course. He made the motif diagonal, thinking about innovation on traditional motifs, and changed the "four" to "for," thinking that weavers work for lines.

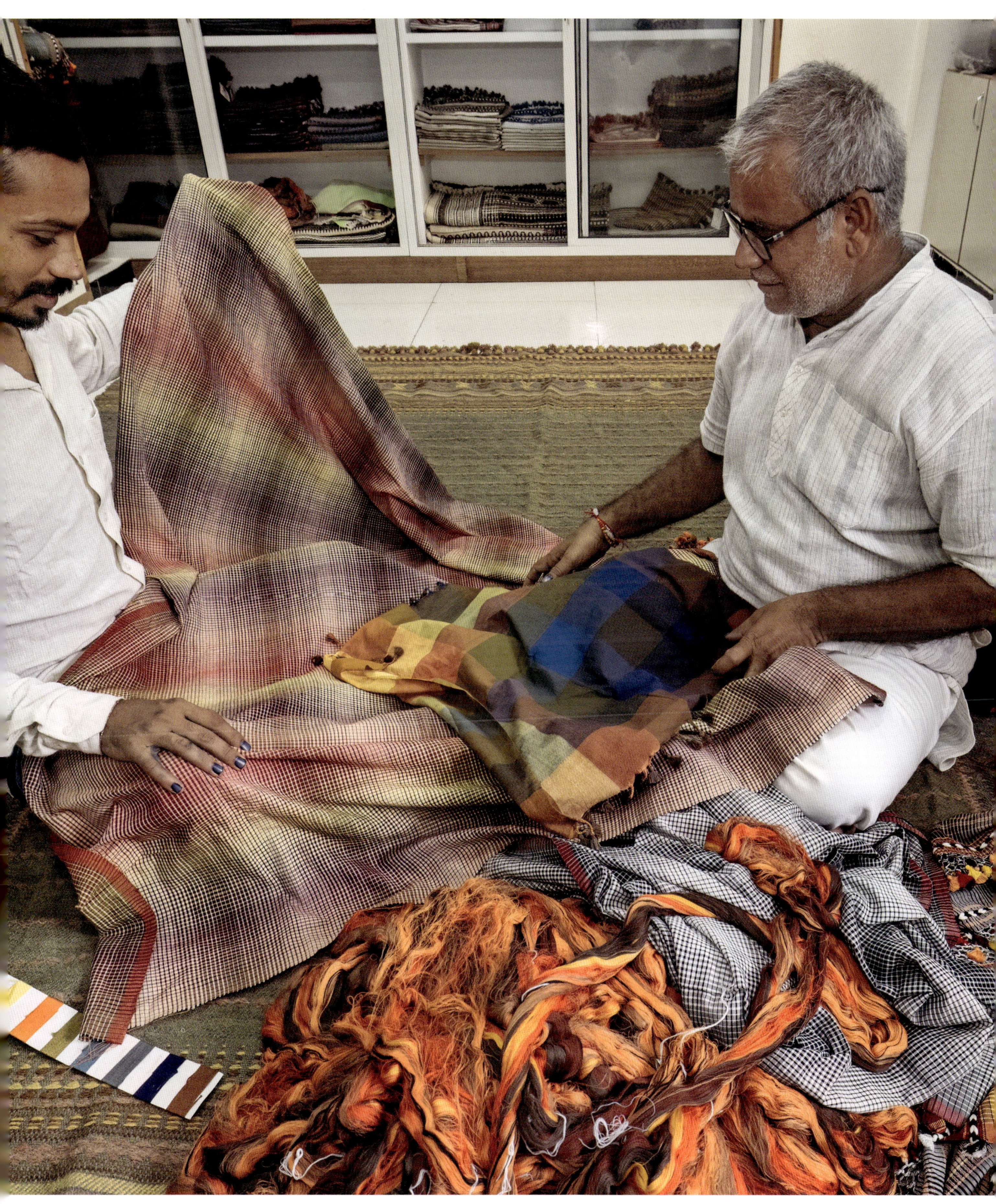

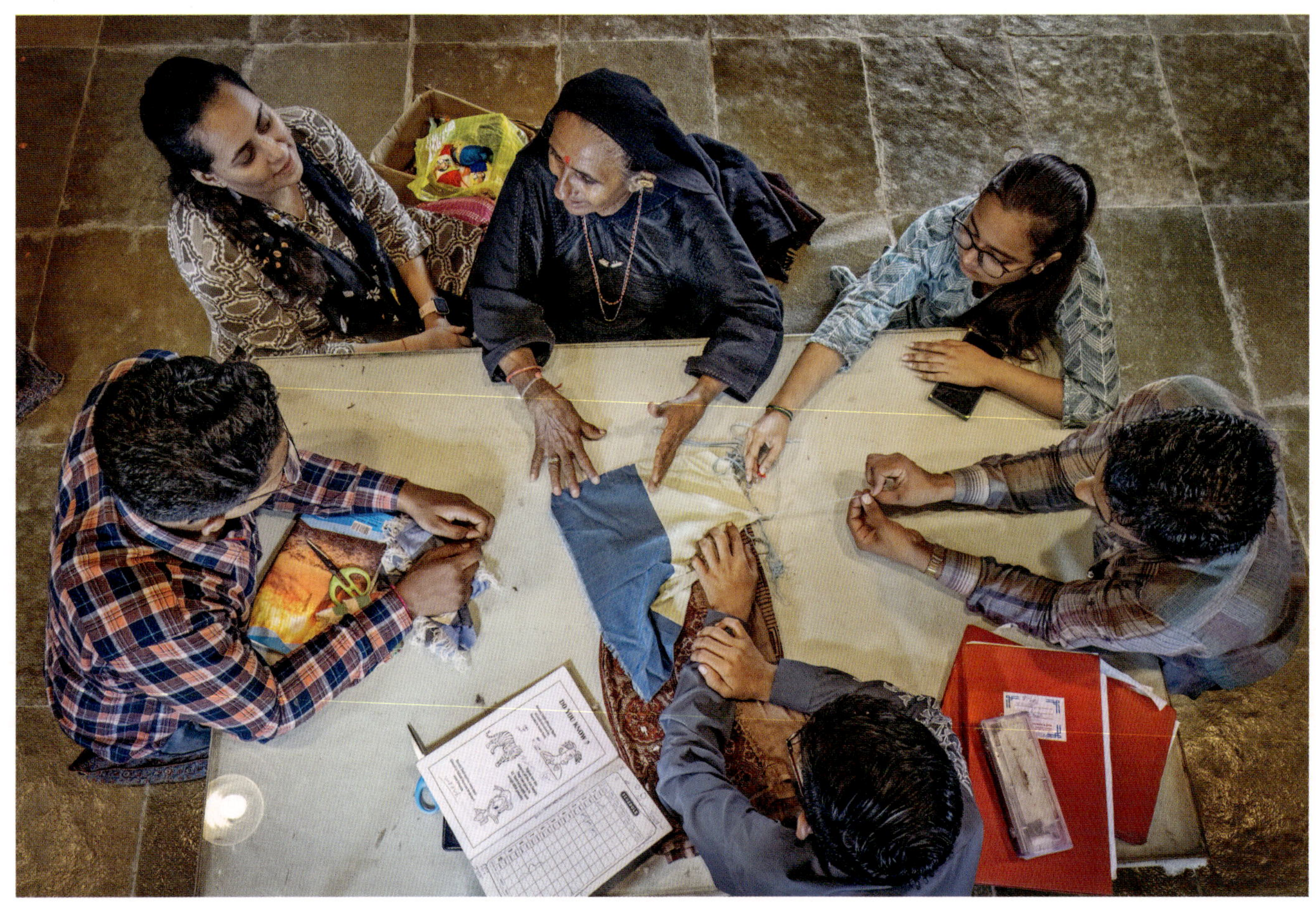

We know the days and nights by the moon and stars. Now I need to learn numbers, calendar, and clock.

~Sajnuben Pachan Rabari

Somaiya Kala Vidya, 2022. Sajnuben sincerely and imaginatively teaches the SKV class of 2022 students finishing techniques. She has become a respected resource. It would not happen outside these walls. The students brush right by social constructions and focus on learning. *Photo: Nevada Wier*

Chapter 21

SAJNUBEN PACHAN RABARI: TRAVERSING TIME AND SPACE

2019

Dressed in the perpetual black mourning of Dhebaria Rabaris, Sajnuben confidently walks into the meeting at Somaiya Kala Vidya. The select group of Ajrakh printers, bandhani artists, and embroiderers is discussing a collection. They will create contemporary work inspired by pieces in the Textile Museum in Washington, DC. Sajnuben listens to the presentations of their concepts and samples, asks for clarifications, and gives some advice. When it's her turn, she pulls some embroideries out of a bright-colored polyester bag festooned with ruffles and glittering trim. Her black blouse is similarly embellished with pencil-fine, bright, shiny trim along the seams, and a broad waistline border of black rick rack lattice over a metallic ribbon. This is style. A few months ago, she dismissed the earnest pondering of design students over whether her blouse was traditional or contemporary. For her, it was a no-brainer. "It's traditional and it's contemporary," she told them. "It's contemporary tradition."

She shows an image of a Rabari embroidery that I collected for the Textile Museum, and her own work from years ago, a half-finished square, to cover a baby in a basket the mother would carry on her head. The group carefully examines the dense, minute work. They have not seen such work in their lifetimes. Artisans understand art, which is deeply gratifying. Then Sajnuben shows the piece she has made for the exhibition: a cushion cover embroidered on red and olive-green silk. Stitched with traditional colors, patterns, and layout, it is nearly as fine as the one decades older. The group appreciates this too.

But Sajnuben is not satisfied. "I want to make something contemporary," she says. "Today, people don't want so much embroidery, and it will be too expensive." She is planning to create a purse with dense embroidery on one side, and just a little on the back. And she will hand-finish it, in the traditional way.

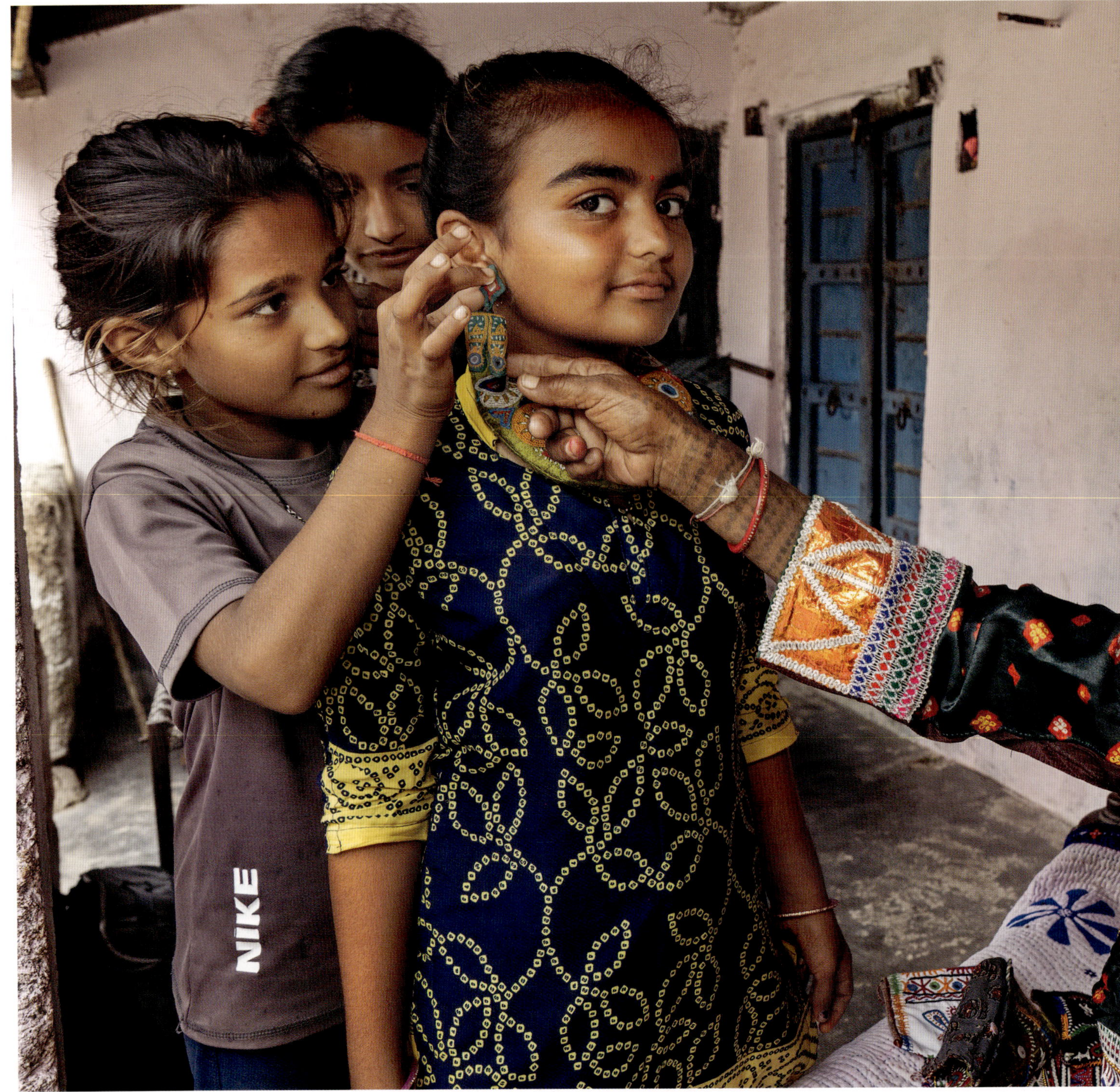

Sajnuben was born almost fifty years ago in Lodai. She married into Kukadsar, and until the end of 2007 she migrated with her husband's family's herd of 250 goats and sheep in the region near the village. But during the monsoon of that year, the entire herd died in an epidemic. The family settled in Kukadsar, and now her husband earns a living doing labor work. Sajnuben has two daughters and a son. All of them were married on April 20, 2015, in a variation of Dhebaria Rabari tradition, at the ages of thirteen to twenty.

Sajnuben learned embroidery from her mother and grandmothers and would embroider at home between migrations. She had completed her dowry when the Dhebaria Nath, the elder men who govern the community, banned embroidery in 1995. Trying to meet increasing requirements for dowry, women often did not transfer to their in-laws' homes until they were in their thirties. The Nath blamed

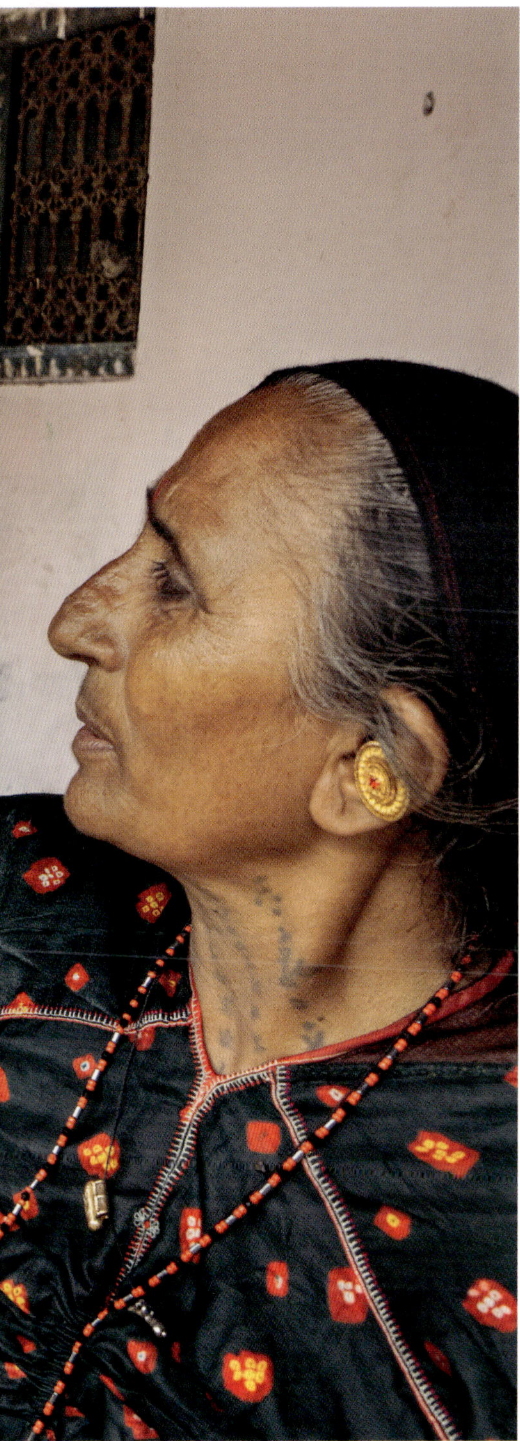

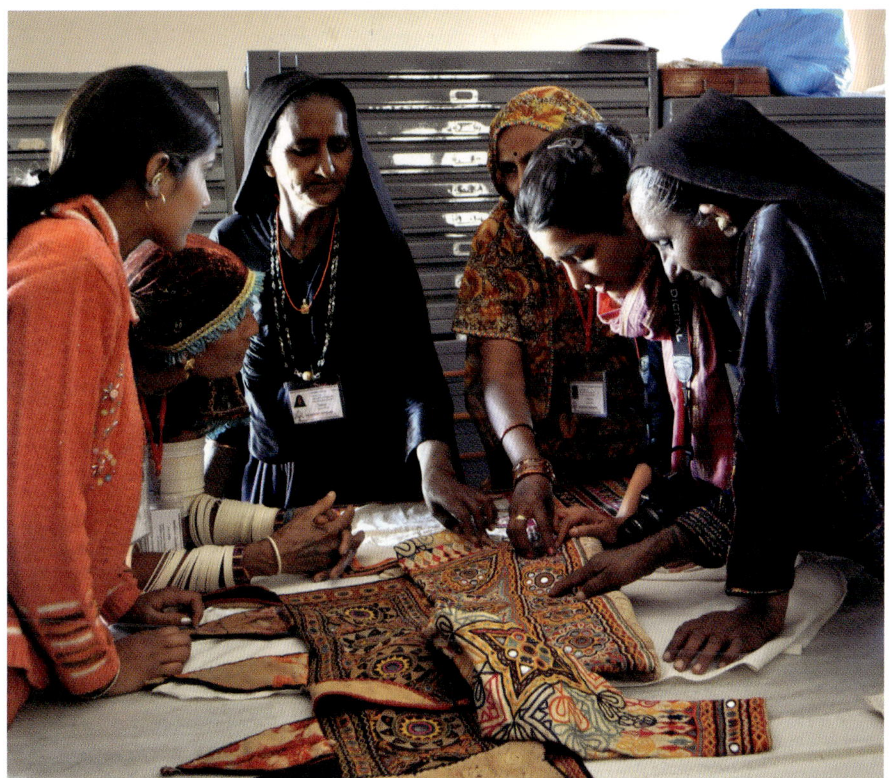

embroidery for the situation. Sajnuben still remembers the dress she had embroidered for a daughter, which was never worn. She recalls how Dhebaria women collectively wondered what to do when the ban was imposed. Embroidery was wealth and joy. How could they have celebrations without embroidery? Traditional jewelry was also banned. They removed their ornaments, but for a year they secretly wore embroidered clothes. They were in constant fear. The Nath would fine them an insurmountable RS 5,000 for infringement of the rule. They thought the ban wouldn't last. But instead, the Nath came to inspect, and they gave up embroidery for good.

Then they thought of trims. No one objected to ready-made rickrack and ribbons applied with a sewing machine. They did one line of trim, then two, then three, diving into the newly invented art form with the passion, creativity, and aesthetic sense that they had expressed with embroidery. "Good design is always innovating," Sajnuben said. "But embroidery was art. It used to be more important than gold and silver." She felt that their heritage was lost. "Our daughters go to school, but they don't know our traditions," she said.

After the earthquake of 2001, Sajnuben started embroidering for Kala Raksha. Commercial work was OK by the Nath, and that was the only future for embroidery that she saw. She dreamed of learning new ways. She participated in Kala Raksha design workshops, and in 2010 she studied at Kala Raksha Vidhyalaya.

"That was the first time I really thought about my work," she said. "We wandered, we embroidered. We did texture, etc., but we didn't know the names—movement, motif, pattern. We learned the names for colors. I liked that we started with tradition. We learned

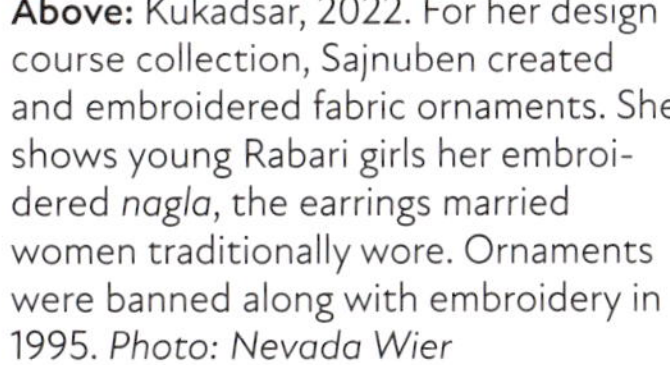

Above: Kukadsar, 2022. For her design course collection, Sajnuben created and embroidered fabric ornaments. She shows young Rabari girls her embroidered *nagla*, the earrings married women traditionally wore. Ornaments were banned along with embroidery in 1995. *Photo: Nevada Wier*

Right: Kala Raksha, 2010. Each year, KRV students visited the Kala Raksha Museum to study textiles from their respective traditions. Sajnuben and her classmates examine Dhebaria Rabari embroidery, which was banned by the community in 1995. *Photo: Judy Frater*

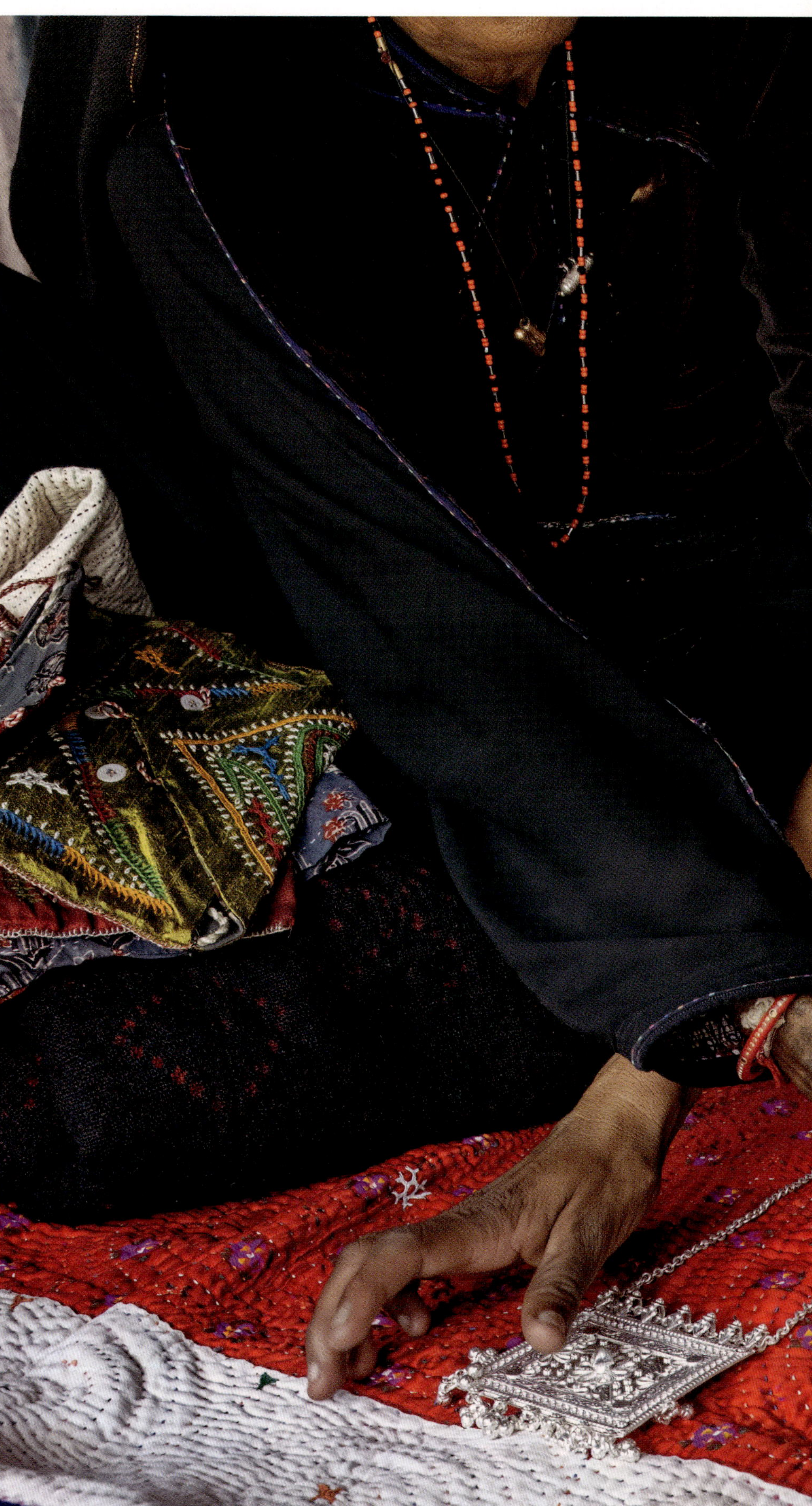

Kukadsar, 2022. With her daughter Harkhi, Sajnuben displays her embroidered *hanso* necklace along with traditional silver ornaments. Although the ornaments have been banned for almost three decades, many women preserve them at home. *Photo: Nevada Wier*

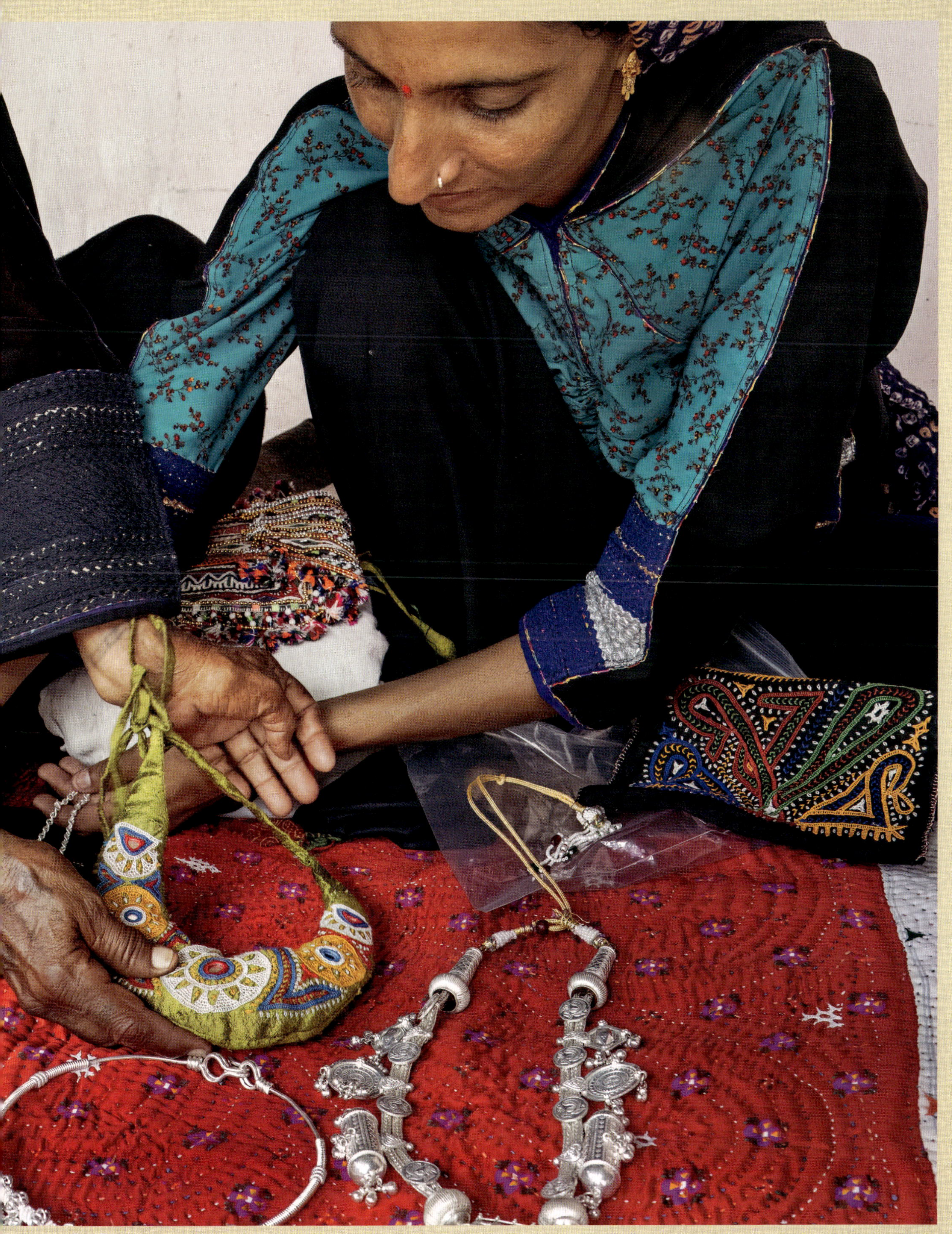

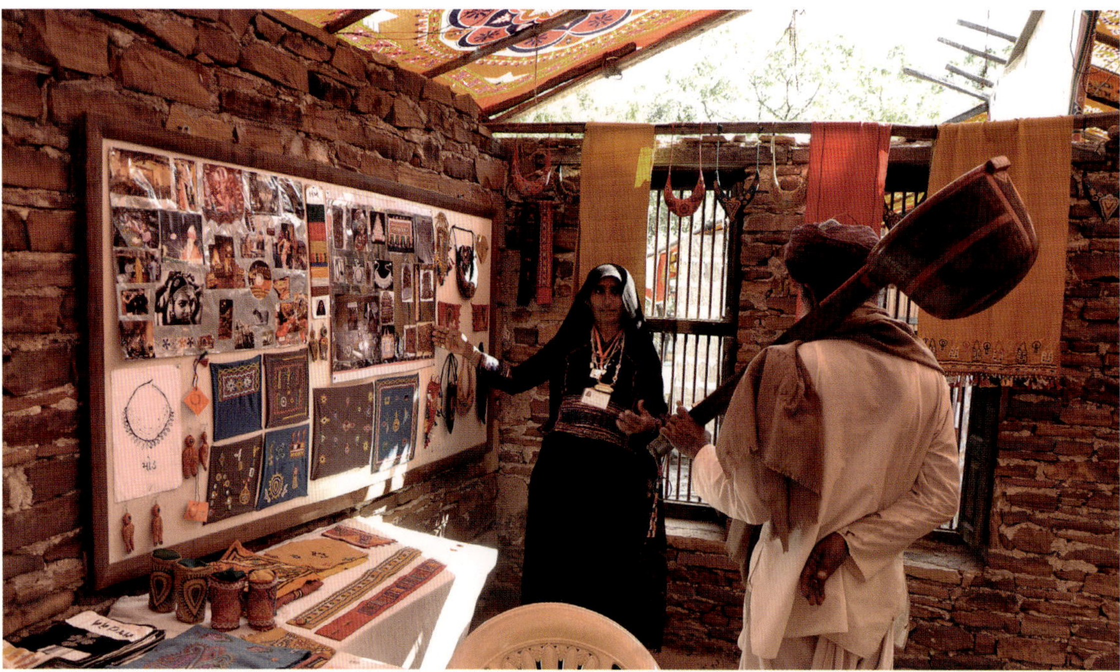

which colors other markets will like, and we learned the value of our work. Rabari work is good but elaborate. In class we learned to simplify. We would have felt it was incomplete. But we did less work and it looked good."

She chose the theme of wedding and, taking inspiration from traditional ornaments, embroidered fabric ornaments and decorated bags and scarves with ornament motifs. Her codesign partner, a student from NIFT, wrote, "Sajnuben was super sincere and very quick with her work. I enjoyed suggesting products for her, and she always chose the best designs. She knew what went with her concept as well as her traditional products. I simply loved the way she made her layouts."

Sajnuben's take was "The embroidery was ours; so were the ornaments. I thought, how to make it new? If we do something new, we can advance."

Family members are invited to the final presentation for the year. Sajnuben's husband, elegant in his traditional *kediyun* jacket and turban, sat in the front row and beamed as she presented her collection. At the tea break, he explained her concept to fellow family members and detailed how she had created the pieces.

Sajnuben graduated with the award for Most Marketable Collection. "Of course, the design course changed my life," she said. "Now I want to make all new things."

She got orders for her ornament collection for a whole year. "Eighty, maybe a hundred orders came from Kala Raksha," she recalled, "and I gave the finished embroideries there." She was a design intern at Kala Raksha; she embroidered new samples and created wonderful works of art to wear. One had elephants of all sizes climbing over a simple jacket, including half an elephant peeping up from the hem. She embroidered the logo for Sangam and created her name for the Akshara calligraphy project. In 2013, she designed and embroidered on garments for a fashion show in Mumbai, Co-Creation Squared.

When I launched the Business and Management for Artisans course at Somaiya Kala Vidya, Sajnuben agreed to enroll. Enterprising, she wanted to grow.

"We need business," she said. "We have been doing embroidery, but we don't value it enough." In the BMA course she learned planning, money management, English, and computers. She also created the SKV logo, a parrot flying with the joy of innovation.

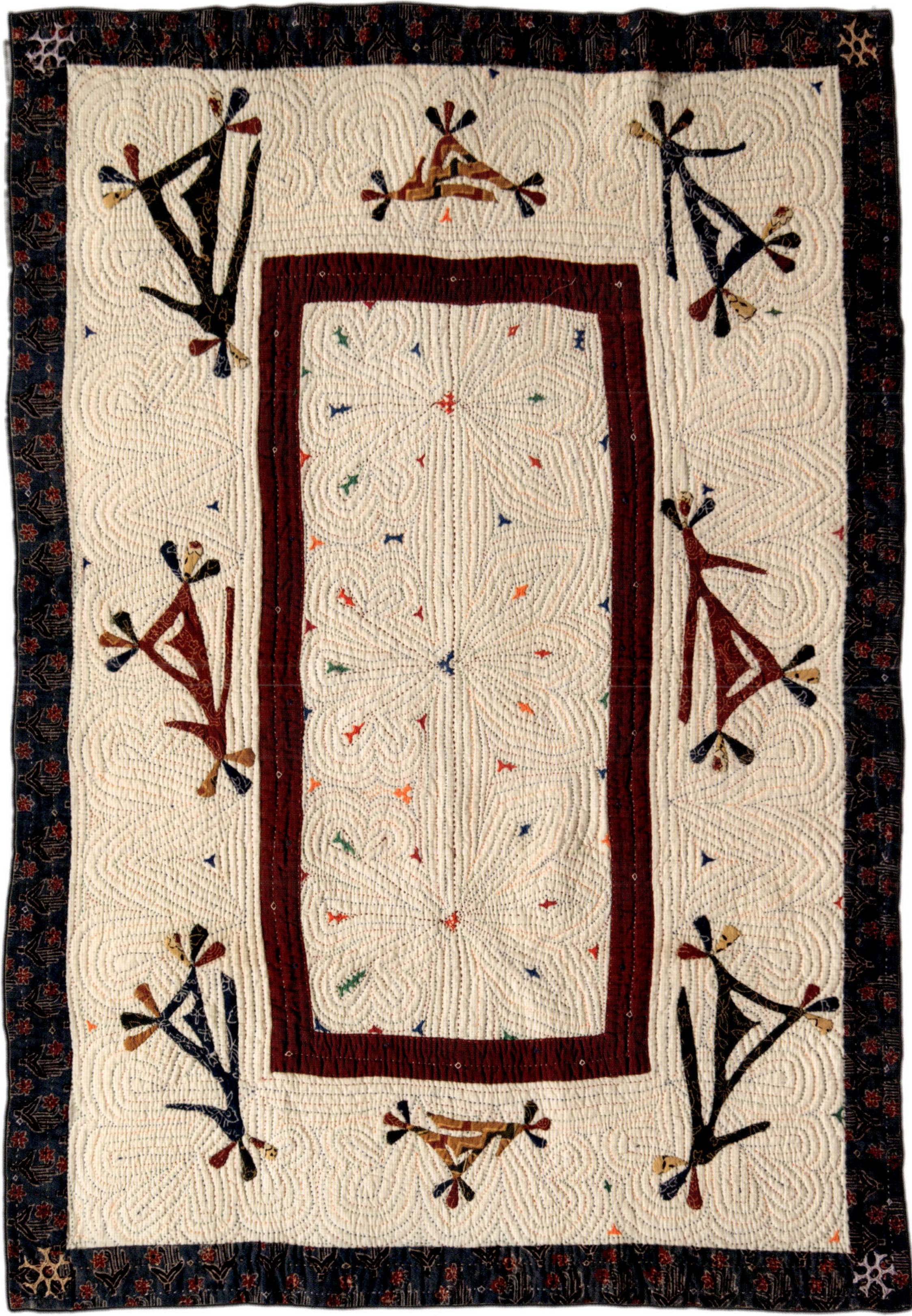

Opposite: Kala Raksha Vidhyalaya, 2010. Sajnuben explains the display of her collection to a Rabari man who has come to play *bhajans*, devotional songs, during the convocation Mela. *Photo: Ketan Pomal, L.M. Studio*

Above: *Popat Quilt*, by Sajnuben Pachan Rabari, 2022. Cotton, applique, hand quilted, embroidered. 30" x 42". Sajnuben had made a large parrot quilt. In that one, there were parrots in the center, she noted. But this is a baby quilt, and the baby will play in the center, so she left it plain. This is design. Decoration follows function. The embroidered motifs in the corners are Sajnuben's signature. *Photo: Schiffer Publishing Ltd.*

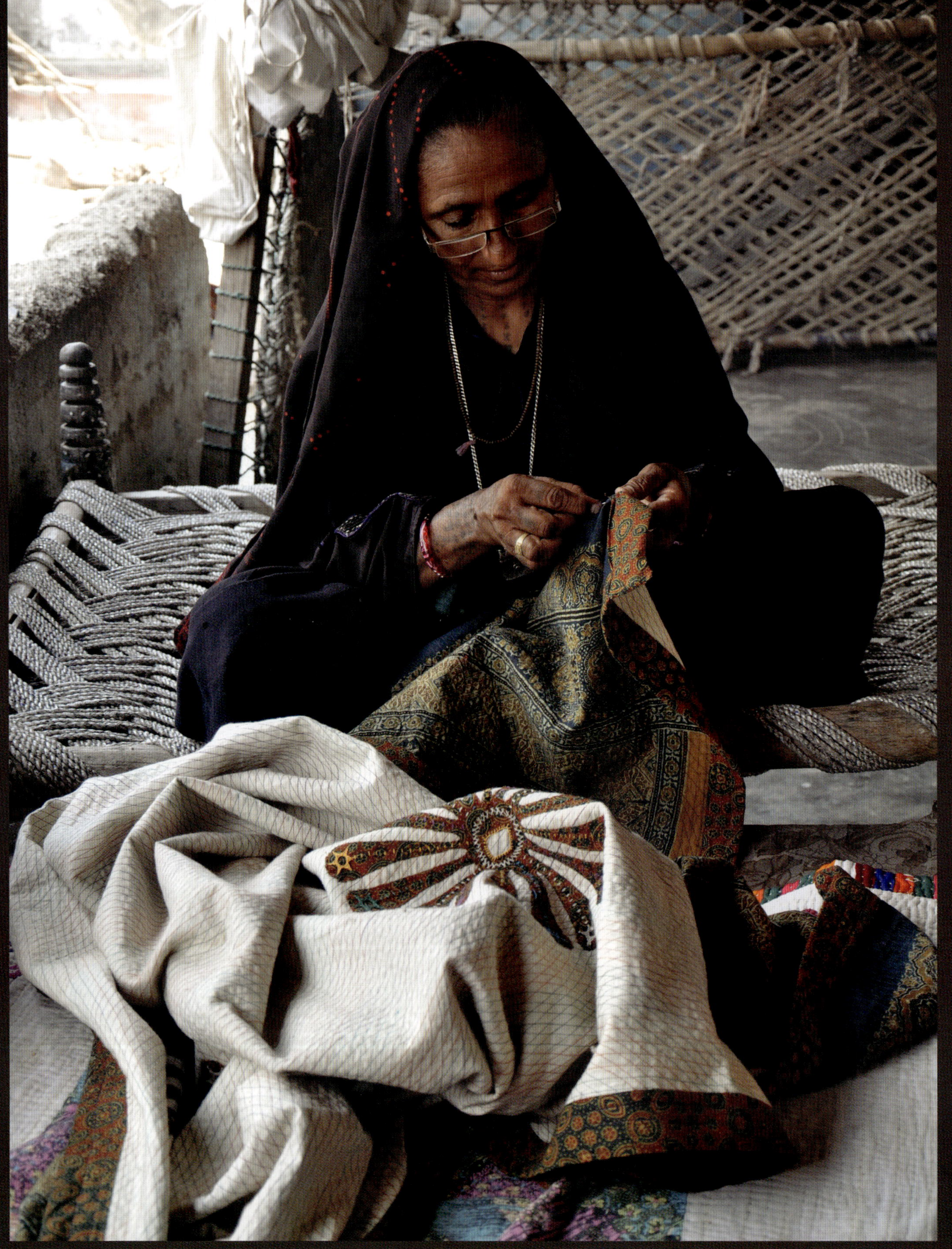

For a new collection for the course, Sajnuben chose the theme "Navratri," the festival of nine nights of dancing for the goddess. She wanted to use bright embroidery and appliqué on dark backgrounds, and she wanted to make what she could fabricate by herself. She planned quilts, a few cushion covers, and bags.

Rabari women were expert at selecting fabrics, thread, mirrors, and trims for their own work—and ensuring the best quality and the lowest prices. But they shut down this capacity in the face of production work. Kala Raksha provided raw materials—and fabrication. Women were paid piecework for embroidering. Simply, it was not their work.

For Sajnuben, the first challenge in the BMA course was to understand that the collection would be her own. She would source the fabrics, invest money and time, and be responsible for the products' sale. Once that was clear, she took a loan from me, went to Ajrakhpur, and purchased natural-dyed plain and printed fabric from Irfanbhai, who she had met in the Co-Creation Squared project.

She created her collection and sold over RS 50,000 in Mumbai. But that was not enough to pay back the loan. And it was not the end of the course. The final session was Analysis / Maximizing Business Performance. She had to do a SWOT analysis of herself and the independent business she wished for. She dreamed of doing tradition-based work and being able to sell it in pop-up exhibitions. She realized that though she had good ideas and family support, she was hindered by illiteracy.

She could manage calculations in daily life. When I told the class I had purchased a RS 20 packet of milk with a RS 100 note and the storekeeper had given me RS 30 change, Sajnuben was the one who, not skipping a beat, asked, "Shouldn't you have gotten a RS 50 note too?" But now, she realized that she would at least have to learn to write numbers. "We know the days and nights by the moon and stars," she said. "Now I need to learn numbers, calendar and clock." She stayed awake at night during this final module, practicing and practicing, so that she would be able to understand the calculations. She realized that her profit from the exhibition was RS 5,958. She set a goal of RS 100,000 profit for the next year, from a total sale of RS 300,000. "By going to Mumbai for the exhibition, I learned to stand on my own feet," she said. "I learned how to show my work to the audience. There is new life in my work."

Still, the sheer isolation of her village posed a huge obstacle. Kukadsar is in a far corner on a rocky coast of southern Kutch, with limited accessibility. One late evening, I visited Sajnuben to pick up quilts she had made for a show. As I was leaving, she asked if I might take her to the next town. She showed me an alarming boil on her foot and said she was running a fever. She directed me through the town's narrow streets to a little pharmacy shop with no doctor's sign. The shopkeeper laughed. Her family has been coming here for decades, he said. He examined her foot and took out ointment, gauze, and scissors. Then he snipped off the top of the boil. I screeched, but Sajnuben did not utter a sound. The man applied the ointment, bound the wound, and gave her some pills. "She will be fine in a day or two," he assured me. And she was.

Sajnuben had family obligations from children and grandchildren to father-in-law. Nonetheless, she rarely passed up an opportunity. She taught SKV artisan design students hand finishing, and international visitors embroidery and appliqué. The international visitors purchased her work at the end of workshops. Slowly, she managed to pay off her BMA loan. But her husband advised her against investing more in new inventory until she had sold all her stock.

Kukadsar, 2014. While Sajnuben was studying in the BMA course, I received an invitation to participate in a pop-up exhibition of quilts. It was an opportunity for women of her class to collaborate, and Sajnuben created a quilt collection. *Photo: Judy Frater*

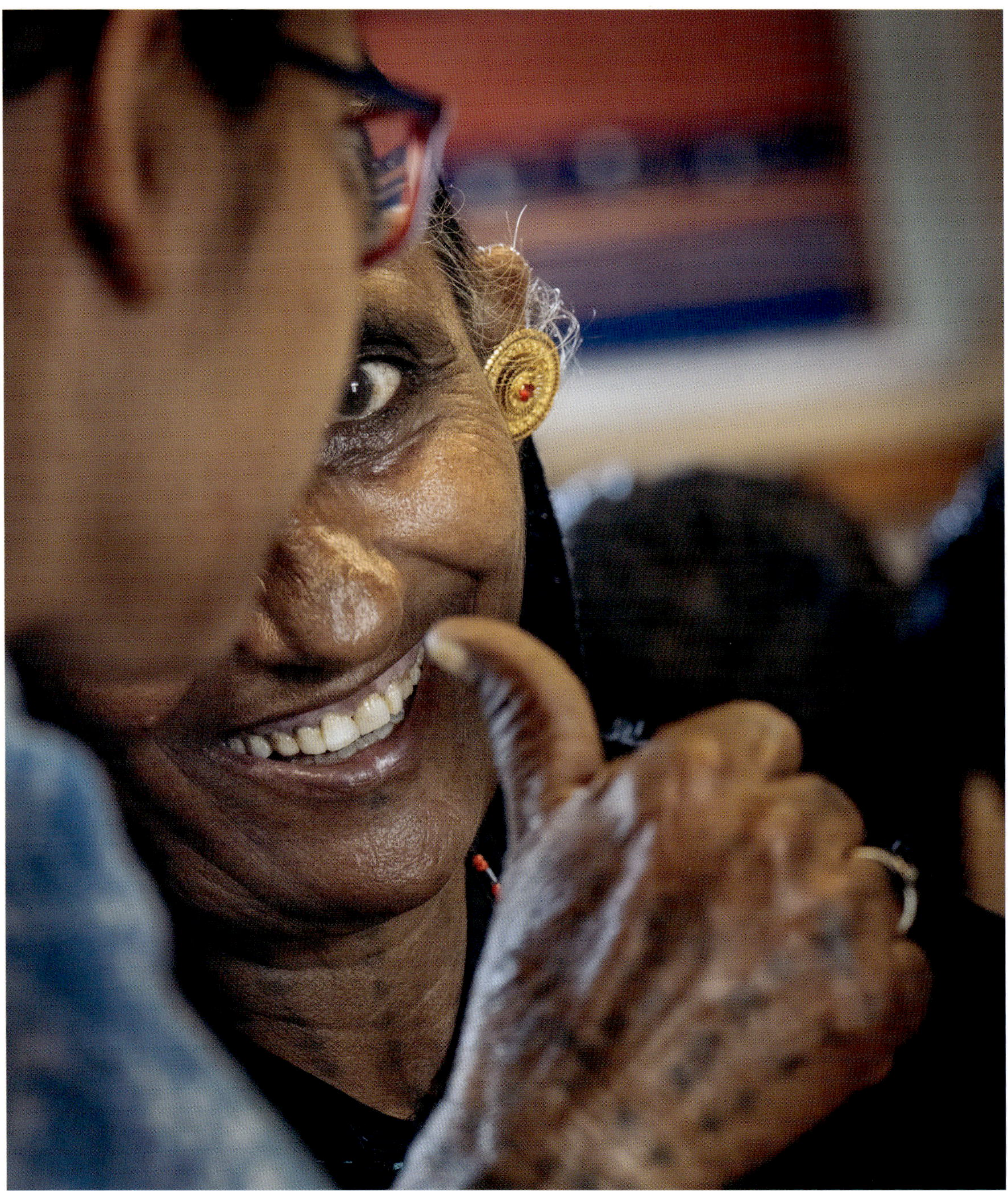

In 2019, she happily participated in a codesign project with Indian design students. When asked what she hoped she would not be asked to do, she quickly, emphatically replied: work with tailors. She had been there and done that; coordinating with a tailor was completely unsatisfactory from start to finish. Her partners understood. They put their heads together to solve her market challenge. Junaidbhai in Ajrakhpur had excess fabric, and visitors frequent his workshop, they said. What if Sajnuben used his fabric to make products and had him sell them in his shop?

Above: Somaiya Kala Vidya, 2022. A student gets a thumbs-up. Sajnuben understands well the importance of positive feedback and recognition. *Photo: Nevada Wier*

Opposite, top: Kala Raksha, 2013. The Co-Creation Squared project was the first time I had women and men design graduates work together. Although Irfanbhai was not Sajnuben's partner, he took a leadership role, and she got to know him during the design workshops for the project. *Photo: Judy Frater*

She visited Junaidbhai in Ajrakhpur with them. Nothing clicked. Then she brightened. Irfanbhai also lives here, she told them. She had an established connection with Irfanbhai. They knew each other's work, had each other's phone numbers, and shared experience and trust. There it was: the personal element of traditional craft, the local market link, and the essential element of ownership. Sajnuben could manage this, with a bit of encouragement. Perhaps she would not get to RS 300,000 the next year, but what she did earn would be her own.

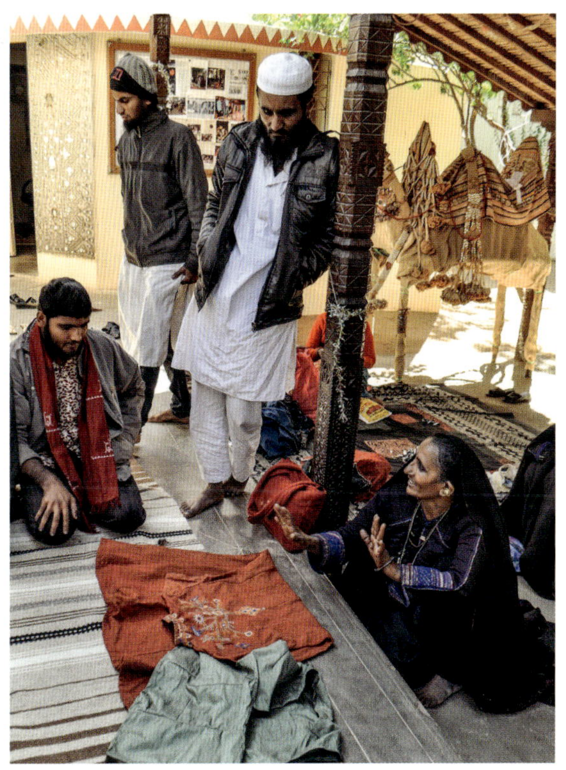

2022

Sajnuben glides over the rough ground, beaming. Without a word, she takes me beyond her house to the house of a relative who is on migration. She has turned it into a studio. The dress form from a project she did during the pandemic is a mannequin, and she has decorated the walls and cot with old and new products. Living traditions.

Sajnuben now has ten women working with her. Her son has a smartphone and, eager to support her, operates her Instagram account. A Rabari man sends her design students for workshops. She's getting orders. Not huge orders, but her needs aren't great, nor is her capacity. Marketing offers come.

She is becoming a magnet for help because she has gained a presence—and because of the persistent perception of artisans as limited. The concept of help is inherently hierarchical, and even when it's well meaning it often keeps people from standing on their own feet. Sajnuben wonders how much help to take. She wants to grow slowly, thoughtfully. She wants to be able to run a business that she can manage.

They show their embroidered necklaces—still selling since 2010! And bags, all hand-finished. They make what they can do themselves—no tailors! Sajnuben needs thicker fabric, and particular colors. She has shown Irfanbhai images, she says. Tuesday she will go to Ajrakhpur to meet him.

Then she brings out a hard-backed notebook. She got this to start her business, she says, and she wants me to write a testimonial to begin. I am honored.

Right: Sajnuben thought of Dhebaria Rabari motifs and her focus on ornaments when she designed her logo. She turned the necklace motif upside down to look like a crown. Originally, she named her brand Dhebaria, but in her BMA course she changed it to Shangar, meaning decoration.

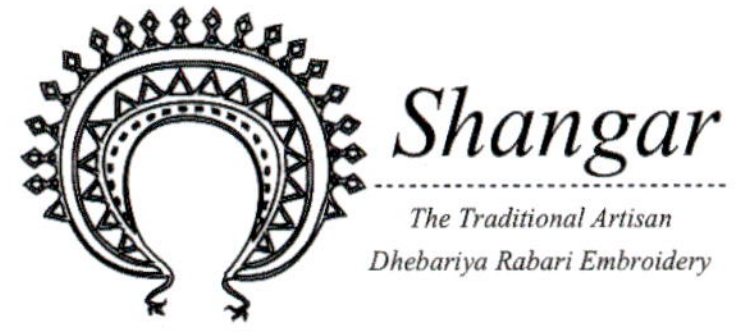

Following pages: Kukadsar, 2022. With years of persistent effort after her courses, Sajnuben has been able to get orders for her signature embroidery. She now has a group of women from Kukadsar working with her, including Meghuben (*right*), who began the design course in 2007 but could not complete it. *Photo: Nevada Wier*

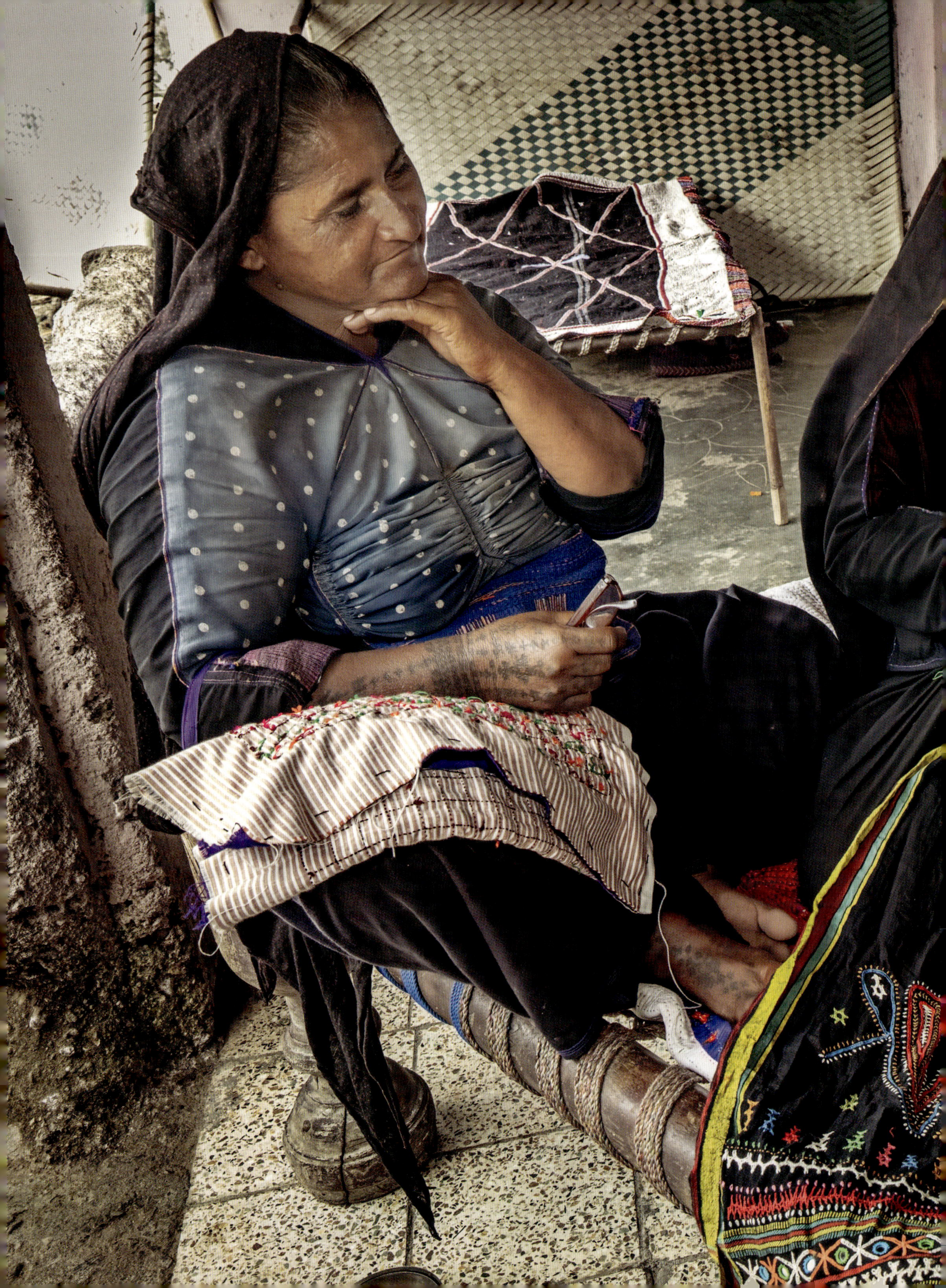

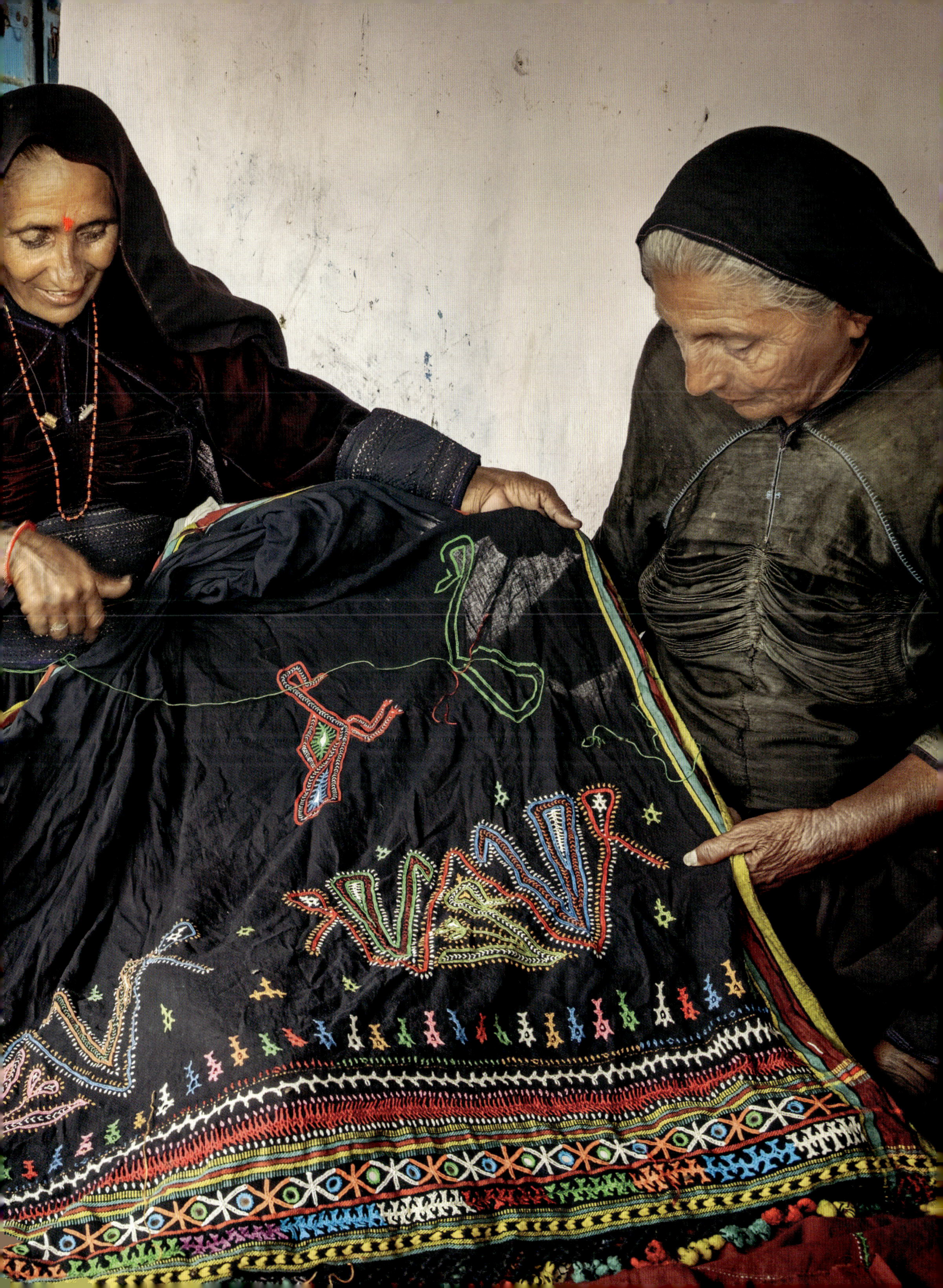

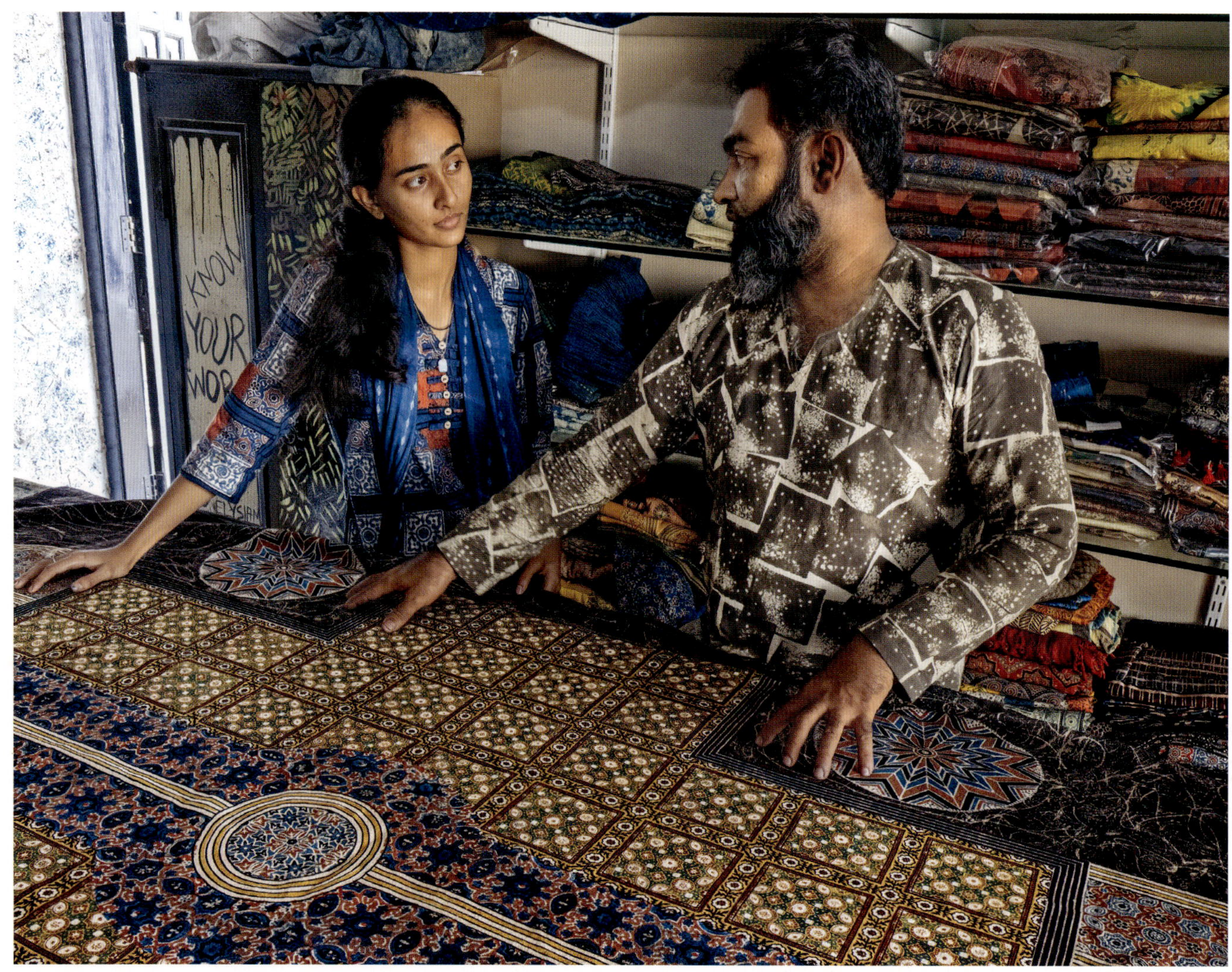

I made a design from which I can create 100 other designs. . . .
The benefit I gained from the course is confidence.

~Khalidbhai Usman Khatri

Above: Ajrakhpur, 2022. Mubassirahben and Khalidbhai discuss *The Story of Ajrakh*. She took up Ajrakh inspired by her father's confidence and self-respect as much as his innovations. In her private studio, she wrote "Know Your Worth" on the cupboard. *Photo: Nevada Wier*

Page 238: *The Story of Ajrakh*, wall hanging by Khalidbhai Usman Khatri, 2022. Cotton, hand block printed and painted, natural dye. 58" x 84". Ajrakh begins with Maldhari cattle herders in bhunga huts in the jungle, Khalidbhai says. The art was in limits; now it has expanded to the world. Khalidbhai uses the formal composition of a traditional Ajrakh for his piece. His virtuosity of colors required an innovation on minakari—processing, washing, reprocessing—three times. Mubassirahben helped a lot, he says. *Photo: Schiffer Publishing Ltd.*

Chapter 22

KHALIDBHAI USMAN KHATRI: CHOOSING ART

2019

"Bring me twenty-four blocks," Khalidbhai tells his young apprentice.

"Twenty-four?!" The boy is taken aback.

"Yes." Twenty-four is the inspiration. There are twenty-four students taking a workshop in Ajrakh hand block print in his workshop, and Khalidbhai feels they need some motivation. He and his fellow tutors will select the best work, and he will present the student with a prize.

The students are at lunch, and the workshop is quiet. The apprentice relishes the chance to choose without guidance. Khalidbhai takes the twenty-four blocks and composes a pattern, printing on the cloth directly, no paper layout needed. He works deliberately and gracefully, using his eyes, his experience, and his heart. And he smiles with pure enjoyment as he works. With some blocks he prints resist paste for white, with others he prints alum mordant for red. The whole team of printers gathers to watch, appreciating the master at work. He brushes iron acetate for a black background, and his team dries it and boils it in alizarin. It is ready in time for a quick jury huddle at the end of the day and presented to the delighted student.

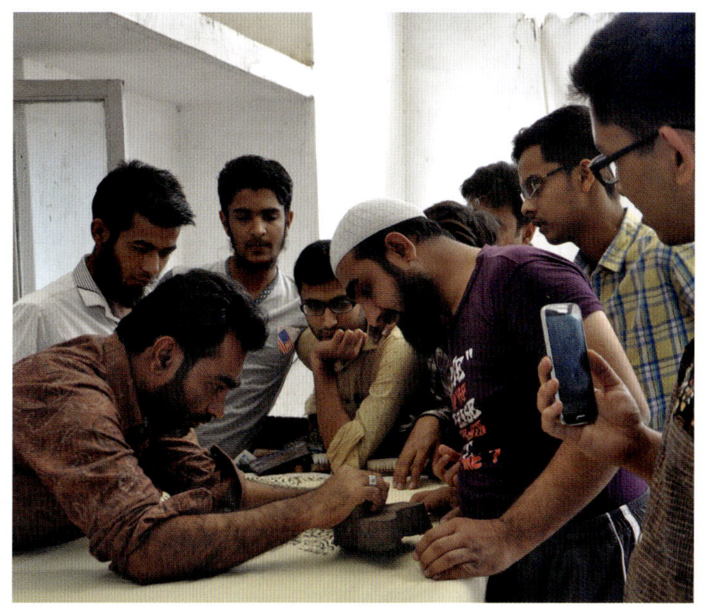

Somaiya Kala Vidya, 2017. Artisans are always fascinated by expertise. In his design class, Khalidbhai was a guide as well as a peer. His classmates affectionately called him "Kaka" (Uncle). *Photo: Judy Frater*

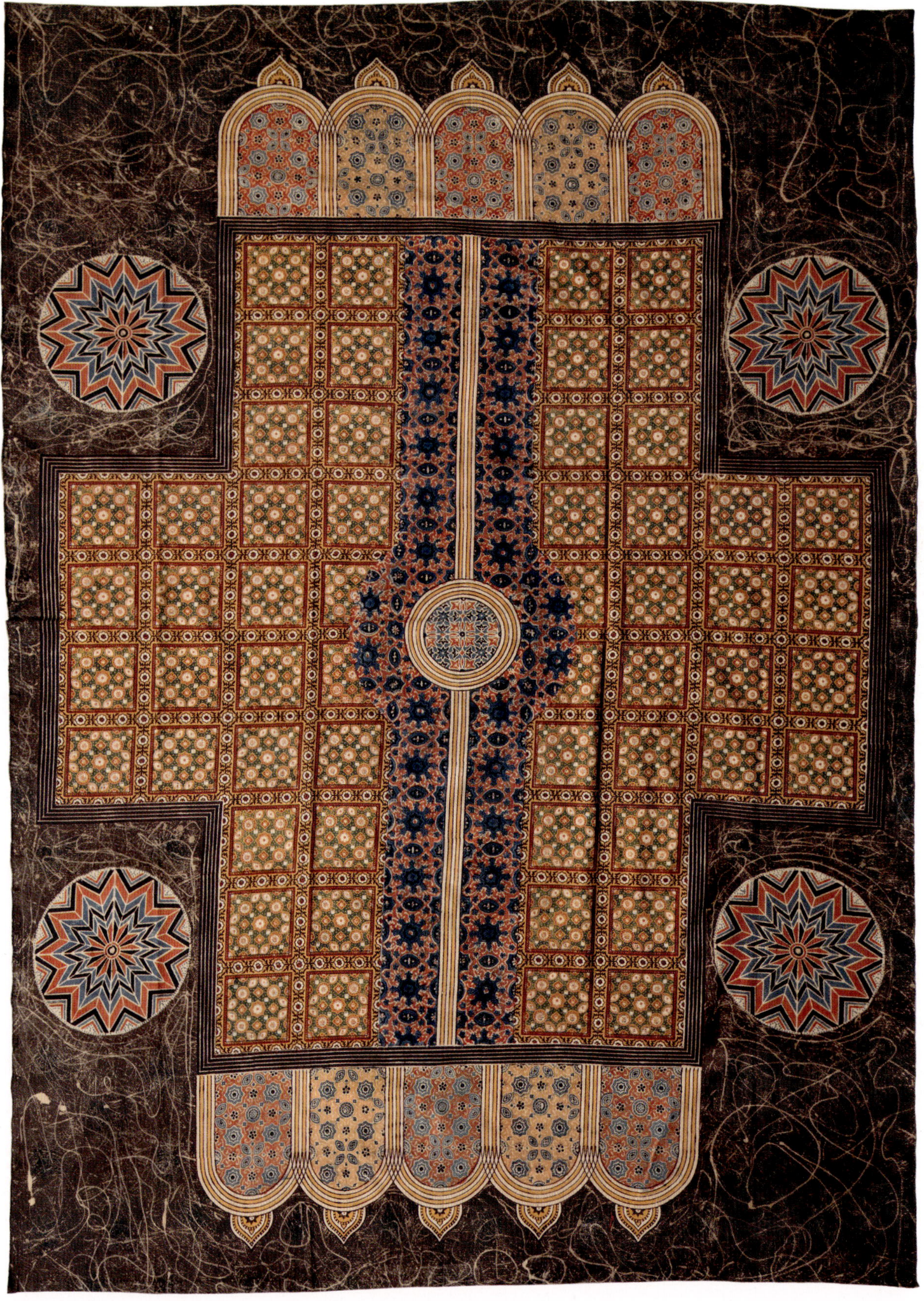

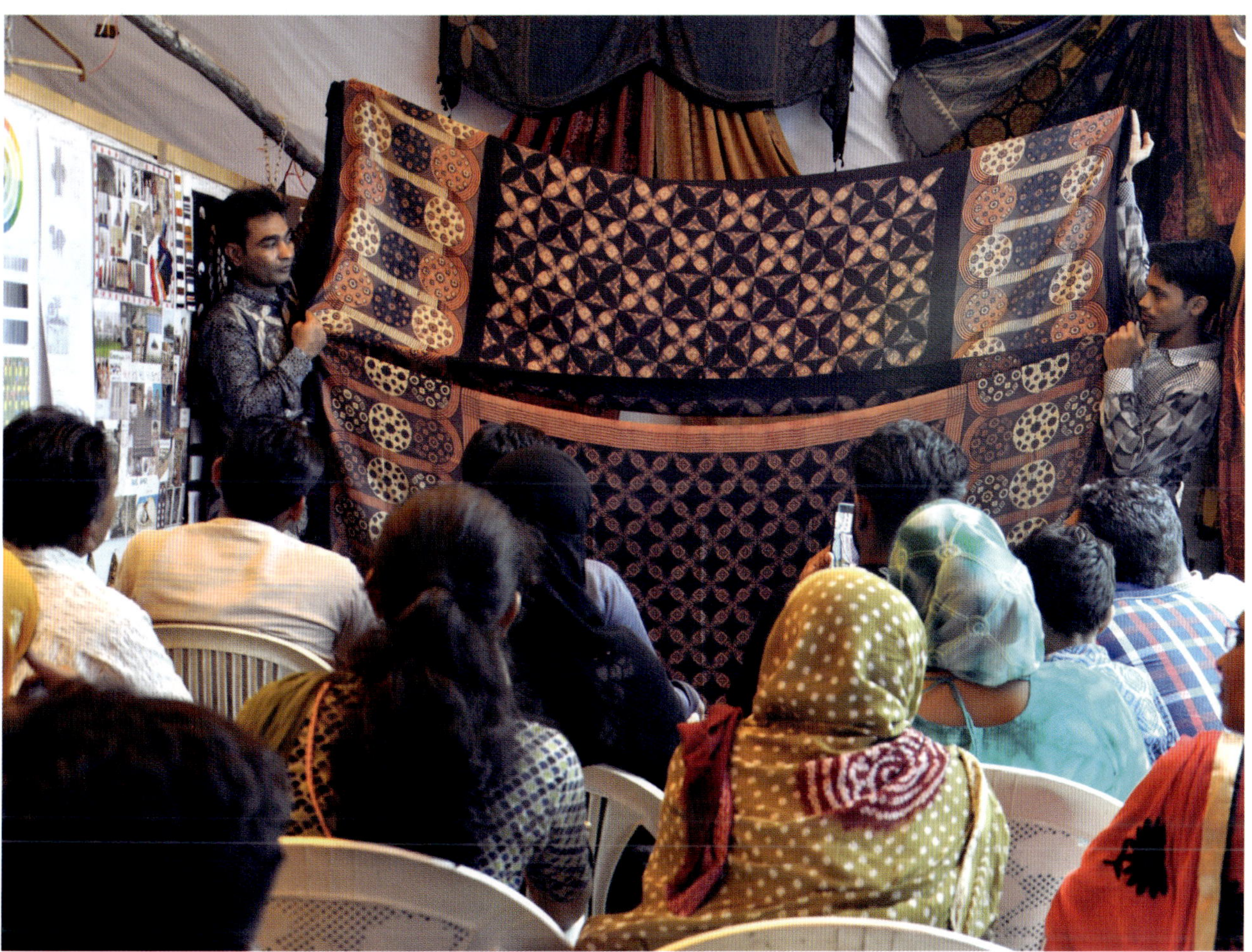

Khalidbhai's family was from Rapar, in eastern Kutch. His father, Usmanbhai, moved to Dhamadka to print Ajrakh and, by the time Khalidbhai was born, moved the family again to Bhuj, where he established a screen print and handprint workshop. U. S. Khatri was skilled and innovative and became well known in his trade.

Khalidbhai went to school until eighth grade but didn't like it. He learned printing from his father when he was fifteen and worked with him for ten years. Then Kutch was struck by a massive earthquake. Khalidbhai lost his father, their workshop, and their home. Their business was destroyed. In a few years, when Ajrakhpur was established, he moved with his wife and two small children to the new village and started over, doing labor work, printing in other artisans' workshops for wages, earning RS 100 per day. When printing work was scarce, he did construction work. A decade passed. Khalidbhai's son Mustafabhai hated to see his father doing labor work. This is not our work, he said, and urged his father to restart their business. Within a year, they built their own workshop and started doing job work, contracts from more-established artisans. But Mustafabhai wanted more autonomy. In 2015, he took Somaiya Kala Vidya's first design course.

Mustafabhai was mature and judicious at the age of eighteen, quick, talented, devoid of teenage self-absorption, cheerful, and helpful. The class elected him president, even though he was not the oldest or most experienced student. He must have good parents, I thought. Khalidbhai brought him to class

Above: Somaiya Kala Vidya, 2017. Presenting to the family jury in the final design course module, Khalidbhai explains perceived value with homework from his Market Orientation module. *Photo: Judy Frater*

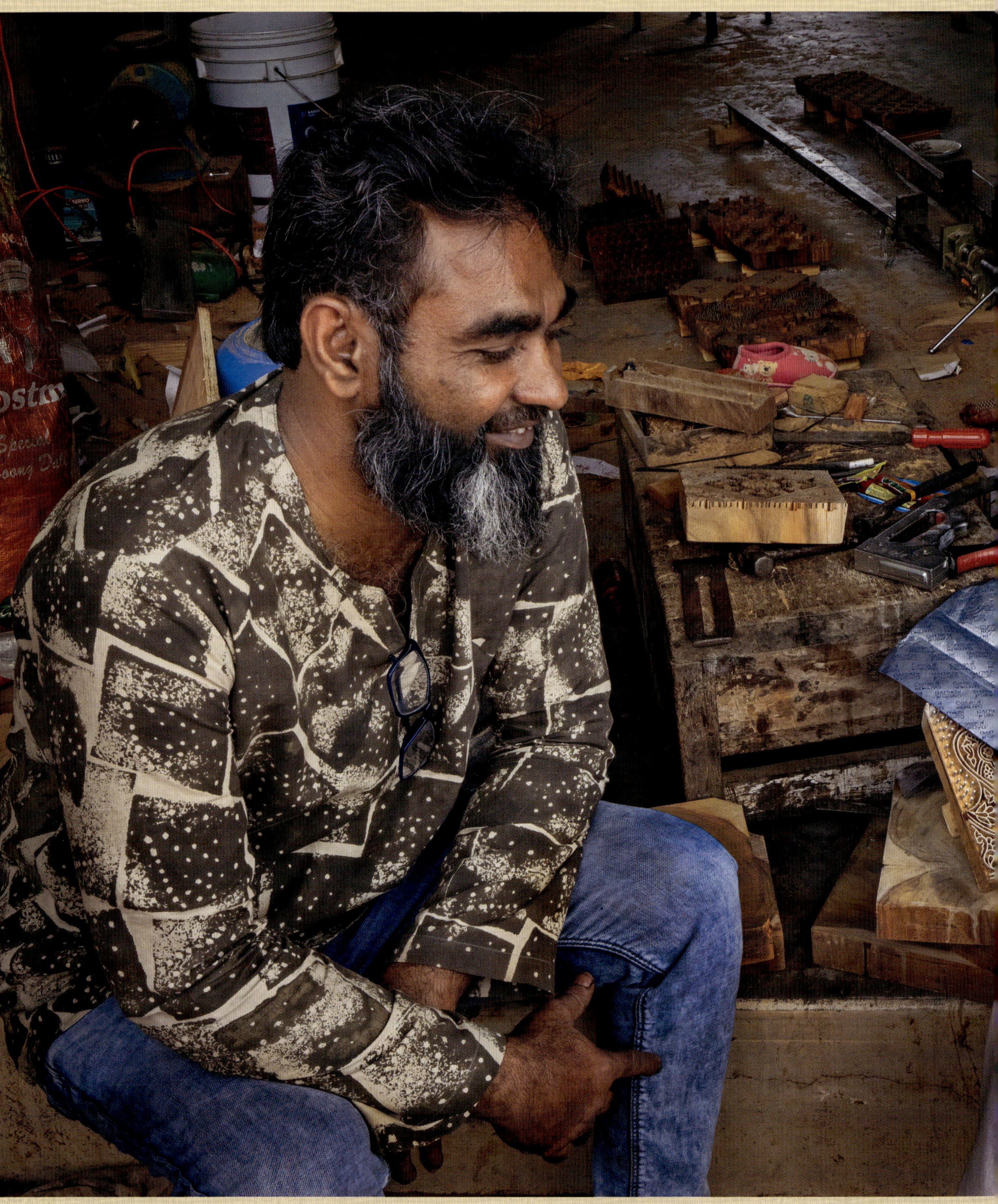

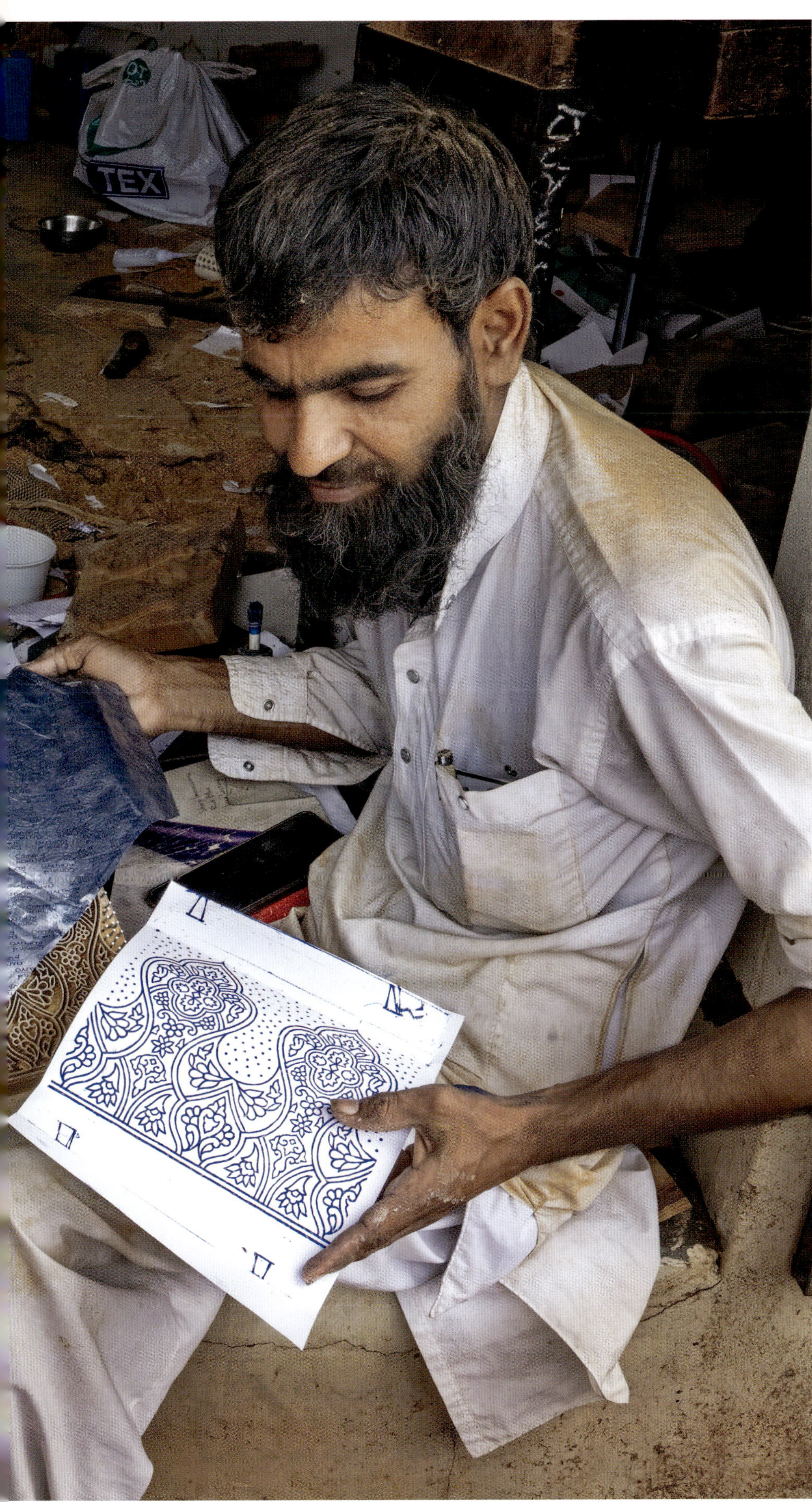

Ajrakhpur, 2022. Hozayfabhai says Khalidbhai doesn't give him orders. Khalidbhai says the real story is that he bothered his friend to learn block making until he told him to make his own. "How much can you teach?" Hozayfabhai asks. "Now it's experience you need. It's good, more people working."
Photo: Nevada Wier

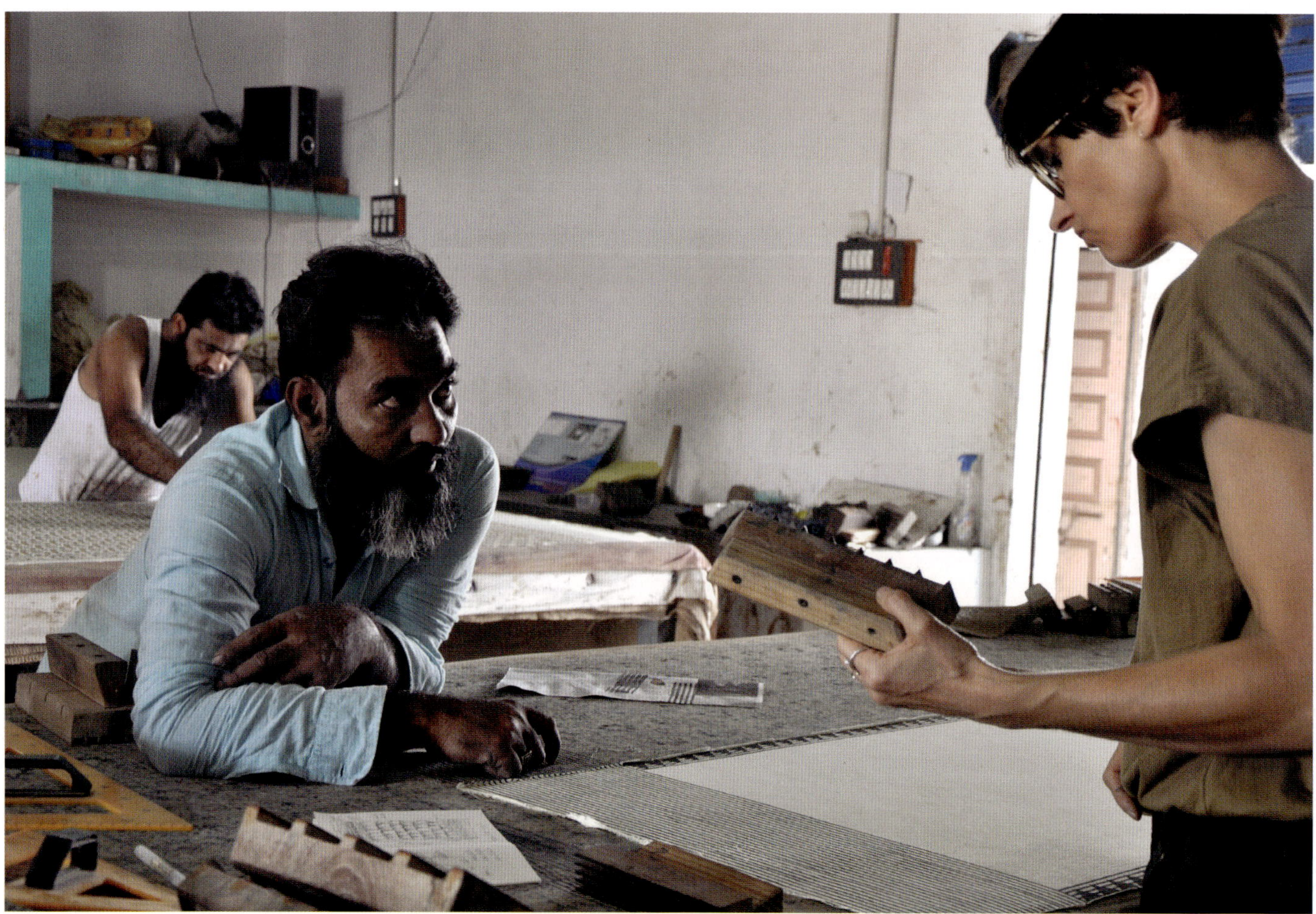

and picked him up at the end of the session. He was retiring and seemed more like Mustafabhai's brother than his father. He lingered in the classroom. At the end of the first course, Color: Sourcing from Heritage and Nature, he quietly sat with the students and alumni to hear each student's presentation. After Mustafabhai presented his first two weeks of design, the teacher asked Khalidbhai, as a parent, what he thought. Tears were streaming down his cheeks.

Mustafabhai designed and produced a collection of home furnishings and graduated with the award for Best Presentation. He gained visibility and contacts at exhibitions in Mumbai and Delhi. They established their business and began getting orders. I urged him to take the Business and Management for Artisans course. He refused twice. The second time, he said, "This year my father wants to take the design course."

Khalidbhai had observed his son at SKV. "I heard him give a presentation, and my heart filled," he said. "He had learned about color—schemes, primary, secondary, and he was talking without fear, with confidence. He was completely changed in one class. Artisans don't know their capacity. At SKV their minds open and they can do new work." And he wanted to do something new.

"Ajrakh was our livelihood," he reflected, "but now it is our identity. That is how we have gone ahead. I am interested only in real Ajrakh. I would rather do construction work than use synthetic dyes. The future of Ajrakh is 100 percent good."

He was forty-one when he took the course. The other students were closer to Mustafabhai's age. But in class, age was easily superseded by the focus on learning design. The students worked together. Khalidbhai was elected president, also for his judiciousness, wisdom, and helpfulness. "Talent is hereditary," he said. "I inherited my father's talent, and now I see it in my son."

The course inspired him. "After the Color course, when I looked at a film song, I was looking at colors!" he said. "I could never draw, but now suddenly I can! It makes me happy. When we went to Ahmedabad to study the market, I saw paintings everywhere and realized that wall hangings can be a new product. I learned how to get design ideas from experience."

He created new blocks. "When we worked with tangrams," he recalled, "I suddenly thought, we always use a four-corner block. But if we have three corners, we can make something else." He also realized that small, discrete motifs offered a skilled printer infinite possibilities in composition. He used a variety of fabrics, created a range of subtle natural dye colors, and overlapped block impressions for texture. His work was complex, labor intensive, and exquisite.

When he began the course, Khalidbhai stated that he had no dreams and no goals. In the final module, Merchandising, Presentation, he created a logo from the signature "eye" motif that he had created. "It is a blowup of a traditional element; I wanted it to have an Ajrakh look," he said. "I called it Ashk, eyes. All eyes should look at my work. This is my deepest desire."

The visiting faculty member wrote, "Khalidbhai tends to work without preparing a layout, which leaves plenty of room for surprises. Despite having helpers, he did his own printing. His work embodies total respect for himself and his tradition." He graduated with awards for Best Collection, Best Student, and Highest Exhibition Sales.

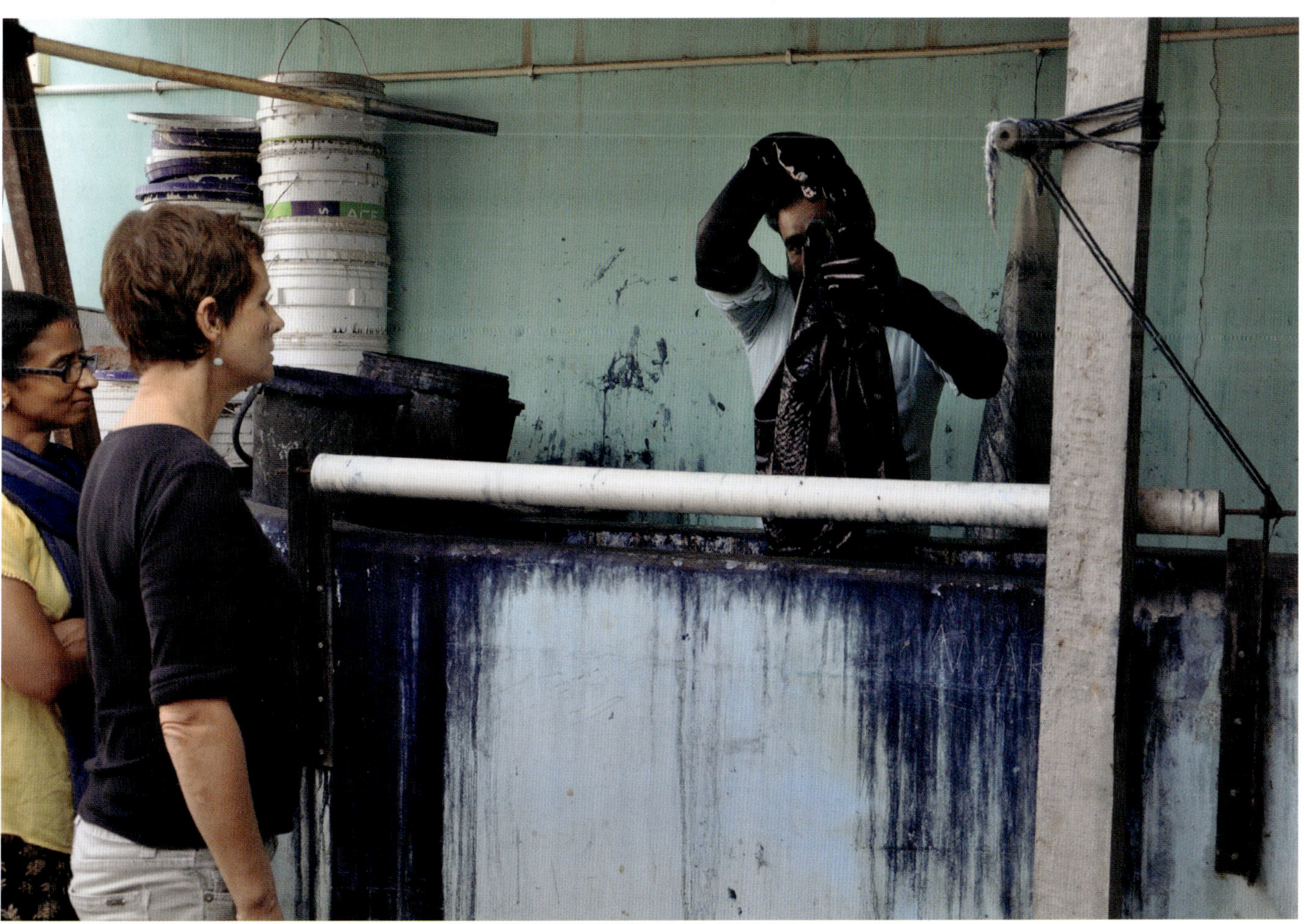

Opposite: Ajrakhpur, 2019. Teaching the advanced session of a three-week course on Ajrakh tradition in his workshop, Khalidbhai solicits feedback. He is as eager to learn as to teach. *Photo: Judy Frater*

Above: Ajrakhpur, 2019. Indigo dyeing is a keystone of Ajrakh. For the students, this part of the course is observation rather than hands on; dyeing is beyond advanced. *Photo: Judy Frater*

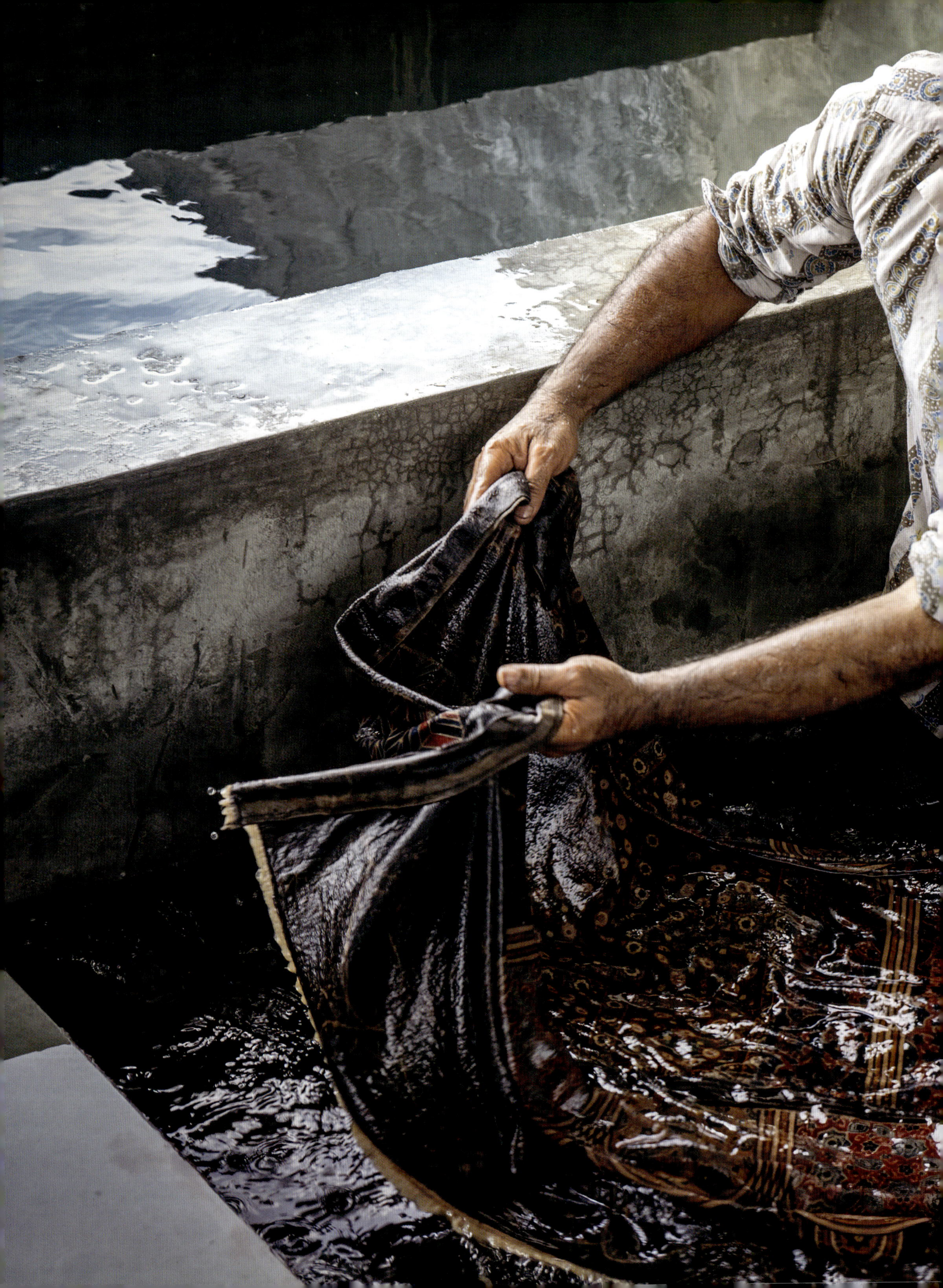

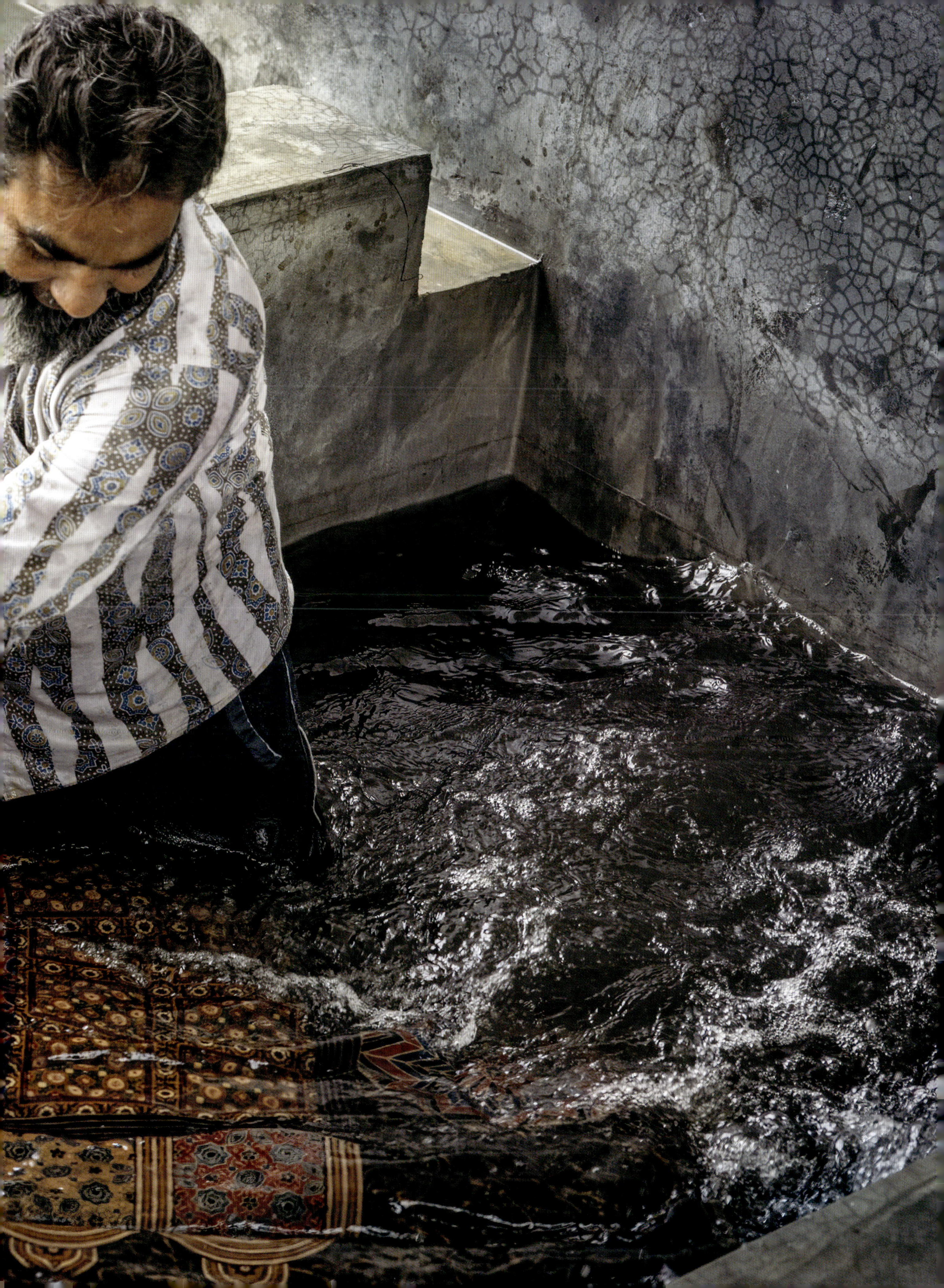

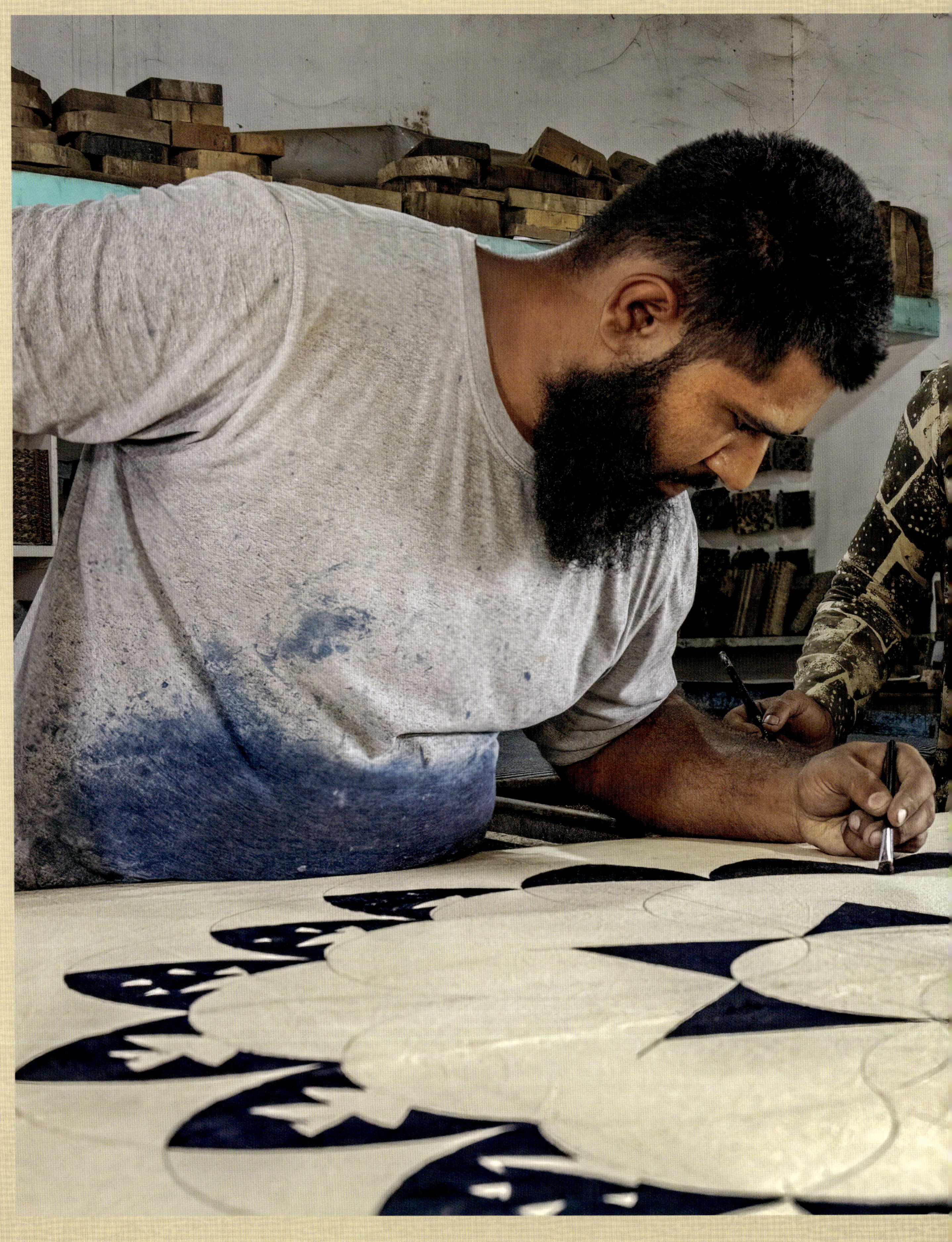

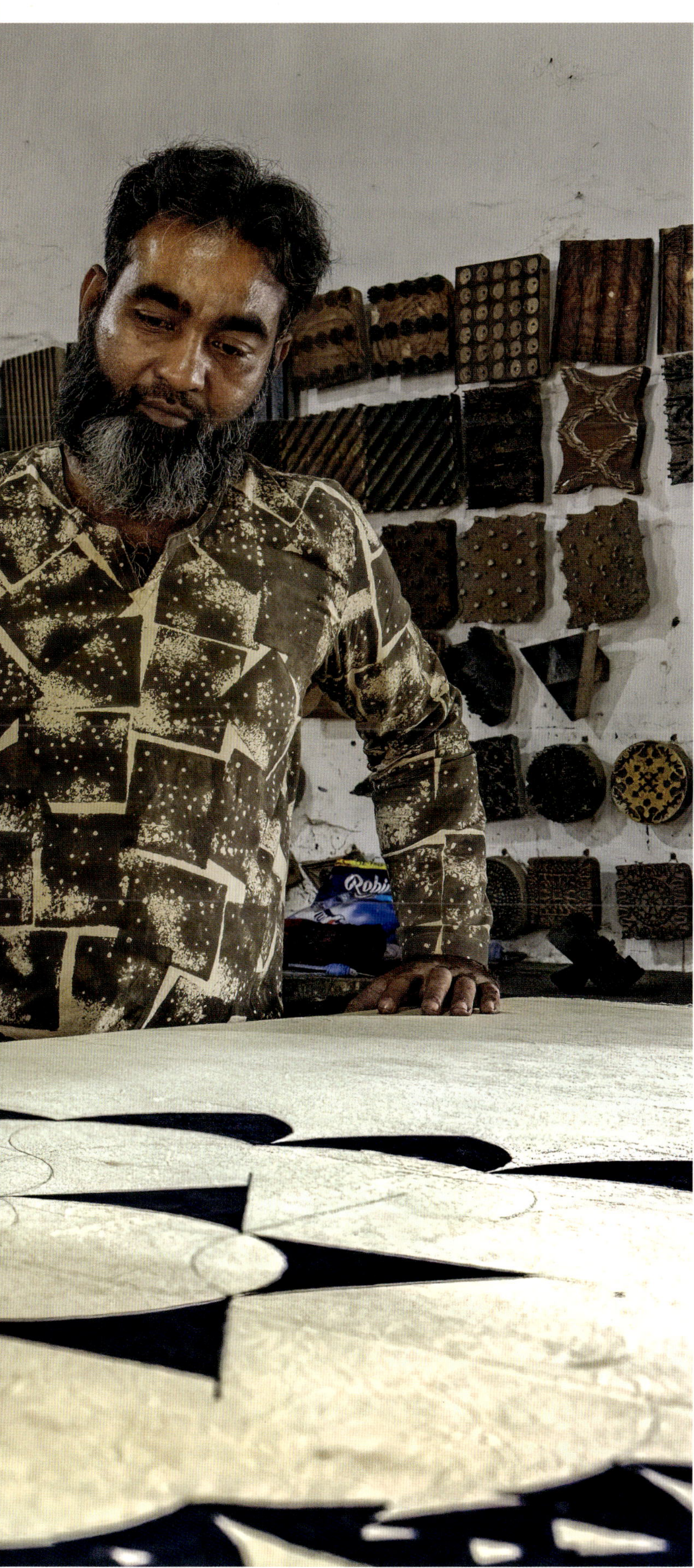

Previous pages: Ajrakhpur, 2022. Khalidbhai washes his wall hanging at his new workshop. An artisan must know all the steps of his work, and proper washing is critical to quality in Ajrakh. *Photo: Nevada Wier*

Left: Ajrakhpur, 2022. The family shares orders and keeps joint accounts, but Mustafabhai runs the family workshop now. Responsibility is a great teacher, and independence signals respect. *Photo: Nevada Wier*

In the first SKV seminar, before he took the course, Khalidbhai asked if an artisan with limited production capacity should take a large order, and if he should let a customer bargain down his price. "If I do not sell it at that price, he will go to another artisan," he said.

In the seminar on copying, after his course, he was first to speak. "I was afraid of being copied until I took this design course," he said. "Now I know that I can make unlimited designs. This year I made a design from which I can create a hundred other designs. If someone copies it, I can make another design, and another. The benefit I gained from the course is confidence."

And in the 2019 course evaluation, he said, "We learned that when we make a product, it is destined for someone. Those who did not study design worry, if I don't sell it, the customer will go to someone else, or the piece will lie in my home. We wait. The one for whom it was made will buy it from us. Our soul has to be content. It's not about a nice car, a nice air-conditioned bungalow. At the least you should be able to sleep peacefully at night."

Observing design graduates over the years, Khalidbhai saw that each student's work was unique. "I liked that best," he said. "Year after year, each one does something new. And now, because they see the benefits I've had, visitors come to me, and people send their children to the course. Before, no one knew me. That's the difference after studying design."

One of Khalidbhai's best friends is Hozayfabhai, an intense, wildly creative, and eccentric man who carves blocks in Ajrakhpur. Hanging out with him, Khalidbhai picked up some skills and a desire to make his own blocks. From there, he experimented further. "There is a future in contemporary looks," he said. "But we can't leave Ajrakh; we need to combine new and traditional." And then, in spite of confidence in being able to continually innovate, Khalidbhai put up a flex sign at the entrance of his workshop. There is a limit to sharing with local artisans who want a free idea. In Gujarati, the sign proclaims that no one is allowed into this workshop without permission.

Another issue was managing scale—how could an artisan with limited production capacity take a large order? Though he loved the satisfaction of printing, as his business grew, Khalidbhai rarely did it. "The master artisan must know his craft," he explained. "But there is a lot of other work. If I have my head down at the printing table, I can't keep track of everything. The issue is how to maintain your artisans.

"And actually, there is an easy solution," he continued. "We have to teach people and treat them well and let them grow." Having worked for others, Khalidbhai managed his staff of ten with an imperceptibly light touch. The artisans were more partners than workers. Sadikbhai, his foreman, and Jusabbhai, his dyer, had been with him since he started his workshop. When the production was their own, for direct sale, he gave them a broad brief, and they printed patterns they liked. They asked for advice when they needed it. Khalidbhai asked for advice from them too. "I choose people who are straight," he explained, "no bad talk, no bad behavior. That is the foundation."

Khalidbhai understood the value of the workshops and Open Studio Tours I launched and was instrumental in developing a structure for them. He created a WhatsApp group to coordinate hosting. The Ajrakhpur artisan designers decided to jury the work before a tour to ensure that it was new. Otherwise, who would come? he asked. And they decided to keep a record of participation and results. "If we want this event to succeed and grow," he said, "we need to make a commitment."

After graduating, Khalidbhai hand-painted and block-printed a large canvas wall hanging to depict his year of design education. It was in the form of a tree, with a frame of traditional Ajrakh. Each branch was a course, and the flowers at the top were created from the new motifs that Khalidbhai had made for his collection. He gave it to SKV in appreciation. Eyeing the tree, Zakiyaben said it looked more like a South Indian Kalamkari than an Ajrakh. Khalidbhai said he needed a form to tell his story, and they discussed how traditions evolve, how to define Ajrakh. And how much compromise is OK?

Khalidbhai said he was thinking of doing a wall hanging to depict the evolution of Ajrakh. He would surely take this discussion to heart. He knows that he is a guardian of his tradition. Respect is his guiding star. His advice to current artisan design students was his own code: keep looking, seeing, analyzing, thinking. And his last word, with his quick Harrison Ford smile, was "Ajrakh is slow. Its meaning is 'Keep it for today.' The slower, more thoughtful you work, the better it is."

2022

Khalidbhai is racing against the rainy weather to get the wall hanging done. It needs to be dried, so he and Mustafabhai take it up to the terrace. And then they take it to the new workshop for washing. He has purchased land and built a state-of-the-art, self-contained workshop, just enough for the family production.

The piece has to dry again. So we visit his daughter Mubassirahben's workshop—converted from the shop during COVID. He slips and says "earthquake" instead of COVID. The pandemic had a similar life-changing impact. Women don't do Ajrakh; they do only the finishing, Khalidbhai had stated in the 2019 evaluation. But Mubassirahben had other ideas. "I watched my father," she says. "And I was inspired." He drew the first piece for her, and she hand-painted it with natural dyes. By now, she is creating yardage and garments stitched by her uncle with fresh abstract patterns hand-painted and printed with kitchen and construction tools—anything but blocks. She has a brand, Elysians, a sophisticated and active Instagram page, and is doing a respectable online business. She's intense like her father. They demo how they work together. Khalidbhai does the structure in blocks. Mubassirahben takes on the texture with a plastic cleaning brush. Khalidbhai steps back. He says he made texture in his wall hanging on the story of Ajrakh but couldn't get balance, so Mubassirahben did that part.

Sadikbhai, the foreman, has started his own independent workshop. Khalidbhai's big workshop is now Mustafabhai's domain. He's working on a large bedsheet with a hand-composed center medallion. He carefully fills in the details. Khalidbhai picks up a brush and does a little filling and steps back again. He gives his son space. "One mistake and it's ruined," Mustafabhai says without looking up. "You need to concentrate." He has his father's decisiveness and confidence, strength as well as great respect.

Within a month, there is one more addition. Above Mubassirahben's workshop, Khalidbhai is constructing another room. It will be his studio, where he can work without disturbance on new collections. His son is happily married and working focused. His daughter is the first Ajrakh woman artist, a rising star and soon to be a student at SKV. He has zeroed in on the idea of doing excellent work, and he has made a commitment.

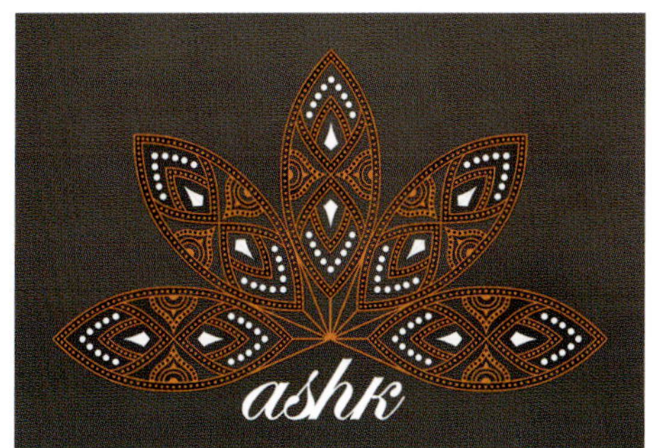

Khalidbhai isolated and enlarged an element of a traditional Ajrakh pattern and repeated it to create a sense of rising sun. He named his logo "Ashk," eyes.

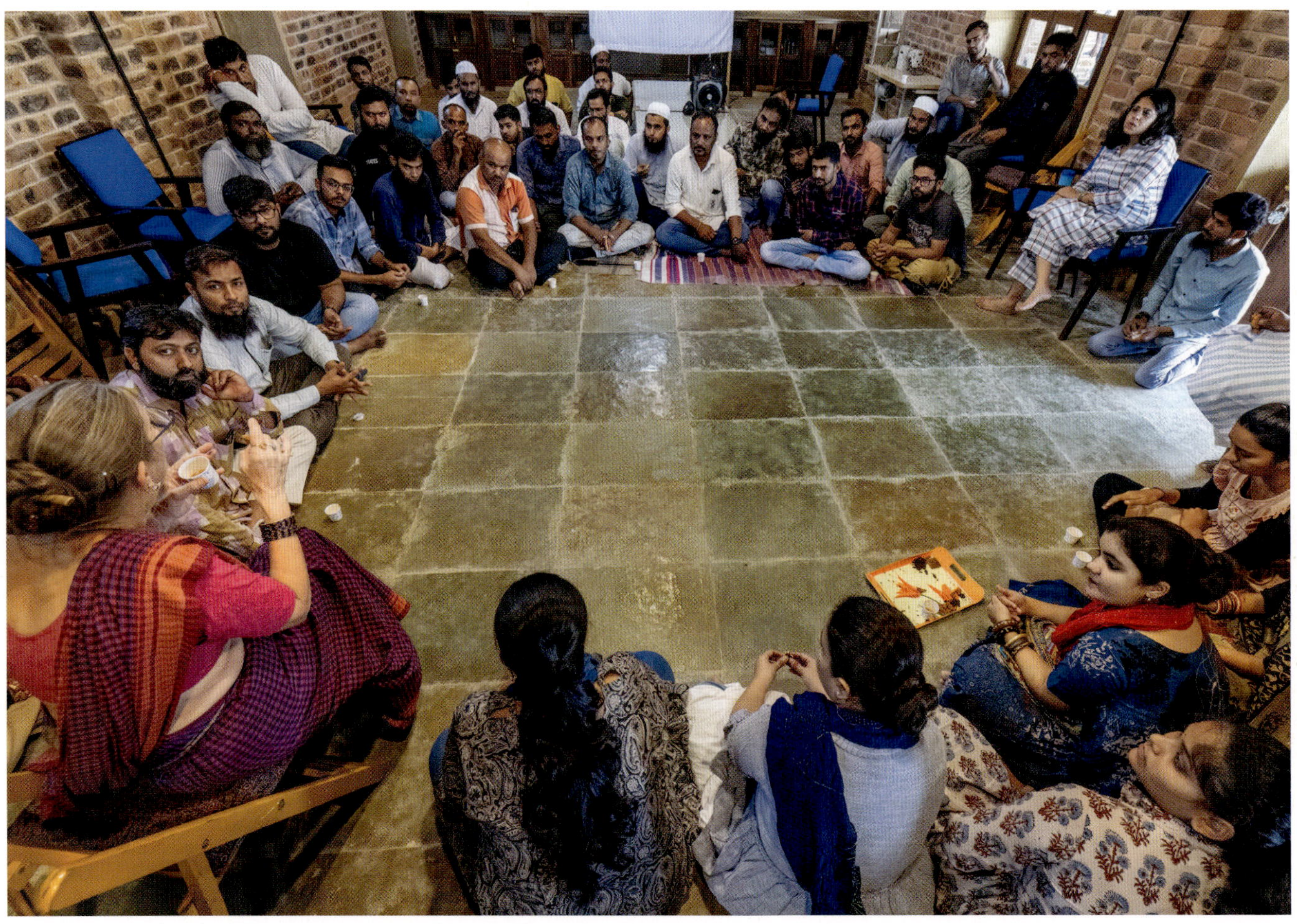

I want to make what is nowhere in the world,
and what everyone will love.

~Akibbhai Ibrahim Khatri, Ajrakh artisan designer

Somaiya Kala Vidya, 2022. Artisan designer alumni share experiences, give feedback and suggestions on the course and programs, and express hopes for the future of craft traditions. *Photo: Nevada Wier*

Chapter 23

WHAT'S NEXT? MAKING CRAFT TRADITIONS WORTH IT

2022

I screen a film on the 2019 impact assessment of the education program for the artisan design alumni. They are the stars of this film; it is their own reflections. I ask them for feedback. Zakiyaben notes there is a commonality in impact. Shakilbhai adds that it wasn't just about income, but a change in thinking.

Long ago, a colleague spoke words that rang true to me: "NGOs have prevented people's movements from happening because they speak the language of funding agencies, not the language of the people." I tried always to speak the language of artisans, not only Gujarati but also the language of their culture and heritage. The program worked because it was based on understanding the socially imposed limitations of artisan communities and believing in their creativity. It built on traditional knowledge and generated confidence.

The graduates care about the institute and want to contribute to the continued efficacy of the course. Don't use design elements already adopted, but invent new ones, they suggest, and don't use internet downloads, but draw from your traditions. I establish an artisan designer advisory board—even as I am leaving.

Aslambhai, ever incisive, says the film should have shown more of the problems they face. They discuss the continuing challenge of involving the next generation. Artisans' children are taking jobs for more money. Adilbhai notes that it's not only money; the status of artisans is still low in India. I ask how many who have children think that they will continue their tradition. A lot of hands are raised—but not all. They know they need to reach better markets, those in which they can explain the value of their work.

Not long ago, I watched Mukhtarbhai, artisan design graduate and faculty at Somaiya Kala Vidya, carefully unwrap a bandhani *abho*. His brother received the President's Award for this piece, the ultimate award for handwork in India. The silk garment was soft shades of red and green natural dye, completely filled with minute textured dots. It equaled historic work in the Calico Museum of Textiles.

Ajrakhpur, 2022. "Regular work," yardage printed quickly and as cheaply as possible, fills Ajrakhpur. Akibbhai's own sign is outside the workshop now. He studies a book on design with me. "Our future is near," he says. *Photo: Nevada Wier*

Will you produce it now? I asked.

"No," answered Mukhtarbhai.

I was stunned.

"It's not worth it," he stated.

Artisans have the capacity to create—or even exceed the work of their forefathers. Finally, the question is, what will make creation worth it?

We can value handwork as industry, or as art. The standards of each are very different. Solutions for a perceived decline in craft focus on skills, product, and production. But what distinguishes craft from industry is that craft is a human expression. Craft in India does not need to be revived; it needs to be revalued.

Crafts Council of England studies demonstrate that people in the UK buy craft as an experience, and a way of signaling connoisseurship.[5] Industrializing handcraft will not meet the needs of these consumers. But UK craftspeople are studio artists. In the tradition-based craft world of India, artisans are not primarily individual artists; they are members of communities.

Traditional artisans in Kutch created for communities that were hereditarily linked to them, for families that they intimately knew. Client and artisan shared standards of evaluation, recognition, and respect. Vishramjji Valji, master weaver of Bhujodi, recalls the world of his youth: "The feeling was that we knew that as the blanket we wove slowly wore away, the user would remember us."

Traditionally, excellence was unquestionably worth making.

What's next is reinventing community-based economies.

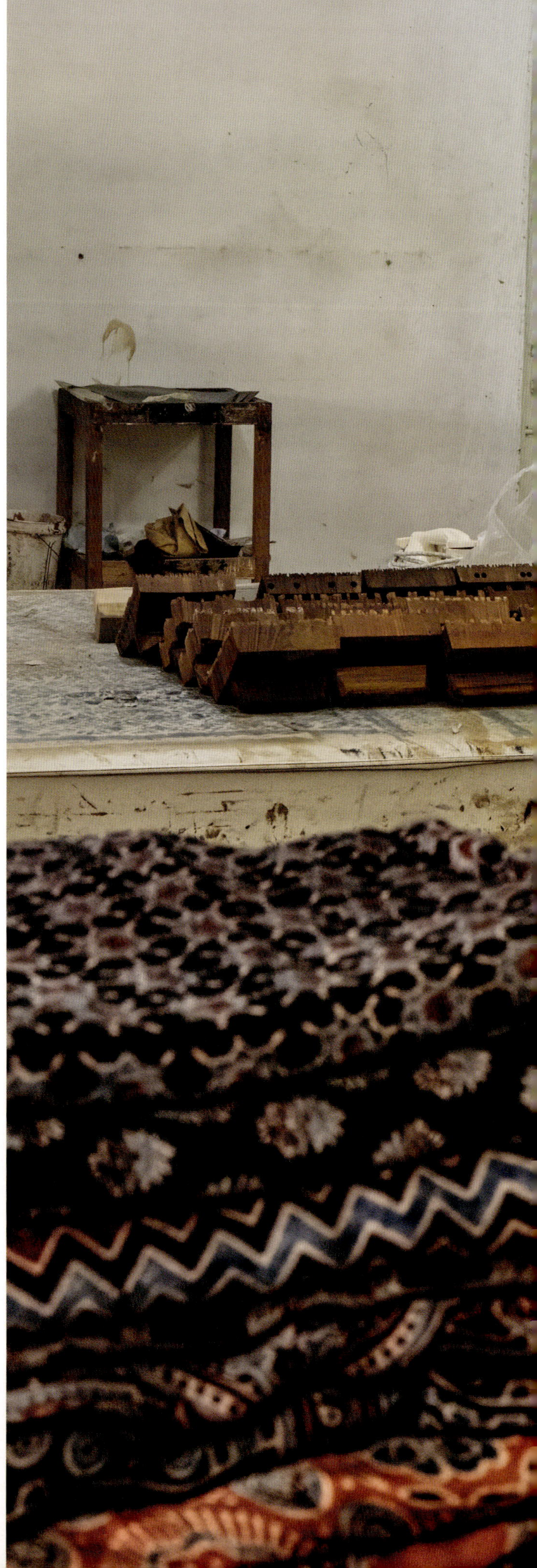

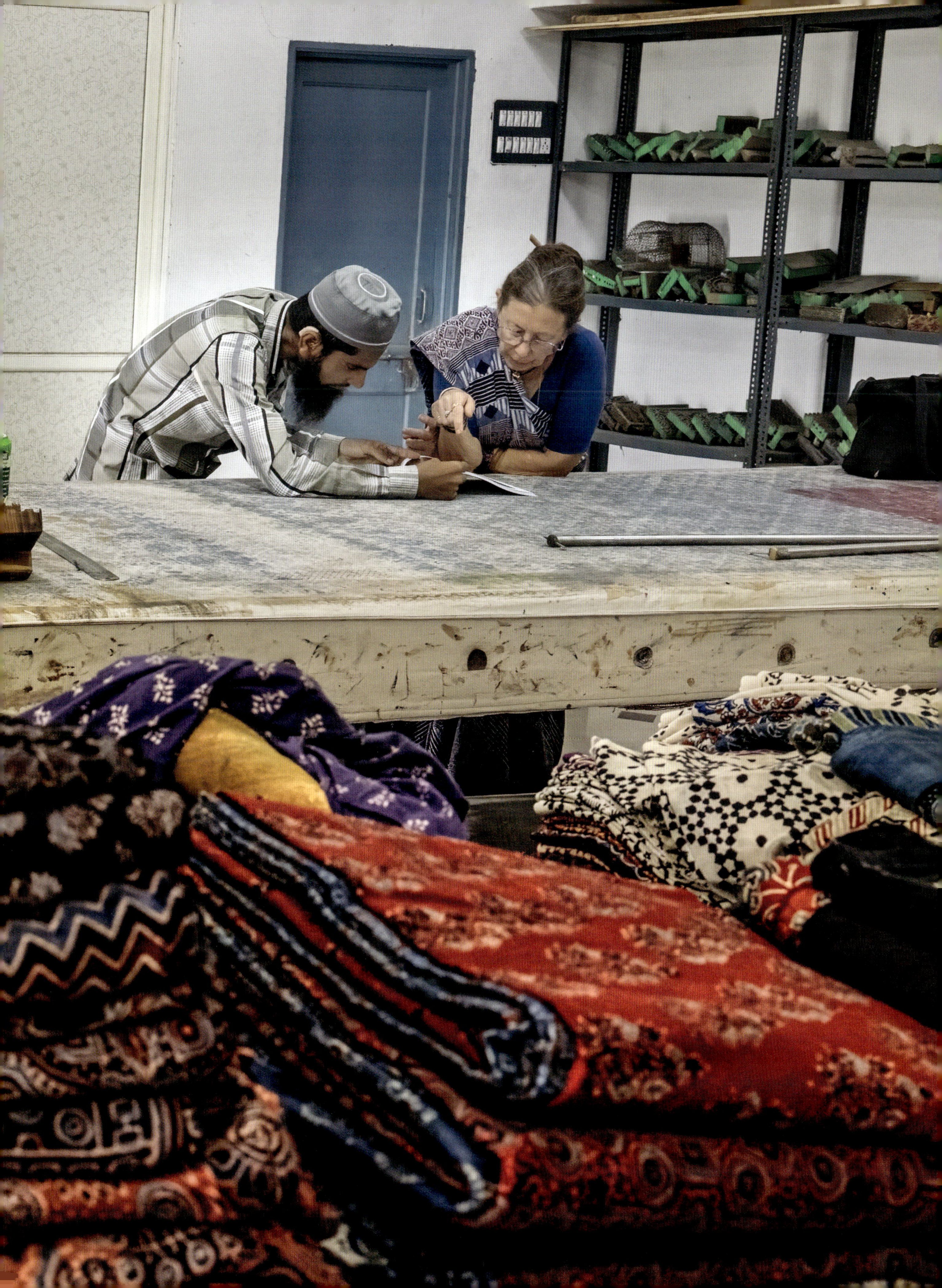

The cultural economist Arjo Klamer writes of a "Creative Craft Culture,"[6] in which artisans have a sense of tradition, mission, innovativeness, and entrepreneurship. They recognize masters, live their values, and share a sense of collegiality. In this ideal scenario, young people view the creative crafts as a career worth striving for. The market in a creative craft culture is commensurate: consumers have a distinctive taste for and appreciation of creative quality and are willing to pay for it.

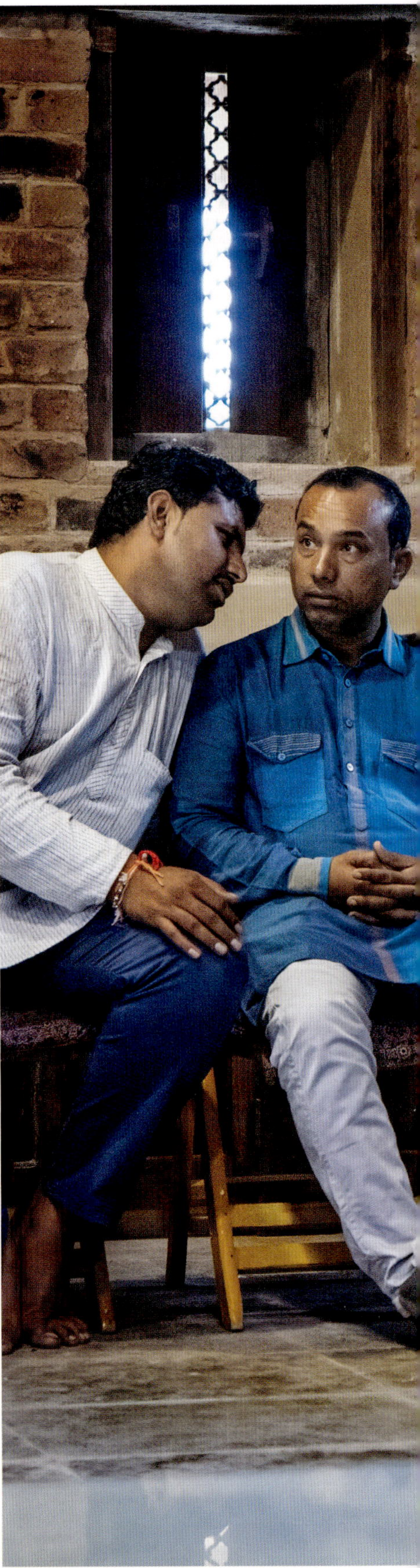

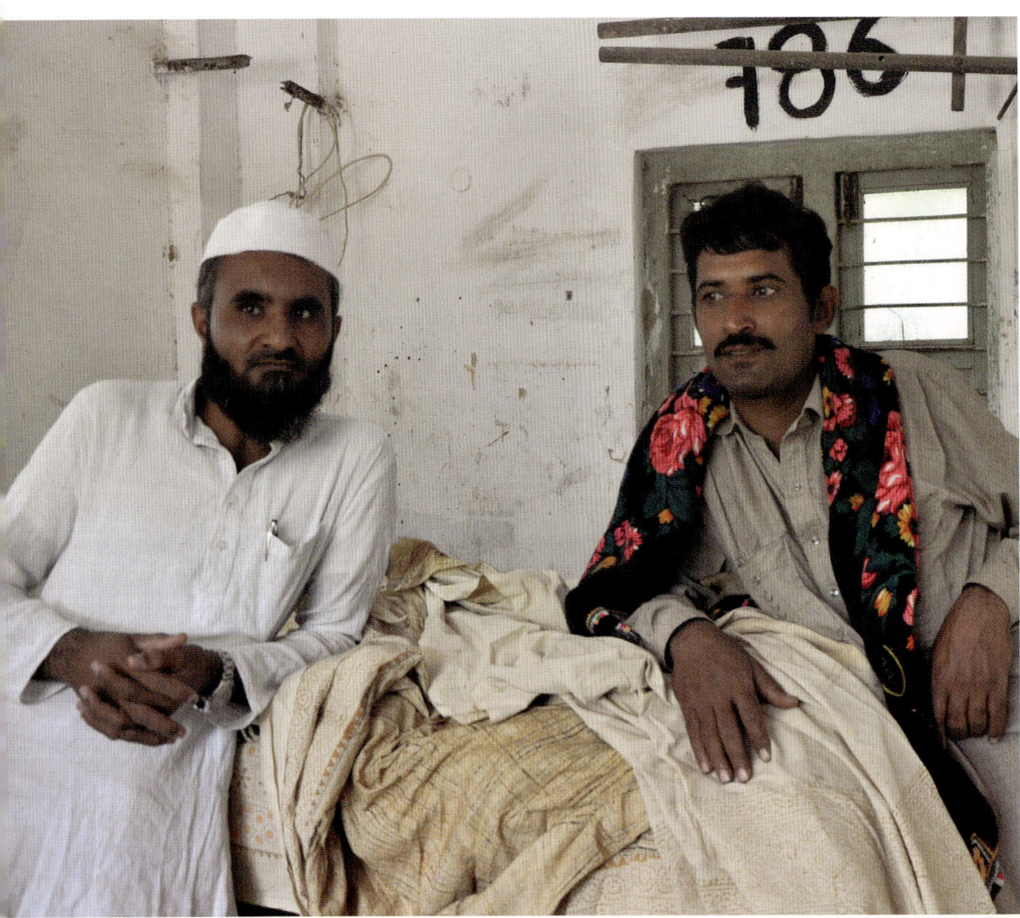

Above: Nani Banni, 2019. Traditionally, artisans of Kutch created for intimately known clients. Irfanbhai's family has worked with Hakimbhai Nodhe's family for generations. Familiarity generates appreciation and respect. Meeting after years, the two men discuss and solicit opinions as if no time has passed. *Photo: Judy Frater*

Right: Somaiya Kala Vidya, 2022. Graduates from different villages and communities enjoy a chance to catch up, momentarily away from their ongoing production work. Building a common community of artisan designers will ensure sustainability of independence, agency, and creativity. *Photo: Nevada Wier*

Following pages: Somaiya Kala Vidya, 2022. Women design graduates are fewer so far, but as social restrictions loosen, women have shown keen interest in the design course as a path to empowerment. *Photo: Nevada Wier*

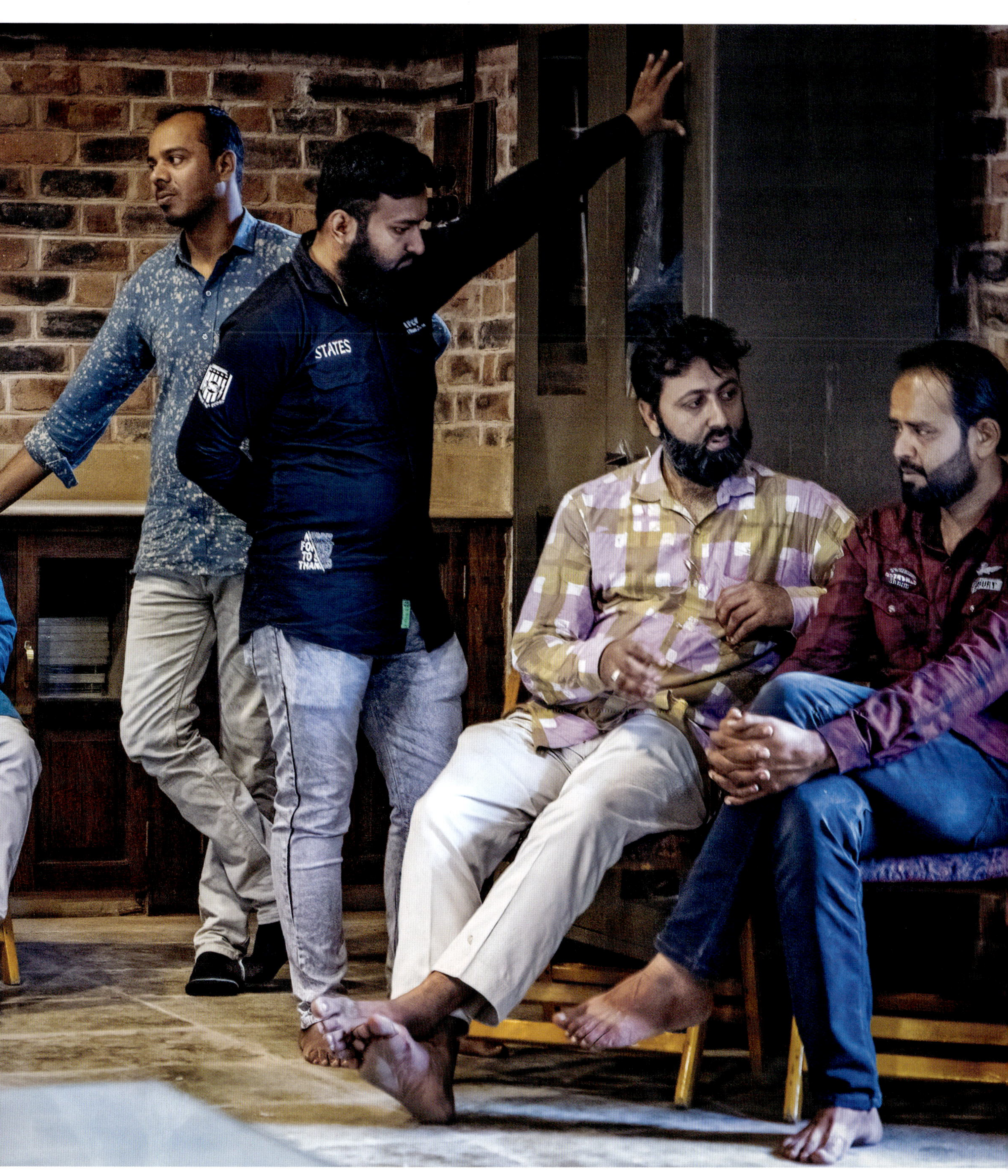
STATES

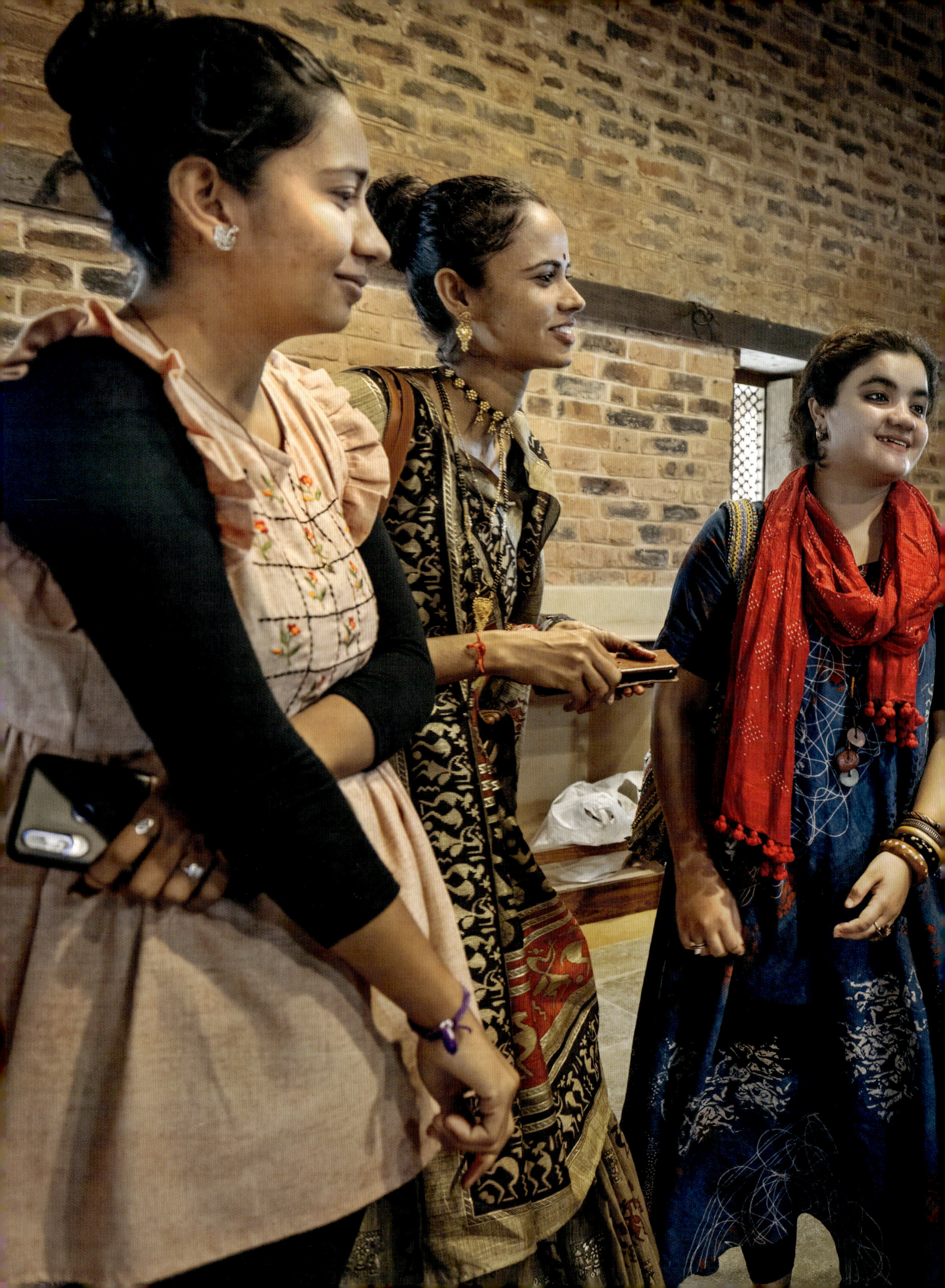

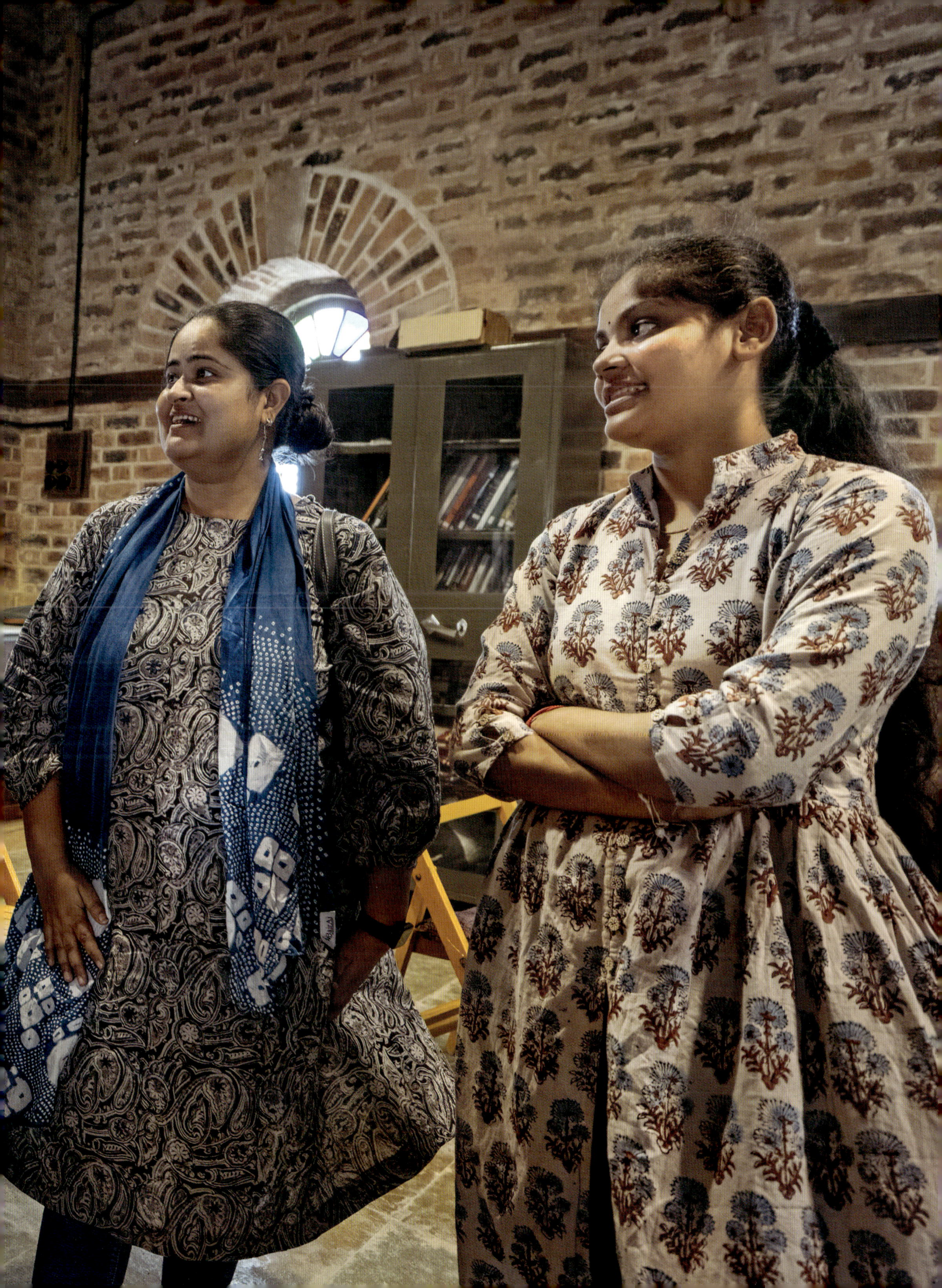

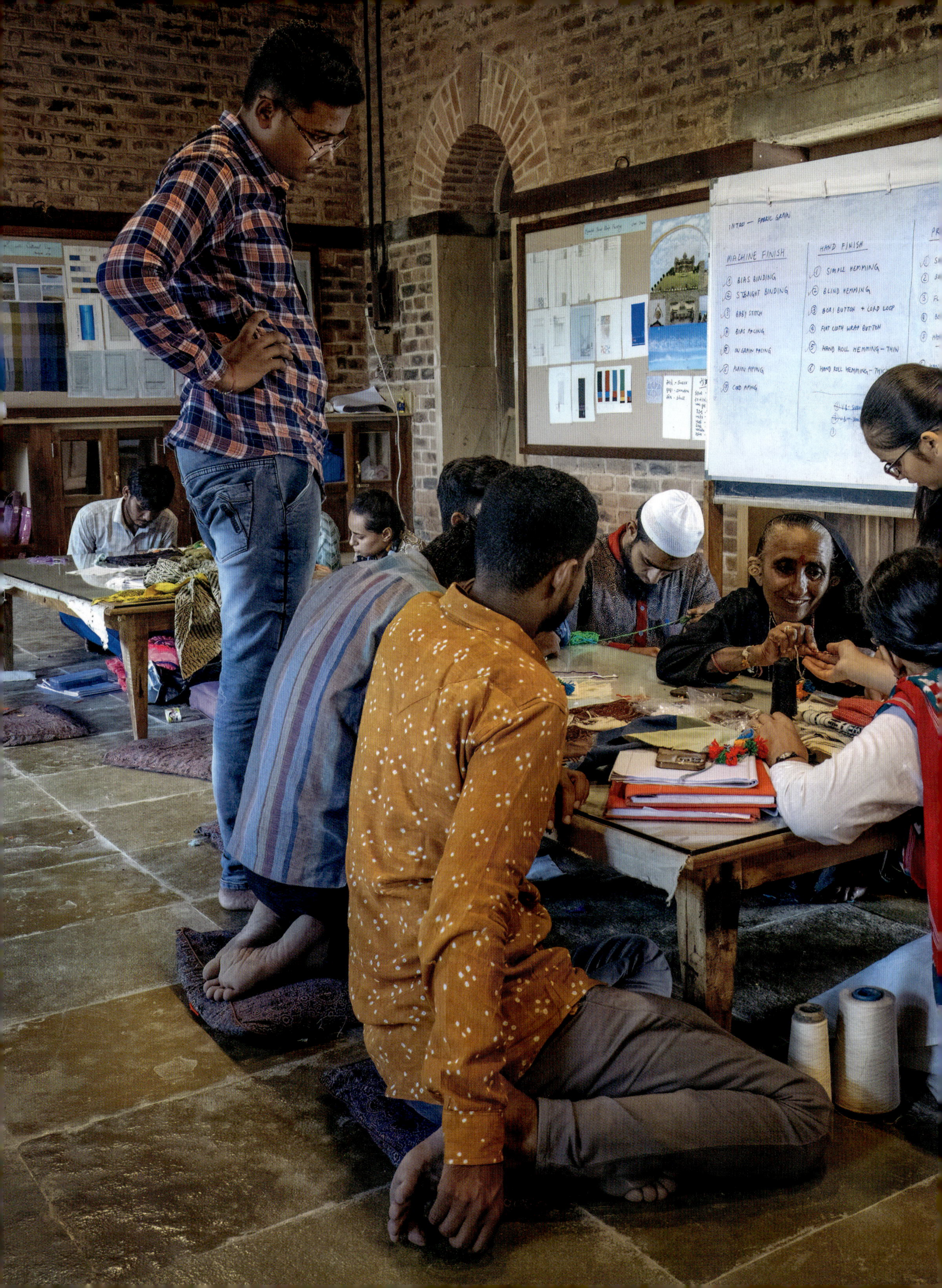
INTRO — FABRIC GRAIN
MACHINE FINISH
① BIAS BINDING
② STRAIGHT BINDING
③ BABY STITCH
④ BIAS FACING
⑤ IN GRAIN FACING
⑥ MAIN PIPING
⑦ CORD PIPING
HAND FINISH
① SIMPLE HEMMING
② BLIND HEMMING
③ BORI BUTTON + CORD LOOP
④ FLAT CLOTH WRAP BUTTON
⑤ HAND ROLL HEMMING – THIN
⑥ HAND ROLL HEMMING – THIC

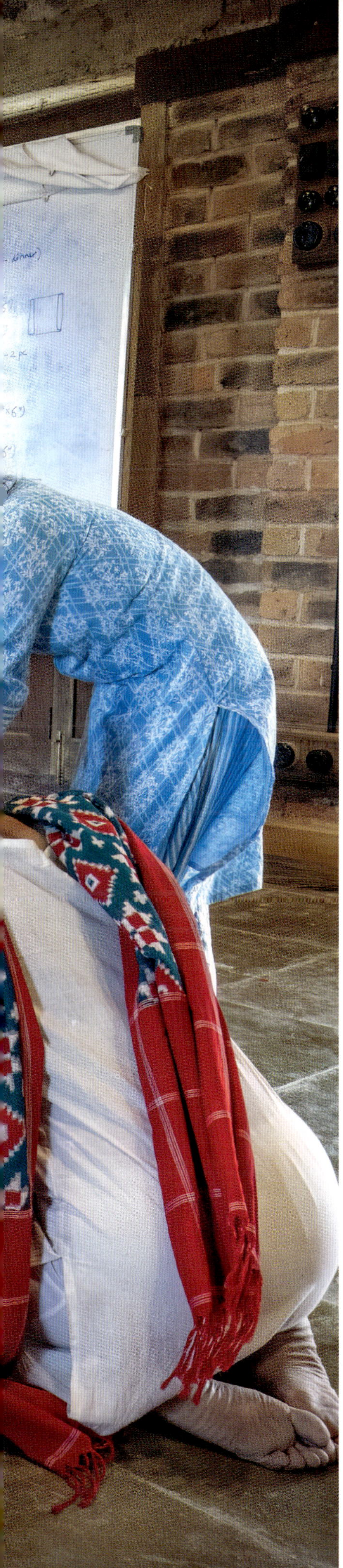

Somaiya Kala Vidya, 2022. Somaiya Kala Vidya's new campus, designed by Hemen Sanghvi with stone, bricks, lime mortar, salvaged antique wood, and foresight, is solid, spacious, and inviting. In 2023, more than fifty men and women artisans applied for the design course. *Photo: Nevada Wier*

The artisan design graduates remarkably embody Klamer's artisans. But the operative word in this vision is "culture." For revaluation, a people's movement, the alumni must work together to build a strong community and create a presence.

"I'll tell you straight out," Mukhtarbhai says. "There is not enough trust among artisans." Shakilbhai adds, "It will take fifteen to twenty years to build trust."

I believe that with sensitive guidance, we can build a community together.

The other critical piece of today's craft world is the crisis of overconsumption. Traditional societies consumed what they needed. Fashion by its nature consumes so much more. I believe that handcraft can offer an alternative in style and meaning that satiates unlimited desire. I envision collectives and communities, loved and appreciated by other communities, a system in which people know each other and craft is valued as a luxury in an increasingly isolated world—a scaling out rather than scaling up.

Ismailbhai, visionary senior Ajrakh artisan, built a studio next to his home, with a big desk, a screening room, and a little workshop where he creates limited editions of traditional textiles—double-sided and minakari Ajrakhs, traditional skirt fabrics—revivals exquisitely printed. When I asked him how to ensure this quality, he grinned and said, "You have to make it with love."

This is the model. This is where craft should go, I said. To which he disdainfully replied, "There's no money in this."

"There are only a few special clients for this work," he explained.

But he does it. Because there is another need: to create and connect to those who appreciate. The third element of a creative craft culture is intermediaries to initiate intensive discussions of the works of creative craftspeople and to connect artisans and their market.

Education must be two way. Through it we can create an upward spiral in which artisans learn to express their creativity, consumers learn to value handcraft, and craft is surely worth it for everyone. Once artisans have prosperity, which today they see as inextricably tied to scale, they do what they love. What's next is developing another way, in which what they love can be valued enough.

I hope that these stories of craft in Kutch and artisans who learned design, and from whom I learned will be a part of the discussions we need.

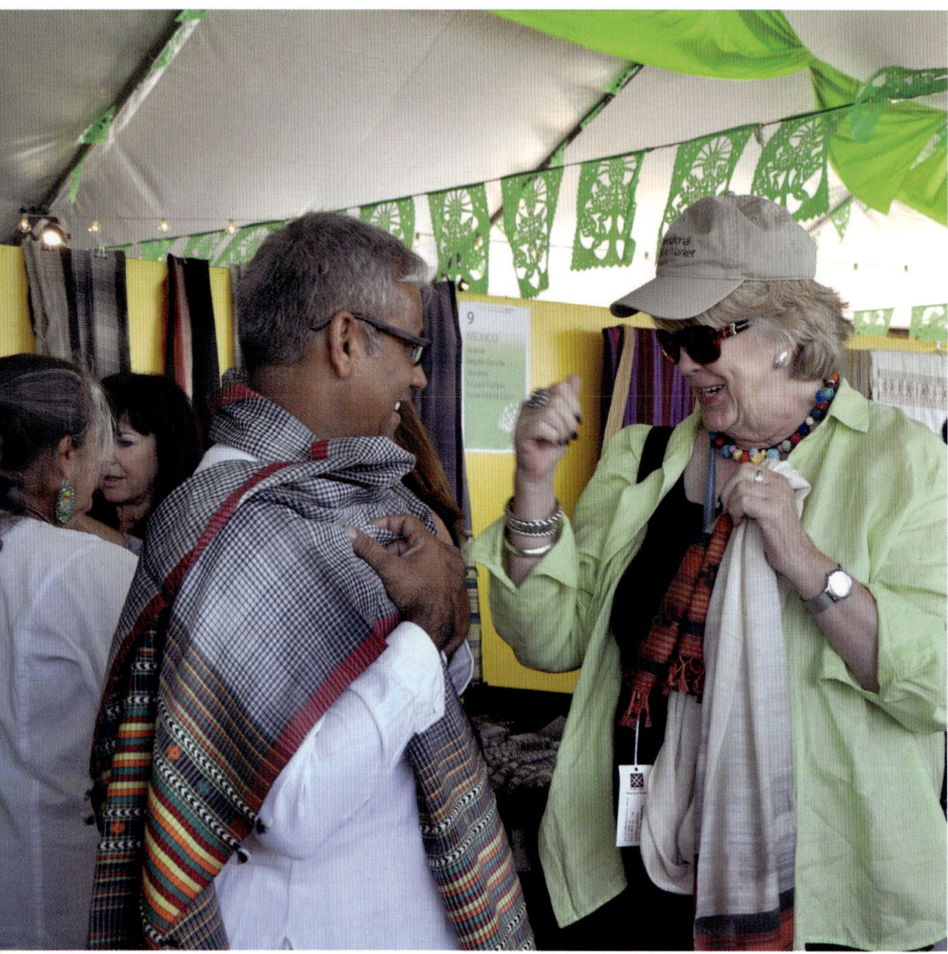

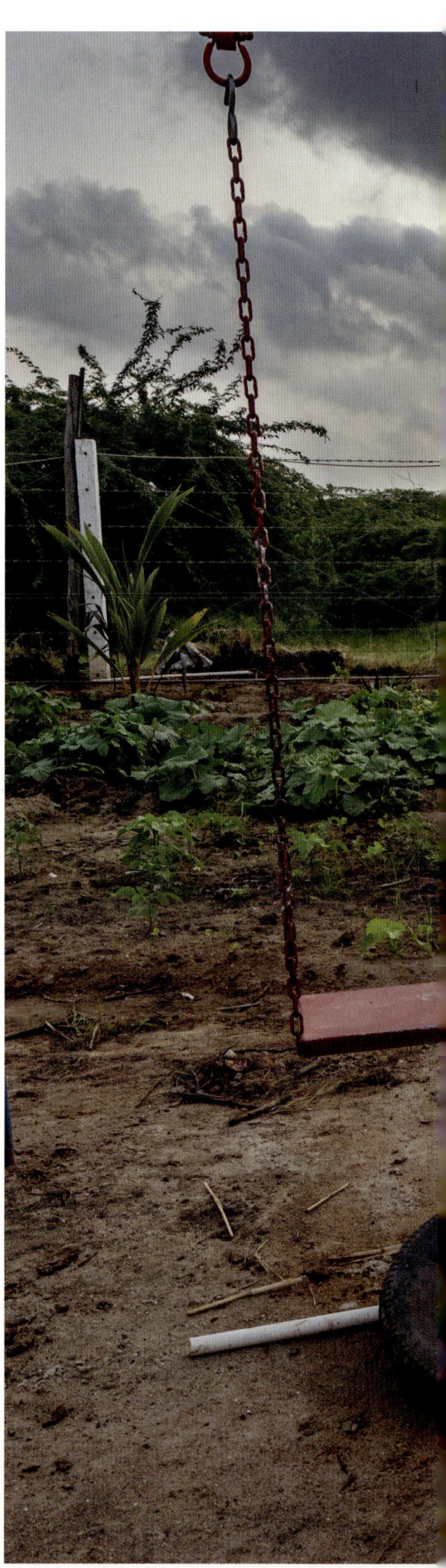

Above: Santa Fe, 2015. Dahyalalbhai meets a customer at the International Folk Art Market. Desire without value threatens contemporary craft, so educating buyers is imperative. Events such as IFAM aim to create value for handwork by emphasizing the artisan. *Photo: Judy Frater*

Right: Ajrakhpur, 2022. Playfulness and joy are unspoken ingredients of a creative life. Exquisite craft is made with love, Ismailbhai says. *Photo: Nevada Wier*

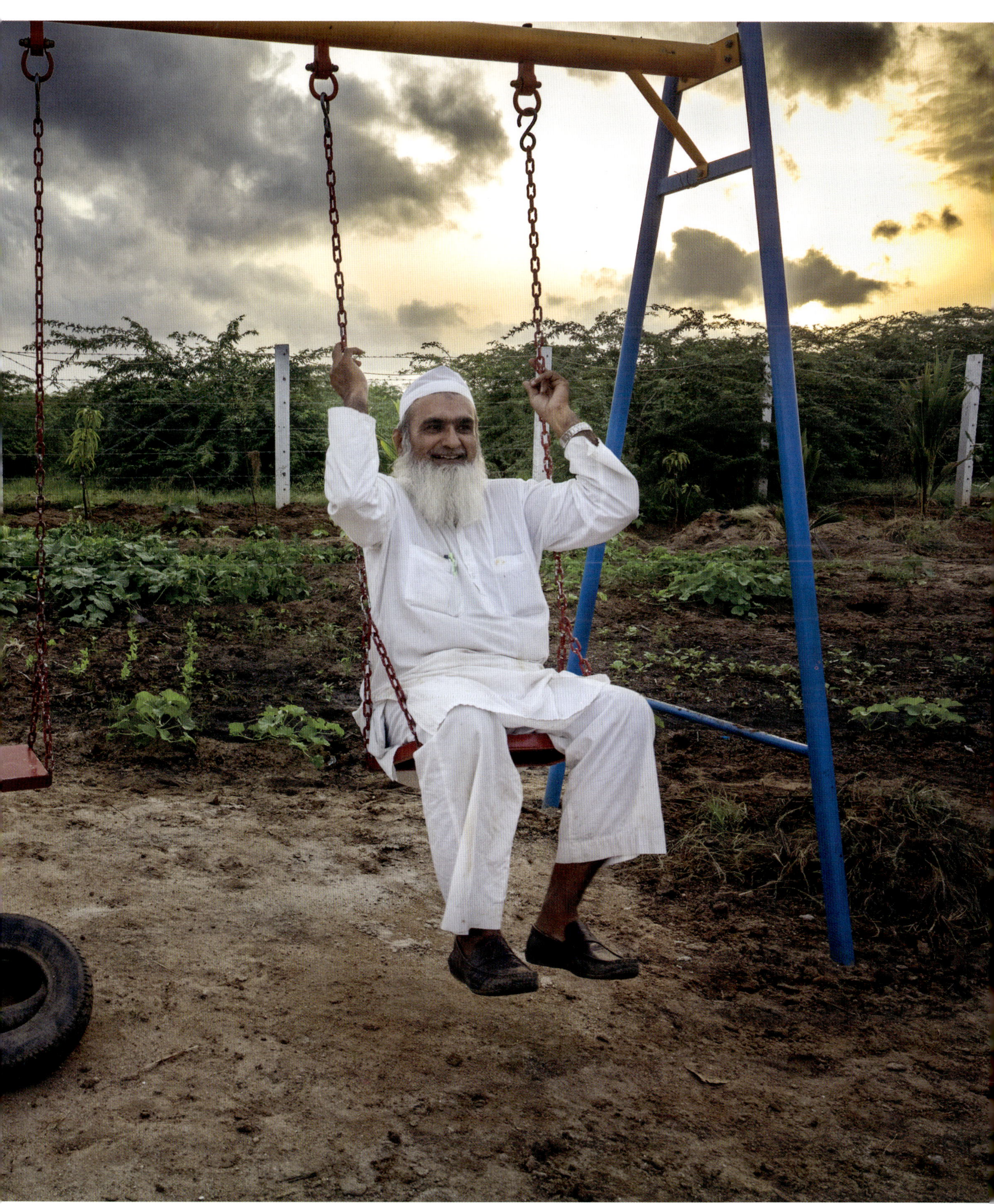

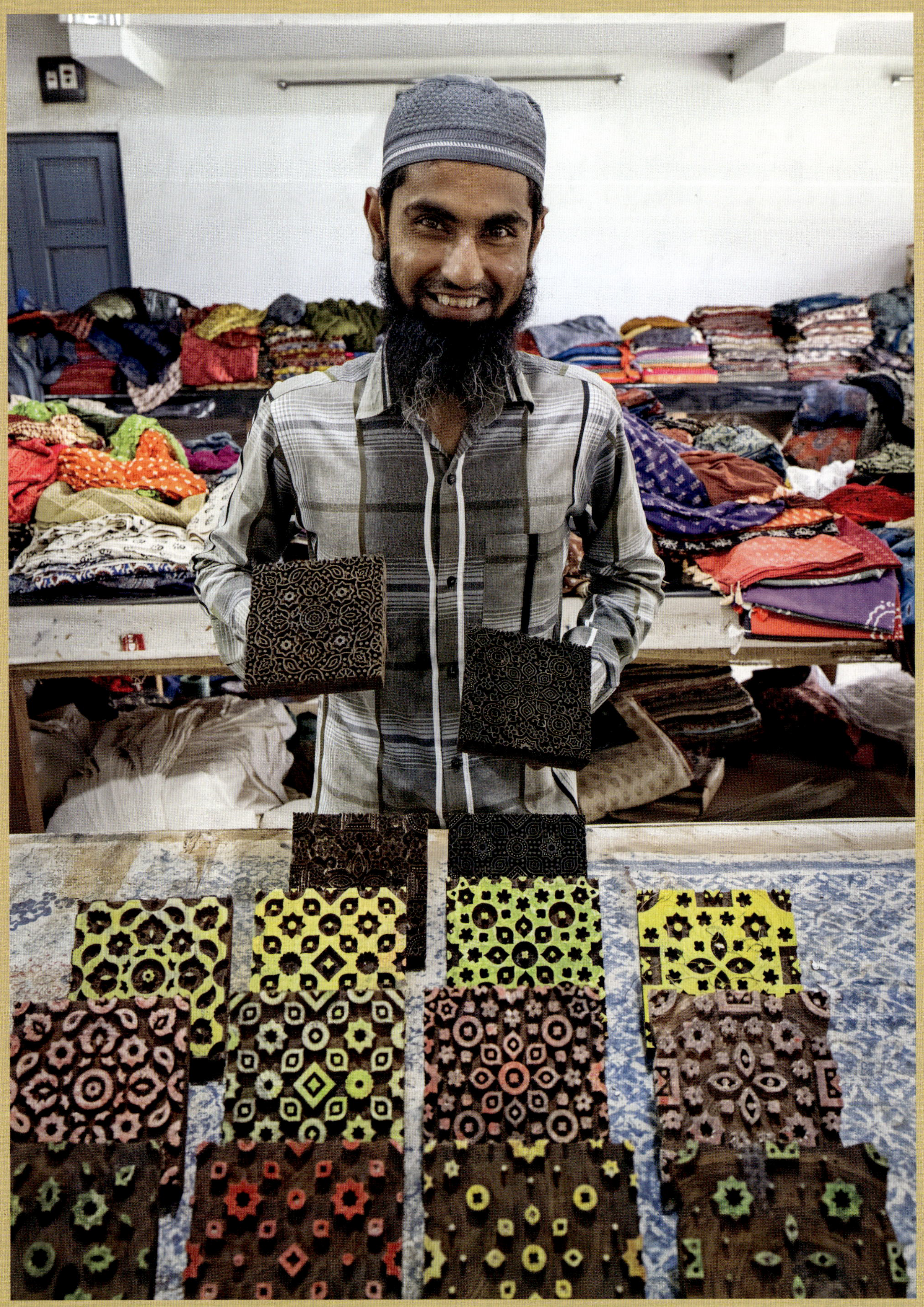

Chapter 24

AKIBBHAI IBRAHIM KHATRI: THE VISIONARY AND THE COMMUNITY

Work to your interest and you will find your way;
find time to do your passion.

~Akibbhai Ibrahim Khatri

2019

The room is jam packed with rainbows of textiles, neatly tied in bundles, ready to go. Akibbhai has to squeeze in a couple of plastic chairs for us to sit.

There must be thousands of meters of yardage, natural and synthetic dyed, handprint and screen print. "We do it all," he says. His father and brother will be taking all of this and more to an exhibition in Delhi. "We are doing big business," he affirms in reply to my look of confusion.

Opposite: Ajrakhpur, 2022. "I compose starting with blocks," Akibbhai says. "If there are many spaces, I need less busy blocks." He also thinks of the size of the block. He just had four sets of blocks made in the original size, before blocks were scaled up for production. *Photo: Nevada Wier*

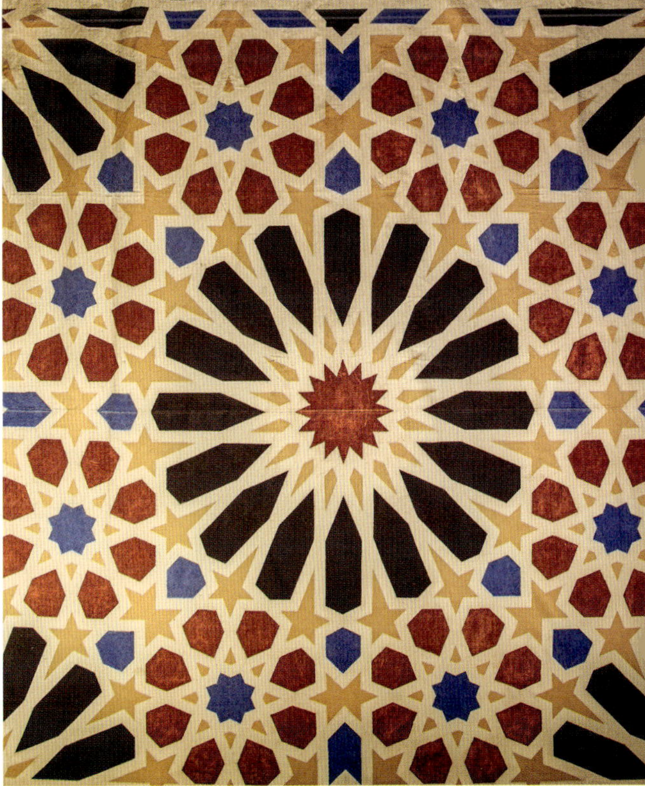

Right: Color block stars, detail. Bed spread by Akibbhai Ibrahim Khatri, 2022. Cotton, hand block printed, natural dyes, 104" x 104". Akibbhai displays his expertise in this deceptively simple piece. Plain areas are more difficult than printed ones, as natural dyes tend to be splotchy. *Photo: Raul Tovar*

Is this the same Akibbhai who spoke to our Business and Management for Artisans class just a few years ago?

Akibbhai comes from a family of visionaries and pioneers. His grandfather was a block printer in Rapar, where he created *sadla* in red with black patterns for Kanbi Patels of the region. But he moved to Dhamadka to be closer to the better markets and raw materials. There, the family started using different colors and creating Ajrakh for the traditional market, and salvar-kamiz-dupatta sets, yardage, and saris for contemporary markets.

When the 2001 earthquake decimated Dhamadka, Akibbhai's mother was injured. She was in a hospital in Pune for two months. During that time, the community decided to build a new village. She recalls how she came back to Kutch and they were the first family to move to the new location. It was wild land. There were no facilities at all—except a water source. They were settlers, living in a tent. Community leaders checked in on them. Others came from Dhamadka and would leave in a month or two. But Akibbhai's family lived there, unafraid.

Finally, seven or eight tin roof huts were built, and the rest of the community came after an NGO built houses. Since there were no schools nearby, Akibbhai and his elder brother Imtiazbhai went to boarding school in Kera District. Akibbhai came back and finished his last years of school and one year of college in Kutch.

In the new village Ajrakhpur, the family rebuilt a business, making printed textiles and selling them in pop-up exhibitions all over India. Akibbhai saw his cousin Irfanbhai's work from the design course and liked it. He was nineteen and had been working in the family business for a year when he took the KRV design course in 2011. "This was a course especially for artisans," he said.

"The fees were minimal, and everything was included except transportation."

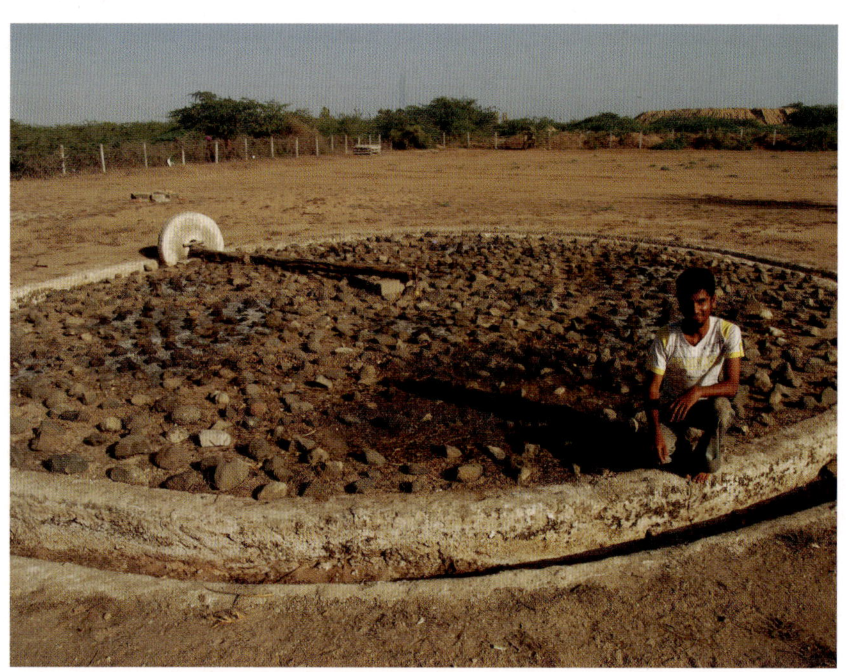

Kala Raksha Vidhyalaya, 2011. After seeing Andy Goldsworthy's nature installations, Akibbhai created his sense of summer: crushing heat, burning to barrenness. *Photo: Shantanu Das*

His dream was to work in block printing on a large scale, break limitations, and use natural colors that had not been possible before. He wanted to begin his own autonomous hand block print business.

Akibbhai struggled with hearing issues. He was shy. When the teacher for the color class personally encouraged him, tears came to his eyes. "I learned that if we try, we can do anything—get all colors from natural dyes," he said. This is my favorite subject, so I never feel it is work."

The faculty for the Concept Development course had the students each choose a season as a theme, write what they felt, draw pictures, and make motifs within their traditions. They worked slowly, with effort. Then one night, he showed them Andy Goldsworthy's film *Rivers and Tides*. As amazed as the students were, the next day he had each one make an installation to evoke his season. Now, the students worked intuitively. Akibbhai had summer. He chose the circular pit with a heavy stone wheel that the architect used for crushing limestone. He filled the center with rocks, piled on leaves and brush, and set it aflame, leaving

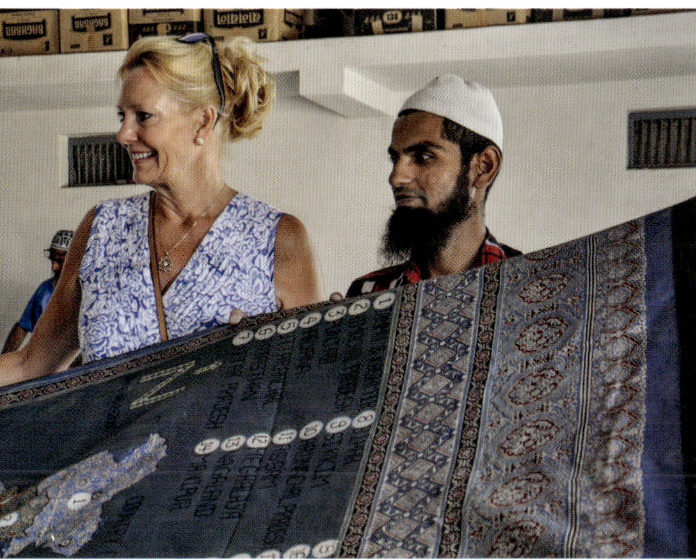

Left: Ajrakhpur, 2017. At an Open Studio Tour, Akibbhai shows a family heirloom, a map of India block-printed and dyed by his father in hopes of receiving a President's Award for craft. *Photo: Judy Frater*

Below: Mumbai, 2017. Akibbhai was among seven graduates who showed collections in Lakme Fashion Week. Although the classic geometry of his indigo saris was a bit overwhelmed by the stylist's zany tops, the experience was a great accomplishment. *Photo: Lakme Fashion Week*

the ash and black ground. Summer is hard, he said. It is crushingly hot and burns away everything. The round area symbolized the sun. He saw the heat as black. His expression was deep, profound, and effective. And it clearly revealed an understanding of summer very different from the conventional Western one.

Collaborating with a student from NID, Akibbhai created a collection of women's garments. "She brought a lot of books," he said. "I believe the more a person reads and observes, the more he can create." His partner rejoined, "Akibbhai thinks twenty-four hours. He is patient, has an eye for detail, and aims for exact specification. And he is conscious about fabric consumption and costing."

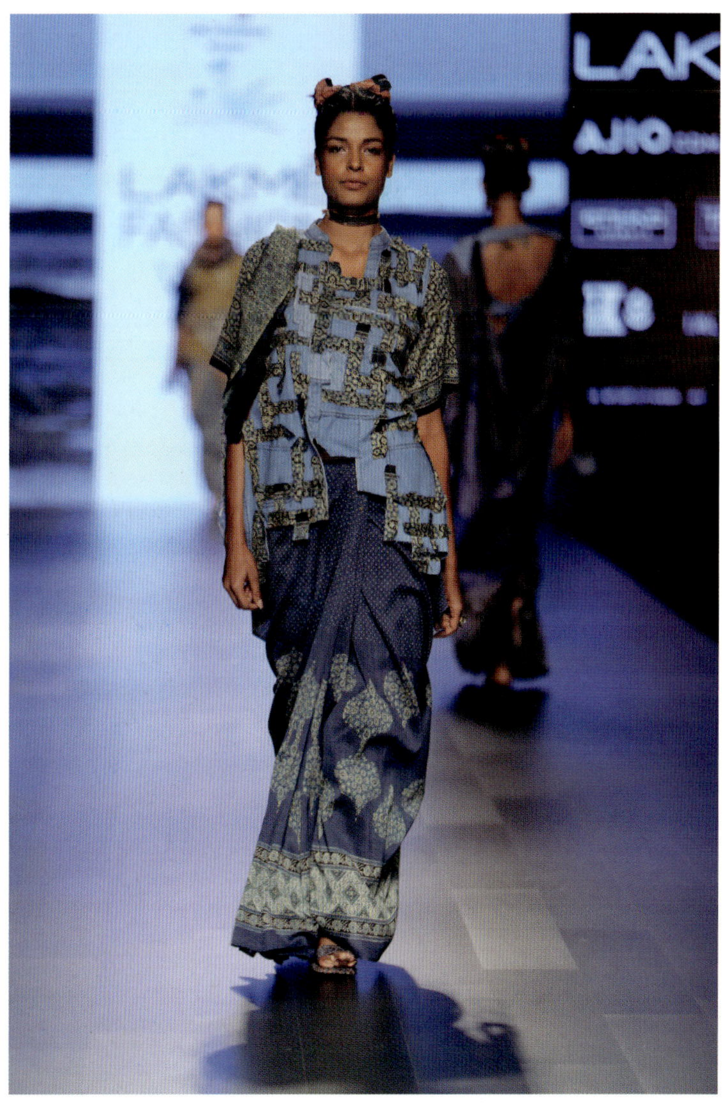

The visiting faculty for the final Presentation course wrote, "Akib creates designs, concepts, etc. after good research and planning. Nothing is impulsive. Yet, he takes a very long time developing his concepts, and he changes his concept completely after he faces a difficult problem. He needs to be able to work within a timeline."

Akibbhai graduated with awards for Most Innovative Artisan and Best Student. Then he began a niche practice, creating small-scale, technically skilled work. His specialization was large, one-of-a-kind complex geometric textiles. And he preferred to sell directly. He taught Ajrakh printing to visitors and students of Somaiya Kala Vidya's Craft Traditions courses. In February 2017, he showed two striking saris inspired by Islamic geometry in Lakme Fashion Week.

I asked him to share his unique business vision with students of the SKV Business and Management for Artisans course. With confidence, Akibbhai told his story and his strategy. "After the design course, I get more ideas than I can do!" he laughed. He told the students to be sure to have bread-and-butter work—regular

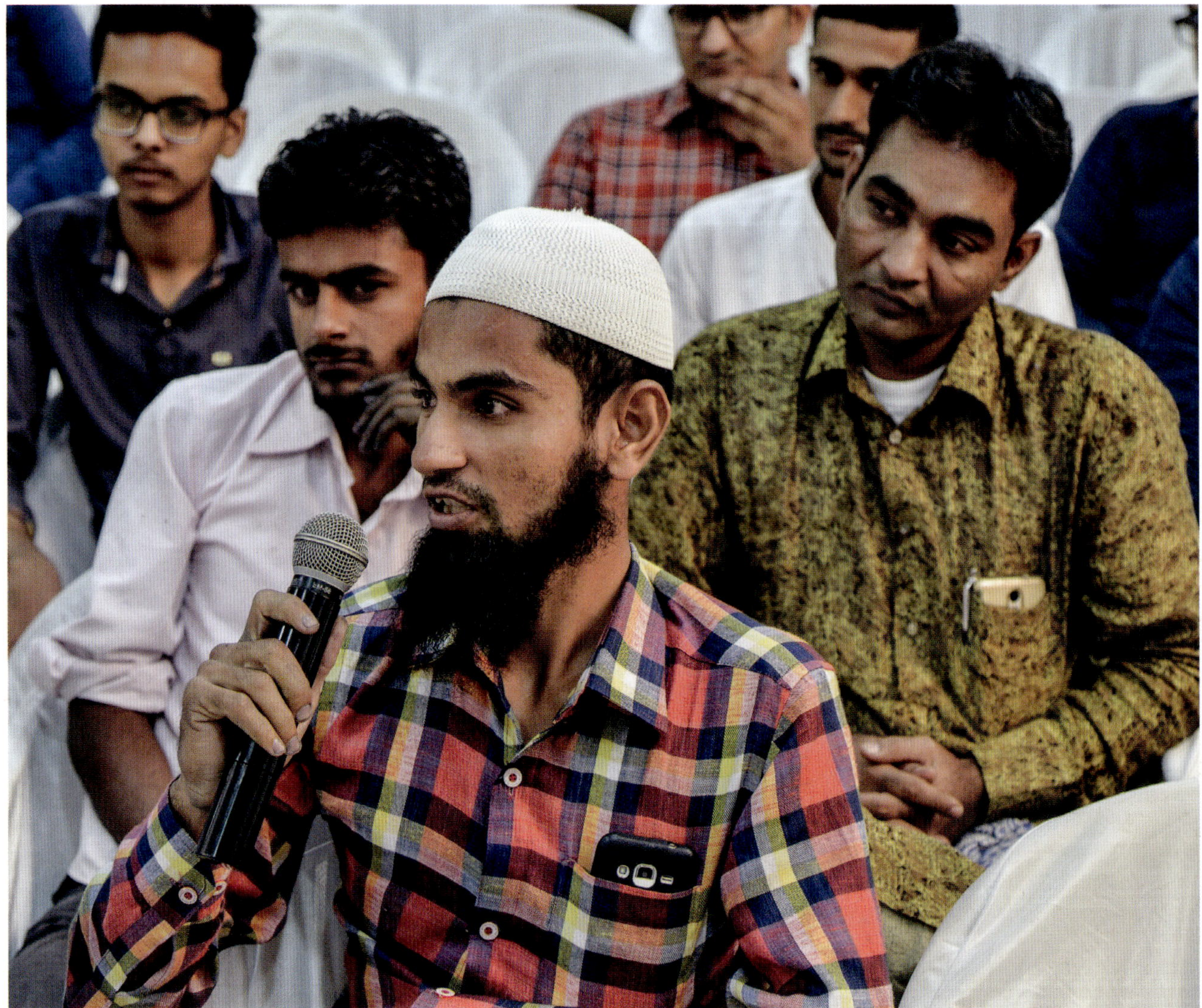

designs but good quality. "You need to stay connected to the market," he said, "not only to earn a livelihood but also so that no one forgets your name. But don't take on work you can't manage. Self-respect, value, respect for family, and faith—these are the bottom lines."

In addition, Akibbhai had the special work that he did in his spare time, exclusive pieces inspired by Islamic art created as his passion. "Work to your interest and you will find your way; find time to do your passion," he said. He wanted to make a name, he told the students. "Today, I earn thirty-five to forty *lakhs* a year. I want to do that in a day." His strategy for such work was to target special clients, only a few a year. "I want to make special pieces so that people will come to me," he said.

A year later at the seminar on copying, Akibbhai listened to the discussion and toward the end took the mic. "If you are to develop a market for yourself," he said, "it should have two parts: one unique and the other commercial. Save money [by] making commercial products, and every year try to make a unique collection through which you can get a platform. Once you make a strong collection, market it well to show your real capacity."

He paused and then continued. "Between unique and commercial collections, there is something called an art-based collection. For that work we can ask as much money as we want, because not everyone can make it. We have to think when to launch these designs. 'Big fish eat small ones.' So we small fish have to think."

The audience applauded his long-term planning, clarity, and passion.

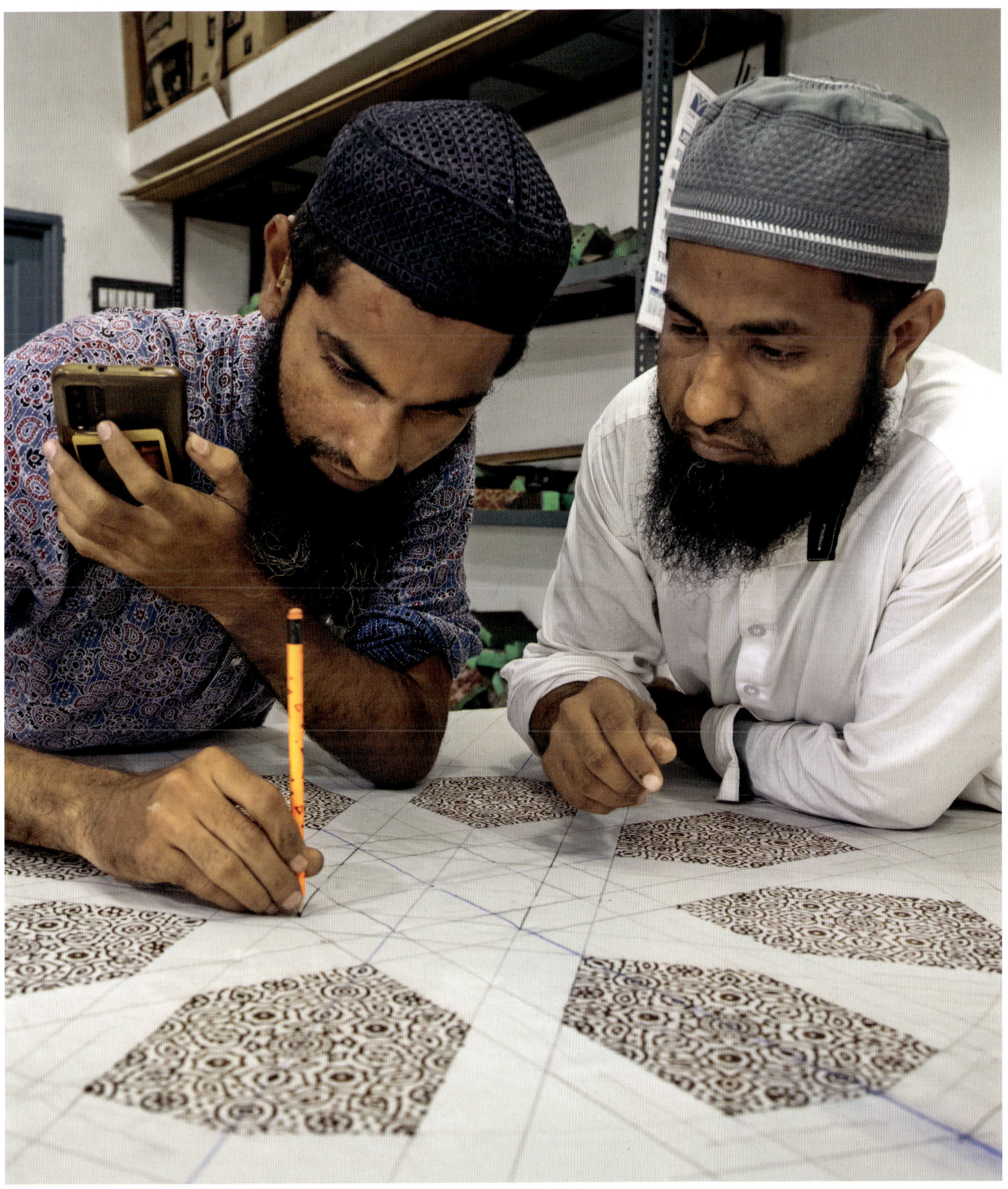

Opposite: Sharma Resorts, 2017. Akibbhai gained confidence through the course. "Besides design, I learned how to talk," he said. "I had done one year of college, but there wasn't anything there to open us up. After KRV, I opened up so much I could go abroad." *Photo: Ketan Pomal, L.M. Studio*

Above: Ajrakhpur, 2022. Although Imtiazbhai prefers production and business, he is a Khatri and can't help but appreciate art. He is always ready to assist his brother. *Photo: Nevada Wier*

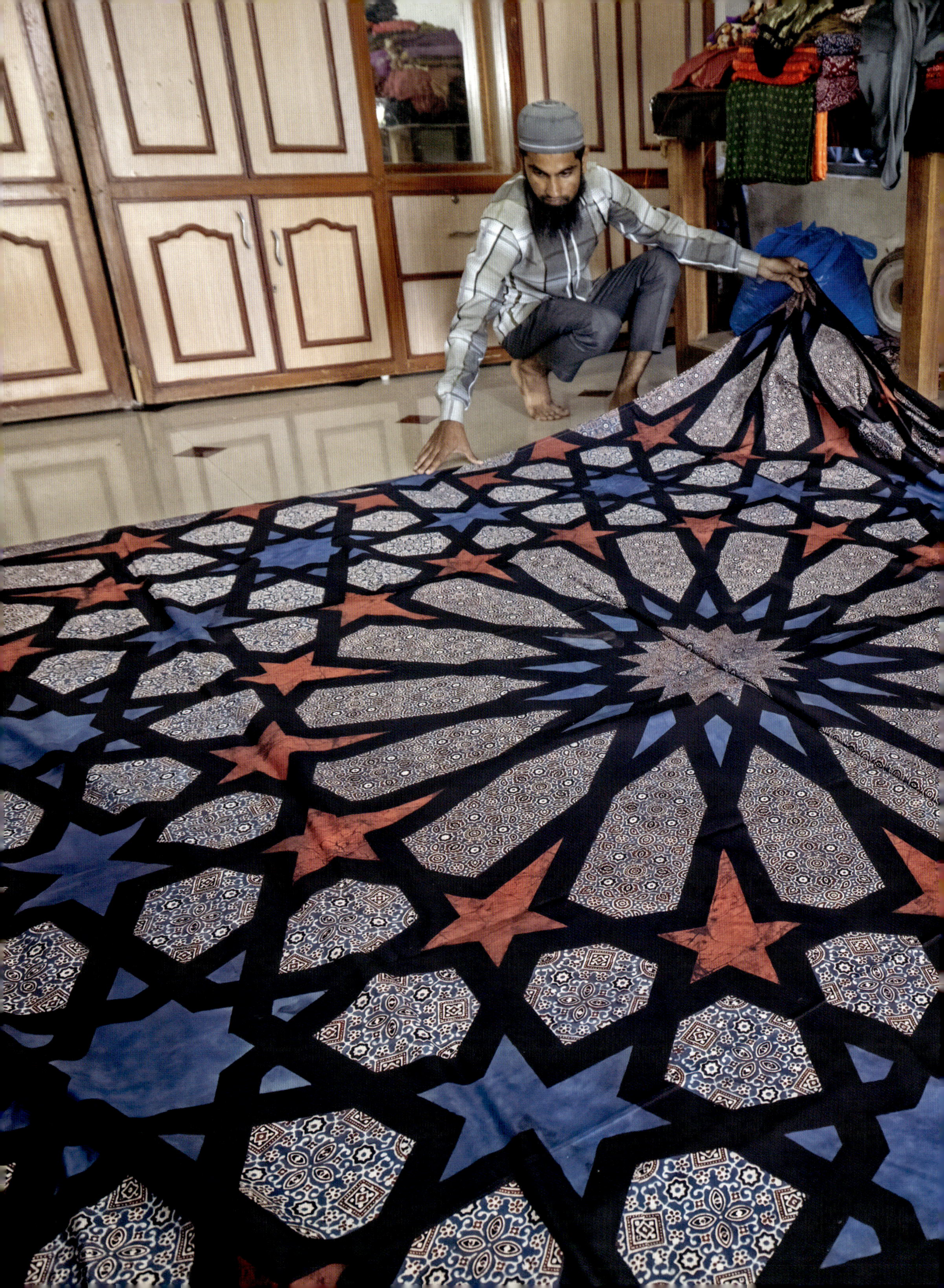

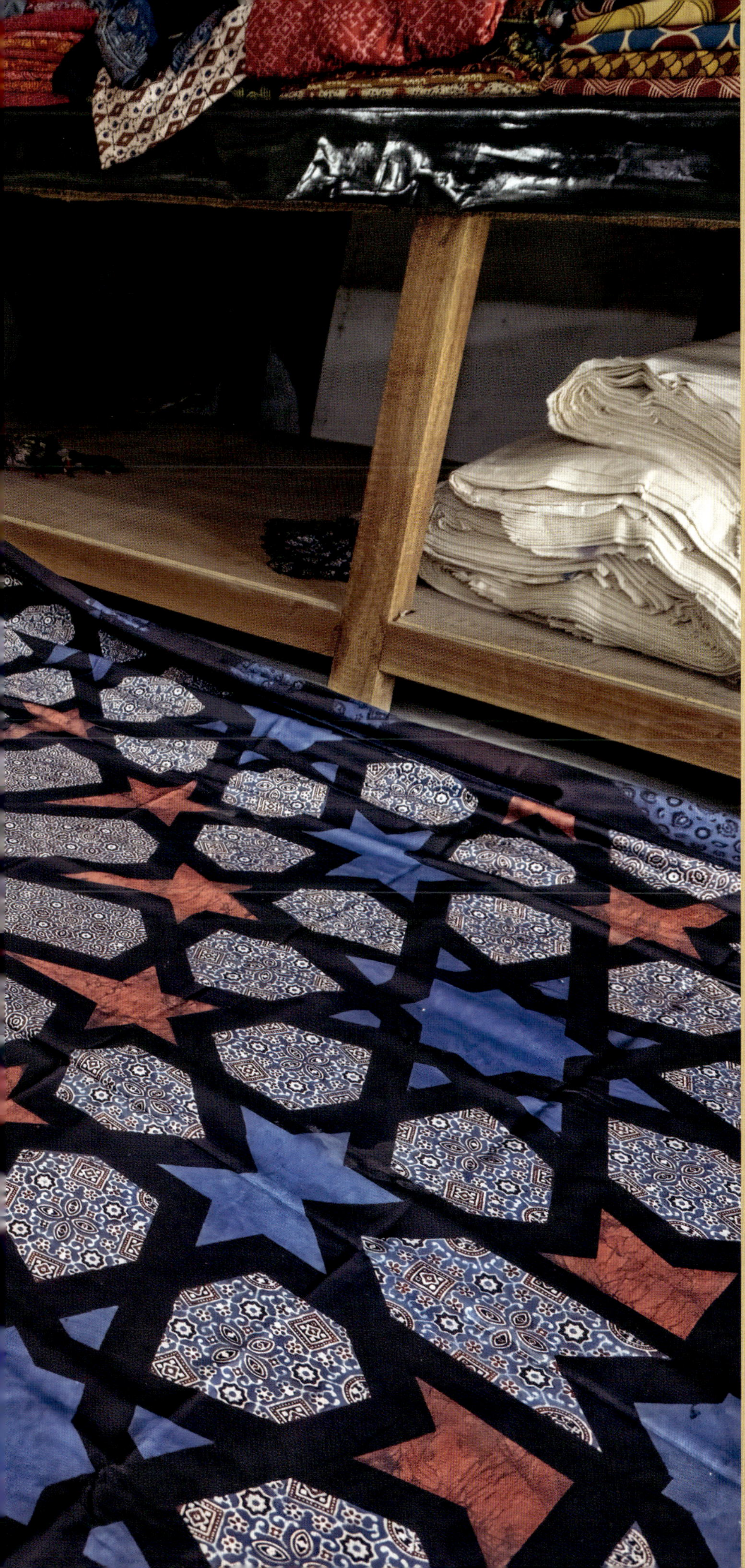

Ajrakhpur, 2022. Akibbhai composes masterpieces by using a giant compass that he made from a selfie stick and a compass. The first one took twenty-two days to print, he says. After that, it was easy. You have to be in a clear-headed, peaceful state. It has to be perfect. *Photo: Nevada Wier*

And then I heard that Akibbhai had closed his workshop. He was the artisan designer, the example that even today an artisan did not have to scale to industrial methods to succeed. I rushed to Ajrakhpur to hear his story.

"It's true," he smiled. "Everyone is going in one direction. It's getting too crowded, and copying is out of hand." He was developing new colors. No sooner had he done swatches than they were copied. "I want to do something different," he said. He decided to study his design books. There was no appreciation in India, he said. Art had to go out of the country first and then come back.

But some months later, when I gave Akibbhai a chance to make a piece for the Textile Museum in Washington, DC, he didn't take it. He was busy restarting his workshop. Sure enough, the signboard appeared: Akib Ibrahim Khatri, Artisan Designer.

And so, I landed in the room filled with bundles of fabric.

Akibbhai waits for family members to slip away, and his amber eyes clear. He never wanted to close his workshop, he confides. It was his elder brother and father. They felt they did not have enough workers to fulfill orders. He lives in a joint family, so he went along. He knew they would not be happy without work. Within a year and a half, they started again. Now they manage many units in Ajrakhpur, and he and Imtiazbhai work in their own workshop.

He made fourteen shades of plain color in synthetic silicate dyes. He got this new idea by listening to women in his home. The plain fabric can match with his prints, and there is a good margin in yardage. "My designs hit the target," he confidently says. "I spent six years observing clients. If we make new products, we can determine the profit." His hearing aid probably cost a few hundred rupees to make, he laughs, but it cost him 10,000 because the company had a new product.

"We have to make new things until they are copied," he continues. The main point is if we don't have the capacity to market, someone else will. He has the patience and focus to create. But he did not have the means to market his art. "You have to decide between quantity and quality. Now our plan is to make money. We need big capital to do something new. We are doing quantity. But we never do big orders. Handwork is not industrial; craft can't do perfect repetition. You run a big risk of client rejection. We need two more years, and then we won't have to do quantity and can connect to outside markets. I want to make what is nowhere in the world, and what everyone will love. The future is outside India.

"We are near our future," he says. He is sure he will get to the international market. He will meet me there.

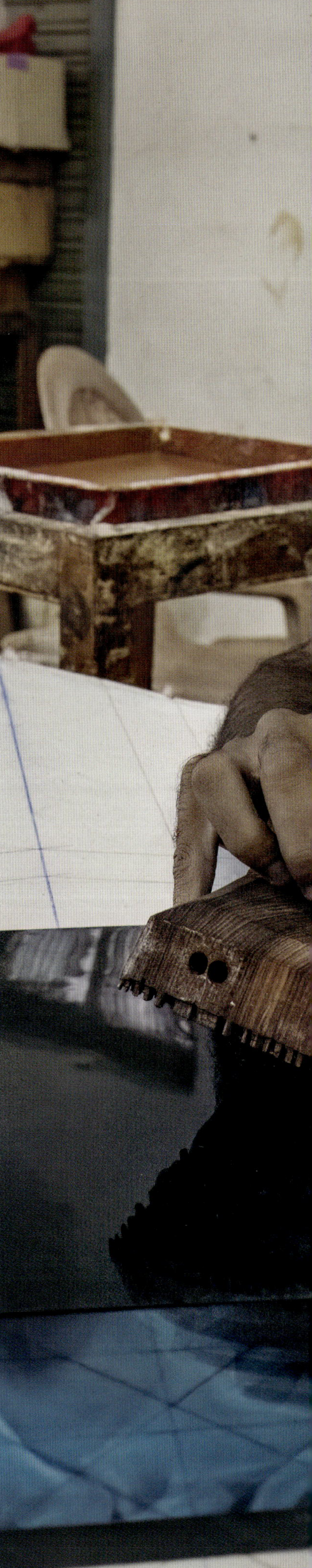

Ajrakhpur, 2022. Artisans shape printed areas by masking—traditionally, laying newspaper on the fabric to prevent a dye impression. Today, they innovate by masking with x-rays, which can be wiped clean and reused. *Photo: Nevada Wier*

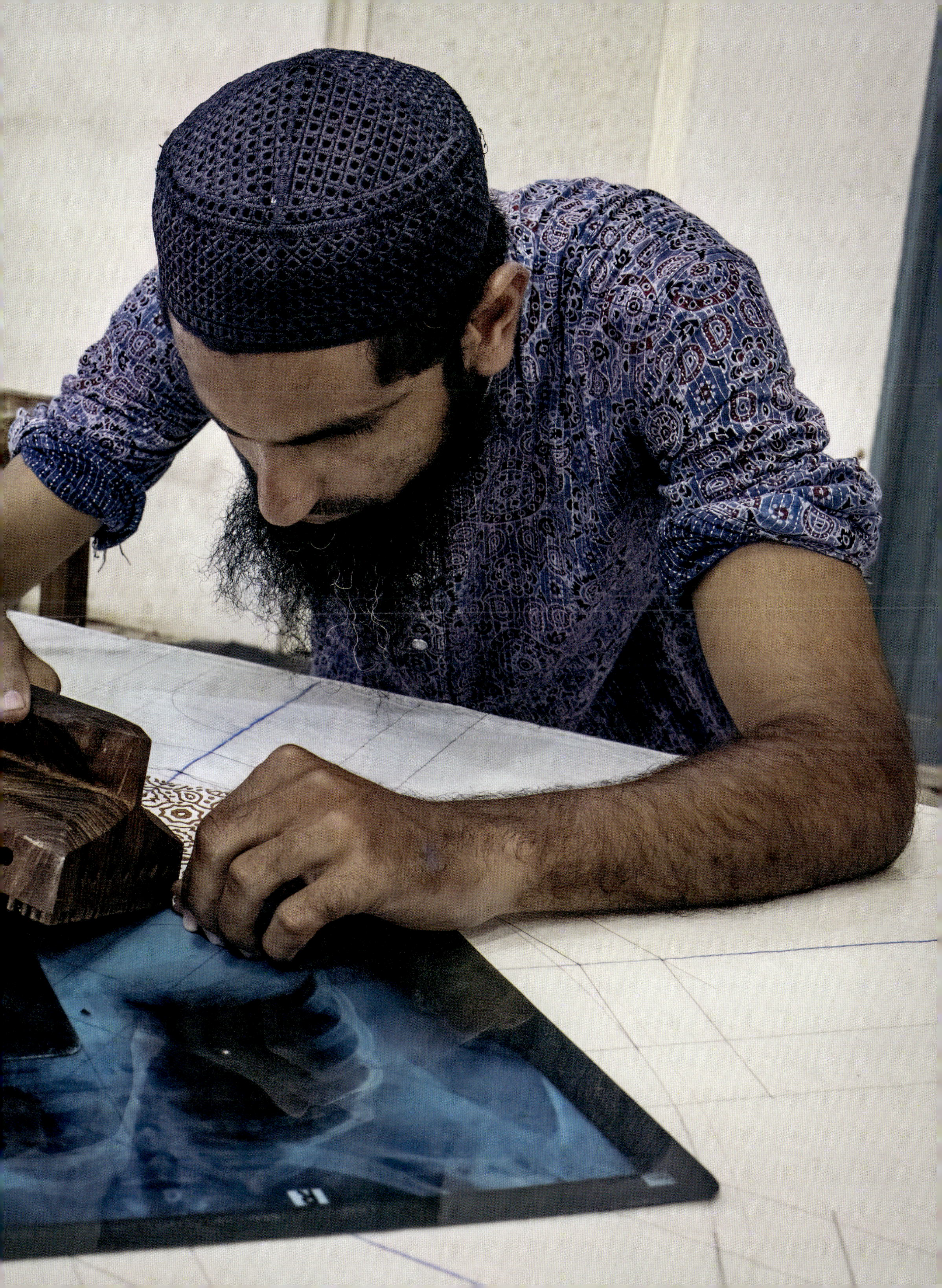

What about the Textile Museum project?

He has not had time to do anything new, he says ruefully. He has one of his Lakme Fashion Week saris. But he is not sure he wants to part with it.

I remember that the year after Akibbhai graduated, he sold a masterpiece bedsheet to an American visitor. It was breathtaking, a perfectly tessellated, radiating medallion embedded in an Ajrakh field. The printing was precise. Each petal was unique, unified by balanced indigo, black, white, and maroon colors. I asked how he felt when he sold a piece like that. He hesitated and then shyly said, "When I sell such a piece, I feel I have lost a little something of myself."

But this sari will give him a chance to have his name in a well-respected American museum. He thinks it over and the next day brings me the piece, carefully wrapped in undyed muslin.

2022

I call Akibbhai from the US and ask him to make a special piece for my book. He says he has many ideas, but he doesn't have time. Then he says I should come. Communication happens in person, not on the phone, he says. He'll get motivated when we meet face to face.

We meet after three years, most of them spent in our respective isolation during the pandemic. Akibbhai's studio is filled with "regular" work—bandhani, yardage, prints on power-loom brocade, synthetic-dyed mashru—anything and everything of mediocre quality. That's Imtiazbhai's work, he says, shaking his head. He's interested only in business now.

Good thing, I note. Akibbhai smiles his sunlight-through-clouds smile. Laughs. Yes. That's the plan. Imtiazbhai can take care of business while Akibbhai does his special work. He has a few contacts now—in India.

He pins a fabric to the table and begins to make a sample of his signature geometric work. He sketches the pattern, using a compass and rulers, precisely, in a trance of concentration. Then he begins to print, carefully masking with x-rays. Imtiazbhai is there for support. Their father, Ibrahimbhai, checks in, watching sternly. "These things are like, one mistake and it's ruined," he says. He, like Imtiazbhai, favors production. Akibbhai is the artist. Matinbhai and Akibbhai's son Mohamed play in and out. Aslambhai comes with his son Hasam on his shoulders.

Meanwhile, a young kitten is wailing its heart out. The family children bring milk. But she's not interested; she's been separated from her family. Akibbhai knows that. There were several, and she was left behind, stuck in the workshop, he says. While he prints, everyone else gets into helping the kitten. Imtiazbhai calls Abdul Rahimbhai—do you have kittens? One missing? Abdul Rahimbhai comes and tries to call her. Nope. And finally, his wife comes. The kitten is no less than one of her children. She coaxes her out, she catches her, and the kitten relaxes into her arms. Happy ending. The community working together.

▼ ▼ ▼

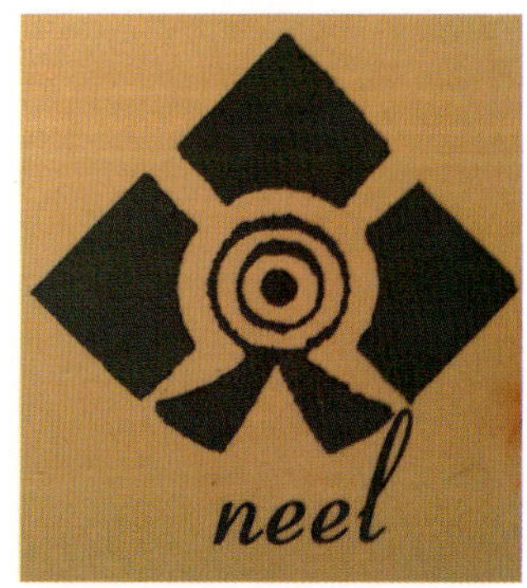

Right: Akibbhai designed his logo Neel, indigo, in his design course. He created a motif that was new yet evoked a traditional block print.

Opposite: Rehnuma, bedspread by Akibbhai Ibrahim Khatri, 2022. Cotton, hand-block printed, natural dyes. 104" x 104". Akibbhai loves Islamic art. He doesn't create by copying images; he studies classic works and absorbs the way geometry is used, the concepts underlying the patterns. It is a way of thinking, he says. He created this piece inspired by Rehnuma, the Guiding Star, for the designer Saloni's project, Connecting for India. *Photo: Raul Tovar*

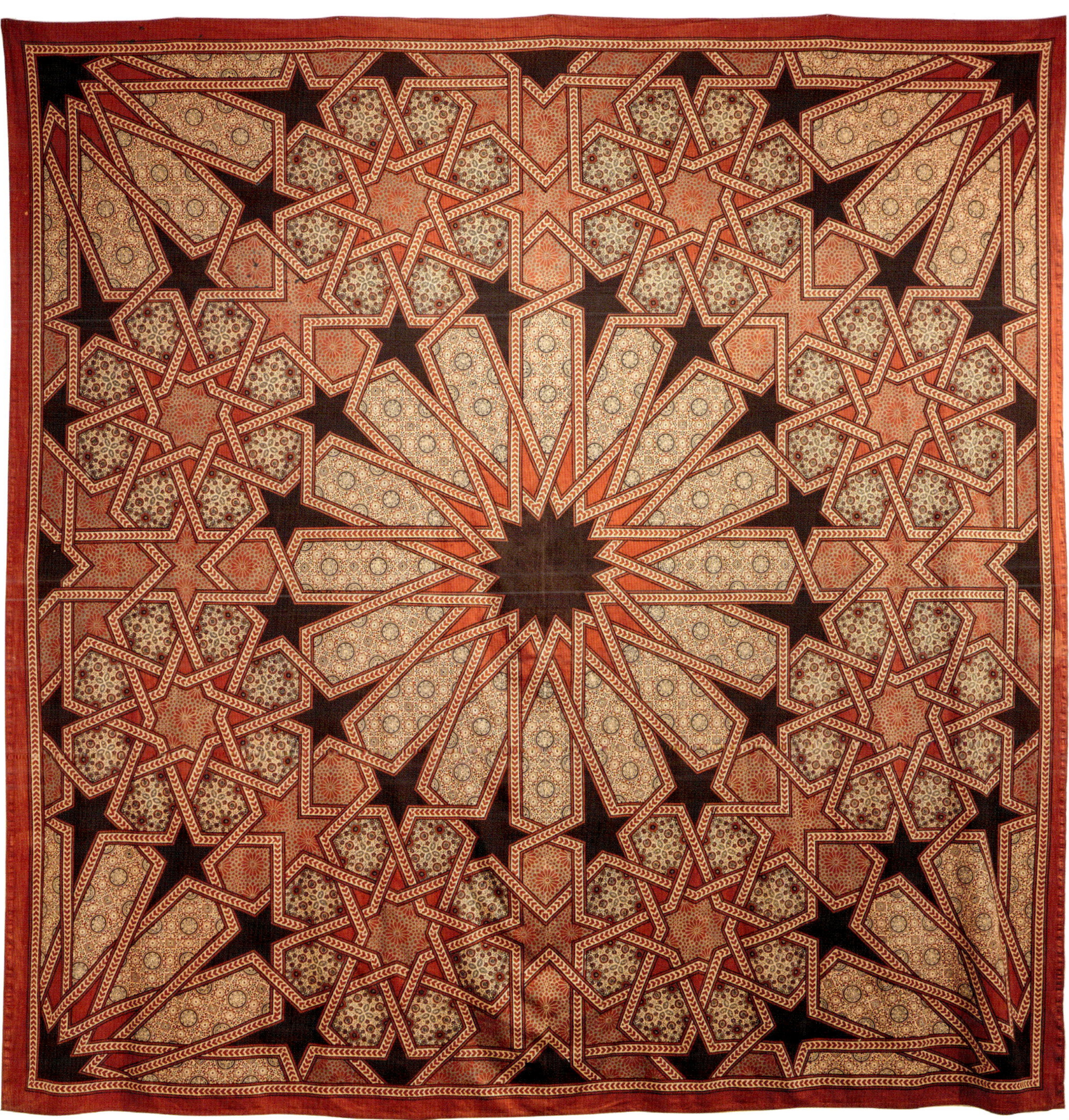

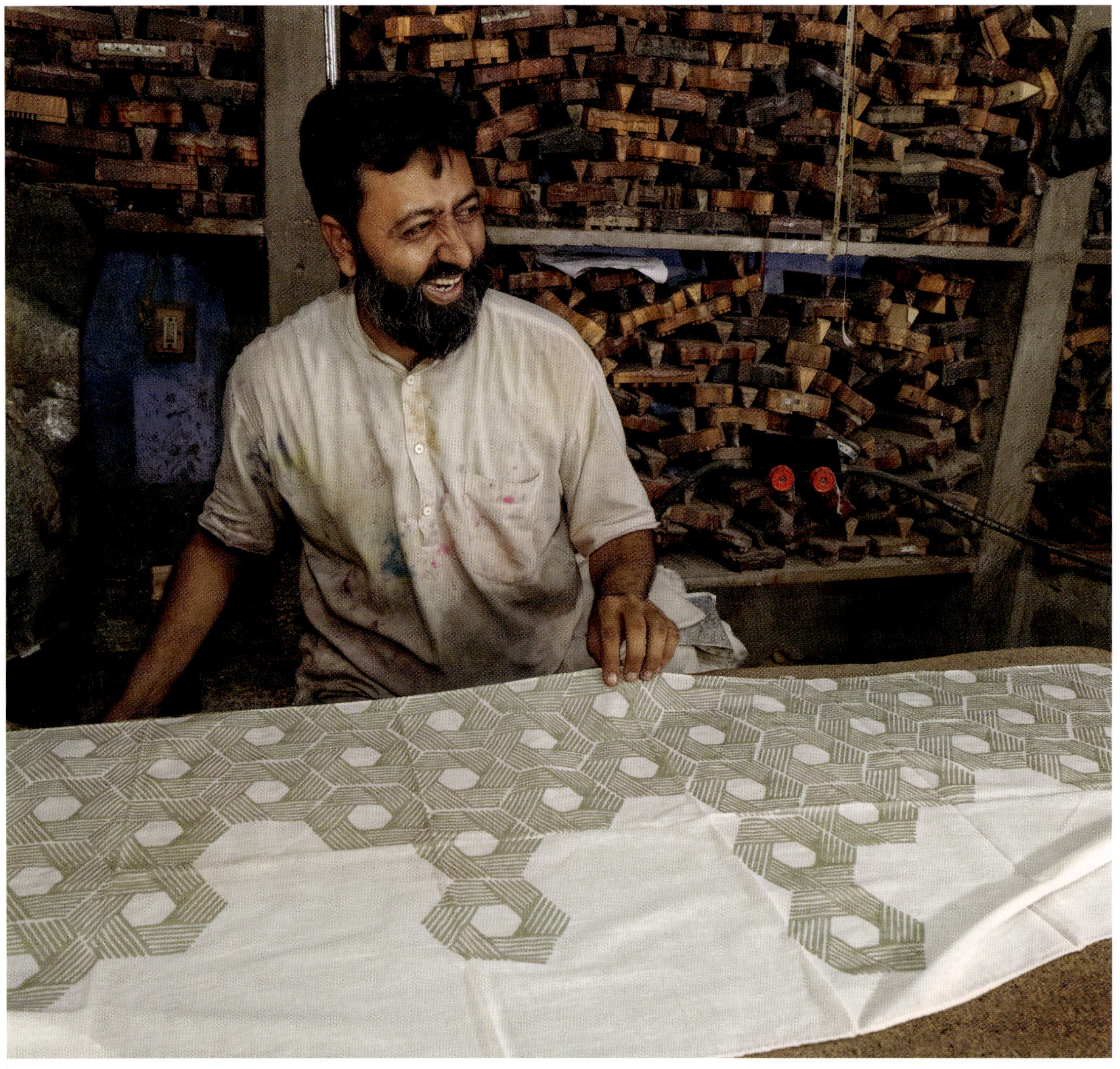

You need the right atmosphere to bring out a skill.
We got the whole atmosphere at the school.

~Shakilbhai Ahmed Qasam Khatri

Above: Mundra, 2022. Work-life balance. Shakilbhai jokes as he prints. Immersed in a craft tradition, artisans realize the sheer joy of expertise. *Photo: Nevada Wier*

Following pages: Mundra, 2022. Chai breaks are an integral part of the daily schedule, strengthening and recharging the team. *Photo: Nevada Wier*

Chapter 25

SHAKILBHAI AHMED QASAM KHATRI: ART AND DEVELOPMENT

2022

Shakilbhai meets me at the gate in the ancient fortress and leads me through the narrow streets of Mundra, only for bikes, cows, people, cats, and dogs now. Mundra city, once the Paris of Kutch, is dilapidated, neglected. It has been eclipsed by the "development" outside. In the last three decades, the seventeenth-century Mundra port has been transformed to the largest private port of India, now Adani Ports and Special Economic Zone Limited. Gautam Adani is the richest person in Asia and the third-richest person in the world. The factories of the Special Economic Zone, trucking lines and truck stops, architectureless cement structures, and toll roads have grown wildly, while the city is as it was centuries ago, and inside it, people are neighbors.

We arrive at a big, rusted door with "Rainbow Textiles" written on it, and a few mobile numbers. Inside, in a compact courtyard, a team of fourteen men are working as they have worked for fifty years. Several people have been here for the duration, turning out hundreds of yards of batik fabric every day. They have a routine. By midday, wax removing is finishing. The removal master is cleaning sand sediment from the bottom of the huge copper vessel, and the team is hanging the finished fabric to dry. They'll press it with a 50-kilogram weight, Shakilbhai says, laughing.

In the tiny, closed room of the workshop, three artisans are printing fabric on small sand-covered tables. Anwar, with bright-orange-hennaed beard and hair, stands at the table in the front, printing rhythmically, like meditation. He's been here since 1986; the date is written on the wall behind him. Shakilbhai says he can tell me a lot about tradition. Head down, quickly placing heavy wood blocks of wax on the fabric, he mumbles in Gujarati, "I don't know Gujarati—only Kutchi."

The other two artisans are newer, one just a year or so in the workshop. He's not good yet, Shakilbhai says. It's been a struggle to keep workers. They are seen as labor, and the burgeoning factories around

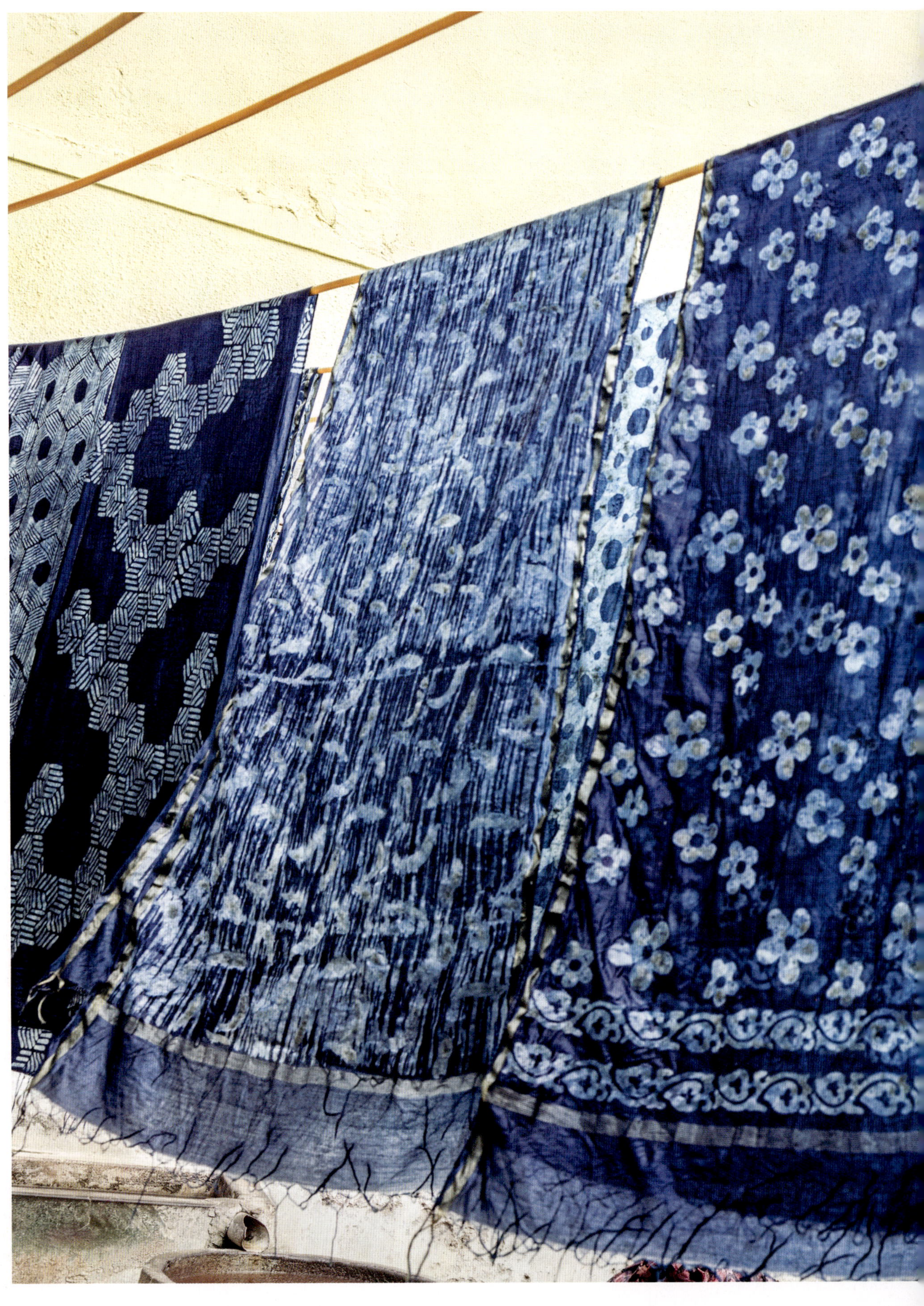

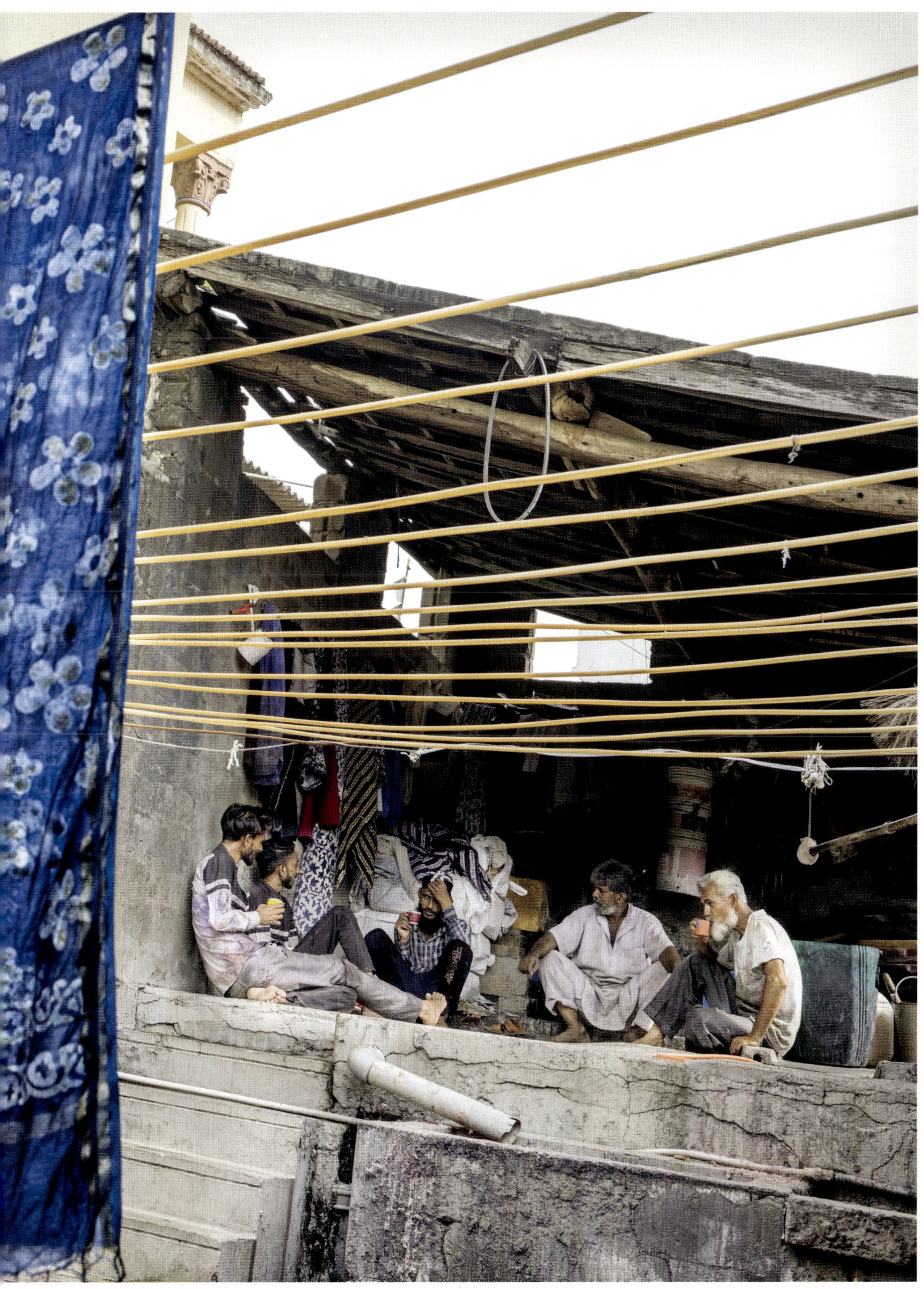

Mundra pay more, exacerbating the problem and lowering the quality of work. I ask Shakilbhai if Anwar could print what he wants. He answers that he prints yardage. I ask, but if he was allowed to riff, like you? "He doesn't have the confidence," Shakilbhai says.

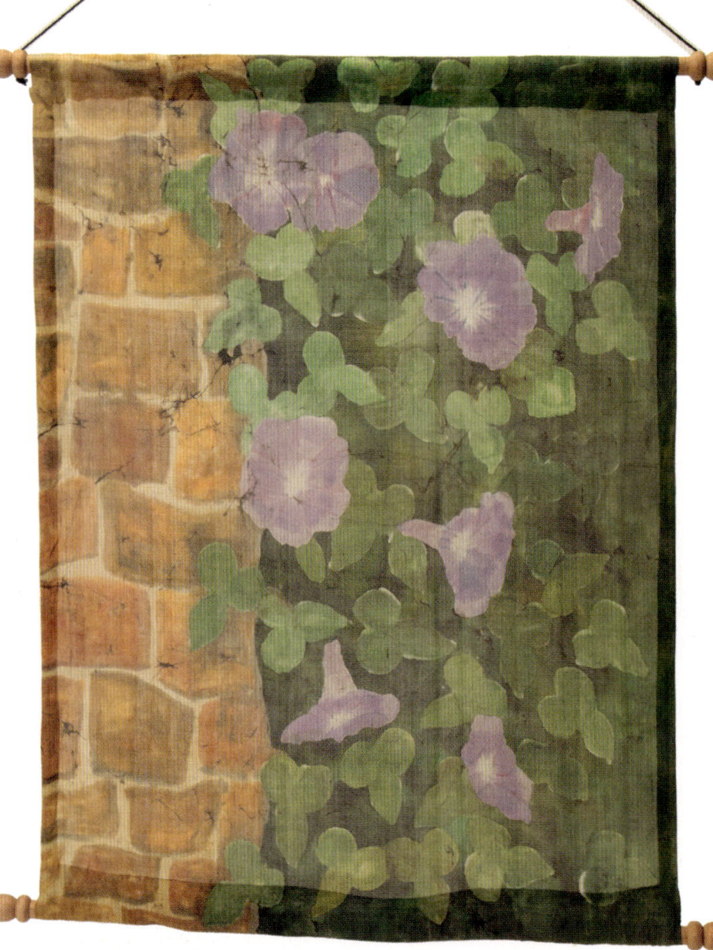

Morning Glories, wall hanging by Shakilbhai Ahmed Qasam Khatri, 2009. Cotton-silk, vat dyes, hand-painted batik. 21" x 25". Collection of the author. Morning glories draped the stone and lime walls of the KRV campus. Capturing them in innovative batik, Shakilbhai created memories. *Photo: Schiffer Publishing Ltd.*

Shakilbhai learned batik from his father and uncle when he was seventeen. He had almost learned printing when the family divided. Until 2005, they had been famous in Mundra as a joint family of sixty-six people. When they split into separate families, Shakilbhai's family chose a new market to avoid competition. They didn't have capital for materials, so they did job work. Slowly they started their own production. We all had to work, Shakilbhai said. "My uncle said, do whatever is in your heart; if you ruin it, we'll absorb it. I got freedom from that and lost fear. He had marketing experience, so I learned that from him too.

"I saw the ad for the design course in the paper in 2006," he continued. "I didn't have confidence; I thought I had nothing in me to learn there. In 2009, my uncle convinced me to go. In the interview, Judyben asked me a strange question: 'Is batik traditional?' It scared me. She had been in Kutch for decades, and there had already been three classes, and she didn't know that batik was traditional here. But I felt happy to be the first batik student. I realized I could lift the veil on batik."

Shakilbhai liked traditional designs and had collected many examples. He said he felt that tradition was a gift of his forefathers, and a way of work and life. "Tradition runs in our blood," he said, "and we can develop it further with the use of new technologies."

He was delighted to find that the design course taught what he was interested in. "We learned first that however modern you do, you can't forget your tradition," he said. "Observation is different from seeing; we learned to observe. We learned color, painting, plus craft. In the first class we sketched early every morning. There were morning glories by Judyben's office, and I painted them. The teacher asked me to do it on fabric. I said it wasn't possible, but she insisted. So I tried. It took nine days and was a trial by fire, but it came out better than I expected. . . . I had been to Ahmedabad, but when we went for the Market Orientation session it was different. My vision had changed. I saw color schemes, cool, warm, primary, and design principles."

The faculty member for the fourth module, Concept/Communication/Projects, noted that Shakilbhai keenly absorbed the inputs and experimented, and his work reflected a fresh combination of the

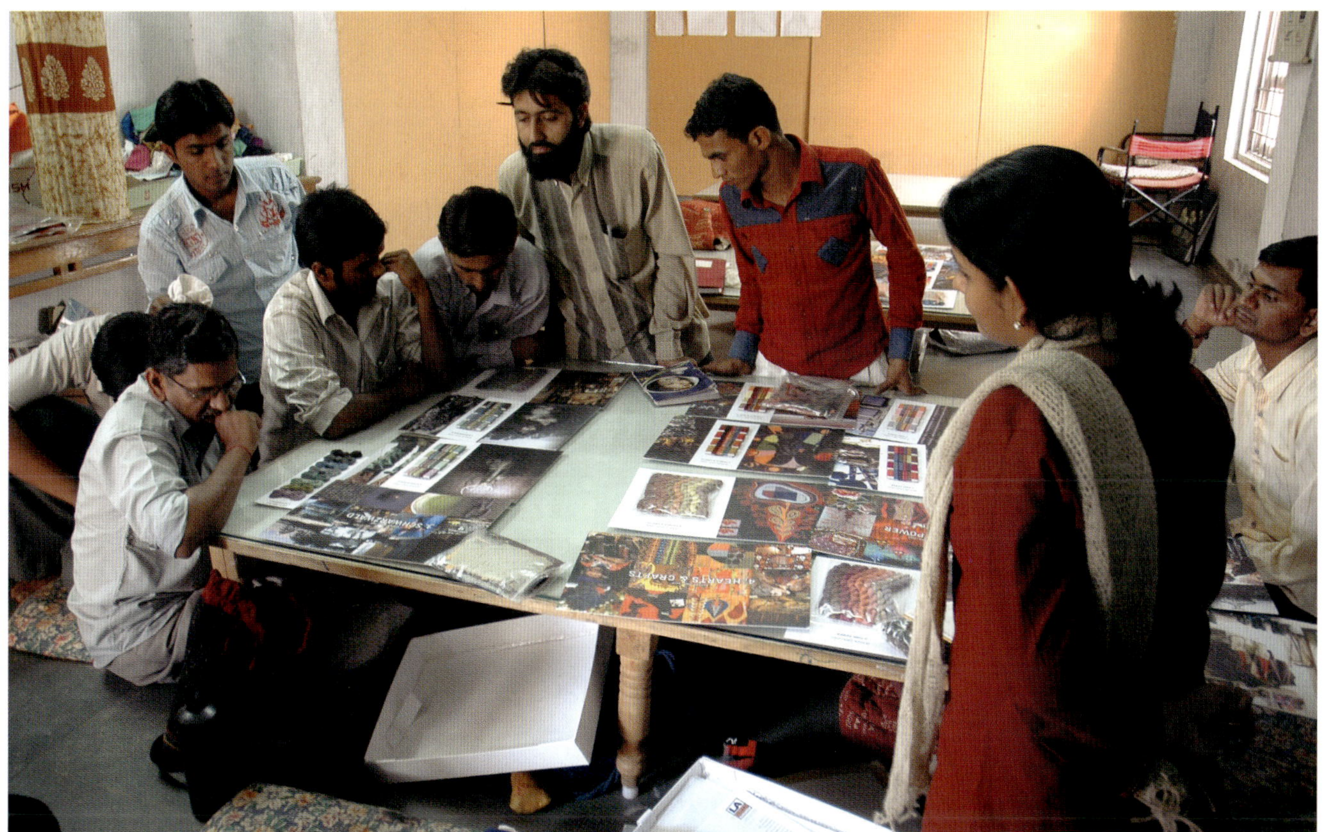

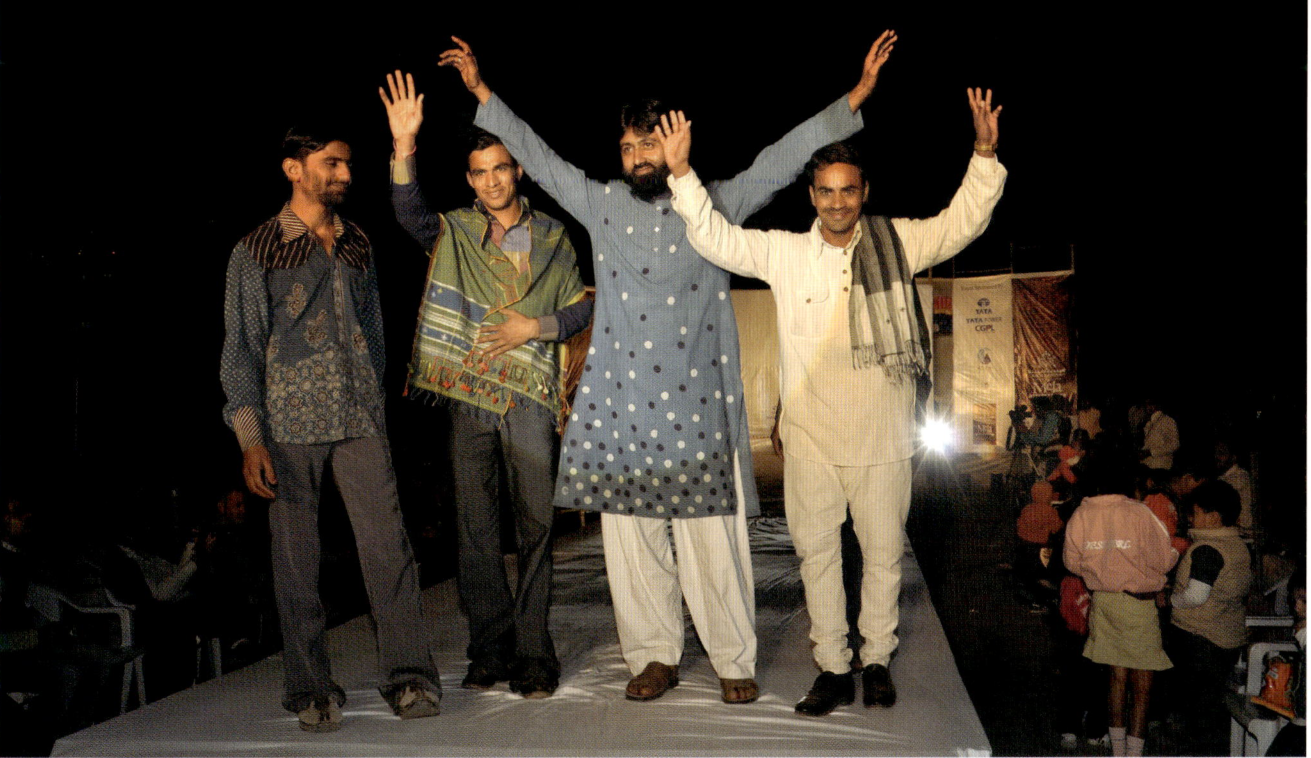

Above: Kala Raksha Vidhyalaya, 2009. Shakilbhai and his classmates study L.A. Colors. Lousmijn van den Acker generously donated her professional trend forecasts to the program. Works of art themselves, the trends inspired students to extend beyond the familiar by using new color combinations. *Photo: Judy Frater*

Below: Kala Raksha Vidhyalaya, 2010. Alumni were invited to present new collections in annual convocation fashion shows. The year after graduating, Shakilbhai and fellow alumni collaborated on a collection inspired by tattoos, and Shakilbhai created a batik kurta to wear on the ramp. *Photo: Ketan Pomal, L.M. Studio*

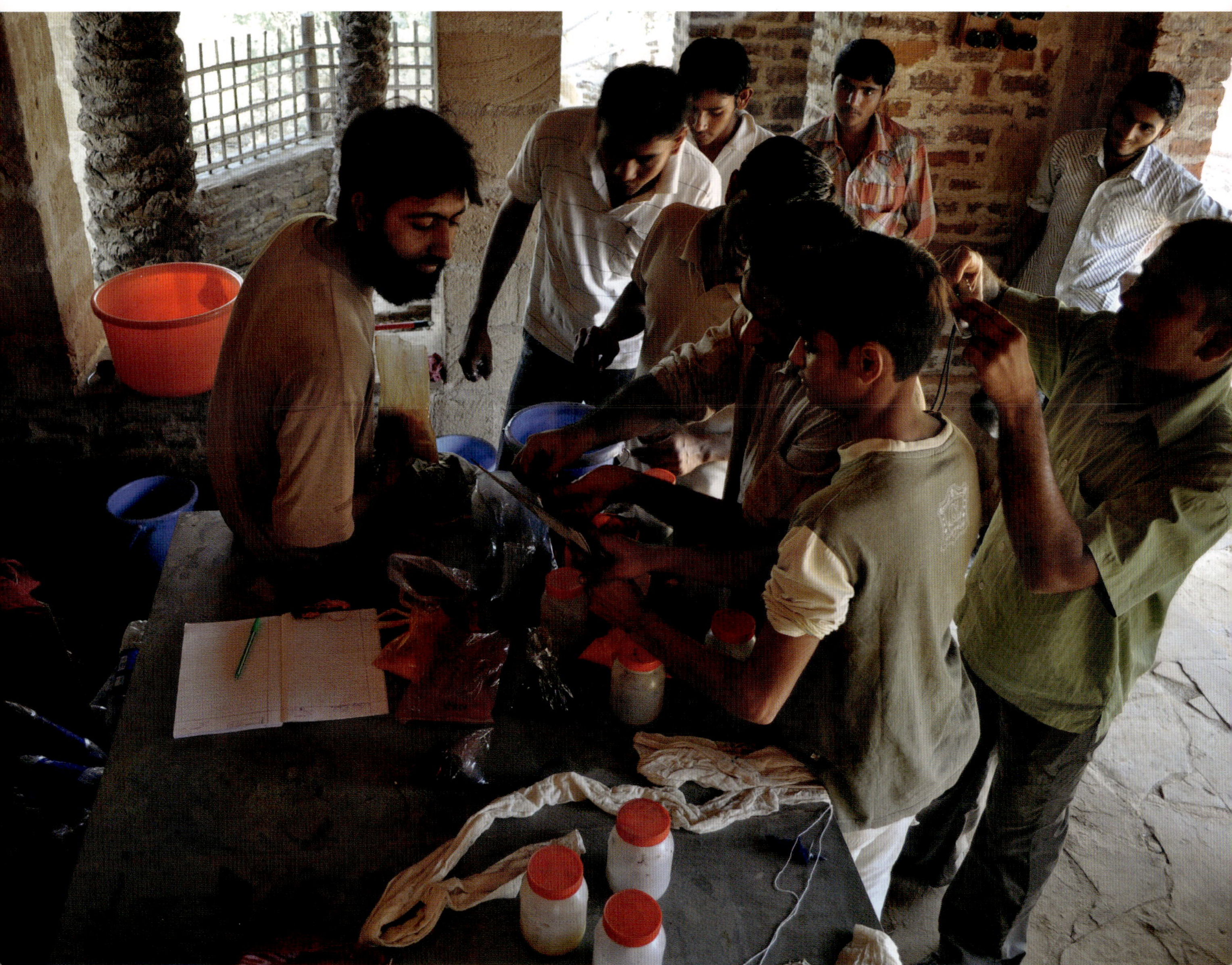

Above: Kala Raksha Vidhyalaya, 2010. Shakilbhai teaches the class of 2010 color theory through dyeing. I invited alumni to mentor students, to build an alumni community, and to ensure that they used what they had learned. *Photo: Judy Frater*

Following pages: Mundra, 2022. Although traditional Kutch batiks were dyed in indigo, Shakilbhai had to rework the process because he now uses synthetic paraffin wax. Oxidizing, the scarves will slowly develop from green to blue. *Photo: Nevada Wier*

traditional and the new. "Shakil carries the responsibility of taking his tradition to greater heights," she wrote, "a journey on which the Ajrakh artisans and weavers are way ahead."

Shakilbhai loved stories, so themes clicked with him. He created an imaginative collection inspired by the Black Hills of Kutch, exploiting the texture of batik to show textures of the forest. He graduated with awards for Best Student and Best Presentation.

Mentoring students in subsequent classes, he told them, "You have to get so into your theme that you see it everywhere. I started buying clothes in the colors of my theme! Limitation gives you a chance to extend yourself. It helps you focus."

He decided to concentrate on handwork to distinguish his work from block printing. "In four generations, this is the first time someone in my family did a batik painting," he said. "At home I couldn't get time to experiment. Now I make time. At night I think of ideas. This is exclusive work—never for wholesale."

It took great effort to fulfill this vow. With the pressure of the family's continual wholesale orders, Shakilbhai spent most of his time directing and supervising. "But sometimes I just have to create," he said.

The rare occasions that he took time to participate in design-school-related activities sometimes left him unrewarded. At a feedback meeting for a codesign project, I heard him mutter something in Kutchi. I asked him to explain in Gujarati. Reluctantly, he confessed that he had lost interest. He and his partner had not clarified a theme, and his partner made their mood board by himself after leaving Kutch. He did not feel that the painted saris they made had enough traditional identity, and they would be easy to copy. He wanted a chance to make layouts in response, keeping in mind the practicalities of batik.

Initial attempts to establish a business to present artisan-designed work as a unique genre were worse. Shakilbhai showed samples of production batik to a buyer who knew little of craft. I urged him to show his exclusive hand-painted work as well. He carefully took his batik morning glories from a briefcase. The buyer said, "Nice; we could make these into cushion covers." He carefully folded his paintings back into the briefcase and never showed samples for this project again.

During the COVID-19 lockdown, Shakilbhai found opportunities. With production all but stopped, he painted, and all of his painted batiks sold. An army doctor tracked him down through his Instagram account, bought several pieces, and commissioned more. The doctor patronizes artists wherever he is stationed, and he begins by commissioning a peacock to assess skill with color. Shakilbhai passed.

He worked on his Instagram account, an arresting view of the textures of his world. Grinding out batik yardage year after year, he sees beauty in drops of wax, crackled fabric, dyes on the floor, piles of firewood, and more.

And he realized his dream of creating a line of natural-dyed batik. In May 2020, he launched Neel Batik.

Shakilbhai shows me the range of natural dye colors that he finally perfected. It took time to figure out the chemistry of mordants and wax. Alum and other acidic substances turn paraffin wax to cement. He has it now, soft subtle shades strikingly different from those of Ajrakh natural dyes. He mostly has saris, dupattas, and salvar-kamiz suits now, because COVID stopped foreign visitors. He knows the market. He sells in Bangalore, Mumbai, and Delhi. The market hasn't fully revived. He wholesales to Ahmedabad, too, but never to local shops. He can't sell at the low value for batik in Kutch.

"My thinking is different," he says. "If they make something for RS 100, I think how can I make it better, so it sells for RS 120? That way, the value for craft will increase, and the value for artisans will increase. At first, everyone feels it's expensive, but once they buy it, their thinking changes."

Shakilbhai has saved all of his work from his 2009 course, systematically. He pulls out his painted morning glories.

"We don't know what skill we have inside," he says. "If you put a seed in a beautiful gold or silver box and put it in a cupboard, will a tree grow? It needs earth, water, fertilizer, light. You need the right atmosphere to bring out a skill. We got the whole atmosphere at KRV."

And then he presents me with a painted batik of morning glories and the stone walls of KRV, stitched on a scroll, covered in a bag he also stitched. I am deeply touched. It is a memory of a time that was special for me too. As the students were learning, I was too. We grew the program together.

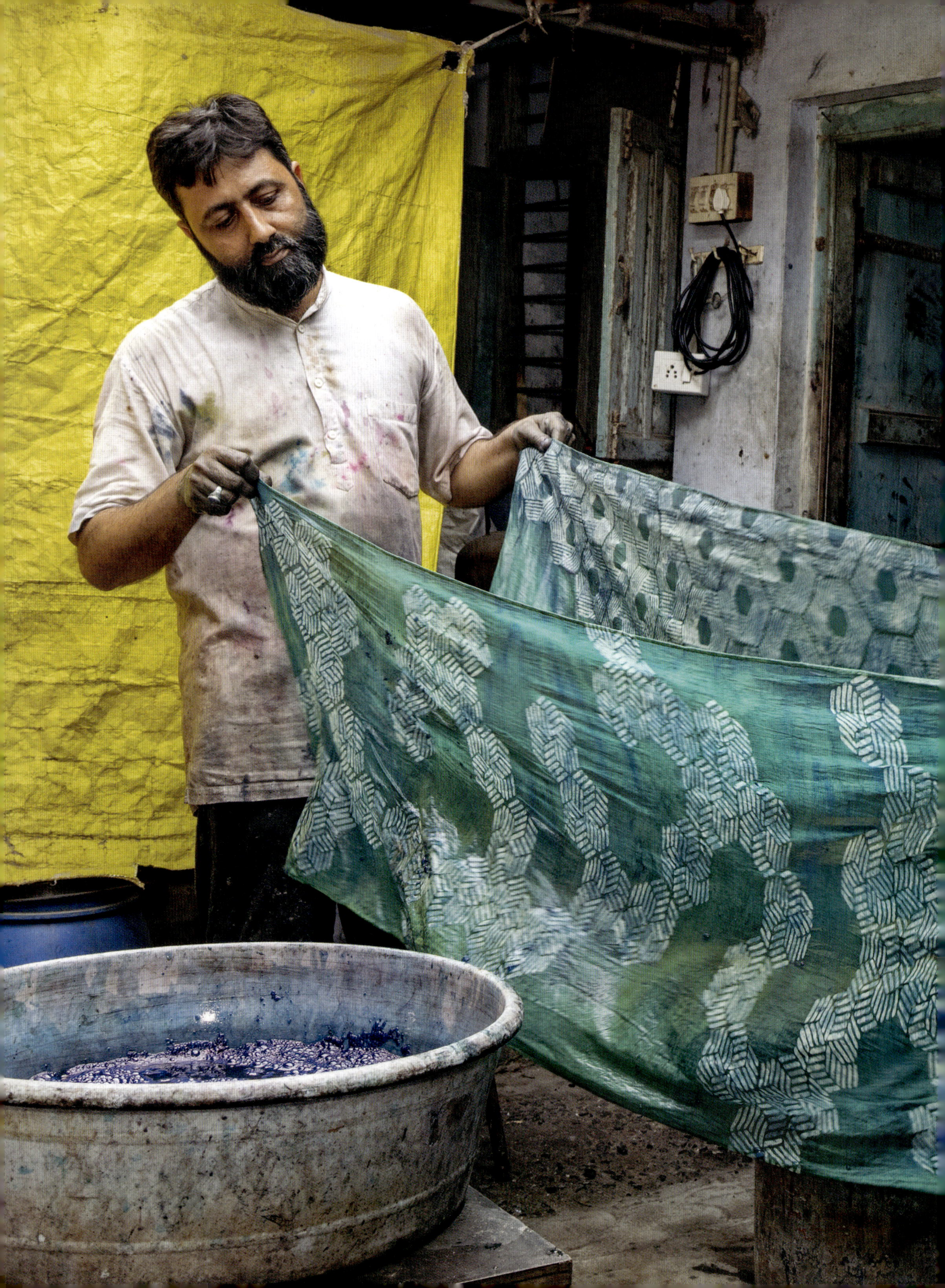

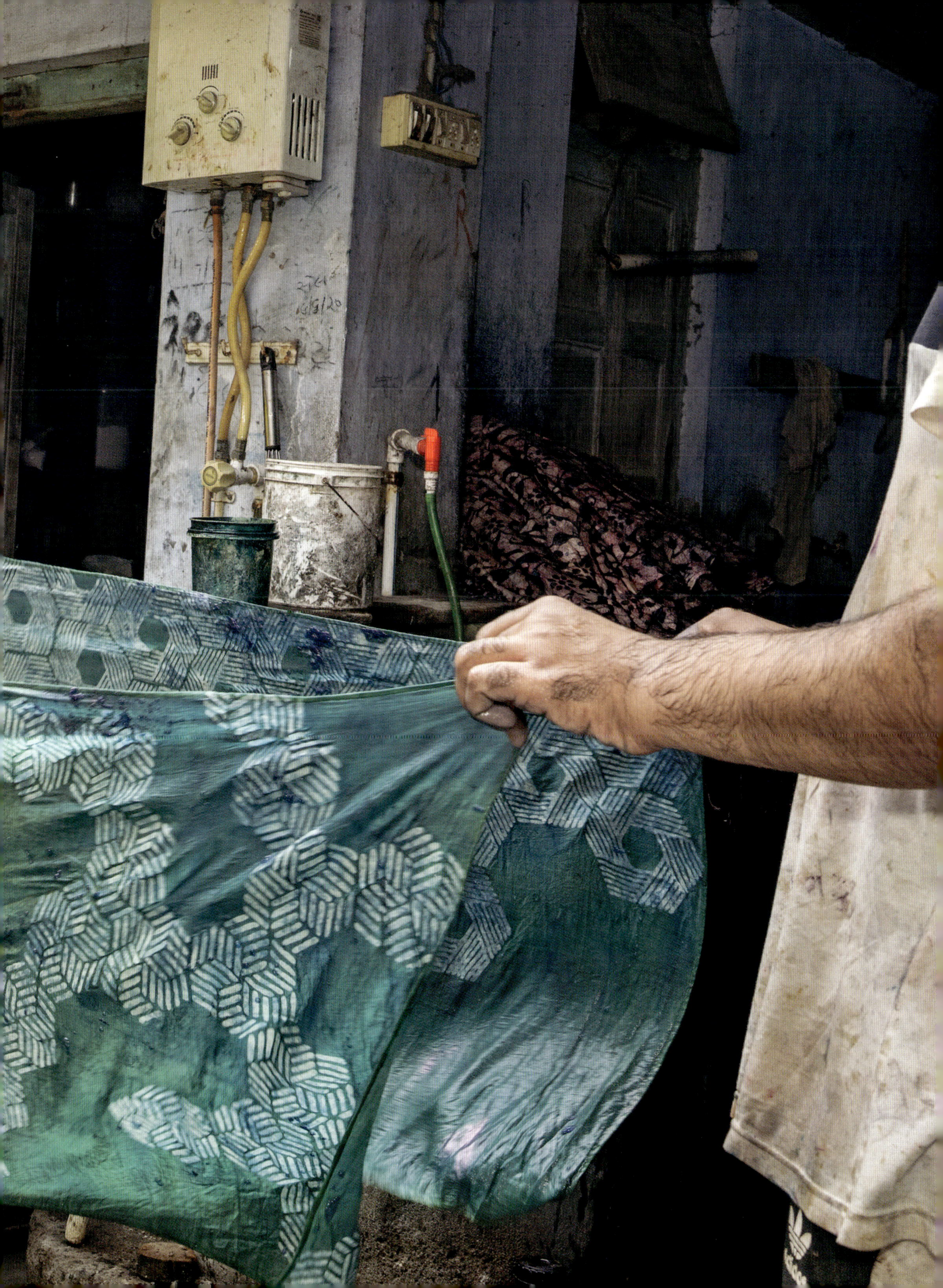

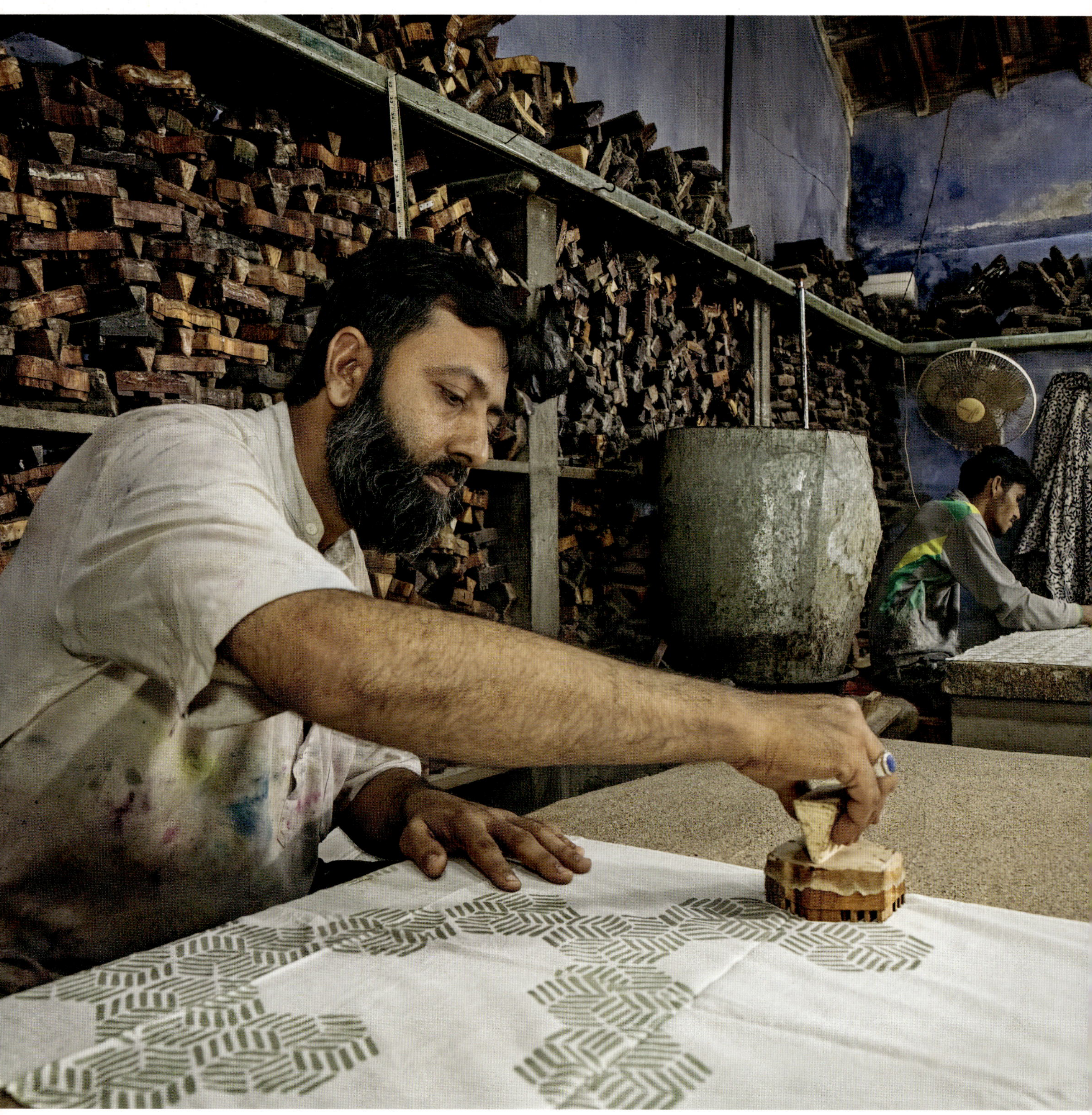

Above: Mundra, 2022. Shakilbhai creates his design as he prints. Students learn to draw layouts on paper, but they are so steeped in their traditions that they can often imagine and work simultaneously. It's not that learning layouts wasn't useful; design principles are incorporated into existing knowledge. *Photo: Nevada Wier*

Opposite: Left, *Coral of the Sea*, scarf by Shakilbhai Ahmed Qasam Khatri, 2022. Silk, natural dye, hand-printed batik. 37" x 102". Right, *Atoms*, scarf by Shakilbhai Ahmed Qasam Khatri, 2022. Cotton, indigo dye, hand-printed batik. 22" x 76". Natural-dyed batik was a challenge and a dream for Shakilbhai. He prints and dyes his limited-edition natural-dye collection himself, under the brand Neel Batik. *Photo: Schiffer Publishing Ltd.*

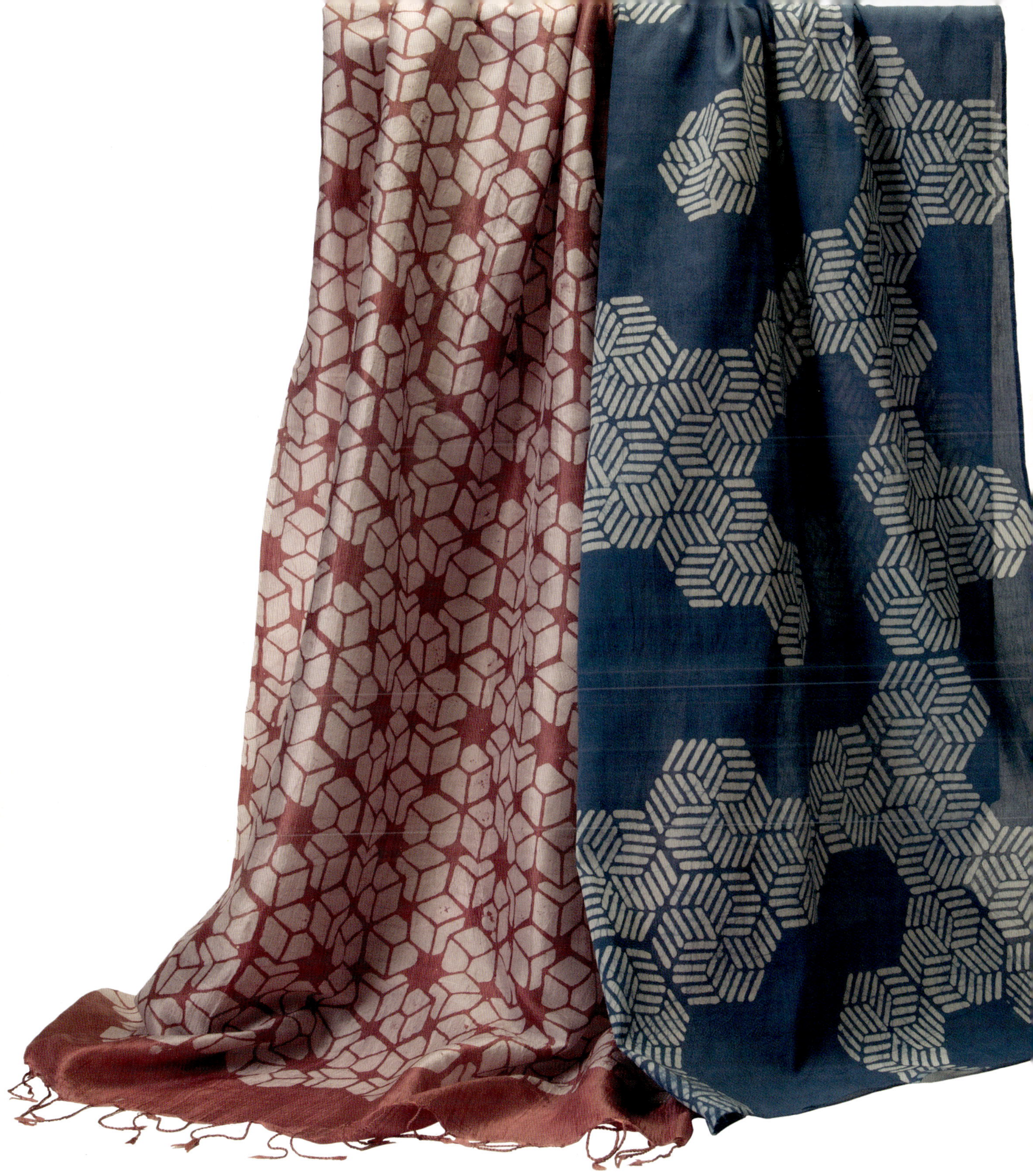

The fourth table in the workshop is Shakilbhai's, left empty until he has the time to work. He moved the table inside to accommodate piles of raw materials. The compact workshop is bursting at the seams. Nafisbhai, Shakilbhai's brother, had worked at Adani Power and returned to help Shakilbhai with accounts. "We want to make a new, bigger workshop outside the city," he says. But the prices of land have skyrocketed, another effect of development.

Shakilbhai says he will make a scarf for my book while I am here. And here is the magic. He lays it out carefully, smooths the fabric on the sand. This is the sketching, planning time. He plans as he goes, he laughs. His theme is atoms . . . and he starts. He prints quickly, as you must with wax, placing the blocks, rhythmically but not regularly. "I like asymmetry," he says. He works instinctively, with hand-eye-heart coordination. It's an extension of mind and body, the way of the artisan that I've revered and never quite captured. This is what we need to nurture or at least not obstruct. It is dance, music, a direct line to God. Then for fun, he does another one, an homage to bees, how the hive looks when half the bees have flown. In an hour and a half, he has printed, indigo-dyed, dewaxed, and created two beautiful scarves—with love.

The call to prayer comes. I say I want to see the Bukhari Dargah, so we go together since mosque and dargah are side by side. According to legend, a Jain merchant asked Pir Hazrat Shah Murad Bukhari to pray for the safety of his sinking cargo ship. Miraculously, the ship was saved. The legend highlights a local custom among seafarers and merchants of visiting the pir's shrine before going to sea. Shakilbhai tells me that there was a mysterious triangular room in the dargah that no one could open for two hundred years. When the 2001 earthquake damaged the dargah, the room opened and a beautiful, sweet fragrance enveloped Mundra. They found a quilt, shreds of robes, copper vessels—the simple possessions of a Sufi, and they enshrined them in the rebuilt dargah.

Outside, the exquisitely carved original walls are crumbling at the base. There's no care, Shakilbhai laments. They cover the damage with plants. He says that NGOs now want to develop batik. But he has figured this out. The batik community recently met to discuss issues, and he told them that if we want batik to progress, each family should send someone to learn design.

For the SKV class of 2023, two batik students are selected.

In class, Shakilbhai created a logo with a bird from a stylized *S* for his name and traditional batik motifs. He continued to work with his family's brand Rainbow Textiles until he launched his natural-dye line. Then he used the logo, adding Neel Batik and characteristic cracks.

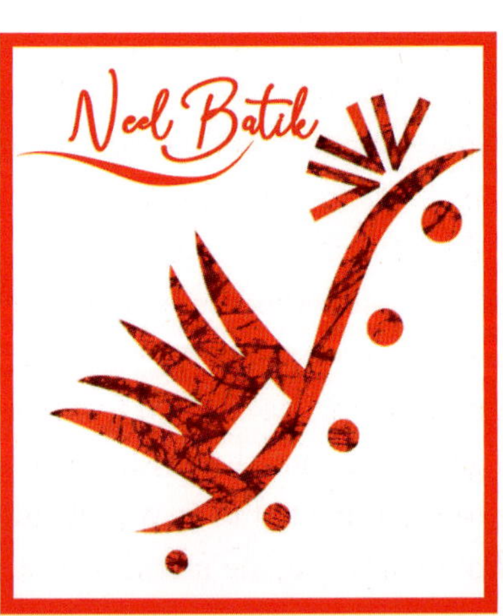

Appendix

STORY OF FATIMA THE SPINNER AND THE TENT

Idries Shah

Once in a city in the Farthest West, there lived a girl called Fatima. She was the daughter of a prosperous spinner. One day her father said to her: "Come, daughter, we are going on a journey, for I have business in the islands of the Middle Sea. Perhaps you may find some handsome youth in a good situation whom you could take as husband."

They set off and traveled from island to island, the father doing his trading while Fatima dreamt of the husband who might soon be hers. One day, however, they were on the way to Crete when a storm blew up, and the ship was wrecked. Fatima, only half conscious, was cast up on the seashore near Alexandria.

Her father was dead, and she was utterly destitute. She could only dimly remember her life until then, for her experience of the shipwreck, and her exposure in the sea, had utterly exhausted her.

While she was wandering on the sands, a family of cloth makers found her. Although they were poor, they took her into their humble home and taught her their craft. Thus it was that she made a second life for herself, and within a year or two she was happy and reconciled to her lot.

But one day, when she was on the seashore for some reason, a band of slave traders landed and carried her, along with other captives, away with them. Although she bitterly lamented her lot, Fatima found no sympathy from the slavers, who took her to Istanbul and sold her as a slave. Her world had collapsed for the second time.

Now it chanced that there were few buyers at the market. One of them was a man who was looking for slaves to work in his woodyard, where he made masts for ships. When he saw the dejection of the unfortunate Fatima, he decided to buy her, thinking that in this way, at least, he might be able to give her a slightly better life than if she were bought by someone else.

He took Fatima to his home, intending to make her a serving maid for his wife. When he arrived at the house, however, he found that he had lost all his money in a cargo that had been captured by pirates. He could not afford workers, so he, Fatima, and his wife were left alone to work at the heavy labor of making masts. Fatima, grateful to her employer for rescuing her, worked so hard and so well that he gave her her freedom, and she became his trusted helper. Thus it was that she became comparatively happy in her third career.

One day he said to her: "Fatima, I want you to go with a cargo of ships' masts to Java, as my agent, and be sure that you will turn a profit." She set off, but when the ship was off the coast of China, a typhoon wrecked it, and Fatima found herself again cast up on the seashore of a strange land.

Once again, she wept bitterly, for she felt that nothing in her life was working in accordance with expectation. Whenever things seemed to be going well, something came and destroyed all her hopes. "Why is it," she cried out, for the third time, "that whenever I try to do something, it comes to grief? Why should so many unfortunate things happen to me?" But there was no answer.

So she picked herself up from the sand and started to walk inland. Now it so happened that nobody in China had heard of Fatima or knew anything about her troubles. But there was a legend that a certain stranger, a woman, would one day arrive there, and that she would be able to make a tent for the emperor. And since there was as yet nobody in China who could make tents, everyone looked upon the fulfillment of this prediction with the liveliest anticipation. In order to make sure that this stranger, when she arrived, would not be missed, successive emperors of China had followed the custom of sending heralds, once a year, to all the towns and villages of the land, asking for any foreign woman to be produced at Court.

When Fatima stumbled into a town by the Chinese seashore, it was one such occasion. The people spoke to her through an interpreter and explained that she would have to go to see the emperor. "Lady," said the emperor when Fatima was brought before him, "can you make a tent?"

"I think so," said Fatima. She asked for rope, but there was none to be had. So, remembering her time as a spinner, she collected flax and made ropes. Then she asked for stout cloth, but the Chinese had none of the kind that she needed. So, drawing on her experience with the weavers of Alexandria, she made some stout tent cloth. Then she found that she needed tent poles, but there were none in China. So Fatima, remembering how she had been trained by the wood fashioner of Istanbul, cunningly made stout tent poles.

When these were ready, she racked her brains for the memory of all the tents she had seen in her travels: and lo, a tent was made. When this wonder was revealed to the emperor of China, he offered Fatima the fulfillment of any wish she cared to name. She chose to settle in China, where she married a handsome prince, and where she remained in happiness, surrounded by her children, until the end of her days.

It was through these adventures that Fatima realized that what had appeared to be an unpleasant experience at the time turned out to be an essential part of the making of her ultimate happiness.

Glossary

Abho (plural abha) – traditional women's tunic

Ajrakh – a traditional hand-block printed cloth with specific patterns and composition, dyed in indigo, madder and iron acetate, used by Muslim Maldhari men

Bagido – a traditional woman's bandhani veil, black and red with 5 central circular motifs

Bandhani – traditional resist dyeing, in which fabric is bound in small knots and dyed to create dotted patterns

Barot – traditional genealogist

Barsang – a pair of hangings at either side of a doorway

Batavo – purse

Batik – resist dyeing with wax. In Kutch, the wax is applied with wooden blocks, then the fabric is dyed in cold dyes. The color cannot penetrate the wax, leaving a pattern of the original fabric color.

Bavaliyun – interlaced embroidery technique

Be-pota – fabrics created in two parts and stitched together to made double width

Bharat – (literally "filled") the word for embroidery

Bharti – a bandhani technique in which tiny knots are tied densely to fill an area

Bhopa – a shaman or intermediary between people and gods. They often go into trance and prescribe advice to the community

Bhopi – female bhopa

Bhungo (plural bhunga) – traditional round mud home

Bokani – (literally "of 2 ears") a long, narrow groom's ceremonial scarf tied over the turban and ears

Brahma Kumaris – a women's spiritual movement that advocates celibacy

Buti – freestanding motif, often floral

Chandrokhani – traditional Khatri woman's bandhani veil , black silk with red dots

Chaini – interlaced motifs

Chaklo (plural chakla) – square hanging

Chaniya-choli – traditional Indian women's ensemble of long gathered skirt and tight-fitting bodice, worn with a veil

Chikan – traditional white on white embroidery of Lucknow

Chamkadi – new name for bavaliyun interlaced technique

Co-Creation Squared – A fashion event held by Kala Raksha in Mumbai in 2013. It was the first time men and women graduates of the design course worked together to co-create ensembles. The garment designs were given by fashion designer Anju Modi; hence the "squared."

Dabeli – vegetarian sloppy Joes

Dalit – (literally "downtrodden") a term that includes a number of ethnic communities or castes formerly called "untouchable" or Harijan (children of God)

Dargah – a shrine or tomb built over the grave of a revered religious figure, often a Sufi saint

Datlo – the filling part of a block printed pattern or motif

Dhablo (plural dhabla) – Traditional hand-woven woolen blanket of Kutch

Double roti – leavened buns

Dungar – (literally "hill") new name for kungari interlaced technique

Dupatta – shawl-sized scarf

Engineered print– a design that is uniquely printed to fit a specific area, such as a garment pattern or a bed spread, rather than a simple repeat pattern

Eri silk – silk from the cocoon of a worm that feeds on castor leaves. Because the worm leaves a hole to escape and the silk can be reeled without killing it, eri is often called ahimsa or non-violent silk. Woven eri silk fabric is matte rather than shiny.

Gadhrang – border in bandhani representing a fort wall

Gajaro – a traditional silver bracelet worn in the Maru Meghval community

Gandho baval – (literally "crazy acacia") the Prosopis juliflora plant introduced to Kutch in the 1950s. The invasive species is so aggressive that it is now impossible to eradicate.

Garasia Jat – one of several communities of Jat, Muslim pastoralists of Kutch and Sindh. Garasia (literally "land holder") Jat women embroider with a unique rendition of cross stitch.

Ghagharo – gathered skirt

Gharanu – food wrap

Gharcholu – (literally "home garment") traditional bandhani characterized by squares created from metallic woven stripes

Gud – raw unrefined sugar from sugar cane

Gulmohar – flame of the forest tree

Gupchi – envelope bag

Hail – set of metal pots

Haveli – a traditional townhouse or manor house

Hem-chandi – (literally "gold and silver") of utmost value

Hindhoni – a ring for balancing pots on the head

Ikat – a yarn dyeing technique in which portions of yarn are tied to resist the dye. This creates patterns that emerge when the yarns are woven.

Jambu – small deep purple fruit

Jharmar – a traditional necklace made of gold leaf-shaped elements strung together; also the inspiration of a border motif

Judio – Rabari name for dowry; traditionally presented at the birth of the first son

Kanchadiyo – unmarried girls' backless blouse

Kanchali – married women's backless blouse

Kanchali kurti – a set of backless blouse and sleeveless vest worn together to cover the body from neckline to waist

Kanda – onion

Kediyun – a jacket worn by men of Rabari and other communities of Gujarat and Rajasthan, characterized by a tied closing on the left and a gathered peplum

Kharakli – a Rabari embroidery motif

Kharek embroidery – (literally "dates") a style of embroidery originating in southern Thar-Parkar, Sindh (Pakistan) characterized by satin stitching in bands, worked by counting warp and weft yarns of the base fabric

Khatri – An ethnic community in Kutch. Some Khatris are Hindu. The Muslim majority are dyers by profession. Over time, Khatri families specialized in different dyeing techniques: block print, batik, bandhani, and roghan hand painting.

Kondi – a traditional technique of North Karnataka weaving that enables creating a cotton sari with a silk end. The cotton warps of the body are hand joined to silk warps of the end.

Kothali – small sack-shaped bag

Kothalo – larger sack-shaped bag made to carry dowry items

Kungari – a crenelated interlaced embroidery technique

Kurti – in communities of the Thar Parkar region, a woman's sleeveless vest

Ladu – a spherical sweet

Laj – (literally "shyness") The custom of women covering their heads and in some communities their faces in front of men of their husband's families for respect

Lakh – 100,000

Latkaniya – a small hanging decorated with square patches of fabric stitched together in a triangular net

Ludi – **Rabari woman's** woolen veil

Majuri kam – labor work

Malir – one of a number of traditional block-printed fabrics of Kutch and Sindh, usually red with specific motifs and composition. The name refers to a town in Sindh.

Mashru – a warp-faced satin fabric traditionally woven with a silk warp and cotton weft. Today rayon is used for the warp.

Master Weaver/ Master Artisan – In Kutch, and elsewhere in India, the term has ambiguous definition. It connotes artisans who have achieved a certain level of skill, recognition, and success, but it more commonly refers to big producers, who usually no longer practice their craft but get it made through other artisans.

Matka silk – handspun silk yarn derived from the outer portion of a mulberry silk cocoon. Slubby and mat rather than shiny, it is usually woven in a plain weave technique.

Meghval – a dalit (low caste) community of Sindh, Gujarat, and Rajasthan regions, traditionally artisans of leather craft and weaving

Minakari – (literally "enameling") In Ajrakh, it is a technique in which printing and dyeing are done a second time after a piece is finished to deepen the indigo and madder or alizarin colors.

Mod – groom's turban ornament. In some ethnic communities, a bride also wears a mod over her veil.

Nala – (literally "canal") a Rabari embroidery motif

Nath – in the Rabari community, a group of elders (men) who govern the community, primarily at a social level

Nolo – (literally "mongoose") a long, narrow money belt

Ola – Indian ride-share company

Oskikun – pillow

Paako – an embroidery style characterized by tight square chain and double buttonhole stitches, often with black slanted satin stitch outlining

Pachedo – traditional Rabari woman's woolen wrapped skirt

Paheranu – Rabari woman's wrapped skirt, usually cotton or synthetic

Paliya – stone memorials to people who die, usually in battle

Pir Saheb – a Sufi saint

Popat – parrot

Poptiyo – a traditional silver bracelet worn in the Maru Meghval community

Rabari – a pastoral nomadic ethnic community of Gujarat and Rajasthan. There are 3 region-based subgroups of Rabaris in Kutch: Kachhis in the west, Dhebarias in central Kutch, and Vagadias in eastern Kutch.

Rekh – the outline of a printed pattern or motif

Rotla – a millet flour flat bread

Sabot – a traditional woman's bandhani veil, similar to the bagido, black and red with 5 central circular motifs, but the motifs are filled with bandhani

Sachi kor – (literally "real border") a hand-woven border created by using an interlocking technique and two hand thrown shuttles

Sadlo (plural sadla) – a woman's wrapped garment, smaller than a sari and larger than a veil, semi-stitched in an "L" shape, worn with a gathered skirt and bodic

Salvar-kamiz-dupatta – traditional dress for women: loose pants, a tunic, and a shawl-sized scarf to cover the bodice and sometimes the head. Sometimes referred to as "suit."

Sameja – one of several mostly endogamous clans of Muslim pastoralists of Kutch and Sindh. Sameja women embroider paako style embroidery, often with metallic threads (a style called muko).

Screen print – a faster way of making hand printed fabric, in which large silk screens rather than smaller wooden blocks are used

Sodha Rajput – one of many clans of traditional warriors and rulers. They were a dominant community in Sindh, but many migrated to India in 1972 after the Indo-Pakistan war.

Suf embroidery – a style of embroidery originating in eastern Thar Parkar, Sindh (Pakistan) characterized by satin or surface satin stitching worked from the back of the fabric by counting warp and weft yarns of the base fabric

Sunnah – an orthodox Muslim man's dress, including white clothes, beard, and cap

Sufi – a follower of Sufism, a mystic body of religious practice found within Islam. One way that Sufis impart wisdom is through teaching stories.

Tassar silk – silk from the cocoon of a worm that is originally wild. The fiber is naturally beige or brownish color with a crisp texture after weaving.

Theli – shopping bag

Toran – hanging over a doorway

Upperlo – washing boy

Vagad – the eastern region of Kutch District

Vinjhano – ceremonial hand fan

Notes

CHAPTER 2

1. In Gujarati, for respectful address "bhai" (brother) is added to men's names, and "ben" (sister) is added to women's names.

CHAPTER 5

2. Very low caste in the Hindu caste system, formerly called "untouchable."

CHAPTER 6

3. Silver and gold.

4. Paliya are memorials to people who die, usually in battle. They are usually stone figures, like which Nek Chand's found art figures looked.

CHAPTER 23

5. M. H. McIntyre, *Consuming Craft: The Contemporary Craft in a Changing Economy* (London: Crafts Council England, 2010).

6. Arjo Klamer, et al. "Crafting Culture: The importance of craftsmanship for the World of the Arts and the Economy at large." Rotterdam: Erasmus University, June 2012.

Index

About the Author

Ashoka Fellow Judy Frater lived in Kutch thirty years. There, she founded Kala Raksha Trust, the Kala Raksha Museum, and Kala Raksha Vidhyalaya, the first design school for artisans. In 2014, she reinvented the school as Somaiya Kala Vidya. She received the Sir Misha Black Medal for Design Education, the Crafts Council of India Kamla award, the George B. Walter'36 Service to Society Award, and the Designers of India Design Guru Award for her work.

Previously Associate Curator at The Textile Museum, she has authored Threads of Identity: Embroidery and Adornment of the Nomadic Rabaris, The Art of the Dyer in Kutch, and numerous chapters in other books.

Since returning to the US, she has been Artist in Residence at the UW, Madison in 2022 and has led annual artisan tours to Kutch. She currently lives in Santa Fe.

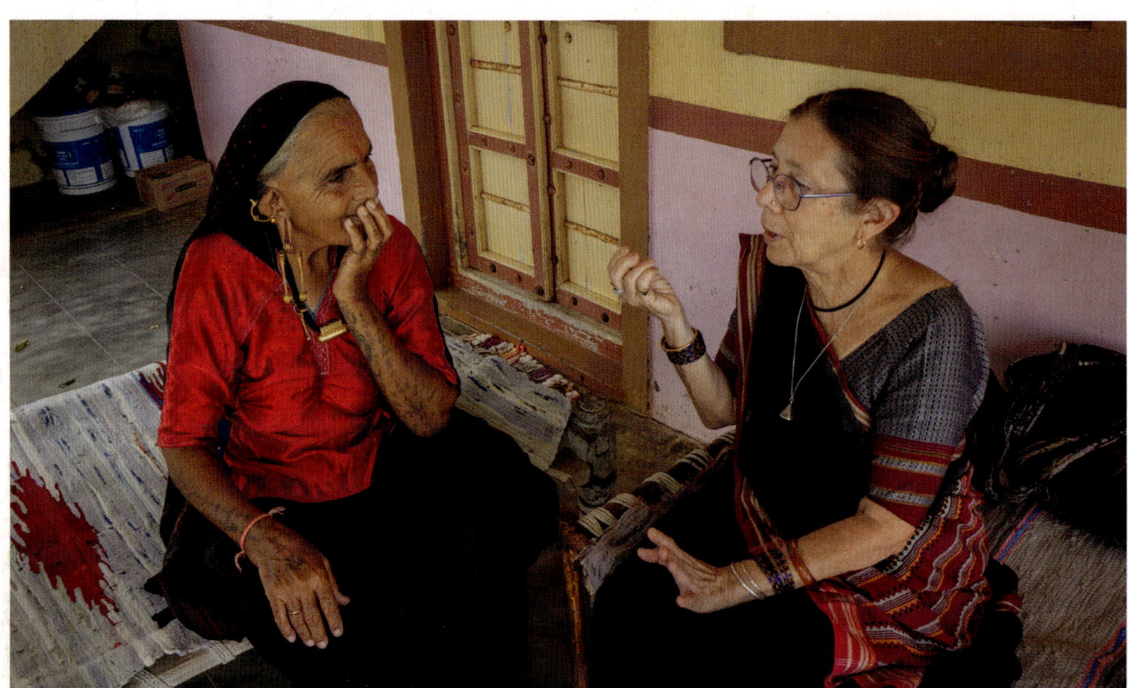